8/68

INORGANIC POLYMERS

INORGANIC

Academic Press·New York·London·1962

POLYMERS

EDITED BY

F. G. A. STONE

Department of Chemistry
Queen Mary College
University of London
London, England

W. A. G. GRAHAM

Arthur D. Little, Inc.
Cambridge, Massachusetts

Contributors

A. J. BARRY, *Dow Corning Corporation, Midland, Michigan*

H. N. BECK, *Dow Corning Corporation, Midland, Michigan*

B. P. BLOCK, *Pennsalt Chemicals Corporation, Wyndmoor, Pennsylvania*

D. C. BRADLEY, *Department of Chemistry, The University of Western Ontario, London, Ontario, Canada*

CLAYTON, F. CALLIS, *Monsanto Chemical Company, St. Louis, Missouri*

HENRY GILMAN, *Iowa State University, Ames, Iowa*

W. A. G. GRAHAM, *Arthur D. Little, Incorporated, Cambridge, Massachusetts*

ROBERT K. INGHAM, *Ohio University, Athens, Ohio*

AMOS J. LEFFLER, *Arthur D. Little, Incorporated, Cambridge, Massachusetts*

A. L. McCLOSKEY, *United States Borax and Chemical Corporation, New York, New York*

MAX SCHMIDT, *Department of Inorganic Chemistry, University of Marburg, Marburg/Lahn, Germany*

F. G. A. STONE, *Department of Chemistry, Queen Mary College, University of London, London, England*

ARTHUR V. TOBOLSKY, *Department of Chemistry, Princeton University, Princeton, New Jersey*

JOHN R. VAN WAZER, *Monsanto Chemical Company, St. Louis, Missouri*

Preface

The object of this book is to provide chemists with a reliable review of current research in several areas of inorganic polymer chemistry. The book is not intended as a comprehensive account of the whole subject of inorganic polymers, but consists of a sequence of reviews of promising areas of research which are being actively studied at the present time by the various authors.

There is now a world-wide interest in inorganic polymers, initiated chiefly by the technological limitations of conventional organic polymers. Those who foot the bill for inorganic polymer research hope that new materials with superior properties will emerge. Interest has centered largely on increased thermal stability, but such factors as resistance to fuels and lubricants, ozone, and radiation are also important. Optimism has been fostered by the rise of the silicones to an important place in technology, suggesting that similarly useful inorganic or semi-inorganic polymers might be found.

The state of knowledge of inorganic polymers is nowhere nearly as well developed as it is for organic polymers. It has been necessary to go back to simple, even nonpolymeric inorganic systems to lay a groundwork, and it might be argued that the most valuable contribution of inorganic polymer research to date is an increased understanding of chemical bonding. Efforts to progress from model compounds to linear polymers of high molecular weight have met with success in only a few instances, and this is perhaps the dominant problem at the present time.

Except for Chapter 1, the order of chapters in this volume is arbitrary. Up to the present, more emphasis in this field has been directed to the preparation of polymers than to their study by physical means. It is, therefore, hoped that inclusion of the material of Chapter 1 will serve to remind those interested in this area of chemistry that inorganic polymers are in no way immune to the laws of physical chemistry, and that many more physical studies on inorganic polymers are required. Thus, the higher bond energies of inorganic systems are frequently offset by the probability of chemical attack involving processes of relatively low activation energy.

We wish to acknowledge our indebtedness to several people, first and foremost to the contributors of the various chapters, to whom credit is due for any value this book may have. We also wish to thank Professor Raymond Fuoss of Yale University and Dr. George Feick and Dr. Norman Wiederhorn of Arthur D. Little, Inc. for many helpful discussions. We acknowledge with gratitude the patience and understanding of our wives Judith Stone and Sydna Graham.

F. G. A. STONE
W. A. G. GRAHAM

Cambridge, Massachusetts
July, 1962

Contents

Introduction   1

F. G. A. STONE AND W. A. G. GRAHAM

1
Properties of Polymers

ARTHUR V. TOBOLSKY

2
Phosphorus-Based Macromolecules

JOHN R. VAN WAZER AND CLAYTON F. CALLIS

3
Sulfur Polymers

MAX SCHMIDT

4

Boron Polymers

A. L. McCLOSKEY

5

Silicone Polymers

A. J. BARRY AND H. N. BECK

6

Organopolymers of Silicon, Germanium, Tin, and Lead

ROBERT K. INGHAM AND HENRY GILMAN

7
Polymeric Metal Alkoxides, Organometalloxanes, and Organometalloxanosiloxanes

D. C. BRADLEY

8
Coordination Polymers

B. P. BLOCK

9
Electron-Deficient Polymers

AMOS J. LEFFLER

Introduction

F. G. A. STONE

Department of Chemistry, Queen Mary College, University of London, London, England

and

W. A. G. GRAHAM

Arthur D. Little, Inc., Cambridge, Massachusetts

The last twenty years has witnessed great progress in most branches of chemistry, and parts of the subject that once appeared to have little connection with each other have converged. Indeed, many of the more remarkable discoveries have occurred on the borderlines of different fields. The new technological advances, such as those which have led to nuclear energy, and jet and rocket travel, have prompted a search for materials able to meet exacting requirements. It is not surprising, therefore, that inorganic chemistry, which has undergone what is popularly described as a renaissance, and polymer chemistry, long a vigorous and exciting branch of chemical science, should have overlapped to provide what is virtually a new discipline, the study of *Inorganic Polymers*.

Even though inorganic polymers are being actively sought and studied in many laboratories there is no general agreement on what is meant by the term "inorganic polymer." That this should be so is entirely reasonable, since both of the terms "inorganic chemistry" and "polymer" have different meanings for different people. Modern inorganic chemistry has been described (*12*) as "the integrated study of the preparation, qualitative and quantitative composition, structure, and reactions of compounds, most of which do not contain carbon," but there are those who would not be prepared to allow inorganic chemists to take over as their domain what is virtually the whole of physical chemistry as well as a considerable fragment of organic chemistry. As for the term "polymer," it too can be defined broadly as a substance in which many structural units are connected by valence bonds in any possible way. If this concept of a polymer is accepted, along with the broad definition of inorganic chemistry mentioned above, then *inorganic polymers* would encompass such diverse substances as most mineral silicates, quartz, phosphates, glasses, diamond, graphite, the cubic and hexagonal forms of boron nitride, phosphonitrilic chlorides, silicones,

1

many organometallic and metal-organic substances,* even giant ionic "molecules" such as a crystal of sodium chloride.

It must be recognized, however, that there are those who believe that the term polymer should have a more restricted use. Physical chemists, in particular, have learned to associate with organic polymers characteristic properties such as high viscosity and long-range elasticity. This in turn led to the realization that the structure of such substances was one in which there was an arrangement of atoms bound by primary valence forces very much greater in spatial extent than the arrangement of atoms in simple compounds. Especially important was the recognition that the structure of the more typical polymer was irregular, in the sense that although cross-linkages between chains or linkages between networks may be many, the number of units between points of cross-linkage varies greatly, thereby introducing *randomness* into the structure. This is very different from the situation in diamond, graphite, or the cubic and hexagonal boron nitrides, for example, where six-membered rings occur with almost perfect regularity, or in sodium chloride where, throughout the structure, every sodium ion is surrounded by six chloride ions and vice versa. Melting disrupts these highly ordered structures, whereas, when conventional polymers melt, continuity of the interunit linkages is not seriously affected (10). This permits them to be extruded and moulded, and in general to behave in a way that fabricators and users of the materials, persons not concerned with technical definitions, have come to regard as being characteristic of a "polymer." It was realized, however, that a certain amount of order (crystallinity) in a solid polymer was acceptable, particularly since regularity can impart a higher melting point and greater strength to the material.† Nevertheless, fusion or crys-

---

* Organometallic (substances with carbon-metal bonds) macromolecules can be of two types. Either carbon can be part of the chain as in certain electron-deficient metal alkyls which possess metal-carbon-metal bridges (Chapter 9), or carbon can form part of a side chain (R) as in organotin compounds of type $(R_2Sn)_n$ (Chapter 6).

The term metal-organic, as here used, refers to substances containing organic groups but which do not possess carbon-metal bonds. Large molecules of this kind include polymeric metal alkoxides (Chapter 7) like $[Ti(OR)_4]_n$ and other coordination polymers (Chapter 8) like $[Cu(NCC_2H_4CN)_2]NO_3$, where succinonitrile molecules act as bridging groups between Cu(I) ions.

† A major advance in polymer chemistry came when it was found possible to make so-called stereoregular polymers, which, because of the regular arrangement of substituent groups on atoms of the polymer chain, are easily packed in the solid state (Chapter 1). Too much regularity, however, as in a completely crystalline material, a common state for inorganic substances, leads to an absence of rubber-like elasticity since there is nothing to unkink. A polymer having elastomeric properties takes on a more crystalline (ordered) state when stretched, and then tends to contract, regaining randomness. Elasticity thus results from entropy effects.

tallization takes place over a relatively wide temperature range and crystallization is never complete, in contrast to typical crystalline solids.

We may summarize the situation by saying that inorganic chemists tend to regard every giant molecule as a polymer, whereas physical chemists tend to regard only linear chain-like giant molecules as polymers, although the important departure from linearity which arises from cross-linking* is accepted so long as some degree of flexibility and elasticity remains. The difference in viewpoint as to what really constitutes a polymer is thus one of degree only, and the reader should not be surprised to find that advocates of both theses have contributed to the following chapters, and furthermore, that certain inorganic substances which would be considered by some as "polymers" are not reviewed in this book.

Reference was made earlier, and in the Preface of this book, to the fact that most of the current interest in inorganic polymers has been brought about by the demands of modern technology. Especially sought have been materials able to withstand severe thermal stress, preferably in the presence of air and moisture, and sometimes in contact with other substances such as hydraulic fluids. Empirically, it has been found that most purely organic polymers begin to break down rather below 250° in air. Brief examination of this stability problem is worthwhile. Oxidative instability of organic polymers is due to conversion of their carbon and hydrogen content to carbon dioxide and water. The latter compounds are the thermodynamically preferred forms in the presence of excess oxygen. The stability of organic materials, even at ambient temperatures, is due to a kinetic effect: the oxidation reaction at low temperatures is very slow. Thus the organic polymer is not in thermodynamic equilibrium but is in a metastable state. As the temperature is raised the oxidation reaction proceeds more rapidly and the polymer decomposes. A question immediately raises itself: Will inorganic polymers do any better?

There is still no certain answer to this question. If thermodynamic factors only were involved, the answer would usually be yes, since there are many bonds which are stronger than those formed by carbon. The silicones (Chapter 5) have become by far the most useful of the polymers with an inorganic backbone, as should be evident after the reader has studied this book. The carbon-carbon single bond strength depends, as do all bond strengths, on the nature of substituent groups, but it may be taken as about 83 kcal (5); this is considerably less than the 106 kcal given (5) for the silicon-oxygen bond.† It is not surprising, therefore, that silicone polymers

---

* Cross-linking in organic polymers is frequently desirable, leading to improvement in properties, as in vulcanized rubber.

† Table XI, Chapter 5, lists the average bond energies for various silicon and carbon bonds.

are in general more stable than those organic polymers having backbones of carbon atoms. Nevertheless, the relative gain in stability in passing from organic to silicone polymers is not as dramatically great as the relative bond strengths might suggest. This is because the same physical principles apply to inorganic polymers as to the organic variety. While the bond energies of inorganic systems may be slightly higher, this is frequently offset by a greater likelihood of chemical attack by processes requiring relatively low activation energies, if other reagents such as air or moisture are present. The silicones provide an excellent example of this difficulty. The molar heat of oxidation of silicon is more than twice that of carbon so that in the presence of an oxygen source and the necessary activation energy the Si—C linkage is destroyed in favor of the Si—O. The ability of silicon to use its vacant 3d orbitals to form favorable transition states opens the way to a low-energy reaction path for decomposition not possible with carbon, which has no vacant low energy orbitals to bond attacking reagents (*9, 17*). Thermal stability of a polymer in the presence of other compounds is thus determined to a very considerable extent by the kinetics of possible degradative reactions, the mechanisms of which are unknown in most cases.

Another aspect of the stability question is the tendency for many inorganic monomers to form four-, six-, or eight-membered rings (I–XII, for example), and the tendency for long chain polymers to depolymerize to small rings at elevated temperatures. Many chain-like silicone polymers, for example, on heating to temperatures in excess of 300° are partially converted to cyclic siloxanes, usually trimers through hexamers, or any mixture of these. However, under other conditions the cyclic siloxanes can be changed to high polymers, emphasizing the ready displacement of the ring/chain equilibrium, a property common to many systems. It can be said that one of the major problems of inorganic polymer chemistry is the existence of small rings rather than long chains. Like any chemical process, polymerization involves an equilibrium between the reactants (monomers, dimers, trimers, etc.) and the products (macromolecules in the form of chains, networks, etc.). At a given temperature the free energy change in passing from a macromolecule to a small ring and vice versa depends on changes in enthalpy and entropy, according to the well-known relationship $\Delta F = \Delta H - T\Delta S$. The tendency for small rings to be preferred in many inorganic systems has as its basis the fact that in these systems entropy effects are playing a dominant role (*3*). Conversion of a few macromolecules into a large number of small molecules of the same material results in an increase in the entropy of the system. Since $\Delta F = \Delta H - T\Delta S$, an increase in entropy leads to a decrease in free energy so that the reaction $(A)_n \rightarrow nA$ is favored. The position of equilibrium (in this instance degree of polymerization), however, is also affected by enthalpy changes and the temperature. Even more important is that in many systems equilibrium is not readily attained and the

$$\begin{array}{c} \text{Me} \\ | \\ \text{O} \\ \text{MeBe} \diagdown \diagup \text{BeMe} \\ \text{O} \\ | \\ \text{Me} \end{array}$$

(I)

$$\begin{array}{c} \text{Me} \\ | \\ \text{S} \\ \text{Me}_2\text{Ga} \diagdown \diagup \text{GaMe}_2 \\ \text{S} \\ | \\ \text{Me} \end{array}$$

(II)

$$\begin{array}{c} \text{CF}_3 \\ | \\ \text{P} \\ \text{CF}_3\text{P} \diagdown \diagup \text{PCF}_3 \\ \text{P} \\ | \\ \text{CF}_3 \end{array}$$

(III)

$$\begin{array}{c} \text{Me} \\ \text{Me}_2\text{Al} \diagdown \diagup \text{AlMe}_2 \\ \text{Me} \end{array}$$

(IV)

$$\begin{array}{c} \text{H} \\ \text{N} \\ \text{HB} \diagup \diagdown \text{BH} \\ | \quad\quad | \\ \text{HN} \diagdown \diagup \text{NH} \\ \text{N} \\ \text{H} \end{array}$$

(V)

$$\begin{array}{c} \text{Me}_2 \\ \text{P} \\ \text{Me}_2\text{B} \diagup \diagdown \text{BMe}_2 \\ \text{Me}_2\text{P} \quad\quad \text{PMe}_2 \\ \diagdown \diagup \\ \text{B} \\ \text{Me}_2 \end{array}$$

(VI)

$$\begin{array}{c} \text{Me}_2 \\ \text{Si} \\ \text{O} \diagup \diagdown \text{O} \\ \text{Me}_2\text{Si} \quad\quad \text{SiMe}_2 \\ \diagdown \diagup \\ \text{O} \end{array}$$

(VII)

$$\begin{array}{c} \text{Cl}_2 \\ \text{P} \\ \text{N} \diagup \diagdown \text{N} \\ \text{Cl}_2\text{P} \quad\quad \text{PCl}_2 \\ \diagdown \diagup \\ \text{N} \end{array}$$

(VIII)

$$\begin{array}{c} \text{Me}_2 \\ \text{N} - \text{P} \\ \text{Me}_2\text{P} \quad\quad \text{N} \\ | \quad\quad\quad | \\ \text{N} \quad\quad \text{PMe}_2 \\ \text{P} - \text{N} \\ \text{Me}_2 \end{array}$$

(IX)

$$\begin{array}{c} \text{N} - \text{S} \\ \text{S} \quad\quad \text{N} \\ | \quad\quad\quad | \\ \text{N} \quad\quad \text{S} \\ \text{S} - \text{N} \end{array}$$

(X)

$$\begin{array}{c} \text{H}_2 \ \text{Me}_2 \\ \text{B} - \text{As} \\ \text{Me}_2\text{As} \diagup \diagdown \text{BH}_2 \\ \text{H}_2\text{B} \quad\quad \text{AsMe}_2 \\ \diagdown \diagup \\ \text{As} - \text{B} \\ \text{Me}_2 \ \text{H}_2 \end{array}$$

(XI)

$$\begin{array}{c} \text{S} - \text{S} \\ \text{S} \quad\quad \text{S} \\ | \quad\quad\quad | \\ \text{S} \quad\quad \text{S} \\ \text{S} - \text{S} \end{array}$$

(XII)

nature of the resulting material is governed by kinetic effects. Since the laws of thermodynamics and kinetics apply equally well to organic substances, the observed degree of polymerization of organic polymers also depends on many factors. Again entropy changes by themselves would favor small rings but depolymerization necessitates rupture of carbon-carbon bonds in the chain, a process requiring considerable activation energy. Hence the change to small rings is not of great importance below temperatures at which other bonds in the polymer break and extensive decomposition ensues. With inorganic polymers, although the bonds forming the backbone may be stronger, reorganization of a chain to a ring is frequently easy because of some reaction path involving little activation energy. This is again well illustrated by the depolymerization of polydialkyl silicones in excess of 300°:

$$
\begin{array}{ccccccc}
& \overset{R}{\underset{R}{|}} & & \overset{R}{\underset{R}{|}} & & \overset{R}{\underset{R}{|}} & \\
-\text{Si}-\text{O}-&\text{Si}-\text{O}-&\text{Si}-\text{O}- & & \longrightarrow
\end{array}
$$

$$
\begin{array}{c}
\overset{R_2}{\overset{\diagup \text{Si} \diagdown}{\quad}} \\
O \qquad O \\
R_2\text{Si} \diagdown \quad \diagup \text{SiR}_2 \\
O
\end{array}
\quad + \quad
\begin{array}{c}
\overset{R_2}{\overset{\diagup \text{Si} - O \diagdown}{\quad}} \\
O \qquad\quad \text{SiR}_2 \\
R_2\text{Si} \qquad\quad O \\
\diagdown O - \underset{R_2}{\text{Si}} \diagup
\end{array}
\quad + \quad \cdots
$$

The reaction involves the rupture and reformation of Si—O (106 kcal) bonds, yet the C—Si (78 kcal) bonds and C—H (98.7 kcal) bonds are not labile, even though they are weaker. Fortunately, conversion of a long chain inorganic polymer once formed into small rings or monomer units often requires elevated temperatures. Thus $[\text{Me}_2\text{PBH}_2]_x$ is not converted to $[\text{Me}_2\text{PBH}_2]_3$ at an appreciable rate below 170°.

   Those working in the area of inorganic polymers are beginning to devise methods for the synthesis of chain structures rather than rings, and for preventing the depolymerization of polymer chains once they have been produced. For example, a judicious amount of cross-linking between chains can impede depolymerization. Other ways of preventing the formation of small rings include the utilization of steric effects, and the selection of types of bonding which do not favor ring formation. The latter approach is much more fundamental, poses exciting possibilities, and is suggested by the behavior of polymers having the P—N backbone (3, 4). Polymeric phosphonitrilic chlorides, $(\text{NPCl}_2)_n$, have long been known (Chapter 2). Indeed, Liebig (13) discovered the trimer $(\text{NPCl}_2)_3$, which is the lowest polymer formed in the reaction:

$$\text{PCl}_5 + \text{NH}_4\text{Cl} \longrightarrow \text{PNCl}_2 + 4\ \text{HCl}$$

Also produced are the tetramer, pentamer, and higher polymers (*14, 15*). There is no doubt that in these materials delocalized π-bonds are formed between nitrogen p orbitals and vacant phosphorus $3d$ orbitals, leading as far as the cyclic polymers are concerned to an inorganic type of aromaticity (*6*). Thus for the trimer $(NPCl_2)_3$ a structure like (VIII), one of two resonance hybrids, accounts for the properties much better than does (XIII). However, in order to make more effective use of the nitrogen lone-pair electrons it is best for the P—N—P bond angle to be large as in linear chains (*3*). It is very interesting, therefore, that the phosphonitrilic chloride trimers, tetramers, and pentamers are converted to high polymers on heating. A number of phosphorus polymers of the type $(NPX_2)_n$ are now known (*11*), and on the basis of π-bonding arguments Burg (*4*) has concluded that polymerizability should increase in the sequence $X = NR_2 >$ Me or Ph $>$ Cl $>$ F.

(XIII)

The concept of p_π–d_π-bonding is also important in considering the structures of polymers based on silicon or sulfur. In R_2SiO polymers, the Si—O—Si angles are far greater than tetrahedral, as would be expected if Si—O p_π–d_π-bonding occurs (*7*). Parenthetically it may be pointed out that p_π–d_π bonding between lone-pair electrons of N or O with vacant d orbitals of Si, P, or S does not lead to the planarity requirements of p_π–p_π-bonding. Thus, whereas in C_6H_6 and (V) there is a coplanar arrangement of ring atoms, in $(NSF_4)_4$, and in (VII) to (XII), there is not.

In addition to the $(NPX_2)_n$ polymers, another all too rare example of chains forming in preference to rings is provided by sulfur trioxide liquid, normally existing mainly as trimer, but which is slowly polymerized by traces of moisture to form asbestos-like crystals $(SO_3)_n$. It is perhaps ironic when one considers present-day efforts to obtain inorganic polymers that, because of the large scale use of sulfur trioxide in industrial sulfonation reactions, much work has been done to inhibit the polymerization of the trimeric liquid form to the linear or cross-linked asbestos-like varieties, which are much less easily handled (*1*).

As examples of new experimental techniques devised to obtain chain-like inorganic polymers we may quote the high pressure polymerization of R_2NBH_2 compounds, and the formation of long R_2PBH_2 chains. The compound Me_2NBH_2 can exist as monomer, dimer, or trimer (*16*), but when the solid dimer is maintained at 3000 atm at 150° an amorphous, insoluble polymer is produced (*8*). Although this material depolymerizes readily its mode of formation represents a refreshing new approach to the problem of obtaining inorganic polymers with high degrees of polymerization. The usual methods for preparing R_2PBH_2 polymers afford mostly trimers and tetramers (Chapter 4). However, if adducts of the type $R_2PH \cdot BH_3$ are made to release hydrogen in the presence of triethylamine or certain other bases (*2, 18*) a respectable yield of high polymer $(R_2PBH_2)_n$ (molecular weight $\sim$6000) can be obtained. Polymerization probably proceeds by successive addition of R_2PBH_2 units to an end group originally consisting of $Et_3N \rightarrow BH_2PR_2$ (*18*).

$$Me_2PH \cdot BH_3 \xrightarrow{\;200°\;} Me_2PBH_2 + H_2$$

$$Me_2PBH_2 \xrightarrow{\;Et_3N\;} Et_3N \cdot BH_2PMe_2$$

$$Et_3N \cdot BH_2PMe_2 + n\ Me_2PBH_2 \longrightarrow (Me_2PBH_2)_nPMe_2BH_2NEt_3$$

It was observed earlier that $(Me_2N)_2BH$ could have a somewhat similar effect on Me_2NBH_2, affording $(Me_2N)_2BH[NMe_2BH_2]_{10}$ (*2*).

The research work of the last decade on inorganic polymers, in spite of a large amount of effort, has not as yet yielded any outstanding products ready for commercial use. The earlier discovered silicones are still the only synthetic inorganic polymers which are widely employed,* although several naturally occurring ones are used, for example asbestos and certain phosphates. It is to be expected that a polymer of the phosphonitrilic chloride family will be the next synthetic inorganic polymer to find commercial use. However, in order to prevent easy hydrolysis it will undoubtedly be necessary to modify the structure in some way, perhaps by copolymerization or condensation with other substances.†

Overemphasis on obtaining materials usable at high temperatures has led chemists to concentrate on the preparative aspects of the field, and to adopt a far too restrictive attitude to this subject. In the future, increasing attention must be given to physical studies. The well-developed area of organic polymers provides the inorganic chemist with a guide in this respect, since it is logical to relate the unknown to the known, and the complex to the simple. However, it is encouraging to recall that people were making automobile tires long before anyone had studied the solution properties of rubber. Finally, as has been noted by others (see, for example, the last paragraph of Chapter 7), it would be undesirable if workers in this field became too concerned with applied chemistry, thereby neglecting contributions that studies in the inorganic polymer field can make to our knowledge of chemistry as a whole.

---

* Glasses, synthetic (fluorinated) micas, diamond, and many other macromolecules are here arbitrarily excluded from mention. See earlier discussion of what is an inorganic polymer.

† *Chem. Eng. News* **39** (Oct. 16) 63 (1961); see, however, *ibid.* **40** (Jan. 15), 29 (1962).

REFERENCES

1. Bevington, C. F. P., and Pegler, J. L., *Chem. Soc. (London) Spec. Publ. No.* **12,** 283 (1958).
2. Burg, A. B., *J. Inorg. & Nuclear Chem.* **11,** 258 (1959).
3. Burg, A. B., *J. Chem. Educ.* **37,** 482 (1960).
4. Burg. A. B., *in* "Inorganic Polymers," *Chem. Soc. (London) Spec. Publ. No.* **15,** 17 (1962).
5. Cottrell, T. L., "Strengths of Chemical Bonds," Butterworths, London, 1958.
6. Craig, D. P., *J. Chem. Soc.* p. 997 (1959); see also references *(14)* and *(15)* for a more general discussion.
7. Craig, D. P., Maccoll, A., Nyholm, R. S., Orgel, L. E., and Sutton, L. E., *J. Chem. Soc.* p. 332 (1954).
8. Dewing, J., Abstracts of Papers presented at the Chemical Society's International Symposium on Inorganic Polymers, Nottingham, 1961.
9. Eaborn, C., "Organosilicon Compounds," Butterworths, London, 1960.
10. Flory, P. J., "Principles of Polymer Chemistry," Cornell Univ. Press, Ithaca, New York, 1953.
11. Haber, C. P., in "Inorganic Polymers," *Chem. Soc. (London) Spec. Publ. No.* **15,** 115 (1961).
12. Lewis, J., and Nyholm, R. S., *Chem. Eng. News* **39,** (Dec. 4), 102 (1961).
13. Liebig, J., *Ann. Chem. Liebigs* **11,** 139 (1834).
14. Paddock, N. L., *Research (London)* **13,** 94 (1960).
15. Paddock, N. L., and Searle, H. T., *Advances in Inorg. Chem. Radiochem.* **1,** 347 (1959).
16. Stone, F. G. A., *Advances in Inorg. Chem. Radiochem.* **2,** 279 (1960).
17. Stone, F. G. A., "Hydrogen Compounds of the Group IV Elements." Prentice-Hall, Englewood Cliffs, New Jersey, 1962.
18. Wagner, R. I., and Caserio, F. F., *J. Inorg & Nuclear Chem.* **11,** 259 (1959).

Properties of Polymers

ARTHUR V. TOBOLSKY

Department of Chemistry, Princeton University, Princeton, New Jersey

TABLE OF CONTENTS

I. The Linear Polymer Molecule

The basic idea in polymer science is the conception of the linear chain molecule, in which the atoms comprising the main chain are united by primary valence forces (covalent, ionic, etc.). A few examples are given below:

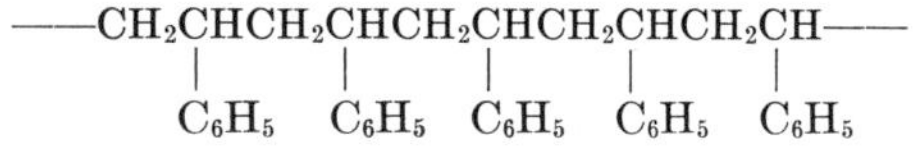

$$—CH_2CHCH_2CHCH_2CHCH_2CHCH_2CH—$$

with C_6H_5 groups attached:

$$\begin{array}{ccccc} | & | & | & | & | \\ C_6H_5 & C_6H_5 & C_6H_5 & C_6H_5 & C_6H_5 \end{array}$$

(polystyrene)

$$—CH_2CH_2CH_2CH_2CH_2CH_2CH_2CH_2CH_2CH_2—$$

(polyethylene)

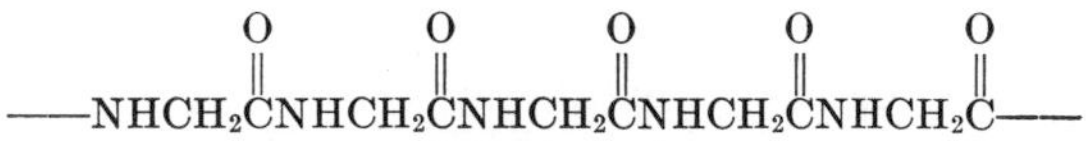

$$\begin{array}{ccccc} O & O & O & O & O \\ \| & \| & \| & \| & \| \\ —NHCH_2CNHCH_2CNHCH_2CNHCH_2CNHCH_2C— \end{array}$$

(polyglycine)

$$\begin{array}{ccccc} CH_3 & CH_3 & CH_3 & CH_3 & CH_3 \\ | & | & | & | & | \\ —Si—O—Si—O—Si—O—Si—O—Si—O— \\ | & | & | & | & | \\ CH_3 & CH_3 & CH_3 & CH_3 & CI'_3 \end{array}$$

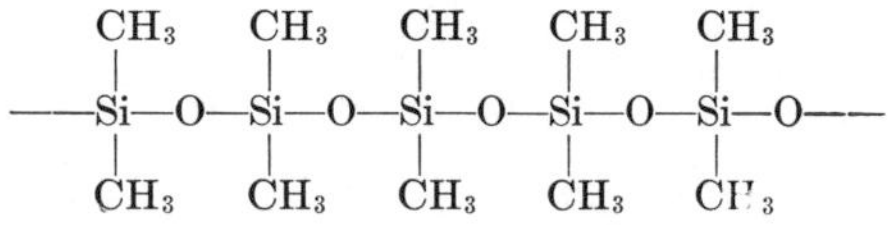

(polydimethylsiloxane)

$$—S—S—S—S—S—S—S—S—S—S—S—S—S—$$

(polymeric sulfur)

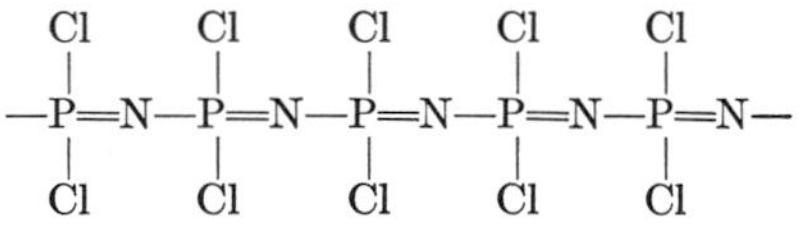

$$
\begin{array}{ccccc}
Cl & Cl & Cl & Cl & Cl \\
| & | & | & | & | \\
—P{=}N—P{=}N—P{=}N—P{=}N—P{=}N— \\
| & | & | & | & | \\
Cl & Cl & Cl & Cl & Cl \\
\end{array}
$$

(polymeric phosphonitrilic chloride)

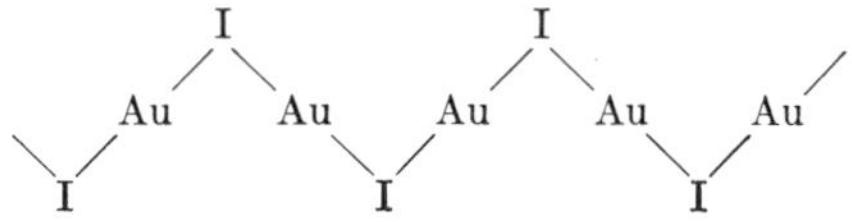

(polymeric gold(I) iodide)

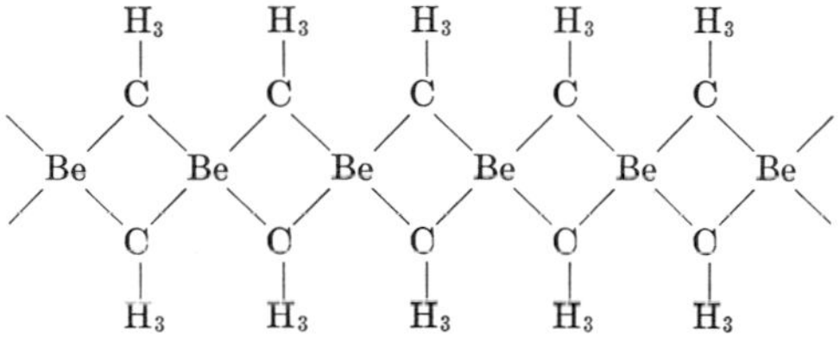

(polymeric dimethylberyllium)

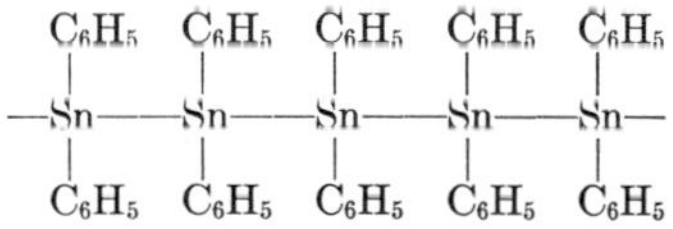

$$
\begin{array}{ccccc}
C_6H_5 & C_6H_5 & C_6H_5 & C_6H_5 & C_6H_5 \\
| & | & | & | & | \\
—Sn—Sn—Sn—Sn—Sn— \\
| & | & | & | & | \\
C_6H_5 & C_6H_5 & C_6H_5 & C_6H_5 & C_6H_5 \\
\end{array}
$$

(polymeric diphenyltin)

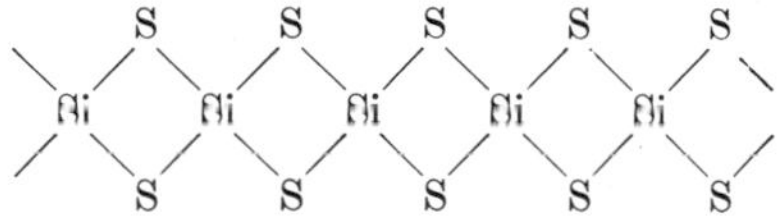

(polymeric silicon sulfide)

It should be noted that the formulation of inorganic compounds as polymers (i.e., infinite linear chains) is often based on a detailed knowledge of the crystal structure, rather than on the properties of their solutions. In other cases, it may rest more tentatively on a consideration of the likely mode of combination of reacting species, supported by the viscosity or insolubility of the product.

A strictly linear representation of the polymer molecule, as we have given above for polystyrene and polyethylene, does not specify an important structural aspect, namely, the stereospecific configuration around optically active chain atoms. This can be accomplished with marginal adequacy by

planar representations. For example, polystyrene can in principle be prepared in three forms, atactic, isotactic, and syndiotactic, as shown below:

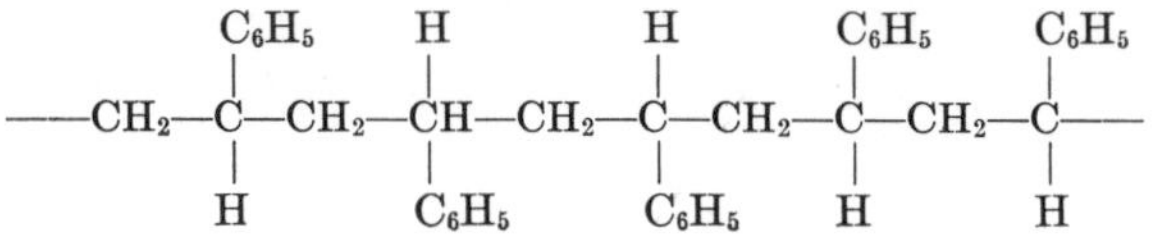

$$
\begin{array}{ccccc}
C_6H_5 & H & H & C_6H_5 & C_6H_5 \\
| & | & | & | & | \\
\text{---CH}_2\text{---C---CH}_2\text{---CH---CH}_2\text{---C---CH}_2\text{---C---CH}_2\text{---C---} \\
| & | & | & | & | \\
H & C_6H_5 & C_6H_5 & H & H
\end{array}
$$

(atactic polystyrene)

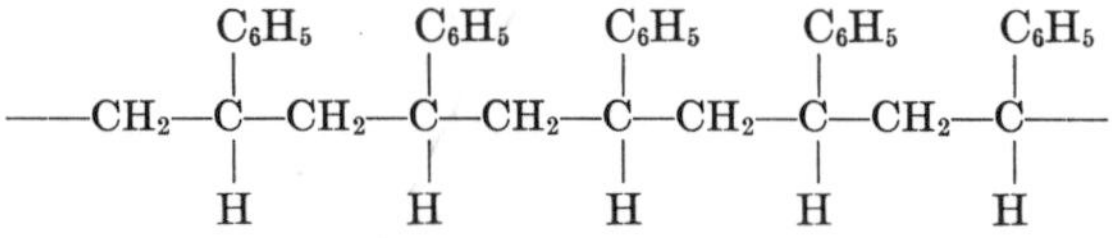

$$
\begin{array}{ccccc}
C_6H_5 & C_6H_5 & C_6H_5 & C_6H_5 & C_6H_5 \\
| & | & | & | & | \\
\text{---CH}_2\text{---C---CH}_2\text{---C---CH}_2\text{---C---CH}_2\text{---C---CH}_2\text{---C---} \\
| & | & | & | & | \\
H & H & H & H & H
\end{array}
$$

(isotactic polystyrene)

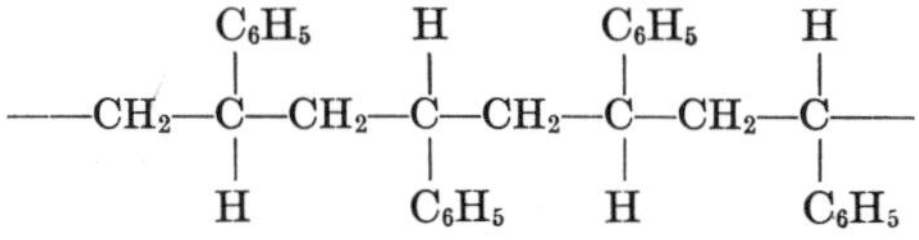

$$
\begin{array}{cccc}
C_6H_5 & H & C_6H_5 & H \\
| & | & | & | \\
\text{---CH}_2\text{---C---CH}_2\text{---C---CH}_2\text{---C---CH}_2\text{---C---} \\
| & | & | & | \\
H & C_6H_5 & H & C_6H_5
\end{array}
$$

(syndiotactic polystyrene)

In atactic polystyrene the phenyl groups are *randomly* "up" and
"down." In isotactic polystyrene the phenyl groups are *all* "up" (or all
"down"). In syndiotactic polystyrene the phenyl groups are alternately
"up" then "down." Atactic and isotactic polystyrene have both been
prepared.

The stereospecific configuration is of great importance since it determines
whether the polymer molecules can pack in regular fashion in the solid
state. Quite recently, a silicone polymer was prepared which is believed
to be stereospecific; this is apparently the first such inorganic polymer. It
consists of phenylsilsesquioxane ($C_6H_5SiO_{2/3}$) units joined together to form
syndiotactic chains, which are joined in turn by *cis* fusion at each unit to
give a ladder-like linear network structure (*1*), as in formula (I).

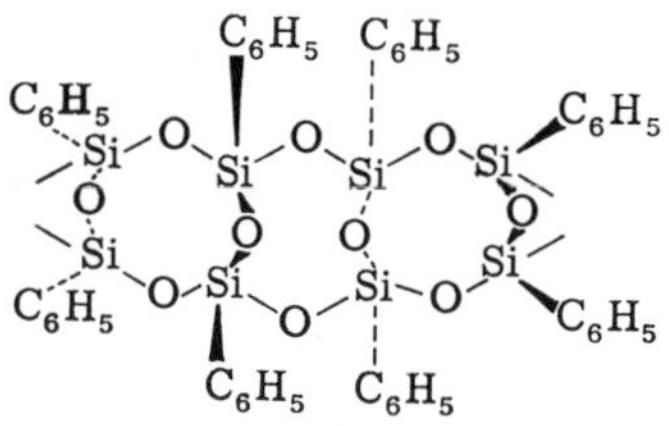

(I)

The structures written above are homopolymers, i.e., they have a continued repetition of a fundamental chemical building block. An immense variety of random copolymers is available, as in formula (II), from styrene

$$CH_2-CH-CH_2-CH-CH_2-CH-CH_2-CH-CH_2-CH-$$
$$\qquad | \qquad\quad | \qquad\qquad | \qquad\quad\; | \qquad\quad |$$
$$\quad C_6H_5 \qquad CN \qquad\; C_6H_5 \qquad C_6H_5 \qquad CN$$

(II)

and acrylonitrile, or formula (III), from the cohydrolysis of dimethyl-

$$(C_6H_5)_3Si \left[\begin{array}{c} \quad CH_3 \quad\; CH_3 \qquad\qquad CH_3 \\ \quad\; | \qquad\quad | \qquad\qquad\;\; | \\ -O-Al-O-Si-O-Si-O-Al-O-Si-O-Al \\ \quad\; | \qquad\quad | \qquad\quad | \qquad\quad\; | \qquad\quad | \qquad\quad | \\ \quad OC_6H_5 \;\; CH_3 \quad CH_3 \quad OC_6H_5 \;\; CH_3 \quad OC_6H_5 \end{array} \right]_n OSi(C_6H_5)$$

(III)

dichlorosilane, phenyltrichlorosilane, and aluminum chloride. Homopolymers have an element of regularity obviously lacking in random copolymers, and this too is important from the point of view of packing in the solid state.

II. Size of Linear Polymer Molecules

The most important characteristic of a linear polymer molecule is its molecular weight or, alternatively, the number of links along its main chain. The only absolute methods available for the determination of molecular weights are methods carried out in dilute solution: osmotic pressure, light scattering, and ultracentrifugation. These methods are in principle exactly the same as those used since the turn of the century for measuring molecular weights of nonpolymeric molecules.

Most synthetic and some natural polymers are available only as a mixture of species of continuously varying molecular weights. The classical methods of molecular weight determination give molecular weight averages: number-average, weight-average and Z-average for osmotic pressure, light scattering, and ultracentrifugation, respectively.

Very fortunately from the point of view of molecular weight determinations, a suitable solvent can be found for most, but not all, organic linear polymers. A notable exception is polytetrafluoroethylene. Most inorganic polymers, however, either are insoluble or react with solvents with breakdown of the polymer chains. An example of the latter behavior is the hydrolysis of the phosphonitrilic chlorides. Since solubility without reaction with solvent is the key to knowledge of colligative properties, the general tendency for inorganic polymers to be insoluble or undergo solvolysis places a heavy restriction on their study. The relative determination of molecular weight of polymers in the solid state will be discussed later.

III. Shape of Linear Polymer Molecules

The shape of linear polymer molecules is again most readily determined in dilute solution. The shape of the polymer depends on (a) the potential energy diagram for the rotation of a chain link with respect to the preceding two or three links, (b) the nature of its interaction with the solvent, and (c) intramolecular interactions such as intramolecular hydrogen bonding or interactions between charged groups attached to the polymer backbone.

Several idealizations have been accepted for the shape of linear polymer molecules, and most polymers conform reasonably closely to one or the other of these idealizations. Perhaps the most common is the random coil, which in its most idealized form consists of a chain of n links, with free rotation of each link with respect to the previous one. Inasmuch as such a chain adopts innumerable conformations, its shape can be described only on a statistical basis. A most useful parameter describing the coil is the mean square distance $\overline{r^2}$ between the first and last chain atom. For a chain of n chain links, each of length l_0:

$$\overline{r^2} = nl_0{}^2 \tag{1}$$

Actual polymer chains such as polyethylene chains in dilute solution are only very roughly described as random coils. Important corrections must be taken into account to describe such chains with greater physical reality. These are (a) the existence of a fixed valence angle between successive chain links,[1] (b) unequal potential energy minima in the potential energy curve describing the hindered rotation of one bond with respect to the plane described by the preceding two bonds, (c) short range and long range steric hindrance, etc., technically known as the excluded volume problem.

The polymer molecule in dilute solution can best be described as existing in various states of rotational isomerism. Generally these rotational isomeric states include highly compact configurations, highly extended configurations, helical configurations, and a variety of intermediate configurations. For this situation, the actual polymer chain may be considered as a modified random coil. For example in Eq. (1), n and l_0 should be replaced by n_e and l_e where:

$$\overline{r^2} = n_e l_e{}^2 \tag{1a}$$

$$r_{\max} = n_e l_e \tag{1b}$$

---

[1] As discussed in Chapter 8, a relatively large variety of geometrical configurations are encountered with inorganic coordination polymers, which may give rise to possibilities unknown to organic polymers.

In Eq. (1a), $\overline{r^2}$ is the actual mean square end-to-end distance of the polymer chain and r_{max} is the extended length of the polymer chain, when taking valence angle restrictions into account.

In certain cases energetic considerations favor special configurations so strongly that certain other idealizations for the polymer molecule in solution other than the modified random coil need to be considered.

A second idealization for the shape of linear polymer molecules is the rigid rod. Cellulose in solution is believed to approximate a rigid rod, and similarly for other linear polymers whose chain linkages resist rotation.

A third idealization for the shape of linear polymer molecules is the helix. Local portions of synthetic polypeptides or protein chains wind up in very regular helices in suitable solvents due to internal hydrogen bonding. These helices may have a definite rod-like axis as in several simple synthetic polypeptides or in collagen, or the axis of the helix may itself twist around in folded convolutions as in the case of globular proteins.

In dilute solutions the physical tools useful for measuring shape have been light scattering, viscosity, diffusion coefficient, sedimentation rate, flow birefringence, and optical activity. The shape of polymer molecules in the solid (pure) state can be determined by X-ray measurements (especially if the polymer is crystalline, as are many inorganic polymers), by stress birefringence, and by infrared dichroism.

IV. Crystalline and Amorphous Polymers

To a certain extent the shapes of polymer molecules in dilute solution are preserved in the solid state of the pure polymer; however, these shapes can also be importantly modified by interchain forces and packing tendencies which may cause crystallization in the solid state. Polymer molecules that exist as random coils in dilute solution may exist in part as helices or as rigid rods (planar zigzags) in the crystalline solid state.

Whereas crystallization in the solid state is a nearly universal tendency among small molecules, this is not true for linear polymers.

Polymers in fact can be divided very sharply into two categories. The amorphous polymers are those that do not show any degree of crystallinity under any conditions. The semicrystalline polymers have regions of crystalline order under certain conditions; however, even the semicrystalline polymers may of course be amorphous above their melting point or if quickly quenched from a molten condition.

The two categories are very readily distinguished from each other by X-ray photographs. The amorphous polymers show the same type of diffuse halo on an X-ray photograph as do simple liquids. From any given point in the structure out to a distance of 15 A, the spatial arrangements of amorphous polymers and those of simple liquids and organic glasses are very similar. From the point of view of longer range distances, the structure of an amorphous polymer might be considered as comparable to the contents of a bowl of cooked spaghetti. The spaghetti-like molecules are in a state of wriggling motion whose amplitude and speed depend on temperature.

The X-ray diagrams of crystalline polymers show a series of sharp diffraction rings superposed on some diffuse scattering. The diffuse scattering comes from the amorphous regions of the polymer; the sharp rings come from regions of crystalline order (crystallites) embedded in an amorphous matrix. The percentage of the polymer involved in regions of crystalline order may be determined by analysis of the X-ray photograph.

It is usual to refer to semicrystalline polymers as crystalline polymers. Both crystalline and amorphous polymers can be oriented, for example by stretching the polymer at a high temperature and maintaining it in the stretched condition while rapidly chilling.

The molecular characteristic that determines whether a given polymer will be crystalline or amorphous is its regularity and symmetry. For instance, homopolymers are much more likely to be crystalline than copolymers, particularly if the latter are random as are most synthetic copolymers. Very few atactic polymers are crystalline, whereas most isotactic or syndiotactic polymers are crystalline. Although an atactic vinyl polymer such as atactic polyvinyl chloride—$CH_2CH(Cl)CH_2CH(Cl)CH_2CH(Cl)$—is slightly (if at all) crystalline with highly imperfect crystallites, the symmetrical polyvinylidene chloride—$CH_2CCl_2CH_2CCl_2CH_2CCl_2$—is highly crystalline.

TABLE I

T_m Values for Several Crystalline Polymers

Polymer	T_m (°C)
Polymethylene	137
Polyethylene oxide	66
Natural rubber	28
Gutta-percha	74
Polychloroprene	80
Polychlorotrifluoroethylene	210
Cellulose tributyrate	207
Polypropylene	176
Polytetrafluoroethylene	327
Polyhexamethylene adipamide	260
Polyethylene terephthalate	267

Crystalline polymers are characterized by a melting temperature T_m above which all crystallites are unstable. Table I gives the values of T_m for several crystalline polymers.

V. Polymer Solubility

There is a universal tendency for substances to mix with or dissolve in other substances, due to the greater randomness of the solution as compared to the unmixed substances. In thermodynamic terms, this greater randomness is expressed as a positive entropy of mixing. For this reason all gases are infinitely miscible in all proportions. In the case of liquids and solids there is in addition a heat of mixing, which occasionally is exothermic and favors solution, but much more frequently is endothermic and opposes solution. Whether a given substance is soluble in a given solvent will depend on the usually opposing balance between entropy of mixing and heat of mixing.

Linear polymers are in no ways immune to the laws of physical chemistry, and the same thermodynamic situation prevails for polymer solutions as for solutions of low molecular weight compounds.

There is, however, a quantitative difference between the solution of linear polymers and that of low molecular compounds. The entropy of mixing which favors solution becomes increasingly smaller with increasing molecular weight. The range of solvents in which a linear polymer will dissolve is much smaller than that for a similar low molecular compound, because fairly small unfavorable heats of mixing will upset the balance between heat and entropy.

Among low molecular weight compounds a liquid substance is frequently more soluble in a given solvent than a crystalline compound of very similar chemical structure. So, too, among linear polymers the crystalline polymers are much more difficultly soluble than are amorphous polymers. For example, amorphous atactic polystyrene is soluble in benzene whereas crystalline isotactic polystyrene is insoluble in benzene.

Linear polymers can be lightly cross-linked by chemical means or by high energy radiation. For example, polyethylene can be cross-linked by beta rays or gamma rays, which knock out hydrogen atoms and produce direct carbon-carbon cross linkage between neighboring chains, and phosphonitrilic chloride chains can be cross-linked by oxygen, which shares electrons with phosphorus atoms in adjoining chains. When more than one cross-link is formed for two polymer chains, "infinite" three-dimensional networks are formed. Another example of cross-linkage is the very well-known vulcanization of natural rubber by sulfur. It is interesting to note that vulcanized rubber may be regarded as a "hybrid" polymer in the sense that it consists of organic chains inorganically cross-linked by sulfur. Cured vinyl silicones, on the other hand, represent inorganic polymers with organic cross-links. Many other types of chemical cross-linking can also be employed. This is especially true of inorganic polymer chains.

These three-dimensional networks are of macroscopic size. For example, a slab of vulcanized natural rubber is in reality a single molecule. Such networks can obviously not be dissolved by solvents. Instead they show a limited equilibrium swelling, the extent of which depends on the nature of the solvent. For a given solvent-polymer system the extent of swelling is smaller the higher the cross-link density of polymer.

VI. Solubility Parameter

Among simple liquids a parameter known as the solubility parameter δ is useful for describing the ability of these substances to dissolve in one another. It is defined as follows:

$$\delta = (E_{\mathrm{vap}}/V_{\mathrm{molar}})^{1/2} \tag{2}$$

In Eq. (2), E_{vap} is the energy of vaporization of the liquid and V_{molar} is its molar volume, both of which are easily measured in low molecular weight liquids. The solubility parameter is obviously a measure of the strength of the intermolecular cohesive forces.

An approximate molecular theory predicts that the heat of mixing of two substances is always endothermic and proportional to the square of the difference of the solubility parameters of these substances:

$$\Delta H_{\mathrm{mix}} \sim (\delta_1 - \delta_2)^2 \tag{3}$$

This indicates that substances whose solubility parameters differ greatly are mutually insoluble. On the other hand, substances whose solubility parameters are equal should be infinitely miscible. Equation (3) is in effect a quantitative statement of the organic chemist's rule that "like dissolves like."

Since polymers cannot be vaporized without decomposition, and inasmuch as they have negligible vapor pressures, E_{vap} cannot be determined by direct measurement or by the Clapeyron-Clausius equation. An indirect determination of the solubility parameter of polymers is required. This is achieved by a study of the equilibrium swelling behavior of the lightly cross-linked polymer in a wide variety of solvents. It is presumed that the solubility parameter of the polymer is the same as that of the solvent in which it achieves maximum swelling.

VII. Glass-Transition Temperature

The glass-transition temperature T_g of a polymer is perhaps its most important characteristic parameter. This parameter is obtained as an inflection point in a plot of specific volume of the polymer versus temperature. For amorphous polymers the importance of the glass-transition temperature is especially noticeable. Below the glass-transition temperature the polymer is in a glassy state. The individual chain segments are frozen on the "lattice sites" of an irregular quasi-lattice. They can execute vibratory motions around these fixed positions, but do not exhibit significant diffusional and translational motion from one "site" to another. In this glassy state the polymer has the high values of elastic modulus (10^{10} to 10^{11} dynes/cm²) that is associated with the solid state.

Above the glass-transition temperature the polymer segments begin to exhibit diffusional motions as do the molecules of a liquid. The velocity of these diffusional motions increases with increasing temperature. If the polymer has a rather small chain length, it will show a rather abrupt change from glassy behavior to viscous liquid behavior within a few degrees of the glass-transition temperature. A linear polymer of high chain length will change from "glassy" to "leathery" at the glass-transition temperature. As the temperature is raised it will change from leathery to rubbery, and finally exhibit the characteristics of a very viscous liquid. For a lightly cross-linked polymer, the change from rubbery state to viscous state does not occur unless the bonds of the network undergo exchange reactions or scission reactions at sufficiently high temperatures.

Above the glass-transition temperature, linear polymers of high chain length exhibit viscoelastic behavior, i.e., they are simultaneously viscous liquids or leathery or rubbery solids, depending on the time scale of the mechanical experiments.

Inasmuch as the glass-transition temperature is such an important characteristic parameter for polymers, it is important to inquire how it depends on the structural and energetic aspects of the polymer.

(A) T_g increases with increasing chain length but, for values of $n > 500$, T_g reaches a limiting value that depends on the nature of the polymer but is independent of chain length.

(B) T_g of a polymer is higher the greater the magnitude of the barrier restricting internal rotation around the chain links.

(C) T_g tends to depend in a direct fashion on the magnitude of δ, i.e., the greater the strength of the intermolecular forces, the higher the value of T_g.

For a copolymer the magnitude of T_g can be obtained from the following approximate formula:

$$1/T_g = w_1/T_{g,1} + w_2/T_{g,2} \qquad (4)$$

where w_1 and w_2 are the weight fractions of components 1 and 2 in the copolymer and $T_{g,1}$ and $T_{g,2}$ are the T_g values of the pure homopolymers. This predicts an intermediate value for the T_g of the copolymer, and this is nearly always true.

Table II gives the T_g values for several polymers.

TABLE II

GLASS-TRANSITION TEMPERATURES FOR SEVERAL POLYMERS

Polymer	T_g (°C)
Silicone rubber	−123
Polybutadiene (emulsion, 50°C)	−85
Polyisobutylene	−70
Natural rubber	−72
Poly(butyl acrylate)	−56
Poly(vinylidene fluoride)	−39
Poly(ethyl acrylate)	−22
Poly(methyl acrylate)	9
Poly(perfluoropropylene)	11
Poly(n-butyl methacrylate)	22
Poly(vinyl acetate)	29
Poly(n-propyl methacrylate)	35
Poly(chlorotrifluoroethylene)	45
Poly(ethyl methacrylate)	65
Poly(vinyl alcohol)	73
Poly(vinyl chloride)	82
Poly(styrene)	100
Poly(methyl methacrylate)	105
Poly(acrylic acid)	106
Poly(methacrylonitrile)	120

VIII. Viscoelastic Behavior (A)

Polymers partake of the properties of both solids and liquids. The most characteristic property of an ideal solid is its modulus of elasticity, defined by Hooke's law:

$$f = Es \qquad (5)$$

We shall consider Eq. (5) as applying to simple tension. In Eq. (5) f is the stress (tensile force per unit area), s is the strain (change in length divided by original length), and E is Young's modulus, a characteristic property of the solid that depends on external properties such as temperature and pressure.

For simple liquids the characteristic property is the viscosity defined by Newton's law:

$$f = \eta(ds/dt) \tag{6}$$

In Eq. (6) f is the shear stress, ds/dt is the rate of shear strain, and η is the viscosity, a characteristic property of the liquid in question, and markedly dependent on temperature and pressure. Although less familiar, a tensile viscosity can also be defined as follows:

$$f = \eta^{(t)}(ds/dt) \tag{7}$$

In Eq. (7) f is the tensile stress, ds/dt is the rate of tensile strain, and $\eta^{(t)}$ is the tensile viscosity.

Polymers can be described neither by Hooke's law nor Newton's law but instead exhibit a combination of viscous and elastic behavior. A very simple experimental approach to this behavior is to consider experiments in which a fixed tensile strain is imposed on a substance as quickly as possible, and the stress necessary to maintain that fixed strain is then measured as a function of time. Hooke's law can then be generalized as follows:

$$f(t) = E_r(t)s_0 \tag{8}$$

In Eq. (8) s_0 is the fixed tensile strain, $f(t)$ is the measured time dependent stress, and $E_r(t)$ is a new property, the time dependent relaxation modulus defined by Eq. (8). The relaxation modulus is a very useful means for characterizing the viscoelastic properties of the material.

The relaxation modulus is a very highly temperature dependent quantity. It has been shown that the temperature dependence of $E_r(t)$ can be simply described by the statement:

$$E_r(t/K(T)) \text{ is the same at all temperatures.} \tag{9}$$

In Eq. (9), $K(T)$ is a characteristic relaxation time of the material, and is a function of temperature. The temperature dependence of $K(T)$ can in fact be approximately expressed by the following equation:

$$\log \frac{K(T)}{K(T_g)} = -17.44 \frac{T - T_g}{51.6 + T - T_g} \tag{10}$$

For cross-linked polymers the relaxation modulus $E_r(t)$ reaches an equilibrium value other than zero for times approaching infinity. For linear amorphous polymers the $E_r(t)$ approaches zero for sufficiently long times.

For linear polymers a plot of $\ln[E_r(t)]$ versus t approaches a straight line as t approaches infinity:

$$\ln [E_r(t)]_{t \to \infty} = \ln E_m - t/\tau_m \tag{11}$$

The quantity τ_m defined by Eq. (11) is called the maximum relaxation time. For linear polymers of long chain length τ_m depends on chain length n and temperature as follows:

$$\tau_m = A [K(T)/K(T_g)] n^{3.4} \tag{12}$$

where A is a constant for a particular polymer.

Equation (12) can be used in conjunction with Eq. (10) to obtain approximate values of the chain length from measured values of τ_m.

IX. Modulus-Temperature Curves

To simplify our discussion we shall for the moment consider the relaxation modulus $E_r(t)$ at a fixed time and discuss its variation with temperature. The fixed value of time shall be 10 sec, and we therefore consider plots of $E_r(10)$ versus T for typical polymers.

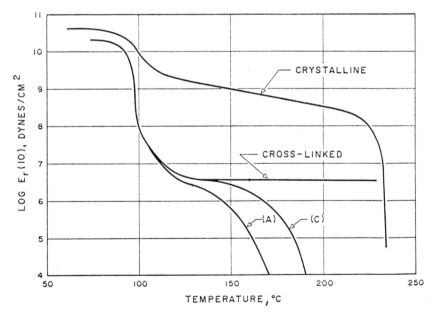

Fig. 1. $E_r(10)$ versus temperature for polystyrene samples of two different molecular weights (A) and (C), for lightly cross linked polystyrene and for crystalline isotactic polystyrene.

Figure 1 shows such a plot for amorphous atactic polystyrene of two different molecular weights, for lightly cross-linked amorphous polystyrene, and for crystalline isotactic polystyrene.

One of the curves for the amorphous linear polystyrene is replotted in Fig. 2, to emphasize that there are in fact five regions of viscoelastic behavior. In order of decreasing modulus values these are: (a) a glassy region, (b) a transition region, (c) a rubbery plateau region, (d) a rubbery flow

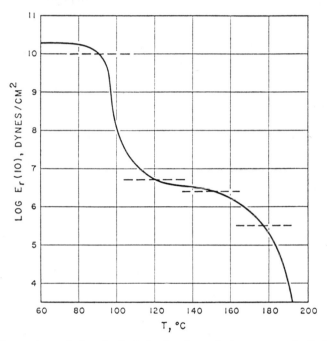

Fɪɢ. 2. Five regions of viscoelastic behavior for polystyrene sample C. [Reprinted with permission from Tobolsky, "Properties and Structure of Polymers." Wiley, New York, 1960.]

region, and (e) a liquid flow region. These regions and the general shape of the modulus temperature curve are characteristic of all amorphous linear polymers. To a first approximation for any of these polymers the curves are as shown in Fig. 2, except that they are displaced along the temperature axis so that the middle of the transition region is centered around the T_g value of the polymer.

It is useful to define several parameters that can be obtained directly from the modulus temperature curve of amorphous polymers. We may readily define E_1, the limiting modulus for the glassy state, and E_2, the modulus for the rubbery plateau region. In addition we may define the inflection temperature T_i at which the value of $\log E_r(10) = \frac{1}{2} (\log E_1 +$

log E_2). For polystyrene the values of E_1, E_2, and T_i are, respectively, $10^{10.35}$ dynes/cm², $10^{6.65}$ dynes/cm², and 102°C. The value of T_i is generally within a few degrees of T_g, which for polystyrene is 100°C.

In the glassy region the segments of the polymer chain are frozen in fixed positions on the sites of a disordered quasi-lattice. They vibrate around these fixed positions just as do the molecules of a molecular crystal. However they undergo little if any diffusional motion from one lattice position to another. This type of diffusional motion, characteristic of liquids, sets in only above T_g.

Young's modulus of a polymer in the glassy state is given by the following approximate formula:

$$E \approx 8.04 \ \delta^2 \tag{13}$$

where δ^2 is the square of the solubility parameter, i.e., the cohesive energy density expressed in units of dynes/cm².

In the transition region the segments of the polymer chain are undergoing short range diffusional motion. The time for diffusion from one "lattice site" to another is of the order of magnitude of 10 sec (our reference time). In the transition region the modulus is changing very rapidly with time as well as temperature.

In the quasi-static rubbery region the short range diffusional motions of the polymer segments are very rapid. However, the long range segmental motions, particularly those involving the motion of entire molecules, are retarded, especially by entanglements between the chains that act as temporary cross-links. The quasi-static rubbery modulus becomes a true rubbery modulus when chemical cross-links are present.

In the region of rubbery flow the motion of molecules as a whole is becoming important. Major configurational changes of the entire molecule, including the slippage of long range entanglements, are taking place in time of the order of 10 sec.

Finally, in the region of liquid flow the long range-configurational changes of the molecules are occurring in less than 10 sec. Elastic recovery is nearly completely negligible in this region for stresses or strains which are maintained for longer than 10 sec.

The regions of rubbery flow and liquid flow can be completely suppressed if chemical cross-links are introduced as permanent network junctures.

X. Flow Viscosity of Linear Polymers

The viscosity of linear polymers of sufficiently long chain length is given by the following approximate formula:

$$\log \eta = 3.4 \log n - \frac{17.44 \ (T - T_g)}{51.6 + T - T_g} + D \tag{14}$$

in Eq. (14) n is the chain length, T_g the glass transition temperature, and D a constant for each polymer.

The fact that the viscosity can be written as a product of a temperature dependent term and a chain length dependent term gave rise to the concept that the flow of polymer molecules involves an activated diffusional jump of polymer segments. This segmental "jump" is common to all members of a homologous series and explains the common temperature dependent factor for chains of all sizes. The chain length dependent factor indicates that for flow to take place there must be a coordinated sequence of segmental jumps. This coordination becomes progressively more difficult with increasing chain length, especially because of entanglements.

XI. Kinetic Theory of Rubber Elasticity

For cross-linked rubber networks at temperatures above the transition region, the rubbery Young's modulus is given by the formula:

$$E = 3\phi NRT = 3\phi \, dRT/M_c \qquad (15)$$

In Eq. (15) N is the number of moles of network chains per cubic centimeter, R the gas constant, T the absolute temperature, and ϕ a constant of order of magnitude unity. Alternatively, the quantity N can be replaced by d/M_c, where d is the density and M_c the average molecular weight of the chains between contiguous network junctures.

This formula is theoretically derived and is based on the conception that a rubbery substance resists stretch for the same reason that a gas resists compression: in both cases the deformed state is a state of lower entropy and in both cases the change of internal energy during stretching might be negligible. The decreased entropy of a stretched rubber is due to the fewer chain conformations consistent with the external restraints.

If a quantitative tetrafunctional cross-linking agent is used to cross-link chains of "infinite" length, the quantity N in Eq. (15) is just twice the moles of cross links per cubic centimeter.

Depending on the concentration of cross-linking agent that is used, one can produce "rubbers" whose modulus varies from 10^6 to $10^{9.4}$ dynes/cm^2. It is only at the lower cross-link concentrations that the rubber networks have long range extensibility. Very highly cross-linked networks still have a "rubbery" modulus given by Eq. (15).

In the absence of crosslinks, the concentration of "entanglements" determine the rubbery modulus:

$$E_2 = 3\phi \, dRT/M_{ent} \qquad (16)$$

In Eq. (16) E_2 is the quasi-static rubbery modulus and M_{ent} is the molecular weight between entanglements.

It is only when the chain length of the polymer is sufficiently large that entanglement can occur to a sufficient extent to produce a quasi-static rubbery modulus. Low molecular weight linear polymers show no region of quasi-rubbery behavior, but change from glassy to liquid behavior in a very narrow temperature range.

Since many inorganic polymers are highly cross-linked networks, it is of interest to consider the properties of such networks more fully at this point. The diamond crystal or cubic boron nitride may be regarded as the ultimate cross-linked network. The force resisting the elongation of a diamond crystal arises from the change of internal energy of the crystal with deformation. The modulus of diamond is exceedingly high (approximately 5.5×10^{12} dynes/cm^2). As far as is known, the elastic properties are relatively unchanged with temperature until decomposition.

On the other hand, such a *relatively* tightly cross-linked polymer as the polymer from tetraethyleneglycol dimethacrylate exhibits a glassy region, a transition region, and a rubbery region at sufficiently high temperatures, even though the modulus in the "rubbery" region is exceptionally high, about $10^{9.4}$ dynes/cm^2. Apparently even a very small linear chain between cross-linkages gives the possibility of a modicum of rubbery behavior.

XII. Viscoelastic Behavior (B)

The viscoelastic behavior of polymer molecules has been idealized as follows. Consider a linear array of n spherical balls of mass m, radius r_0 connected by springs of force constant k and length l_0. The entire array is considered immersed in a liquid of viscosity η_0. The viscoelastic behavior of such an array can be computed exactly by the equations of motion of classical physics. This theory and its various elaborations is generally referred to as the molecular theory of viscoelasticity because the linear array discussed above seems to offer a good analogy to an actual polymer chain either in dilute solution or in the "liquid" consisting of the surrounding molecules of the undiluted polymer.

The molecular theory of viscoelasticity predicts the following equation for the relaxation modulus:

$$E_r(t) = 3\,NkT \sum_{p=1}^{n} \exp\left(-\frac{t}{\tau_{\max}}p^2\right) \tag{17}$$

$$\tau_{\max} = r_0\eta_0 l_0^2 n^2 / \pi kT \tag{18}$$

For undiluted polymers the molecular theory of viscoelasticity appears to agree with experimental results only in the lower modulus portion of the transition region. In the near glassy region internal energy effects must be considered; in the rubbery flow region and liquid flow region the effect of entanglement lends added complication. Whereas the molecular theory of viscoelasticity predicts a flow viscosity proportional to n, the actual flow viscosity is proportional to $n^{3.4}$. In the lower portion of the transition region the molecular theory predicts that a plot of $\log E_r(t)$ versus $\log t$ should have a slope of $-\frac{1}{2}$ and this is in fact found to be approximately true for most amorphous polymers.

XIII. Chemical Flow and Stress Relaxation

At sufficiently high temperatures the viscoelastic properties of polymers are affected by chemical reactions. These can be of two types: (a) reversible interchange reactions that do not change the over-all structure of the polymer and (b) irreversible reactions.

Theoretically speaking, the stress in a sample of silicone rubber maintained at constant stretched length should remain constant indefinitely. In fact there will be a decay of stress to zero at sufficiently elevated temperatures because of interchanges between the Si—O linkages. These interchanges are enormously affected by catalysts. With sufficiently powerful catalysts (e.g., sulfuric acid) the relaxation time of the silicone rubber can be brought down to a value of a few seconds at room temperature. This means that the cross-linked rubber will behave essentially as a liquid because of chemical interchange. By rigorous exclusion of interchange catalysts, the relaxation time of the silicone rubber can be increased to many hours even at 250°C.

When thin strips of cross-linked natural rubber are maintained in a stretched condition at elevated temperatures the stress will decay because of scission of the molecular chains caused by molecular oxygen. This is common to all hydrocarbon-type polymers.

At sufficiently high temperatures the mechanical properties of all polymers are in fact determined by chemical reactions. The problem of finding suitable polymers for high temperature use becomes a problem of chemical stability. Thermochemical bond energies, it should be noted, only set an upper limit to stability. Pathways for decomposition can frequently occur at temperatures far below those required for straightforward bond rupture, if the polymer is exposed to oxygen, water, or other reactive compounds. Thus high bond energies are necessary but are not sufficient for thermally stable polymers.

GENERAL REFERENCES

Tobolsky, A. V., "Properties and Structure of Polymers," Wiley, New York, 1960.
Ferry, J. D., "Viscoelastic Properties of Polymers," Wiley, New York, 1960.

REFERENCE

1. Brown, J. F., *et al.*, *J. Am. Chem. Soc.* **82,** 6194 (1960).

—2—

Phosphorus-Based Macromolecules

JOHN R. VAN WAZER

and

CLAYTON F. CALLIS

Monsanto Chemical Company, St. Louis, Missouri

TABLE OF CONTENTS

I. Introduction

Inorganic chemistry encompasses many macromolecules. Indeed, perhaps the majority of inorganic molecular structures can be considered to be high polymers. These facts have generally not been understood by chemists since most inorganic macromolecules are quite intractable, being either network polymers or otherwise so constituted that they cannot be dissolved or vaporized without breaking up the macromolecular structure, often into fragments of low molecular weight. Iron rust (primarily amorphous, partially hydrated ferric oxide) is a good example of a complicated mixture of what must be extremely high polymers held together by Fe—O bonds. The problem here is that any method of dissolving rust leads to nearly complete depolymerization. This means that the standard methods of polymer physics, which are nearly all carried out on solutions of macromolecules, cannot be applied.

Phosphorus compounds have been found to be outstanding exceptions to the problem of being unable to prove the existence of macromolecular structures in inorganic chemistry by use of the methodology developed for organic polymers. As compared to the majority of completely inorganic polymers, a number of phosphorus macromolecules exhibit good stability and are not highly crosslinked, so that they can be dissolved and studied in solution without gross chemical change. This is related to the fact that phosphorus is covalently bonded to its neighboring atoms in all of its compounds (*118*).

Since this volume deals with inorganic polymers, emphasis will be placed on those molecules having a significantly large number of phosphorus atoms per structure—in most cases at least 100 P atoms per molecule. For further details of phosphorus chemistry not covered here, the reader is referred to the treatise entitled "Phosphorus and Its Compounds" (*117*). Because chain compounds have proven to be of great theoretical and practical importance in the field of organic polymers, the data on phosphorus-based chain structures will be discussed in Section II of this chapter—with emphasis on structure proofs and properties directly related to the high molecular weight. Then, some examples of highly crosslinked structures, primarily sheet and three-dimensional network polymers, will be reviewed in Section III. The amorphous network polymers, of which there are very many in inorganic chemistry, are analogous to the organic thermosetting resins.

A. Structural Reorganization

Some organic macromolecules are found to exchange parts with each other upon being melted. This phenomenon was first studied for the polyesters and was put into rather elegant mathematical form by Flory under the name "random reorganization" (*29*). In the type of reorganization treated by Flory, emphasis was placed upon the exchange of parts between long-chain molecules, and it was assumed that the ends of the chains would retain their monofunctional character and the middles their bifunctional character throughout the reorganization process.

Based on our studies of phosphorus compounds, we have extended Flory's reorganization concepts to include change of functionality of a given building unit during the reorganization process (*76, 121*). Thus, two bifunctional middle groups can be considered as reacting together to form a monofunctional end group plus a trifunctional branching group [see Eq. (1), p. 33]. Such exchange of functionality via ligand-interchange reactions can be treated statistically, and the resulting collection of structural building units can then undergo further statistical sorting into molecules. Size-distribution curves for several ideally random systems involving reorganization of the molecules forming a homogeneous single-

phase fluid are shown in Fig. 1. The calculations given in this figure were
carried out on an IBM-704 computer (*129*) programmed so as to handle the
mathematics for the case of a pure polyphosphoryl-type compound undergoing reorganization involving scission of either (a) only the P—X bond,
(b) only the P—O bond or, finally, (c) both the P—X and P—O bonds.
In these calculations, completely random behavior and no ring formation is
assumed. For the majority of the phosphorus-based macromolecules undergoing structural reorganization as described later in this chapter, complete
reorganization involving change of the functionality of the ligands [i.e.,
case (c) in Fig. 1] is found. The type of reorganization treated by Flory
for the organic polyesters is similar to case (b). Case (a) corresponds to
room-temperature exchange of halogens between polyphosphoryl halides
and is similar to the better-known case of exchange of hydrogen atoms
between hydrocarbons.

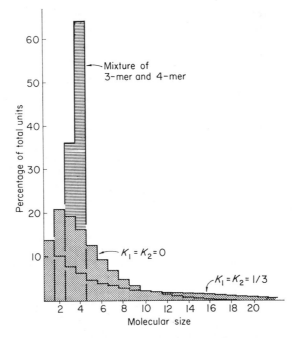

Fig. 1. Size-distribution curves for the composition in the system POX_3—P_2O_5 corresponding to an X/P mole ratio of 1.55. (a) When only P—X bonds undergo scission, a
O O O   O O O O
simple mixture of the 3-mer, XPOPOPX, and 4-mer, XPOPOPOPX, which satisfies the
X X X   X X X X
stoichiometry will remain unchanged. (b) When only P—O bonds make and break
($K_1 = K_2 = 0$), a sharper random distribution results than when both P—O and P—X
bonds undergo scission in a random-reorganization process (c) (*i.e.*, $K_1 = K_2 = \frac{1}{3}$).

1. Exchange of Functionality

If two phosphoryl compounds, OPX₃ and OPZ₃, are mixed together and the mixture is held for a sufficiently long time for ligand interchange to occur, four compounds will result: OPX₃, OPX₂Z, OPXZ₂, and OPZ₃. If there is no preference for the arrangement of the X's and Z's, the distribution of species will be random, as indicated by the dotted lines in Fig. 2. The solid lines in this figure correspond to the equilibrium distribution observed upon heating a fluid mixture of phosphorus oxychloride with phosphorus oxybromide for a few hours at a temperature above 200°C (*37*).

The type of ligand-interchange reaction illustrated in Fig. 2 is not necessarily confined to simple structures based on a single phosphorus atom. Thus, if X stands for a monofunctional ligand and Z for a bridging oxygen atom, a complete family of compounds is achieved, with the average molecular weight increasing as the parameter $R = X/P$ is reduced

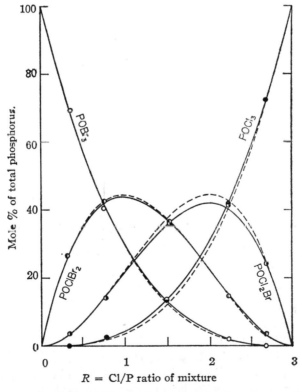

Fig. 2. Equilibria of POCl₃—POBr₃ random reorganization mixtures. The solid lines correspond to $K_{1,0} = 0.406$ and $K_{2,0} = 0.341$; the broken lines correspond to the completely random case in which $K_1 = K_2 = 0.333$.

from its maximum value of 3. Again the concept of ideal random behavior can be applied here. The four compounds, OPX_3, OPX_2Z, $OPXZ_2$, and OPZ_3 now correspond to the following structural building units: the first member of the chemical family or "*ortho* compound," OPX_3; the end group (monofunctional), $OPX_2(O_{1/2}-)$; the middle group (bifunctional), $OPX(O_{1/2}-)_2$; and the branching point (trifunctional), $OP(O_{1/2}-)_3$. When X stands for a chlorine atom, we have the family of polyphosphoryl

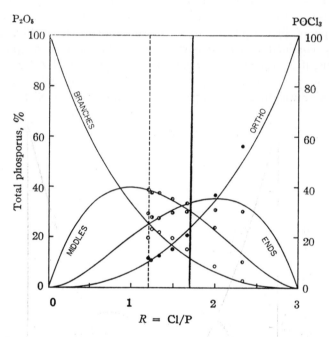

Fig. 3. Distribution of structure building units as a function of composition in the randomly reorganized system $POCl_3$—P_2O_5. The dotted perpendicular line corresponds to the observed gel point, and the solid perpendicular line to the theoretical gel point assuming no rings.

chlorides, for which data (*39*) are shown in Fig. 3. In this system, one end compound OPX_3 is orthophosphoryl chloride, $OPCl_3$, and the other end compound OPZ_3 is phosphorus pentoxide, $P_2O_5 = OP(O_{1/2}-)_3$. The data of Fig. 3 were obtained by dissolving P_2O_5 in $POCl_3$ and equilibrating for several days at 230°C. Essentially identical equilibrium results are obtained when such mixtures are held at room temperature for about a year.

The equilibria between structural building units shown in Fig. 3 correspond quite closely to the random case. These equilibria can be expressed in terms of Eqs. (1) and (2), which are given with their respective equilibrium constants:

2 middle groups = end group + branching group

$$K_1 = [\text{ends}][\text{branches}]/[\text{middles}]^2 = e \cdot b/m^2 \qquad (1)$$

2 end groups = *ortho* molecule + middle group

$$K_2 = [\text{ortho}][\text{middles}]/[\text{ends}]^2 = o \cdot m/e^2 \qquad (2)$$

For the completely random case, $K_1 = K_2 = 0.33$. The curves shown in Fig. 3. represent $K_1 = 0.422$ and $K_2 = 0.639$. The average deviations from these values are ± 0.031 and ± 0.052, respectively.

The perpendicular solid line appearing in Fig. 3 corresponds to the theoretical gel point, assuming no rings. When there is an inappreciable amount of rings in the branched macromolecules, the gel point comes at the value of R for which the number of ends exactly equals three times the number of branches. To the left of the broken line, assuming no rings, there are infinite, highly branched wall-to-wall structures, whereas, to its right, all of the molecules are finite in size. When there are a statistically insufficient number of ends to cap off the third ligand site of each branch, an infinite structure results unless some of the third ligand sites per branch are capped off by each other through ring formation. In other words, the incorporation of rings in the macromolecules will cause the gel point to move to lower values of R *(38)* and this is shown by the perpendicular broken line of Fig. 3.

As will be shown later in Section II,A,1, where the polyphosphoryl chloride macromolecules are discussed in detail, there are considerable changes in properties at the true gel point, which is determined by the number of rings as well as by the ratio of ends to branches. It is interesting to note that distribution curves of structure-building units such as are shown in Figs. 2 and 3, correspond to equilibria that can be reached by heating any mixture having the elemental composition of the equilibrium fluid.

2. Sorting of Building Units into Molecules

In the treatment developed in our laboratory for structural reorganization in which the bonds to all ligands are labile, the process has arbitrarily been divided into the exchange of functionality between building units, as depicted by Eqs. (1) and (2), and sorting of the resulting distribution of building units into molecules so as finally to obtain a distribution of molecules or molecule ions of various sizes and shapes. Obviously the two divisions are simply parts of a single process, with one step not necessarily preceding or following the other. The exchange of functionality between structural units has been treated in terms of chemical equilibrium constants and the sorting of these units into molecules in terms of distribution functions. However, for straight-chain molecules, the process of sorting units can be expressed in terms of Eq. (3) for the redistribution reaction, where E is an end group and M is a middle group:

$$EM_{x-2}E + EM_{y-2}E = EM_{x+z-2}E + EM_{y-z-2}E \qquad (3)$$

where x is the number of building units in one of the reacting molecules and y is the number in the other, with z middle groups being transferred from the molecule containing y units to that containing x units. For large molecules (i.e., $z < x, y \gg 1$) the Flory random-reorganization size-distribution corresponds to an equilibrium constant of unity for Eq. (3). Presumably, more complicated equations involving branch structural units could be set up and equilibrium constants determined from the appropriate size-distribution functions (*38*). This would mean that the entire reorganization process could be expressed in terms of equilibrium constants.

The Flory size distribution for chain molecules (*29*) makes no assumption about molecular geometry and, hence, refers to randomly coiled structures. For ionized species, another distribution function can be derived on the assumption that each molecule-ion is a rigid rod and that rods of a given size are randomly oriented in space (*76*). Although the flexible-chain distribution due to Flory is a relatively straightforward mathematical expression, the rigid-rod distribution function is not and is best solved by use of a computer. The more complicated problems of rings coexisting with chains and of the involved structures that are obtained from inclusion of branching points also are handled best with a computer (*129*).

II. Chain Polymers

A considerable body of literature (*1, 116*) demonstrates that rubberlike elasticity (otherwise known as high elasticity) is a property of primarily amorphous substances (elastomers) consisting of long-chain molecules which are only occasionally crosslinked and are not otherwise bound together by charge interactions or secondary bonds. The moderately low elastic moduli as well as the extremely high degree of deformation without rupture of such substances are due to entropy effects, i.e., the thermal "wreathing" motion of the relatively freely moving chains.

A certain amount of crosslinking is desirable in an elastomer in order to reduce or prevent plastic flow. However, as crosslinking is increased, the deformation at break of the elastomer is reduced while the shear modulus concomitantly increases. Thus, upon crosslinking natural rubber by vulcanization with sulfur, it is found that a small amount of crosslinking eliminates the cold flow and stickiness (due to chain entanglement) of the latex. Somewhat further vulcanization leads to a crumbly rubber, such as in art-gum erasers, which is bouncy and otherwise exhibits obvious elastic properties but cannot be stretched much as compared to a lesser vulcanized rubber, as in a rubber band. Finally, continued crosslinking with sulfur leads to hard rubbers that exhibit mechanical properties not too different from those of steel and glass. The Young's modulus of rubber having only occasional crosslinking through sulfur (as in a rubber band) is around 10^4 dynes/cm^2, whereas, for a typical hard rubber, it is around 10^9 dynes/cm^2.

Chain polymers can crystallize; and elastomers generally show an increasing degree of crystallinity with increasing deformation. The synthetic organic chain polymers that exhibit considerable crystallinity when unstretched are somewhat brittle and do not show high elasticity (*114*). According to theory, high elasticity should not be found for amorphous substances in which molecular chains are strongly attracted to each other by charge interactions or by secondary chemical bonds. The effect of ionization along a molecular chain is exemplified by the salts of organic polyelectrolytes with the ions of multiply charged metals and the inosilicates (*71*), which are rigid and rocklike and do not show elastomeric properties because of the effective multiple crosslinking of the chains by the Coulombic forces between anions and cations.

None of the elastomeric phosphorus-based chain polymers discussed below exhibit good hydrolytic and thermal stabilities. This does not mean that phosphorus-based elastomers and inorganic plastics cannot be developed so as to have such stability. The problem is one of synthesis. The chain polymers described below are those that can be readily synthesized by ligand-interchange reactions—the very same type of reactions that lead to hydrolytic and thermal instability.

A. Families of Compounds Involving Un-ionized Chains

1. *Polymeric Phosphonitrilic Chlorides* (*75*)

Probably the most publicized of all inorganic polymers are the high molecular weight phosphonitrilic chlorides, which are known as "inorganic rubber." These materials, as generally prepared, exhibit high elasticity and may be stretched severalfold with almost complete recovery. They have not found commercial application because they undergo degradation under normal atmospheric conditions more rapidly than do the commercial organic rubbers (both natural and synthetic), and they are about as susceptible to degradation by heating as is natural rubber.

Of the various preparative methods (*3*) described for the phosphonitrilic chlorides, the most common involves the ammonolysis of phosphorus pentachloride by ammonium chloride, according to Eq. (4):

$$x \text{ PCl}_5 + x \text{ NH}_4\text{Cl} \rightarrow (\text{PNCl}_2)_x + 4x \text{ HCl} \qquad (4)$$

This reaction may be carried out in a refluxing solvent, such as *sym*-tetrachloroethane, or a mixture of the solids may be heated in vented tubes. The resulting product, depending on how the reaction is carried out, is a mixture of oil and crystals or a buttery mass containing some crystalline material. By differential solubility, fractions of various molecular weights can be obtained.

All of the lower phosphonitrilic chlorides polymerize upon heating to 250–350°C (*102*). However, when the starting materials have been carefully purified, the reaction is slow. As the elastomeric high polymer is normally prepared, it retains small amounts of the lower cyclic polymers which may be removed by extraction with benzene (*28*). The benzene causes the high polymer to swell and gelatinize; but, upon evaporation of the benzene, the original rubber-like properties of the PNCl_2 polymer are recovered.

The polymerization of the trimer and the tetramer has been studied (*78, 79, 91*) both in bulk and in solution. In bulk polymerization most of the product is insoluble, with the proportion of insolubles increasing at high temperatures (in the range between 250° and 350°C.) and longer conversion periods. In this case, the soluble part exhibited a very low degree of polymerization of 3 to 7. Solution polymerization cannot be carried out in solvents containing hydrogen (e.g., benzene, xylene, and hexane), since there is reaction with the solvent to give organophosphorus compounds plus hydrogen chloride. Chlorinated hydrocarbons, especially carbon tetrachloride, are suitable solvents. Polymerization in solution gives considerably less insoluble material than does bulk polymerization, with degrees of polymerization up to 300 being reached in the soluble part. In both bulk and solution polymerization, the same results were obtained when $(\text{PNCl}_2)_3$ or $(\text{PNCl}_2)_4$ was used as starting material. Polymerization proceeds by a chain reaction in which oxygen plays an important role. Indeed, when oxygen is excluded, polymerization does not occur. In the presence of oxygen, the rate increases with O_2 concentration up to a limiting value of about 1% O_2 and then decreases slightly. Oxygen apparently initiates the polymerization by reacting with the trimer or tetramer ring, thereby breaking the ring and producing a radical. Oxygen apparently also plays the role of a chain terminator and a crosslinking agent. Polymerization-depolymerization equilibrium is not readily achieved at temperatures lower than 250°C; and the kinetic chain length has been calculated (*79*) to be up to 1000 times larger than that determined from the average degree of polymerization, as would be expected in a mechanism involving chain transfer. The kinetic study by Patat and Kollinsky indicates that the polymerization of phosphonitrilic chlorides is of the normal type commonly observed in organic polymer chemistry.

Some of the ways that oxygen can act as a chain terminator and crosslinking agent are shown in electronic structure (5).

$$
\begin{array}{ccccccccccccc}
& \overset{..}{} & & \overset{..}{} & & \overset{..}{} & & \overset{..}{} & & \overset{..}{} & & \overset{..}{} & \\
& :Cl: & & :Cl: & & :Cl: & & :Cl: & & :Cl: & & :Cl: & \\
\overset{..}{} & & \overset{..}{} & & \overset{..}{} & & \overset{..}{} & & \overset{..}{} & & \overset{..}{} & & \overset{..}{} \\
Ⓐ :Cl: & P & :N: & P & :N: & P & :N: & P & :N: & P & :N: & P & :O: Ⓒ \\
\overset{..}{} & & \overset{..}{} & & \overset{..}{} & & \overset{..}{} & & \overset{..}{} & & \overset{..}{} & & \overset{..}{} \\
& :Cl: & Ⓑ :O: & & :Cl: & & :Cl: & & :Cl: & & :Cl: & \\
& \overset{..}{} & & \overset{..}{} & & \overset{..}{} & & \overset{..}{} & & \overset{..}{} & \\
\end{array}
$$

$$
\text{etc.—N} : P : \text{N— etc.}
$$

$$
:Cl:
$$

(5)

In this representation, the terminal chlorine at Ⓐ came from that part of the chain where the crosslinking oxygen, Ⓑ, now shares electrons with the phosphorus. The terminal oxygen, Ⓒ, at the other end of the chain takes the place of a nitrogen atom. According to the role oxygen must play as a chain terminator, it is to be expected that scission of rings will lead to very long chains so that a partially polymerized mixture will consist of rings and long chains without much in the way of short chains—which, indeed, would have chemical compositions quite different from $(PNCl_2)_x$.

The same conclusion, that the chains must be long, is reached if end groups other than oxygen are assumed (even free-radical end groups). It has been shown with some of the lower polymers that PCl_5 can donate end groups to the polymer chains of phosphonitrilic chlorides (*75*). Indeed, there is a series of compounds of the formula $(PNCl_2)_n \cdot PCl_5$ which are logically formulated as chain structures having the formula, $Cl_4P(NPCl_2)_n \cdot Cl$. It is also believed that HCl can furnish end groups to the $PNCl_2$ polymers (*6*). A possible formulation for a chain polymer incorporating hydrogen chloride in the terminal groups is $Cl_3P(NPCl_2)_nNH$.

The molecular weight of the polymerized phosphonitrilic chlorides can be obtained directly from osmotic pressure measurements and indirectly from intrinsic viscosity. The experimentally determined relationship between the intrinsic viscosity and the number-average molecular weight (*79*), obtained from osmotic pressure, is shown in Fig. 4. Solubility frac-

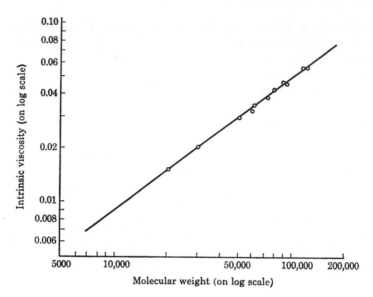

F<small>IG</small>. 4. Relationship of intrinsic viscosity (limiting viscosity number) to the molecular weight of polymeric phosphonitrilic chlorides. The molecular weight was obtained from osmotic data, and both viscosity and osmotic pressure measurements were carried out in the same solvent. [From Van Wazer (*117*).]

tionation of the polymers can be carried out from benzene solution by the stepwise addition of gasoline.

X-ray studies of the elastomeric form of phosphonitrilic chloride indicate that the unstretched material is amorphous but that, upon stretching, it crystallizes to give a fiber diagram (*42, 70*). This behavior is similar to that of rubber and other well-known organic elastomers. Theoretical interpretation of the fiber diagram indicates that there are long spiral chains having the configuration shown in Fig. 5.

The amount of viscous flow in properly prepared fibers of elastomeric phosphonitrilic chlorides is very small, even when the fiber is extended by a factor of 2 or more. Thus the extension was found to be completely reversible (*99*), within a small experimental error, when fibers were stretched to 199% of their original length under a stress of 1 kg/cm² applied for a minute. Such completely elastic behavior was observed throughout the wide temperature range 50–160°C. For periods of extension longer than 75 sec at 1 kg/cm², the fibers did not quite shorten back to their original length, so that a small amount of viscous flow could be detected. However, at room temperature, the deformation is completely reversible even after a period of several hours at moderate extension.

It is interesting to note that phosphonitrilic chloride meets the requirements of an ideal elastomer, based on a stable molecular network, even better than slightly vulcanized, high-grade natural rubber. According to the theory of high elasticity (*1, 116*), the modulus of elasticity should be proportional to the absolute temperature. On one sample of elastomeric phosphonitrilic chloride, Young's modulus was found to be 2.5 kg/cm² at 313°K and 3.2 kg/cm² at 413°K. Superimposed upon this behavior is the reversible crystallization within the structure. Thus, when the polymer is heated under constant deformation (*42, 70*), the stress increases to a degree that is more than proportional to the absolute temperature. On cooling, the tension remains at first higher than it was originally at the lower temperature and then finally decreases to the original value. This is attributed to: (1) "melting" of the crystalline portions as the temperature is raised, with the molten portion then contributing to the stress, and (2) delayed crystallization on cooling. According to the theory of high elasticity, the tendency to contract is produced through thermal agitation of long segments of the flexible chain (the so-called "lattice arcs") in the amorphous portions of the solid. The thermodynamically preferred condition is the relaxed state in which the chains are greatly disoriented and the solid is thus amorphous, instead of the stretched state corresponding to a portion of the chains being so well oriented as to be "crystallized."

From the commonly observed elastic modulus of 2×10^6 dynes/cm² at 25°C, it is estimated (*99*) that the average number of atoms lying between juncture points in the elastic network is approximately 10^8. The lattice-arc length is probably very many times less than the degree of polymerization of a $PNCl_2$ chain in inorganic rubber.

When highly elastic samples of inorganic rubber are stored in the absence of air, there is no change in their elastic properties. However, storage in air results in a considerable increase in the elastic modulus and in the brittleness of the samples, even after a few months. This is explained by the action of water in forming oxygen bridges from chain to chain [Eq. (6)]

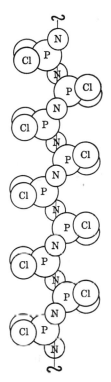

Fig. 5. A stretched chain in a $PNCl_2$ elastomer. The top view, down the axis of the chain, appears as a

$$\begin{array}{ccc} Cl & N & Cl \\ & \diagdown \diagup \diagup \diagdown & \\ & P \qquad P & \\ & \diagup \diagdown \diagdown \diagup & \\ Cl & N & Cl \end{array}$$

rectangle. [From Van Wazer (*117*).]

so as to cause a considerable decrease in the average lattice-arc length, with a concomitant increase in the modulus of elasticity (*99*).

$$
\begin{array}{cc}
\text{Cl} & \text{Cl} \\
\text{—P—N—P—N—} \\
\text{Cl} & \text{Cl}
\end{array}
\qquad
\begin{array}{cc}
\text{Cl} & \text{Cl} \\
\text{—P—N—P—N—} \\
\text{Cl} & |
\end{array}
$$

$$+ \text{H}_2\text{O} \rightarrow \qquad \text{O} \qquad + 2\ \text{HCl} \qquad\qquad (6)$$

$$
\begin{array}{cc}
\text{Cl} & \text{Cl} \\
\text{—P—N—P—N—} \\
\text{Cl} & \text{Cl}
\end{array}
\qquad
\begin{array}{cc}
\text{Cl} & | \\
\text{—P—N—P—N—} \\
\text{Cl} & \text{Cl}
\end{array}
$$

Much more extensive crosslinking of the polymer can be obtained by slowly heating it to a red heat in the presence of some air. In this case, the product is a porous, horny mass. Presumably, the action of heat accelerates oxidation (with some hydrolysis as well), causing partial decomposition, which also results in crosslinking. If heating in an inert atmosphere or vacuum at temperatures above 350°C is properly carried out, the elastomeric form of PNCl₂ can be rather well depolymerized to give a mixture of the lower polymers, predominantly the cyclic trimer and tetramer. On the other hand, slow heating of the polymer to elevated temperatures (around 500°C) in an inert atmosphere leads to quantities of a black, insoluble, infusible residue. In their general behavior upon being heated in an inert atmosphere or a vacuum, the elastomeric phosphonitrilic chlorides are quite similar to the natural rubbers.

Apparently, an equilibrium can be set up between the various polymers of PNCl₂. This equilibrium has been demonstrated in a preliminary fashion since the "same" mixture of polymers including the cyclic trimer and tetramer and higher crystalline and liquid species were obtained by starting with the pure trimer, pure tetramer, or the elastomeric modification (*94*). Since the high-polymer fraction appeared to decrease as the temperature was raised in the region of 600°C, it seems that the polymerization process is exothermic. Further work involving the use of modern techniques such as nuclear magnetic resonance is surely needed on the problem of equilibration between chains and rings.

There is some literature (*75*) on phosphonitrilic fluorides and the mixed chlorofluorides. The chlorofluoride high polymers are stable at room temperature but thermal depolymerization at atmospheric pressure occurs at lower temperatures than with the straight chlorides. Various derivatives of the phosphonitrilic chlorides have been studied recently (*33a, 98a*).

2. Polyphosphoryl Chlorides (*39*)

Although there is a paucity of literature on the chemical family of polyphosphoryl chlorides, they are worthy of inclusion in this chapter because they represent "short" (i.e., crosslinked) elastomeric polymers based on phosphorus. They are highly reactive compounds that combine immediately with the moisture in the atmosphere. However, they are of considerable theoretical interest not only because of their physical properties but because the ligand-interchange reactions between structural building units observed for them correspond reasonably closely to randomness, as described in Section I,A,1.

The simplest way to prepare polyphosphoryl chlorides is by combining the proper proportion of orthophosphoryl chloride with phosphorus pentoxide, according to reaction (7), in which the formula of the product corresponds to ring-free structures:

$$(n + 2) \text{OPCl}_3 + (n - 1) \text{P}_2\text{O}_5 \rightarrow 3\text{P}_n\text{O}_{2n-1}\text{Cl}_{n+2} \tag{7}$$

The distribution of ends, middles, and branches in the equilibrium preparations is shown in Fig. 3. Exploratory studies using a thermal diffusion column coupled with analysis of the fine structure of the P^{31} nuclear-magnetic-resonance spectra of the resulting fractions indicates, at least to a first approximation, the ends, middles, and branches are randomly sorted between molecular structures so that the macromolecules are essentially all highly branched.

The change in viscosity with composition of the equilibrium polyphosphoryl chlorides is shown in Fig. 6. At $R = 1.1$, where the viscosity approaches infinity, the material is a clear amorphous mass exhibiting physical properties similar to those of a 20% gelatin gel at room temperature. This phosphoryl chloride composition is quite elastic and can be flexed considerably without breaking. When squeezed too hard between the fingers, it ruptures to give small pieces such as are obtained by crushing an art-gum eraser. The elastic modulus of the mass is estimated to be around 10^4 to 10^6 dynes/cm².

One of the better methods for estimating the gel point is study of the flow properties of the composition, since the wall-to-wall structure occurring beyond the gel point cannot flow, i.e., it has an infinite viscosity. According to this criterion, the true gel point of the equilibrium system of polyphosphoryl chlorides occurs around $R = 1.1$, at which point there are only 0.88 end groups per branch instead of the value of 3.0 corresponding to random sorting, with no rings. This means that there are many molecular structures containing rings. Of course, ring structures are to be expected, and there may be an appreciable number of conjugated rings because the relative proportion of branch groups is significant above $R = 2.5$. At present, the mathematics describing the gel point in the case in which there are conjugated rings is unclear; however, it seems reasonable to conclude that the shift in gel point from the calculated value of $R = 1.7$ to the

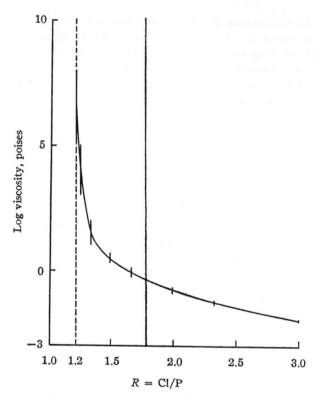

FIG. 6. Viscosity of randomly reorganized phosphoryl chloride compositions at 25°. The broken perpendicular line corresponds to the observed gel point, and the solid perpendicular line to the theoretical gel point assuming no rings.

true value of $R = 1.1$ is due primarily to ring formation and not to non-random sorting of structure building units.

The polyphosphoryl chlorides are strongly acidic, being rather similar in properties to the chlorides of organic acids—such as acetyl chloride. In air, they give off fumes of hydrochloric acid due to reaction with moisture. They are good chlorinating agents for organic reactions and may find commercial use in this area. Presumably, in such an application, the appropriate proportions of $POCl_3$ and P_2O_5 would be combined by the user in the vessel used for chlorination so that the polyphosphoryl chlorides will not be manufactured for sale.

3. Polyphosphoryldimethylamides (97)

Although there is only one paper concerned with the chemical family of polyphosphoryldimethyamides (including the macromolecular structures), this family of compounds is briefly reviewed here because it exemplifies structural reorganization polymers exhibiting different equilibria between the structure building-units and greater stability than the polyphosphoryl chlorides. Preparation of the polyphosphoryldimethylamides is similar to that of the polyphosphoryl chlorides since the monophosphorus compound, hexamethylphosphorylamide, $OP[N(CH_3)_2]_3$, is combined with the desired proportion of phosphorus pentoxide. Equilibrium is achieved by heating the mixture for several minutes at 160–180°C. Equation (8) is for the preparation of ring-free structures in this system:

$$(n + 2)OP[N(CH_3)_2]_3 + (n - 1)P_2O_5 \rightarrow 3P_nO_{2n-1}[N(CH_3)_2]_{n+2} \qquad (8)$$

Equilibrium between structure building units is graphically presented in Fig. 7, in which it should be noted that the distribution is quite far from random, with the middles and ends being present in excessively large amounts. The calculated equilibrium constants for change of functionality

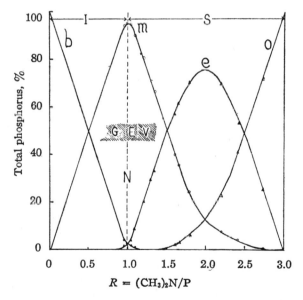

FIG. 7. Distribution of structure building units in the system $[(CH_3)_2N]_3PO-P_2O_5$ at 158°. The symbol o stands for the ortho compound (hexamethylphosphorylamide); e for end groups; m for middle groups; and b for branching groups. For values of $R <$ about 1.05, infinite network polymers should exist. V stands for the range of R values in which the system exhibits high viscosities at room temperature, E for the region of rubberlike elasticities; and G for the glassy region (down to $R = 0$). The composition range denoted by S corresponds to solubility in hot carbon tetrachloride. I stands for insolubility in this solvent. N is the gel-point transition.

between structure units are as follows:

$$K_1 = e \cdot b/m^2 = (6 \pm 2) \times 10^{-4} \qquad (9)$$

$$K_2 = o \cdot m/e^2 = (2.6 \pm 0.3) \times 10^{-2} \qquad (10)$$

As in Fig. 3, the perpendicular line corresponds to the gel point.

Because of the nonrandom distribution of structure-building units, there is a region between $R = (CH_3)_2N/P = 1.4$ and $R = 1.2$ where there are essentially only end and middle structure-building units, so that essentially only straight-chain homologs (such as shown below) are found:

$$\begin{matrix} & O & & O & & O & & O & & O & \\ (CH_3)_2NP & -O-P & -O-P & -O-P & -O-P- & \quad etc. \\ & N & & N & & N & & N & & N & \\ & (CH_3)_2 & & (CH_3)_2 & & (CH_3)_2 & & (CH_3)_2 & & (CH_3)_2 & \end{matrix} \qquad (11)$$

The highest number-average number of phosphorus atoms per chain in this region is about 10. For larger molecules, there is chain branching and crosslinking due to the presence of increasing amounts of branched structural units. Flory-type distribution calculations for an R value of 1.2 (average chain length of 9.78) leads to an estimation of 0.4% of the total phosphorus in straight chains containing 50 or more phosphorus atoms.

The physical properties of the equilibrium reorganized material is of considerable interest. For values of $R = (CH_3)_2N/P$ lying between 3 and 1.5, the mixtures are all relatively fluid. From $R = 1.5$ to $R = 1.3$, there is a noticeable increase in viscosity, which then rises rapidly as R drops from 1.3 to 1.1. At $R = 1.1$, the material exhibits a rubbery appearance and, as R decreases to 0.95, the properties change in the same way as do those of rubber with increased vulcanization. From $R = 0.95$ to $R = 0.70$, and presumably all the way to $R = 0$, the reorganization mixtures are hard and glassy. The transition between the viscous and rubber-like behavior at room temperature is found, within experimental error, to occur at the R value corresponding to the gel point with no rings. This indicates that there are not many rings in the infinite macromolecule occurring at the gel point.

In the range of $0.97 < R < 3$, all reorganization mixtures were found to dissolve in carbon tetrachloride within a few minutes at 100°C. without appreciable reorganization between structural building units being detected by nuclear magnetic resonance. Below the value of $R = 0.97$, complete dissolution could not be achieved. This suggests that the true gel point is at $R = 0.98$ instead of $R = 1.1$ so that there will be a few rings at the gel point.

By using acetone as the precipitant, a freshly prepared aqueous solution of a reorganization mixture for which $R = 0.98$ was fractionated. The average molecular weight obtained by light scattering immediately after dissolution corresponded to 510 phosphorus atoms per molecule. After rapid fractionation, the molecular species were distributed so that the first fraction, which consisted of 22% of the total phosphorus, corresponded to an average molecule based on 800 phosphorus atoms. The second fraction (36% of the total P) corresponded to 610 phosphorus atoms per molecule, the third fraction (16%) to 390 P/molecule, and the residuum (26%) to 134 P/molecule. Since 95.0% of the total phosphorus was present as middle groups, 3.5% as branches, and about 1.5% as end groups in the fractionated mixture before dissolution, the average molecular weight should have been infinity, assuming no rings. The observed value of 510 indicates that about half of the branch points hydrolyzed upon dissolution, if there were no rings, or that the unreasonably large amount of more than ca. 10% of the total phosphorus is involved in rings.

As indicated in the preceding paragraph, branch groups in polyphosphoryldimethylamide molecules are very susceptible to hydrolysis. However, electrical conductivity measurements showed that compositions not containing branch points did not react immediately with water at room temperature or below. Studies on hydrolysis in acidic solution indicate that the P—N bonds hydrolyze somewhat faster than do the P—O—P linkages. It is also interesting to note that rings form concomitantly with P—O—P scission in the hydrolysis of long-chain polyphosphoryldimethylamides. Presumably this ring formation is independent of hydrolytic scission since rings are also formed in carbon tetrachloride, where solvolysis does not occur.

When concentrated (about 30%) solutions of the high-molecular-weight reorganization-equilibrium mixtures exhibiting R values near unity are prepared in carbon tetrachloride by heating at 100° for several hours, they start depositing crystals of the trimeta compound after standing for a day at room temperature. The crystals continue to form for a period of 2 weeks. On the other hand, when dissolution is effected by heating for only 5 min at 100°, no crystals appear upon standing for 2 weeks at room temperature. According to light-scattering measurements, these results are to be interpreted in terms of reorganization in hot carbon tetrachloride of long chains (with or without a small amount of branching) to rings and much shorter chains. Since the trimeta ring compound exhibits moderately low solubility in carbon tetrachloride—with the solubility, perhaps, even being reduced by the presence of chain compounds—crystals are found to form. These results are in accord with the well-known idea that rings are favored in dilute solution. Presumably, the production of rings during hydrolysis is closely related to the formation of rings in carbon tetrachloride.

4. Polyphosphate and Thiopolyphosphate Esters (98)

Another un-ionized family of phosphoryl compounds related to the polyphosphoryl chlorides and the polyphosphoryldimethylamides consists of the esters of the polyphosphoric acids. These compounds are most readily prepared by combining the desired proportions of the monophosphorus compound, trialkylphosphate, $(RO)_3PO$, with phosphorus pentoxide. At 110°C, equilibrium appears to be achieved in a matter of a few hours. Indeed, it occurs immediately upon dissolution of the phosphorus pentoxide in the liquid phase. The curve of the distribution of structural building units is shown in Fig. 8.

By combining trialkyl tetrathioorthophosphate with various proportions of phosphorus pentasulfide, the completely sulfur-substituted analogs of the polyphosphoric esters are obtained. Again, equilibrium seems to be achieved immediately upon formation of a single fluid phase, this time by dissolution of the P_2S_5. As shown in Fig. 8, the end groups are present in

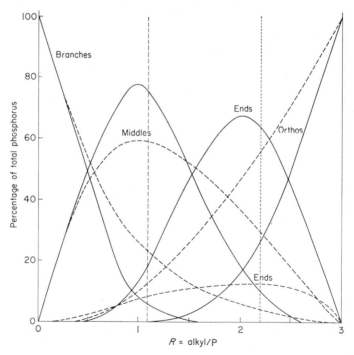

FIG. 8. Distribution of structure building units as a function of composition for the alkyl polyphosphate esters (—) and for the alkyl thiopolyphosphate esters in which all oxygens are substituted by sulfur atoms (---). If we assume no rings, the gel point for the oxygen-based esters comes at $R = 1.1$, whereas, for the completely sulfur-substituted esters, the gel point occurs at $R = 2.2$.

equilibrium in this system in much lesser amounts than would be expected for the ideal random case.

For the ethyl phosphate esters without sulfur: $K_1 = e \cdot b/m^2 = 0.02$ and $K_2 = o \cdot m/e^2 = 0.06$, whereas, for the butyl thiophosphate esters in which all oxygens are substituted by sulfur atoms, $K_1 = 0.06$ and $K_2 = 12$. The difference in K values is not attributable to the substitution of ethyl by butyl since exploratory experiments indicate that all of the short chain alkyl radicals give approximately the same equilibrium constants in the oxygen-based ester system.

It should be noted in Fig. 8 that the gel point calculated for the ring-free oxygen-based esters come at $R = 1.1$, whereas, for the completely sulfur-substituted esters, the gel point, assuming no rings, occurs at $R = 2.2$. Moreover, the completely sulfur-substituted esters apparently represent a much more labile system, in that reorganization involving exchange of functionality between structure-building units seems to progress quite rapidly at room temperature.

B. Families of Compounds Exhibiting Chain Polyanions

1. Vitreous Polyphosphates

Probably the best characterized of all chemical families of phosphorus compounds is the family of sodium polyphosphates. These materials (especially the sodium phosphate glasses) have been the subject of very extensive studies, using the various methods of polymer physics (*15*, *131*) to characterize them. Indeed, the molecular constitution of the sodium phosphate glasses may be as well characterized as that of any of the homologous series occurring in organic chemistry! The polyphosphate anions in these glasses can be confined to only long straight chains. When sodium is the cation occurring with the long-chain polyphosphate anions, the glass is known as Graham's salt.

Vitreous sodium phosphates can be readily prepared for R values less than 1.7 by heating chosen proportions of phosphorus pentoxide with either anhydrous tetrasodium pyrophosphate, $Na_4P_2O_7$, or trisodium orthophosphate, Na_3PO_4. Glasses for which $1.7 > R >$ about 0.9 also may be made by heating together such reagents as sodium carbonate and phosphoric acid, as indicated by Eq. (12) for the straight-chain sodium phosphates:

$$(n+2)Na_2CO_3 + 2n\ H_3PO_4 \xrightarrow{\Delta} 2Na_{n+2}P_nO_{3n+1} + (n+2)CO_2\uparrow + 3n\ H_2O\uparrow \quad (12)$$

A curve showing the distribution of structure-building units for the sodium phosphate glasses is presented in Fig. 9. It should be noted that in this

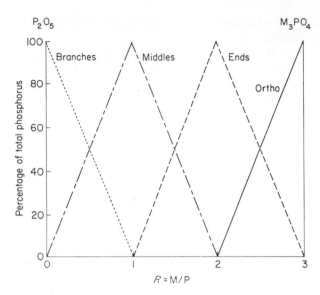

Fig. 9. Distribution of structure-building units as a function of composition in a glass obtained by quenching a melt of an alkali metal phosphate, especially in the $Na_2O-P_2O_5$ system where $M = Na$.

case K_1 and K_2 are extremely small. From work carried out at R values extremely close to unity, it appears that $K_1 \approx 10^{-5}$. From the data obtained at larger R values, it is estimated that $K_2 < 10^{-3}$. When K_1 and K_2 are extremely small, only straight chain molecule-ions will be obtained for R values greater than unity. The longest chains should be obtained for R exactly equal to one (Graham's salt); but, in this region, traces of moisture act very effectively as chain breakers. This is shown by Fig. 10. However, by cycling a metaphosphate melt (metaphosphates are those compositions for which $R = 1$) above and below the liquidus region a number of times over a period of several days and finally quenching the melt from a temperature of around 700° by pouring it onto copper chill plates, a vitreous sodium phosphate can be obtained which averages around 200 phosphorus atoms per anion. On a few occasions when all of the factors were exactly right, as great a number-average chain length as 500 phosphorus atoms per anion was achieved in the vitreous sodium phosphates.

The size distribution of anionic chains in the glasses of high average molecular weight can be obtained by solubility fractionation (*122*). A typical example is shown in Fig. 11. For the shorter chains, paper chromatography gives quantitative separations and, with a two-dimensional chromatogram, individual rings as well as chains may be estimated. Some chromatographic data for the sodium phosphates are given in Fig. 12.

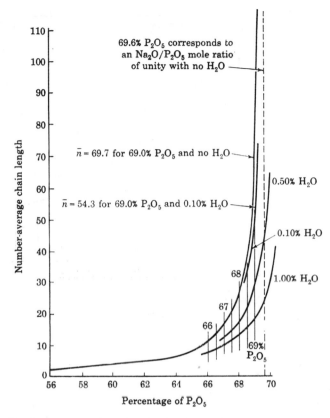

FIG. 10. Number-average chain length of sodium phosphate glasses as a function of P_2O_5 and water content, assuming only chains with no rings, ortho, or branching points. [From Van Wazer (*117*).]

In addition to the chains, there is a small amount of simple ring structures. Thus, a freshly dissolved vitreous sodium phosphate having an average chain length of 100 to 125 phosphorus atoms exhibited about 4% of the total phosphorus as the ring composed of three middle groups (six atoms in all with three phosphorus atoms alternating with three oxygens), 2.5% as the ring consisting of four middle groups, and 0.8% as the ring consisting of five middle groups, with decreasing amounts of the larger rings (*125*). In a very elegant investigation, Strauss *et al.* (*104*, *105*) showed that, for long-chain glasses exhibiting a number-average of several hundred phosphorus atoms per anion, approximately one out of every thousand phosphorus atoms is a branching unit. Although this amount of crosslinking is so small that it cannot be picked up by the usual analytical techniques, it has a pronounced effect on the intrinsic viscosity (*63*), as

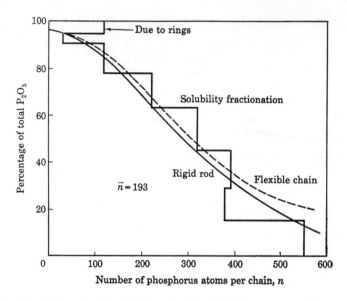

FIG. 11. Cumulative size distribution of chain phosphates in a sodium phosphate glass at the metaphosphate composition—a Graham's salt. [From Van Wazer (*117*).]

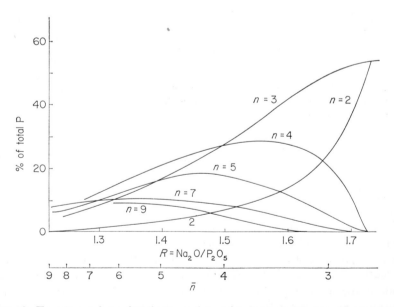

FIG. 12. Experimental size distributions of straight-chain phosphate anions in vitreous sodium phosphates as a function of the Na/P mole ratio. The letter n shows the number of phosphorus atoms in each given chain.

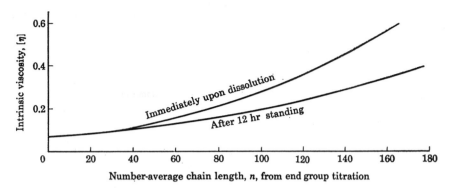

FIG. 13. Hydrolysis at branching points as denoted by the intrinsic viscosity. At $\bar{n}$ = about 50, there are no detectable branches. At $\bar{n}$ = 200, there is about 0.1% of the total phosphorus in branching units. [From Van Wazer (*117*).]

shown in Fig. 13. For the phosphates, it is found that crosslinks are very unstable in neutral aqueous solution, disappearing completely within about 12 hours after the sample is dissolved. It is from this type of data that K_1 for this system is estimated to be around 10^{-5}. It should be noted that straight-chain phosphates are very stable in water at a neutral or alkaline pH.

By methods similar to those used in making the sodium glasses, vitreous lithium, potassium, and calcium phosphates have been prepared. For the short chain glasses ($1.7 > R > 1.2$), measurements using paper chromatography (*131*) have shown a considerable difference between the distribution curves for glasses having different cations, with neither the rigid-rod nor the flexible-chain functions giving a good fit (*119*).

2. Crystalline Metaphosphates

Insoluble crystalline metaphosphates of the alkali metals have been known for over 100 years. As might be expected, the only system in which the alkali metal metaphosphates have been well characterized is the one based on sodium. As is shown in Fig. 14, $NaPO_3$-II, $NaPO_3$-III, and $NaPO_3$-IV are long-chain structures, whereas the other crystalline modifications (the varieties of $NaPO_3$-I) are simple ring structures. The vitrified melt shown in Fig. 14 was discussed previously in Section II,B,1. $NaPO_3$-II and $NaPO_3$-III are known as Maddrell's salt and exhibit an X-ray pattern distinctly different from $NaPO_3$-IV, known as Kurrol's salt. Since much of the literature on these long-chain crystalline phosphates is discussed in terms of Kurrol's and Maddrell's salts, this nomenclature will be used here. Classification of the difficultly soluble metaphosphates into these two

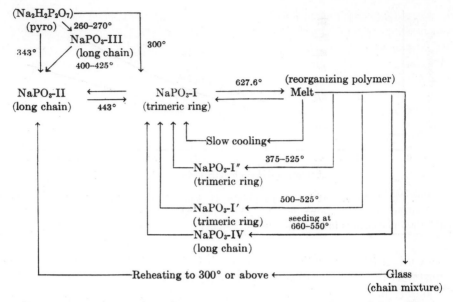

Fig. 14. Transitions in the sodium metaphosphates. It should be noted that all forms can be readily brought to and held at room temperature. Forms I, I′, and I″ all contain the trimetaphosphate ring and easily dissolve to give supposedly identical solutions. Form IV, known as sodium Kurrol's salt, rapidly dissolves in cold salt solutions containing cations other than sodium to give a highly viscous solution. Form III dissolves like form IV in such salt solutions upon warming and form II in such salt solutions upon boiling; both III and II also give viscous solutions. [From Van Wazer (*117*).]

groups has been made on the basis that Maddrell's salts are negligibly soluble in water and saline solutions at room temperature, whereas, Kurrol's salts are negligibly soluble in water but are readily soluble in solutions of salts having other alkali metal cations (*77*). The more modern classification of insoluble metaphosphates as Kurrol's salts has been done by X-ray (*16*). The sodium, potassium, rubidium, cesium, and calcium Kurrol's salts have been found to exhibit the same general powder diffraction pattern. In addition, there appear to be lithium and ammonium versions of this structure.

The difficultly soluble alkali metal metaphosphate that is most readily prepared is potassium Kurrol's salt. It is made by simple thermal dehydration of potassium dihydrogen orthophosphate at temperatures above about 210°C. Unlike the sodium system in which the acid phosphate, $Na_2H_2P_2O_7$, can be made in reasonably pure form by the thermal dehydration of the orthophosphate (see Fig. 14), very little pyrophosphate is generally formed during the dehydration of potassium orthophosphate to Kurrol's salt.

Although a number of different authors have given detailed instructions for making sodium Kurrol's salt, its preparation is still a capricious matter. It is generally necessary to use seed crystals and tempering in order to obtain a reasonable yield of $NaPO_3$-IV, which is usually contaminated with $NaPO_3$-III. Both forms of sodium Maddrell's salt are also rather difficult to obtain reasonably pure. $NaPO_3$-II is generally made by heating monosodium orthophosphate at 400°C in the presence of steam. On the other hand, $NaPO_3$-III is best prepared by heating monosodium orthophosphate in a dry atmosphere at 260°C to give only partial conversion of the intermediate pyrophosphate, $Na_2H_2P_2O_7$, to the metaphosphate and then washing out the excess $Na_2H_2P_2O_7$ with water. The exact conditions of heating are very important in making the various forms of sodium metaphosphate, especially Form III. Water catalyzes the transitions, probably by plasticizing the amorphous-phase intermediates.

a. Dissolution and precipitation. The two varieties of Maddrell's salt, $NaPO_3$-II and $NaPO_3$-III, are, for all practical purposes, insoluble in water, since their rate of dissolution is extremely slow. Thus, at 25°C, Form II dissolves at a rate of 1.8×10^{-2} %/hr when finely powdered, whereas Form III dissolves more rapidly, 0.34 %/hr, under the same conditions (*51*). Both $NaPO_3$-II and $NaPO_3$-III dissolve at a much higher rate in salt solutions based on the ammonium or substituted ammonium ions or alkali metal ions other than sodium. Again, Form III seems to dissolve more rapidly than Form II under the same conditions (*51, 115*). In a solution of lithium chloride—which is especially efficacious in promoting dissolution—Form II dissolves at the rate of 33 %/hr (250°C and a Li/P mole ratio of 1.25), and Form III is all dissolved in a few minutes. Because the rate of dissolution of the Maddrell's salts in pure water is of the same order of magnitude as the rate of hydrolysis of chain phosphates, considerable hydrolysis is to be expected. This is found, because paper chromatograms of the solutions show short chains and rings. However, paper chromatograms of solutions made in aqueous lithium chloride show all nonmoving phosphates (chains or rings exhibiting more than about 10 phosphorus atoms).

$NaPO_3$-IV appears to be somewhat soluble in pure water since, after some days in cold distilled water and after a few hours in hot water, the fibrous crystals swell and become gummy. Eventually they dissolve entirely to give a highly viscous solution. As is the case with the Maddrell's salts, dissolution of sodium Kurrol's salt is greatly speeded up by the presence of salts having cations (especially Li+) other than sodium which do not precipitate phosphates. Potassium Kurrol's salt behaves very similarly to sodium Kurrol's salt in that most preparations dissolve at a very slow rate in distilled water. However, some preparations appear to be more stable than others, since some finely ground asbestos-like fibers of potassium Kurrol's salt have shown no sign of becoming gummy after standing for about a week in distilled water at room temperature. On the other hand, potassium Kurrol's salt dissolves very rapidly in dilute solutions of salts of singly charged cations other than potassium.

The literature concerned with the dissolution of the difficultly soluble alkali metal metaphosphates indicates that the process of dissolution in solutions of simple salts containing cations other than the one appearing in the metaphosphate is an ion-exchange process. It appears that dissolution of the long chains is effected by substitution of a different sized ion in the crystal lattice of the difficultly soluble metaphosphate, so that the long chain anions in these salts are effectively "pried out" of the lattice. This process of dissolution can be extremely fast. Thus, when a finely ground sample of potassium Kurrol's salt having an average chain length of about 500 phosphorus atoms is added to a 0.2 N solution of sodium chloride which is being stirred violently in a Waring Blendor, a 1–5% viscous solution (in which there are no obvious signs of density, inhomogeneities, or undissolved particles) can be produced within several seconds after addition of the phosphate. An interesting example of the ion-exchange type of dissolution is found in mixtures of potassium Kurrol's salt with any of the crude insoluble sodium metaphosphates. These mixtures are found to dissolve at a reasonable, and continuously accelerating, rate in distilled water under conditions in which either of the insoluble materials will not dissolve by themselves. Apparently small amounts of the soluble phosphates present initiate the process by acting on the insoluble phosphate having the other cation.

An excess of singly charged cations other than the one appearing in the insoluble metaphosphate or the low molecular weight quaternary ammonium ions causes the formation of a gelatinous mass instead of a viscous solution. Likewise, the viscous solutions made by dissolving these phosphates in dilute salt solutions can be caused to precipitate a highly viscous, rather rubbery mass by adding additional salt or by adding organic materials soluble in water, such as alcohol or acetone. As might be expected, this salting out is a function of the chain length of the dissolved phosphate and also depends on the exact nature of the salting-out agent. By using relatively insoluble metaphosphates having high-molecular-weight anions, very rubbery masses can be prepared by alternately kneading and then washing the amorphous precipitate with a concentrated salt solution or an organic material, such as alcohol or acetone. Although the salting-out process has not been carefully studied, Malmgren (*65*) has shown that, for a given sample of potassium Kurrol's salt at 20°C, concentrations at which precipitation begins are 0.42 N for NaCNS, 0.90 N for Na_2SO_4, and 0.72 N for $Na_3P_3O_9$, whereas a saturated solution of $Na_4P_2O_7$ (0.82 N) does not salt out the metaphosphate.

Discussions of "double-salt formation" that appear in the very early literature on the condensed phosphates gave proximate analyses of these amorphous precipitates. It appears that various amounts of different cations can be found in the precipitates, depending on the composition of the solution from which the precipitate was formed. Thus, the action of different concentrations of ammonium chloride for various lengths of time (with the ammonium chloride concentration being great enough to cause precipitation of the phosphate) on potassium Kurrol's salt can give a whole series of "mixed salts" varying from a relatively pure amorphous potassium phosphate to a relatively pure amorphous ammonium phosphate. A century ago, it was believed that the proximate analysis of these amorphous compositions gave information as to the structure of the anion.

Multiply charged and heavy metal cations give amorphous precipitates in the form of flocculent solids, rather than as high-viscosity fluids. An interesting study by Thilo (*112*) indicates that the amount of various nitrates required to produce a barely permanent precipitate with a given sample of sodium Kurrol's salt is dependent on the size of the cation, as shown in Table I. Undoubtedly, the larger the size of the ion (and probably the greater its charge), the less of the ion is needed to form a precipitate

TABLE I

<small>Precipitating Action of Various Cations on a Kurrol's Salt Solution</small>

Cation [a]	Required to form permanent precipitates		Radius of cation, σ (A)	$\epsilon\sigma^2$
	ml. 0.1 N nitrate soln./ 20 ml Kurrol's soln.	Equiv. of cation/mole $NaPO_3$, ϵ		
Ag^+	20.5	0.896	1.12	1.12
Sr^{2+}	16.4	0.701	1.27	1.13
Pb^{2+}	13.6	0.585	1.35	1.07
Ba^{2+}	12.6	0.540	1.45	1.10
Bi^{2+}	9.4	0.407	?	—

[a] Large cations (Ba^{2+}, Sr^{2+}, Pb^{2+}, Ag^+, Bi^{2+}, ZrO^{2+}, UO_2^{2+}, and Hg_2^{2+}) in excess give flocculent, solid precipitates, whereas smaller cations for which $\sigma < 1.1$ A (Ca^{2+}, Mg^{2+}, Zn^{2+}, Mn^{2+}, Ni^{2+}, Co^{2+}, Fe^{2+}, Fe^{3+}, Cr^{3+}, Hg^{2+}, and Cu^{2+}) give gummy or oily precipitates or turbidity (*9, 16, 17, 87*). The tetramethylammonium ion does not give a precipitate even at high concentrations (*51*).

with a phosphate of a given molecular weight. Conversely, the higher the molecular weight of the phosphate, the less of the salting-out agent is needed to form a precipitate.

b. Molecular structure. The most complete X-ray diffraction study on a difficultly soluble alkali metal metaphosphate has been done (*9, 17, 87*) on rubidium Kurrol's salt, $(RbPO_3)_n$. This structure consists of continuous —P—O—P— chains, running in the direction of the fibrous cleavage and consisting of interconnected PO_4 groups. Each unit cell contains a portion of two different chains which spiral in opposite ways around the screw axes of the crystal, the pattern repeating itself every two phosphorus atoms in the chain, as shown in Fig. 15. Thus, there are four units of

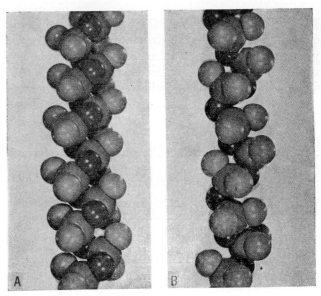

Fig. 15. Portions of the metaphosphate chains running through (A) crystalline rubidium Kurrol's salt and (B) the high temperature form of Maddrell's salt ($NaPO^3$-II). [From Van Wazer (*117*).]

$RbPO_3$ per unit cell. The P—O distances within the chain are 1.62 ± 0.03 A, and the distance between a phosphorus and either one of its pair of isolated oxygen atoms is 1.46 ± 0.05 A. This corresponds to $0.2\ \pi$ bond per σ bond in the chain and $0.9\ \pi$ bond per σ bond leading from the phosphorus to the oxygen atoms not in the chain, so that the over-all amount of two π bonds per phosphorus is unevenly distributed, with the least amount of π character being in the chain-forming bonds. The O—P—O angle between the two isolated oxygen atoms is large (123°) compared to the angle between oxygen atoms in the chain (99.5°). The P—O—P bond angle in the chain is 129°.

It is interesting to note that all of the Kurrol's salts are monoclinic, with two sodium, the rubidium, and the cesium salts exhibiting a $P2_1/n$ space group and the potassium and calcium salts having a $P2_1/a$ space group. The rubidium and cesium salts are isomorphous. It appears that the chains in the cesium and perhaps in the well-known potassium Kurrol's salt exhibit the same configuration as was found for the rubidium salt described above. A preliminary study of one of the forms of sodium Kurrol's salt suggests that the chains repeat every four phosphorus atoms instead of every two, as was found for the rubidium salt.

An X-ray structure study has been carried out ($23, 109$) on the high temperature form of Maddrell's salt, $NaPO_3$-II or "insoluble metaphosphate." According to this work, the Maddrell's salt ($NaPO_3$-II) also consists of long —P—O—P— chains made up of interconnected PO_4 groups. However, the pattern of the chain repeats itself every three units, as shown in Fig. 15, and the chain does not spiral. The structure which is very close to that (13) of β-wollastonite, $CaSiO_3$, can be thought of in terms of a repeating unit of two PO_4 tetrahedra in line with the third tetrahedron placed out of line. The relative placement of the chains in the crystal has been suggested ($23, 109$).

The most careful studies of the molecular constitution of solutions of the difficultly soluble alkali metal metaphosphates have been carried out on potassium Kurrol's salt, probably because of the ease with which this material can be prepared and dissolved. A series of papers from Sweden ($58, 65-67$) report a variety of physicochemical studies on solutions of potassium Kurrol's salts. These studies include measurements by (a) the ultracentrifuge, (b) dialysis, (c) electrophoresis, and (d) dilute solution viscosity in the presence of swamping electrolytes. From this work, it was found that the degree of polymerization of Kurrol's salt depended on the temperature of preparation and the length of time the sample was heated, as shown in Table II.

As can be seen from Table II, the molecular weights of these samples are extremely high, being in the range of 250,000 to several million. Molecular weights determined by the ultracentrifuge are somewhat dependent on the type and concentration of swamping electrolytes. However, the variation is relatively small—being approximately a factor of 2. Although the variation in the calculated degree of polymerization might be attributable to a changing amount of aggregation, it is believed that the effect is probably an artifact introduced by ignoring or imperfectly treating charge interactions in the mathematical interpretation of the data. Present-day studies are unearthing similar anomalies in studies of ionized organic macro-

TABLE II

PHYSICAL DATA ON SOLUTIONS OF KURROL'S SALT PREPARED BY HEATING KH_2PO_4 FOR
VARIOUS PERIODS AT VARIOUS TEMPERATURES [a]

Prepn. temp. (°C)	Time at temp. (hr)	Viscosity [b] in salt soln. (centipoises)	Sedimentation const. S_0 [b] (Svedberg units)	Diffusion const. D [c] (10 cgs units)	Degree of polymerization $\bar{n}$ from equation [d] (zeta av.) (47)
2C0	215–280	1.53	10	1.7	2300
290	120–280	1.93	14	1.4	3900
305	140–190	3.47	26	1.5	6700
382	—	3.47	27	1.0	9300
445	0.5	2.51	—	—	—
445	2.0	3.09	—	—	—
445	4.0	3.36	—	—	—
445	20	4.36	—	—	—
445	115–240	4.60	25	0.6	11,700
495	—	2.60	34	1.2	11,000
665	30–200	4.22	30	0.6	19,500

[a] See references (58), (63), and (65)–(67).

[b] Measurements made on solutions prepared by dissolving 2.36 gm of potassium Kurrol's salt per liter of solution containing 10.2 gm of sodium trimetaphosphate.

[c] Sedimentation and diffusion were studied in a 0.4 M sodium thiocyanate solution.

[d] $M = (s/D)[RT/(1 - V_\rho)]$.

molecules which definitely do not change their degree of polymerization and are not believed to form aggregates.

As described above, the application of the techniques of polymer physics to solutions of potassium Kurrol's salt shows that these materials have extremely high molecular weights. Now the question is whether these are long straight chains—since the metaphosphate composition is a limiting case for the polyphosphates—or whether they are structures containing a considerable number of branching points—since the metaphosphate composition is also a limiting case for certain ultraphosphates. Investigation of the shape of these molecule-ions by flow birefringence (128), anisotropy in electrical conductivity (92, 93), and interpretation of sedimentation and diffusion data in terms of a shape factor (65), all indicate that the molecule-ions are extended rods in aqueous solution which tend to coil up and become less asymmetric on the addition of a swamping electrolyte. Calculation (127) of a chain length from the rotary diffusion constant obtained by flow birefringence agrees quite well with the chain length obtained by intrinsic viscosity. Furthermore, chain lengths obtained from end-group titrations, on the assumption of long straight chains having weakly acidic hydrogens only at the ends, agree reasonably well with the degrees of polymerization obtained by other techniques.

All of this information leads to the conclusion that the usual potassium Kurrol's salt made by dehydrating monopotassium orthophosphate is a straight-chain polyphosphate of a high degree of polymerization. As previously noted, polymerizations ranging from several hundred to several million phosphorus atoms per chain can be obtained by varying the heat treatment of the monopotassium orthophosphate, with higher temperatures and longer heating times resulting in longer chains. As is the case for so many crystalline organic high polymers, the crystal structure is not affected by very large changes in the molecular weight. This is because the individual chains pass through a large number of unit cells and probably terminate at crystal defects and junctures between microcrystallites. For a potassium Kurrol's salt having a molecular weight of 2×10^6, a value at the upper end of the observed range, an average chain will pass through 10^4 unit cells in a crystal! The ultracentrifuge measurements indicate that there is a distribution of molecular sizes, but that the distribution is unusually sharp, as compared to amorphous reorganizing systems involving polymers—systems such as the vitreous polyphosphates.

By varying the K_2O/P_2O_5 mole ratio from values considerably below to values considerably above unity, it is possible to produce a series of potassium Kurrol's salts (*21, 36, 86*), the properties of which point up the chain structure of the Kurrol's salts made by dehydrating potassium orthophosphates for which K_2O/P_2O_5 equals unity. When a potassium orthophosphate mixture containing more than one mole of K_2O to each mole of P_2O_5 is dehydrated, the resulting Kurrol's salt is very similar to the Kurrol's salt made from an orthophosphate for which $K_2O/P_2O_5 = 1$, since the excess potassium remains in the liquid phase and later crystallizes out as $K_5P_3O_{10}$. The viscosity of a salt-free solution of the crude Kurrol's salt formed from a potassium-rich melt decreases with increasing potassium content, but this is due to the tripolyphosphate acting as an added low-molecular-weight electrolyte to cause coiling of the chains. When the $K_5P_3O_{10}$ is washed out of the crushed crude preparation with distilled water, the viscosity of the potassium Kurrol's salt (dissolved by use of an ion-exchange resin) becomes relatively independent of the amount of K_2O in excess of $K_2O/P_2O_5 = 1$ in the original melt. However, for Kurrol's salt preparations made from melts deficient in K_2O, there appears to be crosslinking in freshly prepared solutions. This is demonstrated by a number of different experiments.

The viscosity of salt-free solutions of the crude Kurrol's salt preparations which were dissolved by mixing with Graham's salt ($NaPO_3$ glass)

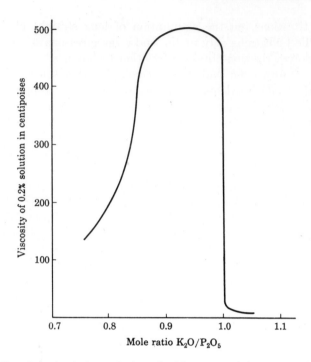

F<small>IG</small>. 16. Viscosity of salt-free solutions freshly prepared from potassium Kurrol's salts exhibiting different K_2O/P_2O_5 ratios. [From Van Wazer (*117*).]

is shown as a function of the K_2O/P_2O_5 mole ratio in Fig. 16. It is seen that the viscosity measured at a 0.2% concentration of the crude Kurrol's salt goes through a maximum at K_2O/P_2O_5 = about 0.9. This effect is attributed to crosslinking in those samples of potassium Kurrol's salt for which K_2O/P_2O_5 is less than unity. The drop in viscosity for K_2O/P_2O_5 ratios greater than unity is attributed to coiling of the chains because of the presence of $K_5P_3O_{10}$.

Added proof that there is crosslinking in these ultraphosphate samples is given by the change in viscosity with time. After keeping a sample of potassium Kurrol's salt for which K_2O/P_2O_5 = 0.99 and another sample for which K_2O/P_2O_5 = 1.01 for one day or longer at pH 8 and 25°C, the viscosity numbers are approximately the same. However, the viscosity number of a freshly prepared solution of the Kurrol's salt for which K_2O/P_2O_5 = 0.99 is more than 10 times higher (at 1% concentration) than the viscosity number of the freshly prepared material having K_2O/P_2O_5 = 1.01. This unusually rapid hydrolysis indicates the presence of branching points in the potassium Kurrol's salt having a deficiency of K_2O.

Because of the preliminary data obtained by X-ray analysis (*23, 109*) and from the small amount of work that has been done on its flow birefringence (*110, 111*) and hydrolysis (*23 109*), it appears that sodium Kurrol's salt contains long, straight-chain molecule-ions, as does potassium Kurrol's salt.

The high viscosity obtained upon dissolving the high temperature form of Maddrell's salt ($NaPO_3$-II) indicates a high-molecular-weight structure for the phosphate molecule-ions in agreement with the X-ray diffraction data. Although the various physical techniques of the solution chemistry of polymers have not been applied to determining the structure of Maddrell's salt, Thilo (*110, 111*) has interpreted some purely chemical data as a proof of the structure of this material. In this work, Thilo made a series of mixed metaarsenatophosphates of which the limiting member on the phosphate side was the high-temperature Maddrell's salt ($NaPO_3$-II). As demonstrated by X-ray diffraction powder diagrams, the crystal structure of the arsenatophosphates appears to be quite similar to the Maddrell's salt. A plot of density versus per cent P_2O_5 and monomeric molecular volume versus per cent P_2O_5 indicated that, for $4 > As_2O_5/P_2O_5$ mole ratio, there is a linear decrease with per cent P_2O_5, and that these linear curves extrapolated in both cases to the measured density or volume for $NaPO_3$-II. As is generally known, the As—O—As and As—O—P bonds hydrolyze immediately upon dissolution of the substance in water, whereas P—O—P bonds not at branching points are extremely stable. Upon dissolving the various metaarsenatophosphates, it was found that all of the arsenic was present in the form of orthoarsenate, and the phosphate appeared as short chains of various lengths. It was then concluded that the arsenatophosphates had long chains in their solid structure, and that this was also the structure of the pure phosphate, Maddrell's salt.

The only structure in the series of metaphosphates known as Maddrell's and Kurrol's salts which has not been shown to be a long chain by some more-or-less acceptable proof is the low-temperature form of Maddrell's salt ($NaPO_3$-III). However, solutions of this material exhibit a relatively high viscosity, which would imply that reasonably high-molecular-weight chains are present. Because of the difficulty in dissolving both forms of Maddrell's salt, the possibility that these materials might represent rings connected by long, straight-chain segments should not yet be completely discounted.

3. Electrical, Mechanical, and Optical Properties of Solutions of Long-Chain Phosphate Salts

The low-molecular-weight phosphates exhibit the properties that might be normally expected from highly charged ions. However, the long-chain phosphates also show properties that depend on their threadlike structure.

For example, the chain phosphates exhibit optical birefringence (*127*) and anisotropic electrical conductivity (*92*) when made to flow. Both the optical and the electrical anisotropy increase with chain length and decrease upon the addition of low-molecular-weight salts, which cause the chains to coil. The evidence of both the optical and the electrical measurements is that the chains line up in the direction of flow. A similar alignment can be achieved by passing an alternating electric current through a solution of long-chain phosphates (*25*). In this case, the chains again tend to line up in the direction of the flow of current. Then conductivity measurements carried out in this direction and at right angles to it show that the conductivity in the direction in which the alternating current had been flowing is greater than normal, and the conductivity at right angles to this direction is smaller than normal. Rotary-diffusion constants for the chains can be calculated from these three kinds of measurements, and the values so obtained are in accord (*127*) with the straight-chain model of the phosphate studied.

Because of the binding of sodium ions with increasing chain length, the transference number of the chain phosphates, as measured by the standard Hittorf technique (*92*), increases with increasing chain length and finally approaches a limiting value of about 2.1 for very long chains. Such transference numbers give no information as to the distribution of the total current between the cation and the anion; but the values do show that, as a result of association, relatively more phosphorus in the long chain phosphates is transported to the anode by a given amount of current than would be possible for a completely dissociated electrolyte. When the measured transference number of the phosphate is greater than unity, the transference number of the counterion must be negative; i.e., the cations must also be carried to the anode. The data shown in Fig. 17 for the transference number of the chain phosphates are somewhat similar to the plot of the transference number of cadmium in cadmium iodide, which at high concentrations also exhibits an anomalously large transference number because of formation of the CdI_4^{2-} complex.

The electrical conductivity of solutions of polyelectrolytes is believed to change with concentration in an approximately logarithmic manner. Such a logarithmic plot is presented in Fig. 18 for a series of phosphate glasses ranging in chain length from 5.8 to 52 and a sample of Kurrol's salt exhibiting an average chain length of 1000 (*92, 93, 130*).

The measurement of the viscosity number, $(\eta_{solution} - \eta_{solvent})/C\eta_{solvent}$, at low concentrations has served as a good tool for unraveling the structure of the chain phosphates (*30, 31, 63, 65, 103, 105, 108, 123*). As is the general case for flexible polyelectrolytes, the viscosity number of the phosphates is

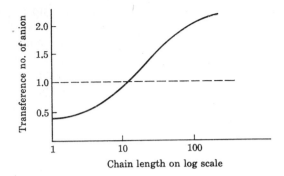

FIG. 17. Hittorf-type transference numbers of the phosphate anion as a function of chain length of chain sodium phosphates. When the values exceed unity (broken line), sodium is building up at the anode as electrolysis proceeds. Concentration in all cases is 0.01 equivalent of sodium per liter. [From Van Wazer (*117*).]

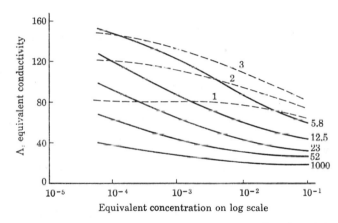

FIG. 18. Equivalent conductivity of chain phosphates as a function of the logarithm of the sodium ion concentration in atomic weights per liter. The numbers to the right of each curve give the number-average number of phosphorus atoms per phosphate chain. Broken lines refer to (1) ortho-, (2) pyro-, and (3) tripolyphosphates. [From Van Wazer (*117*).]

accurately represented by the Fuoss equation (*30, 31, 108*):

$$\frac{\eta_{solution} - \eta_{solvent}}{C\eta_{solvent}} = \frac{A}{1 + B\sqrt{C}} + D \tag{13}$$

The parameters of this equation increase in an approximately linear manner with chain length for the molecular weight range studied (*92, 93*). Thus, for a weight-average chain length of 50, as determined by light scattering,

A is very small, *B* = about 18, and *D* = about 0.05, whereas, for a weight-average chain length of 200, *A* = about 22, *B* = about 40, and *D* = about 0.12 when *C* is measured in grams of phosphate per 100 ml of solution. In the presence of a large amount of added simple salt, the chain phosphates coil and start to obey the usual relationship for the limiting viscosity number of uncharged high polymers. A plot of this type of relationship is given in Fig. 13 for straight-chain polyphosphates (*103, 123*). This plot can be used to determine the molecular weights of long-chain phosphates.

The viscosities of chain phosphates in concentrated solution are Newtonian up to chain lengths of about 500. However, the longer chains, in which there are several thousand phosphorus atoms, begin to show pseudoplastic behavior in flow. This is also true of the steric-hindered, crosslinked phosphates. But the flow properties of all of the chain phosphates produced to date can be closely approximated by a single viscosity coefficient for any one temperature or concentration; i.e., they are essentially Newtonian. In highly concentrated solutions of long-chain phosphates, elastic properties are noticeable. When considered as plastics, the chain phosphates are found to be plasticized the best by a small amount of water.

A considerable number of molecular-weight measurements have been carried out on solutions of chain phosphates with the ultracentrifuge (*56, 57, 65*). In this work, both the sedimentation and equilibrium methods of measuring molecular weight were found to correlate with other techniques; but different molecular weights were calculated for different added electrolytes, the electrolyte being used to obviate the problems of interpretation that arise when polyelectrolytes are studied in a pure solvent. A listing of the various molecular weights found for two samples in the presence of several different electrolytes is given in Table III. Presumably, these differences in the observed chain lengths are due to imperfect mathematical treatment of the data. Present-day studies are unearthing many similar anomalies for ionized organic macromolecules which definitely do not change their degree of polymerization and are not believed to form aggregates. At present, only relative sizes of polyelectrolytes are known with certainty, and most measurements are but guesses as to absolute sizes of the molecule-ions of large polyelectrolytes.

Light scattering has also been employed to characterize the chain phosphates as linear, flexible, polydisperse polyelectrolytes. It is found (*85, 105*) that the light scattering of chain phosphates gives a very good fit to the theoretical equation (*19, 24*):

$$HC/\tau = 1/M + 2Bc \tag{14}$$

This equation for nonionic polymers whose molecules are isotropic and small compared to the wavelength of light is applicable to sodium poly-

TABLE III

CHAIN LENGTHS AND OTHER DATA AS FUNCTION OF ADDED SALTS USED
IN ULTRACENTRIFUGE MEASUREMENTS [a]

Kurrol salt prepara- tion [a]	Medium used	Sedimen- tation const. at infinite diln. (S_0)	Diffusion const. at infinite diln. (D_0)	$\bar{n}$, calc. chain length (zeta av.)	Mol. sym- metry factor (f/f_0)
A	1.1 N NaCl	12	0.87	5400	—
	0.4 N NaCl	34	1.20	11,000	—
	0.2 N Na$_4$P$_2$O$_7$	12	0.86	5500	—
	0.8 N Na$_4$P$_2$O$_7$	17	0.98	6800	—
B	0.1 N NaCl	14	1.05	4100	5.2
	0.4 N NaCl	32	1.08	9300	3.8
	0.1 N NaCl in 5% ethanol	20	1.25	4800	4.1
	0.1 N NaCl in 8% ethanol	25	1.36	5500	3.6

[a] These preparations were made by heating KH$_2$PO$_4$ for several hours at 500°C.
[a] See references (56) and (65).

phosphate in sodium bromide solutions, even though it does not apply to polyelectrolytes under all conditions. In the equation, τ is the excess turbidity of the solution over that of the solvent, c is the concentration of polymer in grams per milliliter of solution, and:

$$ H = \frac{32\pi^3 n_0^2}{3N_0\lambda^4} \left(\frac{n - n_0}{C}\right)^2 \tag{15} $$

where N_0 is Avogadro's number, λ is the wavelength of the light, and n_0 and n are the refractive indices of solvent and solution, respectively. M is the molecular weight, and B is a constant that depends on the interaction of the polymer molecules with one another. The results that Strauss *et al.* (105) obtained for one sample of Graham's salt are shown in Fig. 19. The lines all have a common intercept, which is the reciprocal of the molecular weight of the sample.

At the present time, it appears that light scattering and pH titration for end groups (90) are the most reliable methods for determining the average molecular weights of the longer-chain phosphates. In intercomparing molecular weights obtained by various methods (29a), it should be remembered that end-group titrations and colligative measurements give number averages, viscosity numbers give so-called "viscosity" averages

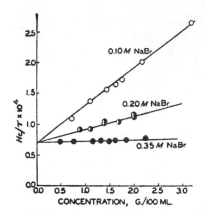

FIG. 19. Light-scattering data from a sample of Graham's salt. The intercept at $c = 0$ gives the reciprocal of the weight-average molecular weight, which is 14,000. [From Van Wazer (*117*).]

(between number and weight averages), light scattering gives weight averages, and ultracentrifuge measurements normally give zeta averages (although the number and weight averages can also be calculated from ultracentrifuge data). The application of polymer physics to chain phosphates has been the subject of a review (*15*).

4. Polyphosphoric Acids

By either adding phosphorus pentoxide to orthophosphoric acid or evaporating water from the acid, the so-called condensed phosphoric acids are prepared. These have been carefully studied by paper chromatography (*43, 49, 74, 131*). From this work, the distribution of building units shown in Fig. 20 is obtained. In addition to the equilibrium between *ortho*, ends, middles, and branches, there is also an equilibrium with unreacted water, as shown by Eqs. (16) and (17):

$$2 \text{ orthophosphate} \rightleftharpoons \text{pyrophosphate} + \text{unreacted } M_2O \qquad (16)$$
$$\text{(M}_3\text{PO}_4) \qquad\qquad \text{(M}_4\text{P}_2\text{O}_7) \qquad\qquad \text{(M}_2\text{O)}$$
$$\text{(2 ends)}$$

$$K_3' = \frac{[M_4P_2O_7][M_2O]}{[M_3PO_4]^2} = \frac{[2 \text{ ends}][M_2O]}{[ortho]^2} \qquad (17)$$

For the condensed phosphoric acids, $K_1 = 10^{-3}$, $K_2 = 0.08$, and $K_3' = 0.02$. The condensed phosphoric acids at R values only slightly greater than unity consist of long straight P—O—P chains. The Flory-type flexible-chain size-distribution function fits the phosphoric acids quite well. This is

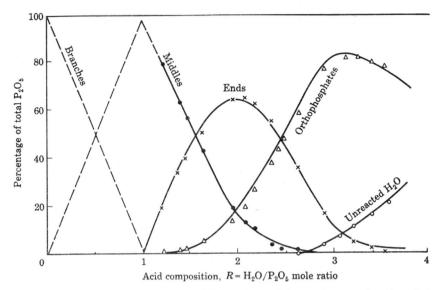

Fig. 20. Distribution of structure-building units and free water as a function of the H_2O/P_2O_5 mole ratio. The curves were calculated on the assumption of $K_1 = 10^{-3}$, $K_2 = 0.08$, and $K_3' = 0.02$. [From Van Wazer (117).]

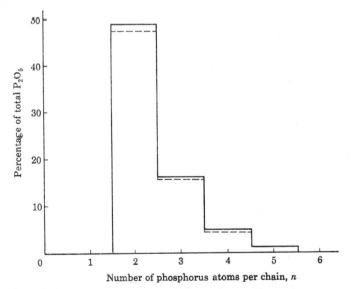

Fig. 21. Size distribution of chain phosphates in a condensed phosphoric acid for which $R = H_2O/P_2O_5 = 2.192$, corresponding to 78.3% P_2O_5. (—) Experimental data (paper chromatography). (– – –) Calculated from the flexible chain theory. [From Van Wazer (117).]

demonstrated by Fig. 21, in which data from paper chromatography are compared with that from calculated size distributions.

The physical properties of the condensed phosphoric acids are very interesting. The amorphous acid exhibiting an H_2O/P_2O_5 mole ratio of unity (where the H_2O is the water of composition) is somewhat flexible but, at the same time, will shatter when hit by a hammer. When pieces of the material are stored in sealed glassware, they slowly flow and assume the shape of the container after a period of several weeks at room temperature. As might be expected, the condensed phosphoric acids are extremely hygroscopic. Condensed phosphoric acids exhibiting H_2O/P_2O_5 mole ratios around 0.8 to 0.7 crackle and pop when a piece is put into water. This is believed to be due to extremely rapid hydrolysis at the branching points and the resulting mechanical strain in the mass. When such an amorphous polyphosphoric acid is put in contact with water, tiny pieces are forcefully ejected from the surface so that, if a chunk is wetted, the impact of the small ejected fragments will cause a strong stinging sensation on a hand held a few inches away.

The mechanical properties of the phosphoric acids are in accord with the chemical evidence, which shows that there is considerable association of the hydrogen atoms. The long chain, amorphous polyphosphoric acids are thus flexible because there is little ionization, and they are tough and not rubber-like because of the hydrogen bonding.

Mixed phosphate glasses containing both sodium and hydrogen have been investigated (*131*). From this work, it appears that the change from the distribution for the strong acid (see Fig. 20) to that for the sodium salt (see Fig. 9) is gradual and continuous. The presence of sodium ion adds considerable rigidity to the polyphosphoric acids. Thus, an acid in which about 20% of the hydrogens are neutralized is rigid and will no longer flow so as to assume the shape of the container, even over a period of many years.

5. Plasticized and Flexible Phosphates

Because of the charge interaction, the pure metal salts of the long-chain polyphosphates are all rigid glasses when in the amorphous state. Likewise, the long-chain phosphoric acids have undesirable properties. However, the soluble polyphosphates can readily be plasticized with water. Thus, when potassium Kurrol's salt is dissolved in a solution of, say, sodium chloride, a gummy mass is readily precipitated by addition of alcohol. By washing this mass in an alcohol-water mixture that is mostly alcohol, a rubber-like solid can be produced. In this case, the water is acting as a plasticizer. Similar results can also be obtained with much shorter phosphate chains. The resulting glob of material bounces readily when dropped onto a hard surface. However, if allowed to remain for any length of time, it will flow out over the surface and adhere to it.

Water is a very poor plasticizer because it is readily removed by exposure to a moist atmosphere. Thus, when a film is made from, say, a solution of Kurrol's salt, it will be very flexible in a moist atmosphere but will dry out to a hard, brittle skin upon dehydration. In this respect, the phosphates are superficially rather similar to gelatin. Attempts have been made to plasticize polyphosphates with polar substances, such as glycerol, which have low vapor pressures. However, the only good solvent for the polyphosphate salts, other than the quaternary ammonium compounds, is water. Some improvement can be made by judicious mixtures of such substances as glycerine with water.

Considerable experimental work has been carried out in various laboratories on the problem of employing unusual cations with the polyphosphates in order to build in flexibility. Although most of this work is unpublished, there is some literature on the subject (*34, 46*). Quaternary ammonium ions exhibiting at least one bulky organic radical contribute sufficient charge separation so that the resulting phosphate is no longer rigid. A certain amount of effective crosslinking can be built into such structures by the use of multiply charged metal ions. Thus, it is reported (*46*) that cetyltrimethylammonium polyphosphates precipitated from a solution of potassium Kurrol's salt are a greasy mass when compacted. However, by substituting the quaternary ammonium ion by 8 to 25 magnesium ions per 100 phosphorus atoms, the material can be made leathery to hard. On the other hand, choice of a proper organic cation will give a leathery material without the use of metal ions. Thus, lauryl pyridinium polyphosphate made from Kurrol's salt exhibits leathery properties; and the molecules can be oriented by stretching a strip severalfold. An interesting flexible polyphosphate is obtained by using 74 equivalents of benzyltrimethylammonium and 26 equivalents of magnesium per 100 phosphorus atoms with a polyphosphate anion derived from potassium Kurrol's salt. This is a nontacky, soft, elastic solid which is soluble in water. Some work has also been done on using chelates of multiply charged metal cations with long-chain polyphosphates. Again, it is possible to obtain more or less elastic, flexible products.

Although several large industrial laboratories have investigated the matter rather thoroughly, they have been unable to obtain commercially suitable products for reasonably large-scale applications. This is because of the hydrolytic instability of the polyphosphates. Exposure of the flexible plastic masses to normally moist air generally results in the formation of a powdery crust or other undesirable changes. This type of degradation may not be pronounced for many months, but it makes these plastics unsuitable except for possibly highly specialized uses. Likewise, there is no particular advantage to such flexible polyphosphates at high temperatures. The hydrocarbon part of the organic cations will char and structural reorganization takes place when the temperature is raised to the softening point. Generally, heating a flexible polyphosphate to around 300°C for a reasonable length of time leads to a product which is no longer flexible when cooled to room temperature.

III. Network Polymers

A. Oxides and Their Derivatives

As has been stated elsewhere in this chapter, the majority of inorganic polymers have been neglected in chemical writings. Some of this neglect has come about due to the fact that classical chemists never wanted to study goos and gunks but threw them down the sink. However, an even more important reason is that a vast number of inorganic polymers are amorphous three-dimensional networks for which adequate methods of study have not yet been developed even in the case of the better known commercial organic polymers of this type. Be this as it may, there is still considerable literature on phosphorus-based network polymers, a few miscellaneous examples of which are given below.

1. Phosphorus Pentoxide and Other Oxides

Phosphorus pentoxide, P_2O_5, is known as a number of modifications in both solid and liquid form. Of the three crystalline modifications, two are sheet polymers, the network structures of which are shown in Fig. 22. In the O form, there are large rings containing ten phosphorus and ten oxygen atoms (*20, 41*), whereas, in the O' form, the interlocking rings are made up of six phosphorus alternating with six oxygen atoms (*64*). In all of the varieties of phosphorus pentoxide, a given phosphorus atom is tetrahedrally surrounded by four oxygen atoms—with three oxygens being shared with adjacent PO_4 tetrahedra, each oxygen with a different tetrahedron. It is interesting to note that the careful X-ray study of the O form shows that the phosphorus and oxygen atoms share electrons and are not ionized (*20*).

The usual stable liquid form of phosphorus pentoxide appears to be a high-polymer modification, as indicated by Fig. 23 (*27*). It can be seen from this figure that the hexagonal crystalline modification, which has the formula, P_4O_{10}, melts to form a limpid liquid of high vapor pressure that

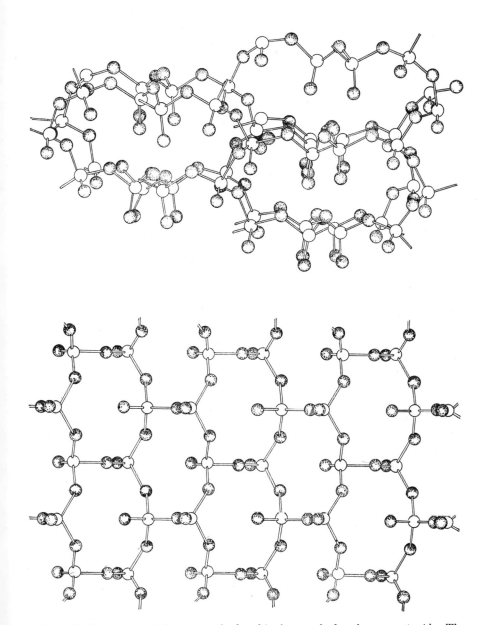

FIG. 22. Structures of the two orthorhombic forms of phosphorus pentoxide. The white balls represent phosphorus atoms and the shaded balls, oxygen atoms. [From Van Wazer (117).]

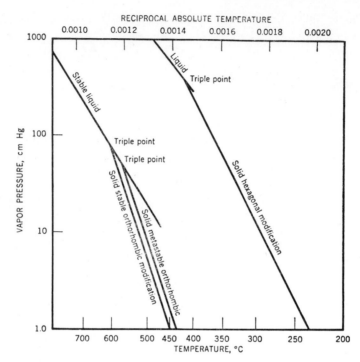

Fig. 23. Vapor pressure of the three crystalline and two liquid forms of phosphorus pentoxide. [From Van Wazer (*117*).]

rapidly converts to the stable liquid exhibiting a considerably higher viscosity. This stable liquid is presumably made up of large molecules. Another high-polymer form of phosphorus pentoxide is the glassy material thought to have a three-dimensional network structure.

When carefully dissolved in ice water, the common hexagonal modification of phosphorus pentoxide, P_4O_{10}, gives predominantly the cyclic trimetaphosphate (*120*). On the other hand, under the same conditions, the high-polymer varieties lead to considerable nonmoving phosphates on a paper chromatogram (i.e., structures having more than about 10 P atoms per molecule).

There is also a high-polymer form of phosphorus trioxide, P_2O_3, which has a yellow color and is amorphous to X-rays (*8, 126*). Phosphorus tetraoxide, which has the empirical formula PO_2, may also exhibit a high polymer modification. In addition, there are a number of amorphous substances of undetermined composition which contain considerable phosphorus and oxygen. These are undoubtedly network polymers that have received little attention because no one knows what to do with them or how to study them. These "lower oxides" generally have a red or yellow color and are insoluble in all known solvents. They can be burned in air at elevated temperatures.

2. Phosphoryl Compounds beyond the Gel Point

As illustrated by Figs. 3, 7, 8, 9, and 20, there are a wide range of network polymers based on the various phosphoryl families of compounds. The limiting case of all of these amorphous systems is vitreous phosphorus pentoxide. As previously noted in this chapter, when structural reorganization involves change of functionality of the structure-building units, every family of compounds will exhibit a region of composition in which network polymers are found. Investigation of the distribution of structure-building units as a function of proximate composition leads to considerable information concerning the network polymers, as is illustrated by the data in Section II.

The transitions occurring at the gel point carry over into the liquid, even when the rate of reorganization in the liquid is high. This is illustrated by Fig. 24, which shows a pronounced change in viscosity at the gel point for both molten sodium phosphates and phosphoric acids. From this figure, it appears that the gel point for the polyphosphoric acids comes at $R =$ about 0.94, and for the sodium polyphosphates at $R =$ about 0.95. These values correspond to some conjugated rings in the infinite network polymers at the gel point.

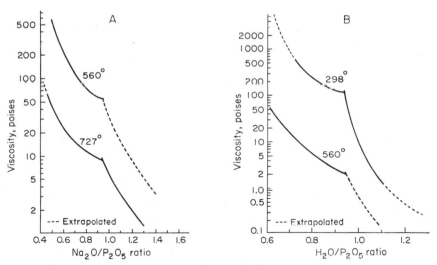

Fig. 24. Viscosities of (A) sodium polyphosphates and (B) polyphosphoric acids as a function of the composition parameter R for two temperatures.

3. Network Orthophosphates

By definition, an orthophosphate is a salt exhibiting the Berzelius formula $3M_2O \cdot P_2O_5$, where M stands for one equivalent of a metal. In many orthophosphates, there are simple $PO_4{}^{3-}$ anions and the metals are cationic, generally exhibiting relatively large coordination numbers (e.g., 8). However, some orthophosphates are truly mixed oxides. This is particularly true of the orthophosphates of Group III elements—for example, boron phosphate, BPO_4 (96), and aluminum phosphate, $AlPO_4$ (107). A similar state of affairs is found with ferric phosphate, $FePO_4$ (14).

In crystalline BPO_4, the P—O distance was found (96) to be equal to 1.55 A and the B—O distance 1.44 A. In $BAsO_4$, which is isostructural with the boron phosphate, the B—O distance is a little larger, being equal to 1.49 A. A reasonable picture of the structure is:

$$
\begin{array}{ccccccc}
 & \text{etc.} & & \text{etc.} & & \text{etc.} & \\
 & \cdot\text{o} & & \cdot\times & & \cdot\text{o} & \\
 & :\ \text{O}\ : & & :\ \text{O}\ : & & :\ \text{O}\ : & \\
 & \times\cdot & & \text{o}\cdot & & \times\cdot & \\
\text{etc.}\ _\cdot^\cdot\ \text{O}\ _\cdot^\cdot\ & \text{P} & _\times^\times\ \text{O}\ :\ & \text{B} & _\cdot^\text{o}\ \text{O}\ _\cdot^\cdot\ & \text{P} & _\cdot^\times\ \text{O}\ :\ \text{etc.} \\
 & \cdot\times & & \cdot\text{o} & & \cdot\times & \\
 & :\ \text{O}\ : & & :\ \text{O}\ : & & :\ \text{O}\ : & \\
 & \text{o}\cdot & & \times\cdot & & \text{o}\cdot & \\
 & \text{etc.} & & \text{etc.} & & \text{etc.} & \\
\end{array}
\tag{18}
$$

where $\times$ = electron donated by P, o = electron donated by B, and $\cdot$ = electron donated by O, all electrons being truly equivalent. By sharing electrons, the boron and phosphorus atoms (each in sp^3 hybridization) can thus be represented as being connected by means of σ bonds (single bonds) to the four oxygen atoms tetrahedrally surrounding each of them. A portion of such a crystal is pictured in Eq. (19) in a two-dimensional projection by the usual single connection notation.

$$
\begin{array}{ccc}
\text{O} & \text{O} & \text{O} \\
| & | & | \\
\text{O—P—O—B—O—P—O} \\
| & | & | \\
\text{O} & \text{O} & \text{O} \\
| & | & \\
\text{O—B—O—P—O etc.} \\
| & | & \\
\text{O} & \text{O} & \\
\end{array}
\tag{19}
$$

The P—O distance of 1.55 A, however, corresponds to about $\frac{1}{3}$ π bond per σ bond. This can be accounted for by a mechanism such as the one shown in Eq. (20) in which the boron atom receives a positive charge and the PO_4 groups receives a negative charge that is undoubtedly located on the oxygen atoms.

$$
\begin{array}{cc}
\text{O} & \text{O} \\
| & | \\
\text{O—B}^+ \left(\begin{array}{c} \cdot\cdot \\ \text{O}\ ::\ \text{P—O} \\ \cdot\cdot \end{array} \right) \\
| & | \\
\text{O} & \text{O} \\
\end{array}
\tag{20}
$$

Such a mechanism allows π bonding in the PO_4 group. Although the σ bond contribution made by boron to a bond length is not so well known as the phosphorus contribution, it appears that the measured B—O bond length of 1.44 A. may be slightly smaller than would be expected for a boron-oxygen σ bond. Although it would be possible to conceive of a similar but considerably smaller π bond shortening of the B—O interatomic distance such as was described for the P—O bond, this does not seem very probable because of the high energy involved in using the d orbitals of first row elements such as boron. The possible shortening of the B—O interatomic distance as compared to a summed B—O σ bond must therefore be mainly attributed to a combination of covalent bonding with the coulombic attraction between the positively charged boron and the surrounding oxygens which bear part of a negative charge. It should be noted that the P—O π bonding and the concomitant positive charging of the boron atoms with distributed negative charging of the oxygen atoms is superimposed upon the basic σ bond structure shown in Eq. (19).

As might be expected, boron phosphate is an unusually stable substance. Thus, although neither B_2O_3 nor P_2O_5 is very refractory, even in their polymerized forms, boron phosphate does not exhibit an appreciable rate of vaporization (45) until temperatures above about 1450°C are reached. Moreover, boron phosphate must have a relatively low free energy, as it is the stable form over a very large area of the ternary system B_2O_3-P_2O_5-SiO_2 (26), and it can also be precipitated from aqueous solution (62). With respect to interactions between borates and phosphates, it is interesting to note that there is some evidence for the existence of borophosphate ions in concentrated aqueous solution (60, 61). Such ions are probably structurally related to the B—O—P network found in boron orthophosphate.

As previously stated, the crystal structure of BPO_4 is similar to that of SiO_2 in that the crystal is recognized as a distorted, high cristobalite type. However, the isostructural relationships (5, 44, 52, 133) between $AlPO_4$ and SiO_2 are much closer, with a direct parallelism between all of the seven crystalline modifications of SiO_2 and similar modifications of $AlPO_4$. As shown in Fig. 25, the transition temperatures are somewhat lower for $AlPO_4$ than for SiO_2. Not only are the equivalent forms similar, but the inversions from one form to another also show a distinct parallelism. Thus, the transformations back and forth from quartz to tridymite to cristobalite are sluggish and exhibit hysteresis effects, whereas the high-low inversions, which do not involve major structural rearrangements, take place readily. Similar results are found for transformations between the equivalent forms of $AlPO_4$. The parallelism between $AlPO_4$ and SiO_2, however, does not continue into the melt. Melts in the Na_2O-($AlPO_4 \cdot P_2O_5$) system are much

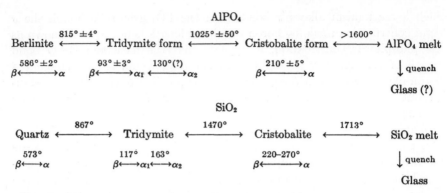

FIG. 25. Transitions in crystalline trialuminum phosphate as compared to those in the completely isostructural silicon dioxide. [From Van Wazer (*117*).]

less viscous than equivalent melts in the Na_2O-SiO_2 system at the same temperature (*22*).

In the investigations concerned with the similarity between $AlPO_4$ and SiO_2, it has often been pointed out that the radius and electron requirements of substituting silicon atoms by aluminum and phosphorus are admirably balanced.

> Since study of the parallelism between $AlPO_4$ and SiO_2 has been carried out in laboratories primarily devoted to crystallography and mineralogy, the jargon of these disciplines has been used in much of the literature. That is to say, the discussions have been couched in terms of hypothetical Al^{3+}, Si^{4+}, and P^{5+} ions so dear to the heart of the crystallographer.

Thus, aluminum has one less electron than silicon and phosphorus has one more. In addition, the aluminum radius is larger than that of silicon by about the same amount as the silicon radius is larger than that of phosphorus. In a recent partial structure study (*11, 12*) it was pointed out that the intensity of the reflection of X-rays from the basal plane (0003) of $AlPO_4$ is almost completely caused by oxygen atoms, with the contributions of Al and P practically cancelling out each other. This behavior is to be expected from the general type of electronic structure described above for boron orthophosphate. In addition, in the case of aluminum orthophosphate, there is the added possibility of some π bonding between the aluminum and oxygen atoms, since the *d* orbitals of aluminum as a second-row atom are reasonably available for bond formation. There should not be so much π bonding to aluminum as to phosphorus in the aluminum phosphates, however, because aluminum has a considerably lower electronegativity than does phosphorus.

Silver orthophosphate (*40*), Ag_3PO_4, is similar to the boron, aluminum, and iron phosphates, in that each silver atom has only four oxygen atoms as nearest neighbors (Ag—O = 2.34 A), but, in addition, two similar silver atoms are rather close to each of these silver atoms (Ag—Ag = 3.00 A, as compared to 2.88 A in metallic silver). The P—O separation is also unusually large, being quoted at 1.61 ± 0.03 A. This distance corresponds to about 0.2 π bond per σ bond as compared to the average value of 0.4 bond per σ bond for the P—O bond in other phosphates.

Silver orthophosphate, Ag_3PO_4, gives considerable evidence of its unusual structure. For one thing, it has a yellow color, although most silver salts and most phosphates are colorless. Moreover, it appears to give an extremely broad absorption peak (*89a, 101*) at 970 cm^{-1} in the infrared without showing the usual fine structure common to most phosphates. This indicates a large amount of mechanical coupling between the constituent atoms.

Another orthophosphate exhibiting (*72*) unusually long P—O distances is vivianite, $Fe_3(PO_4)_2 \cdot 8H_2O$. As expected, the phosphorus atoms are tetrahedrally surrounded by oxygen atoms, and the iron atoms are octahedrally surrounded by the oxygens of the PO_4 groups and of the water molecules. There are complex bands of interconnected phosphorus tetrahedra and iron octahedra extending throughout the crystal, with individual bands apparently being held together only by hydrogen bonding between the water groups. Figure 26 is a representation of such a band. It should be noted that the unshared corners of the FeO_6 octahedra correspond to oxygen atoms from water groups, with the hydrogens not being shown. There are

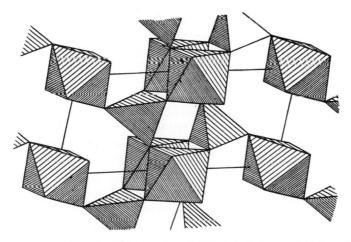

Fig. 26. Part of a band of interconnected PO_4 tetrahedra and FeO_8 octahedra in vivianite. [From Van Wazer (*117*).]

two types of octahedra—a single FeO_6 group [or more properly an $O_2Fe(OH_2)_4$ group] and a double group, Fe_2O_{10} or $O_6Fe_2(OH_2)_4$. The P—O distance to the oxygen atom of a PO_4 group shared with the single $O_2Fe(OH_2)_4$ group is 1.57 A, a normal distance corresponding to 0.3 π bond per σ bond, whereas the P—O distance to the oxygen atom shared between the phosphorus and the two iron atoms of the $O_6Fe_2(OH_2)_4$ double group is 1.62 A. The P—O distances between a given phosphorus and the two separate corners of the $O_6Fe_2(OH_2)_4$ double group are each 1.68 A, a distance corresponding to essentially no π bonding. It is apparent from these data that vivianite represents a transition from the three-dimensional mixed polymer to a simple orthophosphate based on isolated PO_4 groups. Although vivianite is based on a sixfold coordination of iron, the relatively small amount of π bonding per PO_4 group and its unbalanced distribution indicate that the iron must exhibit some covalent bonding (as a d^2sp^3 hybrid), probably with considerable ionic character.

A preliminary study (7) of synthetically prepared crystals of autunite, $Ca(UO_2)_2(PO_4)_2 \cdot nH_2O$, and related minerals (metaautunite, the barium derivative, etc.) has shown that the uranium atoms are each surrounded by six oxygen atoms, and that the crystals are composed of sheets formed by PO_4 tetrahedra and UO_6 octahedra linked together by the sharing of a single oxygen atom between polyhedra. Large cavities exist between the sheets, and these cavities are filled by hydrated calcium ions, which appear to be quite free to move around between the uranium phosphate sheets. In this structure, both the uranium and calcium ions exhibit the large coordination number of a cation, although it could well be argued that this compound is a calcium uranophosphate in which the uranium as a d^2sp^3 hybrid is bonded into a complex anion. In all of the structures mentioned above, the phosphorus has a coordination number of four and hence must be in sp^3 hybridization. The P—O distance in all cases is close to 1.55 A.

B. Other Network Polymers

In this section, several miscellaneous examples will be presented. There are a number of others that could be discussed here, but it is believed that the chosen examples exemplify the general situation.

1. Elemental Phosphorus

Of the three general classes of allotropic forms of elemental phosphorus —white, red, and black phosphorus—two (the red and black varieties) are high polymers. The various allotropic modifications of elemental phosphorus are shown in Table IV. As can be seen from this table, white, red,

TABLE IV

ALLOTROPIC MODIFICATIONS OF PHOSPHORUS

Modification	Crystal structure	Density (gm/cm³)	M.p. (°C)	Heat of sublimation (kcal/mole)	Remarks
α White	Cubic (α = 18.5 A)	1.828	44.1	13.4	Atomic arrangement known: P_4 structure.
β White	Orthorhombic or monoclinic ?? Birefringent	1.88	—	—	Transforms to α white on heating to −76.9°C.
Red I	Amorphous particles	2.16±	—	19.7	Transforms to II at 460°C.
Red II (?)	Hexagonal? Poorly crystalline	2.31	—	24.	Transforms to III at 520°C.
Red III (?)	Hexagonal? Poorly crystalline	2.31	—	—	Transforms to IV at 540°C.
Red IV	Tetragonal (or less probably hexagonal)	2.31	—	28.	Good X-ray powder pattern. More lines than II and III which may be poorly crystallized form IV.
Red V	Triclinic	2.31	590	28.8	Many lines in X-ray powder pattern. Different from IV.
Red VI	? (Deep red color)	?	—	—	Made at 300°C and 8000 atm. Different X-ray pattern than other forms of red P.
Brown	?	?	—	Decomp.	Made from hot P vapor by condensing on liquid nitrogen cold finger. Reverts to 20% red and 80% white P at temps. above about −150°C.
Amorphous black	Amorphous	2.25	—	—	Transition form in prepn. of cryst. black P under pressure.
Black	Orthorhombic a = 3.31, b = 4.38, and c = 10.50 A	2.69	—	30.5	Made by compressing to 12,000 kg/cm² at 200°C. Atomic arrangement known: infinite sheet structure.

and black phosphorus all exhibit submodifications. The common type of red phosphorus is listed in this table as Red I.

Red phosphorus is generally prepared from white phosphorus by heating under various specified conditions. Commercial red phosphorus is almost entirely amorphous, as are laboratory preparations obtained by conversion of liquid white phosphorus below 350°C. As is the case with many network polymers for which various atomic arrangements are possible, red phosphorus prepared by various procedures may exhibit quite different properties. Densities have been found to vary between 2.0 and 2.4 gm/cm³, and the observed melting points range from 585° to 600°C. Once red phosphorus is vaporized or melted, its structure is destroyed. Cooling of the vapor obtained from any form of elemental phosphorus (white, red, or black) always gives white phosphorus, since the liquid and the vapor under normal conditions consist of the same P_4 tetrahedral molecules as are found in white phosphorus.

Because of the fact that catalysts for conversion of white phosphorus to the red variety are taken up by the amorphous red phosphorus as it is formed, it is quite reasonable to assume that the atoms of the catalyst act as end groups on the molecules of red phosphorus, which can be conceived as large, rather randomly arranged arrays of phosphorus atoms, each one of which is bonded to three neighbors (*53, 54*). Variations of this idea have occasionally appeared in the literature on red phosphorus, but the idea has been brought into focus by a relatively recent paper by Kraft and Parini (*53*). These authors explain the observed variety in the forms and properties of red phosphorus in terms of different degrees of polymerization and various terminal groups, which are always due to impurities. They point out that amorphous red phosphorus formed by irradiation of white phosphorus in various solvents has incorporated within it small amounts of impurities derived from the solvent. In the case of organic halides as solvents, the organic radical appears to be strongly affixed to the phosphorus, since it cannot be removed by boiling with water, and oxidation of the phosphorus with nitric acid yields the corresponding alkyl or aryl phosphinic acids.

The existence of forms II and III of red phosphorus is questionable. On the other hand, form IV is generally well crystallized and can be produced as well-formed crystals by slow condensation of phosphorus vapor at 425°C and a pressure of about 1 atm. The crystalline modification of red phosphorus that has been best defined is the triclinic variety denoted as form V in Table IV. This probably represents the violet phosphorus, "metallic" phosphorus, or Hittorf's phosphorus of the early literature. It appears to be the variety of phosphorus which crystallizes from molten metal such as lead or bismuth.

Although thorough structure analyses have not been carried out on the crystalline varieties of red phosphorus, X-ray powder photographs have been obtained and interpreted for amorphous red phosphorus. The radial density distribution curve (*113*) shows two major peaks. The first one at 2.29 A corresponds to the three nearest neighbor phosphorus atoms around a given phosphorus. The second peak at 3.5 A is interpreted as being due to the next nearest neighbors, of which there are, on the average, 6.7 per phosphorus atom. From these two distances, it appears that the P—P—P bond angle is equal to about 99° in amorphous red phosphorus. Pauling and Simonetta (*81*) have suggested that red phosphorus is a three-dimensional network primarily based on the following chains:

$$
\begin{array}{c}
\text{P} \qquad\quad \text{P} \qquad\quad \text{P} \\
-\text{P} \quad \text{P}-\text{P} \quad \text{P}-\text{P} \quad \text{P}-\text{P} \\
\text{P} \qquad\quad \text{P} \qquad\quad \text{P}
\end{array}
\qquad (21)
$$

A random, crosslinked assemblage of such chains with atoms other than phosphorus in terminal positions would be in accord with the ideas of Kraft and Parini (*53*).

Black phosphorus was originally made by compressing white phosphorus under high pressure at an elevated temperature (around 210 to 220°C). Under these conditions, a pressure of 15,000 atm is needed to produce the crystalline variety, whereas, the amorphous variety can be made at around 10,000 atm (*48*). However, preparation of black phosphorus without use of pressure has been reported (*55*).

X-ray data (*43a, 113*) on the two forms of black phosphorus are interpreted in Fig. 27 in terms of radial density distribution curves. The first peak for both crystalline and the amorphous variety are very similar. In the amorphous variety, this first peak corresponds to three neighboring atoms at a distance of 2.27 A. Since the peak goes down to the axis on either side, the neighboring atoms are permanently affixed to the phosphorus atom in question. The second peak at 3.34 A corresponds to next nearest neighbors. From these two atom-center distances, an average P—P—P angle of 95.6° can be calculated for amorphous black phosphorus.

The only form of solid elemental phosphorus in which the atomic parameters have been unequivocally determined is the crystalline black variety. Crystals of this variety are orthorhombic and contain eight atoms in the unit cell. The crystal is composed of corrugated layers made up of phosphorus atoms, each bonded to three neighboring phosphorus atoms. In other words, the phosphorus atoms can be thought of as being in a layer made up of two halves separated by 2.28 A. A representation of this corrugated structure is shown in Fig. 28. Each phosphorus atom exhibits two

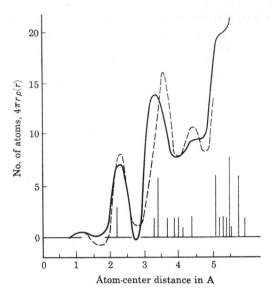

Fɪɢ. 27. Radial density distribution curves for black phosphorus (*68, 113*). The solid curve represents values for the amorphous variety, and the broken curve stands for crystalline black phosphorus. The solid vertical lines indicate the number of atoms to be found for different planes in crystalline black phosphorus. [From Van Wazer (*117*).

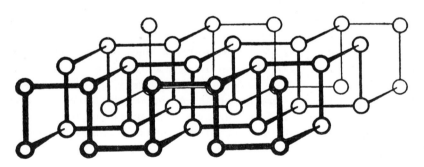

Fɪɢ. 28. The arrangement of atoms in the corrugated planes found in crystalline black phosphorus. [From Van Wazer (*117*).]

bond angles of 99° and one of 103°30″. The two 99° bond angles are in the plane of the layer, whereas the 103°30″ angle connects the layer halves. Thus, each corrugated layer consists of a giant molecule with adjacent layers being bound together less strongly than neighboring rows of atoms in the same layer. As might be expected, crystalline black phosphorus exhibits a flakiness somewhat similar to that of mica and graphite.

2. Polymeric Phosphorus Sulfides

It is well known that there is a plastic-elastic form of sulfur, but the fact that considerable amounts of phosphorus can be incorporated into such sulfur has been discussed very little. In this section, it will be shown that polymeric structures are present in melts (and in amorphous solids obtained by quenching these melts) in the composition range O < P/S mole ratio < about 0.4. However, before discussing the phosphorus-sulfur system, it is necessary to review briefly the available information on the polymeric nature of liquid sulfur and of the sulfur obtained by quenching the liquid.

As shown in Fig. 29, the viscosity (*4, 88*) of molten sulfur goes through a pronounced maximum at about 170°C. When the liquid at temperatures in the range of 160–250°C is rapidly chilled, a highly plastic elastomeric form of amorphous sulfur (called S_μ) is obtained. This plastic sulfur can be drawn into fibers which possess considerable tensile strength. X-ray examination (*69*) of these stretched fibers has revealed a fiber pattern corresponding to a unit cell containing approximately 112 atoms, with a repeat distance along the fiber axis of 9.26 A. In view of the knowledge of other stretched fibers, the fibrous nature of plastic sulfur must certainly be interpreted as being indicative of the presence of long chains of sulfur atoms. Pauling has suggested that the repeating unit in the chains of sulfur atoms found in plastic sulfur is a two-turn spiral of seven atoms (*80*).

The composition of molten sulfur has been calculated as a function of temperature by considering quite a large body of experimental data, and the results of a recent set (*80*) of these calculations are shown in Fig. 30, from which it can be seen that the long-chain sulfur starts to form at a critical temperature of 159°C and increases with rising temperature, leveling off at about 60% of the total sulfur at a temperature of 350° to 400°C. Several estimates have also been made of the average chain length of the sulfur polymer. Since 0.02% of iodine reduces the maximum chain length by approximately 16-fold at the viscosity maximum, the original chain length of the sulfur can be calculated on the basis that iodine is a chain breaker which acts by the mechanism of attaching a single iodine atom at each broken end of the sulfur chain. From this reasoning, it appears that the number-average chain length of the sulfur polymer passes through a maximum of about 10^6 atoms per chain at a temperature of about 170°C (*33*). Although the accuracy was insufficiently high for a precise determination, paramagnetic resonance measurements (*32*) on liquid sulfur showed that the number of free radicals is about 10^{-5} mole/liter at 200°C and increases by a factor of 100 to 200 between this temperature and 375°C. On the assumption that the sulfur polymer chains terminate in free radicals

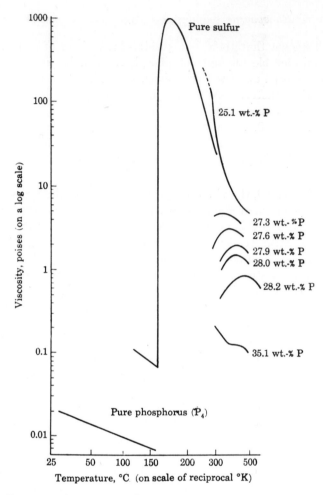

Fɪɢ. 29. Variation of viscosity with temperature for pure sulfur, pure phosphorus, and various phosphorus-sulfur mixtures. (It should be noted that for such mixtures atom percentages are only slightly larger than weight percentages.) [From Van Wazer (*117*).]

—an assumption which has been arrived at theoretically (*33*)—it appears from the paramagnetic data that the number-average degree of polymerization is roughly of the order of magnitude of 10^5.

From viscosity data (*64, 88*), the length of the flow segment in sulfur melts is found to be about 20 atoms; and the over-all weight-average chain length is roughly estimated at 1.2×10^4 sulfur atoms. It is interesting to note that the segment length obtained by applying the Eötvös equation to

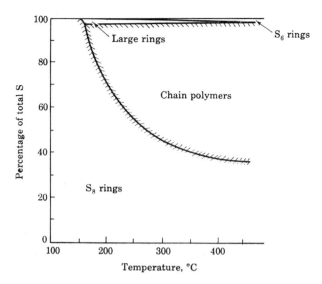

FIG. 30. An area plot showing the composition of liquid sulfur as a function of temperature. [From Van Wazer (*117*).]

surface-tension data on molten sulfur is 18 atoms. Treatment (*89, 99, 100*) of extrapolated elastic data on the quenched sulfur in terms of the theory (*1*) of high elasticity leads to a value of about 10^3 to 10^4 sulfur atoms in the average "free" chain segment between two fixed points in the elastic network (the so-called "lattice arc"). Since quenched sulfur free of additives flows very readily, the elastic data were obtained on sulfur containing varying amounts of phosphorus by extrapolating to zero phosphorus. These results, when taken together, indicate that the sulfur chains are firmly tangled together at about a hundred places along the length of an average chain, which is made up of approximately a million sulfur atoms.

As shown in Fig. 29, the viscosity-temperature curves of phosphorus-sulfur melts (*2*) appear to go through a maximum in the composition range from 0 to about 30% P, corresponding to a P/S mole ratio of 0 to 0.44. Up to a P/S mole ratio of about 0.35, there appears to be very little reduction in the viscosity of the phosphorus-sulfur melt. In the range in which the P/S mole ratio increases from 0.35 to about 0.55, the viscosity maximum vanishes, so that it can be concluded that the long-chain polymers (with or without crosslinking) have practically disappeared, and that the liquid consists primarily of small molecular species, presumably the cage-like structures observed for the crystalline phosphorus sulfides.

As previously noted, the elastic properties of solidified S_μ can be stabilized by the addition of a few per cent of phosphorus. In Fig. 31, the elastic

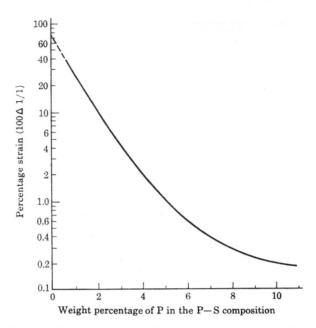

Fɪɢ. 31. The reversible deformation under a stress of 1 kg/cm² of elastic sulfur fibers containing phosphorus. Young's modulus in kg/cm² approximately equals 100/(percentage strain). [From Van Wazer (*117*).]

moduli of fibers made from quenched sulfur-phosphorus mixtures are shown as a function of the phosphorus content (*84*). It should be noted that the modulus decreases quite rapidly with increasing phosphorus content. At the same time, the material becomes more brittle, and plastic flow is greatly reduced so that it appears that phosphorus "vulcanizes" the elastic sulfur in about the same way that sulfur vulcanizes rubber, i.e., through crosslinking of the long chains. The vulcanizing effect of phosphorus is most readily observed in the reduction of plastic flow. Whereas sulfur quenched from a melt held at temperatures above 160°C is so plastic that it is virtually impossible to apply and remove a deforming force without obtaining permanent deformation, the addition of several per cent of phosphorus reduces the cold flow to inappreciably small values at such temperatures, so that, in a normal experiment, the deformation completely disappears when the deforming force is removed.

In Fig. 32, the elastic (reversible) deformation under a stress of 1 kg/cm² is shown as a function of temperature for a number of sulfur-phosphorus mixtures. The curves corresponding to 2 and 3% by weight of added phosphorus exhibit a plateau in which the elastic modulus is roughly proportional to the absolute temperature, as demanded by the theory of high

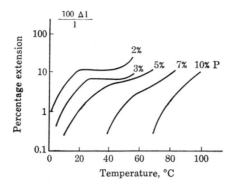

FIG. 32. The deformation of sulfur fibers containing various amounts of phosphorus, as a function of temperature under a stress of 1 kg/cm². [From Van Wazer (*117*).]

elasticity. The curve corresponding to 10% phosphorus represents virtually the end of the transition from an elastomeric to a vitreous type of system.

3. *Miscellaneous Network Polymers*

From the structural reorganization viewpoint used throughout this chapter (e.g., see Fig. 3), the limiting members of the homologous series of hydrocarbons are: methane, the *ortho* compound; and elemental carbon, the completely crosslinked structure. When organic compounds are heated so that structural reorganization involving thorough ligand interchange takes place, lower-molecular-weight compounds volatilize and high-molecular-weight chars are left. Under extreme conditions, one tends to get a mixture of methane and carbon. Since the C—C—C backbone of hydrocarbons predominates throughout organic chemistry, most organic compounds tend to char in the same manner as do the hydrocarbons. Obviously, partial charring of an organic compound is a method of polymerization, with the chars being high-molecular-weight, highly crosslinked macromolecules.

Unlike organic chemistry, which has been primarily concerned with placing various substituents on the hydrocarbon base molecular structure, the chemistry of phosphorus has so developed that there are several basic structures. For example, there are a number of families of phosphoryl compounds based on the molecular segments shown by (I). The limiting

$$
\begin{array}{ccc}
\text{O} \quad\text{O} & \text{.. ..} & \text{| |}\\
\text{—P—O—P—O—} & \text{—P—P—} & \text{—P—N—P—}\\
\text{| |} & \text{| |} & \text{| |}\\
\text{(I)} & \text{(II)} & \text{(III)}
\end{array}
$$

network structure of these families of compounds is phosphorus pentoxide.

On the other hand, a considerable but much lesser amount of study has been devoted to the families of compounds based on the segments shown in (II). In this case, the limiting three-dimensional network structure is elemental phosphorus. The phosphonitrilic chlorides, as well as a considerable variety of derivatives (generally obtained directly from them), exhibit the segments shown by (III) and have the phosphorus nitride P_3N_5 as their limiting network structure.

For any system at temperatures sufficiently high that thorough ligand interchange is taking place, formation of a gaseous reorganization product or of a reorganization product insoluble in the main reorganizing mass will cause the reorganization equilibria to shift in the direction of the gaseous or precipitated product. In the case of hydrocarbons, methane is gaseous and the chars are insoluble in liquid hydrocarbons at the reorganization temperatures of many hundred degrees C. On the other hand, the *ortho* compound of the family of phosphate salts is highly heat resistant, being stable at several thousand degrees centigrade. Moreover, the vapor pressure of P_2O_5 over phosphate salts at, say, 1000°C is very low for values of $R = Na_2O/P_2O_5 \geqslant 1$.

Phosphorus structures based on P—P bonds, where the limiting network macromolecule is elemental phosphorus, behave very much like the hydrocarbons and their derivatives in that a very insoluble "char" is formed on heating. In this type of phosphorus chemistry, the "char" is amorphous red phosphorus (see Section III,B,1). As shown in Fig. 33, the family of condensed phosphoric acids represents the interesting case in which there is an azeotrope. Presumably similar behavior will be found for families of compounds based on other than phosphorus as the backbone element.

The family of polyphosphines in which the *ortho* compound is PH_3 and the network structure is red phosphorus represents an interesting type of behavior. In this system, reorganization involving both P—P and P—H bonds occurs readily at room temperature and below. Thus, when clear, water-white biphosphine, H_2PPH_2, is allowed to stand at, say, 0°C, decomposition occurs quite rapidly according to the following equation:

$$(3x - y)\ P_2H_4 \to (4x - 2y)\ PH_3 \uparrow\ + 2P_xH_y \quad \text{for } x > y \quad (22)$$

As phosphine, PH_3, is released in this reaction, the liquid biphosphine turns noticeably yellow, and subsequently a precipitate forms. Finally, the residue becomes completely solid; and, at room temperature and below, the solid tends to approach a limiting composition, the hydrogen content of which can still be reduced by continuously pumping off the phosphine or by heating. If a sufficient length of time is allowed for removal of the phosphine at room temperature, the resulting amorphous yellow solid has a composition corresponding to one atomic weight of hydrogen for two of

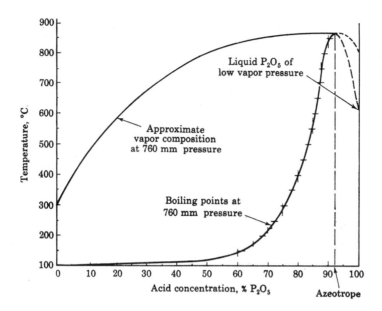

Fig. 33. Temperature composition diagram for the system H_2O-P_2O_5. [From Van Wazer (*117*).]

phosphorus. Upon strong heating, "red phosphorus" results. As might be expected, all of the solids having various ratios of hydrogen to phosphorus are amorphous. For H/P mole ratios around $\frac{1}{2}$, the solid is yellow colored. For values of $\frac{1}{4}$ and below, it is quite red, approaching the color of "red" phosphorus. These solids are all network polymers.

IV. Aggregation Polymers

Cations and anions of reasonably high molecular weight and/or charge tend to agglomerate in solution, and such agglomeration may lead to extremely large assemblages. Long-chain polyphosphates form precipitates with proteins in acid media (*10, 50, 82, 83, 95*), with cationic dyes (*18, 132*), and with reasonably large quaternary ammonium ions (*73*). All of these are examples of association polymers. Since proteins are predominately cationic below their isoelectric point, the interaction between the phosphate anions and proteins are best observed below the isoelectric point. However, if the solution is not too alkaline but is still above the isoelectric point, there may still be enough cationic sites on the protein to result in interaction with the polyphosphate anions. Experiments have shown (*59*) that, even before a precipitate is formed, the interaction of phosphates and proteins can lead to a considerable increase in viscosity. As might be expected, the higher the molecular weight of the protein and the higher the molecular weight of the phosphate at a given pH below the isoelectric point, the less of each is needed to form a precipitate. Likewise, a relatively low-molecular-weight phosphate will give evidence of interaction with a high-molecular-weight protein and vice versa.

Even the simple orthophosphate ion can react with the proper cations to give an aggregation polymer. When approximately 1.0–1.5 moles of Al_2O_3 per mole of P_2O_5 is dissolved in orthophosphoric acid, there results an extremely viscous fluid that can be dried down to an amorphous solid (*35*). It is believed that the interaction between the aluminum ions and the orthophosphate ions leads to three-dimensional networks such as the one indicated in Fig. 34. The stability and degree of polymerization of these

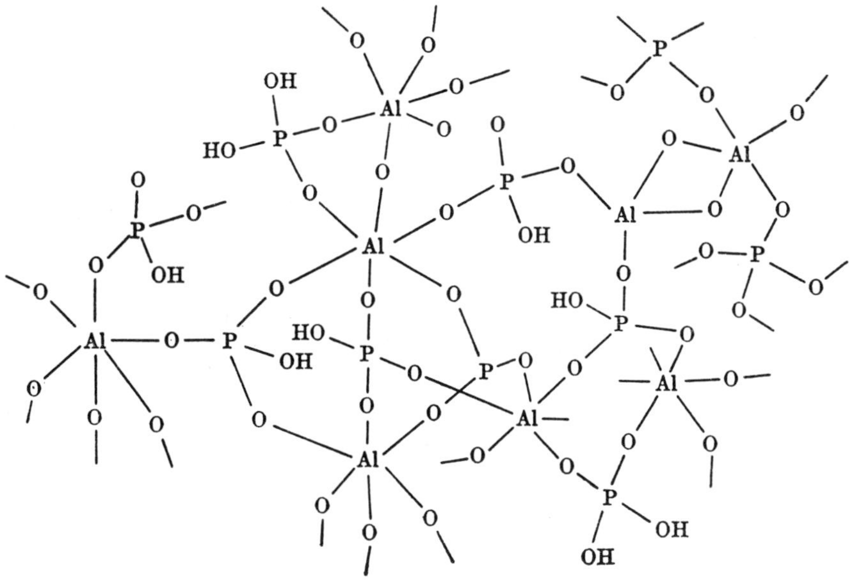

FIG. 34. A schematic representation of an aluminum orthophosphate aggregation polymer. [From Van Wazer (*117*).

aluminum phosphate aggregation polymers are greatly dependent on the pH of the medium, probably in much the same way as is found for the isopoly and heteropoly acids of the chromates, tungstates, and vanadates. Related to this behavior is the fact that the diffusion current measured in a polarographic investigation (*124*) of barium polyphosphates indicated a molar weight of the migrating species ranging from 10^3 to 10^5 for low-molecular-weight polyphosphate anions. On the other hand, the diffusion coefficients of polyphosphato-sodium complexes are found to be only slightly smaller than those of the simple sodium ion. These results presumably indicate that doubly charged barium ions tie different phosphate chains together into aggregations, whereas this is not done by the sodium ions.

V. Practical Applications and Generalizations

A. Stability of the Macromolecules

It is hoped that the discussion of Section III,B,3 has clarified the general picture of the thermal degradation of polymers. It is apparent from the statements in that section that some phosphorus compounds will "char" to give red phosphorus, phosphorus nitrides, phosphorus hydrides, oxynitrides, phospham $(PN_2H)_\infty$, or any of the other materials believed to exhibit network structures and insoluble in the lower homologs of the particular family or families of compounds from which they were obtained. Likewise, those families of compounds for which the *ortho* structure is reasonably volatile will tend to give off gases upon being heated at normal pressures. Other families in which the network structure is quite soluble and the *ortho* compound has a low volatility and there are no side reactions to give volatile products exhibit good stability at extremely high temperatures.

Thus far in discussing stability, interaction with oxygen or moisture of the normal atmosphere has not been considered. This type of behavior for a macromolecule can sometimes be estimated from the properties of a low-molecular-weight homolog. Thus, people studying inorganic polymers often devote the majority of their attention to such "pilot" or "test" structures. However, there are some complications in that, for example, a branching point may have a very different stability than, say, a middle group, end group, or the *ortho* compound. This is true for the phosphates (see Section II,B,1), in which the rate of hydrolytic scission of P—O—P linkages connecting branching points to the rest of the structure is 10^3 to 10^4 times greater than hydrolysis of P—O—P groups connecting ends and middles, under the same conditions. Such behavior would not be predicted from study of a pilot compound. On the other hand, steric hindrance in macromolecules will sometimes make them considerably less reactive. This is exemplified in the part of Section II,A,3 dealing with the hydrolysis of the polyphosphoryldimethylamides.

B. Some Broad Generalizations

The information reviewed in this chapter and covered in considerably greater detail in the book, "Phosphorus and Its Compounds" (*117*), demonstrates not only that rock-like or char-like inorganic network polymers can be made with a phosphorus-based backbone, but that soluble macromolecules, both ionized and un-ionized, can also be made and studied by the standard methods of polymer physics. At the present time, the number and kinds of phosphorus-based macromolecules which have been reasonably well characterized are exceeded only by the number of characterized macromolecules based on carbon (organic polymers). Unfortunately, none of the elastomers based on phosphorus are sufficiently stable under normal use conditions to find application as a structural material. There are, however, possibilities in this regard which are worthy of further investigation. Indeed, the fact that phosphorus compounds have been so much more amenable to study than other inorganic macromolecules indicates that they probably have greater potentialities for development into useable materials than is the case for inorganic polymers based on other elements. The term "useable materials" in the preceding sentence refers to substances that either have elastic properties at room temperature or are sufficiently elastic or flexible under desired use conditions. The preparation of synthetic "rocks" or regular inorganic glasses of somewhat unusual composition does not constitute a solution to the inorganic-polymer problem on which the governments of the U. S. A., U. S. S. R., and other countries are now spending large amounts of money.

From the viewpoint of a polymer chemist, phosphorus chemistry has been particularly valuable in that it has added a new dimension to the study of macromolecules. From the work on phosphorus compounds, it is seen that the type of structural reorganization observed for the organic polyesters is but a special case of the general type of reorganization in which all ligands are labile. Study of such reorganization in phosphorus compounds is leading to an increasingly sophisticated realization of the factors involved in the thermal and degradative stability of polymers.

This realization has also pointed up the fact that much of known inorganic chemistry is based on reactions involving extensive ligand interchange. Unlike organic chemistry in which controlling kinetics often lead to predominance of a given reaction product, inorganic chemistry commonly involves a whole host of products in equilibrium with each other. In the case in which a single product is formed, this is due to phase separation (Le Chatelier Principle). It is because of this that methods for making highly stable inorganic compounds have not yet been developed. Likewise, the families of phosphorus compounds that have been most amenable to study have been those that reorganize reasonably rapidly at several hundred degrees centigrade or below. The synthesis of unusually stable inorganic elastomeric or flexible polymers is probably dependent on development of methods for handling highly stable bonds other than the C—C bond. There is a good chance that this development may come in the chemistry of phosphorus compounds!

C. Present Commercial Uses

From a volume viewpoint, nearly all phosphorus compounds which enjoy commercial application are phosphates. The high-molecular-weight phosphates, however, have only relatively minor uses. Potassium Kurrol's salt is employed in small tonnages in the manufacture of sausages. It reacts with the proteins to prevent water loss, and, at the same time, improves the gumminess of the chopped meats so that they can be properly extruded into the sausage casing. Both straight-chain and crosslinked Kurrol's salts are used in this application.

The largest volume high-molecular-weight sodium phosphate of commerce is Maddrell's salt, $NaPO_3$-II. This material, which is also known as insoluble metaphosphate or IMP, is used as a dentifrice polishing agent. In this application, it exhibits just the right mild abrasive action and is competitive with other dentifrice polishing agents, the significant ones of which are calcium ortho- or pyrophosphates. Vitreous sodium phosphates having a moderately long chain length (a number average of about 60 phosphorus atoms per chain) are employed in several minor food applications, based on the interaction of phosphates with proteins.

The short-chain vitreous phosphates are used commercially for a variety of applications, generally involving sequestration, deflocculation of colloids, or threshold treatment. Thus, large tonnages are sold each year of the sodium phosphate glasses exhibiting $R = Na_2O/P_2O_5$ mole ratios around 1.2. However, an anion exhibiting a number-average chain length of about 15 cannot properly be classed as a macromolecule. A number of phosphorus-based macromolecules other than the phosphates have been made and sold in pound quantities but there is no indication at present that these materials will ever be commercialized on a large scale. An exception is found in red phosphorus, several million pounds of which are sold annually for use in manufacture of the striking surface of match books and of boxes for safety matches.

REFERENCES

1. Alfrey, T., "Mechanical Behavior of High Polymers," pp. 234–237. Interscience, New York, 1948.

2. Atteberry, R. W., Salutsky, M. L., Lefforge, J. W., and Lottes, H. C., Unpublished information from the Monsanto Chemical Company, St. Louis, Missouri.

3. Audrieth, L. F., Steinman, R., and Toy, A. D. F., *Chem. Revs.* **32**, 109 (1943).

4. Bacon, R. F., and Fanelli, R., *J. Am. Chem. Soc.* **65**, 639 (1943).

5. Beck, W. R., *J. Am. Ceramic Soc.* **32**, 157 (1949).

6. Becke-Goehring, M., Private communication.

7. Beintema, J., *Rec. trav. chim.* **57**, 155 (1938).

8. Blaser, B., *Ber. deut. chem. Ges.* **64B**, 614 (1931).

9. Born-Dornberger, K., *Angew Chem.* **67**, 408 (1955).

10. Briggs, D. R., *J. Biol. Chem.* **134**, 261 (1940).

11. Brill, R., and De Bretteville, A. P., *Am. Mineralogist* **33**, 750 (1948).

12. Brill, R., and De Bretteville, A. P., *Acta Cryst.* **8**, 567 (1955).

13. Buerger, M. J., *Proc. Natl. Acad. Sci. U.S.* **42**, 113 (1956).

14. Caglioti, V., *Atti accad. nazl. Lincei* **22**, 146 (1935).

15. Callis, C. F., Van Wazer, J. R., and Arvan, P. G., *Chem. Revs.* **54**, 777 (1954).

16. Corbridge, D. E. C., *Acta Cryst.* **8**, 520 (1955).

17. Corbridge, D. E. C., *Acta Cryst.* **9**, 308 (1956).

18. Damle, S. P., and Krishnan, P. S., *Arch. Biochem. Biophys.* **49**, 58 (1954).

19. Debye, P., *J. Appl. Phys.* **15**, 338 (1944).

20. de Decker, H. C. J., *Rec. trav. chim.* **60**, 413 (1941).

21. Dewald, W., and Schmidt, H., *J. prakt. Chem.* **44**, 196 (1955).

22. Dietzel, A., and Poegel, H. J., *Naturwissenschaften* **40**, 604 (1953).

23. Dornberger-Schiff, K., Liebau, F., and Thilo, E., *Acta Cryst.* **8**, 752 (1955).

24. Doty, P. M., Zimm, B. H., and Mark, H. F., *J. Chem. Phys.* **12**, 144 (1944); *ibid.* **13**, 159 (1945).

25. Eigen, M., and Schwarz, G., *Z. physik. Chem. (Frankfurt)* **4**, 380 (1955).

26. Englert, W. J., and Hummel, F. A., *J. Soc. Glass. Technol.* **39**, 121 (1955); also see **39**, 113 (1955).

27. Farr, T. D., "Phosphorus, Properties of the Element and Some of Its Compounds," Tenn. Valley Author., Wilson Dam, Alabama, 1950, Chem. Eng. Rept. No. 8.

28. Ficquelmont, A. M., *Compt. rend. acad. sci.* **204**, 689 (1937).

29. Flory, P. J., *J. Am. Chem. Soc.* **64**, 2205 (1942); "Principles of Polymer Chemistry," pp. 12–25, 87–91, 320–321, 339, 347. Cornell Univ. Press, Ithaca, New York, 1953.

29a. Flory, P. J., "Principles of Polymer Chemistry," Chapt. 8, pp. 317–398. Cornell Univ. Press, Ithaca, New York, 1953.

30. Fuoss, R. M., *J. Polymer Sci.* **3**, 603 (1948); **4**, 96 (1949).

31. Fuoss, R. M., and Strauss, U. P., *Ann. N. Y. Acad. Sci.* **51**, 836 (1949).

32. Gardner, D. M. and Fraenkel, G. K., *J. Am. Chem. Soc.* **76**, 5891 (1954).

33. Gee, G., *Sci. Progr.* **170**, 193 (1955).

33a. Gee, G., *Nature* **191**, 1046 (1961).

34. Goebel, M. T., and Iler, R. K., *U. S. Patent* 2,592,273 (1948).

35. Greger, H. H., *U. S. Patent* 2,460,344 (1949); *Brit. Patent* 597,169 (1948); *Brick & Clay Record* **117**(2), 63, 68 (1950).

36. Griffith, E. J., Private communication and information presented at the Spring meeting of the American Chemical Society in Cincinnati, Ohio, April 7, 1955, before the Division of Physical and Inorganic Chemistry.

37. Groenweghe, L. C. D., and Payne, J. H., *J. Am. Chem. Soc.* **81**, 6357 (1959).

38. Groenweghe, L. D. C., and Van Wazer, J. R., Material being prepared for publication.

39. Groenweghe, L. C. D., Payne, J. H., and Van Wazer, J. R., *J. Am. Chem. Soc.* **82**, 5305 (1960).
40. Helmholz, L., *J. Chem. Phys.* **4**, 316 (1936).
41. Hill, W. L., Faust, G. T., and Hendricks, S. B., *J. Am. Chem. Soc.* **65**, 794 (1943).
42. Huggins, M. L., *J. Chem. Phys.* **13**, 37 (1945).
43. Huhti, A. L., and Gartaganis, P. A., *Can. J. Chem.* **34**, 785 (1956).
43a. Hultgren, R., Gingrich, N. S., and Warren, B. E., *J. Chem. Phys.* **3**, 351 (1935).
44. Hummel, F. A., *J. Am. Ceramic Soc.* **32**, 320 (1949).
45. Hummel, F. A., and Kupinski, T. A., *J. Am. Chem. Soc.* **72**, 5318 (1950).
46. Iler, R. K., *J. Phys. Chem.* **56**, 1086 (1952).
47. International Union of Pure and Applied Chemistry, Commission on Macromolecules, Subcommission on Nomenclature, *J. Polymer Sci.* **8**, 257 (1952).
48. Jacobs, R. B., *J. Chem. Phys.* **5**, 945 (1937).
49. Jameson, R. F., *J. Chem. Soc.* 752 (1959).
50. Katchman, B., and Van Wazer, J. R., *Biochim. et Biophys. Acta* **14**, 445 (1954); also unpublished data.
51. Kichline, T. P., Watson, L. R., and Stahlheber, N. E., Private communication from the Monsanto Chemical Company, St. Louis, Missouri.
52. Kleber, W., and Winkhaus, B., *Fortschr. Mineral.* **28**, 175 (1949). [A thorough review of isomorphism in the phosphates.]
53. Kraft, M. Ya., and Parini, V. P., *Doklady Akad. Nauk. S.S.S.R.* **77**, 57 (1951).
54. Krebs, H., *Z. anorg. u. allgem. Chem.* **266**, 175 (1951).
55. Krebs, H., Weitz, H., and Worms, K. H., *Z. anorg. u. allgem. Chem.* **280**, 119 (1955).
56. Lamm, O., *Arkiv Kemi, Mineral. Geol.* **17A**(25) (1944); **18A**(8) (1944).
57. Lamm, O., and Malmgren, H., *Z. anorg. Chem.* **242**, 103 (1940); **252**, 256 (1944).
58. Lamm, O., and Malmgren, H., *Z. anorg. u. allgem. Chem.* **245**, 103 (1940).
59. Langguth, R. P., Lyons, J. W., and Siebenthal, C. D., Unpublished results.
60. Levi, G. R., and Curti, R., *Gazz. chim. ital.* **68**, 376 (1938).
61. Levi, G. R., Agussi, A., and Sannicolo, R., *Gazz. chim. ital.* **68**, 179 (1938).
62. Levi, M., and Gilbert, L. F., *J. Chem. Soc.*, p. 2117 (1927).
63. McCullough, J. F., Van Wazer, J. R., and Griffith, E. J., *J. Am. Chem. Soc.* **78**, 4528 (1956).
64. MacGillavry, C. H., de Decker, H. C. J., and Nijland, L. M., *Nature* **164**, 448 (1949).
65. Malmgren, H., *Acta Chem. Scand.* **2**, 147 (1948); **6**, 1 (1952).
66. Malmgren, H., *Acta Chem. Scand.* **3**, 1331 (1949).
67. Malmgren, H., and Lamm, O., *Z. anorg. u. allgem. Chem.* **252**, 256 (1944).
68. Melville, H. W., and Gray, S. C., *Trans. Faraday Soc.* **32**, 271, 1026 (1935).
69. Meyer, K., and Go, Y., *Helv. Chim. Acta* **17**, 1081 (1934).
70. Meyer, K. H., Lotman, W., and Pankow, G. W., *Helv. Chim. Acta* **19**, 930 (1936).
71. Morey, G. W., *in* "Encyclopedia of Chemical Technology" (R. E. Kirk and D. F. Othmer, eds.), Vol. 12, pp. 285–303. Interscience, New York, 1954.
72. Mori, H., and Ito, T., *Acta Cryst.* **3**, 1 (1950).
73. Neu, R., *Z. anal. Chem.* **131**, 102 (1950); *Fette u. Seifen* **53**, 148 (1951); **54**, 682 (1952); **55**, 17 (1953); **56**, 298 (1954).
74. Ohashi, S., Private communication from Kanazawa University, Japan.
75. Paddock, N. L., and Searle, H. T., *Advances in Inorg. Chem. Radiochem.* **1**, 347–383 (1959); also Van Wazer, J. R., "Phosphorus and Its Compounds," Vol. I, pp. 309–324. Interscience, New York, 1958.
76. Parks, J. R., and Van Wazer, J. R., *J. Am. Chem. Soc.* **79**, 4890 (1957).

77. Pascal, P., *Bull. soc. chim. France* **35**, 1119 (1924). [The idea of this author is brought up to date in this chapter.]
78. Patat, F., and Frömbling, K., *Monatsh. Chem.* **86**, 718 (1955).
79. Patat, F., and Kollinsky, F., *Makromol. Chem.* **6**, 292 (1951).
80. Pauling, L., *Proc. Natl. Acad. Sci. U.S.* **35**, 495 (1949).
81. Pauling, L., and Simonetta, M., *J. Chem. Phys.* **20**, 29 (1952).
82. Perlmann, G., *J. Biol. Chem.* **137**, 707 (1941).
83. Perlmann, G., and Hermann, H., *Biochem. J.* **32**, 926 (1938).
84. Pernert, J. C., *U. S. Patent* 2,577,207 (1951); *Brit. Patent* 667,893 (1952 assigned to Oldbury Electrochemical Co.).
85. Pfanstiel, R., and Iler, R. K., *J. Am. Chem. Soc.* **74**, 6062 (1952).
86. Pfansteil, R., and Iler, R. K., *J. Am. Chem. Soc.* **74**, 6059 (1952).
87. Pleith, K., and Wurstner, C., *Z. anorg. u. allgem. Chem.* **267**, 49 (1951).
88. Powell, R. E., and Eyring, H., *J. Am. Chem. Soc.* **65**, 648 (1943).
89. Prins, J. A., and Schenk, J., *Plastica* **6**, 216 (1953).
89a. Pustinger, J. V., Cave, W. T., and Nielsen, M. L., *Spectrochim. Acta*, **1959**, p. 909.
90. Samuelson, O., *Svensk. Kem. Tidskr.* **56**, 343 (1944); **61**, 76 (1949).
91. Schenck, R., and Römer, G., *Ber. deut. chem. Ges.* **57B**, 1343 (1924).
92. Schindewolf, U., *Z. physik. Chem. (Frankfurt)* [N. F.] **1**, 9 (1954).
93. Schindewolf, U., *Naturwissenschaften* **16**, 435 (1953).
94. Schmitz-Dumont, O., *Z. Elektrochem.* **45**, 651 (1939).
95. Schofield, R. K., *Trans. Faraday Soc.* **31**, 390 (1955).
96. Schulze, G. E. R., *Z. physik. Chem.* **B24**, 215 (1934).
97. Schwarzmann, E., and Van Wazer, J. R., *J. Am. Chem. Soc.* **82**, 6009 (1960).
98. Schwarzmann, E., and Van Wazer, J. R., *J. Am. Chem. Soc.* **83**, 365 (1961).
98a. Shaw, R. A., *Ind. Chemist* **37**, 529 (1961)
99. Specker, H., *Angew Chem.* **65**, 299 (1953).
100. Specker, H., *Kolloid-Z.* **125**, 106 (1953); *Z. anorg. Chem.* **261**, 116 (1950).
101. Stock, M. A., and Van Wazer, J. R., Unpublished results at Monsanto Chemical Company, St. Louis, Missouri.
102. Stokes, H. N., *Am. Chem. J.* **19**, 782 (1897).
103. Strauss, U. P., and Smith, E. H., *J. Am. Chem. Soc.* **75**, 6186 (1953).
104. Strauss, U. P., and Treitler, T. R., *J. Am. Chem. Soc.* **77**, 1473 (1955).
105. Strauss, U. P., Smith, E. H., and Wineman, P. L., *J. Am. Chem. Soc.* **75**, 3935 (1953).
106. Strauss, U. P., Woodside, D., and Wineman, P., *J. Phys. Chem.* **61**, 1353 (1957).
107. Strunz, H., *Z. Krist.* **103**, 228 (1941).
108. Therayama, H., and Wall, F. T., *J. Polymer Sci.* **16**, 357 (1955).
109. Thilo, E., *Chem. Tech. (Berlin)* **4**, 343 (1952).
110. Thilo, E., and Kolditz, L., *Z. anorg. u. allgem. Chem.* **278**, 122 (1955).
111. Thilo, E., and Plaetschke, I., *Z. anorg. Chem.* **260**, 297 (1949).
112. Thilo, E., Schulz, G., and Wichmann, E., *Z. anorg. u. allgem. Chem.* **272**, 182 (1953).
113. Thomas, C. D., and Gingrich, N. S., *J. Chem. Phys.* **6**, 659 (1938).
114. Tobolsky, A. V., "Properties and Structure of Polymers," Wiley, New York, 1960.
115. Topley, B., *Quart Revs. (London)* **3**, 345 (1949).
116. Treloar, L. R. G., "The Physics of Rubber Elasticity," Oxford Univ. Press, London and New York, 1949.
117. Van Wazer, J. R., "Phosphorus and Its Compounds," Vol. I. Interscience, New York, 1958.

118. Van Wazer, J. R., "Phosphorus and Its Compounds," Vol. I, p. 26. Interscience, New York, 1958.
119. Van Wazer, J. R., "Phosphorus and Its Compounds," Vol. I, pp. 764–765. Interscience, New York, 1958.
120. Van Wazer, J. R., "Phosphorus and Its Compounds," Vol. I, pp. 693–696. Interscience, New York, 1958.
121. Van Wazer, J. R., *J. Am. Chem. Soc.* **72,** 644 (1950).
122. Van Wazer, J. R., *J. Am. Chem. Soc.* **72,** 647 (1950).
123. Van Wazer, J. R., *J. Am. Chem. Soc.* **72,** 906 (1950).
124. Van Wazer, J. R., and Campanella, D., *J. Am. Chem. Soc.* **72,** 655 (1950).
125. Van Wazer, J. R., and Karl-Kroupa, E., *J. Am. Chem. Soc.* **78,** 1772 (1956).
126. Van Wazer, J. R., and Schwarzmann, E., Unpublished results.
127. Van Wazer, J. R., Goldstein, M., and Farber, E., *J. Am. Chem. Soc.* **74,** 4977 (1952).
128. Van Wazer, J. R., Goldstein, M., and Farber, E., *J. Am. Chem. Soc.* **75,** 1563 (1953).
129. Van Wazer, J. R., Groenweghe, L. C. D., and Matula, D., *J. Am. Chem. Soc.* (Submitted for publication.)
130. Wall, F. T., and Doremus, R. H., *J. Am. Chem. Soc.* **76,** 868 (1954).
131. Westmann, A. E. R., "Modern Aspects of the Vitreous State" (J. D. Mackenzie, ed.), pp. 63–91. Butterworths, London, 1960.
132. Wiame, J. M., *J. Am. Chem. Soc.* **69,** 3146 (1947).
133. Winkhaus, B., Die kistallchemischen Bezeilhungen zwischen Aluminumorthophosphat $AlPO_4$ und Silicumdioxyd SiO_2. Doctoral Dissertation, Bonn, 1951.

—3—

Sulfur Polymers

MAX SCHMIDT

Department of Inorganic Chemistry, University of Marburg, Marburg/Lahn, Germany

TABLE OF CONTENTS

I. Introduction

The pronounced tendency of sulfur to form S—S single bonds leads to
the formation of quite a number of different chain-like compounds. Their

properties and structure reveal a more or less close generic connection with elementary sulfur itself, the simplest substance containing sulfur-sulfur bonds.

Although some of these compounds have been known for a long time, their structure has been the subject of considerable controversy, some authors preferring an unbranched chain structure, others a branched structure, and some even cyclic structures. Today, however, we possess overwhelming evidence, experimental as well as theoretical, that such branched structures are not capable of existence and that polymeric compounds containing sulfur-sulfur linkages all are to be regarded as derivatives of the chain-like sulfanes (hydrogen polysulfides).

The objectives of this review are: (1) to note the major current interests in the formation, reactions, and structures of polymeric compounds characterized by sulfur-sulfur bonds; (2) to summarize and exemplify the most important classes of those compounds; and (3) to try to evaluate the known facts, in each case, in terms of reaction mechanisms of sulfur chains.

This review restricts itself to classes of sulfur-sulfur compounds in which at least one of the sulfur atoms is bivalent. It deals with elementary sulfur, sulfanes, alkyl sulfanes, halogeno sulfanes, sulfane monosulfonic acids, sulfane disulfonic acids, compounds of the Thiokol type, and some new polymeric compounds derived from thio acids.

II. Elementary Sulfur

Oxygen, under normal conditions, forms only a diatomic molecule O_2 with two 3-electron bonds:

$$:O\!:\!:\!:O:$$

In contrast, its homolog sulfur is a standard example of an element which exists in a wide variety of polymeric, allotropic forms. Most of these forms are of limited thermodynamic stability, and can be prepared only by methods involving careful attention to details. Therefore they have not been studied completely, which is the main reason for quite a number of contradictory observations in the literature.

Another reason for some differing results—mainly regarding the physical properties of molten sulfur, such as viscosity—seems to be the fact that it is extremely difficult to obtain the element in a very pure state. Usually sulfur contains varying amounts of impurities (*76*) which influence its properties considerably. Most of the recent measurements have been carried out with sulfur purified by the method of Bacon and Fanelli (*4*): molten sulfur is heated with magnesium oxide. During 120 hr, the black mud formed is repeatedly filtered off. The remaining sulfur is degassed in vacuum. By the newer method of von Wartenberg (*165*), sulfur is heated to 400°C. A red-hot quartz finger in this melt destroys the organic compounds within about two days (CS_2 is evolved) and the carbon content is reduced from about $3 \times 10^{-3}\%$ to less than $10^{-6}\%$. Meyer and Schumacher (*103*) recommend refluxing of prepurified sulfur in a nitrogen atmosphere over a longer period of time, followed by repeated high vacuum distillation. The latest and obviously most effective procedure for purification of sulfur has been published by Murphy *et al.* (*105*): commercial roll sulfur, which contains nonvolatile matter 76, Fe 11, C 140, Se < 1, Te < 1 and As < 0.5 ppm, is purified to 99.999 mole % of sulfur that contains nonvolatile matter 3, Fe 1, C 2, and H_2SO_4 2 ppm. Most of the impurities are removed by oxidation with H_2SO_4—HNO_3 at 150°C. Nonvolatile impurities are removed by distillation, and the remaining sulfuric acid by special extraction with water. Thus far, only the heat capacity from 25° to 450°C, the heat and temperature of transition from rhombic to monoclinic form, and the heat and temperature of fusion have been determined with this purest sample of sulfur (*170*). The melting point is 115.2°C, which is 0.7° higher than the usual accepted value of 114.5°C. This corresponds to a mole fraction of impurity in the older measurements of 0.1% (*170*).

A. Crystalline Forms of Sulfur

1. Well-Known Modifications

a. Rhombic sulfur S_α. The most important variety of sulfur is the orthorhombic form, S_α. It consists of S_8 molecules in the form of staggered, eight-membered rings with mean S—S bond length 2.037 A, mean S—S—S angle 107°48′ and mean dihedral angle 99°16′ (*1, 164*). The rings are stacked together by London forces (*109*). Unit cell dimensions are $a = 10.44$ A, $b = 12.85$ A, and $c = 24.37$ A, each unit cell containing 16 S_8 molecules or 128 atoms.

Rhombic sulfur, S_α, is formed by all other modifications of sulfur on standing because it is the only stable form at room temperature. Commercial roll sulfur and flower of sulfur produce identical Hall patterns, which confirm the identity of their crystalline structures—both S_α (*21*).

Milk of sulfur is described in the literature as an amorphous modification of sulfur. The X-ray powder diagram of freshly prepared milk of sulfur, however, revealed its S_α type of crystalline structure. The good powder photographs obtained without powdering the diffraction specimen indicate that the size of the crystallites in milk of sulfur lies within the limits 10^{-3} to 10^{-4} cm, necessary for ideal powder photographs (*21*).

   b. Monoclinic sulfur S_β. S_β crystallizes monoclinic prismatic. Its crystal form may be very different and depends, among other factors, on the velocity of cooling of the melt and on the kind of solvent. S_β, like S_α, consists of S_8 molecules that are staggered eight-membered rings, stacked together by London forces. It is formed by conversion of more unstable modifications from sulfur melts, solutions of sulfur in S_2Cl_2, $CHCl_3$, diethyl ether, ethyl alcohol, benzene, carbon disulfide etc., and by condensation of sulfur vapor. Slow cooling of a hot solution of sulfur in an organic solvent results in long needles of S_β (*174*).

   No X-ray study of this crystalline variety of sulfur has been reported. Groth (*78*) has recorded its symmetry characteristics. All attempts to obtain an X-ray powder pattern of S_β have been unsuccessful. Even when the diffraction specimen was replaced by freshly prepared ones—one after another—during exposure at quick intervals, in view of its instability, the pattern obtained was clearly of the S_α type. It follows, therefore, that if the needle-shaped crystals formed by cooling molten sulfur contained a new crystalline type, S_β at all, it must have transformed into S_α during the process of powdering and within the short interval of its exposure.

   The enantiotropic transition, $S_\alpha \rightleftharpoons S_\beta$, between the claimed transition point 96.5°C and the melting point formed the subject of a series of investigations (*26, 22, 23*). The most decisive experiment consisted in the study of a sulfur-in-celluloid film, prepared from a quick-drying paste of sufficiently fine sulfur powder added to celluloid in acetone as diluent. The sulfur particles so embedded in celluloid film produced a clear powder pattern of S_α at all temperatures from 80° to 114°C. This proved that S_α does not transform into S_β in the solid state, even if it is kept for hours at a temperature slightly below the melting point (*21*).

   c. Mother-of-pearl-like sulfur S_γ. Monoclinic prismatic crystals of S_γ are formed by slow cooling of a sulfur melt heated above 150°C or by chilling of hot sulfur solutions in alcohols, hydrocarbons, naphthalene, benzene, carbon disulfide, toluene, etc. As a new method for preparing S_γ, Yoshida (*174*) recommends addition of acetone, alcohol, ether, petroleum ether, CCl_4, $CHCl_3$, etc. to a solution of sulfur in carbon disulfide.

   Like S_α and S_β, S_γ consists of staggered S_8 rings. Transformation of S_γ into S_β is accelerated by warming it up to 75°C. Above 95°C this transformation is so fast that a melting point of S_γ cannot be determined. Transformation into S_α is catalyzed by contact with S_α crystals. S_γ sometimes retains its outer form after transformation into S_β or S_α.

   Very interesting studies on the polymorphic transformations of α-, β-, and γ-sulfur have been carried out by Hartshorne and co-workers (*82*).

2. Other Solid Forms of Sulfur

Besides S_α, S_β, and S_γ, a series of other solid forms of sulfur has been reported in the literature. They are thermodynamically unstable at all temperatures, obviously the main reason for their being only poorly characterized. The most important of these forms are (*35*):

S_ρ	rhombohedral	(*31*)
S_ω	hexagonal	(*22*)
S_θ	tetragonal	(*90*)
S_δ	monoclinic	(*90*)
S_η	monoclinic	(*90*)
S_ξ	monoclinic	(*90*)
S	triclinic	(*70*)

a. Rhombohedral sulfur S_ρ. The existence of this form, prepared by acidifying thiosulfate solutions and isolated by extraction with chloroform or toluene, is rather sure (*2, 69, 71*). The orange-yellow crystals (hexagonal prisms terminated by rhombohedra) are rather unstable, forming a surface layer of insoluble sulfur after a few minutes in air; but fairly satisfactory X-ray photographs could be secured. The unit cell was found to contain 18 atoms, and the calculated density of 2.17 g/cm³ is in good agreement with the experimental figure of 2.135. An X-ray crystallographic study indicates that a puckered, six-membered ring is present (*29a*).

b. Hexagonal sulfur S_ω. Hydrolysis of S_2Cl_2 results in a sticky plastic mass, known as white sulfur. It was formerly regarded as amorphous. The X-ray powder diagram of the substance, however, revealed a crystalline structure quite different from S_α (*22*). The same structure was also exhibited by the CS_2-insoluble portion of chilled liquid sulfur, condensed sulfur vapor, and the naturally coagulated deposit of colloidal sulfur carefully prepared near 0°C by the reaction:

$$SO_2 + 2\,H_2S \rightarrow 3\,S + 2\,H_2O \tag{1}$$

Although S_ω has been found unchanged in structure even 12 months after its preparation, it passes on to the stable S_α form at all temperatures, the velocity of transformation being greater at higher temperatures (*26, 25*).

Whenever S_ω is prepared, it is obtained in minute crystallites suitable only for the X-ray powder photograph method of structure analysis. All of the 17 rings in the powder diagram could be identified. An exact coincidence has been obtained for the hexagonal structure with $c/a = 1.11$, $a = 8.24$ A, and $c = 9.15$ A.

c. S_θ, S_δ, S_η, S_ξ *and* $S_{triclinic}$. Four different crystal forms of sulfur, S_θ to S_ξ, were observed by Korinth during the concentration of solutions of sulfur in CS_2 with pyridine, followed by slow evaporation of the solvent (*90*). Friedel (*70*) claims triclinic crystals of sublimed sulfur.

Perhaps some of these forms are only special crystal forms of known modifications. Further experimental studies will be necessary for a final decision in these cases.

B. Molten Sulfur

During the last few years, more attention has been directed to those forms of sulfur, which are formed in the melt, in chilled melts, or in the vapor of sulfur, than to the crystalline forms mentioned above.

Heating monoclinic sulfur, S_β, results at 119.25°C in a yellow liquid even less viscous than water. Although the structure of liquid sulfur at various temperatures has not been fully clarified, all authors agree that the melt contains S_8 molecules immediately above the melting point, and that, with increasing temperature, sulfur molecules containing very many atoms are formed.

When the temperature is kept a little above the "ideal melting point" of 119.25°C for some time, the point of crystallization falls to 114.5°C, the "natural melting point" of sulfur (for the exact value see also Section II,A). This was first observed by Gernez (*75*) and later quantitatively studied by Smith and Holmes (*152*) and Beckmann et al. (*11*). It has been explained on the assumption that, shortly above the melting point, one or more new molecular forms are formed which depress the melting point as an impurity. At present, there is no unanimity in the literature on these new molecular forms. Normally a molecular weight between S_4 and S_6 is assumed for them. Cooling of these melts enables isolation of a form that is less soluble in CS_2 than S_α. Aten (*3*) denoted it by S_π. On standing, S_π is transformed into S_μ.

1. Open Sulfur Chains, S_π

In spite of a large number of investigations S_π had been only poorly characterized until the interesting new results of Schenk and Thümmler (*114*) were reported. S_π is prepared in the form of intensely yellow colored solutions by extracting freshly prepared plastic sulfur with CS_2. Besides S_π such solutions contain common S_λ ($S_\lambda = S_8$ rings), most of which can be separated from the solution as S_α by cooling down to −78°C.

Cryoscopic measurements in CS_2 showed that S_π has the same molecular weight as S_λ (S_8). According to Schenk's experiments the S_8 molecules of

S_π are present to a considerable extent at about 130°C in sulfur melts. The equilibrium:

$$S_\lambda \rightleftharpoons S_\pi \tag{2}$$

therefore corresponds to:

$$S_{8 \text{ ring}} \rightleftharpoons S_{8 \text{ chain}} \tag{3}$$

Log K of the equilibrium constant $K = [S_\pi/S_\lambda]$, plotted against $1/T$ gives a straight line up to about 150°C. Deviations at higher temperatures show a shifting of the equilibrium at the expense of S_λ, through polymerization of S_π.

According to these studies, and in contrast to earlier explanations, the melting point anomaly of sulfur—depression of the "ideal melting point" 119.3°C to the "natural melting point" 114.5°C—is not caused by the presence of high molecular weight S_μ in S_λ, but by establishment of the equilibrium $S_{8 \text{ ring}} \rightleftharpoons S_{8 \text{ chain}}$. At its melting point, sulfur contains about 5.5% S_π (S_8 chains). The heat of the reaction $S_{8 \text{ ring}} \rightleftharpoons S_{8 \text{ chain}}$ in the melt is about 7 kcal/mole.

S_π is not a biradical with unpaired electrons at the chain ends, because sulfur melts show paramagnetism only above 200°C (*72*), whereas, according to Schenk, at 150°C the melt already contains about 10% of S_π. At higher temperatures S_π begins to polymerize. The higher polymers formed are soluble in the melt up to 159°C. At this temperature the $S_{\text{polymeric}}$ dissolved in S_λ changes to S_λ dissolved in $S_{\text{polymeric}}$ (*85*), because the solubility of the polymer in S_λ is exceeded.

2. Molten Sulfur above 159°C

At about 159°C liquid sulfur abruptly changes into a very viscous brown mass. Addition of a halogen in small quantity (about 1%) greatly reduces this increase in viscosity. On the other hand, trivalent elements (e.g., P) stabilize the viscous modifications so that supercooling to room temperature is easy. The mechanism is presumably (*109*) the same as in vulcanization of rubber: chains are cross-linked. The resulting rubber-like mass may be kept at room temperature for many weeks without losing its viscoelastic behavior. X-ray studies of liquid and supercooled liquid sulfur have been reported by Das and Das Gupta (*24*).

a. Anomalous viscosity. The extraordinary rise in viscosity, by a factor of 2000 within 25°C, accompanied by the familiar change of color from yellow to dark red, undoubtedly is caused by a polymerization process. Polymeric sulfur may be obtained from S_8 in various ways: by heating sulfur to temperatures in excess of 160°C, or by irradiation of sulfur solutions.

The interconversion of the forms $S_{polymeric}$, S_8, unstable S_6, and the still more unstable S_2, occurs with very great rapidity.

According to Gee (*73*), in order to interpret these observations it is convenient to regard the polymer as the basic material from which the other forms are made. The polymer is essentially a very long chain of sulfur atoms whose ends are free radicals, in the absence of foreign atoms. Production of S_8 occurs by removal of a ring from the end of a chain:

$$
-S-S-S \diagup \begin{matrix} S-S-S \\ \\ S-S-S \end{matrix} \diagdown S \rightarrow -S-S- + S \diagup \begin{matrix} S-S-S \\ \\ S-S-S \end{matrix} \diagdown S. \qquad (4)
$$

The relationship between S_8 and the polymer can be regarded as a reversible monomer-polymer reaction with S_8 as monomer:

$$
S_8 + S_x \rightleftharpoons S_{(x+8)} \qquad (5)
$$

The over-all heat of reaction should be close to zero, because in this reaction one S—S bond is broken and a new one is formed.

The physical properties of liquid sulfur, notably its viscosity, are not time dependent within the normal duration of an experiment, so that the liquid must represent an equilibrium mixture. The stability of polymer relative to S_8 rises, therefore, with temperature. On irradiation of S_8 solutions at room temperature, polymer is precipitated because of its insolubility.

Gee (*73*) investigated theoretically the molecular complexity of liquid sulfur. By correlating the very sparse experimental data available and making very ingenious assumptions, he was able to obtain a comprehensive semiquantitative description of the sulfur equilibrium. According to this theoretical analysis the extraordinarily mobile ring-polymer equilibrium [Eq. (4)] suggests a heat of polymerization of approximately 4 kcal/mole S_8, and the existence of a critical polymerization temperature below which the concentration of polymer should become vanishingly small.

The viscosity changes in sulfur melts are thus explained as follows: starting from the melting point, the viscosity falls with rise of temperature as long as no polymer is present. At the critical polymerization temperature, polymer begins to appear and, since both its concentration and chain length increase with temperature, a sharp rise of viscosity is to be expected. At higher temperatures, the continued rise of polymer concentration is offset by reductions in both solvent viscosity and polymer chain length. The occurrence of a maximum viscosity is therefore not surprising.

For a quantitative treatment of these arguments the most interesting parameter that enters into the calculations is the heat of scission of polymer chains. As an approximate estimate Gee used $\Delta H = 35$ kcal/mole.

From the viscosity data it may be concluded that the average chain length of the sulfur polymer passes through a maximum of about 10^6 atoms per chain at a temperature of about 170°C.

b. Free radical nature of the polymer. Measurements of the magnetic susceptibility by the Guoy method showed diamagnetism throughout the liquid range of sulfur, so that an upper limit of 0.012 mole liter^{-1} could be placed on the radical concentration near 400°C (*33a*). Measurements by the more sensitive paramagnetic resonance technique, however, give the absolute value of the radical concentration as 1.1×10^{-3} mole liter^{-1}, and show that the value increases by a factor of 100 to 200 between 190 and 375°C (*72*). These findings confirm the free radical nature of the polymer, and agree in order of magnitude with the quantitative estimates of Gee.

c. Large rings. Recent measurements of the specific heat of sulfur have been reported by Braune and Möller (*18*), Fehér and Hellwig (*45*), and West (*170*). These data are very valuable because in addition to the factors which determine the specific heat of a normal liquid, contributions will arise in the case of sulfur from the polymerization process. The results indicate the existence of large sulfur rings in the melt, formed between 150° and 160°C, although they are of negligible importance [see also Fehér (*37*)]. Somewhat tentatively, it has been suggested that the rings could arise through the conversion of about 1% of S_8 to large rings (*73*).

The equilibrium polymerization of sulfur has recently been treated theoretically in a manner similar to Gee, by Tobolsky and Eisenberg (*160*). These authors have presented a simple and unified theory describing the ring-chain equilibrium over the entire liquid range of sulfur. A single formula is given describing the number-average degree of polymerization at any temperature in that range. Calculated ΔH and ΔS values for the initiation and propagation reactions are also given.

3. Plastic Sulfur

Dark colored molten sulfur suddenly poured in a thin stream into cold water yields plastic threads that can be extended like rubber. The threads soon harden into a brittle solid, long regarded as amorphous. Plastic sulfur is in fact no special modification of sulfur, as had long been believed (S_γ). It contains a CS_2-soluble fraction, the amount of which depends mainly on the temperature of heating before chilling, and corresponds to S_λ in the melt, and an insoluble fraction, S_μ, that corresponds to the equilibrium part of the linear polymer in the melt.

Das *et al.* (*22*) established that freshly prepared plastic sulfur is really amorphous since it produces with X-rays a single band with Bragg spacing 3.50 A, whereas the solid obtained on hardening was found to be crystalline and to behave like frozen liquid sulfur. Meyer and Go (*102*) showed that plastic sulfur could be drawn into fibers possessing considerable tensile strength. An X-ray investigation of these fibers revealed a unit cell of 112 atoms with a repeat distance along the fiber axis of 9.26 A.

Pauling (*107*) has discussed the structure of fibrous sulfur and its relation to the ring forms. He has pointed out that the structure of the fiber, and the relative stabilities of various rings, find a common interpretation if it is assumed that sulfur chains tend to form staggered, nonplanar configurations with a preferred dihedral angle of about 100°. If we assume the S—S—S bond angle to be 105°, the dihedral angle in a symmetrical S_8 ring would be 102°6′; in a S_6 ring, 69°34′; in S_{10} and S_{12} rings, 118°59′ and 129°41′, respectively. On this basis alone, the S_8 ring should be the most stable, followed in order by S_{10}, S_6, and S_{12}. On this basis, Pauling suggested that the repeating unit in fibrous sulfur is a two-turn spiral of 7 sulfur atoms. With a bond angle of 106°, a dihedral angle of 76°, and a bond length of 2.08 A, this is consistent with the observed repeat distance of 9.26 A, and the unusual number of atoms per unit cell ($112 = 7 \times 16$).

On standing, plastic sulfur hardens within a short period of time into crystals. Specker (*153*) succeeded in stabilizing the plastic form for some time by adding small amounts of phosphorus or P_2S_5. These experiments seem to be very interesting from the point of view of future technical applications of sulfur as a potential "plastic."

C. Sulfur Vapor

1. Gas Phase

The first comprehensive series of determinations of the density of sulfur vapor between 300° and 850°C were published by Preuner and Schupp (*108*). At the lower end of the temperature range, saturated sulfur vapor has a density approaching that calculated for S_8. As the temperature rises, or at lower pressures, the degree of polymerization tends toward S_2. In order to account for the data it was necessary to postulate the existence of at least one other component than S_8 and S_2 in the "perfect gas mixture," which was assumed to be S_6. Treating the vapor as a gas ternary mixture, the authors deduced equilibrium constants and heats of reaction for the formation of S_6 and S_2 from S_8.

The adequacy of this earlier work has been questioned by Braune and Peter and their co-workers, (*19*), who carried out a very careful and still more extensive series of vapor density measurements. They concluded that there must be at least four constituents of the vapor, and they therefore analyzed their data by assuming perfect gas behavior in a mixture of S_2, S_4, S_6, and S_8. They also calculated equilibrium constants and heats of reaction.

It is very difficult to assess the reliance to be placed on these calculations. Perfect gas behavior is assumed in each case, and specific heat corrections are either ignored or applied quite empirically. S_2 is the only component whose behavior can be studied in the pure state. This is readily achieved at high temperatures, but under other conditions the vapor is always a mixture.

Our knowledge of the composition of sulfur vapor at various temperatures is indirect, based only on measurements of vapor pressure and density. Obviously these do not describe the complicated system in detail. This is shown by the fact that the equilibria between S, S_2, S_4, S_6, and S_8 did allow a rationalization of the measurements; the species S_3, S_5, S_7, and S_9 were not predicted, but were later found by mass spectrometry to exist in sulfur vapor (*17*).

2. Chilled Sulfur Vapor

In 1925 Staudinger (*157*) tried to prepare dark colored condensates from S_2 vapor by analogy with the behavior of O_2, F_2, Cl_2, and Br_2, but without success. In 1953 Rice (*110*) reported condensates differing in color from the yellow of the starting material. They are formed by suddenly cooling sulfur vapor at low pressures to liquid air temperatures. Rice's experiments were repeated by other authors (*112, 68*), who obtained by the same method green, purple, violet, and black sulfur. These colored sulfur condensates contain chilled species from high temperature vapor and are not in thermodynamic equilibrium. Below $-100°C$ they exist for a while, whereas at higher temperatures they are rapidly transformed into plastic sulfur and then into S_8.

A most extensive study of these phenomena has recently been carried out by Meyer and Schumacher (*103*), who were able to prepare at low temperatures deposits of colored sulfur from beams of molecular S_2. Those workers measured the I.R., U.V., E.S.R. spectra of the deposits as well as the electrical resistivity and several other properties. Through I.R. measurements the temperature range of stability and the rate of transformation of the deposits could be quantitatively observed.

The existence of S_2 in these solid deposits was therefore confirmed for the first time by spectroscopic techniques. The color of the deposits is reasonably explained as selective scattering by clusters of roughly equal size, consisting of sulfur chains of variable length formed by S_2 condensation on the low temperature target.

The S_2 molecule, which has the same ground state as O_2, i.e., a biradical with two half-filled antibonding $3p_\pi$ orbitals, is green.

III. Sulfanes (Hydrogen Polysulfides) and Their Salts

It is well known that sulfur compounds, as well as elemental sulfur, form long chain molecules. All these substances can be regarded as derivatives of hydrogen polysulfides H_2S_x. These hydrogen polysulfides have been denoted sulfanes by Fehér and Laue (*49*) because of their analogy with alkanes, silanes, etc. Other long chain sulfur compounds may be named as substituted sulfanes.

A. Free Sulfanes

The sulfanes are the acid parent compounds of the metal polysulfides (see Section III,B). Although this interesting class of compounds has been known since the eighteenth century it has been neglected for a long period of time. The main reason for this is probably the fact that the extremely sensitive sulfanes are very difficult to purify and to handle. Our knowledge of these polymeric compounds is mainly based on a fascinating series of ingenious papers by Fehér and his co-workers which may be regarded as an outstanding example of modern preparative inorganic chemistry.

1. Preparation of Sulfanes

a. From aqueous polysulfide solutions. In 1777 Scheele observed that addition of excess acid to a solution of sulfur in alkali produces an oil (crude hydrogen polysulfide). In 1798 Berthellot fused potash with sulfur, dissolved the polysulfide in water, and added the solution slowly to dilute hydrochloric acid; he recognized the importance of adding the polysulfide to the acid and not vice versa. In 1832 Thenard obtained oils of different viscosities depending upon their sulfur content; he also observed that alkali metal polysulfides decompose hydrogen persulfides, hence the order of addition. But none of these investigators was able to isolate any well-defined compound. This holds also for the work of Sabatier in 1885.

Bloch and Höhn (*14*) were the first to isolate reasonably pure sulfanes. These authors prepared various sodium polysulfides by fusing crude $Na_2S \cdot 9H_2O$ with varying amounts of sulfur. The aqueous polylsulfide solution was allowed to run into dilute hydrochloric acid, which was stirred and kept at $-10°C$ (the reaction is exothermic). The separated crude oil was dried with $CaCl_2$ pretreated with gaseous HCl. Also, the glass vessels were pretreated with HCl gas because of the pronounced alkali sensitivity of the sulfanes. The crude hydrogen polysulfide is a yellow oil having the viscosity of concentrated sulfuric acid and an odor reminiscent of sulfur monochloride and camphor.

Alkali, even the alkali of the glass, catalyzes the decomposition into H_2S and sulfur. The composition of the quite heavy crude oil (its density varies from 1.625 to 1.697) varies with the sulfur content of the starting material. The preparation of crude oil was slightly modified by Walton and Parsons (*163*), who state that hydrochloric acid must be used because other acids such as acetic, phosphoric and sulfuric decompose the oil. They also found that P_4O_{10} was a good drying agent.

Fehér and Laue (*48*) on this basis studied the influence of different factors on yield and composition of the crude oil. They were able to work out a simple method for preparing the crude oil in any amount wanted. Large amounts may be conveniently prepared. Equipment (efficient cooling is important) for continuous or discontinuous preparation is described.

The average sulfur content of the crude oil (prepared from $Na_2S \cdot 9H_2O +$ xS with HCl) is always higher than that of the polysulfide solution due to disproportionation reactions such as:

$$2\ H_2S_3 \rightarrow H_2S + H_2S_5 \tag{6}$$

It is not possible to prepare a crude oil with an average sulfur content below $H_2S_{4.5}$ to $H_2S_{4.0}$. The best yields of crude oil (over 80%) are obtained from $Na_2S_{4.4-4.7}$; its sulfur content is then $H_2S_{6.0-6.5}$. The authors also determined the density, dynamic viscosity, and index of refraction of the crude oil as a function of its average composition.

Bloch and Höhn succeeded in preparing reasonably pure H_2S_2 and H_2S_3 by vacuum distillation of their crude oil. But Fehér and Baudler (*40*) showed by a careful study of the Raman frequencies of the different sulfanes that the crude oil does not contain H_2S_2, H_2S_3, or sulfur, but does contain only H_2S_4, H_2S_5, H_2S_6, and H_2S_7. Its over-all composition varies from $H_2S_{4.5}$ to $H_2S_{6.5}$.

H_2S_2 and H_2S_3 are formed from higher sulfanes in the crude oil by cracking during distillation. By developing a more efficient cracking-distillation apparatus it became possible to obtain from 100 cm^3 crude oil, 30–32 cm^3 H_2S_2 (*37*); or from 120 cm^3 fresh crude oil, 50 cm^3 H_2S_3 plus 8 cm^3 H_2S_2 (*38*). However, the Raman spectrum indicated a contamination of H_2S_3 by H_2S_2 and H_2S_4. Pure H_2S_3 was obtained by "thin layer distillation" (*38*). It disproportionates under the influence of light into H_2S_2 plus $H_2S_4 \cdot H_2S_5$ and H_2S_6 also are found.

Pentasulfane, H_2S_5, and hexasulfane, H_2S_6 have also been prepared from the crude oil by a thin layer distillation (*40*). The Raman spectra proved their purity. They are deep yellow, viscous liquids of irritating odor, soluble in benzene.

In 1956 Fehér *et al.* (*60*) considerably improved the preparation of H_2S_2, H_2S_3, H_2S_4, and H_2S_5 from the crude oil so that large quantities can be prepared. The improvement concerns mainly the equipment used for cracking and thin layer distillation.

b. From anhydrous polysulfides. An impure H_2S_5 was obtained by Mills and Robinson (*104*) from ammonium pentasulfide and anhydrous formic acid. Fehér and Berthold (*44*) reinvestigated this method and found that it works very well provided that polysulfides not of ammonium but of sodium or potassium are used. In particular, sodium tetrasulfide or potassium pentasulfide gives rather pure tetrasulfane or pentasulfane on treatment with formic acid.

c. Electrochemical preparation of sulfanes. Experiments to prepare sulfanes by anodic oxidation of H_2S failed (*46*). However, Fehér *et al.* (*63*) succeeded in reducing SO_2 at the cathode. The primary reduction product is $H_2S_2O_4$, which in strong acid medium decomposes into H_2SO_3 plus sulfanes. When a hydrosulfite solution is treated with excess acid, sulfane oils are formed, their composition varying from $H_2S_{6.5}$ to H_2S_{23} depending on the acid: hydrosulfite ratio. On the other hand, with less acid, hydrosulfite decomposes into H_2SO_3 plus $H_2S_2O_3$ which, in turn, gives H_2SO_3 plus S. The paper describes in detail the electrolytic procedure. A method is also described for preparing simultaneously sulfanes at the cathode and ammonium persulfate at the anode. The method gives mixed sulfanes of medium chain length, e.g., hepta-, octa-, and nonasulfane, which contain 5–15 mole % of dissolved S_8 sulfur.

d. Reaction of sulfanes with chlorosulfanes. The most important method for preparation of higher sulfanes has been worked out by Fehér *et al.* They used a long-known principle for forming S—S bonds by condensing —S—Cl groups with —S—H groups with evolution of HCl:

$$a\ H_2S_n + b\ S_mCl_2 \rightarrow c\ H_2S_x + d\ HCl \tag{7}$$

where $n = 1, 2, 3 \cdots$; $c = a - b$; $m = 0, 1, 2, 3 \cdots$; $d = 2b$; and $x = (na + mb)/(a - b)$. This method may be used for the preparation of larger amounts of higher sulfanes (*56*). It may be illustrated by the preparation of pentasulfane, H_2S_5. The primary reaction is:

$$\text{H—S—S—H} + \text{Cl—S—Cl} + \text{H—S—S—H} \rightarrow \text{H—S—S—S—S—S—H} + 2\ HCl \tag{8}$$

This is accompanied by the secondary reactions:

$$H_2S_5 + SCl_2 + H_2S_2 \rightarrow H_2S_8 + 2\ HCl \tag{9}$$

$$2\ H_2S_5 + SCl_2 \rightarrow H_2S_{11} + 2\ HCl \tag{10}$$

$$H_2S_8 + SCl_2 + H_2S_2 \rightarrow H_2S_{11} + 2\ HCl \tag{11}$$

$$H_2S_8 + SCl_2 + H_2S_6 \rightarrow H_2S_{14} + 2\ HCl \tag{12}$$

etc.

The proportions in which the various products are formed will then depend on the ratio $H_2S_2 : SCl_2$ used. By means of certain assumptions one can calculate these proportions for various ratios of starting material. These calculations show that reasonably pure pentasulfane can be prepared using a reasonable excess of disulfane (about 33 moles H_2S_2 for 1 mole SCl_2).

For this method to be feasible, the starting sulfane, present in excess, must be highly volatile, so that it can be easily removed. This condition is satisfied by H_2S and H_2S_2. In this way, the authors have prepared penta- to octasulfane, starting from H_2S_2, and di- to pentasulfane, starting from H_2S. To avoid side reactions all these experiments were carried out at about $-50°C$ with careful exclusion of moisture.

The reaction of H_2S with Cl_2, a special case of Eq. (7) with $n = 1$ and $m = 0$, has been studied in detail (*122*). This reaction leads in aqueous solution to sulfur and hydrogen chloride:

$$Cl_2 + H_2S \rightarrow 2\ HCl + S + 41.4\ kcal \tag{13}$$

and has been studied in anhydrous medium at $-100°C$ by Stock (*159*) and in the vapor phase by Schenk and Sterner (*113*). These authors did not observe the formation of sulfanes during the reaction.

Chlorine reacts with liquid hydrogen sulfide under proper conditions forming a "new" crude oil with a composition approximating H_2S_4. In contrast to the normal crude oil (Section III,A,1,*a*), it contains considerable amounts of H_2S_2 and H_2S_3. These most important sulfanes may be isolated from it by a simple vacuum distillation on a preparative scale without cracking.

The most important intermediate of this process is HSCl formed by:

$$H_2S + Cl_2 \rightarrow HSCl + HCl \tag{14}$$

HSCl reacts either with H_2S to form H_2S_2:

$$HSCl + H_2S \rightarrow H_2S_2 + HCl \tag{15}$$

or with already formed sulfanes yielding higher sulfanes:

$$HSCl + H_2S_x \rightarrow H_2S_{x+1} + HCl \tag{16}$$

The process may be carried out continuously (higher sulfanes are insoluble in liquid H_2S) and is therefore most suitable for preparing H_2S_2 and H_2S_3 without cracking specially prepared crude oil. Bromine reacts the same way as chlorine but iodine does not react with H_2S under anhydrous conditions (*122*).

e. Methods for preparing higher molecular weight sulfanes. In the reaction of sulfanes with sulfur monochloride, HCl splits out quantitatively (*59*). When equivalent amounts are used, only insoluble sulfur is formed. When the sulfane is used in excess, high molecular sulfanes are formed:

$$H_2S_n + S_2Cl_2 \rightarrow 2\ HCl + H_2S_{2n+2} \qquad (17)$$

The viscosity of products produced from the components in the same ratio varies somewhat depending upon the conditions. While the average composition is the same, the more viscous products contain considerable proportions of high polymers. None of the products is homogeneous; they also contain some elemental sulfur.

An entirely different method for obtaining high molecular weight sulfanes is the reaction of H_2S with high molecular weight chains of sulfur. According to Bacon and Fanelli (*5*), the viscosity of molten sulfur is tremendously decreased by treatment with H_2S. Apparently a chemical reaction with the formation of shorter chains and —SH terminals occurs.

Some products that have been regarded before as modifications of sulfur have been shown to be high molecular weight sulfanes. Von Deines (*28*) found that aqueous sulfurous acid is reduced by hypophosphoric acid. Sulfanes are formed. This mixture of very high molecular sulfanes slowly decomposes into rhombic sulfur and H_2S. The same author (*29*) observed the formation of a sulfane oil in the decomposition of thiosulfate with acid. The oil contained 99% of sulfur and was called "soft sulfur." Fehér and Berthold (*43*) proved that this "soft sulfur" is a high molecular sulfane. They prepared it by pouring hydrochloric acid into a thiosulfate solution and letting the oil settle at 40°C. A yellow nonviscous oil resulted that, however, became more viscous on standing and separated sulfur. The average composition is H_2S_{354}.

2. Properties of Sulfanes

a. Physical properties. The well-characterized sulfanes H_2S_2 to H_2S_8 are yellow liquids, with the exception of H_2S_2, which is colorless. The lower members of the homologous series up to a chain length of 4 to 6 may be purified by vacuum distillation. Sulfanes synthesized by condensation (Section III,A,1,*d*) in general do not need further purification. According to theoretical considerations products of 97% purity may be expected if the correct experimental conditions are employed. Experiments have shown that the purity of the products is even higher. The reason for this is probably the fact that the assumption made in the calculation—equal reaction probability for sulfanes of different chain length—is not fulfilled, and that the higher homologues react more slowly. The purity of the isolated compounds is sufficient for practically all purposes.

The physical constants measured, e.g., molar volume and molar refraction (61), are linear functions of chain length within the homologous series. The relation:

$$\left.\begin{array}{l} \text{Molar volume} \\ \\ \text{Molar refraction} \end{array}\right\} = 2a + (n - 2)b \tag{18}$$

is followed accurately, a being the contribution of the end group, —SH, and b the increment for each inner sulfur atom. For the molar volume $a = 24.8$ and $b = 16.4$, and for the molar refraction $a = 8.9$ and $b = 8.6$ (see Table I).

TABLE I

DENSITY, MOLAR VOLUME, INDEX OF REFRACTION, AND MOLAR
REFRACTION OF THE SULFANES [a]

Sulfane	d^{20}	V	ΔV	n_{D}^{20}	R	ΔR
H_2S_2	1.334	49.6	—	1.631	17.7	—
H_2S_3	1.491	65.9	16.3	1.729	26.2	8.5
H_2S_4	1.582	82.3	16.4	1.791	34.9	8.7
H_2S_5	1.644	98.7	16.4	1.836	43.6	8.7
H_2S_6	1.688	115.2	16.5	1.867	52.2	8.6
H_2S_7	1.721	131.6	16.4	1.893	60.9	8.7
H_2S_8	1.747	148.0	16.4	1.912	69.5	8.6

[a] Reference 61.

b. Constitution. The constancy of the increments b in the above-mentioned relation offers strong support for the view that, in the sulfanes, the sulfur atoms are linked to form unbranched chains. This is also proved by the Raman spectra of the sulfanes, excited by the green mercury line (5461 A): the characteristic S—S stretching frequencies at about 400 to 500 cm^{-1} and the S—S—S bending frequencies at about 150 to 200 cm^{-1} are excellent aids in the identification and characterization of the different members of this homologous series. The Raman spectra further prove the absence of physically dissolved sulfur in the products.

The methods of preparation, the reactions, and the physical properties all point to a straight chain homologous series.

c. Chemical properties and analytical determination of sulfanes. Although the higher sulfanes are unstable thermodynamically with respect to hydrogen sulfide and sulfur (*47*), they are metastable at room temperature because the activation energy of their decomposition is relatively high, about 25 kcal/mole (*55*). In this respect the sulfanes are comparable with the alkanes. The essential difference is that the sulfur chains are more exposed to attack by decomposition catalysts, while the carbon chains are more or less protected by the surrounding hydrogen atoms. Therefore the main difficulty in the preparative chemistry of sulfanes is to eliminate the catalysts. If this is achieved the substances are stable enough for reactions of diverse kinds. They promise to become very interesting and reactive intermediates for various purposes in preparative inorganic and organic chemistry. Until now the chemistry of the sulfanes has been only poorly characterized, except for their reactions with SO_3 and chlorosulfonic acid (see Sections VI and VII), mainly because of the above-mentioned difficulty.

Recently, the acidity of some sulfanes was determined by means of an ingenious special streaming apparatus by Schwarzenbach and Fischer (*151*). They are considerably stronger acids than hydrogen sulfide.

The analytical determination of sulfanes may be carried out by decomposition of the sulfane by quartz powder at 90°C:

$$H_2S_x \rightarrow H_2S + (x - 1)S \tag{19}$$

and weighing the elemental sulfur formed (*39*), or by an argentimetric method:

$$H_2S_x + 2\,AgNO_3 \rightarrow Ag_2S + (x - 1)S + 2\,HNO_3 \tag{20}$$

The fastest and most convenient methods use the degradation processes of sulfanes with sulfite or cyanide, respectively (see also Section X):

$$H_2S_x + (x - 1)SO_3^{--} \rightarrow H_2S + (x - 1)S_2O_3^{--} \tag{21}$$

$$H_2S_x + (x - 1)CN^- \rightarrow H_2S + (x - 1)SCN^- \tag{22}$$

and the iodimetric or colorimetric determination of the formed thiosulfate or thiocyanide, respectively (*139*).

B. Salts of Sulfanes

1. Alkali and Alkaline-Earth Metal Polysulfides

Alkali and alkaline-earth metal polysulfides have been known for a long time. They may be prepared from metal plus sulfur, metal or metal amide plus sulfur in liquid ammonia, metal sulfides plus sulfur in the melt, metal sulfides plus sulfur in water or alcohol, metal hydrosulfides plus sulfur in water or alcohol, metal hydroxides plus sulfur, etc.

Most of these methods do not yield pure products but only mixtures of different polysulfides. A complete series of pure solid polysulfides has been prepared from potassium: K_2S_2, K_2S_3, K_2S_4, K_2S_5, and K_2S_6. For the preparation of X-ray pure substances, liquid ammonia or anhydrous alcohol are the most suitable solvents (*151*). They are decomposed by water to form polysulfide mixtures.

Without any doubt, the polysulfides contain anions S_x^{--}, which are unbranched chains of sulfur atoms. This is proved by X-ray studies and determinations of molar volumes and molar refractions (*151, 34*). The older hypothesis of branched structures for polysulfides therefore can no longer be maintained.

2. Heavy Metal Polysulfides

Polysulfides of the heavy metals Pb, Zn, Cd, Hg, Cu, As, Sb, and Bi have been prepared (*87*). These mostly amorphous substances are formed by reaction of the metal thiophenolates with elemental sulfur in the presence of amines. Their physical and chemical properties have not yet been studied in detail.

3. Polysulfides of Organic Bases

In 1954 Krebs *et al.* (*88*) prepared polysulfides of organic bases by dissolving the amine and the sulfur in a nonpolar solvent and slowly passing in H_2S. The least soluble polysulfide separates. The polysulfide formation is enhanced by the opening of the S_8 ring caused by the amine sulfide, or rather S^{--} ion. Heptasulfides of trimethylamine, *n*-propylamine, piperidine, *n*-hexylamine, *n*-octylamine, *n*-nonylamine, and nonasulfides of triethylamine, di-*n*-propylamine and a hexasulfide of cyclohexylamine were prepared in the crystalline state. They are yellow to orange in color and quite unstable.

By the same method Krebs and Müller (*86*) also prepared polysulfides of diamines. However, since they are much more stable, they could be simply prepared in water or alcohol-water by adding sulfur to the amine solution and saturating with H_2S. The salt crystallized out. They described the trisulfides of ethylenediamine, penta-, hexa-, and heptasulfides of trimethylenediamine, and the hexasulfide of tetramethylenediamine.

IV. Alkyl and Aryl Sulfanes

Organic polysulfides have been known for a long time but their structure has been the subject of considerable controversy, some authors preferring an unbranched chain structure, others a branched structure, and some even cyclic structures. Today, however, we possess an overwhelming evidence, experimental and theoretical, that such branched structures are not capable of existence, but that organic polysulfides are true derivatives of the linear sulfanes (see Section IV,B).

A. Preparation

1. Disulfanes

The most important organosubstituted sulfanes are disulfanes of the general formula R—S—S—R. They may be prepared by the following methods (*150*).

a. Oxidation of mercaptans. The necessary oxidant depends on the redox potential of the thiol-disulfane system. The sensitivity against oxidation decreases in the following order: thiophenols > primary > secondary > tertiary mercaptans > thiourea.

Very often oxidation is possible by air:

$$2 \text{ RSH} + \text{O}_2 \rightarrow \text{RSSR} + \text{H}_2\text{O}_2 \tag{23}$$

$$2 \text{ RSH} + \text{H}_2\text{O}_2 \rightarrow \text{RSSR} + 2 \text{ H}_2\text{O} \tag{24}$$

in alkaline solutions. It is catalyzed by Cu or Fe salts. Also catalyzed by Fe salts is the oxidation of mercaptans to disulfanes by H_2O_2 in alkaline solution [Eq. (24)].

Iodine or bromine oxidize according to:

$$2 \text{ RSH} + \text{I}_2 \rightarrow \text{RSSR} + 2 \text{ HI} \tag{25}$$

In ether, disulfanes are prepared in excellent yields by oxidation of mercaptans by ferric chloride:

$$2 \text{ RSH} + 2 \text{ FeCl}_3 \rightarrow \text{RSSR} + 2 \text{ FeCl}_2 + 2 \text{ HCl} \tag{26}$$

$\text{NO}_2{}^-$, $\text{K}_3[\text{Fe(CN)}_6]$, SO_2Cl_2, HNO_3, or $(\text{NH}_4)_2\text{S}_2\text{O}_8$ may also be used for oxidation of thiols to disulfanes.

Oxidation of equimolar mixtures of two different mercaptans yields a mixture of the three different possible disulfanes. Starting with similar thiols, they are formed statistically, whereas the oxidation of considerably different mercaptans, e.g., primary and tertiary thiols, favors the formation of unsymmetrical disulfanes.

b. Alkylation and arylation of sodium disulfide. Disulfanes may be prepared in good yields by reactions of Na_2S_2 with alkyl or aryl halides:

$$2 \text{ RX} + Na_2S_2 \rightarrow RSSR + 2 \text{ NaX} \tag{27}$$

or with salts of alkylsulfonic acids and with diazonium salts.

c. Disulfanes from thiosulfuric acid esters (Bunte salts). At higher temperatures alkyl thiosulfates may be oxidized with excellent yields by iodine to disulfanes:

$$2 \text{ RSSO}_3\text{Na} + I_2 + 2 \text{ H}_2\text{O} \rightarrow RSSR + 2 \text{ NaHSO}_4 + 2 \text{ HI} \tag{28}$$

Unsymmetrical disulfanes are formed from Bunte salts and mercaptocarbonic acids (*149*):

$$\text{RSSO}_3\text{Na} + \text{NaSR}' \rightarrow RSSR' + Na_2SO_3 \tag{29}$$

d. Other methods. In addition to methods *a–c* a series of other paths leading to disulfanes has been reported which seem to be only of limited interest to preparative chemistry; they include the formation of disulfanes from esters of thiocyanic acid with basic substances, from other sulfur-containing carbonic acid derivatives by oxidative hydrolysis, from sulfonic acid derivatives with HI, by reduction of sulfinic acids, from thiosulfonic acids with alkali, by reduction of sulfonic acid derivatives or by introduction of sulfur by elemental sulfur or S_2Cl_2 into phenols or aromatic amines.

2. Higher Sulfanes

a. Trisulfanes. Trisulfanes RSSSR are formed by the reaction of mercaptans with SCl_2:

$$2 \text{ RSH} + SCl_2 \rightarrow RSSSR + 2 \text{ HCl} \tag{30}$$

in organic solvents or, together with disulfanes, by the oxidation of mercaptans with thionyl chloride:

$$4 \text{ RSH} + SOCl_2 \rightarrow RSSR + RSSSR + H_2O + 2 \text{ HCl} \tag{31}$$

b. Tetrasulfanes. Again the reaction of S—Cl with H—S is the most suitable method for preparing tetrasulfanes, and holds also for all higher organic polysulfides:

$$2 \text{ RSH} + S_2Cl_2 \rightarrow RSSSSR + 2 \text{ HCl} \tag{32}$$

Tetrasulfanes may also be prepared from alkali tetrasulfides plus alkyl or aryl halides:

$$2 \text{ RCl} + Na_2S_4 \rightarrow RSSSSR + 2 \text{ NaCl} \tag{33}$$

or by oxidation of alkyl hydrogen disulfanes with iodine (*16*):

$$2 \text{ RSSH} + \text{I}_2 \rightarrow \text{RSSSSR} + 2 \text{ HI} \tag{34}$$

c. Pentasulfanes. Reactions of potassium pentasulfide with alkyl halides in an anhydrous medium or of S_3Cl_2 with mercaptans yield pentasulfanes.

d. Higher sulfanes. Some hexasulfanes have recently been prepared by the oxidation of alkyl hydrogen trisulfanes with iodine (*16*). According to Fehér *et al.* (*58*), hexasulfanes as well as higher organic polysulfanes are obtained in the reaction of S_4Cl_2 and higher chlorosulfanes (see Section V) with mercaptans.

B. Properties and Structure

At room temperature, organic sulfanes are yellow oils or solids. Except for the disulfanes, which are higher boiling than the corresponding thio ethers, they cannot be distilled without decomposition. They are very toxic and characterized by an extremely unpleasant odor. The extraordinary difficulty of preparing higher sulfanes in a pure state may explain some discrepancies in the literature regarding their properties (it is very difficult to decide among solutions of sulfur in lower sulfanes, sulfane mixtures, and pure sulfanes). Reactions dealing with the scission of sulfur-sulfur bonds in these compounds were recently excellently reviewed by Parker and Kharash (*106*).

As already mentioned, the structure of organosubstituted sulfanes has been the subject of considerable controversy. The fact that the sulfur in excess over the disulfane is easy to remove was the main argument in favor of a branched structure. But today we know that a semipolar bond A → B is possible only if A is more positive than B. If A is sulfur, B must be an element more negative—oxygen, for instance. If B is sulfur, than A must be a more positive element as, for instance, phosphorus in P_4S_{10}. From this point of view S → S seems to be impossible and no compound having such bonds is known.

A few typical examples of arguments for branched or cyclic structures may precede the arguments for unbranched structures. Baroni (*8*) investigated diethylsulfanes. From the parachor he concluded that the disulfane and trisulfane have chain structures but the tetrasulfane has a branched structure (I) and the pentasulfanes have cyclic structures (II, III):

$$\begin{array}{ccc}
\text{R—S—S—S—R} & \text{R—S—S—S—R} & \text{R—S—S—S—R} \\
| & \diagdown\diagup & \diagdown\diagup \\
\text{S} & \text{S——S} & \text{S——S} \\
\text{(I)} & \text{(II)} & \text{(III)}
\end{array}$$

Two isomeric pentasulfides were allegedly prepared. These findings could not stand a critical experimental reinvestigation (*58*). Bezzi (*13*) measured the viscosity of mercaptans, mono-, di-, and tetrasulfanes in ether, benzene, and chloroform and thought they indicated a branched structure.

For polytetrasulfides of the Thiokol type a branched structure was preferred because caustic easily removed two sulfur atoms to give the corresponding disulfides (*100*). Those polytetrasulfides were investigated with X-rays (*84*). They crystallize on stretching and give good crystalline pattern; the patterns fitted a branched formula but allegedly not the general chain formula. It is surprising that it was not realized that sulfur chains are not straight and that the X-ray pattern could not distinguish between the structures (IV) and (V):

$$\begin{array}{cc} \text{R—S—S—R} & \text{R—S} \quad \text{S—R} \\ \downarrow \quad \downarrow & | \qquad | \\ \text{S} \quad \text{S} & \text{S—S} \\ \text{(IV)} & \text{(V)} \end{array}$$

In spite of these arguments, we know today from a number of experimental results as well as of theoretical considerations that organic polysulfides are true derivatives of the linear sulfanes and that the branched structures are not capable of existence. This is shown, for instance, by electron diffraction studies of $(CH_3)_2S_2$ (*158*) and $(CH_3)_2S_3$ (*30*), the Raman spectrum of the same compounds (*74, 162*), and crystallographic and roentgenographic investigations (*161, 27*). They all prove the existence of a puckered chain structure, e.g., the presence of zigzag sulfur chains in those compounds. Also the U.V. spectra indicate such chain structures (*89*).

The most convincing arguments for the unbranched structure of organic sulfanes have been put forward by Fehér *et al.* (*58*), who prepared a series of dimethyl- and diethylsulfanes in a very pure state and measured their densities, viscosities, indexes of refraction, and Raman spectra. The calcu-

TABLE II

DENSITY, MOLAR VOLUME, INDEX OF REFRACTION, MOLAR REFRACTION, AND
DYNAMIC VISCOSITIES η_{20} (CENTIPOISE) OF ALKYL SULFANES

Compound	d_{20}	V_{20}	n_D^{20}	R_D^{20}	η_{20}
$(CH_3)_2S_2$	1.0623	88.7	1.5257	27.2	0.619
$(CH_3)_2S_3$	1.2048	104.8	1.6012	35.9	1.193
$(CH_3)_2S_4$	1.3065	121.2	1.6612	44.8	2.416
$(C_2H_5)_2S_2$	0.9930	123.1	1.5078	36.7	0.8388
$(C_2H_5)_2S_3$	1.1061	139.4	1.5669	45.6	1.6596
$(C_2H_5)_2S_4$	1.1971	155.7	1.6176	54.5	3.2099
$(C_2H_5)_2S_5$	1.2706	171.9	1.6591	63.4	5.9965

lated molar volumes, Lorentz-Lorentz refractions, and logarithms of the dynamic viscosities within a series are linear functions of the number of sulfur atoms. Ring structures or S → S bonds are excluded by these experiments (see Table II). The a and b values in the relation molar volume–molar refraction (see Section III,A,2) for methyl- and ethylsulfanes are $a = 44.3$, $b = 16.3$, $a = 13.6$, $b = 8.8$, and $a = 161.5$ $b = 16.3$, $a = 18.4$, $b = 8.9$.

In addition to the theoretical and physicochemical arguments, the formation of organic tetra-, penta-, hexa-, and higher sulfanes from mercaptans and the linear S_2Cl_2, S_3Cl_2, S_4Cl_2, and higher chlorosulfanes is convincing evidence for an unbranched chain structure for organic sulfanes.

V. Halogeno and Pseudohalogeno Sulfanes

Compounds of the types S_2X_2 and SX_2 have long been known but higher halogeno sulfanes have been prepared only within the last few years.

A. Preparation

1. Chlorosulfanes

a. *From S_2Cl_2 and hydrogen.* The first experimental proof for the existence of higher chlorosulfanes was provided in 1952 by Fehér and Baudler (*41*), who also gave a complete survey of the older literature on the subject. By chilling hot vapor mixtures of S_2Cl_2 and hydrogen the authors prepared orange-yellow viscous oils and light yellow solids of approximate compositions Cl_2S_{20-24} and Cl_2S_{100}, respectively. All substances prepared by this method proved to be mixtures of homologues with different chain lengths, but not solutions of elemental sulfur in lower chloro sulfanes.

b. *From lower chlorosulfanes and sulfanes.* A second and much more convenient method for preparing higher chlorosulfanes has been worked out by Fehér's school (*62, 52*). It uses the reaction of sulfanes with chlorosulfanes already mentioned in Section III,A,1,*d*. With an excess of sulfane it leads to the formation of higher sulfanes, whereas a large excess of chlorosulfane results in higher chlorosulfanes:

$$ClS_n \overline{| Cl + H |} S_m \overline{| H + Cl |} S_nCl \rightarrow ClS_{2n+m}Cl + 2\ HCl \tag{35}$$

By careful, slow addition of the sulfanes H_2S, H_2S_2, H_2S_3, and H_2S_4 to a very large excess of SCl_2 at $-80°C$, the following chlorosulfanes may be prepared in excellent yields and with satisfactory purity without distillation (only the excess of SCl_2 has to be distilled off *in vacuo* at low temperatures): S_3Cl_2, S_4Cl_2, S_5Cl_2, and S_6Cl_2 (*62*). All reactions are carried out without a solvent and with rigorous exclusion of moisture.

Under similar conditions the reactions of excess S_2Cl_2 with H_2S, H_2S_2, H_2S_3, and H_2S_4 yield Cl_2S_5, Cl_2S_6, Cl_2S_7, and Cl_2S_8, respectively (*52*). Table III demonstrates the scope of those reactions by means of some examples.

TABLE III

REACTIONS OF SULFANES WITH EXCESS OF CHLOROSULFANES

S_xCl_2	S_xH_2	Composition of product	Yield (%)
2260 g SCl_2	45 ml H_2S	$S_{3.38}$ Cl_2	84
1200 g SCl_2	26.5 g H_2S_2	$S_{4.00}$ Cl_2	90
900 g SCl_2	19.1 g H_2S_3	$S_{5.01}$ Cl_2	83
550 g SCl_2	19.0 g H_2S_4	$S_{6.04}$ Cl_2	92
450 g S_2Cl_2	10.0 g H_2S	$S_{4.98}$ Cl_2	100
400 g S_2Cl_2	15 g H_2S_2	$S_{6.10}$ Cl_2	100
400 g S_2Cl_2	10 g H_2S_3	$S_{7.04}$ Cl_2	100
500 g S_2Cl_2	15.3 g H_2S_4	$S_{8.03}$ Cl_2	100

2. Bromosulfanes

Chilling a hot vapor mixture of S_2Br_2 and hydrogen resulted in a mixture of higher bromosulfanes S_4Br_2 to $S_{11.4}Br_2$ (*51, 57*). Those mixtures could also be prepared by condensation reactions between S_2Br_2 and H_2S_x (*51, 50*). They cannot be separated into pure compounds by distillation. Pure higher bromosulfanes cannot be prepared according to Eq. (35) from S_2Br_2 and sulfanes, because the boiling point of S_2Br_2 is too high to distill the necessary excess from the higher bromosulfanes.

The pure compounds may be prepared, according to Fehér and Ristić (*53*), by the reaction of pure chlorosulfanes with hydrogen bromide:

$$S_nCl_2 + 2\ HBr \rightarrow S_nBr_2 + 2\ HCl \tag{36}$$

This reaction may be carried out at room temperature with quantitative yields. The following bromosulfanes have been prepared and characterized by this method: S_2Br_2, S_3Br_2, S_4Br_2, S_5Br_2, S_6Br_2, S_7Br_2, and S_8Br_2.

3. Cyanosulfanes

The older literature regarding cyano compounds of sulfur has been summarized by Fehér and Weber (*54*), who proved that these compounds are derivatives of the sulfanes and also were able to prepare a series of definite higher cyanosulfanes. These cyanosulfanes may be synthesized from halogeno sulfanes and mercuric thiocyanate:

$$S_nX_2 + Hg(SCN)_2 \rightarrow S_{n+2}(CN)_2 + HgX_2 \qquad (X = Cl, Br) \qquad (37)$$

The fact that a similar synthesis starting with mercuric cyanide works only with SCl_2 but not with higher chlorosulfanes:

$$SX_2 + Hg(CN)_2 \rightarrow S(CN)_2 + HgX_2 \qquad (38)$$

is a strong hint that the formation of sulfur-sulfur linkages provides the driving force for the reactions.

The following compounds have been prepared according to Eq. (37): $S_3(CN)_2$, $S_4(CN)_2$, $S_5(CN)_2$, $S_6(CN)_2$, $S_7(CN)_2$, and $S_8(CN)_2$.

For synthesis of the trichloromethylsulfanes $(CCl_3)_2S_{3-6}$ see reference *42*.

B. Properties and Structure

1. Chlorosulfanes

The chlorosulfanes Cl_2S_3 to Cl_2S_8 are yellow to orange-yellow viscous liquids of an irritating odor, the color of which deepens with increasing chain length. Only the compounds SCl_2, S_2Cl_2, and S_3Cl_2 may be distilled *in vacuo* without decomposition. They are all relatively stable. At $-80°C$ they may be stored indefinitely; at room temperature they may be stored at least for some weeks. Since they are easily prepared in larger quantities they promise to become very interesting intermediates for quite a number of reactions in both inorganic and organic chemistry.

The Raman spectra as well as the other measured physical properties of the chlorosulfanes (e.g., molar volume, molar refraction, and viscosity) prove unambiguously a chain structure for these compounds. The methods of preparation, the chemical reactions (see Sections III,A,1,c and IV,A,1,b, c, and d), and the physical properties all point to a straight chain homologous series. The a and b values for chlorosulfanes in the relation (18) (Section III,A,2) are $a = 39.9$, $b = 16.2$ for the molar volume and $a = 14.3$, $b = 8.9$ for the molar refraction, respectively.

2. Bromosulfanes

The bromosulfanes Br_2S_2 to Br_2S_8 are dark red-orange viscous liquids. They may not be distilled without decomposition. In contrast to the sulfanes (Section III), the organic sulfanes (Section IV), and the chlorosulfanes (Section V,B,1), the intensity of the color of bromosulfanes decreases with increasing chain length. The Raman spectra, density and viscosity of the different compounds again show the existence of a homologous series of compounds with unbranched chain structure.

The chemical behavior of the bromosulfanes has not yet been evaluated.

3. Cyanosulfanes

Cyanosulfanes form light yellow crystals [up to $S_6(CN)_2$] or yellow-green, very viscous oils [$S_7(CN)_2$ and $S_8(CN)_2$]. They are surprisingly stable and soluble in most organic solvents. At higher temperatures they all polymerize to form amorphous red products. The mechanism of this polymerization is not yet known; the same holds for the chemical reactions of cyanosulfanes.

The preparation of the cyanosulfanes according to Eq. (37), as well as their Raman spectra, prove again the existence of a homologous series of $(NC)S_n(CN)$ with unbranched chain structure.

VI. Sulfane Monosulfonic Acids HO_3SS_xH

This class of compounds was detected only within the last few years after it was realized that thiosulfuric acid is the first member of this new series of acids of sulfur.

A. Preparation

1. Thiosulfuric Acid

Salts of this acid have been known for more than 250 years. But in spite of a great number of experiments it never was possible to prepare the free acid, or stable solutions of it. Instability was regarded as a most characteristic property of $H_2S_2O_3$. Even its decomposition or the decomposition of acidified aqueous thiosulfate was not really understood [for a summary of the literature regarding the large number of experiments dealing with this decomposition see (115)].

In 1957 this acid was prepared (115) for the first time in ether solution free of water as the dietherate, $H_2S_2O_3 \cdot 2(C_2H_5)_2O$, by the reaction of sodium thiosulfate with hydrogen chloride in diethyl ether at $-78°C$:

$$Na_2S_2O_3 + 2\ HCl \rightarrow 2\ NaCl + H_2S_2O_3 \tag{39}$$

The decomposition of the anhydrous acid could then be studied for the first time. Elemental sulfur and sulfur dioxide had been believed to be the main products of this reaction, but the new experiments revealed quite a different, unexpected, and surprisingly simple behavior: anhydrous thiosulfuric acid on warming decomposes quantitatively below 0°C to form monosulfane and sulfur trioxide:

$$H_2S_2O_3 \rightarrow H_2S + SO_3 \tag{40}$$

Under anhydrous conditions the reaction products do not enter a redox reaction but are stable in contact with one another.

This decomposition is completely analogous to the thermal decomposition of sulfuric acid at temperatures above 330°C:

$$H_2SO_4 \rightarrow H_2O + SO_3 \tag{41}$$

and opened up an easy way for the preparation of thiosulfuric acid: stoichiometric amounts of SO_3 and H_2S under anhydrous conditions react at −78°C in ether to form $H_2S_2O_3$ quantitatively (*115*):

$$H_2S + SO_3 \rightarrow H_2S_2O_3 \tag{42}$$

This reaction recently was extended to mercaptans and thiophenols, thus forming for the first time free alkyl or aryl thiosulfuric acids (*135*):

$$RSH + SO_3 \rightarrow RSSO_3H \tag{43}$$

where R is an alkyl or aryl group.

Without a solvent, or in nonpolar solvents such as fluorochloromethanes, H_2S and SO_3 at low temperatures form, not thiosulfuric acid, but only the crystalline white Lewis adduct $H_2S \cdot SO_3$ which is isomeric with the acid and is easily decomposed *in vacuo* even at low temperatures into its components hydrogen sulfide and sulfur trioxide (*136*).

According to its formation [Eq. (42)] and decomposition [Eq. (40)], thiosulfuric acid must be regarded as the monosulfonic acid of monosulfane H_2S, and SO_3 must be regarded as the anhydride of sulfuric acid and at the same time the "ansulfhydride" of thiosulfuric acid. Similarly, chlorosulfonic acid is then the acid chloride of sulfuric acid as well as of thiosulfuric acid, depending upon whether it reacts with water or with hydrogen sulfide.

These considerations opened a third way for the preparation of free thiosulfuric acid—thiolysis of chlorosulfonic acid:

$$HO_3S \!\mid\! Cl + H \!\mid\! SH \rightarrow HO_3SSH + HCl \tag{44}$$

By this method the acid can be synthesized free of any solvent at all (*137*, *133*). Fluorosulfonic acid reacts in the same way but only to a very small extent and very slowly. The same is true for the first pseudohalogenosulfonic acid, thiocyanosulfonic acid $NCSSO_3H$, known in the free state (*134*). The recently prepared bromosulfonic acid, however, like chlorosulfonic acid, is thiolyzed very rapidly and quantitatively according to Eq. (44), and forms thiosulfuric acid and hydrogen bromide (*138*).

2. Higher Sulfane Monosulfonic Acids

The reaction of SO_3 with H_2S [Eq. (42)] can be further extended. SO_3 forms an acid not only with water, but also with hydrogen peroxide. This holds for both the thio analogue of water, H_2S, and the thio analogue of hydrogen peroxide, H_2S_2. According to the reaction:

$$HSSH + SO_3 \rightarrow HSSSO_3H \qquad (45)$$

disulfane and sulfur trioxide react in ether at low temperatures to form the new acid $H_2S_3O_3$ quantitatively. Its constitution is analogous to that of Caro's acid. The $-O-O-$ group of this compound is replaced by a $-S-S-$group (*116*).

Monosulfane monosulfonic acid $H_2S_2O_3$, and disulfane monosulfonic acid $H_2S_3O_3$, are the first two members of the sulfur acid series sulfane monosulfonic acids $H_2S_xO_3$. They are formed according to:

$$HS_xH + SO_3 \rightarrow HS_xSO_3H \qquad (46)$$

H_2S and H_2S_2 yield $H_2S_2O_3$ and $H_2S_3O_3$, as already mentioned. H_2S_3 forms trisulfane monosulfonic acid $H_2S_4O_3$, H_2S_4 tetrasulfane monosulfonic acid $H_2S_5O_3$, H_2S_5 pentasulfane monosulfonic acid $H_2S_6O_3$, and H_2S_6 hexasulfane monosulfonic acid $H_2S_7O_3$ (*116, 123*). $H_2S_7O_3$ is the highest member of this series known at the present time.

Sulfane monosulfonic acids may also be prepared by the reaction of chlorosulfonic acid with higher sulfanes (*137, 133, 64*), as has been shown for monosulfane in Eq. (44).

B. Properties and Structure

Sulfane monosulfonic acids are stable in ethereal solution at low temperatures. At room temperature they are decomposed more or less quickly. With the exception of thiosulfuric acid, which is dibasic, they are all strong monobasic acids. They may be isolated from their solutions as mono-etherates $H_2S_xO_3 \cdot (C_2H_5)_2O$ ($H_2S_2O_3$ forms a dietherate).

Again with the exception of the first member, $H_2S_2O_3$, they are stable at room temperature for some time in concentrated hydrochloric acid and in glacial acetic acid. Water and especially aqueous alkali decompose the acids very rapidly, thiosulfate, sulfur dioxide, and elemental sulfur being the main decomposition products.

Except for the thiosulfates, the salts $Me^IO_3SS_xH$ of sulfane monosulfonic acids are very unstable thermally as well as reactive toward water, and especially toward alkali. They may be prepared from alcoholic solutions of the acids.

In neutral or weakly basic aqueous solutions, the compounds react with excess sulfite to form thiosulfate:

$$H_2S_xO_3 + (x - 2)H_2SO_3 \rightarrow (x - 1)H_2S_2O_3 \qquad (47)$$

These reactions are quantitative and may therefore be used to analyze the acids by determining iodimetrically the thiosulfate formed during the reaction.

A similar degradation of the sulfane monosulfonic acids occurs with excess cyanide, whereby thiocyanate and thiosulfate are formed:

$$H_2S_xO_3 + (x - 2)HCN \rightarrow H_2S_2O_3 + (x - 2)HCNS \qquad (48)$$

This cyanide degradation also is quantitative and therefore very useful for analytical purposes.

For reactions of these acids with chlorosulfonic acid, chlorosulfanes, iodine, and chlorine see Section VII,A, 2.

The structure of the sulfane monosulfonic acids has not yet been established by physical measurements but follows from their formation from SO_3 and the linear sulfanes as well as from their oxidation to linear polythionic acids $H_2S_xO_6$ (see Section VII). They are built up from unbranched skewed sulfur chains with a —SO_3H group on one end and a hydrogen atom on the other end. Hexasulfane monosulfonic acid, according to this, appears to be:

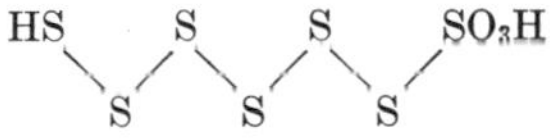

$$\begin{array}{ccccccc} HS & & S & & S & & SO_3H \\ \diagdown & \diagup & \diagdown & \diagup & \diagdown & \diagup & \\ & S & & S & & S & \end{array}$$

VII. Sulfane Disulfonic Acids $H_2S_xO_6$

According to the findings of the last few years, it is known that a very close genetic connection exists between the sulfanes, the sulfane monosulfonic acids $H_2S_xO_3$, and the polythionic acids $H_2S_xO_6$ (*117*); the polythionic acids therefore should be designated as sulfane disulfonic acids. This nomenclature should replace the established and customary older names, at least in cases in which the genetic relationship of polythionic acids to the class of sulfanes and their monosulfonic acids is emphasized, as in this review.

Anhydrous sulfane disulfonic acids have only recently been prepared (*137, 133, 64, 148, 146*), whereas the history of their salts and dilute aqueous solutions (their nature as derivatives of sulfanes not being recognized) is a long one, and fraught with problems as to chemical behavior and structure. As early as 1808, Dalton commented on the chemical nature of the constituents of the liquid (which later came to bear the name of Wackenroder) formed by the interaction of hydrogen sulfide and excess sulfur dioxide in water. The acids $H_2S_3O_6$, $H_2S_4O_6$, and $H_2S_5O_6$ were discovered in 1840 to 1846, and Debus in 1888 isolated from Wackenroder's liquid a salt that analyzed for potassium hexathionate; the existence of hexathionic acid was later doubted, and was not definitely established until the work of Weitz and Achterberg (*166*) in 1928. The literature on sulfane disulfonates (polythionates) up to 1927 has been reviewed by Kurtenacker (*91*); an excellent later review was given by Goehring in 1952 (*79*).

According to the older definitions, polythionates are salts of the acids $H_2S_xO_6$ with $x = 3$ to 6. The acids themselves were supposed for some time to be nonexistent in the anhydrous state, but to occur only in dilute aqueous solution. In spite of a number of studies giving some hints as to the existence of higher polythionates than hexathionates (*166, 93, 167, 172, 171, 173*), it is very improbable that these products represent pure individuals and not mixtures of homologues. Definite polythionates higher than hexathionates were prepared for the first time in 1957 (*118*).

A. Sulfane Disulfonates $Me_2^IS_3O_6$ to $Me_2^IS_6O_6$

Because of the unusually large number of papers on this group of compounds, and the confusing multiplicity of their reactions, only a very abbreviated summary can be given here. The fact that the many publications not infrequently are contradictory shows that there existed no real understanding of the essential nature of these compounds until the last few years, when it was realized that they were derivatives of the sulfanes. For details of the older literature see reference *79*.

1. Preparation

Sulfane-disulfonates are formed with different yields and purity mainly in the following ways:

Interaction of sulfur halides or other derivatives of S_2^{++} *and* S^{++} *with* HSO_3^- *and* $S_2O_3^{--}$, *respectively.* These reactions have been studied in detail by Stamm and Wintzer (*155*), Stamm and Goehring (*154*), and Goehring and Stamm (*81*), as well as other authors. As a consequence of later studies, the theoretical explanation of the course of these reactions given by the authors seems to be very doubtful. They assume as a common intermediate either $S_2(OH)_2$, S_2^{++}, or S_2O, whereas according to the more modern conception the undissociated species react with each other in a condensation reaction to form two moles of HX (X = halogen, —OR, etc.), the driving force being the formation of a sulfur-sulfur linkage (*147, 130*).

Interaction of hydrogen sulfide with excess sulfur dioxide in aqueous solution (Wackenroder's liquid). In spite of innumerable hypotheses regarding the various reactions occurring in this liquid (*79*), the formation of sulfane disulfonic acids by this method is not yet understood completely. Recently, it was pointed out that the reactions of elemental sulfur with sulfurous acid may play an important part (*125*). But altogether, Wackenroder's liquid still represents a "classical" problem in inorganic chemistry.

Oxidation of thiosulfates (monosulfane monosulfonates) with I_2, Cu^{++}, ICN, BrCN, $S_2O_8^{--}$, NO_2^-, *or* H_2O_2, *or at the anode.*

Disproportionation of sulfurous acid and its derivatives at higher temperatures.

Interaction of thiosulfates with acids in the presence of special catalysts such as As *or* Sb *salts.* These reactions are not yet understood.

a. Monosulfane disulfonates (trithionates). The potassium salt, $K_2S_3O_6$, may be prepared in satisfactory yield and purity by the interaction of $K_2S_2O_3$ with SO_2 in water (*99*).

b. Disulfane disulfonates (tetrathionates) are easily obtained in a pure state by the oxidation of thiosulfates by iodine (*111*) on a preparative scale. A method not yet published for the preparation of disulfane disulfonates seems to be very interesting, not only because of the high yields of pure product without further purification, but also because of its theoretical aspects: a large number of experiments has been carried out in the hope of forming sulfur chains in which an inner sulfur atom forms one or two linkages to oxygen (*124*):

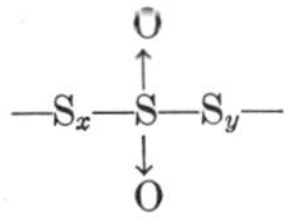

$$-S_x-\overset{\displaystyle O}{\underset{\displaystyle O}{S}}-S_y-$$

They were all unsuccessful. The only compound containing such a configuration that could be prepared was sulfuryl thiocyanide:

$$\overset{\displaystyle O}{\underset{\displaystyle O}{NCSSSCN}}$$

but this molecule decomposes at very low temperatures according to reaction (49):

$$SO_2(SCN)_2 \rightarrow SO_2 + (SCN)_2 \tag{49}$$

Other compounds could not be isolated at all. They immediately split off SO_2 (*124*). This holds also for the reaction of sulfuryl chloride with thiosulfates (*130*), which results in practically quantitative yields of pure disulfane disulfonates and sulfur dioxide:

$$HO_3SS-H + Cl-\overset{\overset{O}{\|}}{\underset{\underset{O}{\|}}{S}}-Cl + H-SSO_3H \rightarrow HO_3S-S-\overset{\overset{O}{\|}}{\underset{\underset{O}{\|}}{S}}-S-SO_3H + 2\ HCl \qquad (50)$$

$$HO_3S-S-\overset{\overset{O}{\|}}{\underset{\underset{O}{\|}}{S}}-S-SO_3H \rightarrow HO_3S-S-S-SO_3H + SO_2 \qquad (51)$$

This reaction, which is carried out in acid solution, proves that undissociated or unsolvolyzed molecules, respectively, react with each other rather than with ionic species.

c. Trisulfane disulfonates (pentathionates). Absolutely pure potassium trisulfane disulfonate $K_2S_5O_6$ may be made on a preparative scale by an improved method (*131*), worked out principally by Foerster (*67*). It is based on the acid decomposition of thiosulfate in the presence of As_2O_3.

A discrepancy in the literature exists in regard to the water of crystallization in $K_2S_5O_6$. Most authors describe the salt $K_2S_5O_6 \cdot 1.5H_2O$ (*80, 92, 99*), whereas Weitz (*167*) found a composition $K_2S_5O_6 \cdot 1H_2O$. The latter formula was established recently (*131*). Since this salt attracts water even from concentrated H_2SO_4 up to the constitution $H_2S_5O_6 \cdot 1.5H_2O$, the discrepancy is explained.

d. Tetrasulfane disulfonates (hexathionates). $K_2S_6O_6$ is best prepared by the oxidation of thiosulfate with HNO_2, first proposed by Weitz and Spohn (*167*), improved by Stamm *et al.* (*156*), and recently much further improved with respect to yield and purity by Sand (*131*).

2. Properties and Structure

Except for $K_2S_3O_6$ and $K_2S_4O_6$, the sulfane disulfonates are very difficult to prepare in a really pure state. The ions decompose in alkaline solutions and also, more or less rapidly, in strong acid solutions. Their most important reactions are the decomposition with an excess of sulfite:

$$S_xO_6^{--} + (x - 3)SO_3^{--} \rightarrow S_3O_6^{--} + (x - 3)S_2O_3^{--} \qquad (52)$$

forming monosulfane disulfonate and thiosulfate in stoichiometric amounts, and a similar cyanide degradation:

$$S_xO_6^{--} + (x - 3)CN^- + OH^- \rightarrow S_2O_3^{--} + (x - 3)CNS^- + HSO_4^- \qquad (53)$$

forming thiosulfate and thiocyanate, respectively.

A characteristic of sulfane disulfonates is their instability in aqueous solution in the presence of traces of sulfite or thiosulfate, normally present from the preparation. This decomposition, like most of the other reactions of these compounds, is very confusing and was not understood at all for a long time in spite of a large number of investigations.

The irritating complexity of the reactions of sulfane disulfonates could be systematized and understood for the first time on the hypothesis that they were sulfites or thiosulfites of S^{++} or S_2^{++}, respectively. This view was developed mainly by the schools of Foss and Fava (*79*). But measurements of the molar refraction by Grinberg (*77*) showed that this hypothesis cannot be correct. New methods of synthesis for the sulfane disulfonic acids proved definitely that they are true derivatives of the sulfanes (see Section VI,B,1) and not of S^{++} or S_2^{++}.

The very complicated analytical methods for a qualitative identification and quantitative determination of the different sulfane disulfonates have been worked out mainly by Kurtenacker (*93*). These ingenious chemical methods can be used only with reservation, especially in mixtures whose composition is continuously changing, because of the unavoidable interactions of the added reagents with the extremely labile sulfane disulfonates.

Regarding these difficulties, it seemed to be desirable to develop methods for a physical identification and separation of the sulfane disulfonates without any chemical influence on the salts in aqueous solution. Such methods appear to be a fundamental requirement for any further studies of the complicated formation and degradation reactions of the salts under discussion. They were recently developed by Sand (*131*), who first studied the crystal forms of the potassium salts and worked out a method of identifying the different compounds microscopically on the basis of the characteristic crystalline forms. For tetrasulfane disulfonate (hexathionate) two forms were observed. This observation led to the detection of the previously unknown acid salt KHS_6O_6 besides the normal $K_2S_6O_6$. This acid salt is formed by the normal preparative methods and may easily be differentiated from $K_2S_6O_6$ by chemical methods, as well as by its macroscopic crystal form and its X-ray pattern.

Exact measurements of the extinction in the ultraviolet region in combination with an error calculation enabled Sand to identify single sulfane disulfonates and to analyze quantitatively a mixture of sulfane disulfonates, if the components of the mixture were qualitatively known, without a chemical analysis.

An identification of solid salts is also possible by means of the infrared spectrum. Impurities higher than 5% may be detected by this method, which also permits the identification of sulfane disulfonates in aqueous solution within plastic sheets.

Determination of the dielectric constant of sulfane disulfonates permits a definite characterization of the different members of the homologous series. In the case of trisulfane disulfonate (pentathionate) these measurements show that the bound water is definitely not true water of crystallization fixed within the lattice.

Polarographic studies have shown that the method of oscillographic polarography is suitable for qualitative and quantitative analysis of sulfane disulfonates.

The quantitative separation of sulfane disulfonates by means of anionic exchangers has been studied in detail. It is suitable for the separation of SO_3^{--}, $S_2O_3^{--}$, $S_3O_6^{--}$, $S_4O_6^{--}$, and $S_5O_6^{--}$.

The scope and limits of a chromatographic separation of sulfane disulfonates have been carefully studied by Steinle (*132*). His experiments show that the power of this method was sometimes overestimated within the last few years due to the instability of the salts studied and a lack of knowledge of their various interactions with impurities (mainly sulfite and thiosulfate, which are practically always present when the salts are prepared by conventional methods). Paper chromatography, because of the instability of sulfane disulfonates and their rapid interactions with all sorts of compounds, even with water, seems to be of no use in elucidating the state of affairs in sulfane disulfonate mixtures. The time necessary for separation by this method is far too long for any valid statement. This holds also for any chromatographic "separations" of radioactive sulfane disulfonates labeled with ^{35}S. These separations may be carried out much more sensitively than ordinary separations, but not faster. What is not realized in these cases is the fact that, not the sensitivity, but the speed of the determination is decisive. Valid statements as to the composition of mixtures in the case of sulfane disulfonates are only possible when analysis of the composition is carried out within small fractions of a second but not within a couple of hours. Sulfane disulfonates, therefore, are not well suited for testing out new analytical procedures. Their very complicated chemistry seems to be too difficult for this purpose.

Structure. Blomstrand (*15*) in 1869 and, one year later, Mendelejeff (*101*) formulated the sulfane disulfonates with unbranched sulfur chains. Later, however, many authors preferred formulas with branched sulfur chains, mostly on the ground that the sulfur atoms of di-, tri-, and tetrasulfane disulfonates, which are so readily given off by the action of basic reagents such as hydroxide, sulfite, and cyanide ions must be bonded differently from the others and therefore could not be part of unbranched chains.

Today we know with certainty that the sulfane disulfonic acids possess an unbranched structure, not only from their chemical behavior but also from a number of physical measurements such as determination of refraction, viscosity, and electrical conductivity (*83*), of the Raman spectra (*32*), and of the K_α X-ray fluorescence (*33*). The most convincing arguments for the unbranched structure are structure determinations of the salts by X-ray methods, mainly carried out by Foss, who very recently wrote an excellent review on this subject (*66*). According to Foss:

> Two types of sulfur-sulfur bonds occur in the polythionates, namely, between divalent sulfur atoms in the middle of the chains and between one divalent and one sulfonate sulfur atom at the ends. The weighted average of the observed values for the length of the terminal bonds, in nine different salts, is 2.11 A, with an average deviation of 0.01 A. The middle bonds have within the errors the same length as the S—S bonds in orthorhombic sulfur, 2.04 A, which is also the value found for S—S bonds in organic di- and trisulfides.
>
> The difference in length between the two types of bonds indicates, apart from a possible effect of different hybridization of σ-bond orbitals at divalent and sulfonate sulfur, that bonds between divalent sulfur atoms possess some pd π-bond character, or, what is less probable, that the terminal bonds are longer than single bonds.

B. Free Sulfane Disulfonic Acids $H_2S_xO_6$

Only the following members of the series are known in dilute aqueous solution: $H_2S_3O_6$, $H_2S_4O_6$, $H_2S_5O_6$, and $H_2S_6O_6$. They are for the most part formed in more or less complicated mixtures by uncertain reaction paths, and may be separated only by tiresome fractional crystallization of their salts.

1. Preparation

The discovery of the sulfane monosulfonic acids (Section VI) in 1957 opened up a number of new and especially clear paths into the field of sulfane disulfonic acid chemistry. Sulfane monosulfonic acids react with sulfur trioxide in ethereal solution in a simple, straightforward reaction (*118*) to form anhydrous sulfane disulfonic acids in quantitative yields:

$$HO_3SS_xH + SO_3 \rightarrow HO_3SS_xSO_3H \qquad (54)$$

The following compounds have been prepared by this method: $H_2S_3O_6$, $H_2S_4O_6$, $H_2S_5O_6$, $H_2S_6O_6$, $H_2S_7O_6$, and $H_2S_8O_6$. One may just as well start out directly from the sulfanes as from their monosulfonic acids; the corresponding stoichiometric amount of sulfur trioxide must then be used, that is, $H_2S_x:SO_3 = 1:2$:

$$HS_xH + 2 SO_3 \rightarrow HO_3SS_xSO_3H \tag{55}$$

The above-mentioned acids are formed in an anhydrous state in a clearly defined manner, free from side products or other impurities.

A third route for the formation of sulfane-disulfonic acids was found in the oxidation of the monosulfonic acids with iodine in aqueous medium:

$$HO_3SS_xH + I_2 + HS_xSO_3H \rightarrow HO_3SS_{2x}SO_3H + 2 HI \tag{56}$$

With thiosulfuric acid, this oxidation has been known for a long time and is used for iodine titration in quantitative analysis. This method yields the highest members of the sulfane disulfonic acid series known at the present time as well-defined individuals. The following acids have been synthesized by it: $H_2S_4O_6$, $H_2S_6O_6$, $H_2S_8O_6$, $H_2S_{10}O_6$, $H_2S_{12}O_6$, and $H_2S_{14}O_6$. Stoichiometric amounts of chlorine instead of iodine as oxidant [Eq. (56)] permits the preparation of these acids in anhydrous medium (*123*).

Two further ways also lead from sulfane monosulfonic acids to sulfane disulfonic acids—their condensation with chlorosulfanes (*146, 64, 148*):

$$HO_3SS_x\text{--}H + Cl\text{--}S_y\text{--}Cl + H\text{--}S_xSO_3H \rightarrow HO_3SS_{2x+y}SO_3H + 2 HCl \tag{57}$$

and with chlorosulfonic acid (*137, 64*):

$$HO_3SS_x\text{--}H + Cl\text{--}SO_3H \rightarrow HO_3SS_xSO_3H \tag{58}$$

Recently the existence of higher sulfane disulfonic acids in Wackenroder's liquid up to a chain length of 12 has been reported by Barbieri and Bruno (*6, 7*).

Some results of Weitz and co-workers indicate that the sulfane disulfonate series extends up to and including the hydrophilic Odén sulfur sols. These appear to be sodium salts, $Na_2S_xO_6$ with x from 50 to 100. The stability of the salts with respect to liberation of sulfur decreases up to x about 20 and then increases as the properties approach those of the sulfur sols.

2. Properties and Structure

Sulfane disulfonic acids are soluble in water as well as in ether. Aqueous solutions are readily decomposed, whereas anhydrous ether solutions are stable at room temperature for some time. From those solutions the strong diprotic acids may be isolated as dietherates $H_2S_xO_6 \cdot 2(C_2H_5)_2O$, which are colorless oily liquids at normal temperature. Because of the open sulfur chain, the higher members (above $H_2S_5O_6$) are extremely sensitive to traces of alkali, while the stability to aqueous acids seems to pass a maximum in $H_2S_6O_6$. Some of the most important chemical reactions of sulfane disulfonic acids, such as their reactions with nucleophilic reagents will be discussed in Section X.

As to structure, there is no doubt that they are built up from unbranched sulfur chains with two SO_3H groups on the ends.

VIII. Thiokol-Type Compounds

Polymeric compounds of the composition $(C_xH_{2x}\text{---}S_y)_n$ are called Thiokols. In this formula the hydrogen atoms may be partly or completely substituted by a large number of organic groups.

A. Alkyl Polysulfide Polymers

The basic reaction in the preparation of alkyl polysulfide polymers may be written as:

$$n \text{ YRY} + n \text{ Na}_2S_x \rightarrow (RS_x)_n + 2n \text{ NaY} \tag{59}$$

This is essentially a nucleophilic displacement of the reactive terminal by the polysulfide anion. The rules for the reaction of monomeric reagents by this mechanism may be applied also to the polymer-forming system.

The products formed by those reactions are rubber-like materials. Because of their high resistivity to solvents they have found practical applications as concrete tank liners, fuel tank sealers, industrial maintenance coatings, vulcanizing agents, and many others.

Most of the work on Thiokols deals with their technical preparation and the application of these polymers. Though very interesting and important in many respects, it is far beyond the scope of this review, which deals only with the fundamental chemistry of polymeric compounds containing sulfur-sulfur linkages, and not with their technical aspects. The reader may find an extraordinarily carefully collected history of this interesting class of compounds from its beginning in 1838 up to the latest literature in 1958 in the report of Berenbaum and Panek (12), who refer to more than 800 papers. Most of the Thiokols used today are substituted ethylene tetrasulfides $-(-RCHCH_2\text{---}S_4-)-_x$.

In spite of the huge number of publications (12), surprisingly little is known of the fundamental chemical reactions leading to these polymers. This holds especially for the formation of polymeric methylene polysulfides.

The fundamental reaction of the most simple bifunctional hydrocarbon halide, methylene chloride, with sulfides and polysulfides had been studied only in mixtures with formaldehyde before the detailed work of Schmidt and Blaettner (*120, 121*). With this reviewer, Blaettner studied the reaction:

$$n \text{ RCHCl}_2 + n \text{ Me}_2\text{S}_x \rightarrow (\text{R—CH—S}_x\text{—})_n + 2n \text{ MeCl} \qquad (60)$$

for methylene chloride CH_2Cl_2, benzal chloride $C_6H_5CHCl_2$, and ethylidene chloride CH_3CHCl_2 with Me_2S to Me_2S_8 (Me = H, Na, and K). In the simplest case, with $x = 1$ and R = H, thioformaldehyde is formed which is not stable as a monomer but immediately polymerizes after its formation. Trimeric thioformaldehyde $(CH_2S)_3$ and some high molecular weight forms $(CH_2S)_n$ have long been known. They were prepared by the interaction of formaldehyde with hydrogen sulfide. The new method allows the preparation of pure crystalline $(CH_2S)_3$ or homogeneous high polymeric material $(CH_2S)_n$ in excellent yields from methylene chloride and MeSH, the degree of polymerization depending in a reproducible manner on the conditions of the reaction.

In the course of these studies a new low molecular weight species of thioformaldehyde could be detected and isolated: $(CH_2S)_4$. The white crystals melt at 42°C. They are derived from the S_8 ring by a symmetrical replacement of four sulfur atoms by four CH_2 groups.

In the presence of triethylamine, liquid hydrogen sulfide at room temperature and under pressure reacts with CH_2Cl_2 to form polymeric products of the composition $(CH_2S_{1.1})_n$. Their properties are similar to those of the polymeric thioformaldehydes, the difference being a content of about 10% disulfide bridges —C—S—S—C— instead of normal —C—S—C— linkages.

Reactions of methylene chloride with alkali polysulfides in homogeneous organic aqueous media yield polymers of the following average composition: $(CH_2S_2)_n$, $(CH_2S_3)_n$, $(CH_2S_4)_n$, $(CH_2S_5)_n$, $(CH_2S_6)_n$, $(CH_2S_7)_n$, and $(CH_2S_8)_n$. These products form rubber-like, insoluble masses. Whereas $(CH_2S_2)_n$ and $(CH_2S_8)_n$ are nearly brittle, the other members are softer, $(CH_2S_5)_n$ behaving almost like a very viscous liquid. On warming above 100°C the polymers first soften and then decompose at about 150° to 200°C.

Benzal chloride with polysulfides reacts more easily than methylene chloride. The following compounds could be obtained: $(C_6H_5CHS_2)_n$, $(C_6H_5CHS_3)_n$, $(C_6H_5CHS_4)_n$, $(C_6H_5CHS_5)_n$, $(C_6H_5CHS_6)_n$, $(C_6H_5CHS_7)_n$, and $(C_6H_5CHS_8)_n$. They form red materials of very high viscosity. With increasing sulfur content they become more brittle. Obviously, small amounts of unreacted benzal chloride function as softeners. They may be removed by a long treatment with water vapor. By this method the polymers remain as glassy, brittle materials. Similar products are also obtained by reactions of benzaldehyde with sulfanes.

In contrast to the methylene polysulfides some benzal polysulfides are soluble in carbon disulfide to a slight extent. This fact allows a determination of the order of magnitude of their molecular weight by means of Staudinger's viscosity method. The average degree of polymerization is about 50 units per molecule, the molecular weight between $\sim$ 8000 and $\sim$ 17,000.

Whereas benzal chloride is more easily attacked by polysulfides than methylene chloride, the contrary is true for ethylidene chloride, CH_3CHCl_2. This compound does not react with polysulfides in aqueous alcoholic solutions under normal conditions but only in very concentrated solutions at high temperatures in sealed tubes. Then, however, the products are pure and the degree of polymerization of $(CH_3CHS_x)_n$ is low. For instance, $(CH_3CHS_2)_n$ is octameric.

The experiments of Blaettner and Schmidt revealed a clear difference in the reactivity of geminal hydrocarbon halides with respect to polysulfides of the following order:

$$C_6H_5CHCl_2 > CH_2Cl_2 \gg CH_3CHCl_2$$

The knowledge derived from these studies of the behavior of methylene chloride and substituted methylene chlorides toward sulfides and polysulfides was recently used for the synthesis of a new class of polymeric compounds which seems to be considerably interesting insofar as practical uses are concerned (*143, 145*).

Thiokols and silicones represent two completely different classes of plastics with different properties and different applications. A combination of their properties could be attained by reactions of chlorinated siloxanes with sulfides and polysulfides. So symmetrical bischloromethyltetramethyldisiloxane reacts with sulfides to form the very interesting new compound, cyclization being preferred to linear polymer formation in this case:

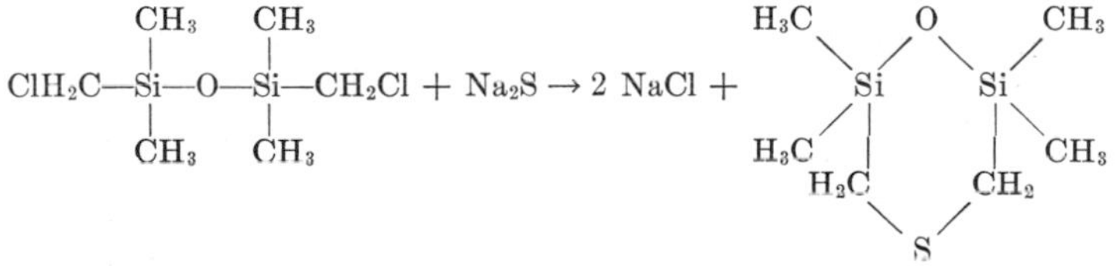

$$
\begin{array}{c}
\underset{\underset{CH_3}{|}}{\overset{\overset{CH_3}{|}}{ClH_2C-Si}}-O-\underset{\underset{CH_3}{|}}{\overset{\overset{CH_3}{|}}{Si}}-CH_2Cl + Na_2S \rightarrow 2\,NaCl + \quad\quad\quad (61)
\end{array}
$$

Whereas this reaction yields a low molecular weight product, polymers of very interesting properties may be obtained by interaction of chlorinated siloxanes with sulfides or polysulfides. A vulcanization of silicones in the real meaning of the word may so be achieved, that is, a linking of siloxane chains or rings over C—S—C or C—S$_x$—C bridges. The number of sulfur bridges, and with this the properties of the resulting plastics, can be varied with the number of C—Cl groups in the starting material. The following picture shows part of one of these newly prepared macromolecules—in this example, a transparent, very hard and chemically as well as thermally very stable product, with 100% sulfur linkages:

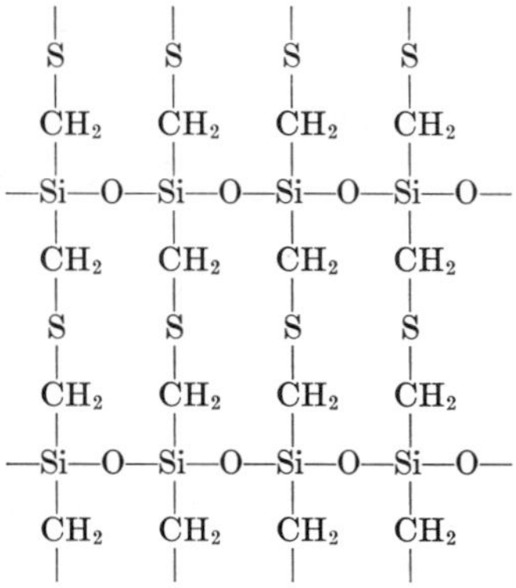

$$
\begin{array}{cccc}
| & | & | & | \\
S & S & S & S \\
| & | & | & | \\
CH_2 & CH_2 & CH_2 & CH_2 \\
| & | & | & | \\
-Si-O-Si-O-Si-O-Si-O- \\
| & | & | & | \\
CH_2 & CH_2 & CH_2 & CH_2 \\
| & | & | & | \\
S & S & S & S \\
| & | & | & | \\
CH_2 & CH_2 & CH_2 & CH_2 \\
| & | & | & | \\
-Si-O-Si-O-Si-O-Si-O- \\
| & | & | & | \\
CH_2 & CH_2 & CH_2 & CH_2 \\
| & | & | & |
\end{array}
$$

B. Phenylene Polysulfides

Although nuclear-substituted halogens are normally very unreactive, Macallum (*96–98*), by using very drastic reaction conditions, was able to prepare polymers from such compounds as *p*-dichlorobenzene. The polymerization was carried out in an evacuated sealed tube containing a mixture of powdered sulfur and sodium carbonate together with the dihalide. Treatment for 20 hr at 300° to 400°C resulted in substantially complete reaction. These products were quite hard though not brittle at room temperature, becoming plastic enough to mould at 180° to 200°C. The melting points are in the 250°–350°C range. Notwithstanding the difficulty of the reaction, respectable molecular weights up to 20,000 were obtained. These experiments naturally attracted the interest of polymer chemists because a phenylene linkage repeated in the backbone of a polymer chain is a very desirable moiety that imparts regularity and rigidity to the chain.

The mechanism of the Macallum polymerization and the structure of polymers obtained by it have been studied in detail by Lenz *et al.* (*94, 95*). According to this study, the Macallum polymerization is a polycondensation of an aryl halide and an inorganic sulfide or polysulfide in the absence of solvents. The monomer system studied most thoroughly is represented by the following, unbalanced equation:

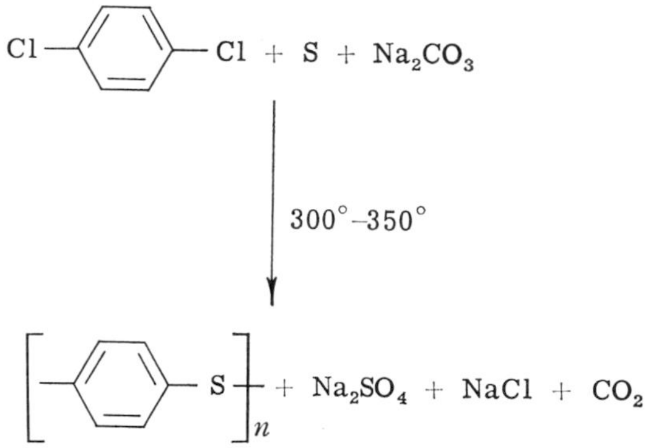

$$Cl-\langle\bigcirc\rangle-Cl \ + \ S \ + \ Na_2CO_3$$

$$\downarrow 300°\text{--}350° \qquad\qquad (62)$$

$$\left[-\langle\bigcirc\rangle-S-\right]_n + \ Na_2SO_4 \ + \ NaCl \ + \ CO_2$$

In this system, sulfur and sodium carbonate are believed to react in the melt to form sodium sulfide which, in turn, combines with *p*-dichloroben-zene to form the polymers. The complicated inorganic and organic reactions believed to occur in the melt polymerization are considered both separately and in conjunction with the over-all polycondensation. The reactions discussed include: the nucleophilic substitution type of oxidation-reduction reactions of polysulfides and oxysulfur compounds, e.g.:

$$Na_2CO_3 + S\!-\!S\!-\!S\!-\!S \rightarrow S\!-\!S^-Na^+ + Na^+\ ^-OS\!-\!S + CO_2 \qquad (63)$$

free-radical substitution on aromatic rings:

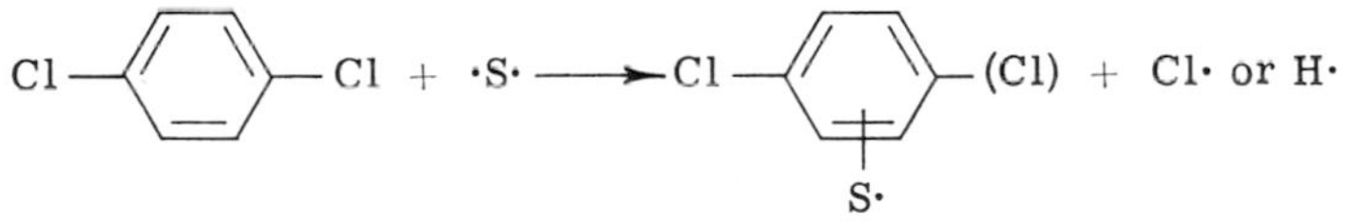

$$Cl-\langle\bigcirc\rangle-Cl \ + \ \cdot S\cdot \longrightarrow Cl-\langle\bigcirc\rangle-(Cl) \ + \ Cl\cdot \text{ or } H\cdot \qquad (64)$$
$$\qquad\qquad\qquad S\cdot$$

and nucleophilic substitution of unactivated, aryl halides:

$$ArCl + Na_2S \rightarrow ArS^-Na^+ + NaCl \qquad (65)$$
$$Ar'Cl + ArS^-Na^+ \rightarrow ArSAr' + NaCl \qquad (66)$$

The over-all polycondensation is believed to consist of a combination of these reactions in the form of more or less distinct initiation and propagation steps.

Polymers prepared by the Macallum homopolymerization and copolymerization were compared to a linear phenylene sulfide polymer prepared by the self-condensation of sodium *p*-chlorothiophenoxide. The properties compared included solubility, softening point, melting point, X-ray diffraction pattern, infrared spectrum, and thermal stability. For the last named, both differential thermal analyses and thermal gravimetric analyses were carried out. The linear polyphenylene sulfide and the Macallum polymers were found to be essentially identical in all of these properties, even though the sulfur contents of the latter were generally higher by 15 to 20% than the amount present in the linear polymer. Consideration of this identity and of the probable mechanism of the Macallum polymerization led to the postulation of a structure for the Macallum polymers consisting of a cross-linked core to which are attached more or less extended linear chains.

Under the conditions of the Macallum polymerization, some as yet un-described polymeric phenylene sulfides were recently isolated which are for the most part soluble in organic solvents and have only low molecular weights (*129*), such as a decameric *m*-phenylene sulfide, $(C_6H_4S)_{10}$, or trimeric, pentameric, heptameric, and nonameric *o*-phenylene sulfides, $(C_6H_4S)_{3, 5, 7,}$ and $_9$. On heating they may be further polymerized into insoluble species of very high thermal stability.

IX. Polymeric Compounds Derived from Thio Acids

The well-established method of condensing HS groups with ClS groups for the formation of sulfur-sulfur linkages:

$$-S-\overline{-H + Cl-}-S- \rightarrow HCl + -S-S- \tag{67}$$

has been very useful for the preparation of quite a number of substances such as sulfanes, chlorosulfanes, alkyl sulfanes, etc. The reaction of thio-sulfuric acid with chlorosulfanes to form sulfane disulfonic acids is an example in which a thio acid is used as the —SH bearing substance.

Thioacids are the thio analogs of the oxygen acids, one or more oxygen atoms being replaced by sulfur atoms. Normally those acids do not exist in the free state, or at least are much less stable than their oxygen analogs. An important exception to this rule is trithiocarbonic acid H_2CS_3 which, in contrast to H_2CO_3 is stable for some time in the free state.

The examples in this section drawn from still unpublished work show that other thio acids than $H_2S_2O_3$ may also be used for condensation reactions with chlorosulfanes, forming new polymeric sulfur compounds with interesting properties (*128, 126*). They all are derivatives of the sulfanes.

A. Compounds of the Type $(CS_x)_n$

Free thiocarbonic acid, H_2CS_3, may be prepared by careful decomposition of $BaCS_3$ [formed from $Ba(SH)_2$ and CS_2] with hydrochloric acid in about

50% yield. The dry acid is soluble in the organic solvents ether, chloroform, carbon disulfide, etc. These solutions are stable at room temperature for some hours.

Slow addition of a solution of the stoichiometric amount of a chlorosulfane in ether or chloroform to a vigorously stirred solution of H_2CS_3 in the same solvent, with careful exclusion of moisture and cooling to $-78°C$, results in the evolution of hydrogen chloride and the formation of an orange-yellow colored deposit. The reaction takes from 2 to 20 hr depending on the chain length of the chlorosulfane. If the deposit is separated too early it becomes a soft, plastic mass at room temperature, but after condensation is completed it stays dry and powdery indefinitely. What happens in these reactions is the formation of polymeric carbon-sulfur compounds:

$$ClS_x\!-\!|\!-\!Cl + H\!-\!|\!-\!S\overset{\overset{\text{S}}{\|}}{C}S\!-\!|\!-\!H + Cl\!-\!|\!-\!S_x\!-\!|\!-\!Cl + H\!-\!|\!-\!S\overset{\overset{\text{S}}{\|}}{C}S\!-\!|\!-\!H + Cl\!-\!|\!-\!S_x\!-\!|\!-\!Cl + H\!-\!|\!-\!S\overset{\overset{\text{S}}{\|}}{C}SH,\ \text{etc.}$$

$$\rightarrow\ ClS_x S\overset{\overset{\text{S}}{\|}}{C}SS_x S\overset{\overset{\text{S}}{\|}}{C}SS_x S\overset{\overset{\text{S}}{\|}}{C}SH \quad (68)$$

This condensation polymerization goes on until very long chains or large rings are formed that are insoluble.

The over-all reaction may be written as:

$$n\ H_2CS_3 + n\ S_xCl_2 \rightarrow (CS_{x+3})_n + 2n\ HCl \quad (69)$$

The following compounds have been prepared in excellent yields and satisfactory purity from SCl_2, S_2Cl_2, S_3Cl_2, S_4Cl_2, S_5Cl_2, S_6Cl_2, and thiocarbonic acid, respectively: $(CS_4)_x$, $(CS_5)_x$, $(CS_6)_x$, $(CS_7)_x$, $(CS_8)_x$ and $(CS_9)_x$. They all form orange-colored dry powders at room temperature; the color deepens with increasing chain length. In organic solvents as well as in water they are completely insoluble. Soluble low molecular weight forms have not been isolated in spite of many experiments aimed at the formation of small rings of the type:

$$S{=}C\overset{\overset{\displaystyle S_x}{\diagup\quad\diagdown}}{\underset{\diagdown\quad\diagup}{\underset{\displaystyle S_x}{}}}C{=}S$$

The formation from the linear chlorosulfanes, the chemical behavior, and the infrared spectra of the new polymers indicate their structure as long sulfur chains or large rings, respectively, with $-\overset{\overset{\text{S}}{\|}}{C}-$ groups built in regularly, always between 3, 4, 5, 6, 7, or 8 sulfur atoms.

The compounds are thermally decomposed between 150° and 200°C, quantitatively, according to the reaction:

$$(CS_x)_n \rightarrow n\, CS_2 + (S_{x-2})_n \qquad (70)$$

and form carbon disulfide and plastic sulfur.

They are very stable against water and aqueous acids, and are attacked only slowly by alkaline solutions.

B. Compounds of the Type $(PS_x)_n$

Similar condensation reactions have also been observed by the interaction of chlorosulfanes with thiophosphoric acids (*128*).

1. Sulfane Phosphonic Acids

Monothiophosphonic acid H_3PO_3S contains only one HS group capable of condensation reactions and therefore should lead to the formation of well-defined, low molecular weight compounds by reaction with chlorosulfanes. This is indeed the case. In ethereal solution, H_3PO_3S reacts at low temperatures quantitatively with SCl_2 and S_2Cl_2, respectively:

$$(HO)_2OPS{-}{\mid}{-}H + Cl{-}{\mid}{-}S{-}{\mid}{-}Cl + H{-}{\mid}{-}SPO(OH)_2 \rightarrow (HO)_2OPS{-}S{-}SPO(OH)_2 + 2\,HCl \quad (71)$$

and:

$$(HO)_2OPS{-}{\mid}{-}H + Cl{-}{\mid}{-}SS{-}{\mid}{-}Cl + H{-}{\mid}{-}SPO(OH)_2 \rightarrow (HO)_2OPS{-}S{-}S{-}SPO(OH)_2 + 2\,HCl$$

$$(72)$$

thus forming the first two members of the new class of sulfane phosphonic acids, $H_4P_2O_6S_x$.

$H_4P_2O_6S_3$ and $H_4P_2O_6S_4$ are deposited from ether in the form of oily dietherates. The ether may be completely removed *in vacuo* at 0°C, the free acids remaining as very viscous, colorless liquids. *In vacuo* they are stable for some time at room temperature but in air they decompose to deposit elemental sulfur. In aqueous solutions they form phosphoric acid, hydrogen sulfide, and sulfur. This decomposition goes on comparatively slowly so that from freshly prepared solutions the barium salts $Ba_2O_6P_2S_3$ and $Ba_2O_6P_2S_4$ may be precipitated by the addition of barium hydroxide. These salts are stable except against acids.

The molecular weights of the acids may be determined cryoscopically because of the solubility of sulfane phosphonic acids in benzene.

2. High Polymeric Sulfane Derivatives of Phosphorus

In contrast to monothiophosphoric acid, tetrathiophosphoric acid H_3PS_4 contains three HS groups capable of condensation with chlorosulfanes; this led to the prediction of the formation of polymers $(PS_x)_n$ in these reactions. Free tetrathiophosphoric acid had long been described in the literature as nonexistent. Only within the last few years has it been prepared for the first time (*127*, *144*).

This acid reacts in ether at low temperatures with SCl_2 and S_2Cl_2 according to the equations:

$$2x \ H_3PS_4 + 3x \ SCl_2 \rightarrow (PS_{5.5})_{2x} + 6x \ HCl \tag{73}$$

and:

$$2x \ H_3PS_4 + 3x \ S_2Cl_2 \rightarrow 2(PS_7)_x + 6x \ HCl \tag{74}$$

The reaction path may be symbolized as:

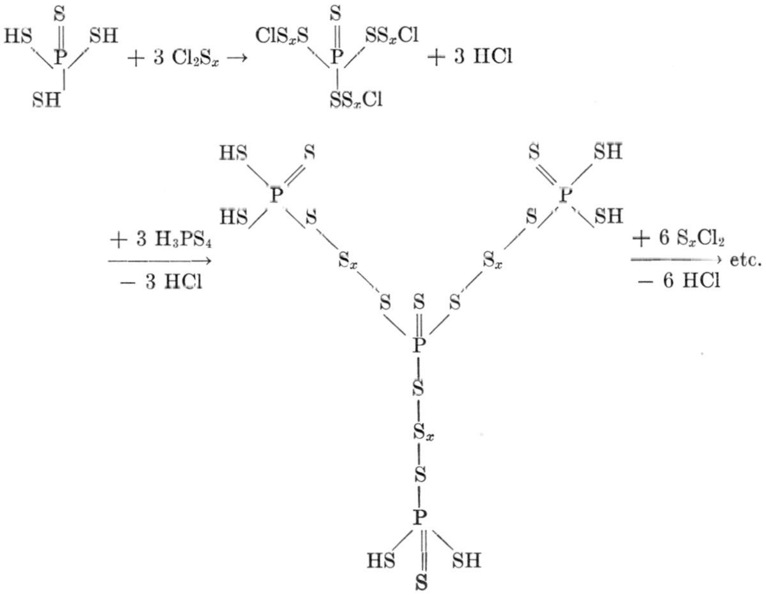

The plastic products are light yellow in color and stable at room temperature *in vacuo*. In air they slowly evolve some hydrogen sulfide. In organic solvents as well as in water they are insoluble. Aqueous alkali decomposes the polymers. Thermally, they are decomposed above temperatures of about 220°C.

X. Reactions of Chain-Containing Sulfur Compounds with Nucleophilic Agents

The detection of the sulfane monosulfonic acids (Section VI) (*116*) and the revealing of their close genetic connection with the sulfanes (Section III) on the one hand and the sulfane disulfonic acids (polythionic acids) (Section VII) on the other cast an essentially new light on many branches of sulfur chemistry, earlier believed to be quite different from each other. These findings serve as a new starting point for the understanding not only of the confusing diverse and complicated reactions of the sulfane disulfonates, but also of many other reactions in sulfur chemistry, as will be shown by means of some more or less arbitrarily chosen examples in the following part of this section.

A. Reactions of Sulfane Sulfonic Acids with Nucleophilic Agents

Many reactions of sulfane disulfonates which could formerly be explained with difficulty (or not at all) can now be rationalized without difficulty on the basis of the new concept, according to which the polythionates are not sulfites or thiosulfates of positive sulfur S_2^{++} or S^{++}, but rather the disulfonates of the sulfanes, H_2S_x. A consequent nomenclature has already been applied in this review. (In the case of dithionic acid $H_2S_2O_6$, this nomenclature logically offers no name at all. Thereby it is clearly expressed that this acid stands in no direct chemical relationship to the higher members of the series $H_2S_xO_6$, even though according to its name it still frequently is designated as a "polythionic acid.")

The study of the chemical behavior of sulfane monosulfonic acids revealed the important fact that these acids are formed as intermediates in quite a number of mostly very complicated reactions in sulfur chemistry. It was only natural that the reactions that had been experimentally observed a long time ago could not be explained satisfactorily without a knowledge of an important link of the logical chain, the sulfane monosulfonic acids.

On the basis of the observation that treatment of the sulfane monosulfonic acids with sulfite, cyanide, sulfide, alkali, etc., produces exactly the same degradation products as are formed from sulfane disulfonic acids, it may be concluded that the monosulfonic acids always are the first degradation products of the disulfonic acids. All the numerous single reactions of the disulfonic acids may then be explained as a sort of cleavage process of these compounds by means of H_2SO_3, HCN, H_2S, HOH, etc., functioning as cleaving agents. The sulfur chain is cleaved by the addition of the nucleophilic agent to the incipient free ends of the sulfur chain. In all these reactions, which proceed without exception in a stepwise manner, a sulfane monosulfonic acid is formed by the primary cleavage. From the large number of these degradation processes, attention will be focused on only a very few examples in this review.

1. Sulfite Degradation of Sulfane Sulfonic Acids

It has long been known and also used for analytical purposes that sulfane disulfonates react with excess sulfite in aqueous solution:

$$S_xO_6^{--} + (x - 3)SO_3^{--} \rightarrow S_3O_6^{--} + (x - 3)S_2O_3^{--} \tag{76}$$

forming, quantitatively, thiosulfate and monosulfane disulfonate (79). A number of hypotheses has been put forward to explain the path of these reactions (79), which are mostly contradictory to each other and do not fit into the modern interpretation. According to this interpretation, the reaction of sulfane disulfonates with sulfite proceeds in the way shown for the example of tetrasulfane disulfonic acid as:

$$+ \text{H}\vdots\text{—SO}_3\text{H}$$
$$\text{HO}_3\text{S—S—S—S—}\vdots\text{S—SO}_3\text{H} \rightarrow \text{HO}_3\text{S—S—S—S—H} + \text{HO}_3\text{S—S—SO}_3\text{H} \tag{77}$$
$$+ \text{H}\vdots\text{—SO}_3\text{H}$$
$$\text{HO}_3\text{S—S—S—}\vdots\text{SH} \rightarrow \text{HO}_3\text{S—S—SH} + \text{HSSO}_3\text{H} \tag{78}$$
$$+ \text{H}\vdots\text{—SO}_3\text{H}$$
$$\text{HO}_3\text{S—S—}\vdots\text{SH} \rightarrow \text{HO}_3\text{S—SH} + \text{HSSO}_3\text{H} \tag{79}$$

$$H_2S_5O_6 + 3 H_2SO_3 \rightarrow H_2S_3O_6 + 3 H_2S_2O_3 \tag{80}$$

According to this, tetrasulfane disulfonic acid is degraded by sulfite through the stages of trisulfane monosulfonic acid $H_2S_4O_3$ and disulfane monosulfonic acid $H_2S_3O_3$ to thiosulfate and monosulfane disulfonate.

This interpretation of the sulfite decomposition of sulfane disulfonates explains quite simply the results of Christiansen (20), who carried out experiments using radioactively labeled sulfur. Earlier, the sulfite degradation of sulfane disulfonates was explained on the basis that sulfite has a strong tendency to combine with sulfur and thereby to form a coordinate tetravalent state. In the case of disulfane disulfonate, for example, the reaction was therefore interpreted as the loss of a sulfur atom from disulfane disulfonate, thereby forming monosulfane disulfonate, and the acceptance of sulfur by sulfite, thus forming thiosulfite.

If this simple scheme is correct, one would expect that, if the reaction were carried out using radioactively labeled sulfite, all the activity would be found in the thiosulfate:

$$S_4O_6^{--} + {}^*SO_3^{--} \nrightarrow S_3O_6^{--} + {}^*S_2O_3^{--} \tag{81}$$

Exactly the opposite is the case. The total activity is found in the monosulfane disulfonate, whereas the thiosulfate is free of labeled sulfur. This initially surprising result follows necessarily from the new interpretation, as is shown by the following equation:

$$\begin{array}{l} \qquad\qquad + \text{H}\vdots\text{—}^*\text{SO}_3\text{H} \\ \text{HOS}_3\text{—S—}\vdots\text{S—SO}_3\text{H} \rightarrow \text{HO}_3\text{S—SH} + \text{HO}_3\text{S}^*\text{SSO}_3\text{H} \end{array} \qquad (82)$$

Clearly the total activity must be found only in the monosulfane disulfonate and none at all in the thiosulfate, as is actually found to be the case.

2. Cyanide Degradation of Sulfane Sulfonic Acids

The long known cyanide degradation of sulfane disulfonates according to:

$$S_xO_6^{--} + (x - 3)CN^- \rightarrow S_2O_3^{--} + (x - 3)SCN^- + HSO_4^- \qquad (83)$$

may be satisfactorily explained by the following steps (in the case of tetrasulfane disulfonic acid):

$$\begin{array}{l} \qquad\qquad\qquad\qquad + \text{H}\vdots\text{—CN} \\ \text{HO}_3\text{S—S—S—S—S—}\vdots\text{SO}_3\text{H} \rightarrow \text{NCSO}_3\text{H} \; (\xrightarrow{+\text{H}_2\text{O}} \text{HCN} + \text{H}_2\text{SO}_4) + \text{HO}_3\text{S—S—S—S—SH} \end{array} \qquad (84)$$

$$\begin{array}{l} \qquad\qquad\qquad + \text{H}\vdots\text{—CN} \\ \text{HO}_3\text{S—S—S—S—}\vdots\text{SH} \rightarrow \text{HO}_3\text{S—S—S—SH} + \text{HSCN} \end{array} \qquad (85)$$

$$\begin{array}{l} \qquad\qquad + \text{H}\vdots\text{—CN} \\ \text{HO}_3\text{S—S—S—}\vdots\text{SH} \rightarrow \text{HO}_3\text{S—S—SH} + \text{HSCN} \end{array} \qquad (86)$$

$$\begin{array}{l} \qquad\quad + \text{H}\vdots\text{—CN} \\ \text{HO}_3\text{S—S—}\vdots\text{SH} \rightarrow \text{HO}_3\text{S—SH} + \text{HSCN} \end{array} \qquad (87)$$

$$H_2S_6O_6 + 3\ HCN + H_2O \rightarrow 3\ HSCN + H_2S_2O_3 + H_2SO_4 \qquad (88)$$

This formulation is in complete agreement with the behavior of sulfane disulfonic acids, as well as of sulfane monosulfonic acids, against excess cyanide in aqueous solutions.

3. Arsenite Degradation of Sulfane Sulfonic Acids

The reaction of arsenite with sulfane disulfonates had not been studied in detail until the work of Wägerle (*141*). According to his experiments, sulfane disulfonic acids react with arsenite in aqueous solutions:

$$S_xO_6^{--} + (x - 1)AsO_3^{3-} \xrightarrow{+OH^-} 2\ S_2O_3^{--} + (x - 2)AsO_3S^{3-} + HAsO_4^{--} \qquad (89)$$

These experiments indicate that the same stepwise degradation reactions of sulfane disulfonates as with sulfite and cyanide also take place in the presence of arsenite ions, yielding thiosulfate and monothioarsenate in stoichiometric amounts.

The same reaction mechanism obviously holds also for the reactions of sulfane mono- and disulfonic acids with —SH and —OH ions.

4. Self Decomposition of Sulfane Sulfonic Acids

It is known that every sulfane disulfonate solution which contains sulfurous acid or thiosulfate decomposes by a great number of reactions to form all sorts of other sulfane disulfonates. If one formally includes sulfurous acid H_2SO_3 in the series of sulfane monosulfonic acids $H_2S_xO_3$, then all these various reactions are explained quite simply by the two following general equations:

$$H_2S_xO_6 + H_2S_yO_3 \rightleftharpoons H_2S_{y+2}O_6 + H_2S_{x-2}O_3 \tag{90}$$

$$H_2S_xO_3 + H_2S_yO_3 \rightleftharpoons H_2S_{x-1}O_3 + H_2S_{y+1}O_3, \tag{91}$$

again assuming the previously mentioned cleavage processes. The first equation applies to the first reaction step. If a sulfane monosulfonic acid is formed that contains more than two sulfur atoms in the molecule, this compound is further cleaved according to the second equation, which also applies to all the following steps. With the aid of these two equations, practically all the reactions of sulfane disulfonates in the presence of sulfite or thiosulfate in aqueous solution may be interpreted essentially as equilibrium reactions between the members of the classes of sulfane monosulfonic acids and sulfane disulfonic acids.

In order further to test this hypothesis of a stepwise degradation of sulfur chains, it seemed desirable to investigate still other compounds that contain chains of sulfur atoms in the molecule.

B. Reactions of Sulfanes with Nucleophilic Agents

As model compounds for the above-mentioned research, the sulfanes themselves were available since Fehér and his students had unequivocally proved that these compounds possess unbranched chain structures. In this connection, the behavior of some sulfanes toward sodium sulfite in aqueous solution has been studied.

1. Sulfite Degradation of Sulfanes

If one compares the stepwise sulfite degradation of sulfane disulfonic acids and sulfane monosulfonic acids on the one hand with sulfite degradation of sulfanes on the other, all of which proceed by the same principle, one arrives at the following picture (in the case of tetrasulfane and its sulfonic acids) :

$$+ \text{ H}\vdots\text{SO}_3\text{H} + \text{ H}\vdots\text{SO}_3\text{H}$$

$$\text{HO}_3\text{S}\!-\!-\!\text{S}\!-\!-\!\vdots\text{S}\!-\!-\!\text{ S}\!-\!-\!\vdots\text{S}\!-\!-\!\text{SO}_3\text{H} \rightarrow 3 \text{ H}_2\text{S}_2\text{O}_3 + \text{H}_2\text{S}_3\text{O}_6 \qquad (92)$$

$$+ \text{ H}\vdots\text{SO}_3\text{H}$$

$$+ \text{ H}\vdots\text{SO}_3\text{H} + \text{ H}\vdots\text{SO}_3\text{H}$$

$$\text{HO}_3\text{S}\!-\!-\!-\!\text{S}\!-\!-\!\vdots\text{S}\!-\!-\!-\!\vdots\text{S}\!-\!-\!\vdots\text{SH} \rightarrow 4 \text{ H}_2\text{S}_2\text{O}_3 \qquad (93)$$

$$+ \text{ H}\vdots\text{SO}_3\text{H}$$

$$+ \text{ H}\vdots\text{SO}_3\text{H} + \text{ H}\vdots\text{SO}_3\text{H}$$

$$\text{H}\!-\!-\!-\!\text{S}\!-\!-\!\vdots\text{S}\!-\!-\!-\!\vdots\text{S}\!-\!-\!\vdots\text{S}\!-\!-\!\text{H} \rightarrow \text{H}_2\text{S} + 3 \text{ H}_2\text{S}_2\text{O}_3 \qquad (94)$$

$$+ \text{ H}\vdots\text{SO}_3\text{H}$$

Accordingly, as is actually found to be the case, from 1 mole of sulfane disulfonate, the sulfite degradation always must lead to 1 mole of monosulfane disulfonate and a quantity of thiosulfate that depends upon the chain length of the sulfane disulfonate.

In the degradation of sulfane monosulfonic acids, however, according to this scheme no monosulfane disulfonate is formed; in agreement with the experimental findings only thiosulfate is formed, quantitatively, according to the chain length, as in Eq. (93).

If the above formulation is correct, the reaction of any sulfane with sulfite will result in the formation of 1 mole of hydrogen sulfide and a quantity of thiosulfate determined by the sulfur content of the starting material. This is, in fact, the case. If an ethereal sulfane solution is shaken with an excess of aqueous Na_2SO_3, decomposition of the sulfane proceeds extremely quickly with the formation of thiosulfate and sulfide. After a short time the sulfide may be precipitated by the addition of CdCO_3 or ZnCO_3. The precipitate (CdS and excess CdCO_3) is filtered and the sulfide may be determined by titration of the precipitate with iodine solution. The excess sulfite in the filtrate may be complexed with formalin solution, while the thiosulfate arising from the sulfite degradation is determined directly by iodine titration.

The experiments show that, in the case of a given sulfane, the same ratio of iodine for the titration of the CdS to iodine for the titration of thiosulfate always obtains. This ratio with disulfane H_2S_2 is 2:1, with trisulfane H_2S_3, 2:2, and with tetrasulfane H_2S_4, 2:3. Generally, a ratio of $2:(x-1)$ results for a given sulfane of formula H_2S_x. (Naturally no thiosulfate is formed from monosulfane H_2S by treatment with sulfite.)

The sulfite decomposition of sulfanes yields 1 mole of sulfide and 1 mole of thiosulfate per mole of disulfane. One mole of trisulfane gives 1 mole of sulfide and 2 moles of thiosulfate; 1 mole of tetrasulfane gives 1 mole of sulfide and 3 moles of thiosulfate.

This is, however, exactly as anticipated for a stepwise sulfite decomposition of sulfane itself, which previously had been derived in analogy with the sulfite decomposition of the di- and monosulfonic acids of sulfane. It appears, therefore, that the reaction of linear hydrogen polysulfides with sulfite in aqueous solution proceeds by the same stepwise degradation mechanism that occurs in the sulfite decomposition of sulfane disulfonic acids (polythionic acids) and sulfane monosulfonic acids, that is, by the action of a nucleophilic reagent in bringing about the cleavage of the S—S bonds of the chain. Since the newly discovered reaction of sulfanes with sulfite proceeds quickly and quantitatively, it may be applied with excellent results to the quantitative determination of very small quantities of sulfanes simultaneously with the determination of sulfur content per mole. This procedure requires no expenditure for equipment and is rapidly carried out.

2. *Cyanide Degradation of Sulfanes*

The same considerations as for the sulfite degradation of sulfanes also holds for the corresponding cyanide degradation, which has been found to proceed according to:

$$H_2S_x + (x-1)CN^- \rightarrow H_2S + (x-1)SCN^- \tag{95}$$

following the steps (for the example of H_2S_4):

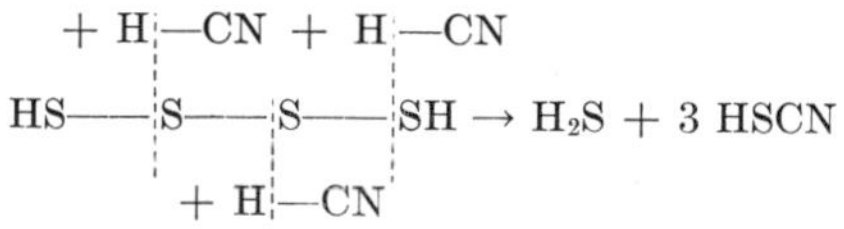

$$\begin{array}{c} + \; H\!\!-\!\!CN \; + \; H\!\!-\!\!CN \\ HS\!\!-\!\!S\!\!-\!\!S\!\!-\!\!SH \rightarrow H_2S + 3\;HSCN \\ + \; H\!\!-\!\!CN \end{array} \tag{96}$$

This reaction, as well as sulfite degradation, may be used for a fast and simple quantitative determination of the sulfanes (*139*).

C. Reactions of Sulfur with Nucleophilic Agents

After the successful application of the hypothesis set up to explain the sulfite decomposition of sulfane disulfonic acids and sulfane monosulfonic acids to the reaction of sulfanes with sulfite, this line of reasoning was taken with the simplest compound containing an S—S bond, namely elemental sulfur. It has long been known that elemental sulfur dissolves in boiling aqueous sodium sulfite solution with the formation of sodium thiosulfate.

Indeed, this reaction has been used for the preparation of $Na_2S_2O_3$. The literature, however, offers no convincing indication as to the actual course of this reaction. Usually, it is formulated as follows:

$$Na_2SO_3 + S \rightarrow Na_2S_2O_3 \tag{97}$$

That this formulation is not the true reaction course, and merely represents the starting materials and end products, follows from the fact that sulfur, under the conditions of the thiosulfate synthesis, is present not as atomic sulfur but in the S_8 ring form. Since sulfur exists in its S_8 molecular state, the equation for the formation of thiosulfate from sulfide and sulfur would have to be written:

$$S_8 + 8\ Na_2SO_3 \rightarrow 8\ Na_2S_2O_3 \tag{98}$$

If the thiosulfate formation actually did proceed according to this equation, then we would have a 9th order reaction, which is unlikely. It is therefore clear that the long known formation of thiosulfate from sulfur and sodium sulfide must proceed through intermediate stages. If we now apply the above-mentioned hypothesis concerning the cleavage of the sulfur chain by means of nucleophilic agents to the reaction of elementary sulfur with sulfite, we arrive at the following picture:

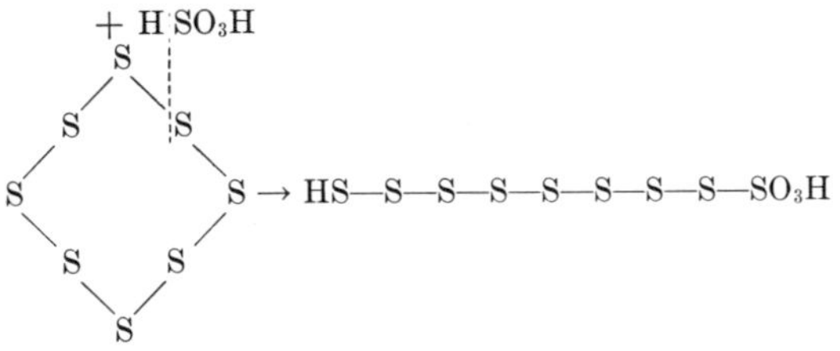

(99)

$$\begin{array}{l} \quad + HO_3S{\vdots}H + HO_3S{\vdots}H + HO_3S{\vdots}H + HO_3S{\vdots}H \\ HS{\vdots}—S{\vdots}—S{\vdots}—S{\vdots}—S{\vdots}—S{\vdots}—S{\vdots}—S—SO_3H \rightarrow 8\ H_2S_2O_3 \\ \qquad + HO_3S{\vdots}H + HO_3S{\vdots}H + HO_3S{\vdots}H \end{array} \tag{100}$$

Accordingly, first an S—S bond is cleaved with the addition of H^+ and SO_3H^- as well as SO_3^{--} to the resulting free end, forming a sulfane monosulfonic acid. This octasulfane monosulfonic acid, in the presence of excess sulfite, undergoes further stepwise degradation, as is known from investigations of the behavior of sulfane monosulfonic acids toward sulfite.

Thus, application of knowledge drawn from the study of the behavior of the newly discovered sulfane monosulfonic acids to the reaction of elemental sulfur with sulfite led to the first experimental proof for part of an ingenious concept put forward by Foss (*65*) on theoretical grounds in 1950.

Foss was right in his prediction of the first step of this reaction [a similar first step has also been found on the basis of kinetic measurements for the reactions of sulfur with tertiary phosphines (*10*) and cyanide (*9*) by Bartlett *et al.*], but not in his conclusion that "the sulfur chains bearing sulfite groups at one end must, of course, be pictured as unstable intermediates only." In contrast to this, the then unknown sulfane monosulfonic acids are stable and may be isolated during the reactions under proper conditions. According to this scheme, 8 molecules of thiosulfate must arise from 1 molecular S_8 ring. The rate-determining step of this reaction is undoubtedly the cleavage of the S_8 ring to form the octasulfane monosulfonic acid, while further steps in the degradation of this compound proceed more rapidly, through the heptasulfane, hexasulfane, pentasulfane, tetrasulfane, trisulfane, disulfane, and finally monosulfane sulfonic acid (thiosulfuric acid).

From this interpretation of the formation of thiosulfate from elementary sulfur and sodium sulfite, we may conclude, in contrast to the usual belief, that the reaction does not proceed by simple addition of sulfur to the sulfite ion, the driving force for which is the desire of the central atom to achieve a coordination number of 4; rather, it is a cleavage process of the S_8 ring by sodium sulfite. If this is true, then the reaction must proceed quantitatively. This is the case. If elemental sulfur and excess aqueous sodium sulfite are boiled together for 1 hr in neutral or weakly alkaline solution, as would result from hydrolysis of sodium sulfite, complete conversion to thiosulfate occurs. The thiosulfate may be determined, after the excess sulfite is complexed with formalin, by direct iodimetric titration.

In the cold, however, practically no reaction occurs between sulfur and sulfite. This is not primarily a question of reaction rate, as was first thought, but can be explained by the fact that sulfur is far too hydrophobic to be able to react with sulfite in aqueous solution. It was shown that the reason for the extremely slow reaction of sulfur with sulfite at room temperature is that sulfur is only poorly wetted. If, however, the sulfur is first dissolved in an organic solvent such as chloroform or carbon tetrachloride and then an aqueous solution of excess sodium sulfite, along with a sufficient amount of a second organic solvent such as acetone or methanol to homogenize the aqueous and organic phases is added, then all the sulfur reacts with the sulfite within 30 sec quantitatively to form thiosulfate. This method for the reaction of sulfur with sulfite to form thiosulfate, which may then be iodimetrically determined, offers itself preeminently for the determination of elementary sulfur or of sulfur solutions in organic solvents, as, for example, are often found in the rubber industry. This method is far superior to the oxidation of sulfur to sulfate followed by weighing as barium sulfate. The reaction of sulfur with sodium sulfite in an aqueous solution can, more-over, be strongly accelerated by the addition of a wetting agent such as is contained in any modern detergent. Based upon this reaction, it has been possible to work out a quantitative method for determination of sulfur in organic and inorganic compounds. The same quantitatively very useful degradation also occurs with cyanide at room temperature in the same manner.

The behavior of several other nucleophilic reagents such as nitrite, Grignard reagents, metal alkyls, etc., toward sulfur and sulfur-chain com-pounds has been studied (*119*). These studies revealed a complete analogy to the above reactions, clarified the mechanism of some long known reac-tions, and enabled the prediction of new reactions important for preparative and analytical purposes. For instance, the interaction of the very weakly nucleophilic nitrite ion with sulfur in anhydrous medium leads to cleavage of the S_8 ring, followed by a stepwise degradation of the intermediates, primarily to thionitrites (*142*):

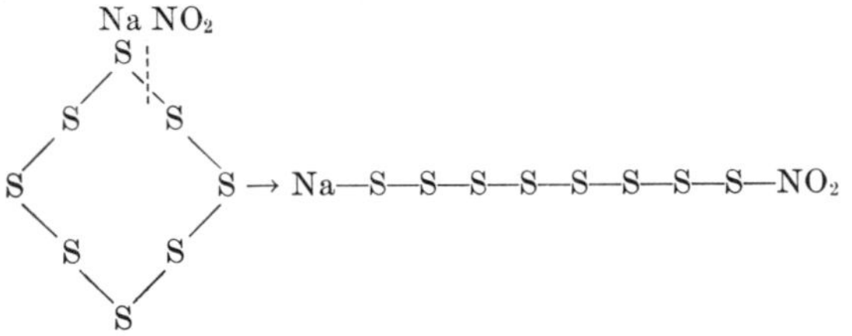

$$\text{Na}\,S\!-\!S\!-\!S\!-\!S\!-\!S\!-\!S\!-\!S\!-\!S\!-\!\text{NO}_2 \tag{101}$$

$$\text{Na}\!-\!\text{S}\!-\!\text{S}\!-\!\text{S}\!-\!\text{S}\!-\!\text{S}\!-\!\text{S}\!-\!\text{S}\!-\!\text{NO}_2 \rightarrow 8\ \text{NaNO}_2\text{S} \tag{102}$$

These unstable compounds decompose according to:

$$2\ \text{NaNO}_2\text{S} \rightarrow \text{Na}_2\text{S}_2\text{O}_3 + \text{N}_2\text{O} \tag{103}$$

thus forming in a very simple preparative reaction pure and anhydrous thiosulfates in 100% yield (*142*).

We believe that this hypothesis of a stepwise degradation of the sulfur chain by means of basic materials makes possible a simple, uniform way of looking at all the reactions of the sulfane disulfonic acids (polythionic acids), sulfane monosulfonic acids, and sulfanes, as well as derivatives of these substances and of elemental sulfur, with reagents such as S^{--}, SH^-, CN^-, OH^-, $S_2O_3^-$, HSO_3^-, etc. It furthermore points out new connections between many reactions. We conceive of the cleavage of the S—S bond as occurring by an initial polarization brought about by the approach of the nucleophilic agent X^-. The next step would be the formation of a partial bond between S and X^-, accompanied by the simultaneous weakening of the S—S bond, followed by the formation of a true bond between S and X^- and the cleavage of the S—S bond.

This representation of the reaction between compounds with sulfur chains and basic reagents makes many unexplained facts easily understandable. As an example, we have the conditions that prevail in a polysulfide solution. It is well known that elemental sulfur dissolves readily in alkali sulfide solutions with formation of alkali polysulfides. One might at first expect that the sulfur simply adds to the sulfide ion, with the formation of a polysulfide ion, which would be constructed analogously to the sulfite or sulfate ion. It is, however, clearly evident from the work of Fehér and his students, that this is not the case. The polysulfides are built up completely from unbranched sulfur chains, although there is to date no convincing explanation for this. Furthermore, it is not clear why the polysulfide solutions are stable at all.

It is known that the hydrogen polysulfides are extremely unstable, so that they can be prepared only by carefully pouring a polysulfide solution into a large excess of cold hydrochloric acid, and never in the reverse way, as with other acids or hydrogen sulfide. On the other hand, polysulfide solutions react by hydrolysis to form strongly alkaline solutions, which can arise only from the fact that, in spite of the alkaline reaction, the solution contains free sulfane (arising from the reaction: $S_x^{--} + 2\,HOH \rightarrow H_2S_x + 2\,OH^-$).

This apparent contradiction may be understood through the new concept of this reaction. Elemental sulfur dissolves in sulfide solution because the S_8 ring is cleaved by S^{--} or SH^- according to:

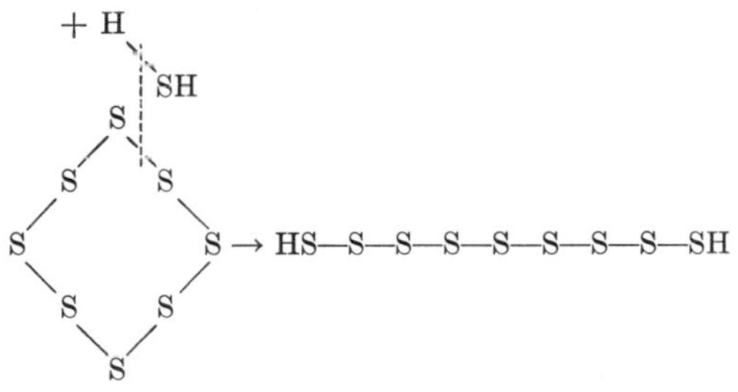

$$\rightarrow HS—S—S—S—S—S—S—S—SH \tag{104}$$

with the formation of a nonasulfide, which then disintegrates to smaller chains. At the same time longer chains are formed from the S^{--} ion, such as S_2^{--}, S_3^{--} and so on, which themselves can engage further in the decomposition process. One may then consider the processes in aqueous polysulfide solution as a continuous "sulfite decomposition" of polysulfide and a simultaneous polysulfide synthesis of sulfides, which can be schematically represented by Eqs. (105) and (106).

$$+ \text{ HS}|\text{H} \quad + \quad \text{HS}|\text{H} \quad + \quad \text{HS}|\text{H} \quad + \quad \text{HS}|\text{H}$$

$$\text{HS}|\!\!-\!\!-\text{S}|\!\!-\!\!-\text{S}|\!\!-\!\!-\text{S}|\!\!-\!\!-\text{S}|\!\!-\!\!-\text{S}|\!\!-\!\!-\text{S}|\!\!-\!\!-\text{S}\,-\text{SH} \rightarrow 8 \text{ H}_2\text{S}_2 + \text{H}_2\text{S} \qquad (105)$$

$$+ \text{ HS}|\text{H} \quad + \quad \text{HS}|\text{H} \quad + \quad \text{HS}|\text{H} \quad + \quad \text{HS}|\text{H}$$

$$+ \text{ HS}_2|\text{H} \quad + \quad \text{HS}_2|\text{H} \quad + \quad \text{HS}_2|\text{H} \quad + \quad \text{HS}_2|\text{H}$$

$$\text{HS}|\!\!-\!\!-\text{S}|\!\!-\!\!-\text{S}|\!\!-\!\!-\text{S}|\!\!-\!\!-\text{S}|\!\!-\!\!-\text{S}|\!\!-\!\!-\text{S}|\!\!-\!\!-\text{SH} \rightarrow 8 \text{ H}_2\text{S}_3 + \text{H}_2\text{S} \qquad (106)$$

$$+ \text{ HS}_2|\text{H} \quad + \quad \text{HS}_2|\text{H} \quad + \quad \text{HS}_2|\text{H} \quad + \quad \text{HS}_2|\text{H}$$

Since the reactions, as indicated, proceed in steps, the degradation of nonasulfanes proceeds through octa-, hepta-, hexa-, and pentasulfane, etc., parallel with the synthesis of monosulfanes through di-, tri-, tetrasulfane, etc., whereby a dynamic equilibrium is set up. We have, therefore, in an aqueous polysulfide solution of the type which might be formed by the action of alkali sulfide solution on sulfur, no statically existing compounds in the presence of each other but rather a complicated dynamic equilibrium involving sulfides of various chain lengths. Naturally, only unbranched sulfur chains may take part in this equilibrium. Such a solution may be called "pseudostable." This interpretation explains the fact that in no instance could an aqueous solution of polysulfide of definite chain length be obtained by treatment of stoichiometric quantities of sulfur and sulfide, and from which by subsequent treatment with acid a pure sulfane could be obtained. In every case, only a mixture of hydrogen polysulfides was found.

This arbitrarily chosen example demonstrates how many obscure reactions may be logically explained by this scheme. Furthermore the scheme allows the grouping of a large number of diverse reactions under one unifying viewpoint and makes the chemistry of sulfur and its compounds somewhat better understood.

REFERENCES

1. Abrahams, S. C., *Chem. Abstr.* **50**, 2233h (1956); *Acta Cryst.* **8**, 661 (1955).
2. Aten, A. H. W., *Z. physik. Chem.* **84**, 1 (1913).
3. Aten, A. H. W., *Z. physik. Chem.* **81**, 257 (1913); **83**, 442 (1913); **86**, 1 (1914); **88**, 321 (1914).
4. Bacon, R. F., and Fanelli, F., *Ind. Eng. Chem.* **34**, 1043 (1942).
5. Bacon, R. F., and Fanelli, R., *J. Am. Chem. Soc.* **65**, 639 (1943).
6. Barbieri, R., and Bruno, M., *J. Inorg. & Nuclear Chem.* **14**, 148 (1960).
7. Barbieri, R., and Bruno, M., *Ricerca sci.* **30**, 3 (1960).
8. Baroni, A., *Atti accad. nazl. Lincei Rend. Classe sci. fis. mat. e nat.* **14**, 28 (1931).
9. Bartlett, P. D., and Davis, R. E., *J. Am. Chem. Soc.* **80**, 2513 (1958).
10. Bartlett, P. D., and Meguerian, G., *J. Am. Chem. Soc.* **78**, 3710 (1956).

11. Beckmann, E., Paul, R., and Liescke, O., *Z. anorg. u. allgem. Chem.* **103**, 189 (1918).
12. Berenbaum, M. B., and Panek, J. R., "The Chemistry and Application of Polysulfide Polymers." Thiokol Chemical Corp., Trenton, New Jersey, 1958.
13. Bezzi, S., *Gazz. chim. ital.* **65**, 704 (1935).
14. Bloch, I., and Höhn, F., *Ber. deut. chem. Ges.* **41**, 1961 (1908).
15. Blomstrand, C. W., "Chemie der Jetztzeit," p. 157. 1869.
16. Böhme, H., and Zinner, G., *Ann. Chem. Liebigs* **585**, 142 (1954).
17. Bradt, P., Mohler, F. L., and Dibeler, V. H., *J. Research Natl. Bur. Standards* **57**, 223 (1956).
18. Braune, H., and Möller, O., *Z. Naturforsch.* **9a**, 210 (1954).
19. Braune, H., Peter, S., and Neveling, V., *Z. Naturforsch.* **6a**, 32 (1951); Braune, H., and Steinbacher, E., *Z. Naturforsch.* **7a**, 486 (1952); Peter, S., *Z. Elektrochem.* **57**, 289 (1953).
20. Christiansen, J. A., and Drost-Hansen, W., *Nature* **164**, 759 (1949).
21. Das, S. R., "Colloquium der Sektion für Anorganische Chemie der Internationalen Union für Reine und Angewandte Chemie," Münster/Westf., September, 1954, p. 103. Verlag Chemie, Weinheim/Bergstrasse, 1955.
22. Das, S. R., *Indian J. Phys.* **12**, 163 (1938); Das, S. R., *Sci. and Cult.* VI, **1**, 784 (1936); Das, S. R., and Ray, K., *Sci. and Cult.* VI, **2**, 12 (1937).
23. Das, S. R., *Sci. and Cult.* **4**, 11 (1939).
24. Das, S. R., and Das Gupta, K., *Nature* **143**, 332 (1939).
25. Das, S. R., and Ghosh, K., *Indian J. Phys.* **13**, 91 (1939).
26. Das, S. R., and Ray, K., *Sci. and Cult.* VI, **2**, 12 (1937).
27. Dawson, I. M., Mathieson, A. M. L., and Robertson, J. M., *J. Chem. Soc.*, pp. 322, 1556 (1948).
28. von Deines, O., *Ann. Chem. Liebigs* **440**, 213 (1924).
29. von Deines, O., *Z. anorg. u. allgem. Chem.* **177**, 13 (1928).
29a. Donohue, J., Caron, A., and Goldfish, E., *J. Am. Chem. Soc.* **83**, 3748 (1961).
30. Donohue, J., and Schomaker, V., *J. Chem. Phys.* **16**, 92 (1948).
31. Engel, R., *Compt. rend. acad. sci.* **112**, 866 (1891).
32. Eucken, M., and Wagner, J., *Acta Phys. Austriaca* **1**, 339 (1948).
33. Faessler, A., and Goehring, M., *Naturwissenschaften* **39**, 169 (1952).
33a. Fairbrother, F., Gee, G., and Merrall, G. T., *J. Polymer Sci.* **16**, 459 (1955).
34. Fehér, F., "Colloquium der Sektion für Anorganische Chemie der Internationalen Union für Reine und Angewandte Chemie," Münster/Westf., September 1954, p. 80. Verlag Chemie, Weinheim/Bergstrasse, 1955.
35. Fehér, F., "Colloquium der Sektion für Anorganische Chemie der Internationalen Union für Reine und Angewandte Chemie," Münster/Westf., September 1954, p. 81. Verlag Chemie, Weinheim/Bergstrasse, 1955.
36. Fehér, F., "Colloquium der Sektion für Anorganische Chemie der Internationalen Union für Reine und Angewandte Chemie," Münster-Westf., September 1954, p. 112. Verlag Chemie, Weinheim/Bergstrasse, 1955.
37. Fehér, F., and Baudler, M., *Z. anorg. Chem.* **253**, 170 (1947).
38. Fehér, F., and Baudler, M., *Z. anorg. Chem.* **254**, 251 (1947).
39. Fehér, F., and Baudler, M., *Z. anorg. Chem.* **254**, 289 (1948).
40. Fehér, F., and Baudler, M., *Z. anorg. Chem.* **258**, 132 (1949).
41. Fehér, F., and Baudler, M., *Z. anorg. u. allgem. Chem.* **267**, 293 (1952).
42. Fehér, F., and Berthold, H. J., *Chem. Ber.* **88**, 1634 (1955).
43. Fehér, F., and Berthold, H. J., *Z. anorg. u. allgem. Chem.* **267**, 251 (1951).

44. Fehér, F., and Berthold, R., *Z. anorg. u. allgem. Chem.* **290**, 251 (1957).
45. Fehér, F., and Hellwig, E., "Colloquium der Sektion für Anorganische Chemie der Internationalen Union für Reine und Angewandte Chemie," Münster/Westf., September 1954, p. 95. Verlag Chemie, Weinheim/Bergstrasse, 1955.
46. Fehér, F., and Heuer, E., *Angew. Chem.* **A59**, 237 (1947).
47. Fehér, F., and Heuer, E., *Z. anorg. Chem.* **255**, 185 (1947); Fehér, F., and Winkhaus, G., *Z. anorg. u. allgem. Chem.* **292**, 210 (1957).
48. Fehér, F., and Laue, W., *Z. anorg. u. allgem. Chem.* **288**, 103 (1956).
49. Fehér, F., and Laue, W., *Z. Naturforsch.* **8b**, 687 (1953).
50. Fehér, F., and Rempe, G., *Z. anorg. u. allgem. Chem.* **281**, 161 (1955).
51. Fehér, F., and Rempe, G., *Z. Naturforsch.* **8b**, 688 (1953).
52. Fehér, F., and Ristić, S., *Z. anorg. u. allgem. Chem.* **293**, 307 (1958).
53. Fehér, F., and Ristić, S., *Z. anorg. u. allgem. Chem.* **293**, 311 (1958).
54. Fehér, F., and Weber, H., *Z. Elektrochem.* **61**, 285 (1957).
55. Fehér, F., and Weber, H., *Chem. Ber.* **91**, 642 (1958).
56. Fehér, F., and Winkhaus, G., *Z. anorg. u. allgem. Chem.* **288**, 123 (1956); Fehér, F., and Kruse, W., *Z. anorg. u. allgem. Chem.* **293**, 302 (1958).
57. Fehér, F., Kraemer, J., and Rempe, G., *Z. anorg. u. allgem. Chem.* **279**, 18 (1955).
58. Fehér, F., Krause, G., and Vogelbruch, K., *Chem. Ber.* **90**, 1570 (1957).
59. Fehér, F., Laue, W., and Kraemer, J., *Z. Naturforsch.* **7b**, 574 (1952).
60. Fehér, F., Laue, W., and Winkhaus, G., *Z. anorg. u. allgem. Chem.* **288**, 113 (1956).
61. Fehér, F., Laue, W., and Winkhaus, G., *Z. anorg. u. allgem. Chem.* **290**, 52 (1957).
62. Fehér, F., Naused, K., and Weber, H., *Z. anorg. u. allgem. Chem.* **290**, 303 (1957).
63. Fehér, F., Schliep, E., and Weber, H., *Z. Elektrochem.* **57**, 916 (1953).
64. Fehér, F., Schotten, J., and Thomas, B., *Z. Naturforsch.* **13b**, 624 (1958).
65. Foss, O., *Acta Chem. Scand.* **4**, 404 (1950).
66. Foss, O., *Advances in Inorg. Chem. Radiochem.* **2**, 237 (1960).
67. Foerster, F., and Centner, K., *Z. anorg. u. allgem. Chem.* **157**, 45 (1926).
68. Freund, T., *J. Chem. Phys.* **21**, 180 (1953).
69. Friedel, C., *Compt. rend. acad. sci.* **112**, 834 (1891).
70. Friedel, C., *Bull. soc. chim. france* **32**, 113 (1879).
71. Frondel, C., and Whitfield, R. E., *Acta Cryst.* **3**, 242 (1950).
72. Gardner, D. M., and Fraenkel, G. K., *J. Am. Chem. Soc.* **76**, 5891 (1954); **78**, 3279 (1956).
73. Gee, G., *Sci. Progr.* **43**, 193 (1955).
74. Gerding, H., and Westrik, R., *Rec. trav. chim.* **61**, 412 (1942).
75. Gernez, D., *Compt. rend. acad. sci.* **82**, 1152 (1876).
76. "Gmelin's Handbuch der anorganischen Chemie, 8. Auflage, System-Nummer 9, Teil A, Verlag Chemie, Weinheim [1953], p. 512–16.
77. Grinberg, A. A., *Zhur. Priklad. Khim.* **21**, 425 (1948).
78. Groth, P., "Chemische Kristallographie," Vol. I, pp. 22, 26, 28. 1906.
79. Goehring, M., *Fortschr. chem. Forsch.* **2**, 444 (1952).
80. Goehring, M., and Feldmann, U., *Z. anorg. Chem.* **257**, 223 (1948).
81. Goehring, M., and Stamm, H., *Z. anorg. Chem.* **250**, 56 (1942).
82. Hartshorne, N. H., *Chem. Soc. Symposia Bristol 1958 Spec. Publ. No.* **12**, 253 (1958).
83. Hertlein, H., *Z. physik. Chem.* **19**, 287 (1896).
84. Katz, J. R., *Trans. Faraday Soc.* **32**, 77 (1936).
85. Krebs, H., *Angew. Chem.* **65**, 293 (1953).
86. Krebs, H., and Müller, K. H., *Z. anorg. u. allgem. Chem.* **281**, 187 (1955).

87. Krebs, H., Fassbender, H., and Jörgens, F., *Ber. deut. chem. Ges.* **90**, 425 (1957).
88. Krebs, H., Weber, E. F., and Balters, H., *Z. anorg. u. allgem. Chem.* **275**, 147 (1954).
89. Koch, H. P., *J. Chem. Soc.*, p. 394 (1949).
90. Korinth, E., *Z. anorg. u. allgem. Chem.* **174**, 57 (1928).
91. Kurtenacker, A., *Abegg's Handb. anorg. Chem.* **4**(1), 541 (1927).
92. Kurtenacker, A., and Fluss, W., *Z. anorg. u. allgem. Chem.* **210**, 125 (1933).
93. Kurtenacker, A., and Matejka, K., *Z. anorg. u. allgem. Chem.* **229**, 19 (1936).
94. Lenz, R. W., and Carrington, W. K., *J. Polymer Sci.* **41**, 333 (1959).
95. Lenz, R. W., and Handlovits, C. E., *J. Polymer Sci.* **43**, 167 (1960).
96. Macallum, A. D., *J. Org. Chem.* **13**, 154 (1948).
97. Macallum, A. D., *U. S. Patent* 2,513,188 (1950).
98. Macallum, A. D., *U. S. Patent* 2,538,941 (1951).
99. Martin, F., and Metz, L., *Z. anorg. u. allgem. Chem.* **127**, 83 (1923).
100. Martin, S. M., and Patrick, S. P., *Ind. Eng. Chem.* **28**, 1144 (1936).
101. Mendelejeff, D. I., *Chem. Ber.* **3**, 870 (1870).
102. Meyer, K. H., and Go, Y., *Helv. Chim. Acta* **17**, 1081 (1934).
103. Meyer, B., and Schumacher, E., *Helv. Chim. Acta* **43**, 1333 (1960).
104. Mills, H., and Robinson, P. L., *J. Chem. Soc.*, p. 2326 (1928).
105. Murphy, T. J., Clabough, W. S., and Gilchrist, R., *J. Research Natl. Bur. Standards* **64A**, 355 (1960)
106. Parker, A. J., and Kharash, N., *Chem. Revs.* **59**, 584 (1959).
107. Pauling, L., *Proc. Natl. Acad. Sci. U.S.* **35**, 495 (1949).
108. Preuner, G., and Schupp, W., *Z. physik. Chem.* **68**, 129 (1910).
109. Prins, J. A., "Colloquium der Sektion für Anorganische Chemie der Internationalen Union für Reine und Angewandte Chemie," Münster/Westf., September 1954, p. 102. Verlag Chemie, Weinheim/Bergstrasse, 1955.
110. Rice, F. O., and Sparrow, C., *J. Am. Chem. Soc.* **75**, 848, 6066 (1953).
111. Sander, A., *Z. angew. Chem.* **28**, 273 (1915).
112. Schenk, P. W., *Angew. Chem.* **65**, 325 (1953).
113. Schenk, P. W., and Sterner, S., *Monatsh. Chem.* **80**, 117 (1949).
114. Schenk, P. W., and Thümmler, U., *Z. Elektrochem.* **63**, 1002 (1959).
115. Schmidt, M., *Z. anorg. u. allgem. Chem.* **289**, 141 (1957).
116. Schmidt, M., *Z. anorg. u. allgem. Chem.* **289**, 158 (1957).
117. Schmidt, M., *Z. anorg. u. allgem. Chem.* **289**, 193 (1957).
118. Schmidt, M., *Z. anorg. u. allgem. Chem.* **289**, 175 (1957).
119. Schmidt, M., *in* "Zehn Jahre Fonds der Chemischen Industrie" (ed. Verband der Chemischen Industrie), p. 135. (1960) Düsseldorf.
120. Schmidt, M., and Blaettner, K., Thesis K. Blaettner, University Munich, 1960.
121. Schmidt, M., and Blaettner, K., *Angew. Chem.* **71**, 407 (1959).
122. Schmidt, M., and Dersin, H., Diplomarbeit H. Dersin, University Munich, 1958.
123. Schmidt, M., and Dersin, H., *Z. Naturforsch.* **14b**, 735 (1959).
124. Schmidt, M., and Eichelsdörfer, D., Thesis D. Eichelsdörfer, University Munich, 1960.
125. Schmidt, M., and Heinrich, H., *Angew. Chem.* **70**, 572 (1958).
126. Schmidt, M., and Moisdorfer, H., Unpublished work.
127. Schmidt, M., and Resch, K., Diplomarbeit K. Resch, University Munich, 1957.
128. Schmidt, M., and Rankl, F., Thesis F. J. Rankl, University Munich, 1960.
129. Schmidt, M., and Ruf, H., Diplomarbeit H. Ruf, University Munich, 1960.
130. Schmidt, M., and Sand, T., Unpublished work.
131. Schmidt, M., and Sand, T., Thesis T. Sand, University Munich, 1960.

132. Schmidt, M., and Steinle, K., Thesis K. Steinle, University Munich, 1962.
133. Schmidt, M., and Talsky, G., *Chem. Ber.* **92,** 1526 (1959).
134. Schmidt, M., and Talsky, G., *Chem. Ber.* **93,** 719 (1960).
135. Schmidt, M., and Talsky, G., *Chem. Ber.* **94,** 1352 (1961).
136. Schmidt, M., and Talsky, G., Unpublished work.
137. Schmidt, M., and Talsky, G., *Angew. Chem.* **70,** 312 (1958).
138. Schmidt, M., and Talsky, G., *Z. anorg. u. allgem. Chem.* **303,** 210 (1960).
139. Schmidt, M., and Talsky, G., *Z. anal. Chem.* **166,** 274 (1959).
140. Schmidt, M., and Wägerle, R. R., *German Patent* 1,085,507 (1961).
141. Schmidt, M., and Wägerle, R. R., Thesis R. R. Wägerle, University Munich, 1960.
142. Schmidt, M., and Wägerle, R. R., *Z. Angew. Chem.* **70,** 594 (1958).
143. Schmidt, M., and Wieber, M., *Chem. Ber.* **94,** 1426 (1961).
144. Schmidt, M., and Wieber, M., Diplomarbeit M. Wieber, University Munich, 1960.
145. Schmidt, M., and Wieber, M., Thesis M. Wieber, University Munich, 1961.
146. Schmidt, M., and Wirwoll, B., *Z. anorg. u. allgem. Chem.* **303,** 184 (1960).
147. Schmidt, M., and Wirwoll, B., *Z. anorg. u. allgem. Chem.* **303,** 184 (1960).
148. Schmidt, M., Wirwoll, B., and Fliege, E., *Angew. Chem.* **70,** 506 (1958).
149. Schöberl, A., and Bauer, G., *Angew. Chem.* **69,** 478 (1957).
150. Schöberl, A., and Wagner, A., "Methoden der organischen Chemie" (Houben-Weyl), 4th ed., Vol. 9, p. 59. Georg Thieme, Stuttgart (1955).
151. Schwarzenbach, G., and Fischer, A., *Helv. Chim. Acta* **43,** 1365 (1960).
152. Smith, A., and Holmes, W. B., *Z. physik. Chem.* **42,** 469 (1903).
153. Specker, H., *Z. anorg. Chem.* **261,** 116 (1950); *Angew. Chem.* **65,** 299 (1953).
154. Stamm, H., and Goehring, M., *Naturwissenschaften* **27,** 317 (1939).
155. Stamm, H., and Wintzer, H., *Chem. Ber.* **71,** 2212 (1938).
156. Stamm, H., Becke-Goehring, M., and Schmidt, M., *Angew. Chem.* **72,** 34 (1960).
157. Staudinger, H., and Kreis, W., *Helv. Chim. Acta* **8,** 71 (1925).
158. Stevenson, D. P., and Beach, J. Y., *J. Am. Chem. Soc.* **60,** 2872 (1938).
159. Stock, A., *Chem. Ber.* **53,** 837 (1920).
160. Tobolsky, A. V., and Eisenberg, A., *J. Am. Chem. Soc.* **81,** 780 (1959).
161. Toussaint, J., *Bull. soc. chim. Belges* **54,** 319 (1945).
162. Vogel-Högler, R., *Acta Phys. Austriaca* **1,** 311 (1948).
163. Walton, J. H., and Parsons, L. B., *J. Am. Chem. Soc.* **43,** 2539 (1921).
164. Warren, B. E., and Burwell, J. T., *J. Chem. Phys.* **3,** 6 (1935).
165. von Wartenberg, H., *Z. anorg. u. allgem. Chem.* **286,** 243 (1956); **297,** 226 (1958).
166. Weitz, E., and Achterberg, F., *Chem. Ber.* **61,** 399 (1928).
167. Weitz, E., and Spohn, K., *Chem. Ber.* **89,** 2332 (1956).
168. Weitz, E., Becker, F., Gieles, K., and Alt, B., *Chem. Ber.* **89,** 2353 (1956).
169. Weitz, E., Gieles, K., Singer, J., and Alt, B., *Chem. Ber.* **89,** 2365 (1956).
170. West, E. D., *J. Am. Chem. Soc.* **81,** 29 (1959).
171. Yanitskji, I. V., and Valanchunas, I. N., *Sbornik Stateĭ Obshcheĭ Khim. Akad. Nauk. S.S.S.R.* **1,** 732 (1953); *Chem. Abstr.* **49,** 8023 (1955).
172. Yanitskji, I. V., and Valanchunas, I. N., *Zhur. Obshcheĭ Khim.* **24,** 790 (1954); *Chem. Abstr.* **48,** 13510 (1954); *J. Gen. Chem. U.S.S.R.* (*Engl. Transl.*) **24,** 793 (1954).
173. Yanitskji, I. V., Valanchunas, I. N., and Tuchaite, O. Y., *Zhur. Neorg. Khim.* **3,** 2087 (1958).
174. Yoshida, K., *Chem. Abstr.* **51,** 11141g (1957); *Bull. Chem. Research Inst. Non-Aqueous Solutions Tohoku Univ.* **6,** 17 (1956).

Boron Polymers

A. L. McCLOSKEY

United States Borax and Chemical Corporation, New York, New York

TABLE OF CONTENTS

I. Introduction

There are many "polymers," that is, high molecular weight materials, with regularly spaced boron atoms as integral parts of chains, layers, or three-dimensional networks. Several of these giant molecules have been known for years. For example, under normal conditions the structure of boric oxide consists of a three-dimensional framework of distorted BO_4 tetrahedra. Hexagonal boron nitride, sometimes called white graphite, has a layer structure:

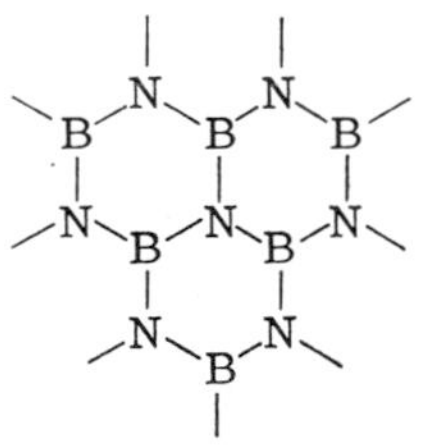

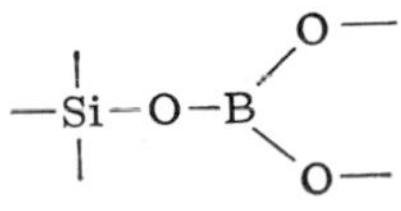

Crystalline boron consists of an infinite three-dimensional arrangement of boron atoms. Borosilicate glasses must have groups incorporated in the

$$-\overset{|}{\underset{|}{Si}}-O-\overset{|}{\underset{|}{Si}}-$$

framework. The forementioned materials have excellent thermal stability and other useful properties which make them of some commercial value. They have, therefore, stimulated the quest and on occasion acted as models for other high molecular weight polymers based on boron.

These examples also illustrate two problems which arise again and again. The first concerns cyclization. Organic chemists are accustomed to an unwritten rule that "formation of ring structures is likely to occur." Boron chemists are likely to restate this rule as "formation of ring structures cannot be avoided."

The tendency to form rings is related in part to changes in entropy, which in turn effect changes in free energy. The entropy of a system is greater if it is composed of many small molecules instead of a few macromolecules. Entropy is related to free energy by the equation $\Delta F = \Delta H - T\Delta S$, so that an increase in ΔS leads to a decrease in ΔF, making the formation of small molecular units more probable. Fortunately, thermodynamic factors are frequently offset by activation energy requirements, and, moreover, depolymerization can be inhibited in a number of ways, for example by ensuring that small rings are not favored energetically. Chemists have learned to open carbocyclic rings, and it should be possible to cleave the rings of borocyclic compounds, to give useful substances. In several instances this has been done with production of polymers. Of course, it might also be possible to link or otherwise join borocyclic rings one to another into giant molecules which still retain structural features leading to desirable physical properties.

The second problem concerns the reactivity of tricoordinate boron. The art of synthetic organic chemistry depends to a great extent on selective reactivity and "blocking groups," with C—H bonds acting as blocking groups in many reactions. A boron atom having three ligands is fundamentally a more reactive group than a saturated carbon atom, probably because the boron can readily become four-coordinate as a prelude to reaction, whereas four-coordinate carbon cannot expand its valence shell. Hence the problem of retarding undesired reactions while engaged in functional group chemistry is fundamentally more difficult for boron. It is frequently desirable to seek a group, R, which will give a series of RBY_2 compounds wherein Y represents a center of reaction, the R—B site being very stable and unreactive. For example, since benzeneboronic acid has long been known as a stable boron compound, it is not surprising that a great deal of effort in this field has been concentrated on the chemistry of phenylboron compounds. It always remains to be proved by experiment which will be the best blocking groups for each particular type of polymer synthesis. Without the use of stable blocking groups, control of reactivity, in particular avoidance of cross-linking, would appear to be extremely difficult or impossible.

Some have thought that boron polymers would have commercial utility, because certain aspects of boron chemistry find their counterparts in silicon chemistry, and silicone polymers have great technological importance (Chapter 5). Furthermore, the energies of boron-oxygen ($\sim$130 kcal) and of boron-nitrogen ($\sim$100 kcal) bonds are high, leading one to think of high temperature applications for boron polymers based on these linkages. Interest in the general area of inorganic polymers has recently become an honorable academic pursuit, and from these separate stimuli there have developed numerous studies concerned with boron-containing polymers.

In many instances, however, the properties of polymeric boron compounds have been inadequately described, frequently no information being given on molecular weight, solubility, resistance to heat, or chemical attack. Only in the last decade have workers tended to evaluate the properties of their polymeric products in a reasonable way. Even so, this field is still in its infancy.

The reader is referred to three important recent reviews (*20, 53, 112*) of boron polymers for further discussion of the subject.

II. Boron-Nitrogen Polymers

The boron-nitrogen skeleton appears to be a particularly attractive choice on which to base an inorganic polymer. The possibility of forming chains of alternate boron and nitrogen atoms has been recognized since the discovery of borazole (*87*) and the relatively high B—N bond strength has been mentioned above. Partly because of this (*73, 74*) borazole chemistry has received intensive study (over one hundred publications) in recent years, and although a complete review of the borazoles is not in order here (*83*) certain features of borazole chemistry have a direct bearing on the subject of boron polymers. Stock and Pohland (*87*) observed that borazole was thermally stable at 500°. Indeed, the relatively high thermal stability of many borazoles has been substantiated recently (*66*). High thermal stability alone is not necessarily the overriding requirement for a new polymer system, but it is certainly a desirable characteristic. Very little is known about the actual mode of borazole ring formation. It is just possible that the several synthetic methods known (*83*) for the synthesis of borazoles have as a common intermediate a monomeric species containing the —B≡N— group, e.g.,

$$BCl_3 + NH_3 \rightarrow [BCl_3 \cdot NH_3] \rightarrow [H_2NBCl_2] \rightarrow [HN{=}BCl] \rightarrow [HNBCl]_3 \dagger$$

Although this possibility has been suggested in several publications (*105*), it has not been confirmed experimentally.

Based on present knowledge of borazole chemistry there would appear to be three main avenues for possible boron-nitrogen polymerization. The first would involve attempts to produce high polymers by ring-opening reactions of various borazoles, and the second avoidance of ring closure in reactions between difunctional boron and nitrogen molecules. Ruigh (*73, 74*) has discussed the possibility of ring opening followed by polymerization in connection with some resinous material formed from tris(β-chlorovinyl)borazole (I). This material was not investigated further, and

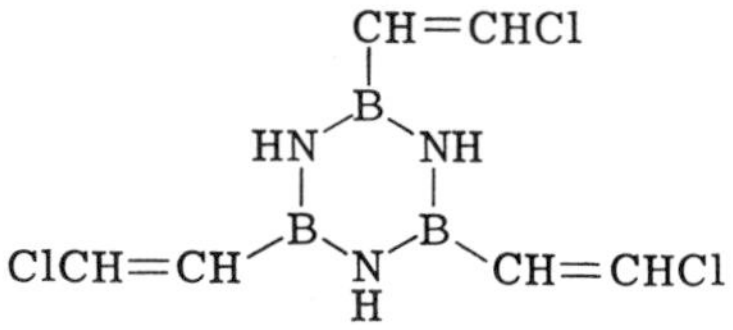

(I)

it now appears unlikely that it was a polymer derived in this manner. A third method for production of B—N polymers could involve attempts to join rings of borazole in some fashion, to form linear molecules with sufficient flexibility between rings to impart useful properties. The hexagonal form of boron nitride exemplifies a B—N ring system in which cross-linking is so great that the material does not have the flexibility, elasticity, and workability properties that tend to be considered synonomous with the term "polymer." It is interesting to note that the structure of hexagonal boron nitride differs in an important respect from that of graphite. Localization of electrons on the nitrogen atoms in hexagonal boron nitride leads to a different mode of layer packing with boron atoms in one layer directly under nitrogen atoms in another. In accordance with this, this form of boron nitride is a poor electrical conductor, although it has other useful properties. One of these involves its transformation into a cubic form at 1800° and 85,000 atm. The "diamond"-like boron nitride obtained in this manner surpasses diamond in mechanical strength, suffers only surface oxidation in air up to 2000°, and is a good dielectric (*103*). The properties

---

† A compound best obtained from boron trichloride and ammonium chloride in boiling chlorobenzene (*16*).

of hexagonal boron nitride suggest that the major problem in joining or fusing of borazole rings is the avoidance or control of crosslinking. Some preparative approaches to this problem are mentioned below.

The problem of cyclization to afford borazoles in reactions which could have led to polymers with long chains of boron and nitrogen atoms was mentioned above. A partial solution to this dilemma is suggested by some recent work of Gerrard and Mooney (*38*). Using phenylboron dichloride and *n*- or isobutylamines as starting materials, it was possible to prevent ring formation by steric hindrance to give a linear polymer $[C_6H_5BNC_4H_9]_x$, containing 20–40 atoms of boron and nitrogen in the chain. Such polymers melt near 150°, but like most boron-nitrogen compounds are readily hydrolyzed.

The products of the reaction between primary amines and boron trihalides are very much dependent on the substituents on the α-carbon atom of the amine. When the α-carbon is fully substituted, compounds which probably contain an eight-membered boron-nitrogen ring are obtained (*92a*). These tetrameric species, of which $[t\text{-BuNBCl}]_4$ is an example, are much less reactive than the trimeric B-chloroborazoles, evidently as a result of steric effects.

Historically the study of boron-nitrogen polymers resembles developments in other areas of chemistry in that in many cases nonvolatile products of reaction were arbitrarily classed as polymers (either before or after analysis) and then cast out as not worthy of further study. Thus borazole, $(HBNH)_3$, deposits solids on standing or on being heated, and gives off hydrogen under these same conditions (*87*). It was noted (*87, 107*) that the nonvolatile residue which remained after 12 hours at 500° (19% of the original borazole was recovered) had the empirical formula BNH. These residues have not since been investigated. It is not known whether formation of solids is dependent on the production of hydrogen, or whether bonding of the polymer is through boron-boron bonds, boron-nitrogen bonds, or both. It is clear that the residues from Stock's 500° pyrolysis may have boron-boron bonds, but little is known of these polymers or the ones formed at other temperatures. Volatile products from the pyrolysis of borazole have recently been investigated (*54, 63*). Volatile materials were obtained to which structures (II) and (III) were assigned. It remains to be

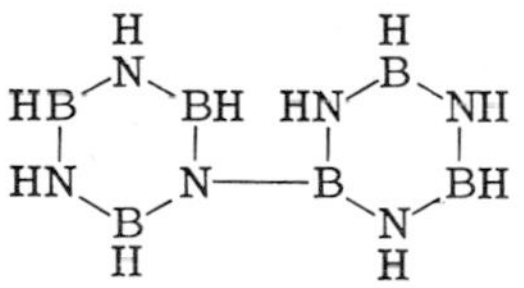

(II) 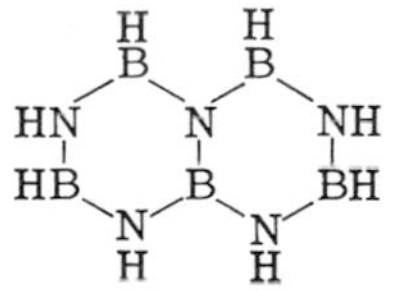   (III)

seen whether the loss of hydrogen is in all cases accompanied by borazole polymerization, or if boron-boron or boron-nitrogen bonds are formed thereby. The formation of the naphthalene analog (III) would require some fragmentation of the borazole ring, perhaps to —B≡N— monomer units, as proposed by Wiberg and Bolz (*106*), a mechanistically complicated reassembly process.

The very interesting aminoborane, $(H_2NBH_2)_x$, is another material thought to be highly polymeric. It was obtained (*79*) as a product of the decomposition of aminodiborane (B_2H_7N):

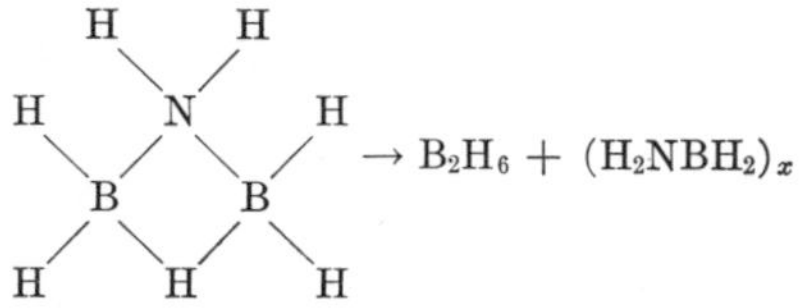

$$\rightarrow B_2H_6 + (H_2NBH_2)_x$$

The polymer was a nonvolatile solid which was not further investigated. The reaction of diborane with lithium amide (*78*) gave lithium borohydride and a material also formulated as polymeric aminoborane:

$$B_2H_6 + LiNH_2 \rightarrow LiBH_4 + (H_2NBH_2)_x$$

The "diammoniate of diborane" dissolved in liquid ammonia reacts with sodium, lithium, or potassium to give the alkali metal borohydride and also the ether-insoluble aminoborane (*77*). A polymeric nature apparently has been attributed to the substance because of its insolubility (*76*). The nature of this material and its possible crosslinking by loss of hydrogen are well worth further investigation. Up to now it has been ignored as of no interest because of its nonvolatile, insoluble character. The well-established dimers and trimers—(IV) (*17*), V (*29*), (VI) (*11*), and (VII) (*31*)—which contain tetracovalent boron and nitrogen, lend support to the view that $(H_2NBH_2)_n$ is a boron-nitrogen analog of polyethylene.

Related to the material $(H_2NBH_2)_x$ is the well-known compound N,N-dimethylaminoborane, which is dimeric as a solid but exists in the vapor phase as a monomer-dimer equilibrium, the latter disturbed by some disproportionation of the Me_2NBH_2 species into diborane, $(Me_2N)_2BH$, and $(Me_2N)_3B$ (*24, 25*). The interesting observation has recently been made that dimethylaminoborane at 150° and 3000 atm forms what is believed to be a chain polymer (*32*). This polymer is amorphous, insoluble, and stable to hydrolysis, but not to heat. At ambient temperatures it reverts to the dimer $(Me_2NBH_2)_2$ over a period of months, but this reversion is inhibited by ether. It is apparent from this work that studies of the effect of high pressures on boron polymers with low degrees of polymerization might be very profitable.

A chemical system of historical interest is based on the reaction of boron chloride with ammonia. Mention of the polymers from phenylboron dichlorides and the butylamines was made above. However, it was observed

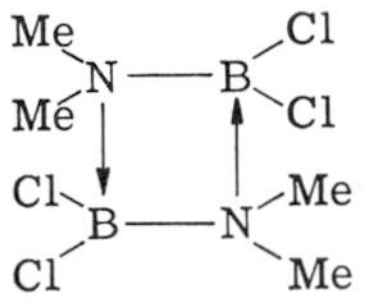

(IV)

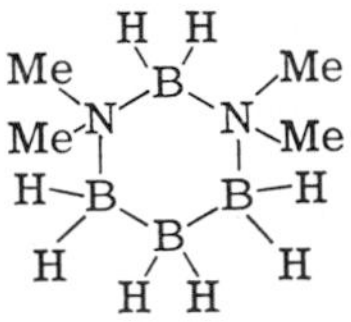

(V)

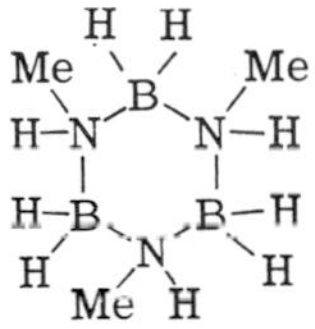

(VI)

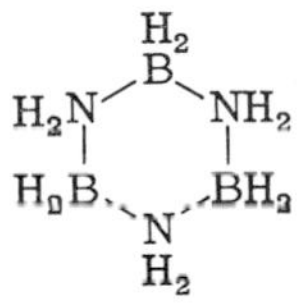

(VII)

long ago that reaction of boron chloride or bromide at low temperatures with excess of ammonia led to ammonolysis, giving material which was identified as trisaminoborane, $B(NH_2)_3$ (*50, 86*). This compound has never been isolated in the pure state because it releases ammonia at room temperature and gives boron imide, $B_2(NH)_3$, on moderate heating (*50*). Further heating of the boron imide gave, as expected, ammonia and hexagonal boron nitride. Stock (*85*) has also observed the formation of $B_2(NH)_3$ from the reaction of an excess of ammonia with either diborane or borazole. This is admittedly not a particularly attractive system to study, but it is one of the fundamental ones related to boron-nitrogen chemistry and it has not been seriously investigated.

A somewhat similar case, still to be resolved, involves a material of composition $(MeNBF)_x$. Wiberg and Horeld (*108*) reported preparation of *N*-trimethyl-*B*-trifluoroborazole by the reaction of dimethylfluoroborane with methylamine at 400°:

$$3 \ Me_2BF + 3 \ CH_3NH_2 \xrightarrow{400°} 6 \ CH_4 + (MeNBF)_3$$

The decomposition of bis(dimethylamino)fluoroborane, $(Me_2N)_2BF$, on the other hand, gave trimethylamine and a polymer of empirical composition

(MeNBF)$_x$, which was stated not to be the trimer (*21*), mostly on the basis
of a lower melting point than Wiberg and Horeld's material, and perhaps
too low a volatility. The decomposition of methyl silyl aminoboron di-
fluoride apparently gives the *B*-fluoroborazole (*92*), although the physical
constants do not agree with those given in reference (*108*). There is thus
some possibility that one or more of these preparations of (MeNBF)$_x$ has
given a polymer other than a cyclic trimer.

Monoisopropylaminoborane, *i*-PrH$_2$N·BH$_3$, was reported to form polymeric materials of formula (*i*-PrNBH)$_x$ when heated at 300° for 1 hour
(*46*). This polymer was formed in 88% yield, and was presumed to have a
very high molecular weight because it was not soluble in any of the common
solvents. The material was a clear viscous oil at 300°, and formed a glass
when cooled to room temperature. Short heating (3–15 minutes) of the
intermediate *i*-PrNHBH$_2$ at 300°C was said (*46*) to form a crystalline
polymer with about the same stability as an amorphous polymer formed
by 1 hour of heating at the same temperature. Attempts to repeat this
work (*57*) have given the expected amount of hydrogen, but the degree of
polymerization of the polymer obtained in highest yield was 3. The reason
for this discrepancy is not clear, but it is probably related in some manner
to impurities. Either the polymer of the original work (*46*) was formed
directly from impurities in the isopropylaminoborane, or the formation of
the polymer was catalyzed by impurities. The recent attempt (*57*) to prepare the polymer was performed with quite pure starting material.

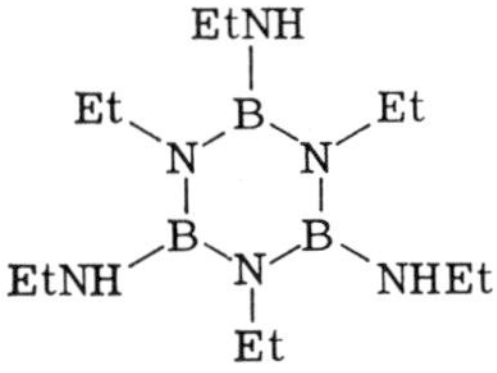

(VIII)

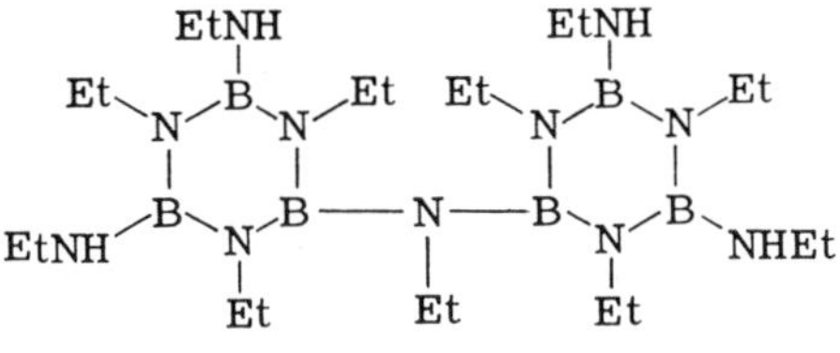

(IX)

Methoxy derivatives of hydroxylamine form complexes with diborane (10). The complex from O-methylhydroxylamine, $MeONH_2 \cdot BH_3$ was found to give methyl borate and a polymeric residue of approximate composition BNH, which because of its apparently highly cross-linked nature was not further studied. The N-methyl-O-methylhydroxylamine complex $(MeO)MeNH \cdot BH_3$ was decomposed similarly, affording several products, including one whose composition was $(HBNH)_x$, but which was obviously not borazole.

The compound tris(ethylamino)borane, $B(NHEt)_3$, heated at 200° for $3\frac{1}{2}$ hours loses ethylamine and forms an aminoborazole (VIII) by a transaminative condensation (5, 52). This aminoborazole (VIII) on heating at 300° for 4 hours lost ethylamine until the composition of the residue corresponded to that of the biborazole (IX). Heating of (IX) at higher temperatures resulted in loss of ethylamine so that the residue corresponded to a polymer of 10 borazole units, and additional heating of this material for 9 hours at 600°C gave further evolution of ethylamine and a material which was formulated as (X), a completely cross-linked material of composition

(X)

$[B(NEt)_2]_x$. Rubbery characteristics were ascribed to some of the intermediates of these processes, but the polymers themselves have not yet been studied thoroughly (5). Analogous syntheses have been described by other workers (41, 67). The possibility of obtaining linear polymers by use of suitable blocking groups has been recognized, and indeed N-tert-butyl-B-tert-butylaminoborazole could not be formed, a "linear" dimer (XI) being isolated instead (59).

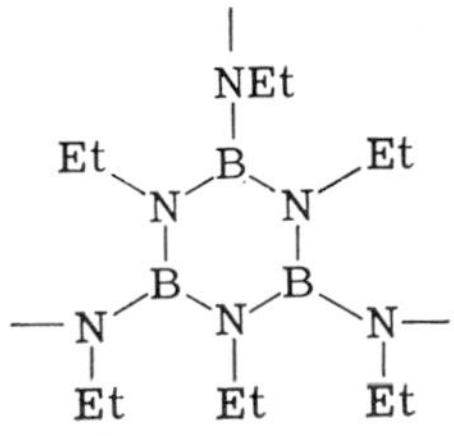

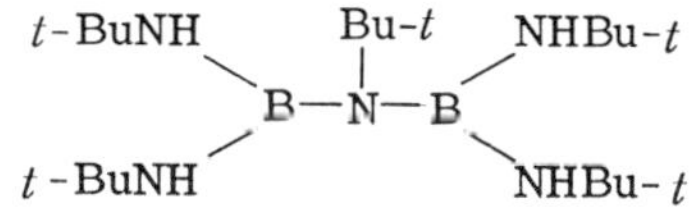

(XI)

The reaction of acetonitrile with diborane has been shown to give, as well as the expected N-triethylborazole (XII), a high boiling material

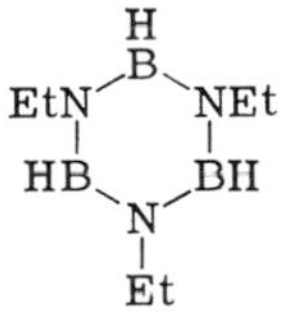

(XII)

$[EtNBH]_{5 \text{ to } 6}$

(XIII)

(XIII) having the same composition by elemental analysis but a higher molecular weight. However, hydrolysis produced ammonia as well as ethylamine, which indicates that the structural arrangement of (XIII) is not that of higher cyclic or linear composition. Thus the molecular weight reported is at present not meaningful (*34*).

Propionitrile was found to react with diborane to produce an adduct which on careful warming (up to 20°C) gave *N*-tri-*n*-propylborazole and a second fraction which corresponded to the empirical formula (*n*-PrNBH)$_x$. The value of x was 4 or 6 depending on determination by either a cryoscopic (M.W. 300) or vapor density (450) method. Again hydrolysis produced both propylamine and ammonia, highly indicative that the substance, in spite of analysis in agreement with theory, was a mixture (*34*). Both acrylonitrile and cyanogen gave, on reaction with diborane, amorphous brown solids which contained carbon, hydrogen, nitrogen, and boron. They have not been further characterized (*34*).

It has been postulated (*57*) that borazoles of optimum thermal stability with suitable substituent groups on boron and nitrogen could be opened by nucleophilic reagents to produce equilibrium mixtures of trimeric borazole and linear polymer [reaction (1)]. It was also considered possible

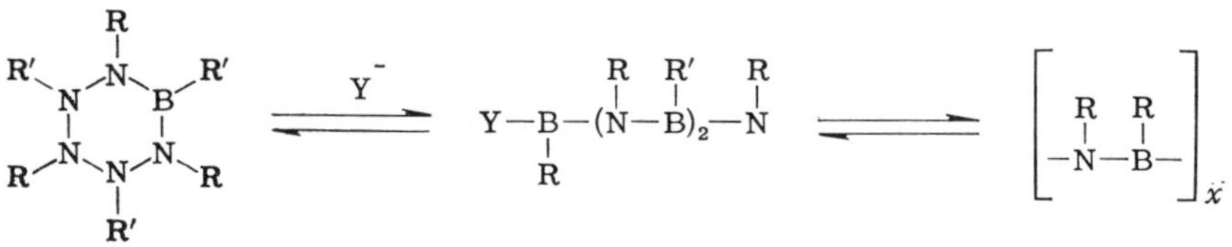

$$\tag{1}$$

that a similar reaction could be initiated by an electrophilic, radical, or solvolytic reagent. Several of the more thermally stable borazoles have been screened for such behavior by stepwise heating at temperatures up to about 400°C in the presence of various possible catalysts. At lower temperatures, high yields of the starting borazoles were recovered; at higher temperatures some of the borazoles produced resins, apparently by

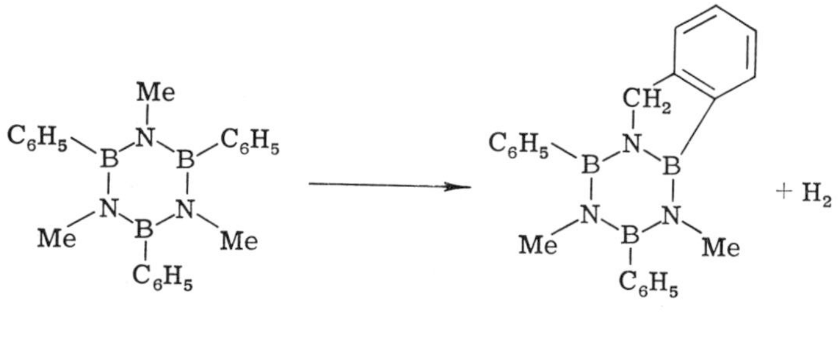

$$\tag{2}$$

reactions other than simple linearization. These resins were thermally stable, suffering very little weight loss at temperatures of 400° and above. So far, two general types of reaction have been shown to be operating in these high temperature reactions, although there are probably other important ones remaining to be sorted out. The first of these reactions is of the type shown in reaction (2). This reaction has been demonstrated for the intramolecular case, and there is evidence that its intermolecular counterpart is involved in resin formation. The second type of reaction is illustrated by the copolymerization of N-trimethyl-B-triphenylborazole with B-triphenylborazole. This produces benzene, probably by a B—N-forming dephenylation process [reaction (3)]. The resin produced had good

$$(3)$$

thermal stability above 400° in an inert atmosphere, although its molecular weight was below 1000. At least two new polymerization reactions of borazoles were thus discovered, although neither led to the linear polymers desired. Both the new polymerization reactions suffer from difficulties inherent in controlling such complex reactions. However, the products are of fused and/or joined borazole nuclei, and it begins to appear that such polymers, in spite of their complexity, will be the first borazole polymers to be obtained having high molecular weight.

A number of miscellaneous reactions have yielded what are apparently boron-nitrogen polymers. Thus Burg and Kuljian (*23*) refer to nonvolatile residual materials suspected of being B—N polymers from the decomposition of $(SiH_3)_2BNH_2$ or $(SiH_3)_2NBCl_2$. Steindler and Schlesinger (*84*) reported reactions of hydrazine and *sym*-dimethylhydrazine with diborane to form the bisborane complexes. These complexes lost hydrogen and produced polymers when heated. Stout and Chamberlain (*91*) described formation of a polymer from benzeneboronic acid and *m*-phenylenediamine. Gould (*40*) attempted to form polymers by treating boron chloride with ethylenediamine or hexane-1,6-diamine. The polymers formed retained large amounts of chloride, and it was stated that this was present as hydrochloride end-blocking groups. Cross-linking B—N—H functional groups with isocyanates was attempted in this study project, as was the reaction between boric acid and isocyanates. It is possible that Gould (*40*) was the originator of this idea (*1*). McLeod (*61*) has described the formation of stable, water-soluble resins from the reaction between boric acid and biurets. Rust (*75*) has described the preparation of water-soluble resinous products by reaction between boric acid and polyamines. Morgan

(64) has described the preparation of water-soluble urea resins by reaction between boric acid and ureas or substituted ureas. Although resins may be produced in some of these cases (61, 64, 75), each of these systems has been reexamined for B—N bond formation (39) but no evidence was found that they exist. Water-soluble, water-reactive polymers can be formed from many polyamine systems and boric acid esters (12), but no extensive examination of such polymers has been reported.

Ruigh (73, 74) has made a significant contribution in this area of chemistry by establishing the trimeric nature of polymeric $(BuBNH)_x$, reported by Booth and Kraus (12) and by a workman-like sorting out of the myth of B—N bond formation from the reaction between B—OH groups and isocyanates (93, 94), which has recently been reperpetrated on the patent-reading public (1). The nature of reactions between organic isocyanates and boric or boronic acids has not yet been published in primary literature sources. Reactions (4) (73, 74), (5) (15, 73, 74), and (6) (15) have been observed:

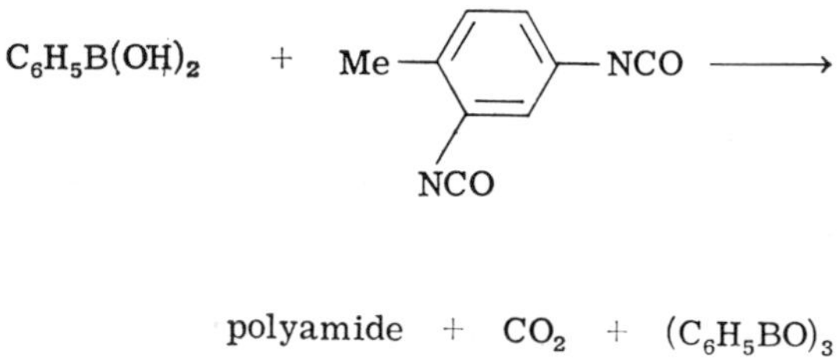

$$C_6H_5B(OH)_2 \quad + \quad \text{Me}—\langle\text{ring}\rangle—NCO \longrightarrow$$

with NCO substituent

$$\text{(4)}$$

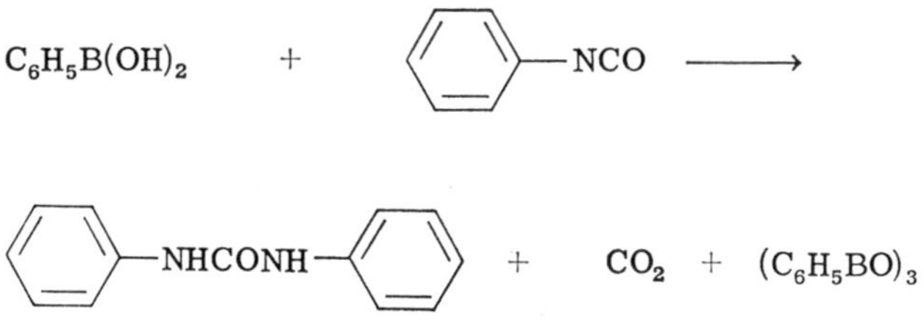

$$\text{polyamide} \; + \; CO_2 \; + \; (C_6H_5BO)_3$$

$$C_6H_5B(OH)_2 \quad + \quad \langle\text{ring}\rangle—NCO \longrightarrow$$

$$\text{(5)}$$

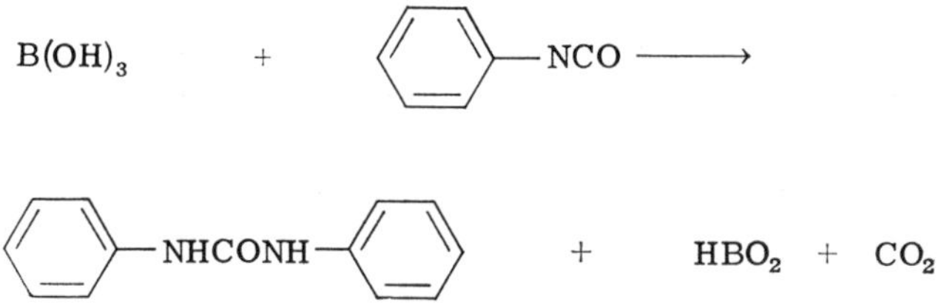

$$\langle\text{ring}\rangle—NHCONH—\langle\text{ring}\rangle \; + \; CO_2 \; + \; (C_6H_5BO)_3$$

$$B(OH)_3 \quad + \quad \langle\text{ring}\rangle—NCO \longrightarrow$$

$$\text{(6)}$$

$$\langle\text{ring}\rangle—NHCONH—\langle\text{ring}\rangle \; + \; HBO_2 \; + \; CO_2$$

A study of the formation of boron-nitrogen polymers with intervening aromatic groups was performed by Schupp and Brown (15, 81). A substance produced from forced reaction of boron chloride and *o*-phenylene-diamine must have been polymeric.

Quill and co-workers (*72*) have reported a reaction between equimolar concentrations of (MeOBO)$_3$ and aniline which produced a polymer formulated as:

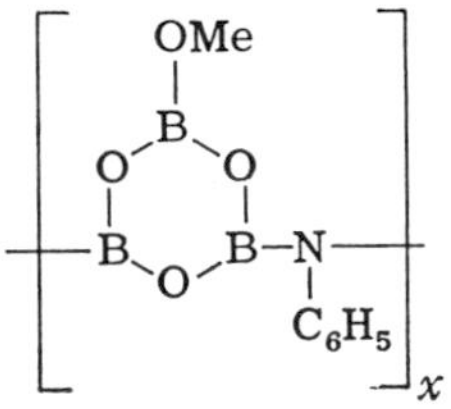

III. Boron-Phosphorus Polymers

Somewhat analogous to the boron-nitrogen bonded systems would be boron-phosphorus compounds, and many such substances with alternating boron and phosphorus bonds are known.

The first boron-phosphorus compound, "diborane diphosphine," $B_2H_6 \cdot 2PH_3$, was prepared by Gamble and Gilmont (*36*). This complex, which has a high dissociation pressure at ambient temperatures, on heating underwent loss of hydrogen. As was later pointed out (*27*), the product is intractable, as expected, for loss of hydrogen can hardly be expected to occur selectively at only one or two of the three sites on each phosphorus and boron atom. The formation of a noncross-linked polymer in an idealized process would be represented by the following sequence:

$$B_2H_6 + 2\ PH_3 \rightarrow 2\ H_3B \cdot PH_3$$

$$H_3B \cdot PH_3 \rightarrow H_2 + (H_2B \cdot PH_2)_x$$

Further loss of hydrogen from the above polymer would undoubtedly lead to crosslinking in a haphazard fashion.

A development of major significance in boron-phosphorus chemistry came when Burg and Wagner (*27*) studied the reaction of diborane with dimethylphosphine. The initial product was an adduct, $Me_2PH \cdot BH_3$, which lost one mole of hydrogen on heating at 150° to produce a mixture of polymers:

$$Me_2PH \cdot BH_3 \rightarrow H_2 + (Me_2P \cdot BH_2)_x$$

The product was predominantly ($\sim$90%) trimer ($x = 3$) and ($\sim$9%) tetramer ($x = 4$), but a trace of higher polymer was formed. It was immediately recognized that the trimer and tetramer were six-membered and eight-membered ring structures, and this was confirmed for the trimer by an X-ray crystallographic study (*44*). It was found that both the tetramer and the higher polymer could be converted to the trimer (or the trimer-tetramer mixture) by heating. The trimer and tetramer have remarkable chemical and thermal stabilities. Trimeric dimethylphosphinoborane is thermally stable at 350° and reacts only slowly with concentrated hydrochloric acid at 300°. Since such stability is far greater than that of the dimer [Me_2NBH_2]$_2$, Burg and Wagner (*27*) attributed the greater stability of the phosphorus compounds to strengthening of the P—B bonds by delocalization of B—H bonding electrons into vacant $3d$ orbitals of adjacent phosphorus atoms. Such supplementary bonding would be impossible in the aminoboranes because nitrogen has no d orbitals of low enough energy to partake in chemical bonding. Subsequently, however, the cyclic trimer [Me_2NBH_2]$_3$ became known (*29*) and proved to have almost the same degree of stability as dimethylphosphinoborane trimer. Nevertheless, if classical structures (XIV) and (XV) are by themselves supposed

(XIV)　　　　　　　　　　　　　　　　　(XV)

to account for the bonding in these trimers, it is difficult to understand why the phosphorus compound is so stable. Usually, N → B dative bonds are much stronger than P → B (*88*). For example, the N—B bond in $Me_3N \cdot BF_3$ has a strength of about 30 kcal while the P—B bond in $Me_3P \cdot BF_3$ has a strength of about 19 kcal. Furthermore, the donor power of an element is greatly reduced by attachment of electronegative groups. Nevertheless, trimers and tetramers of $(CF_3)_2PBH_2$ were made, and these polymers were thermally stable to 200° (*22*). In view of the effect a CF_3 group has on the donor power of an atom to which it is attached (*7*), it is difficult to see why $(CF_3)_2PBH_2$ groups polymerize at all, since the phosphorus atom should not have sufficient base strength. If, however, one recognizes that in a polymer of $(CF_3)_2PBH_2$ the classical dative σ-bonds are weak but the nonclassical π-bonding is strengthened* over what it is in polymers of

---

* Replacement of groups on a donor atom possessing vacant d orbitals by groups which are more electronegative (i.e., Me replaced by CF_3) results in contraction of the d orbitals with a consequential increase in the use of these orbitals for π-bonding. See reference (*30*).

Me$_2$PBH$_2$, the polymerization is accounted for. It is evident that whatever are the causes for the relative stabilities of certain aminoboron and phosphinoboron compounds, and they may be many, studies in this area have led to development of much novel chemistry. The discovery that boron-phosphorus polymers could have high thermal stabilities gave an extra impetus to the study of these systems, although they are of a great deal of scientific interest, regardless of their high temperature properties.

Burg and Slota (*26*) developed a method for preparing dialkylphosphinoboranes from more conveniently handled starting materials than phosphines and diborane. The method involved treatment of diorgano-substituted phosphorus trihalides with sodium borohydride in diglyme, followed by pyrolysis [reaction (7)]:

$$R_2PCl + NaBH_4 \rightarrow R_2PH \cdot BH_3 + NaCl \downarrow$$
$$\left. \right\downarrow \text{heat} \tag{7}$$
$$(R_2P\dot{B}H_2)_n$$
$$R = \text{Et, Ph, etc.}$$

Wagner and his co-workers (*98, 99, 100, 102*) have prepared many different kinds of phosphinoboranes and have examined their chemical properties. About 35 phosphinoborane polymers with degree of polymerization of 3 or above and about half a dozen "copolymers" (mixed polymers prepared from two or more phosphinoborines) have been synthesized since 1953. These are listed in Table I. Very recently, the dimeric phosphinoborane derivatives [(C$_6$H$_5$)$_2$PBBr$_2$]$_2$ and [(C$_6$H$_5$)$_2$PBI$_2$]$_2$ have been reported (*37a*).

Studies apparently directed at possible commercial utilization of boron-phosphorus polymers were reported by Yolles (*111*). Complexes of mono-alkyl- and monoaryl-phosphines with borane lost hydrogen to produce polymers:

$$RPH_2 \cdot BH_3 \rightarrow H_2 + \text{polymer}$$
$$ArPH_2 \cdot BH_3 \rightarrow H_2 + \text{polymer}$$

These polymers had molecular weights (cryoscopic) only in the 600 range, but films could be cast on metals and glass with them. These films were stated to have excellent protective properties except that they were degraded by atmospheric oxidation, perhaps of the PH bonds. It was further stated that the elemental analysis of the polymers showed that the polymerization was not straightforward. This may be connected with the possibility that elimination of two molecules of hydrogen can occur with subsequent irregularity and cross-linking in the resultant polymer.

Leffler (*55*) has reported the preparation of aliphatic difunctional phosphines. These phosphines formed adducts with diborane which on pyrolysis lost hydrogen; the polymers obtained in this manner were highly cross-linked and brittle, but exhibited considerable thermal stability up to 300°C.

TABLE I

SOME PHOSPHORUS-BORON POLYMERS

Composition	Polymeric character	Ref.
Me_2PBH_2	Trimer	*27*
	Tetramer	*27*
	High polymer, thermoplastic	*19, 27*
	High polymer, M.W. $\sim$6000	*101, 102*
	High polymer, M.W. $\sim$14000	*98*
$H_{<2}PBH_{<2}$	Cross-linked, degree of polymerization $\sim$28	*27, 36*
Me_2PBMe_2	Trimer	*27*
H_2PBMe_2	Monomer forms high polymer on standing	*27*
$HMePBMe_2$	Not isolated pure	*27*
$HMePBH_2$	High polymer	*27*
$HRPBH_2$, $HArPBH_2$	Polymers which form films on glass or metal, M.W. $\sim$600	*111*
$EtMePBH_2$	Translucent plastic polymer, M.W. $\sim$1850	*101*
$HBPH(CH_2)_3HPBH$	Highly cross-linked brittle foam	*55*
H_2PBBu_2	Polymeric	*37*
$HEtPBH_2$	Glass	*99*
Me_2PBF_2	Trimer	*99*
Me_2PBCl_2	Trimer, linear polymer	*98, 99, 102*
Me_2PBBr_2	Trimer	*99*
Me_2PBI_2	Trimer	*99*
$(C_6H_5)_2PBBr_2$	Dimer	*37a*
$(C_6H_5)_2PBI_2$	Dimer	*37a*
$H_2BP(Me)(CH_2)_3(Me)PBH_2$	Highly cross-linked insoluble material	*100*
$(p\text{-}MeC_6H_4)_2PBH_2$	Trimer	*100*
Et_2PBH_2	Brittle translucent, insoluble white solid	*102*
$n\text{-}PrMePBH_2$	Linear polymer, viscous colorless liquid, M.W. $\sim$1050	*102*
$i\text{-}PrMePBH_2$	Linear polymer, viscous liquid	*102*
$(CH_2)_4PBH_2$	Linear polymer, viscous liquid	*102*
$C_6H_5MePBH_2$	Linear polymer, viscous liquid, M.W. $\sim$800	*102*
$(C_6H_5)_2PBH_2$	Trimer	*102*
$CH_2{=}CH{-}CH_2(Me)PBH_2$	May consist of phosphinoborane rings cross-linked by saturated carbon chains	*102*
$C_6H_5(Me)PBMe_2$	Trimer	*102*
$EtMePBH_2 + HMePBH_2$	Fused-ringed copolymer	*99*
$EtMePBH_2 + EtPBH$	Copolymer	*99*
$H_2BP(Me)(CH_2)_3(Me)PBH_2$	Copolymer with Me_2PBH_2	*100*

TABLE I—*Continued*

Composition	Polymeric character	Ref.
EtMePBH$_2$ + *i*-PrMePBH$_2$	Copolymer	*100*
EtMePBH$_2$ + C$_6$H$_5$HPBH$_2$	Copolymer	*100*
C$_{12}$H$_{25}$(Me)PBH$_2$	Waxy copolymer with Me$_2$PBH$_2$	*102*
CH$_2$=CH—CH$_2$(Me)PBH$_2$ + EtMePBH$_2$	Saturated copolymer which may consist of phosphinoborane rings cross-linked by saturated carbon chains	*102*
HMePBH$_2$ + Me$_2$PBH$_2$	Copolymer	*102*
EtMePBH$_2$ + HMePBH$_2$	Copolymer	*102*

Two methods of formation of high molecular weight and probably linear polymers have recently been disclosed. Burg (*19*) described the decomposition of the borane complex of tetramethylbiphosphine at 174° to produce dimethylphosphine, dimethylphosphinoborane trimer and tetramer, and a thermoplastic white residue described as being a high linear polymer. This residue was largely converted to the dimethylphosphinoborane trimer-tetramer mixture by heating for 20 hours at 330°. Wagner and Caserio (*101*) found that the addition of 10 to 45 mole % of a base such as tri-ethylamine during the pyrolysis of phosphine-borane complexes increased the amount of high molecular weight polymer formed. In the case of dimethylphosphinoborine, a 45% yield of polymer of molecular weight 6000 was obtained in the presence of triethylamine, and the evidence was in accord with a linear structure for this polymer. Linearity was presumed to arise by successive addition of the (as yet unisolated) phosphinoborane monomer units to an end group consisting of a triethylamine-phosphino-borine monomer complex:

$$Me_2HP \cdot BH_3 \xrightarrow{200°} Me_2PBH_2 + H_2$$

$$Me_2PBH_2 + Et_3N \longrightarrow Me_2PBH_2 \cdot NEt_3$$

$$Me_2PBH_2 \cdot NEt_3 + n\ Me_2PBH_2 \longrightarrow (Me_2PBH_2)_n Me_2PBH_2 \cdot NEt_3$$

If, as presumed, the terminal BH$_2$ unit of the growing chain is tied up by coordination with amine, it is reasonable to assume that cyclization to trimer or tetramer is rendered more difficult (*101*). An alternative polymerization mechanism cannot be ruled out, however.

The highest molecular weights obtained with phosphinoborines correspond to a degree of polymerization of about 100 (*98, 102*). The structure of these high molecular weight polymers is assumed to be linear, but this has not yet been proved. Numerous copolymers, some with fused ring structures, have been prepared by Wagner and co-workers, but none appear to have any advantage over the polymers from a single monomer. Although the apparently uncatalyzed reversion of the linear polymers to trimer-tetramer mixtures at temperatures slightly above 300° would seem to limit their utility in high temperature applications, the success in developing the chemistry of this polymer system based on inorganic skeletal atoms must be recognized as a step of great importance.

IV. Polymeric Materials with B—B Bonds

Boron hydride polymers, which are mostly irregular materials but contain boron-boron bonds, are discussed in Section V. The discussion here is limited to those molecules containing trigonal boron-boron bonds with alkyl, halogen, alkoxy, and amino groups as substituents. Apparently hydrogen, alkyl, and aryl groups on boron do not offer enough electron density to prevent disproportionation so that the R_2B—BR_2 type of compounds are unstable. However, reactions which might produce such compounds (where R = H, alkyl, aryl) have not been studied enough to ascertain if disproportionation can be inhibited.

Attempted formation of tetraalkyldiborons either by the reaction of diboron tetrachloride with organometallic reagents (*95*) or by the reduction of dialkylmonohaloboranes with active metals has always given triorganoboron compounds and dark-colored residues, the analysis of which sometimes corresponded to $(RB)_x$. There is the suspicion that tetraalkyldiborons are formed as intermediates only to disporportionate as shown in reaction (8). These residues, polymeric by inference, have

$$n \begin{bmatrix} \text{Me} & & \text{Me} \\ & \diagdown \quad \diagup & \\ & B\text{—}B & \\ & \diagup \quad \diagdown & \\ \text{Me} & & \text{Me} \end{bmatrix} \rightarrow n\ \text{Me}_3\text{B} + (\text{MeB})_n \qquad (8)$$

never been studied, and one is tempted to believe that a study of them would be about as difficult as a study of the polymeric boron hydrides, $(BH_x)_n$.

The halodiboron compounds disproportionate to produce BX_3 and $(BX)_n$ materials. Thus, diboron tetrachloride disproportionates above 0° to produce boron trichloride and B_4Cl_4. The structure of this molecule (X-ray diffraction) has been found to be a tetrahedron of boron atoms each attached to a chlorine atom (*4*). The halide B_8Cl_8, which has also been isolated from B_2Cl_4 decomposition residues, has a structure (*49*) consisting of a polyhedron of boron atoms each bonded to a chlorine atom. Diboron tetrafluoride has been prepared (*35*), but nothing is known of its (possible) disproportionation products.

Diboron tetrabromide (*95, 104*) has not been studied, but an attempt to prepare it by an electrodeless discharge afforded lower boron bromides (*71*). These materials of higher molecular weight than B_2Br_4 have not been investigated. Diboron tetraiodide (*50*) was found to disproportionate in a similar fashion to diboron tetrachloride except that polymerization was complicated by loss of molecular iodine. A boron monoiodide, BI, has been stated to be polymeric (*80*), but no other studies of this polymer have been made. Thus, most of the reliable experimental work on polymeric boron subhalides is that concerning the chlorides B_4Cl_4 and B_8Cl_8, which have cyclized structures, and are electron deficient in a manner somewhat reminiscent of the higher boron hydrides (*89*). (See Chapter 9 for a further discussion of electron-deficient polymers.) Very recently, derivatives of the ions $B_{10}H_{10}^{-2}$ and $B_{12}H_{12}^{-2}$ have been shown to form the basis of a vast new field cf boron chemistry (*47a*). The remarkable thermal and chemical stability of these species suggests that they may play a useful role in inorganic polymers, providing that satisfactory methods of linking the polyhedral units can be found.

Early data on tetraalkoxydiboron compounds (*37, 109*) led to the belief that they disproportionated easily to produce orthoborate and elemental boron (*37*) or possibly a polymeric aggregate of BOR units [reaction (9)].

$$
\begin{array}{c}
\text{OR} \qquad \text{OR} \\
\diagdown \qquad \diagup \\
\text{B—B} \qquad \rightarrow \text{B(OR)}_3 + \text{B } or \text{ BOR} \\
\diagup \qquad \diagdown \\
\text{OR} \qquad \text{OR}
\end{array}
\tag{9}
$$

Preparation of tetraalkoxydiborons from difficultly accessible B_2Cl_4 was recently circumvented by the discovery of a facile synthesis of tetra(dimethylamino)diboron (*14*), $[(Me_2N)_2B—B(NMe_2)_2]$, and the subsequent development of methods for the exchange of alkoxy or phenoxy groups for the amino groups (*13*). The compounds tetramethoxydiboron and tetraethoxydiboron were then shown to be considerably more stable when pure than previously thought (*37, 109*). In fact, tetramethoxydiboron could not be induced to disproportionate below 130°C, a temperature at which a secondary reaction involving ether formation sets in [reaction (10)]. The

$$
\begin{array}{c}
\text{MeO} \qquad \text{MeO} \\
\diagdown \qquad \diagup \\
\text{B—B} \qquad \xrightarrow{130°C} \text{(MeO)}_3\text{B} + \text{Me}_2\text{O} + \text{polymer} \\
\diagup \qquad \diagdown \\
\text{MeO} \qquad \text{MeO}
\end{array}
\tag{10}
$$

formation of ether dictates that cross-linking must be occurring according to a reaction similar to (11). The B=O double bond is written purely for convenience, it being expected that larger than two-membered rings are formed in any condensed phase. Tetraethoxydiboron could be induced to decompose at a lower temperature, producing a polymer whose boron content indicated that chains of up to 10 boron atoms had been formed

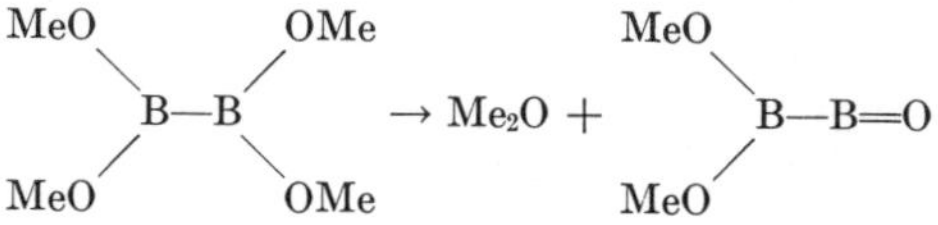

$$\underset{\text{MeO}}{\overset{\text{MeO}}{\diagdown}} \text{B}-\text{B} \underset{\text{OMe}}{\overset{\text{OMe}}{\diagup}} \rightarrow \text{Me}_2\text{O} + \underset{\text{MeO}}{\overset{\text{MeO}}{\diagdown}} \text{B}-\text{B}{=}\text{O} \tag{11}$$

[reaction (12)]. These polymers had neither oxidative nor hydrolytic stability and decomposed, releasing ethers at temperatures above 150°. Since the original objective of the work was to obtain polymers of high stability, it is not surprising that the study was terminated. Nevertheless, it is ap-

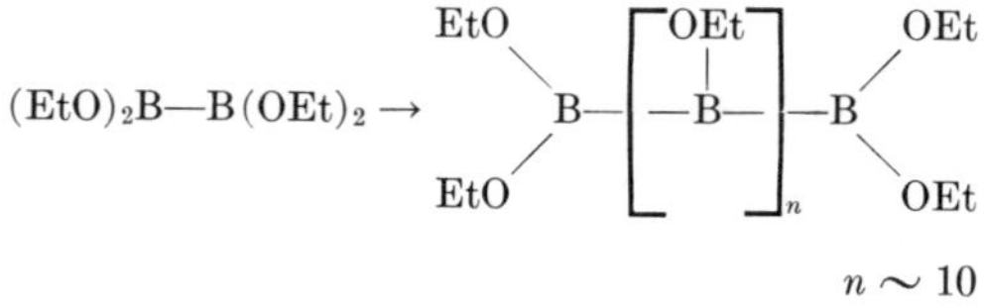

$$(\text{EtO})_2\text{B}-\text{B}(\text{OEt})_2 \rightarrow \underset{\text{EtO}}{\overset{\text{EtO}}{\diagdown}} \text{B}-\left[-\underset{}{\overset{\text{OEt}}{\mid}}\text{B}-\right]_n -\text{B} \underset{\text{OEt}}{\overset{\text{OEt}}{\diagup}} \tag{12}$$

$$n \sim 10$$

parent that compounds having B—B bonds are of great interest, their study providing new information on the chemistry of covalent boron compounds.

Finally, it may be noted that the synthesis of polymers of type (XVI) suggested that polymers of type (XVII) would be of interest. However, no

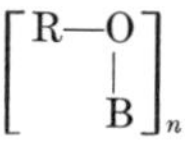

$$\left[\overset{\text{R}-\text{O}}{\underset{\text{B}}{\mid}}\right]_n \qquad \left[\overset{\text{R}_2\text{N}}{\underset{\text{B}}{\mid}}\right]_n$$

$$\text{(XVI)} \qquad\qquad \text{(XVII)}$$

method of disproportionating tetra(dimethylamino)diboron has yet been developed.

V. Boron Hydride Polymers

Stock and his co-workers were the first to observe that the volatile boron hydrides lose hydrogen on standing for long periods at room temperature or on heating, forming a series of nonvolatile materials, evidently polymeric in character. Stock's observations were casual, since, as he stated (85), "We have not as yet undertaken any systematic work in this field, because it seems to offer no adequate return for the effort that would be required." This still appears to be the general viewpoint, with some notable exceptions recently. Mild heating of lower boron hydrides forms colorless hydrides, which lose hydrogen at higher temperatures, changing to yellow; the color deepens as further heating leads to loss of additional hydrogen. For example, tetraborane, B_4H_{10}, was reported to give a yellow hydride of empirical composition $BH_{0.8}$, which was infusible and insoluble in carbon disulfide (85).

A recent kinetic study of the pyrolysis of decaborane by Beachell and Haugh (8) sheds some light on the nature of the polymeric product. Only hydrogen was formed in the reaction, and there was no evidence that other volatile boron hydrides were involved as intermediates. In the over-all reaction, about 4 moles of hydrogen were lost per mole of decaborane, corresponding to a residue of composition $BH_{0.6}$. In the early stages of the pyrolysis, however, much less hydrogen was evolved per mole of decaborane consumed, which the authors suggested was due to a chain process initiated by decaborane diradicals. The initial pyrolysis products were soluble in decaborane, in which solvent molecular weights were determined by vapor pressure lowering; values up to 915 were observed.

Another interesting study of the nonvolatile $(BH_x)_n$ solids was made by Shapiro and Williams (82). At 100°, diborane and decaborane evolved hydrogen much more rapidly than either compound alone at that temperature, forming the polymer. In this case, as well as in the work mentioned above, no other intermediate volatile boron hydrides were detected, and it was suggested that the B_2H_6 molecule might complete the partial icosahedron formed by $B_{10}H_{14}$, with further loss of hydrogen from the unstable $(BH)_{12}$ unit:

$$B_2H_6 + B_{10}H_{14} \xrightarrow{100°} 4\ H_2 + (BH)_{12} \xrightarrow{-H_2O} (BH_x)_n$$

Infrared spectra indicated the absence of B—H—B bridges, consistent with this view (82). The B_{12} structure unit is found, for example, in boron carbide.

Burg has attempted to use chemical means to control and promote the formation of polymeric boron hydrides. He treated pentaborane-9 with trimethylamine, dimethylamine, or dimethylaminoborane (18). These reactants give rise to unsymmetrical cleavage of pentaborane-9. In the case of reaction with trimethylamine, one product isolated in high yield was trimethylamine-borane complex $Me_3N \cdot BH_3$. The over-all reaction has been described as an abstraction of two borane (BH_3) molecules from pentaborane-9, followed by the rapid polymerization of the remaining B_3H_3 units. This polymerization reaction was investigated in further detail by Campbell (see reference 57), who found that less than two moles of trimethylamine-borane could be obtained and that the polymerization was attended by some loss of hydrogen. The polymers retained varying amounts of amine, probably intimately involved in the polymer bonding. The materials produced are of reasonably high molecular weight, are resistant to solvolysis by methanol or hydrochloric acid, and begin to degrade by loss of methane above 200°. These, then, are probably boron hydride polymers of complex structures and mechanisms of formation. The polymerization reaction may be simpler than straight boron hydride pyrolysis. These materials await further investigation. Studies with other basic reagents such as tertiary phosphines have given similar results.

VI. Boron-Oxygen Polymers

Polymeric compounds having boron-oxygen links in a chain include polymers and anhydrides of boric acids. Although these materials have relatively high thermal stability, most of them are easily hydrolyzed, thereby reducing their utility. Anhydrides of alkyl- or arylboronic acids, the so-called boroxoles, usually occur as cyclic trimers or dimers, viz., $(RBO)_3$, $(ROBO)_3$, or $(RBO)_2$. Such substances are thermally very stable; tri-n-butylboroxole (b.p. 259°) is not appreciably decomposed at 600°, but above this temperature affords ethylene (*70*). (It should be noted that pyrolysis experiments of reference (*70*) were carried out at low pressure in a flow system, in terms of which this thermal stability seems less astonishing.)

A number of benzenediboronic acids have been prepared as starting points for polymer synthesis. Benzene-1,3- and benzene-1,4-diboronic acids have been prepared and it was found that neither melted below 410°, although it was believed that anhydride formation (the anhydrides would have to be polymeric) was taking place (*68*). Musgrave (*65*) prepared benzene-1,4-diboronic acid and observed that it dehydrated above 230° to give a very stable anhydride. Polyesters from diboronic acid derivatives have been mentioned (*6*) but no molecular weights or other properties were given.

It has been found (*9*) that mixtures of boric acids and glycols or glycerol become progressively more viscous as water is removed by distillation. The reaction of boric acid with alcohols is rapid and reversible so high molecular weights may be built up with polyalcohols by exhaustively removing the water produced by esterification. No structure determinations have been made on such products and no doubt the structures are far from simple. Cross-linking of chains is inevitable because of the trivalent character of boron. Rings within the polymeric structure are likely, and the extreme mobility of boron-oxygen exchange reactions makes the distribution of structure types dependent not only on the details of the method of preparation, but also on the total history of the material. Inclusion of small amounts of water, for example, will greatly diminish the molecular weights of the resins. Both Stout and Chamberlain (*91*) and Gould (*40*) attempted to get ordered polymers from glycol and boric acid systems, but met with no particular success.

Boric oxide will dissolve in either alkyl borates, $(RO)_3B$, or trialkyl-boranes, R_3B. A one-to-one stoichiometry leads to the formation of six-membered ring species by partial or complete disruption of the B_2O_3 network and shuffling of R or OR groups (*43*):

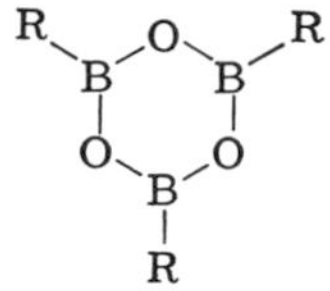

Higher amounts of boric oxide can be dissolved in borate esters to give materials which must be regarded as modified boric oxides. The structures of these materials are not known, but it is reasonable to assume an increase in complexity as the mole ratio of dissolved boric oxide is increased [reactions (13) and (14)]. The preservation of the six-membered rings in these postulated structures is based on intuition rather than experimental evidence, any even-numbered ring size being possible in the reorganized structures. The molecular structures may be random in size, and reach limits

$$B(OR)_3 \ + \ B_2O_3 \quad \longrightarrow \qquad\qquad\qquad\qquad \tag{13}$$

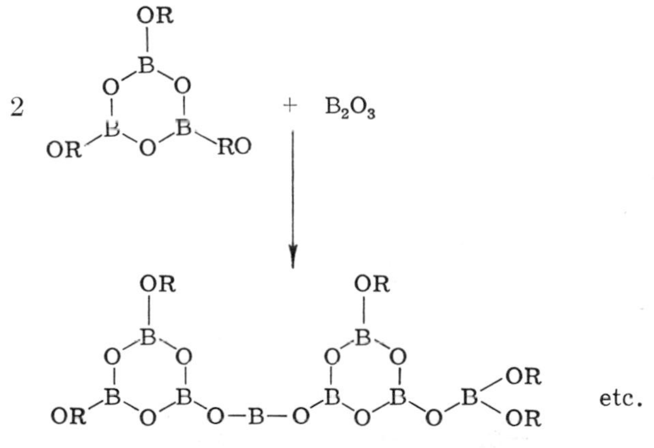

$$(14)$$

depending on the tendency for crystallization of products or reactants from the reaction media. These materials, like the glycol borates, are quite sensitive to water, and this and the possible mobility of their reactions make structure and property studies difficult.

Polymers containing the B—O—Si linkage have been studied most recently by Vale (*97*), who gives references to earlier work in this field. By reaction of boric acid and dimethyldichlorosilane, Vale obtained materials of molecular weight 500–1000, to which he assigned the structure:

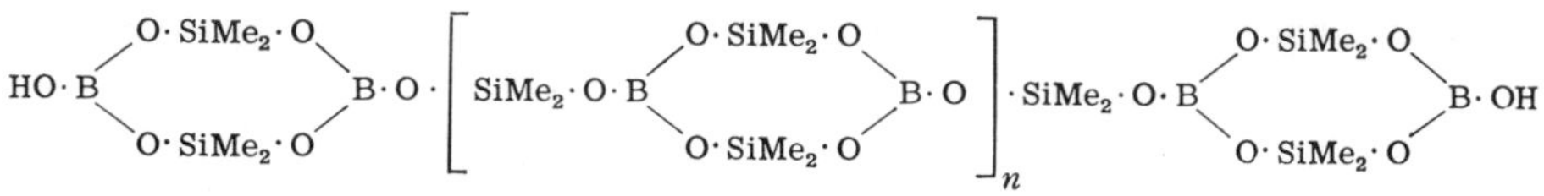

$$\text{HO} \cdot \text{B} \underset{\text{O} \cdot \text{SiMe}_2 \cdot \text{O}}{\overset{\text{O} \cdot \text{SiMe}_2 \cdot \text{O}}{<}} \text{B} \cdot \text{O} \cdot \left[\text{SiMe}_2 \cdot \text{O} \cdot \text{B} \underset{\text{O} \cdot \text{SiMe}_2 \cdot \text{O}}{\overset{\text{O} \cdot \text{SiMe}_2 \cdot \text{O}}{<}} \text{B} \cdot \text{O} \right]_n \cdot \text{SiMe}_2 \cdot \text{O} \cdot \text{B} \underset{\text{O} \cdot \text{SiMe}_2 \cdot \text{O}}{\overset{\text{O} \cdot \text{SiMe}_2 \cdot \text{O}}{<}} \text{B} \cdot \text{OH}$$

Despite the rather low molecular weights, the products had interesting thermal and elastic properties. Cross-linking was accomplished with high energy electrons, resulting in improved resistance to hydrolysis.

VII. Boron-Carbon Polymers

Polymers with only boron and carbon in the chain are at present relatively rare. The decomposition of trimethylboron (*42*) at about 400° gave methane, hydrogen, and some less volatile boron- and carbon-containing materials. It was expected that loss of methane would lead to the unsaturated compound CH_3—B=CH_2. No substance of this composition was detected in the volatile fractions, but its tetramer, 1,3,5,7-tetramethyl-

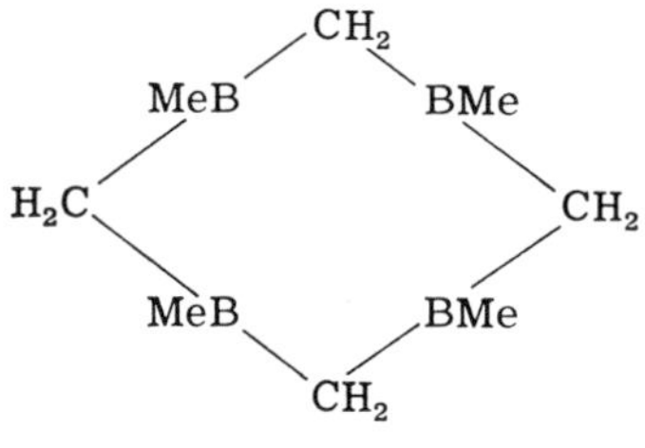

(XVIII)

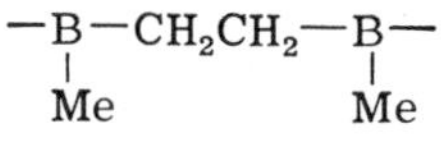

$$-\text{B}-\text{CH}_2\text{CH}_2-\text{B}-$$
$$\overset{|}{\text{Me}} \qquad \overset{|}{\text{Me}}$$

(XIX)

$$-\text{CH}_2\text{CH}_2-\text{B} \underset{\text{CH}_2\text{CH}_2}{\overset{\text{CH}_2\text{CH}_2}{<}} \text{B}-$$

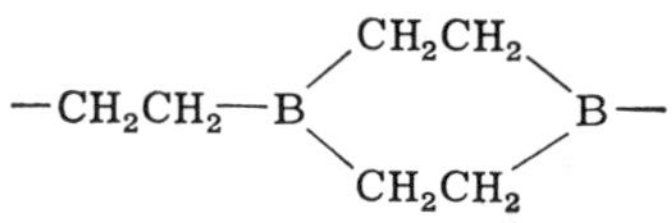

(XX)

1,3,5,7-tetraborocyclooctane, assumed to have the cyclic structure (XVIII), was isolated from the less volatile portion. No high molecular weight polymer of composition $(BC_2H_5)_n$ was found. The existence of the cyclic tetramer is by no means proof of the existence of an unsaturated B=C intermediate, but it is an interesting possibility to contemplate. The higher molecular weight substances from the pyrolysis of trimethylboron were shown by analyses to be products of further loss of methane and hydrogen, which are necessarily cross-linking reactions. The decomposition of other trialkylboron compounds is also accompanied by formation of polymeric materials. Tri-*n*-hexylboron, for example, decomposes under reflux according to the equation:

$$x\ (C_6H_{13})_3B \rightarrow [(C_6H_{13})B]_x + 2x\ C_2H_{12} + x\ H_2$$

In a side reaction, 1-*n*-hexyl-2-methylboracyclohexane, $B(C_6H_{13})(C_6H_{12})$, was produced. Continued heating of the polymer $[B(C_6H_{13})]_x$ produced a dark solid and a viscous liquid for which analysis suggested the formulations $[-B(C_6H_{13})BH-]_x$ and $[-B(C_6H_{13})-(C_6H_{12})-B(C_6H_{13})-]_r$. respectively (*110*).

Treatment of the compound $Cl_2BCH_2CH_2BCl_2$ with dimethylzinc affords $Me_2BCH_2CH_2BMe_2$, which on pyrolysis releases trimethylboron and forms materials assigned structures (XIX) and (XX) (*96*). Other reactions which lead to materials with boron-carbon atom chains include (15) (*48*), (16) (*33*), and (17) (*62*):

$$(C_6H_8C{\equiv}C)_3B \cdot O(CH_2)_4 \xrightarrow{85°} (CH_2)_4O + \text{reddish-violet polymer} \quad (15)$$

$$n\ (C_6H_5)_2BCl \xrightarrow[\text{AlCl}_3]{\text{heat}} C_6H_5[B(Cl)C_6H_4]_{n-1}B(Cl)C_6H_5 + (n-1)\ C_6H_6 \quad (16)$$

$$(CH_2{:}CHCH_2)_3B + (\text{iso-Bu})_3B$$

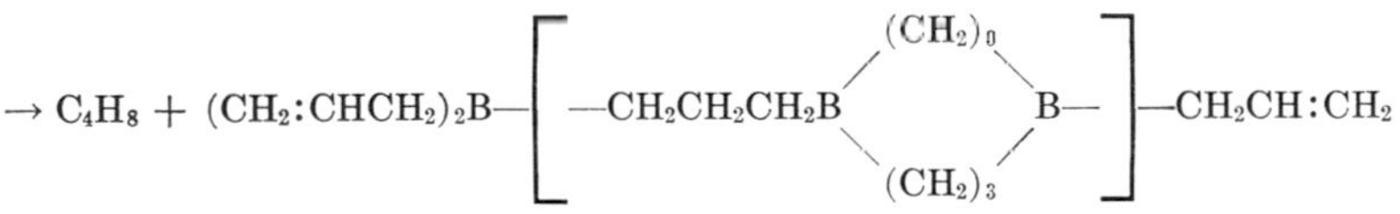

$$\rightarrow C_4H_8 + (CH_2{:}CHCH_2)_2B{-}\left[{-}CH_2CH_2CH_2B \overset{\textstyle (CH_2)_9}{\underset{\textstyle (CH_2)_3}{\diagup\!\!\diagdown}} B{-} \right]{-}CH_2CH{:}CH_2 \quad (17)$$

A recent patent (*69*) reveals a new method for synthesis of a resinous polymer by treating a boron halide or ester with the di-Grignard reagent derived from *p*-dibromobenzene. The polymer presumably has a structure:

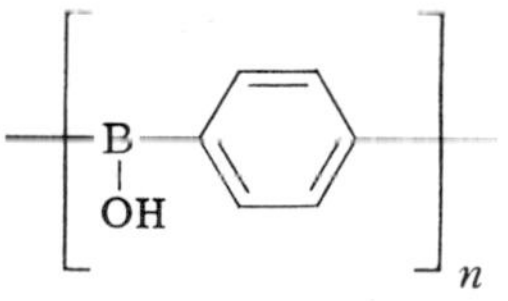

Some cross-linking is to be expected, but such polymers may have interesting and useful properties. Wartik and Rosenberg (*105*) reported that boron trichloride and carbon monoxide in an ozonizer-type discharge (11,000 volts, 160 hours) reacted to give a polymer which was stable to water and had other properties reminiscent of a high polymer. Such compounds could contain boron-carbon bonds.

Polymers containing —B—C— linkages can usually be oxidized by atmospheric oxygen, and suffer a fundamental disadvantage in this respect.

VIII. Boron Polymers of Miscellaneous Types

In a number of instances boron monomers have been copolymerized with conventional organic monomers. Bis(*p*-vinylbenzene)boronic acid has been copolymerized with styrene and other vinyl compounds yielding resins (*56*). Copolymerization of β-chlorovinylboronic acid with vinyl monomers is mentioned in a patent (*2*). Copolymerization of *B*-substituted borazoles with hexamethylene diisocyanate yields copolymers of linear or three-dimensional character, depending on the stoichiometry [reaction (18)]. The materials are transparent with softening temperatures depending on the nature of the substituent on boron (*51*).

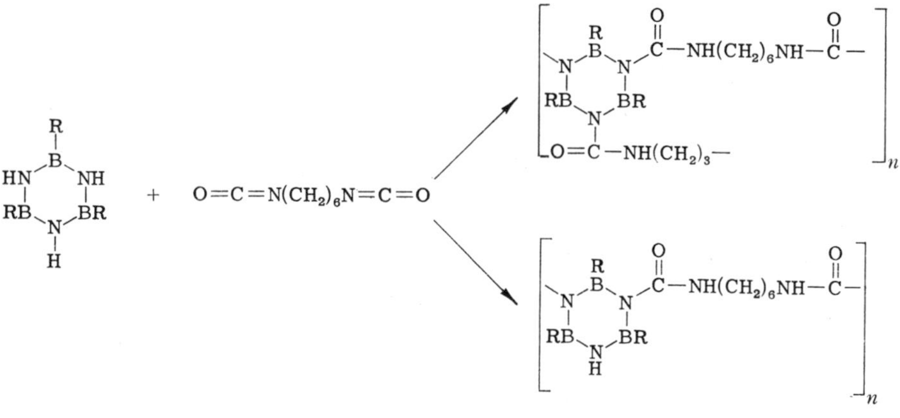

(18)

From the reaction [reaction (19)] between boron triacetate and triethyl phosphate, an infusible, very hygroscopic mixed polyanhydride has been obtained (*45*).

$$x \; B(OCOCH_3)_3 + x \; (C_2H_5O)_3PO \rightarrow \left[-O-B-O-\overset{\overset{O}{\|}}{P}- \right]_x + 3x \; CH_3COOC_2H_5 \qquad (19)$$

Andrianov and co-workers (*3*) have carried out heterofunctional poly-condensation of alkyl- and aryl-dialkoxysilanes with triacetoxyboron, and of alkyl- or aryl-diacetoxysilanes with butyl borate to give organobora-siloxanes:

$$(-SiR_2-O-B-O-SiR_2-O-)_n$$
$$|$$
$$OC_4H_9$$

These polymers are unfortunately easily hydrolyzed, although they have good thermal stability.

A number of compounds of boron containing sulfur or arsenic have been obtained which are polymeric in nature. Diborane and dimethylarsine react to give an adduct $Me_2AsH \cdot BH_3$, which on heating forms trimer, tetramers, and higher polymers of composition $(Me_2AsBH_2)_n$, analogous to phosphinoboranes, but less stable to heat and chemical degradation (*90*). Diborane and hydrogen sulfide react slowly at room temperature to afford a colorless transparent film $(BHS)_n$ and hydrogen. The unstable complex $MeSH \cdot BH_3$ releases hydrogen on slow warming above $-78°$ to give low polymers $(McSBH_2)_n$ (*28*). Sulfur-boron dative bonding between monomer units is weak, the polymers being much less stable than the arsinoboranes.

IX. Modification of Properties of Conventional Polymers by Boron Compounds

Boron compounds are sometimes incorporated commercially into natural and synthetic polymers in order to modify properties. Boric acid (and borax) are added to cellulosic materials, and synthetic polymers of the polyvinyl alcohol type. The chemical phenomenon involved here is the rapid reversible esterification of boric acid by certain glycols. This use of boric acid has been reviewed (*47*). "Bouncing putty" (*60*), a silicone polymer with small amount of boric oxide added, probably depends for its properties on the rapid exchange of oxygen atoms at a boron atom. Thus the boron atom may act as a "mobile" cross-linking agent, but with the degree of cross-linking remaining the same.

REFERENCES

1. Aires, R. S., U. S. Patent 2,931,831 (April 5, 1960).
2. Arnold, H. R., U. S. Patent 2,402,590 (June 25, 1946).
3. Andrianov, K. A., and Volkova, L. M., *Isvest. Akad. Nauk S.S.S.R. Otdel. Khim. Nauk* p. 303 (1957).
4. Atoji, M., and Lipscomb, W. N., *J. Chem. Phys.* **21**, 172 (1953).

5. Aubrey, D. W., and Lappert, M. F., *J. Chem. Soc.* p. 2927 (1959).
6. Bamford, W. R., and Fordham, S., Paper presented at Symposium of the Plastics and Polymer Group, Society of Chemical Industry, London, 1960.
7. Banks, R. E., and Haszeldine, R. N., *Advances in Inorg. Chem. Radiochem.* **3,** 337 (1961).
8. Beachell, H. C., and Haugh, J. F., *J. Am. Chem. Soc.* **80,** 2939 (1958).
9. Bennett, H., U. S. Patent 1,953,741 (April 3, 1934).
10. Bissot, T. C., Campbell, D. H., and Parry, R. W., *J. Am. Chem. Soc.* **80,** 1868 (1958).
11. Bissot, T. C., and Parry, R. W., *J. Am. Chem. Soc.* **77,** 3481 (1955).
12. Booth, R. B., and Kraus, C. A., *J. Am. Chem. Soc.* **74,** 1415 (1952).
13. Brotherton, R. J., McCloskey, A. L., Boone, J. L., and Manasevit, H. M., *J. Am. Chem. Soc.* **82,** 6245 (1960).
14. Brotherton, R. J., McCloskey, A. L., Peterson, L. L., and Steinberg, H., *J. Am. Chem. Soc.* **82,** 6242 (1960).
15. Brown, C. A., ONR Contract Nonr 1439(02), Project NRO52–355, September 1956.
16. Brown, C. A., and Laubengayer, A. W., *J. Am. Chem. Soc.* **77,** 3699 (1955).
17. Brown, J. F., Jr., *J. Am. Chem. Soc.* **74,** 1219 (1952).
18. Burg, A. B., *J. Am. Chem. Soc.* **79,** 2129 (1957).
19. Burg, A. B., *J. Inorg. & Nuclear Chem.* **11,** 258 (1959).
20. Burg, A. B., *J. Chem. Educ.* **37,** 482 (1960).
21. Burg, A. B., and Banus, J., *J. Am. Chem. Soc.* **76,** 3903 (1954).
22. Burg, A. B., and Brendel, G., *J. Am. Chem. Soc.* **80,** 3198 (1958).
23. Burg, A. B., and Kuljian, E. S., *J. Am. Chem. Soc.* **72,** 3103 (1950).
24. Burg, A. B., and Randolph, C. L., *J. Am. Chem. Soc.* **71,** 3451 (1949).
25. Burg, A. B., and Randolph, C. L., *J. Am. Chem. Soc.* **73,** 953 (1951).
26. Burg, A. B., and Slota, P. J., Jr., *J. Am. Chem. Soc.* **82,** 2145, 2148 (1960).
27. Burg, A. B., and Wagner, R. I., *J. Am. Chem. Soc.* **75,** 3872 (1953).
28. Burg, A. B., and Wagner, R. I., *J. Am. Chem. Soc.* **76,** 3307 (1954).
29. Campbell, G. W., and Johnson, L. F., *J. Am. Chem. Soc.* **81,** 3800 (1959).
30. Craig, D. P., Maccoll, A., Nyholm, R. S., Orgel, L. E., and Sutton, L. E., *J. Chem. Soc.* p. 351 (1954).
31. Dahl, G. H., and Schaeffer, R., *J. Am. Chem. Soc.* **83,** 3032 (1961).
32. Dewing, J., Abstracts of Papers presented at the International Symposium on Inorganic Polymers, Nottingham, July, 1961.
33. Dandegaonker, S. H., Gerrard, W., and Lappert, M. F., *J. Chem. Soc.* p. 2076 (1959).
34. Emeleus, H. J., and Wade, K., *J. Chem. Soc.* p. 2614 (1960).
35. Finch, A., and Schlesinger, H. I., *J. Am. Chem. Soc.* **80,** 3573 (1958).
36. Gamble, E. L., and Gilmont, P., *J. Am. Chem. Soc.* **62,** 717 (1940).
37. Gardner, D. M., Ph.D. Thesis, University of Pennsylvania, Philadelphia, Pennsylvania, 1955.
37a. Gee, W., Shaw, R. A., Smith, B. C., and Bullen, G. J., *Proc. Chem. Soc.* p. 432 (1961).
38. Gerrard, W., and Mooney, E. F., Abstracts of Papers presented at the International Symposium on Inorganic Polymers, Nottingham, July, 1961; see also *Soc. Chem. Ind. Monograph No.* **13,** 332 Macmillan, New York, 1961.
39. Goldsmith, H., and McCloskey, A. L., Unpublished results.
40. Gould, E. S., *et al.*, Final Report, Contract No. DA 36–039 s c 5492 Department of the Army Project No. 3–93–00–500, April 30, 1952.

41. Gould, J. R., U. S. Patent 2,754,177 (July 10, 1956).
42. Goubeau, J., and Epple, R., *Chem. Ber.* **90,** 171 (1957).
43. Goubeau, J., and Keller, H., *Z. anorg. u. allgem. Chem.* **267,** 16 (1951).
44. Hamilton, W. C., *Acta Cryst.* **8,** 199 (1955).
45. Henglein, F. A., Lang, R., and Schmack, L., *Makromol. Chem.* **22,** 103 (1957).
46. Hough, W. V., and Schaeffer, G. W., U. S. Patent 2,809,171 (Oct. 8, 1957).
47. Irany, E. P., *Ind. Eng. Chem.* **35,** 1290 (1943).
47a. Knoth, W. H., Miller, H. C., England, D. C., Parshall, G. W., and Muetterties, E. L., *J. Am. Chem. Soc.* **84,** 1056 (1962).
48. Krüerke, U., *Z. Naturforsch.* **11b,** 364 (1956).
49. Jacobson, R. A., and Lipscomb, W. N., *J. Am. Chem. Soc.* **80,** 5571 (1958).
50. Joannis, A., *Compt. rend. acad. Sci.* **135,** 1106 (1902).
51. Korshak, V. V., Zamyatina, V. A., Bekasova, N. I., and Ma Zhuizhan', *Vysoko-molekulyarnye Soedineniya* p. 1287 (1960).
52. Lappert, M. F., *Proc. Chem. Soc.* p. 59 (1959).
53. Laubengayer, A. W., *Chem. Soc. (London) Spec. Publ. No.* **15,** 78 (1961).
54. Laubengayer, A. W., Moews, P. C., Jr., and Porter, R. F., *J. Am. Chem. Soc.* **83,** 1337 (1961).
55. Leffler, A., Groch, R., and Teach, E., *Abstr. 136th Nat. Am. Chem. Soc. Meeting, Atlantic City, New Jersey, 1959* p. 10N.
56. Letsinger, R., and Hamilton, S., *J. Am. Chem. Soc.* **81,** 3009 (1959).
57. McCloskcy, A. L., *et al., WADC (Wright Air Develop. Center) Tech. Rept.* **59–761** (1959).
58. McCloskey, A. L. *et al., Abstr. 135th Natl. Am. Chem. Soc. Meeting Boston, Mass. 1959* p. 34M.
59. McCloskey, A. L., and Goldsmith, H., *Abstr. 132nd Natl. Am. Chem. Soc. Meeting, N. Y. 1957* p. 54P.
60. McGregor, R. R., and Warrick, E. L., U. S. Patent 2,431,878 (Dec. 2, 1947).
61. McLeod, F. D., U. S. Patent 2,352,796 (July 4, 1944).
62. Mikhailov, B. M., and Tutorskaya, F. B., *Izvest. Akad. Nauk S.S.S.R. Otdel. Khim. Nauk* p. 1127 (1959).
63. Moews, P. C., and Laubengayer, A. W., *Abstr. 136th Natl. Am. Chem. Soc. Meeting, Atlantic City, New Jersey 1959* p. 53N.
64. Morgan, W. L., U. S. Patent 2,501,783 (March 28, 1950).
65. Musgrave, O. C., *Chem. & Ind. (London)* p. 1152 (1957).
66. Newsom, H. C., English, W. D., McCloskey, A. L., and Woods, W. G., *J. Am. Chem. Soc.* **83,** 4134 (1961).
67. Niedenzu, K., and Dawson, J. W., *J. Am. Chem. Soc.* **81,** 3561 (1959).
68. Nielsen, D. R., and McEwen, W. E., *J. Am. Chem. Soc.* **79,** 3081 (1957).
69. Pearce, C. A., British Patent 858,817 (Jan. 18, 1961).
70. Perrine, J. C., and Keller, R. N., *J. Am. Chem. Soc.* **80,** 1823 (1958).
71. Pflugmacher, A., and Diener, W., *Angew. Chem.* **69,** 777 (1957).
72. Quill, L. L., Ogle, P. R., Kallander, L. G., and Lippincot, W. T., *Abstr. 129th Natl. Am. Chem. Soc. Meeting, Dallas, Texas 1956* p. 40N.
73. Ruigh, W. L., *et al., WADC (Wright Air Develop. Center) Tech. Rept.* **55–26,** Parts I and II.
74. Ruigh, W. L. *et al., WADC (Wright Air Develop. Center) Tech. Rept.* **52–26,** Parts III and IV (1956).
75. Rust, J. B., U. S. Patent 2,366,129 (Dec. 26, 1944).
76. Schaeffer, G. W., and Adams, M., Canadian Patent 586,522 (Nov. 3, 1959).

77. Schaeffer, G. W., Adams, M. D., and Koenig, F. J., *J. Am. Chem. Soc.* **78,** 725 (1956).
78. Schaeffer, G. W., and Basile, L. J., *J. Am. Chem. Soc.* **77,** 331 (1955).
79. Schlesinger, H. I., Ritter, D. M., and Burg, A. B., *J. Am. Chem. Soc.* **60,** 2297 (1938).
80. Schumb, W. C., Gamble, E. L., and Banus, J. D., *J. Am. Chem. Soc.* **71,** 3225 (1949).
81. Schupp, L. J., and Brown, C. A., *Abstr. 128th Natl. Am. Chem. Soc. Meeting, Minneapolis, Minn. 1955* p. 48R.
82. Shapiro, I., and Williams, R. E., *J. Am. Chem. Soc.* **81,** 4787 (1959).
83. Sheldon, J. C., and Smith, B. C., *Quart. Revs. (London)* **14,** 200 (1960).
84. Steindler, M. J., and Schlesinger, H. I., *J. Am. Chem. Soc.* **75,** 756 (1953).
85. Stock, A., "Hydrides of Boron and Silicon," Cornell Univ. Press, Ithaca, New York, 1933.
86. Stock, A., and Holle, W., *Ber. deut. chem. Ges.* **41,** 2096 (1908).
87. Stock, A., and Pohland, E., *Ber. deut. chem. Ges.* **59B,** 2215 (1926).
88. Stone, F. G. A., *Chem. Revs.* **58,** 101 (1958).
89. Stone, F. G. A., *Endeavour* **20,** 61 (1961).
90. Stone, F. G. A., and Burg, A. B., *J. Am. Chem. Soc.* **76,** 386 (1954).
91. Stout, L. E., and Chamberlain, D. F., *WADC (Wright Air Develop. Center) Tech. Rept.* **52–192** (1952).
92. Sujishi, S., and Witz, S., *J. Am. Chem. Soc.* **79,** 2447 (1957).
92a. Turner, H. S., and Warne, R. J., *Proc. Chem. Soc.* p. 69 (1962).
93. Upson, R. W., U. S. Patent 2,511,310 (June 13, 1950).
94. Upson, R. W., U. S. Patent 2,517,944 (Aug. 8, 1950).
95. Urry, G., Wartik, T., Moore, R. E., and Schlesinger, H. I., *J. Am. Chem. Soc.* **76,** 5293 (1954).
96. Urry, G., Kerrigan, I., Parsons, T. D., and Schlesinger, H. I., *J. Am. Chem. Soc.* **76,** 5299 (1954).
97. Vale, R. L., *J. Chem. Soc.* p. 2252 (1960).
98. Wagner, R. I., *WADC (Wright Air Develop. Center) Tech. Rept.* **57–126,** Part IV (1960).
99. Wagner, R. I., *et al.*, *WADC (Wright Air Develop. Center) Tech. Rept.* **57–126,** Part I (1957).
100. Wagner, R. I., *et al.*, *WADC (Wright Air Develop. Center) Tech. Rept.* **57–126,** Part II (1958).
101. Wagner, R. I., and Caserio, F. F., *J. Inorg. & Nuclear Chem.* **11,** 259 (1959).
102. Wagner, R. I., Caserio, F. F., and Freeman, L. D., *WADC (Wright Air Develop. Center) Tech. Rept.* **57–126,** Part III (1959).
103. Wentorf, R. H., *J. Chem. Phys.* **26,** 956 (1957).
104. Wartik, T., Moore, R., and Schlesinger, H. I., *J. Am. Chem. Soc.* **71,** 3265 (1949).
105. Wartik, T., and Rosenberg, R. M., *J. Inorg. & Nuclear Chem.* **3,** 388 (1957).
106. Wiberg, E., and Bolz, A., *Ber. deut. chem. Ges.* **73B,** 209 (1940).
107. Wiberg, E., and Bolz, A., *Ber. deut. chem. Ges.* **73B,** 202 (1940).
108. Wiberg, E., and Horeld, G., *Z. Naturforsch.* **6b,** 338 (1951).
109. Wiberg, E., and Ruschmann, W., *Ber. deut. chem. Ges.* **70B,** 1393, 1583 (1937).
110. Winternitz, P., and Carotti, A., *J. Am. Chem. Soc.* **82,** 2430 (1960).
111. Yolles, S., *Abstr. 136th Natl. Am. Chem. Soc. Meeting, Atlantic City, New Jersey 1959* p. 9N.
112. Zamyatina, V. A., and Bekasova, N. I., *Russ. Chem. Revs.* **30,** 22 (1961).

—5—

Silicone Polymers

A. J. BARRY and H. N. BECK

Dow Corning Corporation, Midland, Michigan

TABLE OF CONTENTS

I. Introduction

The publication date of this book marks roughly the centennial of organosilicon chemistry, for it was in 1863 that Friedel and Crafts (*160*) reported the synthesis of tetraethylsilane, the first organosilicon compound. This stirred the interest of many researchers, who, armed only with difficult and poorly rewarding synthetic methods, nevertheless by the turn of the century provided the science with a foundation of about 27 compounds. These silicon derivatives were rather simple structures made in order to compare them with the analogous carbon compounds. The work of Frederic S. Kipping and his colleagues at Nottingham, England, made possible by the discovery of the Grignard reagent, contributed monumentally to the knowledge of organosilicon chemistry. During the period 1901–1944 they reported in over 50 papers (*180*) a quest directed toward elucidation of the elementary chemistry of silicon compounds and of the concept of optical activity about the silicon atom, the asymmetry of which had not yet been demonstrated. The work was fruitful beyond these ends, for in their experiments on the condensation of silanols they obtained polysiloxanes, described by them as large molecules with alternating silicon-oxygen backbones. In spite of his accurate perception of their Si—O—Si chain structure (*242, 244*), Kipping named the products "silicones," since he had expected elimination of water from silanediols to give silicon analogues of ketones ($R_2Si{=}O$). Though they were not then considered significant, these compounds were the prototypes for today's commercially important polysiloxane fluids, rubbers, and resins; the term "silicones" has persisted as their trivial name.

The next important phase in the history of organosilicon chemistry embraced the intensive study of high polymer silicones and their commercial development, for which the stage was set in America. Commencing in 1931, J. F. Hyde and his co-workers (*219*) at Corning Glass Works in Corning, New York, built on the groundwork laid by Kipping when they set about synthesizing the resins essential for use with the newly developed glass-fiber fabrics in the manufacture of high temperature electrical insulation. The need for a temperature-resistant resin was met by Hyde and his co-workers when they prepared a variety of organopolysiloxane resins of thermal stability far greater than that of the available organic resins and of more than adequate dielectric strength. A number of interesting silicone fluids were obtained as rewarding by-products of this work. These were complemented by a series of poly(dimethylsiloxane) fluids developed by R. R. McGregor and his co-workers (*274*) under Corning Glass Works sponsorship at Mellon Institute of Industrial Research in Pittsburgh, Pennsylvania, in 1938 and succeeding years. The heat-resistant organosiloxane resins and fluids not only met military needs in 1942, but, together with the subsequently developed elastomers, offered the promise of a new and important field of industrial chemistry surely destined to serve worthwhile purposes in the postwar world. In 1942 the silicone knowledge of Corning Glass Works and the industrial organics experience of The Dow Chemical Company were brought together to expedite production of the first commercial silicone—an ignition-sealing compound for aircraft. This led to the creation of the jointly owned Dow Corning Corporation in Midland, Michigan, in 1943 and the immediate construction of its plant facility, initially based upon the Grignard process. The growing importance of this field of chemistry was marked by the entry of General Electric Company and its construction of a plant at Waterford, New York, in

1947. Its operation was based upon the synthesis of methylchlorosilanes from methyl chloride and silicon metal, first published by Rochow (*353*) which, along with other direct processes discovered elsewhere, afforded improved production convenience and economics. Eight years later, Union Carbide and Carbon Company built its plant at Long Beach, West Virginia. In the Soviet Union, K. A. Andrianov conducted research in this field as early as 1938 (*7*), but industrial production of silicones was not begun until sometime after 1947. Contributions of significance to the field of organosilicon polymer chemistry from elsewhere than America and Russia only began to appear after the close of World War II.

A. Definition

The chemical constitution of the silicones can be represented broadly by the generic polymer formula:

$$[R_a SiO_{(4-a)/2}]_n$$

where n is large and a can be varied from 0 to 4. At the extremes, if a is 0, the formula reduces to that of silica and the polymer is inorganic; if a is 4, the formula is that of a tetraorganosilane, virtually an organic compound (and not a polymer in the usual sense). Between these limits, it is difficult to decide whether silicones should be described as inorganic or organic polymers. From the standpoint of physical properties, they possess inorganic characteristics due to the high percentage of ionic character in the Si—O bonds, and organic characteristics due to the substituent groups and to the low intermolecular forces resulting from their shielding of the siloxane skeletons. It would be well to consider these obvious hybrids in the light of both lines of parentage.

1. *As Inorganic Polymers*

The silicones embrace an extensive variety of polymers based on chains or networks of alternating silicon and oxygen atoms, matching many of the structures found in the mineral kingdom, but, whereas the polysiloxane skeletons in natural minerals are crosslinked by means of metalloxy groups, the corresponding backbones in silicones are isolated by substitution of organic groups at the silicon sites. The siliceous minerals are cross-linked structures so involved that the *whole* specimen of a pure mineral may be but *one* continuous molecule, insoluble, infusible, and intractable within reasonable temperature limits. On the other hand, the silicone chains are laterally blocked by organic substituents and can merely associate with each other by weak van der Waals' forces. Accordingly, the silicones are

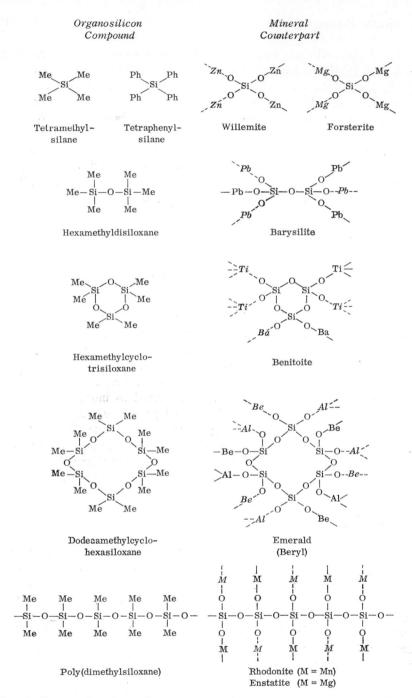

FIG. 1. Structural analogies between organopolysiloxanes and mineral silicates. (See also pp. 194 and 196)

liquids varying in viscosity and volatility, or, if they are gums or solids because of extremely high molecular weight, crystallinity, or cross-linking, still they remain soluble in appropriately selected organic media. As a preface to the extended study of their chemistry and physical characteristics, it is instructive at this point to preview a number of organosilicon polymers and to note their structural counterparts in the mineral kingdom as portrayed in Fig. 1.

To afford a complete analogy, the first organosilicon compound in the illustration is included even though it is a simple silane, incapable of forming a polymer. Tetramethylsilane is a liquid boiling at 25°C; the analogous tetraphenylsilane is a crystalline solid, melting at 236°C and boiling at 430°C, and is soluble in many common organic solvents. The mineral counterpart of these, willemite, is zinc orthosilicate, a crystalline solid not fusible below 1500°C, nor soluble in anything short of a chemical reagent which will destroy it. The same is true of forsterite (magnesium orthosilicate), zircon (zirconium orthosilicate), and the related minerals olivine and garnet.

The first organosiloxane illustrated is hexamethyldisiloxane, in which each silicon is triply substituted; it is a mobile liquid (b.p. 100°C). The comparable mineral structure is found in the pyrosilicates (sorosilicates), of which the zinc mineral, hemimorphite, and the lead mineral, barysilite, are representative. The longest siloxane moiety in any of these is comprised of two silicons bridged with one oxygen atom.

Among the organosiloxanes having two alkyl or aryl groups on each silicon will be found ring compounds, the simplest of which contain three silicon atoms and three oxygen (cyclotrisiloxanes); others containing four, five, six, seven, and eight of each atom in the ring are very common. Whether they are liquid or solid depends on the types of organic groups present, but regardless of the substitution these ring compounds are easily soluble in appropriate organic solvents. While the penta-, hepta-, and octasiloxane ring compounds have no known mineral counterparts, the cyclic trimer, tetramer, and hexamer structures are respectively represented by benitoite, axinite, and emerald in the mineral kingdom. As expected, these minerals are difficultly fusible and are insoluble.

Up to this point the insolubility of the simple classes of minerals mentioned has been emphasized, but many of them are decomposed by hydrochloric acid; this removes the metal atoms as soluble chlorides. With the metalloxy bridges so destroyed, the residual siloxane moieties are free to disperse as orthosilicic acid or simple polysilicic acids, so that for a short time the mineral is completely dissolved in the acid before the silicic acids condense to silica gel. This somewhat circumscribed solubility of the simple minerals is a physical manifestation of their analogy to the lower organosiloxanes, as far as the —Si—O— backbone structure is concerned.

The linear diorganosiloxane polymers, illustrated by poly(dimethyl-siloxane) in Fig. 1, are rather simple molecules except that they may reach exceedingly great chain lengths. Depending on the length of the chain they vary from thin liquids to gums so viscous that it is difficult to perceive flow in cut chunks—yet they are true fluids and, in contrast to their mineral counterparts, dissolve completely in appropriate solvents. Their inorganic analogues, exemplified by the manganese and magnesium minerals rhodonite and (clino)enstatite, are infusible at 1300°C and do not even form gels in acids. They belong to the broader class known as inosilicates; the prefix "ino," signifying fiber-like, is aptly descriptive also of the extended linear structure of the polyorganodisiloxanes.

Organosilsesquioxane
Polymers

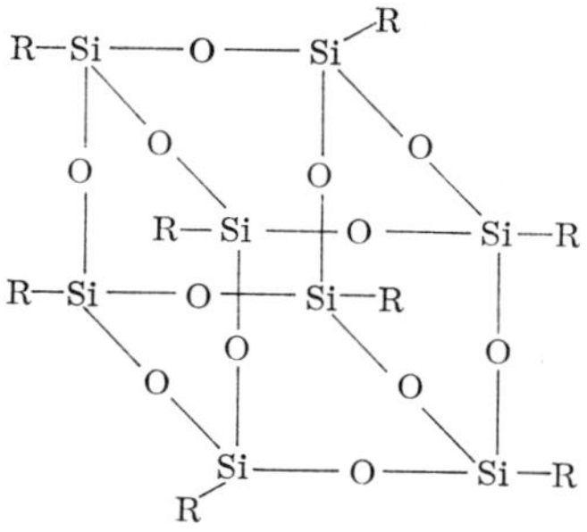

Cubical octamer

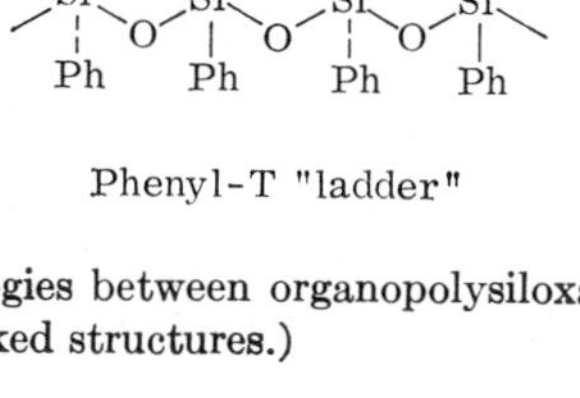

Phenyl-T "ladder"

FIG. 1a. Structural analogies between organopolysiloxanes and mineral silicates (see p. 196 for random cross-linked structures.)

In the case of organosiloxane polymers having but one organic group on each silicon the attendant trifunctionality of the building units would be expected to result in complicated structures. One example is the cubical octamer, an orderly three-dimensional array, block-like in structure. Another is a two-dimensional fused-ring system which forms the double-chain "ladder" polymer shown in Fig. 1a. In both, the higher crosslinking capacity of the building units is expended within the molecule in a well-ordered manner and the polymers remain fusible and soluble in organic media. These siloxane structures have no known counterparts among the silicate minerals. Where branching and cross-linking become extensive in three dimensions and occur randomly rather than in orderly array, the organosiloxane polymer will be a resin of involved and infinite network, corresponding to Warren's concept for the structure of glass (*459*) pictured in the last part of Fig. 1b. Here the glass is shown in only two dimensions and should be viewed as a puckered plane with a fourth valence on each silicon tetrahedrally directed below or above the plane to project a three-dimensional structure. When the metalloxy groups in the glass are replaced by organic groups, the structure represents an organopolysiloxane resin.

With progressively fewer organic groups in the resin structure, as with fewer metalloxy units (MO— termini or labile —OMO— bridges) in the glass, the product will become richer in SiOSi bridges and hence more difficultly fusible, and ultimately insoluble. In either case the end product will be some form of silica. At this point organosiloxane and inorganic silicate chemistry come together.

2. As Organic Polymers

The organic side of the silicone family is represented in the groups bonded to the silicon atoms. The physical properties and therefore the specific usefulness of any organopolysiloxane are determined by the kind and number of organic groups on each silicon as well as by the way the siloxane building units are hooked together.

The varying effects of different organic groups are apparent in the range of substituents that have received extensive academic and commercial attention: methyl, phenyl, hydrogen, vinyl, ethyl, stearyl, and trifluoropropyl—in about that order. A comparison of the first two in their effect on physical properties of the polymer shows that methyl groups promote fluidity, low viscosity-temperature index, low melting point, and high liquid compressibility, whereas phenyl groups induce contrasting effects. The methylpolysiloxanes and phenylpolysiloxanes show distinctive solubility parameters, and may even be incompatible with one another. At higher temperatures this effect is minimized and they both are more gen-

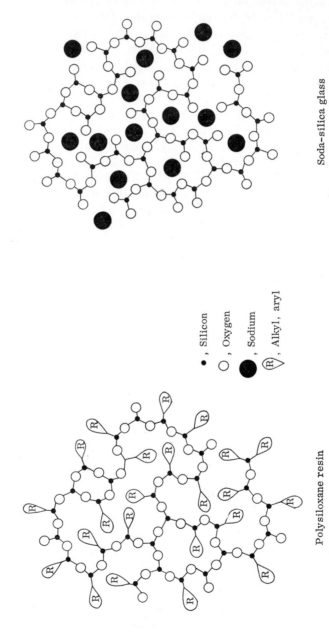

Random Cross-Linked Structures

Soda–silica glass

Polysiloxane resin

● , Silicon
○ , Oxygen
⬤ , Sodium
Ⓡ , Alkyl, aryl

Fig. 1b. (continued from pp. 192 and 194). Structural analogies between organopolysiloxanes and mineral silicates.

erally soluble in organic media. Substitution by fluoroalkyl groups results in resistance to hydrocarbon solvents, important in polymers for low swelling rubbers. The foregoing properties and many others are sensitively affected by the molecular weight of the polymer. This is typical of organic polymers and so reflects the organic heritage of the silicones.

The organic substituents play another important role in that their very number, regardless of type, establishes the functionality of the individual siloxane building units and thereby controls the linearity or complexity of the polysiloxane and is a factor in determining its molecular size. Disubstituted units (R_2SiO—) provide the building blocks for linear polymers of any length. Trisubstituted units (R_3SiO—) are monofunctional end-blocking or terminal groups in the polysiloxane chains, controlling their lengths and molecular weights. Monosubstituted ($RSiO$—) and unsubstituted units generally increase the molecular weight of the polymer by affording sites for chain branching and cross-linking. These effects were apparent in the preceding discussion relating the structures of certain organopolysiloxanes to those of their mineral counterparts.

In the same discussion, it was seen that the manner in which the siloxane units were linked together influenced the ultimate design, molecular weight, and properties of the polysiloxane. Thus the diorganosiloxane polymers, whose linear structures are of potentially infinite length, may be limited to very low molecular weight by cyclic closure. The manner of polymer linkage shows its effect even more dramatically in network structures built upon organosilsesquioxanes, whose trifunctionality can lead to polymers so highly cross-linked that they are generally insoluble, as well as to the simple, usually soluble cubical octamers.

These observations project themselves into fundamental and practical considerations of organosiloxane copolymers. Whereas the copolymers of mono- and di-functional units are linear molecules of predictable character, copolymers of average functionality greater than two become more complex and less predictable as one loses control of how the functionality is utilized. Thus in the realm of elastomers, a certain degree of cross-linking might afford a rubber of good elasticity—or alternatively a weak jelly or a leathery plastic; in the realm of resins, the necessarily higher degree of crosslinking might afford a product of desirable flexibility—or the identical formulation might give an asphalt-like resin or a brittle glass as extremes, depending on the mode of cross-linking. These characteristics reflect those of the fluids, rubbers, and plastics among the organic high polymers.

B. Nomenclature

The naming of the simpler organosilicon compounds in this chapter will adhere to the IUC rules (*123*). These rules are definitive for many organosilicon compounds, but lead to bulky terminology for polymeric structures. In such cases it is convenient to represent siloxane polymers by a widely accepted "shorthand" method (*203*) which designates functionality of the monomer building units by letters:

M	monofunctional	$R_3SiO_{1/2}$
D	difunctional	$R_2SiO_{2/2}$
T	trifunctional	$RSiO_{3/2}$
Q	quadrifunctional	$SiO_{4/2}$

In the fractional subscripts of the formulas, the denominators show that each oxygen atom is shared by two silicon atoms and the numerators indicate the number of oxygen atoms so shared. Unless otherwise stated, the siloxanes are methyl substituted. To illustrate the use of this system, the linear decamethyltetrasiloxane:

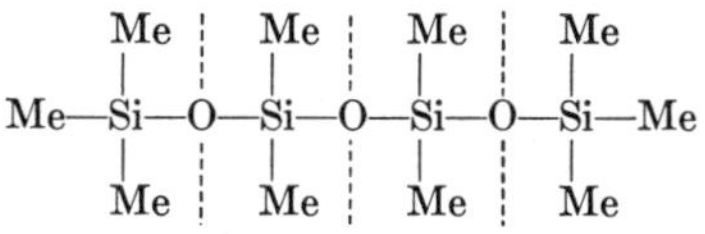

$$
\begin{array}{ccccccc}
 & \text{Me} & & \text{Me} & & \text{Me} & & \text{Me} \\
 & | & & | & & | & & | \\
\text{Me—Si—O—Si—O—Si—O—Si—Me} \\
 & | & & | & & | & & | \\
 & \text{Me} & & \text{Me} & & \text{Me} & & \text{Me} \\
 & \text{M} & & \text{D} & & \text{D} & & \text{M}
\end{array}
$$

would simply be written as MD_2M; and the hexamethyldisiloxane and the two cyclics of Fig. 1 (Section I,A,1) as MM, D_3, and D_6 in order. Some siloxane polymers can become so complex, especially where polyfunctionality of building units and a variety of substituent groups appear in the same macromolecule, that it is clearer and simpler to write their structural formulas than to attempt to name them.

II. Preparative Methods

A. Organosilicon Intermediates

Intermediates for the preparation of organopolysiloxanes may be produced by any of several methods. Synthesis by way of organometallic compounds may be accomplished using Grignard reagents, organo-sodium, -lithium, or -potassium reagents, and alkyls or aryls of zinc, mercury, aluminum, and cadmium. These methods offer convenience in laboratory preparations but all are costly on any scale; only the Grignard method has achieved industrial importance. More important industrially are the direct processes which avoid the preparation of organometallic intermediates:

"Direct" silicon process

Aromatic silylation

Silane-olefin addition

Rearrangement and disproportionation reactions of organo-chlorosilanes and -alkoxysilanes afford practical means for converting some of them to more useful compounds.

1. Production of Elemental Silicon

Silicon metal, the prerequisite to today's synthesis of organosilicon intermediates, is a gray-black solid with a metallic luster. It melts at 1410°C, boils at approximately 2677°C, and has a density of 2.0–2.5 depending on the temperature and the crystalline or allotropic form. It is prepared by the reduction of quartz or silica with coke in an electric furnace at about 1500 to 1600°C; the over-all reaction is shown in Eq. (1):

$$SiO_2 + 2\ C \rightarrow Si + 2\ CO \tag{1}$$

This process is used also in the commercial production of silicon carbide by controlling the balance of raw materials [Eq. (2)]. To favor the yield of

$$SiO_2 + 3\ C \rightarrow SiC + 2\ CO \tag{2}$$

$$SiO_2 + 2\ SiC \rightarrow 3\ Si + 2\ CO \tag{3}$$

silicon metal excess silica is employed (Eq. 3). The silicon is generally of greater than 95% purity; iron and aluminum, the principal contaminants, do not adversely affect the use of the silicon in the chemical processes to be considered in this text.

Among the simple compounds of silicon, two chlorides are key source materials for organosilicon synthesis. Silicon tetrachloride is prepared by the chlorination of silicon carbide:

$$SiC + 2\ Cl_2 \rightarrow SiCl_4 + C \tag{4}$$

Trichlorosilane is prepared by the reaction of hydrogen chloride with powdered silicon at about 300°C:

$$Si + 3\ HCl \rightarrow HSiCl_3 + H_2 \tag{5}$$

The partial reversal of this reaction at higher temperatures occurs in one process for the current production of ultrahigh purity silicon for use in transistors, rectifiers, and other semiconductor applications.

2. Organometallic Processes

a. Grignard Reagent. The silicone industry was founded upon the Grignard process. In fact, the synthesis of organosilicon compounds was the first large industrial application of the Grignard reaction (*272*). Various alkyl- and aryl-chlorosilanes and the corresponding alkoxysilanes can be prepared by this method. A common starting material is silicon tetrachloride; it will react with a Grignard reagent in successive steps to give a mixture of products which must be separated by fractional distillation [Eq. (6)] (*180*). Alkoxysilanes react similarly [Eq. (7)]. Mixed alkylaryl-

$$\text{SiCl}_4 + \text{MeMgX} \rightarrow \left\{ \begin{matrix} \text{MeSiCl}_3 + \text{Me}_2\text{SiCl}_2 \\ + \\ \text{Me}_3\text{SiCl} + \text{Me}_4\text{Si} \end{matrix} \right\} + \text{MgXCl} \tag{6}$$

$$\text{Si(OEt)}_4 + \text{RMgX} \rightarrow \text{R}_x\text{Si(OEt)}_{4-x} + \text{MgX(OEt)} \tag{7}$$

chlorosilanes may be prepared as shown in Eq. (8). Organochlorosilanes

$$\begin{matrix} \text{MeMgCl} + \text{PhSiCl}_3 \\ \\ \text{PhMgCl} + \text{MeSiCl}_3 \\ \\ \text{PhMgCl} + \text{MeMgCl} + \text{SiCl}_4 \end{matrix} \quad \searrow \atop \nearrow \quad \rightarrow \text{PhMeSiCl}_2, \text{ mainly} \tag{8}$$

$$\text{HSiCl}_3 + \text{RMgX} \rightarrow \text{R}_x\text{HSiCl}_{3-x} + \text{MgXCl} \tag{9}$$

containing Si—H bonds are obtained from trichlorosilane [Eq. (9)]. The main products that are isolated from the Grignard process depend on the particular organic groups involved, the activity of the organometallic compound, the concentrations of the reagents, the solvent, and the temperature. Coordinating compounds such as diethyl ether, tetrahydrofuran, or the polyethylene glycol diethers are commonly used as solvents for the reaction. *In situ* techniques may be used.

Several practical disadvantages are inherent in the Grignard process. Moisture must be rigorously excluded. The volume efficiency is low. The mixture must be freed of sticky semisolid magnesium salts, which tenaciously retain organosilicon compounds. The mixture of products and solvent must then be separated, usually by distillation; a serious fire hazard is always present. In addition, the process is inapplicable to organic groups that contain functions, such as carbonyl, nitrile, and hydroxyl, that are sensitive to the Grignard reagent. Many of these disadvantages are overcome in the direct processes.

b. Other Organometallic Reagents. Chlorosilanes or alkoxysilanes may be alkylated by organoalkali compounds prepared separately or *in situ* (*331*):

$$\text{SiCl}_4 + \text{EtLi} \rightarrow \text{Et}_4\text{Si} + 4 \text{ LiCl} \tag{10}$$

$$\text{SiCl}_4 + 4 \text{ PhCl} + 8 \text{ Na} \rightarrow \text{Ph}_4\text{Si} + 8 \text{ NaCl} \tag{11}$$

Organolithium compounds are more reactive than Grignard reagents;

organo-sodium and -potassium compounds react even more vigorously. Because of the difficulty in controlling them, reactions using organoalkali compounds are commonly limited to the preparation of tetra-alkyl- and -arylsilanes.

Organochlorosilanes may be prepared by passing a mixture of vapors of an alkyl halide and a halosilane over finely divided aluminum or zinc at 300 to 500°C [Eqs. (12) and (13)] (*204, 206*). Although they are not

$$SiCl_4 + MeCl \xrightarrow[350-400°C]{Al} Me_xSiCl_{4-x} + AlCl_3 \qquad (12)$$

$$MeSiCl_3 + MeCl \xrightarrow[450°C]{Al} Me_3SiCl + Me_2SiCl_2 + AlCl_3 \qquad (13)$$
$$\phantom{MeSiCl_3 + MeCl \xrightarrow[450°C]{Al} } 21\% \qquad\quad 11\%$$

isolated, aluminum- and zinc-alkyls are probably the reactive intermediates:

$$2\,Al + 3\,MeCl \to [MeAlCl_2 + Me_2AlCl] \xrightarrow{2MeSiCl_3} Me_2SiCl_2 + Me_3SiCl + 2\,AlCl_3 \quad (14)$$

Dialkylzinc and diarylmercury reagents made possible the first syntheses of organosilicon compounds, but are little used at present.

3. Direct Process Methods

a. Silicon Process. The silicon direct process is general for the preparation of many alkylchlorosilanes, (*39, 210, 353, 359*), but is particularly useful in the production of methylchlorosilanes. When methyl chloride is passed through powdered silicon, preferably containing a copper catalyst, at about 300°C, a complex mixture of products consisting mainly of dimethyldichlorosilane and methyltrichlorosilane is obtained [Eq. (15)].

$$MeCl + Si \xrightarrow[300°C]{Cu} Me_2SiCl_2 + MeSiCl_3 + others \qquad (15)$$

$$2\,MeCl + Si \to Me_2SiCl_2 \qquad (16)$$

The optimum reaction would produce only dimethyldichlorosilane [Eq. (16)], and indeed this is the principal product ($>50\%$ theoretical) when copper or other catalyst is used. But, with or without catalyst, side reactions occur which form MeSiCl$_3$ as a major by-product along with smaller yields of other compounds such as Me$_4$Si, Me$_3$SiCl, Me$_2$HSiCl, MeHSiCl$_2$, SiCl$_4$, HSiCl$_3$, H$_2$SiCl$_2$, H$_2$, hydrocarbons, polysilanes of the general formula Me$_x$Si$_2$Cl$_{6-x}$, silmethylene compounds, and some higher alkylchlorosilanes. The products depend upon the temperature, the gas flow rate (contact time), gaseous diluents or coreagents, the type and amount of catalyst and the manner in which it is associated with the silicon, and upon many other factors.

A complex mechanism would be predicted for the direct process, since it involves the reaction of a vapor with a solid, catalyzed by another solid. A mechanism has been proposed for the copper-catalyzed system based upon the following reaction sequence (*210*):

$$MeCl + 2\ Cu° \rightarrow MeCu + CuCl \tag{17}$$

$$MeCu \rightarrow Cu° + Me· \tag{18}$$

$$CuCl + Si° \rightarrow Cu° + (SiCl) \tag{19}$$

$$Me· + (SiCl) \rightarrow (MeSiCl) \tag{20}$$

At the reaction temperature the methylcopper formed in the first step is unstable, decomposing as shown in Eq. (18) to regenerate copper, then available to react with more methyl chloride, and to yield methyl radicals, the active methylating species. Because they have been proved nonreactive with silicon metal and chlorosilanes, the methyl radicals are assumed to combine with a highly reactive subchloride of silicon as shown in the last step. The formation of this subchloride, perhaps little more than a monomolecular layer formed upon the silicon surface, may be justified on the basis that CuCl is known to react with silicon at about 265°C to give ultimately $SiCl_4$ and copper metal. The unstable (MeSiCl) shown in Eq. (20) would be expected to react further with MeCu and CuCl, or even with MeCl to satisfy the residual valences of the silicon. The catalyst therefore functions to generate and prolong the lives of methyl radicals and to transport them, as well as chlorine atoms, from methyl chloride to silicon.

The over-all reaction is exothermic and once it starts the process must be cooled; the optimum temperature is the lowest at which the reaction will proceed with reasonable speed and economy. Higher temperatures increase the reaction rate, but this advantage is offset by an increased proportion of by-products rich in hydrogen and chlorine and correspondingly poor in organic groups. This is attributable to the pyrolysis of some of the methyl free radicals [Eq. (21)], aggravated by the autocatalytic effect of

$$CH_3· \rightarrow ·CH_2· + H· \rightarrow [H\overset{·}{C}· + H_2] \rightarrow \underline{C} + H_2 + H· \tag{21}$$

the pyrophoric carbon generated. The loss of methyl groups in this manner results in fixation of progressively greater amounts of chlorine and hydrogen than of methyl groups, yielding excessive amounts of $MeSiCl_3$ and other silanes. Methyl chloride is an expensive source of chlorine, and if $MeSiCl_3$ is a preferred product, as for instance in the manufacture of resins, the chlorine is supplied more economically by introducing HCl along with the MeCl feed [Eq. (22)]. Such a modification results also in increased yields

$$MeCl + 2\ HCl + Si \xrightarrow[300°C]{Cu} MeSiCl_3 + H_2 \tag{22}$$

benzene with the products of reaction (27). The formation of some $SiCl_4$ as a minor by-product may be accounted for by thermal rearrangement of

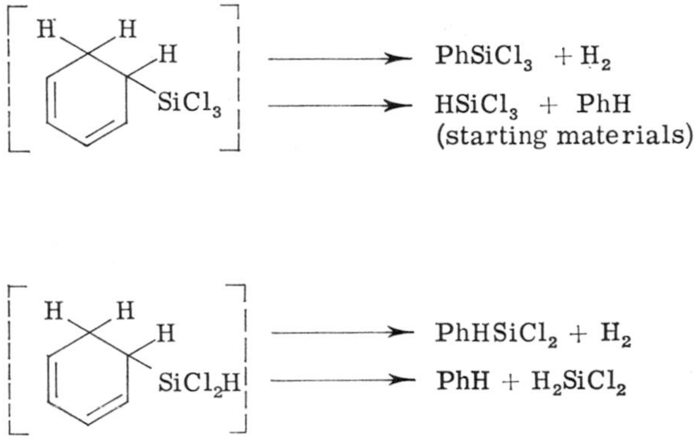

$$PhSiCl_3 + H_2$$
$$HSiCl_3 + PhH$$
(starting materials)

$$PhHSiCl_2 + H_2$$
$$PhH + H_2SiCl_2$$

(27)

$HSiCl_3$, as in Eq. (28); this in turn may be initiated by a cross-over recombination of Cl^- and $^+SiCl_3$ ions in reaction (25).

$$4\ HSiCl_3 \rightarrow 2\ H_2 + Si + 3\ SiCl_4 \tag{28}$$

This process can be adapted to the synthesis of a wide range of arylsilicon compounds by varying either or both of the starting materials. Organochlorosilanes may be used in place of $HSiCl_3$; thus methylphenyldichlorosilane may be prepared from benzene and methyldichlorosilane as in Eq. (29), using BCl_3 as catalyst. The methyl substitution on the silicon lowers

$$PhH + MeHSiCl_2 \rightarrow MePhSiCl_2 + H_2 \tag{29}$$

the threshold temperature of this reaction to 130°C—considerably below the limit for the analogous reaction of $HSiCl_3$. Diphenyldichlorosilane is obtained from the corresponding reaction of phenyldichlorosilane. Almost all aromatic hydrocarbons and many of their derivatives may be used in place of benzene: toluene, ethylbenzene, xylene, biphenyl, terphenyl, naphthalene, chlorobenzene, and many others. With naphthalene the expected naphthyl compound is obtained but, in addition, hydronaphthyl compounds analogous to the cyclohexadiene structures hypothesized in reactions (26) and (27) may be isolated from the reaction products (*48*). The BCl_3-catalyzed reaction of chlorobenzene with SiH-containing halosilanes affords the corresponding chlorophenyl silicon compounds (*32*). Aside from its versatility, this direct process is industrially important because it is economical with respect to raw material costs and volume efficiency.

c. Silane-Olefin Addition. A third important direct synthesis involves
the addition of unsaturated organic compounds to halosilanes or organo-
halosilanes containing one or more hydrogens on the silicon (*40, 49*). This
synthesis is represented in Eqs. (30) and (31). In the thermal version of this

$$\text{HSiCl}_3 \quad + \quad \text{H}_2\text{C}=\text{CH}-\text{R} \longrightarrow \text{Cl}_3\text{SiCH}_2\text{CH}_2-\text{R}$$

(30)

(31)

process equimolar mixtures of an olefin and the appropriate chlorosilane
are heated in an autoclave for a few hours at 200–400°C. The reaction
proceeds at lower temperature (even room temperature), but the rates
become impractically low; on the other hand, temperatures much in excess
of 300°C promote decomposition of the desired products. Kinetic data
indicate second-order bimolecular reaction of about 19-kcal activation
energy for addition of a variety of olefins to HSiCl$_3$ or MeHSiCl$_2$. At 300°C,
the system pressure reaches a maximum of 300 psi for the reaction of
octadecene; it may exceed 1500 psi for ethylene, but drops to the vapor
pressure of the product, EtSiCl$_3$, as the reaction nears completion. Normally yields are in the range of 75–95% of theoretical values.

In the case of 1-alkenes, the silyl group adds to the terminal olefinic
carbon to afford principally the normal alkylchlorosilane as indicated in
Eq. (30), but reverse addition occurs to a small extent; for example, the
reactions of propylene and 1-butene with HSiCl$_3$ give 3 and 1.4% of the
respective 2-alkylsilicon compounds. The reaction of 2-butene gives the
expected *sec*-butyl adduct, but it gives also an equal amount of the normal
isomer derived from 1-butene formed *in situ* by thermal migration of the
double bond. This is more marked in higher olefins, but may be minimized
by using lower reaction temperatures. The desired product is accompanied
also by higher boiling compounds formed by limited polymerization of
the olefin used; thus, the equimolar reaction of ethylene with HSiCl$_3$ gives
up to 15% BuSiCl$_3$ and lesser quantities of C$_6$H$_{13}$- and C$_8$H$_{17}$-SiCl$_3$. In
practice, formation of these by-products is suppressed by employing a
moderate excess of the chlorosilane.

Many types of hydrocarbons are useful in the process: linear, branched,
and cyclic monoolefins; diolefins; polyolefins; terpenes; alkynes. The order
of reactivity of the olefins has not been ascertained, except that addition
to terminal bonds is the most rapid. A wide variety of halosilanes may be

employed. Their reactivities are quite sensitive to structure; typical reactivities toward propene at 300° and 1100 psi are:

$$HSiCl_3 > MeHSiCl_2 > Me_2HSiCl$$

Methyl substitution in the chlorosilanes decreases the reaction rate, nearly one order of magnitude for each group present, and is accompanied by an increase in the amount of polymer formed.

The mechanism proposed (*37*) for these thermal syntheses comprises the (a) formation of a metastable intermediate adduct by imposition of the electron-rich terminal carbon atom of the olefin upon the electrophilic silicon atom of the silane accompanied by (b) simultaneous or rapid sequential migration of hydride ion from the pentacovalent silicon to the electron-poor carbon of the adduct to give the stable end product. That the reaction does not depend upon initial stretch of the H—Si bond to give a siliconium ion seems evident from the fact that BCl_3 is not a catalyst in these reactions, quite in contrast to its positive effect in the foregoing benzenoid reactions. That the reaction rate decreases sharply with methyl substitution on the chlorosilane is compatible with the proposed mechanism since electron feed from the methyl groups would be expected to decrease the susceptibility of the silicon to nucleophilic attack by the olefin.

Many types of initiators will promote these reactions at low temperatures and pressures and thereby extend the utility of the process to systems in which the unsaturated organic raw material, or its reaction product, might be thermally unstable. Such initiators are peroxides (*94, 251, 325, 406, 415, 417*), azo compounds (*264*), ultraviolet light (*325, 406*), gamma radiation (*142*), organic bases (*303, 304, 319*), metals such as palladium and platinum, alone or supported on porous solids (*416, 454, 456*), and metal compounds such as chloroplatinic acid and platinum, ruthenium, and indium chlorides (*161, 318, 364, 367, 416, 438, 449*).

The reactions initiated by peroxide and azo compounds and by radiation are generally believed to proceed by a free radical path (Eq. 32). The

Initiation:

$$H—Si\equiv \xrightarrow{\text{radiation}} H\cdot + \cdot Si\equiv \qquad \text{or}$$

$$(MeCOO)_2 \xrightarrow{\Delta} 2\ MeCOO\cdot \to Me\cdot + CO_2$$

$$Me\cdot + H—Si\equiv \to CH_4 + \cdot Si\equiv$$

Propagation: (32)

Telomer formation:

$$\underset{/ \, \cdot \;\; |}{\overset{\backslash \quad |}{C}-\underset{|}{C}-Si\!\equiv} \; + \; \underset{/}{\overset{\backslash}{C}}\!=\!\underset{\backslash}{\overset{/}{C}} \;\; \xrightarrow{\;k_2\;} \; \underset{/ \, \cdot \;\; | \;\; | \;\; |}{\overset{\backslash \quad | \;\; | \;\; |}{C}-\underset{|}{C}-\underset{|}{C}-\underset{|}{C}-Si\!\equiv} \;\; \xrightarrow{\;HSi\equiv\;}$$

$$H\underset{|}{C}-\underset{|}{C}-\underset{|}{C}-\underset{|}{C}-Si\!\equiv \; + \; \cdot Si\!\equiv$$

telomerization shown is generally not desired and will affect the yield of desired adduct to an extent depending on k_1/k_2. Thus unsaturated compounds which are easily polymerized by peroxides, such as styrene, 1-alkenes, vinyl acetate, and acrylonitrile, yield mostly telomers and are not suitable for such reactions. Olefins that do not polymerize readily, such as cyclohexene and 1,2-disubstituted olefins, react satisfactorily. Alkenylation may also be carried out using alkynes and can be controlled to give vinyltrichlorosilane or the bis(trichlorosilyl)ethane shown in Eq. (33) (*94*):

$$\text{HSiCl}_3 + \text{HC}\!\equiv\!\text{CH} \xrightarrow{\text{Bz}_2\text{O}_2} \text{Cl}_3\text{SiCH}\!=\!\text{CH}_2 \xrightarrow[\text{Bz}_2\text{O}_2]{\text{HSiCl}_3} (\text{Cl}_3\text{SiCH}_2)_2 \qquad (33)$$

The most important applications of the free radical reaction embrace silane additions to hendecenoic acid (*165*), alkenyl esters and ethers (*412, 417*), and other unsaturated organic compounds (*417*) which are unstable at the high temperatures required when no catalyst is used. The free radical reaction also permits the use of triphenylsilane (*165*) and presumably other silanes which have not been shown to react thermally. Silicon hydrides containing alkoxy groups do not react satisfactorily.

Platinum and the related Group VIII metals are efficient catalysts for olefin additions to silanes in that extremely small amounts, as low as 10^{-8} mole of platinum per mole of olefin, generally effect rapid reaction at

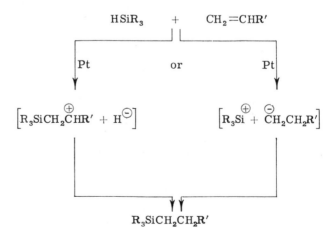

$$\qquad (34)$$

temperatures under 100°C. An ionic mechanism has been proposed for the reaction (*141*, p. 52), as represented in Eq. (34). A free radical mechanism is excluded by the failure of free radical inhibitors to suppress the reaction. The reactivities of several olefins and silicon hydrides have been correlated on the basis of semiquantitative measurements (*413*):

Chlorohydrosilanes:

$$HSiCl_3, \ MeHSiCl_2 > H_2SiCl_2 > Me_2HSiCl > MeH_2SiCl$$

Hydrosil(ox)anes:

$$MeHSiCl_2 > (MeHSiO)_n > O(SiMe_2H)_2, \ (EtO)_3SiH > R_3SiH > SiH_4$$

Hydrocarbons:

$$HC\equiv CH > CH_2=CH_2 > RCH=CH_2,$$

$> CH_2=CRR' > MeCH=CRR' >$

In these reactions the addition is oriented to favor bonding of the silicon atom to the terminal carbon atom. This is true not only for olefins with terminal unsaturation but also for those having internal double bonds (*364*); platinum apparently causes migration of the reactive site in the hydrocarbon.

The addition reactions catalyzed by platinum and related metals are more versatile than those promoted by peroxides or induced by heat alone. Almost any silicon hydride may be alkylated using a wide variety of unsaturated compounds which, in addition to hydrocarbons of the types shown in the reactivity series above, include styrene, haloolefins, alkenyl cyanides, alkenyl ethers, unsaturated esters, and other compounds containing organofunctional groups as well as unsaturated moieties, illustrated in Eqs. (35)–(38). In reactions such as (37) and (38), involving

$$PhCH=CH_2 + HSiCl_3 \xrightarrow{Pt} PhCH_2CH_2SiCl_3 \qquad (35)$$

$$\overset{O}{\overset{\|}{CH_3COCH}}=CH_2 + MeHSiCl_2 \xrightarrow{Pt} \overset{O}{\overset{\|}{CH_3CO}}CH_2CH_2\overset{Me}{\overset{|}{Si}}Cl_2 \qquad (36)$$

$$CH_2=CHC\equiv N + HSiCl_3 \xrightarrow{Pt} Cl_3SiCH_2CH_2C\equiv N \qquad (37)$$

$$CH_2=\overset{}{\underset{Me}{C}}-\overset{O}{\overset{\|}{C}}OR + HSiCl_3 \xrightarrow{Pt} Cl_3SiCH_2\overset{}{\underset{Me}{CH}}\overset{O}{\overset{\|}{C}}OR \qquad (38)$$

conjugated double bonds, the silicon may bond to the α carbon; this is repressed by substitution at that site as in Eq. (38). The four reactions shown cannot be realized using free radical catalysts because the unsaturated components in these systems would polymerize at extremely high rates. Furthermore, reactions (36)–(38) are not possible by thermal means alone because the organofunctional moiety in each case would be destroyed by pyrolysis or at least reduced by the hydrosilane.

In summary, the thermal and catalytic additions of silanes to olefinic compounds represent simple methods, employ relatively cheap raw materials, afford high yields of products, and make possible the synthesis of special compounds unobtainable by other methods.

4. Redistribution of Organochlorosilanes and Organoalkoxysilanes

The direct processes and Grignard reactions yield a spectrum of materials of varying degrees of usefulness. For instance, $MeSiCl_3$, Me_3SiCl, and $SiCl_4$ are required in limited amounts, and excesses of these and other chlorosilanes may be converted into the more desirable Me_2SiCl_2 by redistribution reactions catalyzed usually by $AlCl_3$ (*45, 372, 374, 496*) or $NaAlCl_4$ (*67, 70*). The reactions involve the interchange of organic groups and halogen; the products contain the same total number of silicon-halogen and silicon-carbon bonds as the reactants. For example, an equimolar mixture of Me_3SiCl and $MeSiCl_3$ or a mixture of 2 moles Me_3SiCl and 1 mole $SiCl_4$ will rearrange in the presence of $AlCl_3$ at 350°C under pressure to give preponderantly Me_2SiCl_2 [Eq. (39)] (*45, 372*). In the same way an equimolar mixture of Me_4Si and Me_2SiCl_2 will give Me_3SiCl [Eq. (40)].

$$Me_3SiCl + MeSiCl_3 \underset{\substack{350°C \\ pressure}}{\overset{AlCl_3}{\rightleftharpoons}} 2\ Me_2SiCl_2 \tag{39}$$

$$Me_4Si + Me_2SiCl_2 \underset{\substack{350°C \\ pressure}}{\overset{AlCl_3}{\rightleftharpoons}} 2\ Me_3SiCl \tag{40}$$

A proposed mechanism (*496*) involves the formation of rather stable intermediate complexes [Eq. (41)]. The equilibrium distribution of groups at-

$$Me_2SiCl_2 + AlCl_3 \overset{rapid}{\longrightarrow} Me_2SiCl_2 \cdot AlCl_3$$

$$Me_2SiCl_2 + Me_2SiCl_2 \cdot AlCl_3 \rightleftharpoons Me_3SiCl + MeSiCl_3 \cdot AlCl_3 \tag{41}$$

$$Me_2SiCl_2 + MeSiCl_3 \cdot AlCl_3 \rightleftharpoons MeSiCl_3 + Me_2SiCl_2 \cdot AlCl_3$$

tached to silicon shows considerable deviation from the random distribution shown by methylethyllead compounds (*98*). The equilibria lie con-

siderably to the right, with increasing temperature favoring the reverse
reaction:

Equation	Equilibrium constant 350°C	Equilibrium constant 420°C
(39)	39.9	29.8
(40)	74.3	54.9

Generally, higher temperatures favor decomposition and demethylation
with accompanying formation of methane and silmethylene linkages.

Phenyl groups also migrate under suitable conditions; $SiCl_4$ and Ph_4Si
yield Ph_2SiCl_2 and $PhSiCl_3$ (*302*). Mixed arylalkylchlorosilanes may be
prepared by redistribution of mixtures of organochlorosilanes containing
the required organic groups in almost any combination (*112, 373*). For
example, $PhSiCl_3$ and Me_3SiCl rearrange to yield $PhMeSiCl_2$ as well as the
expected Me_2SiCl_2 and $MeSiCl_3$ [Eq. (42)]. The same products are simi-

$$PhSiCl_3 + Me_3SiCl \underset{\substack{325°C \\ 600 \text{ psi}}}{\overset{AlCl_3}{\rightleftharpoons}} PhMeSiCl_2 + MeSiCl_3 + Me_2SiCl_2 \tag{42}$$

larly obtained along with some Ph_3SiCl by redistribution of a mixture of
Ph_2SiCl_2 and $Ph_2MeSiCl$. The rearrangement of phenyldichlorosilane
shown in Eq. (43) is of particular interest because it occurs at an unusually

$$PhHSiCl_2 \underset{185°C}{\overset{AlCl_3}{\rightleftharpoons}} Ph_2SiCl_2 + H_2SiCl_2 \tag{43}$$

low temperature and also because it illustrates the migration, from one
silicon atom to another, of hydrogen and of phenyl groups (*455*, cf. *111*).

Alkoxysilanes undergo similar redistribution reactions in the presence of
bases such as sodium alkoxides (*23, 25*) or amines (*283*, p. 104):

$$2 \ C_3H_5Si(OEt)_3 \xrightarrow{NaOEt} (C_3H_5)_2Si(OEt)_2 + Si(OEt)_4 \tag{44}$$

$$2 \ HSi(OEt)_3 \underset{}{\overset{amines}{\rightleftharpoons}} H_2Si(OEt)_2 + Si(OEt)_4 \tag{45}$$

5. *Preparation of Alkoxysilanes, Acyloxysilanes, and Silazanes*

Alkoxy- and acyloxy-silanes and silazanes find only limited use in the
production of organosiloxane polymers. Nevertheless, they are of importance in the synthesis of certain organosilicon compounds and serve to
indicate the variety of intermediates available for the preparation of
polymers.

Alkoxy- and aryloxy-silanes are readily prepared by the reaction of alcohols or phenols with chlorosilanes [Eqs. (46) and (47)]. The reactions are

$$\text{SiCl}_4 + 4 \text{ EtOH} \rightarrow \text{Si(OEt)}_4 + 4 \text{ HCl} \tag{46}$$

$$\text{Me}_2\text{SiCl}_2 + 2 \text{ MeOH} \rightarrow \text{Me}_2\text{Si(OMe)}_2 + 2 \text{ HCl} \tag{47}$$

reversible, but may be carried to completion by continuous removal of hydrogen chloride by purging with dry air or nitrogen (especially in high boiling solvents in which the hydrogen chloride is poorly soluble) or by using an acid acceptor such as pyridine or triethylamine. If the HCl concentration becomes too high, it will convert the alcohol to an alkyl halide; the water given off will hydrolyze the chlorosilane and the alkoxysilane to give undesirable polysiloxane residues.

Acetoxysilanes may be prepared by the reaction of a chlorosilane with sodium acetate in an anhydrous solvent [Eq. (48)], with acetic acid [Eq. (49)], or with acetic anhydride [Eq. (50)] (*14, 381*). Equations

$$\text{Me}_3\text{SiCl} + \text{NaOAc} \rightarrow \text{Me}_3\text{SiOAc} + \text{NaCl} \tag{48}$$

$$\text{Me}_2\text{SiCl}_2 + 2 \text{ HOAc} \rightarrow \text{Me}_2\text{Si(OAc)}_2 + 2 \text{ HCl} \tag{49}$$

$$\text{MeSiCl}_3 + 3 \text{ Ac}_2\text{O} \rightarrow \text{MeSi(OAc)}_3 + 3 \text{ AcCl} \tag{50}$$

(49) and (50) represent reversible reactions which may be driven to completion by continuous removal of the more volatile product by distillation. An acid acceptor also is effective for removal of liberated hydrogen chloride.

Silazanes and silylamines are prepared by allowing a chlorosilane to react with an excess of ammonia or mono- or di-substituted organic amine [Eqs. (51)–(53)], usually in solvents such as ether, benzene, or petroleum ethers (*147, 308*).

$$2 \text{ Me}_3\text{SiCl} + 3 \text{ NH}_3 \rightarrow (\text{Me}_3\text{Si})_2\text{NH} + 2 \text{ NH}_4\text{Cl} \tag{51}$$

$$\text{Me}_2\text{SiCl}_2 + 4 \text{ Me}_2\text{NH} \rightarrow \text{Me}_2\text{Si(NMe}_2)_2 + 2 \text{ Me}_2\text{NH} \cdot \text{HCl} \tag{52}$$

$$\text{Me}_3\text{SiCl} + 2 \text{ PhNH}_2 \rightarrow \text{Me}_3\text{SiNHPh} + \text{PhNH}_2 \cdot \text{HCl} \tag{53}$$

6. *Separation and Purification*

Table I lists many of the common organosilicon intermediates and their physical properties. Most of the processes discussed thus far yield mixtures containing many of these compounds which must be carefully separated by fractional distillation before they can be used in preparing polysiloxanes. For example, the direct reaction of methyl chloride with silicon-copper yields a mixture of products; seven of them, found in Table I, boil between 25° and 70°C, and the two major constituents, Me_2SiCl_2 and MeSiCl_3, boil only three degrees apart. It is obvious that highly efficient continuous distillation columns are required to separate the large amounts of ·chloro-

TABLE I

COMMON ORGANOSILICON INTERMEDIATES[a]

Compound	M.p. (°C)	B.p. (°C)	Refractive Index, n_D	Density (gm/ml)
$SiCl_4$		57.6	1.412[b]	1.476[c]
$Si(OMe)_4$		123	1.368[d]	1.018[c]
$Si(OEt)_4$		168	1.383[b]	0.933[c]
$HSiCl_3$	−128	32	1.398[b]	1.336[c]
$MeSiCl_3$	−78	66.4	1.407[b]	1.276[c]
$MeSi(OMe)_3$		103	1.369[b]	0.949[c]
$MeSi(OEt)_3$		143	1.381[b]	0.891[c]
$MeSi(OAc)_3$	∼40	95/9 mm	1.408[d]	1.165[c]
$ViSiCl_3$		91	1.433[b]	1.270[c]
$EtSiCl_3$	−106	99	1.426[b]	1.235[c]
$PhSiCl_3$		201	1.524[b]	1.321[c]
$HMeSiCl_2$	−93	41	1.398[b]	1.113[c]
Me_2SiCl_2	−76	69.6	1.402[b]	1.073[c]
$Me_2Si(OMe)_2$		82	1.371[b]	0.858[d]
$Me_2Si(OEt)_2$		113	1.381[b]	0.848[c]
$Me_2Si(OAc)_2$		45/3 mm	1.404[d]	1.052[d]
$ViMeSiCl_2$		92	1.427[b]	1.080[c]
$EtMeSiCl_2$		100	1.418[d]	1.059[c]
Et_2SiCl_2	−97	129	1.431[b]	1.055[c]
$HPhSiCl_2$		185	1.524[d]	1.193[c]
$MePhSiCl_2$		205	1.518[d]	1.176[c]
Ph_2SiCl_2		304	1.577[b]	1.220[c]
HMe_2SiCl		36	1.382[d]	0.870[c]
Me_3SiCl	−58	57.7	1.389[b]	0.856[c]
Me_3SiOMe		57	1.368[d]	0.764[c]
Me_3SiOEt		75	1.371[b]	0.752[c]
Me_3SiOAc		103	1.388[d]	0.894[d]
$ViMe_2SiCl$		82	1.414[b]	0.874[b]
$EtMe_2SiCl$		90	1.404[b]	0.875[c]
$Et_2MeSiCl$		119	1.421[d]	0.885[c]
Et_3SiCl		146	1.431[d]	0.893[c]
$Me_2PhSiCl$		193	1.508[b]	1.027[c]
$PhMeHSiCl$		176	1.516[b]	1.038[c]
Ph_2HSiCl		270	1.581[b]	1.113[c]
$Ph_2MeSiCl$		295	1.573[b]	1.107[c]
Ph_3SiCl	94	378		

[a] Extensive tabulations of organosilicon compounds may be found in more comprehensive surveys (*179, 141*).

[b] 25°C.

[c] Specific gravity (25°/15°C).

[d] 20°C.

silanes needed for industry. The separation of methylchlorosilanes is further complicated by their ability to form closely boiling azeotropes with some hydrocarbons and with one another, such as Me_3SiCl and $SiCl_4$ (*375*). Some alkoxysilanes also form azeotropes (*370*).

The purity of the intermediates is critical in the preparation of long linear polymers for silicone rubbers. A poly(dimethylsiloxane) of about 8000 —Me_2SiO— units in the chain is suitable for this purpose and can be obtained starting with the hydrolysis of pure Me_2SiCl_2. If the latter contains only 0.05 mole % Me_3SiCl, however, this impurity will limit the polymer to but half the desired chain length. Furthermore, the presence of only very small amounts of tri- and tetrafunctional impurities ($MeSiCl_3$ and $SiCl_4$) give cross-linked polymers that may be useless gels.

B. Silanol Intermediates

Although rarely isolated in pure form, silanols comprise some of the most important intermediates in the preparation of organopolysiloxanes. They may be prepared by careful hydrolysis of halides (*91, 131, 172, 243, 267, 279*), silazanes (*147, 370, 393*), acyloxysilanes (*393*), and alkoxysilanes (*216, 234, 445*) (Eqs. 54–57). Their extreme sensitivity to acid- or base-

$$Et_2SiCl_2 + 2 H_2O \rightarrow Et_2Si(OH)_2 + 2 HCl \qquad (54)$$

$$(Me_3Si)_2NH + 2 H_2O \rightarrow 2 Me_3SiOH + NH_3 \qquad (55)$$

$$Et_3SiOAc + H_2O \rightarrow Et_3SiOH + HOAc \qquad (56)$$

$$PhSi(OMe)_3 + 3 H_2O \rightarrow PhSi(OH)_3 + 3 MeOH \qquad (57)$$

catalyzed condensation to siloxanes requires that the hydrolysis be accomplished under essentially neutral conditions and preferably in the cold. Sodium bicarbonate or other salts may be added to buffer the HCl from the first reaction, and carbon dioxide or acetic acid to scavenge the ammonia from the second. The last reaction is inherently neutral; a trace of acetic acid may be used to promote the hydrolysis.

In general, silanols appear to be much more strongly acidic and only slightly less basic than carbinols of analogous structure (*476, 477*). The stability of the silanols and accordingly their ease of isolation increase with the number and sizes of the organic groups on the silicon atoms:

$$R_3SiOH > R_2Si(OH)_2 > RSi(OH)_3 \gg Si(OH)_4$$

$$Ph_3SiOH \gg Et_3SiOH > Me_3SiOH$$

A number of silanols which have been isolated and characterized are represented in Table II.

TABLE II

COMMON SILANOLS[a]

Silanol	M.p. (°C)	B.p. (°C)	Refractive Index, n_D	Density (gm/ml)
PhSi(OH)₃	130			
Me₂Si(OH)₂	101			
EtMeSi(OH)₂	80			
Et₂Si(OH)₂	97			
MePhSi(OH)₂	75			
Ph₂Si(OH)₂	Variable[b]			
Me₃SiOH		99	1.388[c]	0.811[c]
Et₃SiOH		154	1.434[c]	0.865[c]
Ph₃SiOH	151			
(HOMe₂Si)₂O	68			
(HOPhMeSi)₂O	111, 84			
(HOPh₂Si)₂O	114			

[a] Extensive tabulations of organosilicon compounds may be found in more comprehensive surveys (*179, 141*).

[b] 115–155°C (*431*).

[c] 20°C.

C. Simple Polysiloxanes

1. Preparation

a. Condensation of Silanols. Organopolysiloxanes are readily prepared by hydrolysis of chlorosilanes (*314*), alkoxysilanes (*202, 274*), acetoxysilanes, or silazanes (*147*), followed by condensation of the resulting silanols (Eq. 58) (*219*). The hydrolysis of chlorosilanes is industrially by far the most

$$
\begin{array}{c}
2 \equiv\!SiCl \qquad\qquad\qquad 2\ HCl \\
2 \equiv\!SiOR \qquad\qquad\qquad 2\ HOR \\
\xrightarrow{\ 2\ H_2O\ } 2 \equiv\!SiOH + \qquad \rightarrow \equiv\!SiOSi\!\equiv + H_2O \qquad (58) \\
2 \equiv\!SiOAc \qquad\qquad\qquad 2\ HOAc \\
2 \equiv\!SiN\!\equiv \qquad\qquad\qquad 2\ HN\!\equiv
\end{array}
$$

important of these processes. No precautions are taken to ensure either neutral or cold conditions, and the intermediate silanols are not isolated, but rapidly undergo thermal or acid- or base-catalyzed condensation to yield polysiloxanes and water.

The hydrolysis of monofunctional silanes yields disiloxanes. For example, in the presence of hydrogen chloride the trimethylsilanol resulting from the hydrolysis of trimethylchlorosilane condenses at once to hexamethyldisiloxane (Eq. 59). It is possible to obtain mixed disiloxanes by

$$2 \text{ Me}_3\text{SiCl} + \text{H}_2\text{O} \rightarrow 2 \text{ Me}_3\text{SiOH} + 2 \text{ HCl} \rightarrow \text{Me}_3\text{SiOSiMe}_3 + \text{H}_2\text{O} \qquad (59)$$

hydrolysis of a mixture of two chlorosilanes and cocondensation of the resulting silanols [Eq. (60)].

$$4 \text{ Me}_3\text{SiCl} + 4 \text{ Et}_3\text{SiCl} + 8 \text{ H}_2\text{O}$$

$$\downarrow$$

$$8 \text{ HCl} + 4 \text{ Me}_3\text{SiOH} + 4 \text{ Et}_3\text{SiOH} \qquad (60)$$

$$\downarrow$$

$$2 \text{ Me}_3\text{SiOSiEt}_3 + \text{Me}_3\text{SiOSiMe}_3 + \text{Et}_3\text{SiOSiEt}_3 + 4 \text{ H}_2\text{O}$$

The hydrolysis of a difunctional silane such as a diorganodichlorosilane (or other related and easily hydrolyzed compound) yields the corresponding silanediol, as illustrated in Eq. (61). Under the conditions of the hydrolysis the diol undergoes rapid condensation [Eq. (62)], to yield a com-

$$\text{R}_2\text{SiCl}_2 + 2 \text{ H}_2\text{O} \rightarrow \text{R}_2\text{Si(OH)}_2 + 2 \text{ HCl} \qquad (61)$$

$$\text{R}_2\text{Si(OH)}_2 \xrightarrow{\text{H}^+} \underset{\textit{linear}}{\text{HO(R}_2\text{SiO)}_x\text{H}} + \underset{\textit{cyclic}}{\text{(R}_2\text{SiO)}_{3-6}} + \text{H}_2\text{O} \qquad (62)$$

plex mixture consisting of both linear and cyclic polysiloxanes in a wide distribution of molecular weights (*201, 202, 219, 274, 314*). The distribution of products depends on the nature and purity of the compounds undergoing hydrolysis and the reaction conditions, especially the hydrolysis medium and the temperature. For example, the slow addition of dimethyldichlorosilane to excess water at 15 to 20°C yields a mixture consisting of 0.5% hexamethylcyclotrisiloxane (D_3), 42.0% octamethylcyclotetrasiloxane (D_4), 6.7% decamethylcyclopentasiloxane (D_5), 1.6% dodecamethylcyclohexasiloxane (D_6), 49.2% residue of linear polymer, and also higher molecular weight cyclics in amounts too small to be readily isolated (*314*). The hydrolysis of dimethyldiethoxysilane gives a higher proportion of linear polymers (*272*, p. 272; *274*) and accordingly a higher average viscosity for the mixture. Hydrolysis in strongly acid medium or in the presence of a water-miscible solvent favors the production of cyclics or low molecular weight linear polymers, while an alkaline medium has the opposite effect (*314*). Hydrolysis at elevated temperatures tends to give polymers of higher viscosity, presumably by promoting the condensation of silanol end groups. The cocondensations of different diols to produce copolymers and mixed cyclics are more thoroughly discussed in Section II,D.

Trifunctional silanes undergo rapid hydrolysis to yield unstable silanetriols [Eq. (63)]. Like the diols, the triols undergo rapid intermolecular

$$RSiCl_3 + 3 H_2O \rightarrow RSi(OH)_3 + 3 HCl \tag{63}$$

condensation to yield, in this case, random resinous structures. Depending upon the size of the substituent group and upon the conditions of hydrolysis, the hydroxy-end-blocked polymers initially formed may undergo intramolecular condensation to yield orderly crystalline organosilsesquioxanes of relatively low molecular weight [Eq. (64)], (*38, 41, 382, 419*), as the cage structure (Fig. 1).

$$RSi(OH)_3 \rightarrow \underset{\text{resin}}{(RSiO_{3/2})_n} + \underset{\text{crystalline}}{(RSiO_{3/2})_{6,8,12}} + H_2O \tag{64}$$

Analogously, tetrafunctional silanes would be expected to yield silane-tetrol, or orthosilicic acid, but this acid has never been isolated because the tetrol undergoes immediate condensation to yield silica or a hydrated form of silica:

$$SiCl_4 + 4 H_2O \rightarrow 4 HCl + [Si(OH)_4] \rightarrow SiO_2 + 2 H_2O \tag{65}$$

The structure and therefore the usefulness of polysiloxanes may be widely varied through cocondensation of silanols of various functionalities. The reaction between a diol and a silanol [Eq. (66)], will give a mixture

$$2 R_3SiOH + x Me_2Si(OH)_2 \xrightarrow{H^+} R_3SiO(Me_2SiO)_xSiR_3 + (x + 1) H_2O + \text{cyclics} \tag{66}$$

of linear polysiloxanes. The molecular weight distributions obtained from this condensation depend to a great extent on the type and number of end-blocking monofunctional groups present.

In general, the molecular weights of polysiloxanes prepared directly by hydrolysis of dichlorosilanes are low and the products are fluids, because total hydrolysis and condensation are difficult to achieve. Hydrolysis of dichlorosilanes in the presence of excess water yields polymers containing some silanol end groups (I) while a deficiency of water results in polymers that contain a considerable number of chlorosilyl end groups (II) (*314*).

$$\underset{(I)}{HOMe_2SiO(Me_2SiO)_xSiMe_2OH} \qquad \underset{(II)}{ClMe_2SiO(Me_2SiO)_xSiMe_2Cl}$$

Similar considerations apply to the hydrolysis of alkoxysilanes. The molecular weights and therefore the viscosities of such polymers are unstable since, upon exposure to moisture, further hydrolysis may occur followed by condensation to polymers of higher molecular weight. The viscosities of siloxanes produced by hydrolysis techniques may be stabilized by deliberate introduction of monofunctional end groups and controlled by varying the proportion of these groups to the difunctional units in the hydrolysis mixture. Functional end groups such as HMe_2SiO- or

ViMe₂SiO— may be introduced into the polymer to be used later for further reactions. A list of many of these common siloxane building units and their properties may be found in Table III.

Chain branching is introduced into a polysiloxane by cocondensation of tri- and/or tetra-functional silanols with other silanols, as illustrated schematically in Eq. (67). It is apparent that the inclusion of only small

$$3\ R_3SiOH + R_2Si(OH)_2 + RSi(OH)_3 \xrightarrow{H^+}$$

$$R_3SiOSiR_2SiOSiR_3 + 4\ H_2O$$

$$\underset{\displaystyle \overset{|}{O} \atop \displaystyle \overset{|}{SiR_3}}{}$$

(67)

amounts of tri- and/or tetra-functional building units can vastly change the molecular architecture of the polymer obtained. This is illustrated by the hydrolysis of mixed chlorosilanes in Eq. (68), which but for the pres-

$$(a + b + c + d)\ Me_2SiCl_2 + SiCl_4 \xrightarrow[\ (OMe_2Si)_bOH\ ]{H_2O}$$

$$HO(Me_2SiO)_a\!\!-\!\!Si\!\!-\!\!(OMe_2Si)_cOH + HCl$$

$$(OMe_2Si)_dOH$$

(68)

ence of SiCl₄ could yield only linear or cyclic polymer molecules. Instead, the cruciform polymer molecule shown not only represents in itself a high degree of branching but may produce much greater branching and crosslinking by further condensation with other molecules of the same type. The end result may be an infinite network, but the process is limited by a steric effect, which results in some natural termination by silanol end groups. Control of the ultimate structure is better insured by incorporating the appropriate monochlorosilane in the original hydrolysis mixture. Structures ranging from branched polymers through slightly cross-linked gums to rigid solids may be obtained depending on the relative numbers of the four functional types of silanols made available for cocondensation. It must be borne in mind, or course, that a spectrum of structures and products is always obtained—never a single chemical entity.

The hydrolysis of chlorosilanes to produce silanols is an extremely fast reaction; the relative rates depend on the number and nature of the substituent groups. For a given group, R, the rates of hydrolysis decrease with increase in the number of such groups (*390*):

$$SiCl_4 > RSiCl_3 \gg R_2SiCl_2 > R_3SiCl$$

For a given degree of substitution the rate is determined by the inductive effects of the substituent groups. This is reflected, for example, in a series

TABLE III

COMMON SILOXANE BUILDING UNITS

Unit	x	M.p. (°C)	B.p. (°C)	n_D	Density (gm/ml)
$(Me_2SiO)_x$	3	64.5	134	—	—
	4	17.5	175	1.3935^a	0.9497^a
	5	−44	205	1.3958^a	0.9531^a
	6	−3	236	1.3996^a	0.9613^a
	7	−32	147/20 mm	1.4018^a	0.9664^a
	8	31.5	168/20 mm	1.4039^a	1.177^h
$(PhMeSiO)_x$	3	α 45.5	—	1.540^b	1.106^b
		β 100	—	—	—
	4	99	—	—	—
$(Ph_2SiO)_x$	3	190	295/1 mm	—	—
	4	201	335/1 mm	—	1.185^c
$(MeHSiO)_x$	3		94	1.3770^d	0.963^e
	4	−69	135	1.3870^a	0.991^e
	5	108	169	1.3912^d	0.994^e
	6		196	1.3944^a	1.006^e
$Me_3SiO(Me_2SiO)_xSiMe_3$	0	−68	100	1.3748^a	0.761^f
	1	−86	152	1.3822^a	0.818^f
	2	−76	194	1.3872^a	0.852^f
	3	−84	229	1.3902^a	0.871^f
	4	−59	142/20 mm	1.3922^a	0.887^f
	5	−78	184.5/40 mm	1.3940^a	0.900^f
	6	−63	202/39 mm	1.3952^a	0.908^f
	7		199/16 mm	1.3980^d	0.918^d
	8		203/10 mm	1.3988^d	0.025^d
	9		202/5 mm	1.3994^d	0.930^d
$(HMe_2Si)_2O$			72	1.369^d	0.756^d
$(ViMe_2Si)_2O$			140	1.410^a	0.803^a
$(PhMe_2Si)_2O$		< −80	292	1.515^a	0.971^a
$(Ph_2MeSi)_2O$		51	418	1.587^g	1.076^g
$(Ph_3Si)_2O$		226	494	—	—

[a] 25°C.

[b] 20° on supercooled liquid.

[c] 20–25°C.

[d] 20°C.

[e] Specific gravity (25°/15°C).

[f] Specific gravity (25°/25°C).

[g] At 25° on supercooled liquid.

[h] For crystals.

of monochlorosilanes whose equilibrium constants decrease with decrease in electron-withdrawing character of the variant group (*217*):

$$ClCH_2Me_2SiCl > PhMe_2SiCl > F_3C(CH_2)_2Me_2SiCl > MeMe_2SiCl > EtMe_2SiCl$$

Degree of substitution is generally the dominant factor but may be over-balanced in the case of substituent groups having very high inductive effects; thus $ClCH_2Me_2SiCl$ shows a slightly higher rate constant than Me_2SiCl_2 (*217*). In any chlorosilane which contains two or more chlorines, the first chlorine is hydrolyzed much faster than the others. This difference in reactivity makes possible the preparation of chlorosiloxanes by careful hydrolysis (*380*). An S_N2 reaction mechanism has been proposed [Eq. 69)],

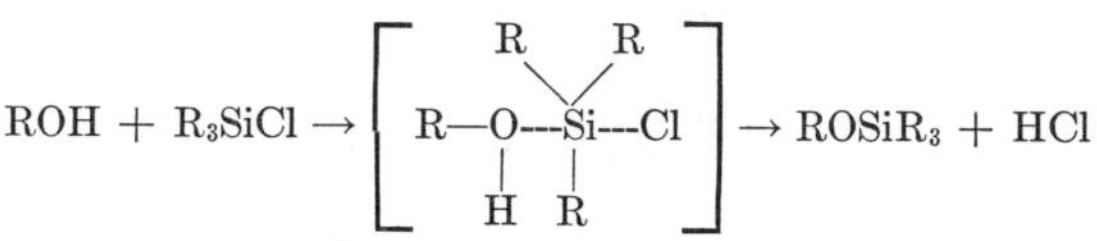

$$ROH + R_3SiCl \rightarrow \left[\begin{matrix} & R & R & \\ R{-}O{-}{-}{-}Si{-}{-}{-}Cl \\ & | & | & \\ & H & R & \end{matrix} \right] \rightarrow ROSiR_3 + HCl \qquad (69)$$

transition state

based upon the rates of solvolysis of sterically hindered chlorosilanes in various solvents (*4, 5*). The reaction is strongly promoted by polar solvents and shows a dependence upon the size of the alkyl group present in the series:

$$HOH > MeOH > EtOH \gg i\text{-PrOH}$$

The rate-controlling step in hydrolysis is the condensation of silanols to siloxane linkages (*185, 390*); acids and bases catalyze this condensation and, in methanol solution, HCl is five hundred times as effective as KOH (*185*).

The hydrolysis of chlorosilanes involves an equilibrium between the chlorosilane, water, siloxane, and hydrogen chloride, which lies to the right as written:

$$2\,R_3SiCl + H_2O \rightleftharpoons (R_3Si)_2O + 2\,HCl \qquad (70)$$

favoring formation of siloxane and acid; no intermediate silanol has been detected. Like the reaction rate, the position of equilibrium varies with the nature and number of the substituent groups. The equilibrium constant is slightly greater at 25°C than at higher temperatures, but the significant advantage of low temperature hydrolysis is that it minimizes group loss by scission of the R—Si bond, to which phenyl and hydrogen on silicon are particularly susceptible [Eqs. (71) and (72)]. For such compounds high

$$2\equiv\!SiH + H_2O \xrightarrow{\text{OH}^-} 2\,H_2 + \equiv\!SiOSi\!\equiv \qquad (71)$$

$$2\equiv\!SiC_6H_5 + H_2O \xrightarrow{\text{H}^+} 2\,C_6H_6 + \equiv\!SiOSi\!\equiv \qquad (72)$$

dilution and the presence of buffering agents are helpful devices in the laboratory but are of limited value in larger scale operation.

b. Other Condensation Methods. Siloxane bonds also result from the reactions of silanols with halosilanes in the presence of an acid acceptor such as pyridine:

$$\equiv\text{SiOH} + \text{X—Si} \xrightarrow[\text{acceptor}]{\text{acid}} \equiv\text{SiOSi}\equiv + \text{HX} \tag{73}$$

Alkali metal silanolates and halosilanes yield siloxane bonds in a similar manner [Eq. (74)], as do silanols and alkoxysilanes in the presence of an alkali metal silanolate catalyst [Eq. (75)]. The reactions of a chlorosilane

$$\equiv\text{SiONa} + \text{X—Si} \rightarrow \equiv\text{SiOSi}\equiv + \text{NaX} \tag{74}$$

$$\equiv\text{SiOH} + \text{ROSi}\equiv \xrightarrow{\text{Me}_3\text{SiONa}} \equiv\text{SiOSi}\equiv + \text{ROH} \tag{75}$$

with an ethoxysilane in the presence of ferric chloride [Eq. (76)] (*386*), or with a metal oxide such as that of silver, mercury, copper, iron, cadmium, or lead [Eq. (77)], likewise produce siloxane bonds.

$$\equiv\text{SiCl} + \text{EtOSi}\equiv \xrightarrow[\Delta]{\text{FeCl}_3} \equiv\text{SiOSi}\equiv + \text{EtCl} \tag{76}$$

$$2 \equiv\text{SiCl} + \text{HgO} \rightarrow \equiv\text{SiOSi}\equiv + \text{HgCl}_2 \tag{77}$$

The removal of organic groups by acid and base catalysis to give siloxanes [Eqs. (71) and (72)] represents an inefficient but sometimes practical condensation method. The oxidation of organic groups on silicon by oxygen or ozone, especially at elevated temperatures, also produces siloxane bonds [Eqs. (78) and (79)]. These reactions have practically no preparative

$$2 \equiv\text{SiCH}_3 + 2 \text{O}_2 \rightarrow \equiv\text{SiOSi}\equiv + \text{H}_2\text{O} + 2 \text{CH}_2\text{O} \tag{78}$$

$$6 \equiv\text{SiCH}_3 + 8 \text{O}_3 \rightarrow 3 \equiv\text{SiOSi}\equiv + 9 \text{H}_2\text{O} + 6 \text{CO}_2 \tag{79}$$

value, but have been investigated in evaluating the oxidative and hydrolytic stability of polysiloxanes and in determining mechanisms for group loss.

2. Chemical Properties

a. Cleavage of Siloxane Bond. Organometallic compounds such as organolithium or Grignard reagents (*370*) cleave silicon-oxygen bonds to give more highly substituted products, as illustrated in Eq. (80). Lithium aluminum hydride reduces siloxanes to silanes [Eq. (81)] (*192*). Halides

$$
\begin{array}{c}
\text{R} \\
| \\
\xrightarrow{x\,\text{R}'\text{MgX}} x\,\text{R}'\text{SiOMgX} \quad\quad\quad \text{H}_2\text{O} \\
|\\
\text{R}
\end{array}
$$

$$
-\left(\begin{array}{c}\text{R}\\|\\\text{Si}-\text{O}\\|\\\text{R}\end{array}\right)_x
\qquad\qquad
\begin{array}{c}\text{R}\\|\\x\,\text{R}'\text{SiOH}\\|\\\text{R}\end{array}
$$

$$
\begin{array}{c}
\xrightarrow{x\,\text{R}'\text{Li}} \\
\begin{array}{c}\text{R}\\|\\x\,\text{R}'\text{SiOLi}\\|\\\text{R}\end{array}
\qquad \text{H}_2\text{O}
\end{array}
$$

$$\tag{80}$$

of aluminum, boron, and phosphorus give halosilanes (Eq. 82), (*177, 215, 271, 306, 452, 478*).

$$4 - \left(\begin{array}{c}\text{R}\\|\\\text{Si}-\text{O}\\|\\\text{R}\end{array}\right)_x + 2x\ \text{LiAlH}_4 \rightarrow 4x\ \text{H}-\!\!\begin{array}{c}\text{R}\\|\\\text{Si}\\|\\\text{R}\end{array}\!\!-\text{H} + x\ \text{Li}_2\text{O} + x\ \text{Al}_2\text{O}_3 \tag{81}$$

$$\equiv\!\text{SiOSi}\!\equiv + \text{AlX}_3 \rightarrow \equiv\!\text{SiX} + \equiv\!\text{SiOAlX}_2 \rightarrow \equiv\!\text{SiX} + \text{AlOX} \tag{82}$$

Siloxanes undergo hydrolysis and alcoholysis reactions, especially in the presence of acids or bases. The SiOSi bond may be broken with water at elevated temperatures [Eq. (83)]. Siloxanes react reversibly with alcohols, yielding alkoxysilanes [Eqs. (84) and (85)]. Siloxanes react with alkalies giving silanols and silanolates [Eq. (86)], and with anhydrous or concentrated acids [Eqs. (87) and (88)]. Reactions (83), and (86)–(88) are

$$\equiv\!\text{SiOSi}\!\equiv + \text{H}_2\text{O}\ (\text{high pressure steam}) \rightarrow 2 \equiv\!\text{SiOH} \tag{83}$$

$$\equiv\!\text{SiOSi}\!\equiv + \text{ROH} \underset{}{\overset{\text{H}^+\ \text{or B}^-}{\rightleftharpoons}} \equiv\!\text{SiOR} + \text{HOSi}\!\equiv \tag{84}$$

$$\text{HOSi}\!\equiv + \text{ROH} \rightleftharpoons \equiv\!\text{SiOR} + \text{H}_2\text{O} \tag{85}$$

$$\equiv\!\text{SiOSi}\!\equiv + \text{KOH} \rightarrow \equiv\!\text{SiOH} + \text{KOSi}\!\equiv \tag{86}$$

$$\equiv\!\text{SiOSi}\!\equiv + \text{HCl} \rightarrow \equiv\!\text{SiOH} + \text{ClSi}\!\equiv \tag{87}$$

$$\equiv\!\text{SiOSi}\!\equiv + \text{H}_2\text{SO}_4 \rightarrow \equiv\!\text{SiOH} + \equiv\!\text{SiHSO}_4 \tag{88}$$

equilibria really inclined much more to the left than to the right, but may be upset by proper choice of conditions. Thus the Flood reaction (*156*) for the preparation of a trialkylchlorosilane by action of sulfuric acid and a metal halide upon the appropriate disiloxane [Eq. (89)] is essentially an

$$R_3SiOSiR_3 \xrightarrow[\text{NaX or NH}_4\text{X}]{\text{concd. H}_2\text{SO}_4} 2\ R_3SiX + H_2O \qquad (89)$$

embodiment of reaction (87), which is made almost quantitative by volatilization of the chlorosilane from the system and dehydration of the system by use of a large excess of concentrated sulfuric acid.

In general the more highly substituted the silicon atoms in the polymer, the more resistant the siloxane to attack by alkali; the relative ease of salt formation is in the order:

$$SiO_{4/2} > RSiO_{3/2} > R_2SiO > R_3SiO_{1/2}$$

In contrast, increasing substitution on silicon renders the polymer more susceptible to attack by acid; thus, the relative reactivities with HCl are in the order:

$$R_3SiO_{1/2} > R_2SiO > RSiO_{3/2}$$

The inductive effects of the substituent groups are responsible for these reversed orders of susceptibility toward alkali and acid attack (*217, 235*). Each substitution of a methyl group for an electron-withdrawing oxygen atom increases the concentration of electrons around the silicon atom; this hinders nucleophilic attack upon the silicon by bases and facilitates electrophilic attack upon the oxygen by acids. The effect is greater for a methyl group than for a substituent group, like phenyl or trifluoropropyl, that is itself electron withdrawing.

b. Siloxane Redistribution and Equilibration. Susceptibility of siloxane bonds to attack by either acid or base results in siloxane redistribution, a useful device for preparing an extensive variety of siloxane structures. Since these reactions are equilibria, it remains necessary merely to provide for more than one species of silanol on the right-hand side of Eqs. (86) and (88) to obtain a mixed siloxane on recondensation. With a properly selected *mixture* of siloxanes in the presence of acid or base, it is possible to prepare many *mixed siloxanes* by what is commonly referred to as equilibration. *Equilibration* is defined as the process of breaking and reforming of siloxane linkages until thermodynamic equilibrium is reached. The acid or base is referred to as the *equilibration catalyst*. Equilibration is useful not only in preparing mixed siloxanes but, within a single system, may be used to readjust the molecular sizes of the polymer species represented. Further consideration of this technique will be directed immediately to the preparation of disiloxanes and the lower cyclic polysiloxanes because of their important role in precision structuring of higher siloxane polymers.

Preparation of disiloxanes: The equilibration method is useful in the preparation of an unsymmetrical disiloxane from a mixture of two symmetrical species. Thus phenylpentamethyldisiloxane is obtained from hexamethyldisiloxane and symmetrical diphenyltetramethyldisiloxane as shown in Eq. (90) (*131*). After the base has been neutralized, the desired

$$(Me_3Si)_2O + (PhMe_2Si)_2O \overset{KOH}{\rlap{\longrightarrow}\raisebox{-3pt}{\longleftarrow}} 2\ Me_3SiOSiMe_2Ph \qquad (90)$$

product is isolated, usually by distillation. For practical purposes the product distribution varies statistically and a 50% yield of the desired product will be obtained from the equimolar starting mixture of Eq. (90). The amount of the desired product may be varied according to the law of probability by adjusting the initial reactant ratios. Undesirable side reactions such as shown in Eq. (72) or the phasing-out of any species, of course, upset the equilibrium.

A wide choice of catalysts is available for the equilibration process; the most common are strong mineral acids (*235, 314, 383*), inorganic acid anhydrides, Lewis-type acids (*383*), alkali metal hydroxides (*213, 214, 463*), alkali metal silanolates such as Me_3SiOK or $(NaOMe_2Si)_2O$ (*213, 214*), and tetramethylammonium hydroxides (*214, 235*). The catalyst must be selected with regard for possible sensitivity of functional groups other than $\equiv SiOSi\equiv$ in the compounds to be equilibrated. The type of catalyst used may markedly affect the path and rate to equilibrium, but not the end state (*235*).

Equations (91)–(94) (*118, 344, 371*) illustrate the preparation by

$$(Me_3Si)_2O + (Et_3Si)_2O \overset{H_2SO_4}{\rlap{\longrightarrow}\raisebox{-3pt}{\longleftarrow}} 2\ Et_3SiOSiMe_3 \qquad (91)$$

$$(Me_3Si)_2O + (N\equiv CCH_2Me_2Si)_2O \overset{H_2SO_4}{\rlap{\longrightarrow}\raisebox{-3pt}{\longleftarrow}} 2\ Me_3SiOSiMe_2CH_2C\equiv N \qquad (92)$$

$$(Me_3Si)_2O + (MeSO_2CH_2SiMe_2)_2O \overset{H_2SO_4}{\rlap{\longrightarrow}\raisebox{-3pt}{\longleftarrow}} 2\ Me_3SiOSiMe_2CH_2SO_2Me \qquad (93)$$

$$(Me_3Si)_2O + \left(\overset{\overset{\displaystyle O}{\displaystyle \|}}{CH_2=CMeCOCH_2SiMe_2} \right)_2O \overset{H_2SO_4}{\rlap{\longrightarrow}\raisebox{-3pt}{\longleftarrow}}$$

$$2\ Me_3SiOMe_2SiCH_2O\overset{\overset{\displaystyle O}{\displaystyle \|}}{C}CMe=CH_2 \qquad (94)$$

equilibrium reactions of several compounds that would be difficult to prepare otherwise, particularly the last three, because they contain organofunctional groups. The organofunctional siloxane, pentamethyldisiloxanylmethyl methacrylate [Eq. (94)], may be obtained in good yields from the bisester by equilibration with relatively large amounts of hexamethyldisiloxane, the excess of which is easily removed by distillation after the catalyst is washed from the mixture.

Preparation of cyclic siloxanes: It was shown that cyclic siloxanes may be prepared by hydrolysis of chlorosilanes [Eq. (62)], followed by fractional distillation to separate them from the linear polymers (*201, 314*). In the case of the dimethylsiloxanes, the yield of cyclic structures amounts to about 50%, and most of that is one species, the cyclic tetramer (D_4). The higher polymers obtained from the hydrolysis can be reequilibrated by heating alone (*314*), or in the presence of a catalyst, preferably an alkali metal hydroxide (*201*), giving an enhanced yield of cyclic siloxanes, which again can be separated from the equilibrium mixture by distillation. When the equilibration and distillation are carried on simultaneously, the process is commonly referred to as "cracking," perhaps an appropriate term when elevated temperatures (350–400°) are employed. Under these conditions, the volatile cyclics are favored because they are removed from the mixture as fast as formed and before equilibrium can be established. The cracking of the polymer portion of Eq. (62) yields 44% D_3, 24% D_4, 9% D_5, 10% D_6, and 13% cyclics larger than the hexamer (*314*). (Compare with the original distribution in the hydrolyzate, Section II,C,1,*a*). Any of these cyclics, any polymer, or even the original hydrolyzate in its entirely could be appropriately "cracked" to obtain ultimately a single cyclic species.

D. Fluid Polysiloxanes by Equilibration

Fluid polymers of any desired viscosity may be prepared by equilibrating mixtures of cyclic polysiloxane and a disiloxane or other source of monofunctional groups. The cyclic siloxane may be a single species, usually from trimer through hexamer (D_3–D_6), or any mixture of these; the source of the monofunctional groups may be an appropriate disiloxane (MM) or a short linear polymer already end blocked by the desired monofunctional units. The average molecular weight and therefore the viscosity of the equilibrated fluid will be determined by the ratio of monofunctional to difunctional groups present. The ideal reaction might be written as in Eq. (95), but the equilibrium mixture will still contain some of the initial MM

$$MM + 3\ D_4 \xrightarrow[\text{base}]{\text{acid or}} MD_{12}M \tag{95}$$

and D_4 as well as other cyclics formed by equilibration; furthermore, the product formed will be a mixture of polymers of various chain lengths instead of a single species. Despite these complications, after the catalyst has been inactivated and the low boiling siloxanes distilled from the system, the final ratio of M/D and consequently the viscosity and average molecular weight of the product will be some consistent function of the proportions of M and D units initially present. In Table IV, the product distributions are shown for two typical equilibrations starting with equimolar mixtures of $(Me_3Si)_2O$ and $(Me_2SiO)_4$, one catalyzed by acid and the other by base.

TABLE IV

PRODUCTS FROM EQUILIBRATION OF EQUIMOLAR AMOUNTS OF
$(ME_3SI)_2O$ AND $(ME_2SIO)_4$

Compound	Using concd. H_2SO_4 at 25°C (*383*) (wt. %)	Using Me_4NOH at 80°C (*235*) (wt. %)
MM	6.5	8.6
MDM	8.7	8.2
MD_2M	9.7	8.8
MD_3M	10.0	8.0
MD_4M	8.3	8.3
MD_5M	7.8	7.1
MD_6M	6.6	—
D_4	3.1	3.3
D_5	~0.8	1.3
Higher M.W. polymers	~38.5	39.6

The base-catalyzed rearrangement of organopolysiloxanes involves two nucleophilic attacks upon silicon: first, the entry of the catalyst molecule [Eq. (96)] and, second, the continued action of the catalyst molecule or some part of it in the rearrangement [Eq. (97)]. The nearly equivalent

$$SiOSi + KOH \rightleftharpoons SiOK + HOSi \qquad (96)$$

$$\overset{*}{Si}\overset{*}{O}Si + SiOK \rightleftharpoons \overset{*}{Si}OSi + \overset{*}{Si}OK \qquad (97)$$

catalytic effects of potassium hydroxide and potassium silanolate indicate that the equilibrium in reaction (96) lies far to the right. The assumption that the silanolate ion is the active species is supported by kinetic data. The catalytic activity of bases has been correlated:

$$CsOH > RbOH > KOH > NaOH > LiOH$$

This order of reactivity is probably due to decreasing ionization of the active silanolate catalyst with decreasing size of the alkali metal atom (*186, 209, 213, 214*).

The base-catalyzed polymerization of any mixture of $(Me_3Si)_2O$ and $(Me_2SiO)_4$ exhibits a viscosity maximum (*235*). The viscosity initially rises sharply to a maximum value and then drops and approaches the value obtained in acid equilibration. The maximum is attributed to the differences in reactivity of Me_3SiO- and $-OMe_2SiO-$ linkages. Because the more electropositive silicon in the latter type of compound is more susceptible to nucleophilic attack (cf. Section II,C,2,a), the order of activity of siloxanes toward bases is:

$$D_3 > D_4 > MD_2M > MDM > MM$$

Thus the trimer and tetramer units polymerize to a high degree before the less reactive disiloxane end-blocking units can enter the reaction to lower the average molecular weight.

The exact mechanism of the acid-catalyzed equilibration of siloxanes is not so well understood as that of the base-catalyzed equilibration. It is known, however, that strong mineral acids such as sulfuric acid will attack siloxane linkages to produce easily hydrolyzed sulfate and bisulfate end groups (*340, 404*) as shown for hexamethyldisiloxane and octamethylcyclotetrasiloxane in Eqs. (98) and (99) (*340*):

$$(Me_3Si)_2O + 3 H_2SO_4 \rightleftharpoons 2 Me_3SiHSO_4 + H_3O^+ + HSO_4^- \tag{98}$$

$$D_4 + H_2SO_4 \rightleftharpoons H(OMe_2Si)_4HSO_4 \tag{00}$$

Reaction with a polysiloxane probably produces a bisulfate end grouping [Eq. (100)] (*314*), which is able to cause redistribution with other silanol end groups as shown in Eq. (101):

$$SiOSi + H_2SO_4 \rightleftharpoons SiOH + HSO_3OSi \tag{100}$$

$$HSO_3O\overset{*}{S}i + SiOH \rightleftharpoons HSO_3OSi + \overset{*}{S}iOH \tag{101}$$

Here, in contrast to base-catalyzed rearrangements and polymerizations, the silanol end groups appear to be the active intermediates (*208*). The catalyst could be regenerated by hydrolysis of a bisulfate end group; the water arises from condensation of two silanol end groups to yield a new polymer [Eqs. (102) and (103)]. Similar equations could be written in-

$$\overset{*}{S}iOH + SiOH \rightleftharpoons H_2O + \overset{*}{S}iOSi \tag{102}$$

$$H_2O + SiOSO_3H \rightleftharpoons H_2SO_4 + SiOH \tag{103}$$

volving chlorine end groups for equilibration with hydrochloric acid; many other acid catalysts could perform in the same way.

No maximum is observed in the acid-catalyzed polymerization of cyclics as in the base-catalyzed process, and a reverse order of reactivity is observed:

$$D_3 > MM > MDM > MD_2M > D_4$$

(*185, 235*). The apparently anomalous high reactivity of the cyclic trimer is due to great strain in the ring.

E. High Polymer Organosiloxanes

High molecular weight polysiloxane gums may be prepared by equilibration of cyclic siloxanes in the absence of monofunctional groups. The resulting linear polymers are end blocked by the catalyst, as illustrated by Eq. (104) for a base-catalyzed system:

$$D_4 + KOH \rightleftharpoons HO(Me_2SiO)_xK + D_{4,5,6} \tag{104}$$

The reaction is believed to take place by hydroxyl or silanolate ion attack upon silicon according to the sequence shown in Eqs. (105) and (106):

Initiation:

$$(Me_2SiO)_4 + KOH \rightleftharpoons HO(Me_2SiO)_3Me_2SiO^- + K^+ \tag{105}$$

Propagation:

$$(Me_2SiO)_4 + HO(Me_2SiO)_3Me_2SiO^- \rightleftharpoons HO(Me_2SiO)_7Me_2SiO^- \tag{106}$$

The rates of reaction and the average molecular weights of the polymers obtained depend on many factors such as reaction temperature, type of cyclic siloxane, and the type and concentration of catalyst. The following experimental data, illustrative of these relationships, are all taken from polymerizations of cyclic dimethylsiloxanes using potassium trimethylsilanolate or KOH as catalysts; the reactions were quenched by "killing" the catalysts by addition of dry ice and washing out the salts.

The average molecular weight of the polymer obtained is independent of the temperature of reaction, but varies inversely with the concentration of the catalyst (*220, 463*). These observations are supported by the data of Table V. Experimentally the reaction times were variable, but all exceeded the requirements for complete equilibration at the temperature given.

As might be expected, the rate of polymerization increases with increase in temperature (*220*). This is indicated in Table VI, particularly by com-

TABLE V

Dependence of Molecular Weight upon Catalyst Concentration in Polymerization of $(Me_2SiO)_4$ with Me_3SiOK^a

Si/K	Temp. (°C)	Time	M.W.[b]
51.9	120	129 min	6400
189	77	70 hr	34,800
428	120	122 hr	58,800
1230	100	72 hr	164,000

[a] Reference (*220*).

[b] Calculated from intrinsic viscosity data according to Barry's equation (*30*).

TABLE VI

EFFECT OF TEMPERATURE UPON RATE OF POLYMERIZATION OF
$(Me_2SiO)_4$ WITH $Me_3SiOK^{a,b}$

Temp. (°C)	Time	Per cent cyclic polymerized
77	6 hr	60
77	18 hr	86
100	3 hr	72
120	45 min	86
171	5 min	85

[a] Reference (*220*).
[b] Ratio of Si/K = ~190.

parison of the three experiments that were carried to the same conversion of octamethylcyclotetrasiloxane to polymer.

The rate of polymerization is proportional to the square root of catalyst concentration (*186, 254*). This is documented by the data of Table VII for the polymerization of $(Me_2SiO)_4$ using KOH as catalyst; a reasonably constant value is obtained when the rate constants are divided by the square root of the catalyst molality.

The rate of polymerization depends also on the particular cyclic used because of variations in the degree of ring strain in the molecule, steric factors, and electronic influences. As already mentioned, the six-membered cyclics such as hexamethylcyclotrisiloxane are considerably strained and, therefore, react more rapidly than the higher membered cyclics (*220, 383*).

TABLE VII

RATE OF POLYMERIZATION OF $(Me_2SiO)_4$ WITH KOH AT 152.6°C AS A FUNCTION OF CATALYST CONCENTRATION^a

Si/K	Rate const. k (min^{-1})	$C^{\frac{1}{2} \, b}$	$k/C^{\frac{1}{2}}$
34,400	0.021	1.98×10^{-2}	1.06
10,700	0.038	3.5×10^{-2}	1.09
5620	0.047	4.8×10^{-2}	0.979
3600	0.0625	6.1×10^{-2}	1.03
2440	0.076	7.4×10^{-2}	1.03

[a] Reference (*186*).
[b] C = molal concentration of KOH.

TABLE VIII

RATE OF POLYMERIZATION OF DIMETHYL CYCLICS AT 77°C[a]

Cyclic	Si/K	Time	Per cent polymerized
D₃	188	3 min	96
D₄	190	6 hr	60
D₄	190	18 hr	86

[a] Reference (220).

The data in Table VIII show that the hexamethylcyclotrisiloxane is more than a hundred times as reactive as the octamethylcyclotetrasiloxane. The effect of electronic influences as well as ring strain is illustrated by the polymerization of 1,3,5-trifluoropropyl-1,3,5-trimethylcyclotrisiloxane, $(F_3CCH_2CH_2MeSiO)_3$, which under comparable conditions is about four to five times as reactive as $(Me_2SiO)_3$ and about four hundred times as reactive as $(Me_2SiO)_4$ in base-catalyzed polymerizations (324). The strong electron-withdrawing effect of the trifluoropropyl group facilitates nucleophilic attack at the silicon atom (see also Sections II,C,1,a and 2,a).* Additional evidence for the effect of electronegative groups upon reactivity of cyclics has been shown in copolymerization studies (287). For example, hexaphenylcyclotrisiloxane is about 25 times as reactive as hexamethylcyclotrisiloxane toward base-catalyzed polymerization at 25°C.

In many instances, the molecular weights of hydroxy-end-blocked gums may be increased still further by azeotropic removal of water with toluene or by heating the polymer under vacuum. Catalysts such as amine salts or metal salts like lead octoate or dibutyltin dilaurate also increase the molecular weight by promoting condensation.

F. Copolymerization

Linear organosiloxane copolymers are prepared by the same methods as the homopolymers, i.e., direct hydrolysis and condensation of mixtures of the appropriate dichlorosilanes, or equilibration of mixtures of cyclic siloxanes (218), or mixtures of linear polysiloxanes (218) as summarized in Eq. (107). The mechanism of reaction and factors governing copolymerization are essentially the same as for homopolymer formation but two complications peculiar to copolymer systems become evident. Any marked

---

* Similar electronic effects have been observed in silanes, RR_aR_bSiH, which contain electronegative groups. Their alkali-catalyzed hydrolyses proceed at rates proportional to the electron-withdrawing ability of the substituent groups (422, 423).

differences in reactivities, due to steric effects, inductive effects, and ring strain in the species to be equilibrated, may favor homopolymerization of the more reactive species rather than copolymerization of the mixture;

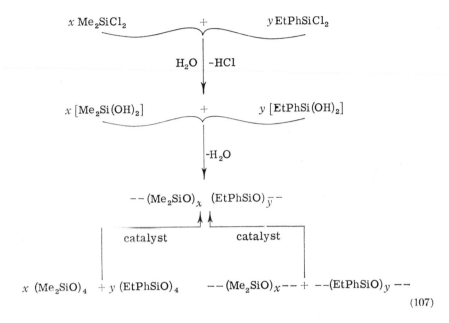

$$(107)$$

also, any physical inhomogeneity, due to incompatibility of the initial components or separation of a second phase during the equilibration, may interfere with the formation of copolymers. Some of these difficulties may be expediently controlled, for example, by using a strained cyclic to compensate for weak inductive effect or unfavorable geometry of the substituent groups (*225*), or by employing a mutual solvent and/or higher reaction temperature to ensure homogeneity of the system. Perhaps the best method for the preparation of uniform copolymers resides in the polymerization of a cyclic of mixed structure (III) containing the desired

$$\begin{array}{c}
R_1 \diagdown \quad O \diagdown \quad \diagup R_3 \\
\quad Si \quad \quad Si \\
R_2 \diagup \; | \quad \quad | \; \diagdown R_4 \\
O \diagdown \quad \diagup O \\
\quad Si \\
\diagup \quad \diagdown \\
R_3 \quad \quad R_4
\end{array}$$

(III)

building units. The required starting material may be prepared by any of several methods usually used for making cyclosiloxanes (*369, 444, 492*).

G. Elastomers

The largest single use of high molecular weight polysiloxane gums is in the preparation of silicone elastomers. The manufacture of silicone rubber is divided essentially into two steps—*compounding* and *cross-linking*. The first step consists of the intimate mixing under high shear or milling of the polysiloxane gum, a filler, and usually a crosslinking agent, together with miscellaneous additives for obtaining desired physical properties; a typical formulation would include 100 parts of a benzene-soluble polymer, 20–50 parts silica filler, up to 6 parts peroxide vulcanizing agent, and 10 parts or less miscellaneous additives (*461, 462, 469, 488*). The second step involves the cross-linking and curing processes that connect the polymer molecules with one another into an elastomeric mass of the desired properties.

The polysiloxane gum should be a linear polymer of high molecular weight; the tensile strength of the elastomer increases with the size of the polymer up to a molecular weight of about $1\frac{1}{2}$ million, at which point it appears to level off (*469*). For best thermal stability, the gum should be free of catalyst residues; cyclic siloxanes, solvents, and any other low boiling materials should be removed in a devolatilization step.

Fillers are added in order to reinforce the polysiloxane gum which, by itself, is soft and weak even at high molecular weight. To avoid degradation of the polymer, the filler must be neutral. Fillers are divided into weakly reinforcing or "dead" fillers and highly reinforcing or active fillers. Stocks containing the first type of fillers may yield rubbers with tensile strengths of 300 to 800 psi, whereas use of the latter type may give 1200–1400 psi.

Among the weakly reinforcing fillers are natural silicas, titanium dioxide, zinc oxide, ferric oxide, or calcium carbonate.

The active fillers are synthetic silicas made by two quite different processes, wet and dry. The wet process starts with waterglass, which is acidified to give first a silica sol and then an incompletely condensed and highly hydrated gel:

$$Na_2O \cdot 3\ SiO_{4/2} \cdot x\ H_2O + 2\ HCl_{aq.} \rightarrow 3\ SiO_{4/2} \cdot x\ H_2O + 2\ NaCl \qquad (108)$$

The silica aquagel is dehydrated by techniques that guard against collapse or shrinkage of the structure. Alternatively, calcium chloride may be added to the waterglass to give a complex hydrated calcium polysilicate, from which the calcium is then leached by hydrochloric acid. The dry process comprises "burning" silicon tetrachloride in a mixture of hydrogen and oxygen [Eq. (109)], which is virtually a high temperature vaporphase

$$SiCl_4 + 2\ H_2O \rightarrow SiO_2 + 4\ HCl \qquad (109)$$

hydrolysis. Both methods yield dry powders with very high surface areas, in the range of 300 square meters per gram. In commerce they are often referred to as "silica soots." To a small extent, carbon blacks are also used as reinforcing fillers.

The mechanism of filler action is still incompletely understood. The interaction between polysiloxane and an active silica filler is affected by the structure of the filler, its state of subdivision, the nature of its surface, especially the number and kinds of reactive groups like hydroxyl present on it, as well as by possible other factors not yet recognized. The reinforcement could involve scission of the polymer chain by the filler, condensation of silanol groups in the filler with those of the polymer, van der Waals' forces, or possibly other factors. Polymer-filler interaction may be strong and rapid, so much so that the useful shelf life of the raw stocks may be quite short because of "crepe aging," the development of rubbery properties prior to intentional vulcanization.

In order to control "crepe aging," additives such as diphenylsilanediol or certain pinacols are included in silicone-rubber stocks (*188, 487*). Addition of certain other materials to the compounds results in improvements in specific physical properties of the resulting rubbers. Among these miscellaneous additives are: compounds that increase thermal stability, as ferric oxide or octoate; those that reduce compression set, as cadmium oxide; and pigments, as colored inorganic oxides.

The final physical properties of a silica-filled polysiloxane depend greatly upon the amount of shear or milling it has undergone. The data of Table IX show how the milling of such a mixture results in degradation of the polymer. In contrast, prolonged milling of unfilled polysiloxane gum has little effect upon its molecular weight.

TABLE IX

EFFECT OF MILLING ON PROPERTIES OF SILICA-FILLED POLYSILOXANES[a]

Composition		Milling time (min)	Polymer M.W.
$(Me_2SiO)_x$ polymer	Aerosil[b]		
5 gm	—	None	458,000
5	2	6.5	232,000
5	2	36.5	108,000
5	2	120.0	69,000

[a] Reference (*211*).
[b] Approximately 200 meters^2/gm surface area.

The compounded stock may be cross-linked by any of several methods, the most common of which is the action of an organic peroxide, usually benzoyl peroxide, 2,4-dichlorobenzoyl peroxide, or *tert*-butyl perbenzoate. With benzoyl peroxide, vulcanization is carried out at 120 to 130°C; the substitution of two chlorine atoms on the benzene ring permits lowering the vulcanization temperature to 110°C. The perester requires a temperature of 150°C. With these catalysts, the mechanism of cross-linking utilizes phenylcarboxy and phenyl free radicals successively generated by the thermal decomposition of the peroxides [Eq. (110)]. Either of these may abstract hydrogen from methyl groups on silicon, leading to the formation of $\equiv SiCH_2\cdot$ free radicals as illustrated in Eq. (111). Two such

$$\left(\underset{PhC-O-}{\overset{O}{\underset{\|}{}}}\right)_2 \rightarrow 2\ Ph\overset{O}{\overset{\|}{C}}O\cdot \rightarrow 2\ Ph\cdot + 2\ CO_2 \qquad (110)$$

$$Ph\overset{O}{\overset{\|}{C}}-O\cdot + \left(\underset{CH_3}{\overset{CH_3}{-Si-O-}}\right)_x \rightarrow \left(\underset{CH_2\cdot}{\overset{CH_3}{-Si-O-}}\right)_x + PhCO_2H \qquad (111)$$

radicals unite to form a primary crosslink through a silethylene bridge (Eq. 112). Since the crosslinking reaction is not a chain reaction, one cross-

$$\left(\underset{CH_2\cdot}{\overset{CH_3}{-Si-O-}}\right)_x + \left(\underset{CH_2\cdot}{\overset{CH_3}{-Si-O-}}\right)_y \rightarrow \left(\underset{}{\overset{O}{CH_3Si-}}\right)_x CH_2CH_2\left(\underset{}{\overset{O}{-SiCH_3}}\right)_y \qquad (112)$$

link at most can be formed by the decomposition of one molecule of peroxide, so that the number of cross-links can be controlled by varying the amount of peroxide used. A major disadvantage of peroxides as vulcanization initiators is the formation of by-products, among them benzene, carbon dioxide, and benzoic acid. The first two are volatilized in postcuring, sometimes leaving voids; carbon dioxide can also contribute to siloxane rearrangements (*307*). Benzoic acid remains in the elastomer, resulting in poor electrical properties and in polymer degradation detected by stress-relaxation studies (*228, 307, 437*, p. 260).

A decrease in the amount of peroxide needed and better control of cross-linking, with resulting improved physical properties in the elastomer, are obtained by introducing into the polymer less than 1% of vinyl groups, either as difunctional (IV) or as monofunctional (V) groups (*239, 278, 333, 338*). Vinyl-specific cross-linking agents are di-*tert*-butyl peroxide, which requires a vulcanizing temperature of 170°C, dicumyl peroxide, which requires 150°C, and a newer diperoxide, 2,5-dimethyl-2,5-di(*tert*-butyl-

ing by gamma radiation from Co^{60} (*149*) or by accelerated electrons from a Van de Graaff generator (*150*). Cross-linking by irradiation gives elastomers whose ultimate physical properties are comparable to or slightly better than those of peroxide-vulcanized stocks. No foreign materials are added to the stocks, and thus no harmful residues remain in the finished rubber. The cross-links formed may be through oxygen or carbon bridges, depending on the environment during irradiation and cure. The number of cross-links (as measured by modulus) increases with dose received. The tensile strengths depend upon the total dose and upon the relative amounts of chain scission and cross-linking which occur.

The efficiency of cross-linking (cross-links formed per unit of radiation received) with gamma radiation is strongly dependent upon sample composition; for instance, the presence of vinyl groups on silicon increases the efficiency, whereas that of aromatic groups (free radical sinks) has the opposite effect, as does the presence of air or of crystalline species within the samples. Time effects are observed due to the presence of somewhat stable active sites, but subsequent heat curing increases the efficiency and gives reproducible ultimate properties. Since gamma rays are highly penetrating, relatively thick samples may be cross-linked in this manner.

Accelerated electrons are much more efficient in producing cross-links in polysiloxanes than is gamma radiation. Oxygen inhibition is no problem in this method, because the high intensities that may be obtained from a Van de Graaff generator and the high localized heating of the sample combine to give cross-linking rates much greater than the rate of diffusion of air into the samples. Unfortunately, since accelerated electrons have poor penetrating power, this method is limited to use on relatively thin samples.

The silicon-hydride addition reaction to vinyl-containing siloxanes (Section II,A,3) may also be used to crosslink polysiloxanes [Eq. (120)]

$$(-MeHSiO-)_x + \left(\begin{array}{c} | \\ MeSi-CH=CH_2 \\ | \\ O \\ | \end{array} \right)_y \xrightarrow{\text{catalyst}} \left(\begin{array}{c} | \\ O \\ | \\ MeSi- \\ | \end{array} \right)_x \left(\begin{array}{c} | \\ O \\ | \\ -CH_2-CH_2-SiMe \\ | \end{array} \right)_y$$

(120)

(*414*). The hydride and vinyl groups may be on terminal or chain silicons; they can both be in the same molecule or each in a different one. The catalyst may be platinum or peroxides.

Of commercial importance is the room temperature-vulcanizing method which utilizes reactive groups such as silanol or alkoxysilyl groups (*60, 246, 334, 396, 453*). Suitable catalysts such as organo-lead and -tin compounds promote condensation of silanols to give elastomers which are cross-linked through siloxane bridges. Equation (121) illustrates a reaction capable of yielding a cross-linked elastomer at room temperature. The remaining

$$3 \text{ HO}(\text{Me}_2\text{SiO}{-})_x\text{H} + \text{RSi}(\text{OR}')_3 \xrightarrow{\text{catalyst}} \underset{\underset{\displaystyle \text{O}(\text{Me}_2\text{SiO})_x\text{H}}{\diagdown}}{\overset{\overset{\displaystyle \text{O}(\text{Me}_2\text{SiO})_x\text{H}}{\diagup}}{\text{R}{-}\underset{}{\text{Si}}{-}\text{O}(\text{Me}_2\text{SiO})_x\text{H}}} + 3 \text{ R}'\text{OH} \qquad (121)$$

silanol groups are available for further similar reactions with more $\text{RSi}(\text{OR}')_3$.

H. Resins

Silicone resins are characterized by the presence of ring structures and by much higher density of cross-linking than is found in siloxane elastomers. In a stressed elastomer the molecular chains uncoil through rotation about the siloxane bonds; in a resin such rotation is highly restricted, and response to stress occurs mostly by bending and stretching of the bonds.

The contribution of the siloxane skeleton to the properties of the resin is determined by two factors: the functionality, determined by the ratio of substituent groups to silicon atoms, R/Si, and the extent to which the functionality is used in cross-linking. As the R/Si ratio is lowered from 2.0 to 1.0, the polymers become progressively less fluid, less fusible, and less soluble, depending on the effective crosslinking. When R/Si is 1.0, if all the functionality were used in random crosslinking, a brittle, infusible, and insoluble product would be obtained; when, at the same R/Si ratio, special techniques give systematically ordered intramolecular SiOSi bonds, "cage" structures and the quasilinear "ladder" polymers (87,) shown in Fig. 1 may be obtained as flexible, fusible, and soluble products. Most resins have R/Si ratios between 1.0 and 1.6, and structures resembling that drawn in Fig. 1, in analogy to the structure of glass, with part of the functionality used in formation of ring structures, and part in cross-linking. Accordingly, their properties are intermediate between those of a fluid and those expected of a highly cross-linked structure with R/Si equal to 1.0.

The first silicone resins were prepared by partial oxidation of difunctional structures (*212, 219*), but this method is now of historical interest only. The availability of individual organochlorosilanes in commercial quantities made possible the preparation of resins by direct hydrolysis of known mixtures of RSiCl_3 and R_2SiCl_2 in the desired ratios, with subsequent condensation of silanol groups (*356*). The process can be summarized as follows: the chlorosilane mixture is hydrolyzed, the hydrolyzate is separated, and the organic layer is washed, stripped to the desired solids content, and sometimes treated to induce further condensation of silanols.

In the hydrolysis step the chlorosilanes most used are $MeSiCl_3$, $PhSiCl_3$, Me_2SiCl_2, $PhMeSiCl_2$, and Ph_2SiCl_2. Equations (67) and (68) (Section II,C,1,a) illustrate such a reaction. Hydrolysis of mixtures of chlorosilanes having an average functionality greater than 2.0 is difficult to effect without the occurrence of at least some gelation through rapid and premature condensation of silanol groups. To minimize it the chlorosilane mixture is hydrolyzed slowly by addition to water, usually in the presence of a solvent, and the temperature during hydrolysis is controlled. The presence of a solvent helps also to control condensation in subsequent treatment of the resin and to facilitate handling and application of the finished resin. The solvents most used are toluene and xylene.

During the hydrolysis reaction about 90% of the silanol groups condense to siloxane linkages. In this process of random condensation some ring closure must occur, because of the extreme flexibility of SiOSi chains. To a slight extent this may result in the formation of cyclic siloxanes such as D_4 and D_5, or of various modifications of cage structures having molecular weights low enough that they are volatilized during cure. Clearly the probability of the formation of such materials is low when R/Si is low. Sometimes a trifunctional unit may take part in a ring closure of the type:

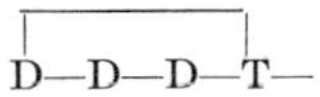

$$D-D-D-T-$$

Such structures may act as effective monofunctional components, limiting the molecular weights of the resins. In many cases, difunctional (VI) or polyfunctional (VII) rings may form parts of the polymer chains, giving

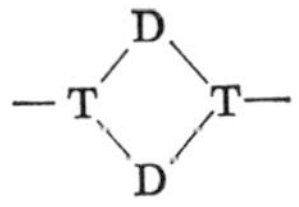

(VI) 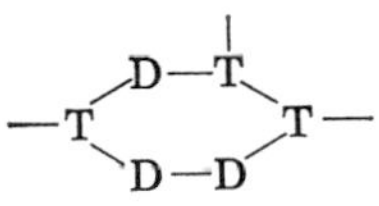   (VII)

multicyclic structures like that shown for glass in Fig. 1. Such modified chains lack the flexibility characteristic of purely linear chains, but because of their presence any silicone resin is much more flexible than would be the hypothetical one of the same average functionality, with all of the functionality used in cross-linking.

The remaining 10% of the silanol groups condense more slowly, with increasing difficulty. From a physical standpoint, as the number of silanol groups decreases, it becomes more difficult to effect condensation. Statistically, fewer fruitful molecular collisions can occur, and the increased viscosity hinders molecular motion. Furthermore, with growing polymer size the remaining hydroxyls become fixed in the network too far apart to condense with one another. For different silanol structures such as (VIII) to (XII) the condensation is in general faster for the more highly functional

```
        Me                              Me
        |                               |
  ---OSi---                      ---OSi—OH
        |                               |
        OH                              OH

      (VIII)                           (IX)
```

```
              Me
              |
       ----OSi—OH
              |
              Me

             (X)
```

```
        Ph                              Ph
        |                               |
  ---OSiO---                     ---OSi—OH
        |                               |
        OH                              OH

       (XI)                            (XII)
```

units and for those containing methyl rather than phenyl substitution. In any case, some silanol groups remain.

At the completion of the hydrolysis step the separated organic layer is washed free of chloride, both dissolved HCl and chemically bound chlorine. Though the equilibrium lies far to the right, the hydrolysis of chlorosilanes is a reversible reaction, and therefore in the presence of HCl some chlorine end blocking of the polymer persists. Exhaustive washing with water converts residual chlorosilane bonds to silanols.

The concentration of these residual silanol groups, both from the initial hydrolysis and the water washing, may be lowered by further treatment. In some cases, depending on the formulation and on the end use, the resin is "bodied" by heating at 120 to 200°C with or without a catalyst. In this step more silanol groups are condensed to siloxane linkages, with resulting increase in molecular weight and viscosity through formation of more cross-links.

The silanol groups remaining in the finished resin are critical for its properties. They contribute to the viscosity. Different applications require resins of various viscosities; a laminating resin is usually relatively thin so that it will better impregnate glass fibers, whereas a paint resin must be thicker so that it will adhere to a surface instead of running off. The silanol groups also determine the stability, or shelf life, of the resin. In storage, resins are constantly undergoing condensation and cross-linking reactions, at a rate determined by the temperature, the resin concentration, and the nature and number of substituent groups on silicon. In dilute solutions silanol condensations occur more slowly than in concentrated solutions, but in dry, solventless resins they are minimized due to relative immobility of the silanol groups.

The final cure of the resin involves further reaction of residual silanol groups; their ultimate condensation occurs after the resin is applied. This may be hastened by heating with suitable catalysts. Those most commonly used are metal salts of organic acids that are soluble in organic media, especially the 2-ethylhexoates and naphthenates of tin, lead, cobalt, zinc, and iron. Certain organic amines and quaternary compounds have also been used. Peroxides are not generally used to cure silicone resins. Since many cross-links are required, which is not the case for an elastomer, and one peroxide molecule produces at most only one cross-link, an exorbitant amount of peroxide would be required and the properties of the resin would be drastically impaired. Resins that contain allyl and, especially, vinyl groups on silicon, however, may be cured with minor amounts of peroxides at moderate temperatures.

The properties of silicone resins depend on the ratio of R/Si, the nature of R, and the method of hydrolysis and curing. With increasing R/Si values, the decreasing degree of cross-linking may give properties varying from glass-like to rubbery. Methyl substituents in the difunctional portion of the formulation give flexibility to a resin and thus are unsuitable components for a rigid resin. Increasing the chain length of alkyl substituents makes the resin softer, increases its solubility in organic solvents and its water repellency, and decreases its stability to heat. Phenyl substituents impart heat stability to a resin but, except for the "ladder" polymers, pure phenyl resins generally are solids too fusible and too brittle for most applications. Improved properties can be obtained in copolymeric resins which contain both phenyl and methyl groups.

The general properties of silicone resins are summarized in Table X. Many of these properties are obviously attractive for practical purposes and need not be elaborated upon at this point. In many instances, the qualities noted as "poor" can be improved by blending with conventional organic resins with little, if any, sacrifice of some other desirable properties. Thus the appropriate hybrid of a silicone resin and an alkyd resin may show quite improved hardness, toughness, and adhesion yet retain satisfactory thermal stability, intermediate between the parent values. Some silicone resins, especially those rich in phenyl groups, are compatible with organic

TABLE X

GENERAL PROPERTIES OF SILICONE RESINS

Excellent	Satisfactory	Poor
Thermal resistance	Moisture resistance	Hardness
Oxidative resistance	Flexibility	Toughness
Chemical resistance	Electrical properties	Adhesion
Color	Gloss	Solvent resistance
Color retention		
Gloss retention		
Weatherability		

resins and the two types may simply be mixed together for many uses. When they are incompatible, copolymerization may be necessary to afford a satisfactory product.

Copolymers may be prepared by the reaction of residual silanol groups or alkoxy groups in polysiloxanes with suitable functional groups in organic resins or organic compounds. For example, silanol groups in a silicone resin will react with the hydroxyl groups in an organic resin as illustrated in Eq. (122) for an alkyd of glycerine and phthalic acid. The two resins are heated together with or without a solvent until compatibility and the desired viscosity is achieved. Condensation of silanol groups to siloxane

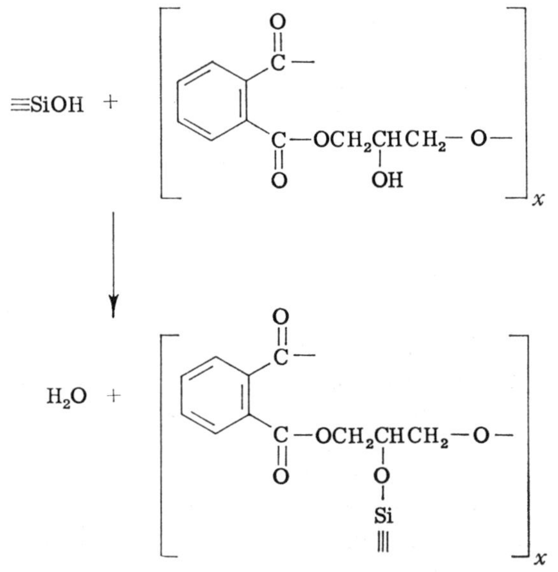

$$(122)$$

linkages instead of to Si—O—C bonds may complicate this method. This difficulty may be overcome by using an alkoxy group in place of the hydroxyl group on silicon [Eq. (123)]. By use of this type of ester inter-

$$\equiv\text{SiOR} \quad + \quad \begin{bmatrix} ---\text{CH}--- \\ | \\ \text{OH} \end{bmatrix}_x \quad \longrightarrow \quad \begin{bmatrix} ---\text{CH}--- \\ | \\ \text{OSi}\equiv \end{bmatrix}_x \quad + \quad \text{ROH}$$

(123)

change, silicone resins may be copolymerized with phenolic, polyester, epoxy, cellulosic, and other functional resins. It is apparent that from a few ingredients it is possible to prepare many modified resins whose properties should vary depending on the nature of the polysiloxane, the organics, the order of reaction, and the degree of condensation.

III. Properties of Organopolysiloxanes

Organopolysiloxanes are characterized by combinations of chemical, mechanical, and electrical properties not common to any other class of polymers. Particularly true of the polysiloxanes containing methyl and phenyl groups on silicon, their high thermal and oxidative stabilities, insolubility in water, relative inertness to many ionic reagents, unique rheological properties, high dielectric strength, and low power loss, among other desirable properties, arouse interest from the academic as well as the technological point of view. These properties can be explained by examining both the nature of the chemical bonds and the geometry of the structures involved.

A. Properties Dependent upon Chemical Bond Considerations

1. General Considerations

Both carbon and silicon have a normal valence of 4, but here the similarity between the two elements ends. Unlike carbon, silicon can expand its octet and in some compounds such as the hexafluorosilicate ion, SiF_6^{2-}, has a coordination number of 6. The bond strengths, bond lengths, and ionic nature are different for carbon and silicon compounds. Table XI lists the average bond energies for various silicon and carbon bonds. It is apparent that bonds of silicon to oxygen, nitrogen, and the halogens are all stronger than corresponding bonds involving carbon. The silicon-oxygen bond, especially, is much stronger than the carbon-oxygen bond

TABLE XI

BOND ENERGIES (KCAL/MOLE)[a]

Bond[b]	Energy	Bond	Energy
Si—Si	53	C—C	82.6
Si—C	78	—	—
Si—O	106	C—O	85.5
Si—H	76	C—H	98.7
Si—N	—[c]	C—N	72.8
Si—F	135	C—F	116
Si—Cl	91	C—Cl	81
Si—Br	74	C—Br	68
Si—I	56	C—I	51

[a] Reference (*121*); cf. also (*316*).

[b] The difficulties in securing complete oxidation to SiO_2 in combustion bomb calorimetry may subject the silicon bond energies to minor revisions.

[c] Recent work suggests that the value of the silicon-nitrogen bond is 80–85 kcal/mole.

and is partially responsible for the high thermal stability of polysiloxanes. The silicon-carbon bond is intermediate in strength between a silicon-silicon bond and a carbon-carbon single bond, but its strength approaches that of the latter more closely and the difference is not sufficiently great to account for the differences in the properties of silicones and hydrocarbons. The ease of oxidation of polysilanes compared to hydrocarbons is illustrated by the release of about 53 kcal/mole in going from a silicon-silicon bond to a silicon-oxygen linkage, while only about 3 kcal/mole is released in going from a carbon-carbon single bond to a carbon-oxygen bond. The relatively large energy release in going from silicon-chlorine, -bromine, or -iodine bonds to silicon-oxygen bonds accounts in part for the greater sensitivity to hydrolysis of these halosilanes as contrasted to the corresponding organic halides. The energy input necessary to transform a silicon-fluorine bond to a silicon-oxygen bond (29 kcal/mole) accounts also in part for the relative difficulty of hydrolysis of fluorosilanes compared to the other halosilanes.

Silicon in most of its compounds is decidedly electropositive when compared to carbon and oxygen. Pauling has estimated the relative electronegativities of silicon 1.8, carbon 2.5, and oxygen 3.5 (*316*). Based upon the assumption that the ionic character of a covalent bond is caused by an unequal sharing of electrons, two empirical equations have been suggested which relate the ionic character of a covalent bond to the electronegativity differences of the bonded atoms. Table XII shows the relative ionic character of silicon and carbon bonds to other atoms as developed by Pauling

TABLE XII

PARTIAL IONIC CHARACTER OF VARIOUS SILICON AND CARBON BONDS

Bond	$(X_A - X_{Si})$	Ionic character (%)		Bond	$(X_A - X_C)$	Ionic character (%)	
		a	b			a	b
Si—C	0.7	12	13	—		—	—
Si—O	1.7	51	37	C—O	1.0	22	20
Si—H	0.3	3	5	C—H	−0.4	4	7
Si—N	1.2	30	24	C—N	0.5	7	9
Si—F	2.2	70	52	C—F	1.5	43	32
Si—Cl	1.2	30	24	C—Cl	0.5	7	9
Si Br	1.0	22	20	C—Br	0.3	3	5
Si—I	0.7	12	13	C—I	0	0	0

[a] Pauling (*316*): amount of ionic character $= 1 - \exp\{\frac{1}{4}(X_A - X_B)^2\}$.

[b] Hannay and Smyth (*189*): amount of ionic character $= 0.16(X_A - X_B) + 0.035(X_A - X_B)^2$, where X_A and X_B are the relative electronegativity values of Pauling (*316*).

(*316*) and Hannay and Smyth (*189*). The pronounced ionic character of silicon-element bonds when compared to the corresponding carbon-element bond is at once apparent. Most noteworthy is the predicted high partial ionic character of the silicon-oxygen bond, 37–51%, especially when compared to the carbon-oxygen, 20–22%, and the essentially nonionic carbon-carbon bond. This large fraction of ionic character has been suggested as the source of many of the properties of polysiloxanes such as thermal stability, ease of acid- and base-catalyzed rearrangements, and optical properties (*202, 468, 489*). However, the silicon-oxygen bond, although much more polar than the carbon-oxygen bond, is probably less ionic than predicted, because of oxygen-silicon dative p_π, d_π bonding. The latter effect, which must be important (see Introduction to this book), is not allowed for in the empirical equations used to estimate relative ionic character.

Additional evidence for the ionic nature of silicon-oxygen and silicon-carbon bonds in siloxanes may be found upon examining the corresponding bond distances. The atomic radii are silicon 1.17, carbon 0.77, and oxygen 0.66 (*316*). (A value of 0.74 A has also been reported for the atomic radius of oxygen (*293*, p. 135; *379*).) Table XIII shows the calculated bond distances for silicon-oxygen, silicon-carbon, and carbon-carbon bonds based upon the additivity of atomic radii. The value found for the silicon-oxygen bond in a siloxane is considerably less than the calculated value and is

TABLE XIII

BOND DISTANCES

Bond	Calcd. (A)	Found (A)
Si—O	1.83	1.63,[a] 1.64,[b] 1.65,[c] 1.66[d]
Si—C	1.94	1.88,[a,d,e] 1.92,[c] 1.93[f]
C—O	1.43	1.36–1.47[g]
C—C	1.54	1.52–1.55[h]

[a] In $(Me_3Si)_2O$ *(490)*.
[b] In $Si(OMe)_4$ and $(Cl_3Si)_2O$ *(490)*.
[c] In $(Me_2SiO)_4$ *(420)*.
[d] In $(Me_2SiO)_3$ *(420)*.
[e] In octamethylspiro[5.5]pentasiloxane *(362)*.
[f] In Me_4Si *(293, p. 133)*.
[g] In paraffinic, heterocyclic, and aromatic compounds and epoxides *(426)*.
[h] In many saturated hydrocarbons *(293, p. 133)*.

indicative of the presence of considerable ionic and/or double bond character. The great intensity of the infrared spectral bands for the Si—O linkage also confirms the large ionic character of this bond *(489)*. A small amount of ionic character is similarly indicated for the silicon-carbon bond in several siloxanes, but not in the cyclic tetramer or the symmetrical compound Me_4Si, as might have been expected from electronegativity values. Although no compound has been reported in which a p_π, p_π double bond is attached to silicon, partial double bond character (d_π, p_π) has been attributed to the bonds in halosilanes in order to explain the discrepancies between calculated and observed bond lengths *(316, p. 310 ff.)*. Such resonance considerations might also contribute to bond shortening in polysiloxanes. (A silacyclopentadiene anion, an aromatic system containing silicon, has been reported recently *(57a)*. It presumably owes its existence to considerable resonance stabilization and consequent partial double bond character between silicon and carbon.)

2. High Temperature Properties

a. Thermal and Flame Resistance. Outstanding thermal stability is one of the most important properties of polysiloxanes. The bond energies presented in Table XI suggest the large amount of thermal resistance contributed to a polysiloxane by the "backbone" of the polymer. The large amount of ionic character in the silicon-oxygen bond also contributes to the thermal stability. Under high vacuum or in an inert atmosphere and under rigorously clean conditions highly pure polysiloxanes are stable to about 350 to 400°C, where the siloxane bonds are ruptured and then recombine to give volatile products. For example, in a platinum container, a pure poly(dimethylsiloxane) may show less than 10% weight loss after eight hours at 363°C under high vacuum (*261*). From a practical standpoint, however, the thermal stability is considerably less. For example, commercial grade poly(dimethylsiloxanes) with a viscosity of 100 cs (= centistokes) or greater are stable for long periods of time to about 200°C. The practical thermal stability depends not only upon the energies and ionic strengths of the bonds involved but also upon the cross-link densities of the polymer (i.e., fluid, elastomer, or resin), the environment, and the time limit of stability. The environment embraces several parameters such as moisture (hydrolytic stability), oxygen and other oxidizing species, oxidation inhibitors, rearrangement catalysts, and trace impurities (*261, 262*). Phenyl substituents in place of methyl on silicon improve the heat stability of the polymer (*296*).

The flash points and autoignition temperatures for several siloxane fluids are listed in Table XIV. Siloxanes, even the most simple ones, are not readily burned under ordinary conditions. They possess definite flash points but not definite flame points, i.e., external heat must be supplied

TABLE XIV[a]

DIMETHYLSILOXANE FLASH POINTS[b] AND AUTOIGNITION TEMPERATURES[c]

Siloxane	Viscosity at 25°C (cs)	Flash point minimum (°C)	Autoignition temp.	
			Vol.[d]	°C
MM	0.65	−1	e	—
MDM	1	43	10	418
MD$_2$M	1.5	71	—	—
MD$_3$M	2	79	3	430
—	3	102	3	438
—	5	135	0.5	443
—	10	163	0.5	452
—	20	271	0.5	476
—	50	279	0.5	488
—	100	302	0.5	>490
—	>100	316	—	—

[a] Based upon Dow Corning Corporation 200 Fluids.
[b] Open cup, ASTM D92–33.
[c] ASTM D286–30.
[d] Smallest volume in ml that will ignite at autoignition temperature.
[e] Evaporated before ignition.

constantly for them to burn. This is not too surprising when one considers that the silicon in a polysiloxane is already one half oxidized to SiO_2. The high molecular weight polysiloxanes themselves do not burn but undergo thermal depolymerization to yield more volatile siloxanes which can be burned. Substitution of hydrogen for methyl groups greatly increases the ease of combustion, as shown by the flammability of *sym*-tetramethyldisiloxane.

b. Boiling Points and Volatility. The lower members of the polysiloxane series are volatile liquids easily separated by distillation at atmospheric pressure (Table III). The boiling points of the cyclic polymers are somewhat lower than the corresponding linear siloxanes containing the same number of silicon atoms. This difference is probably due not to the difference in molecular shape but to the slightly higher molecular weight of 14 units for each linear molecule. Figure 2 compares the boiling point variation with molecular weight for representative hydrocarbons and dimethylsiloxane polymers. Clearly for polymers of the same molecular weight the poly(dimethylsiloxane) exhibits the lower boiling point. The silicone polymers exhibit smaller coefficients of boiling point elevation with molecu-

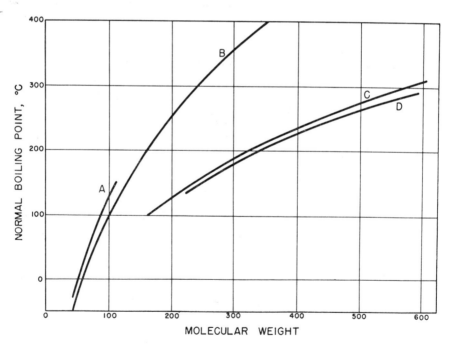

Fig. 2. Boiling point dependency on molecular weight (*202*): (A) cyclic alkanes, (B) normal hydrocarbons, (C) linear $Me_3SiO(Me_2SiO)_xSiMe_3$, (D) cyclic $(Me_2SiO)_x$.

lar weight than do the hydrocarbon polymers. Vapor pressure curves have been obtained for the lower siloxane members (*479*):

For cyclics D_n where $n = 4$ to 8 and T is °K,

$$\log p_c = 7.07 - \frac{1190}{T} + \left[0.265 - \frac{294}{T}\right]n$$

For linear siloxanes $MD_{n-2}M$ where $n = 5$ to 11,

$$\log P_l = 6.28 - \frac{1030}{T} + \left[0.443 - \frac{360}{T}\right]n$$

The latent heats of vaporization were determined to be, in kcal/mole:

for cyclics, D_n, $\Delta H_{vap} = 5.45 + 1.35n$

for linears, $MD_{n-2}M$, $\Delta H_{vap} = 4.70 + 1.65n$.

With increasing number of dimethylsiloxy units the boiling points of the different linear polymers approach each other, and separation becomes increasingly more difficult. The polymeric mixtures are then referred to according to their viscosity. The fluids of 10- to 50-cs viscosity are difficult to distil even under very high vacuum. Those above 50-cs viscosity are practically nonvolatile and have no true boiling points; depolymerization to more volatile fragments occurs before the boiling points are reached. Figure 3 illustrates the relationship between relative volatility and vis-

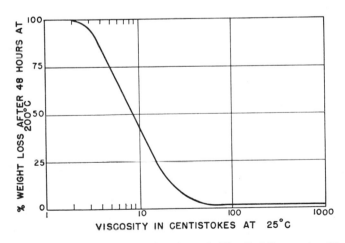

FIG. 3. Volatility-viscosity relationship for poly(dimethylsiloxanes) with a 35-gm sample in a 150-ml beaker having a bottom area of 3 in².

TABLE XV

EFFECT OF CHAIN COMPOSITION CHANGES ON BOILING POINTS OF ME₃SI—X—SIME₃

X	B.p. (°C at 760 mm)
—O—	100
—	113
—NH—	126
—CH₂—	134
—S—	163
o,*m*,*p*-Phenylene	About 230 to 240

cosity for linear polysiloxanes up to 1000 cs. Of interest is the sharp drop of volatility with increasing viscosity; polymers possessing viscosities above 50 cs have negligible vapor pressures and are essentially nonvolatile. Polysiloxanes with viscosities from 30,000 to greater than 1,000,000 cs at 25°C have less than 2% weight loss after 48 hr at 200°C—probably residual volatile cyclics.

It is of interest to observe the effect of the oxygen atom upon the boiling point of a silicon compound when compared to the effect of other groups. The data listed in Table XV show the effect on the boiling point when the oxygen atom in a disiloxane is replaced by amino, methylene, sulfur, and phenylene. Clearly the replacement of oxygen by any of the other groups raises the boiling point (*402, 441*). This behavior has been interpreted in the light of the helical structure and reduced external force fields mentioned previously (*468*).

c. Specific Heat. Table XVI shows the specific heats of several siloxane polymers as compared to water and representative organic liquids. Be-

TABLE XVI

SPECIFIC HEATS OF LIQUIDS

Poly(dimethylsiloxane)[a] viscosity (cs[b])	Specific heat (cal/gm/°C)	Compound[c]	Specific heat (cal/gm/°C)
2	0.323	Water	0.9988[20°]
10	0.360	MeOH	0.600[20°]
100	0.352	EtOH	0.581[25°]
350	0.340	Glycerine	0.57[25°]
1000	0.349	Aliphatic hydrocarbons	0.49–0.60
		Aromatic hydrocarbons	0.39–0.41

[a] Reference (*51*).
[b] At room temperature.
[c] Reference (*194*).

tween 0° and 100°C the specific heats of dimethylsiloxane polymers of 0.65- to 50-cs viscosity lie between 0.32 and 0.35 cal/gm/°C. For those polymers of viscosity 100 to 1000 cs, they lie between 0.35 to 0.37 cal/gm/°C (*434*). These values are about one third that of water and somewhat lower than those of the common alcohols and hydrocarbons.

d. Thermal Expansion. The coefficients of cubical thermal expansion of polysiloxanes decrease with increasing viscosity as shown in Fig. 4, and are of the same order of magnitude as those of benzene and ethanol and considerably greater than those of mercury and water. Substitution of phenyl groups for about half the methyl groups decreases the coefficient of thermal expansion as illustrated by curve b of Fig. 4. Ethyl substitution causes a similar decrease (*158*). Figure 5 illustrates the decrease of expansion coefficient with increasing viscosity of linear dimethylsiloxane polymers. A sharp decrease of expansion coefficient is noted with increasing viscosity until 100 cs, above which the coefficient decreases only slightly with increasing viscosity. Such behavior possibly serves to illustrate the effect upon viscosity of "diluting" the trimethylsiloxy end groups (*51*, *202*; see also *203*).

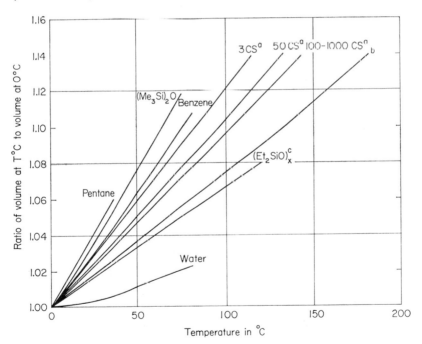

F̲ɪ̲ɢ̲. 4. Volume expansion of polysiloxanes and other liquids: (a) poly(dimethylsiloxane) fluid; (b) poly(methylphenylsiloxane) fluid, 475–525 cs; (c) poly(diethylsiloxane) fluid, 158-cs viscosity.

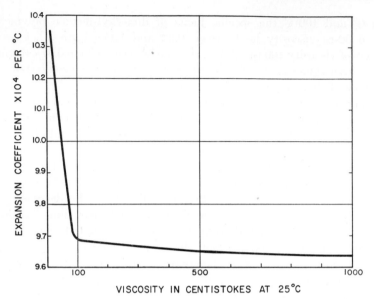

FIG. 5. Viscosity dependency of expansion coefficient for Me₃SiO(Me₂SiO)ₓSiMe₃ at 25 to 100°C.

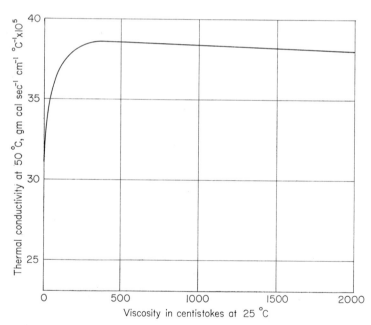

FIG. 6. Variation of thermal conductivity of poly(dimethylsiloxanes) at 50°C with viscosity.

e. Thermal Conductivity. The thermal conductivity of poly(dimethyl-siloxanes) rises with increasing viscosity up to about 200 cs. With further increasing viscosity the thermal conductivity becomes essentially constant with a maximum occurring at 350-cs viscosity. Figure 6 shows representative data for change of thermal conductivity with viscosity (*51, 71*). The thermal conductivities of poly(dimethylsiloxane) fluids of 0.65- to 12,500-cs viscosity are 2.36–3.86 $\times$ 10^{-4} gm cal sec^{-1} cm^{-1} °C^{-1} at 50°C and may be obtained from the following empirical equation for thermal conductivity as a function of viscosity and temperature:

$$K_{t\gamma} = \left[0.2387\left(\frac{4.66 + \gamma_{25} - 0.000003\ \gamma_{25}^2}{8.00 + \gamma_{25}}\right)(1663 - t°C)\right]10^{-6}$$

$$\times\ \text{gm cal sec}^{-1}\ \text{cm}^{-1}\ °\text{C}^{-1}$$

where γ_{25} is the kinematic viscosity at 25°C in centistokes (*51*). The values for the thermal conductivities of other liquids are listed in Table XVII. Thus the thermal conductivities for dimethylsiloxane polymers are of the same order of magnitude as that of benzene, slightly less than those of common alcohols, and only about one-fourth that of water. The thermal conductivity of silicone rubber has been stated to be about twice that of ordinary rubber (*283*, p. 60). The temperature coefficient of thermal conductivity of dimethylsiloxane polymers is small as contrasted to those of other liquids, and for those polymers between 0.65 and 12,500 cs it is relatively constant at about −0.06% per degree centigrade.

3. Hydrolytic and Chemical Stability

The bond energies in Table XI indicate the following order of stability for silicon-element bonds:

$$\text{SiF} > \text{SiO} > \text{SiCl} > \text{SiC, SiH}$$

TABLE XVII

THERMAL CONDUCTIVITIES OF COMMON LIQUIDS[a]

Liquid	Temp. (°C)	K(gm cal sec^{-1} cm^{-1} °C^{-1})
Water	20	1.43×10^{-3}
Benzene	5	3.33×10^{-4}
Methanol	—	4.95×10^{-4}
Ethanol	—	4.23×10^{-4}
Glycerine	9–15	6.37×10^{-4}

[a] Reference (*194*).

This order of stability, indicating that the silicon-halogen bonds are more stable than silicon-carbon bonds, holds for *homolytic* scission of the bonds and indicates relative thermal stability, but it does not explain the hydrolytic or chemical stability of polysiloxanes. Table XVIII lists the ionic bond energies for silicon-element bonds. These energies are an index to the relative ease of *heterolytic* scission. Thus, an order of stability is obtained that agrees more closely with observed chemical stability:

$$SiH > SiC > SiO > SiF > SiCl$$

For example, a chlorosilane is more readily hydrolyzed than a fluorosilane, which in turn is more readily hydrolyzed than a siloxane or silcarbane linkage. Inconsistencies in reported ionic bond energies permit only qualitative correlations.

The highly ionic character of the siloxane bond, as well as the ability of silicon to expand its valence shell, render polysiloxanes susceptible to attack by certain reagents. For example, strong bases and concentrated acids such as sulfuric, phosphoric, and hydrochloric acids cause depolymerization. Water under the extremes of heat and pressure, especially in the presence of catalyst, causes depolymerization. Some solid salts such as aluminum and ferric chlorides cleave both siloxane and silicon-carbon bonds, causing an increase in viscosity followed by ultimate gelation. Other reagents, especially under severe conditions, also cleave the carbon-silicon bond. For example, concentrated nitric acid completely oxidizes the polymer, especially at elevated temperatures. Cleavage of aromatic substituent groups by concentrated sulfuric acid may cause ultimate gelation. Dry chlorine attacks the organic groups on silicon, rendering them more unstable through chlorination, and increases the viscosity due to increased molecular weight and interactions between chains.

Polysiloxanes are relatively inert to most chemicals, with the exceptions noted above, which are rather drastic treatments. In general, aqueous

TABLE XVIII

Ionic Bond Energies[a]

Bond	Ionic bond energy (kcal/mole)	Bond	Ionic bond energy (kcal/mole)
Si—H	245.8	Si—S	187.0
Si—C	235.2	Si—Cl	186.9
Si—O	228.4	Si—Br	172.4
Si—F	220.0	Si—I	162.2

[a] References (*140*, *391*).

solutions of any kind have little effect on polysiloxanes. This behavior is more likely due to the great insolubility of water in silicones and poor wetting properties (Section III,B,5) than to the inertness of the siloxane or silicon-carbon bonds to the solutes. Thus dilute acids, metal salt solutions, dilute hydrogen peroxide, and ammonium hydroxide have little effect on the polymers. Weak acids and bases such as acetic acid, phenol, fatty acids, and liquid ammonia likewise have little effect. Sulfur dioxide, hydrocarbons, chlorinated solvents, alcohols, and ketones also do not chemically attack polysiloxanes, although many of the organic liquids may effect swelling or solution of the polymer (Section III,B,3). In general, polysiloxanes are not affected by metals at elevated temperatures and are noncorrosive to them. The effects of various metals and alloys on the stability of poly(dimethylsiloxanes) have been determined after 7 days exposure at 200°C in the presence of air by noting the viscosity changes and the amounts of formaldehyde and formic acid liberated (*20*). Copper and selenium inhibit viscosity changes, and copper, lead, and selenium inhibit oxidation. Tellurium accelerates oxidation at 200°C, but acts as an inhibitor at 225°C. Antimony, cadmium, nickel, platinum, silver, tin, zinc, Duralumin, and cold-rolled and stainless steel have no effect. Similar tests at 225°C on poly(methylphenylsiloxane) show that lead, selenium, and tellurium accelerate oxidation, while copper, antimony, Duralumin, silver, nickel, steel, zinc, and tin have no effect (*296*).

Stress-relaxation studies offer a sensitive means of studying chemical reactions of materials with polysiloxanes under various conditions in which no visible change is observed. Such delicate methods have been used to detect the reactions of residual polymerization and cross-linking catalysts, carbon dioxide, water, and filler with polysiloxane elastomers (*228, 307, 437*, p. 260).

4. Stability toward Oxygen, Ozone, and Corona Discharge

Closely associated with thermal stability (Section III,A,2) is oxidative stability, for most uses of polysiloxanes are in the presence of oxygen. As stated previously for thermal stability, oxidative stability depends upon the type of bonds, type of polymer, the environment, and the time limit of stability and should be stated in terms of a standard test.

In general, polysiloxanes are quite resistant to attack by oxygen. No significant changes attributable to oxidation occur in poly(dimethylsiloxanes) at 175°C (*20*), but oxidation takes place at 200°C as shown by viscosity changes and the evolution of formaldehyde and formic acid; even here, the higher molecular weight polymers show less than 10% change in viscosity after 16 hours (*434*). Above 200°C, susceptibility to oxidation increases greatly with increase in temperature and, at 250°C, a poly-(dimethylsiloxane) fluid will cross-link to a rubbery gel in a few hours. Under comparable conditions, a resin will exhibit much less perceptible change because it is already highly cross-linked.

The oxidative stability of polysiloxanes depends to a large extent upon the organic parts of the molecules. Aromatic groups substituted in place of methyl groups increase the oxidative stability (*12, 296*). Poly(methyl-phenylsiloxanes) show no appreciable oxidative changes at 225°C, but at 250°C the viscosities increase and the evolution of volatile oxidation products becomes significant (*296*); the composition of the volatile products indicates that the methyl groups are attacked preferentially to the phenyl groups. Oxidative stability of polysiloxanes also decreases with increasing chain length of alkyl substituents. Vinyl and hydrogen substituents also introduce oxidative instability.

Other factors may also affect the oxidative stability. The rate of oxidative degradation of certain silicone resins has been shown to be proportional to the rate of diffusion of oxygen into the sample and to the degree of crosslinking of the surface (*138*). Oxidative degradation may be inhibited for a time by the addition to the polysiloxane of small amounts of antioxidants; these presumably function as free radical "sinks" or chain stoppers (transfer agents), thereby stopping autocatalytic degradation before it progresses to the extent of seriously altering the desirable physical properties of the polymer. Chelate compounds such as the copper chelate of acetoacetic ester (*429*) and various amines and polyols (*275*) are examples of such materials.

Poly(dimethylsiloxanes) are quite resistant to attack by ozone. Such polymers show no detectable evidence of attack when treated with 1% by volume (10^4 parts per million) of ozone in oxygen for about 20 hours at temperatures up to 40 to 50°C (*56*). Above these temperatures ozone attack and degradation, detected by tensile and swelling measurements, increase with increasing temperature. The rate of ozone attack on solid samples is dependent also on the rate of diffusion of ozone into the samples. Due to the different mechanisms of attack by ozone (Section II,G) and oxygen, aromatic groups do not increase ozone resistance as they do oxygen resistance. Ozone readily attacks poly(methylphenylsiloxanes) at room temperatures, presumably by destroying the aromatic ring. As might be expected from the electrophilic mechanism of ozone attack (*26*), electron-withdrawing substituents on the phenyl rings tend to inhibit ozone attack somewhat, and electron-donating groups tend to enhance it. Vinyl and hydrogen on silicon are susceptible to ozone attack, the former reacting quickly with ozone even at −55°C.

Dimethylsiloxane polymers are resistant to corona discharge. Their resistance is almost as good as that of mica, and they have the added advantage of flexibility. The silica-filled polymers have been exposed to the ionizing effect of about 15,000 volts at room temperature as a sealant in an ozonator for several years with no apparent change in properties.

5. *Radiation Stability*

High energy radiation affects polysiloxanes, the extent of reaction depending on the type of polymer, the radiation dose, and other variables (*73, 103, 148, 259*). Molecular weight increase and cross-linking are the predominant reactions observed—fluids increase in viscosity and eventually gel; elastomers and high polymers cross-link as shown by reduced elongations and increased moduli. Tensile strengths increase initially, followed by decreasing strengths upon prolonged exposure (*149, 150, 443, 464*). Many types of radiation have been used, such as cyclotron (*464*), gamma from Co^{60} (*149, 151, 464*), X-ray (*464*), beta or accelerated electrons (*29, 88, 134, 150, 259, 288, 290, 464*), and pile radiation consisting of gamma radiation and fast and slow neutrons (*103*).

The susceptibility of polysiloxanes to radiation attack is governed to a large extent by the type of substituent groups on silicon (*148, 149, 151, 168, 190, 247, 425, 464, 494*). Polymers containing methyl, vinyl, hydrogen, or trifluoropropyl groups are relatively easily attacked by radiation, while those containing phenyl or aromatic groups are considerably more resistant to radiation. Several investigators (*151, 494*) have shown that a linear relationship of positive slope exists between logarithm of G (noncondensable gas)[*] and the electron fraction methyl[†] for liquid polysiloxanes (Fig. 7). In other words, the radiation stability of silicones increases with the number of phenyl groups in the polymer molecule. Comparative radiation stabilities have shown that dimethylsiloxane polymers are slightly more resistant to cross-linking by 2-Mev electrons than is polyethylene to 0.8-Mev electrons (*464*). A sample of $(PhMeSiO)_x$ which received 186 Mrep was crosslinked to about the same extent as a sample of $(Me_2SiO)_x$ which had received 10 Mrep. This large variation in susceptibility has made possible the use of radiation for vulcanization of elastomeric polysiloxanes, affording silicone rubbers of improved physical properties (*149, 150, 464*) as well as permitting their use close to high energy radiation sources (*148, 464*).

---

[*] Molecules of noncondensable gases, mainly hydrogen and methane, evolved per 100 ev of energy absorbed.

[†] Number of electrons associated with all the atoms of the methyl groups divided by the total number of electrons of the atoms in the entire molecule.

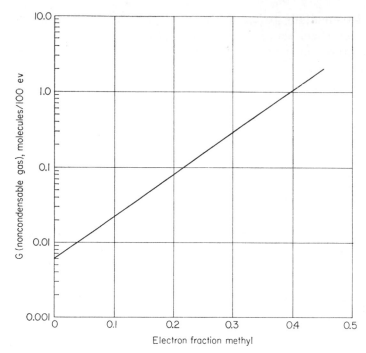

FIG. 7. Dependence of radiation stability of polysiloxanes upon composition.

The amount of cross-linking which occurs upon radiation is proportional to the dose received and is independent of the molecular weight (except for very low viscosity oils) (*88, 103, 259*). The extent of radiation attack is also governed to a somewhat lesser extent by the type of filler used (*148*), the presence of antirads (*148*), the temperature, dose rate, amount of crystallinity present (i.e., the physical state), type of radiation (i.e., relative energy, penetration, and mechanism), and the presence of oxygen (*138, 149, 150, 258, 259, 288, 289, 425, 464*).

Many reactions identified with the irradiation of an organic material (*425*) are found also in the irradiation of polysiloxanes: gas evolution, chain scission, crosslinking, and branching (*102, 134, 241, 464*). Crosslinking predominates over chain scission for polysiloxanes (*88, 134, 135, 289*), but the opposite is true for polysilanes (*56*). The reactions proceed by homolytic bond scission, and it would be expected that the weakest bonds would be broken preferentially (Table XI). Irradiation of hydrocarbons, such as polyethylene, yield hydrogen and ultimately result in complete degradation of the polymer, because the weakest bond is the carbon-carbon bond that constitutes the polymer backbone (*290*). The silicon-carbon bond, the weakest bond in poly(dimethylsiloxanes), ruptures, preferentially to the siloxane linkage. Thus cross-linking predominates over chain scission, and methane and ethane are observed along with hydrogen in the evolved gases (*134, 135, 288, 368, 464*). Radicals of the type shown in Eq. (124) are produced (*134*) and in some cases have

$$
\left(
\begin{array}{c}
CH_3 \\
| \\
-Si-O- \\
| \\
CH_3
\end{array}
\right)_x
\xrightarrow{\gamma \text{ or } \beta}
\left\{
\begin{array}{l}
-(Me\dot{S}i-O-)_x + CH_3\cdot \\[2mm]
\left(
\begin{array}{c}
-MeSi-O- \\
| \\
CH_2\cdot
\end{array}
\right)_x + H\cdot \\[3mm]
-(Me_2Si-O\cdot)_y + (\cdot SiMe_2-)_z
\end{array}
\right.
\tag{124}
$$

been detected by mass spectrometer (*135*) and electron paramagnetic resonance (*442, 443, 494*) studies. These radicals may combine in a variety of ways. The following linkages and compounds have been observed: SiSi, SiCH$_2$Si, SiCH$_2$CH$_2$Si, and SiOOSi (especially in the presence of oxygen), hydrogen, methane, and ethane. Irradiation of MM with β particles has yielded SiCH$_2$Si, SiSi, and SiCH$_2$CH$_2$Si in the ratio 2:1:0.6 (*134*), while D$_4$ yielded the same products in the ratio 2:1:0 (*88*). The reactions in Eq. (124) also are capable of yielding SiOCH$_3$, SiMe$_3$, SiOH, SiH, SiOCH$_2$Si, SiOSi, and (with oxygen) SiOOH linkages, some of which would be susceptible to further attack and reaction. Residual active sites, especially at low temperatures, have been used to obtain cross-links upon warming (*149*). It is conceivable that such sites could be utilized to prepare graft copolymers (Section IV,A,4).

G values (previously defined) are a measure of the susceptibility of a material to attack by radiation. High G values indicate poor radiation resistance, while low values indicate higher radiation resistance. G values have been reported for poly(dimethylsiloxanes) (*29, 88, 103, 134, 288, 289, 368, 464*): G (cross-linking) 2.2–3.1; G (H$_2$) 0.65–0.7; G (CH$_4$) 1.0–1.4; G (C$_2$H$_6$) 0.4–0.46. Slight discrepancies may be attributed in part to different types of radiation.

Ultrasonic radiation will also degrade poly(dimethylsiloxanes) (*58, 59*). The rate of polymer scission depends on the ultrasonic intensity, type of solvent, medium (i.e., air or argon), and solution concentration.

6. *Dielectric Properties*

The dielectric properties (*27, 50, 129, 191, 376, 430, 434, 493*) of poly-(dimethylsiloxanes) together with their other desirable properties have led to their widespread use as electrical insulators. Their dielectric constants are a measure of the recoverable energy stored within the polymer, and their power factors are a measure of energy both stored and dissipated as heat. The dielectric constants of linear poly(dimethylsiloxanes) are func-

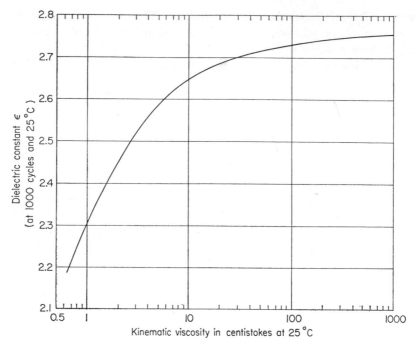

FIG. 8. Variation of dielectric constant ϵ with viscosity for poly(dimethylsiloxanes) (*27, 50, 376, 434, 493*).

tions of molecular weight and temperature but are only slightly dependent upon frequency. The values of ϵ at 20° to 25°C increase with increasing viscosity from 2.17 for MM to 2.82 for 12,500-cs viscosity (Fig. 8). For higher polymers of viscosities 30,000 to over 1,000,000 cs, ϵ lies between

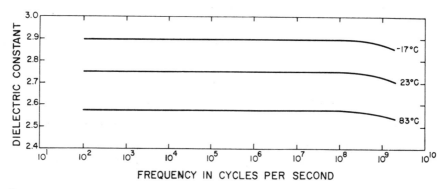

FIG. 9. Variation of dielectric constant ϵ with temperature and frequency for poly(dimethylsiloxanes), 1000 cs.

2.63 and 2.77 (*434*). The cyclics D_n, where n is 4 to 8, have dielectric constants from 2.39 to 2.74 (*376*). Thus $(Me_2SiO)_x$ polymers have dielectric constants much lower than water (80) and methanol (33), about the same as benzene (2.28), toluene (2.39), and transformer oil (2.24), and somewhat higher than hexane (1.87) and octane (1.96) (*194*). The dielectric constants decrease with increasing temperature, probably because of slight viscosity-density changes (Fig. 9), and remain practically unchanged with change in frequency up to 10^8 cps. A slight decrease with increasing frequency is noted beyond 10^8 cycles per second.

The power factors of poly(dimethylsiloxanes) are low and lie below those of typical transformer oils (*50*). At frequencies of 10^3 to 10^7 cps and from $-35°$ to $+150°C$ the power factors are essentially zero and certainly less than 10^{-4}, while at about 50 cps they are around 3×10^{-4} (*191*). At frequencies higher than 10^7 or 10^8 cps a considerable increase in power factor is observed due to a strong absorption in the microwave region characteristic of linear siloxane systems (*191*). The peak appears to lie at 10^{10} to 10^{11} cps (Fig. 10). Power factors vary somewhat with temperature and polymer chain length, but the changes are insignificant in contrast to those observed with frequency (*50, 191*).

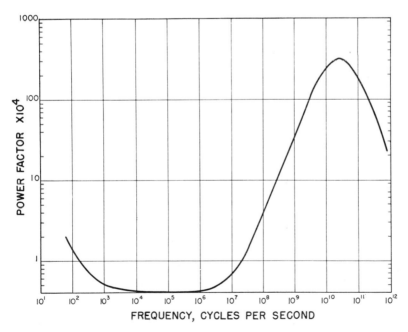

FIG. 10. Effect of frequency upon power factor of poly(dimethylsiloxanes), 1000 cs, at 20°C.

Volume resistivities are of the order of 10^{14} to 10^{15} ohm cm and vary only slightly with viscosity, but they do decrease somewhat with increasing temperature to around 10^{13} at 200°C. Dielectric strength at room temperature is on the order of 250 to 300 volts/mil when measured at 100 mils, and 500 volts/mil at 10 mils.

7. *Light Transmission*

Poly(dimethylsiloxanes) show 100% transmittance of all visible wavelengths of light and in the near infrared up to 1000 mμ (10,000 cm^{-1}). Their ultraviolet transmittance decreases with decreasing wavelength and at 280 mμ they show about 50% transmittance. The ultraviolet absorption spectra of poly(dimethyl- and methylphenylsiloxanes) have been reported both for the pure liquids and in isooctane solution and show four to six absorption maxima between 246 and 270 mμ (*95*).

The infrared (*115, 125, 250, 253, 350, 395, 436, 489, 492*) and Raman (*99, 253, 294, 295, 377, 394, 446, 470*) spectra of polysiloxanes have been investigated and a thorough discussion of the former presented by Bellamy (*57*). Table XIX lists the main absorption frequencies exhibited by common polysiloxanes. Polysiloxanes are characterized by a very strong absorption at 9.5 μ (1053 cm^{-1}) due to siloxane stretching. It is about five times as strong as absorptions due to carbon-oxygen stretching (*489*). Increasing cyclic ring size or increasing chain length of linear polymers causes a small but steady bathochromic shift in the siloxane bands, while branching produces a slight hypsochromic shift. The other main absorption bands of interest for poly(dimethylsiloxanes) are those at 1259 and 814–800

TABLE XIX

INFRARED ABSORPTION FREQUENCIES FOR POLYSILOXANES[a]

Group	Wave number[b] (cm^{-1})
SiMe$_3$	1250, 841, 756–4
SiMe$_2$	1259, 814–800
SiMe	1259, near 800
SiPh	1429, 1130–1090
SiOSi (cyclic)	Trimers 1020–1010
	Tetramers 1090–1080
	Higher rings 1080–1050 (strong)
SiOC and SiOSi (open chain)	1090–1020
SiH	2300–2100

[a] Reference (*57*).
All absorptions are very strong.

cm⁻¹ due to the SiMe₂ group and at 1250, 841, and 756–4 cm⁻¹ due to the SiMe₃ group. Those at 841 and 756–4 cm⁻¹ vary in intensity with concentration and hence may be used to estimate the chain length of trimethylsilyl end-blocked polymers. The relative intensities of the Me—Si and Ph—Si bands near 1263 and 1435 cm⁻¹ may be used to determine quantitatively the Me/Ph ratio in such polysiloxanes (*18, 256*).

8. Additive and Constitutive Properties

a. Refractive Index. The refractive indices at 25°C for the dimethylsiloxane polymers range from 1.394 to 1.404 for the cyclics, tetramer through octamer, and from 1.387 to 1.395 for the linear members, dimer through hexamer (*201, 202*). With increasing molecular weights the indices of the linear polymers increase to the asymptotic value of 1.4035 (Fig. 11). Substitution of other groups for methyl tends in general to raise the refractive index, as does replacement of the oxygen atoms by methylene groups (*402, 441*). Stress-optical studies on polysiloxanes indicate that the amount of birefringence depends on the nature of the polymer and the amount of applied stress and may be positive or negative in value (*321, 322*).

b. Density. The densities of polysiloxanes are not far different from those of organic compounds and are somewhat higher than corresponding silmethylene compounds (*402, 441*). The cyclics, D₄₋₇, have densities of

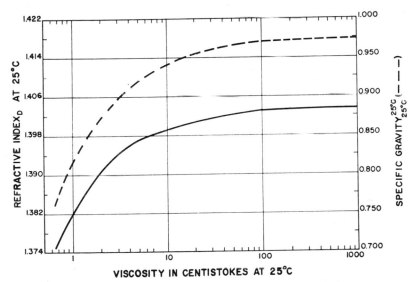

FIG. 11. Variation of refractive index and specific gravity of linear poly(dimethylsiloxanes) with viscosity.

0.950 to 0.966 at 25°C (*201*), somewhat larger than those of the corresponding linear polymers containing the same number of silicon atoms. The linear polysiloxanes vary in specific gravity from 0.761 for hexamethyldisiloxane to 0.908 for MD_6M (*202*). The gravities of the polymers increase with increasing molecular weight in a manner analogous to the refractive indices (Fig. 11).

The molar volumes of poly(dimethylsiloxanes) have been found to be large (*203, 376*); the fact that the molecules are relatively large and bulky is consistent with the known low intermolecular forces. The average molar volume for a linear Me_2SiO unit has been calculated to be 75.5 ml (*203*). The constant contribution of the end groups $[CH_3 + SiMe_3]$ is 137.3 ml. Thus, the molar volume at 20°C for a polymer MD_xM may be calculated from: $V = 137.3 + 75.5 (x + 1)$. The ring structure itself contributed a small amount to the molar volume of cyclic polymers ranging from 8.0 ml in D_4 down to 4.8 ml in D_7. Attempts to relate the specific volume and viscosity using Batschinski's equation [Eq. (125)] (*52*) have been made for several polysiloxanes (*203*).

$$\eta = c/(V + w), \text{ where } c \text{ and } w \text{ are constants} \tag{125}$$

c. Parachor. The parachor for organosilicon compounds has been investigated thoroughly (*154, 158, 201, 202, 291, 471*). Its use is rendered cum-

TABLE XX

BOND REFRACTION VALUES[a]

Bond	Bond refraction (ml/mole)	Bond	Bond refraction (ml/mole)
Si—O	1.75	C—O	1.51
Si—Si	5.65	C—C	1.25
Si—C$_{aliphatic}$	2.50	C$_{ar}$—C$_{ar}$	2.73[b]
Si—C$_{aromatic}$	2.56	C$_{na}$—C$_{na}$	2.78[c]
Si—H	3.20	C—H	1.69
Si—F	1.50	C—F	1.72
Si—Cl	7.20	C—Cl	6.53
Si—Br	10.20	C—Br	9.37
—	—	C—I	14.55
Si—N	2.00	C—N	1.54
Si—S	6.25	C=O	3.38
N—H	1.81	O—H	1.73
C=C	4.16	C≡C	6.40

[a] References (*132, 460*).
[b] In benzene and its derivatives.
[c] In naphthalene and its derivatives.

bersome and unreliable, especially when compared with the use of bond refractions, due to variation of the bond parachors with different substituents on silicon and to the variation of the carbon-carbon bond parachor in different alkyl groups on silicon (*291*). Parachor equivalents for silicon have been determined in a variety of polysiloxanes and simple organosilicon compounds and range from 25 to 38.2 with no regular variation with structure evident.

d. Bond Refractions. The comparison of observed molar refractions, readily calculated from density and refractive index measurements, and those calculated from bond refractions yields reliable evidence for the determination of structures of organosilicon compounds. Several systems of bond refractions have been worked out for silicon and carbon compounds (*132, 371, 450, 460*) and also for silicon, tin, lead, germanium, and mercury compounds (*450*). Table XX lists bond refractions worked out for silicon compounds (*460*) based upon those established for organic systems (*132*). The data are based upon 72 compounds and are correct to within an average error 0.62%.

The average composition of a polymer of the type $Me_xSiO_{(4-x)/2}$ may be determined by using Eq. (126) (*371*).

$$x = \frac{60.06R_D - 7.005}{5.822 - 7.034R_D}, \text{ where } R_D = \frac{n_D^2 - 1}{n_D^2 + 2} \cdot \frac{1}{d} \qquad (126)$$

If one assumes the presence of only dimethyl- and trimethylsiloxane units in the polymer, it is possible to calculate a molecular weight with limitations (*460*).

e. Dipole Moment. Dipole moments have been determined for the lower molecular weight polysiloxanes (*27, 116, 162, 187, 196, 255, 376*). The dipole moments of linear poly(dimethylsiloxanes), MD_nM, where n is 0 to 4, are reported to range from 0.73 to 1.58 D, and those of the cyclics, D_n, where n is 4 to 8, from 1.09 to 1.96 D, the values in both series increasing with increasing molecular weight (*376*). The dipole moments of the linear MD_nM polymers agree with the equation $\mu = 0.70(n + 1)^{\frac{1}{2}}$, while those values of the larger cyclic polymers appear to approach the values predicted by this equation (*376*). It must be noted that these values are high because the methods used could not exclude the atomic polarization, which is very high for these compounds. For example, the dipole moment of hexamethyldisiloxane has been reported as 0.73–0.80 D (*162, 187, 255, 376*), but methods that permit exclusion of the atomic polarization give 0.43–0.46 D (*27, 196*). Values similarly obtained for higher linear polymers exhibit no orderly variation with molecular weight (*27*).

f. Magnetic Rotatory Power. Poly(dimethylsiloxanes) rotate the plane of polarized light when placed in a magnetic field (Faraday effect). The

Verdet constants vary from 16.23 to 16.93 $\times$ 10^{-3} min/gauss/cm for liquids of 0.65- to 1000-cs viscosity when measured at 25°C and at the sodium D line (5893 A) (*257*). Slightly higher values have been obtained using the mercury 5461 A line. The Verdet constant increases with molecular weight and tends to approach an asymptotic value of about 16.9 $\times$ 10^{-3}. For comparison, Verdet constants for ethanol, water, and benzene are 11.12, 13.08, and 29.7 $\times$ 10^{-3}, respectively (*194*).

g. *Diamagnetic Susceptibility.* The diamagnetic susceptibility is also an additive property, and values have been obtained for the lower poly-(dimethylsiloxanes) (*19, 280, 281, 282, 310*). The atomic susceptibility of silicon χ_{Si} has been determined to be -12.4 to -12.78×10^{-6} cgs units in several low molecular weight cyclic and linear polymers. However, the values of χ_{Si} vary somewhat, decreasing with increasing polymer chain length, increasing number of oxygen atoms attached to silicon, and increasing length of alkyl chain substituents on silicon.

B. Properties Dependent on Macromolecular Structure

1. *General Considerations*

Many of the observed physical properties of polysiloxanes, such as compressibility, small viscosity-temperature coefficients, and surface properties, have been attributed to more or less regularly coiled ("helical") structures of the macromolecules (*30, 158, 298, 315, 468*) and the low forces of attraction between them (*201, 358, 360, 362*). The low temperature coefficient of viscosity for poly(dimethylsiloxanes) has been explained on the basis that the molecules are of kinked and coiled structure, more pronounced at low temperatures where the concommitant low order of molecular interaction results in a relatively low viscosity; upon raising the temature the kinked structures open out, invoking greater interaction and entanglement. This favors an increase in viscosity that partially compensates the normal decrease in viscosity caused by the thermally increased molecular motion and thus the viscosity of the fluid changes relatively little with temperature change (*30*). Increasing substitution of bulky groups hinders coiling and may be the source of the larger temperature coefficients of viscosity obtained for the higher phenyl content polysiloxanes (*126*).

The reductions of intermolecular forces by coiling of poly(dimethylsiloxanes) may be attributable to the internal compensation of dipoles and to the outward orientation of the methyl groups, capable of only weak interactions with those of neighboring molecules. As expected, elevated temperature and high pressure offset this effect by uncoiling the molecules and exposing them to greater interaction with one another.

The ability of polysiloxanes to coil, in contrast to analogous linear hydrocarbon or ether-type polymers possessing relatively rigid structure, may be attributed to the larger diameter of the silicon atom as compared with carbon (*158*). Furthermore, helical coiling is undoubtedly facilitated by the "softness" of the siloxane bond angles. The bond angles between the bonds attached to silicon are fairly constant and well known (*2, 362, 420, 426, 490*). The O—Si—O angle appears to be fairly constant at 108–110°, but is somewhat higher for D_3 at 110 to 120°; the C—Si—C angle generally lies between 106° and 118°. On the other hand, values as divergent as 104–180° have been reported for the Si—O—Si bond angle, as determined by electron and X-ray diffraction, infrared and Raman spectra, and dipole moment measurements (*2, 125, 157, 159, 162, 176, 196, 266, 268, 277, 354. 360–362, 376, 420, 426, 490*). The wide range of values reflects the great flexibility of this readily deformed angle and can be accounted for by oxygen-silicon p_π, d_π bonding and by the relatively large polar character of the bond.

Opposition to the helix structure has been voiced because: (i) in order to achieve the observed properties of polysiloxane elastomers a helix of so many siloxane units per turn would be required that the distinction between coils and chains would become clouded, (ii) the viscosity of liquid polysiloxanes varies not only with temperature but also with chain length so that the thermal coefficient of uncoiling would have to vary regularly with chain length, and (iii) although the molar volume of Me_2SiO units in small cyclics is about the same as in linear molecules, a helical structure cannot be applied to them even though they possess temperature coefficients of viscosity similar (somewhat higher) to those of the linear polymers (*358*). The objection to the helical arrangement on the grounds that it "represents an improbably high degree of order (low entropy)" (*283*, p. 18) seems poorly grounded when one considers the many naturally occurring helical structures (*317, 327*).

Aside from the helical structure, the low intermolecular attractive forces may be due to the large molar volume of the Me_2SiO group and the free rotation about the silicon-carbon and silicon-oxygen bond. Since attractive forces between molecules vary inversely with the distance separating them, anything that tends to give a large intermolecular distance and, therefore, large molar volume, should markedly decrease the attractive forces. The molar volume is determined to a large extent by the protruding methyl groups (*358, 360, 362, 420*). Nuclear magnetic resonance experiments have shown that the methyl groups rotate about the silicon-carbon bond somewhat like an umbrella with an unusual amount of freedom, and that this motion persists and is still extensive even at $-195°C$, whereas analogous organic compounds present a rigid lattice at considerably higher temperatures (*358*). Because of this rotation the methyl groups require more space than if they did not rotate and, therefore, occupy a larger molar volume with correspondingly smaller intermolecular attractions. Studies on octamethylspiro[5.5]pentasiloxane have shown that the methyl groups are quite free to rotate about the silicon-oxygen bond in a manner similar to a ball-and-socket joint. This type of motion prevents close packing of the polymer chains (*360, 362*).

2. Low Temperature Properties

The freezing points of pure dimethylsiloxane cyclics, D_{3-8}, and trimethylsiloxy end-blocked linear polymers, $MD_{0-6}M$, may be found in Table III. Those of the cyclics vary from $+65°$ to $-44°C$ and those of the

TABLE XXI

LOW TEMPERATURE PROPERTIES OF POLYSILOXANES

Siloxane	Viscosity at 25°C (cs)	Pour pt,[a] (°C)
Me$_2$	3	-65
Me$_2$	5	-65
Me$_2$	10	-65
Me$_2$	20	-60
Me$_2$	50	-55
Me$_2$	100	-55
Me$_2$	200	-53
Me$_2$	500	-50
Me$_2$	1,000	-50
Me$_2$	2,000	-48[b]
Me$_2$	10,000	-46[c]
Me$_2$	30,000	-44[d]
Me$_2$	100,000	-46[c]
Me$_2$	30,000 to 10^6	-40 to -45[e]
10% PhMe	100	-62[f]
25% PhMe	100–150	-50[f]
45% PhMe	500	-22[f]
Chlorinated PhMe	40–60	-73[f]

[a] Pour point ASTM D97–39, Sections 5 to 7 (*434*).
[b] Freezing point (*51*).
[c] Freezing point (*283*, p. 20).
[d] Solidification temperature (*434*).
[e] Freezing point (*434*).
[f] Reference (*283*, p. 22).

linears from $-59°$ to $-86°C$. The tendency of these compounds to super-
cool makes it difficult to obtain precise freezing point values. In general,
a linear polymer freezes at a lower temperature than the corresponding
cyclic containing the same number of silicon atoms. In contrast to the
boiling points, these differences are probably due to molecular shape rather
than molecular weight differences. No regular pattern of change in freezing point is observed in going from one member to another in each series.
The melting points of the lower siloxane polymers are affected by pressure
and show abnormal behavior. This abnormality has been explained through
large supercooling effects connected with their abnormally large increase of
viscosity under pressure (84).

Table XXI lists the pour points, freezing points, and solidification temperatures for several poly(dimethylsiloxanes) and four polymers which
contain phenyl and chlorophenyl groups. The solidification temperatures
slowly rise with increasing viscosity to about $-40°$ to $-45°C$ for viscosities
between 30,000 and 1,000,000 cs.

The data in Table XXI and Fig. 12 show the effect of substituent phenyl
groups on the freezing point of polysiloxanes. Figure 12 shows the effect
upon the freezing point of a poly(dimethylsiloxane) of molecular weight of
about 2000 when phenyl groups are substituted for some of the methyl
groups. Thus the introduction of a small number of bulky phenyl groups
interrupts the regularity of the siloxane chain and impedes crystallization.
Beyond a certain limit, however, overpopulation of phenyl groups promotes
their probability of interaction, which raises the freezing point of the co-

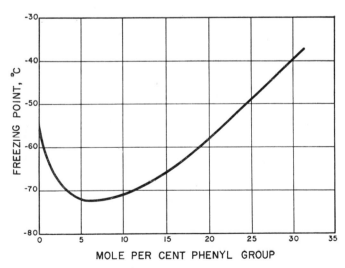

FIG. 12. Freezing point lowering of poly(dimethylsiloxanes).

polymer (*335*). Similar effects upon the freezing point are also caused by ethyl, chloromethyl, and other bulky side groups (*77, 468*).

The low temperature characteristics of the siloxane fluids are reflected again in polysiloxane elastomers. Upon cooling, many cross-linked silicone rubbers tend to crystallize and pass through second-order transitions. Crystallization is a time-consuming process involving a phase change and a sharp change or discontinuity in the primary thermodynamic properties of a material at the crystallization temperature (*485*). A second-order transition involves a change in slope occurring at the second-order transition temperature (glass temperature) when variables such as hardness, brittleness, coefficient of thermal expansion, heat capacity, dielectric constant, and thermal conductivity are plotted against temperature (*75, 486*). A second-order transition involves neither a phase transition nor a change in molecular orientation. It is complete as soon as temperature equilibrium is reached at a temperature sufficiently low to greatly hinder or prohibit rotation of groups or molecular segments of the polymer molecules. Thus at its glass temperature a polymer may change from a viscous or rubbery polymer to a hard, brittle glass. The ratio of the glass temperature to the

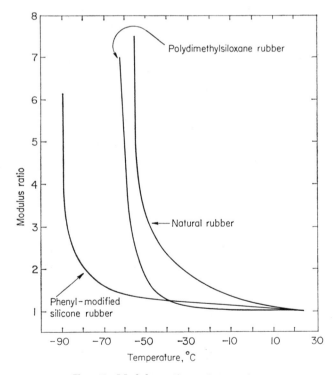

FIG. 13. Modulus ratio vs. temperature.

melting point for linear poly(dimethylsiloxanes) has been shown to be about 0.70, and for natural rubber, 0.67 (*55*). The average T_g/T_m for eight polymers including these two is 0.665. The glass temperature of poly-(dimethylsiloxane) rubber is $-123°C$, the lowest yet recorded for any polymer (*335, 472, 486*); that for natural rubber is $-72°C$ and butyl rubber (polyisobutylene), $-70°C$. The glass temperature rises slowly with increasing temperature to a limiting value of about $-86°C$ when PhMeSiO groups are substituted for the Me$_2$SiO groups in poly(dimethylsiloxanes) (*335*).

Substituent groups on the silicon atoms in polysiloxane rubbers have a pronounced effect upon their crystallization behavior (*248, 335, 337, 472*). Poly(dimethylsiloxane) rubbers crystallize rapidly without supercooling at about $-54°C$. The substitution of small numbers of bulky phenyl groups in place of the methyl groups interrupts the regularity of the polymer molecule and thus impedes crystallization. For example, a poly(dimethyl-siloxane) rubber containing 3.5 mole % of the Me$_2$SiO groups replaced by PhMeSiO groups crystallizes at $-70°C$; one containing 7.5 mole % PhMeSiO groups does not crystallize. There is a great tendency to super-cool when phenyl groups are present in the rubber. Figure 13 shows modu-lus-temperature data for natural rubber, poly(dimethylsiloxane) rubber, and a phenyl-modified low temperature silicone rubber. Substitution of PhMeSiO groups for Me$_2$SiO groups causes a decrease in the coefficient of thermal expansion from 9.44×10^{-4} for poly(dimethylsiloxane) to 4.6×10^{-4} for 99.858 mole % poly(methylphenylsiloxane) (*335*).

The crystallinity and orientation of crystallites in stressed, silica-filled poly(dimethylsiloxane) rubber has been investigated at low temperatures by X-ray diffraction methods (*305*). As the sample is stretched, the crystal-lization temperature rises and preferential orientation of the crystallites with respect to the direction of stress increases. The crystallinity increases with decreasing temperature and appears to be independent of the extension ratio below $-60°C$. An over-all crystalline fraction of 0.42 was measured at $-60°C$ and an extension ratio of 6.3. Crystallization at low temperatures in silicone rubber causes a rise in tension in contrast to natural rubber (*465*). This phenomenon is attributed to the ability of the chain elements in silicone rubber to crystallize in all states of orientation as contrasted with natural rubber, which crystallizes with the chain segments oriented in the direction of stress.

The ability of silicone rubber to crystallize without altering the orienta-tion of chain segments, the rapidity of crystallization, and the low tem-perature of freezing and second order transition have been accounted for by the low intermolecular forces in the polymers, the flexibility of and free rotation around bonds, and the low temperature coefficient of viscosity

(*335, 337, 465, 468*). At low temperatures the molecules of silicone rubber are *relatively* mobile due to the low temperature coefficient of viscosity (Section III,B,4); after nucleation, the crystals form and grow quickly and equilibrium is rapidly reached. In contrast, the molecules of natural rubber have low mobility at low temperatures and thus crystallize slowly. Complete crystallinity is not achieved in either polymer because segments of a single macromolecule may belong to several different crystallites; their growth places a strain upon the noncrystalline parts of the polymer and thereby limits the extent of crystal formation.

3. Solubility Characteristics

In general, poly(dimethylsiloxanes) show the solubility behavior of nonpolar liquids. Several representative solvents and nonsolvents are shown in Table XXII. The solubility varies somewhat with chain length; the low polymers are more soluble than the high polymers in a given solvent. Their solubilities are depressed by the presence of small amounts of water in the solvent. Replacement of methyl groups on silicon by larger alkyl and aryl groups increases the solubility of the polysiloxane in nonpolar solvents; the presence of polar groups like trifluoropropyl or cyanoethyl decreases the solubility in such solvents.

The solubility properties of polysiloxanes are most significantly reflected in the swelling behavior of the silicone elastomers made from them. In many cases, the practical utility of an elastomer will depend on its resistance to swelling in certain liquids. The swelling of an elastomer is a complex phenomenon influenced by many factors: solvent/polymer interaction, density of cross-links, type and amount of filler used, temperature, contact time, and others. The first of these is the most important, and the most subtle.

TABLE XXII

SOLUBILITY OF POLY(DIMETHYLSILOXANES) IN SOLVENTS

Miscible	Partially soluble	Insoluble
Benzene	Acetone	Water
Toluene	Dioxane	Methanol
Diethyl ether	Ethanol	Cyclohexanol
Methyl ethyl ketone	Isopropanol	Ethylene glycol
Carbon tetrachloride	Butanol	Dimethyl phthalate
Chloroform		Cellosolve
Perchloroethylene		Carbitol
Kerosene		

The relationship between polymer structure and solvent can be expressed quantitatively in terms of cohesive energy density and solubility parameters. The cohesive energy density (CED) is a measure of the cohesive forces in a unit volume of the liquid; it is defined as the molar energy of vaporization divided by the molar volume. The solubility parameter, δ, is defined as the square root of the cohesive energy density, (Eq. 127). Table XXIII lists the solubility parameter for several classes of solvents. The solubility parameter for a polymer cannot be calculated from Eq. (127)

$$\delta = \sqrt{CED} = \sqrt{E_{vap}/V} \qquad (127)$$

but must be determined experimentally by observing the amount of swelling exhibited by the cross-linked elastomer in solvents of various cohesive energy densities. The relative amounts of swelling are plotted against the solubility parameters of the solvents to yield a Gaussian distribution curve; the maximum represents the solubility parameter of the polymer.

Table XXIV lists the cohesive energy densities, solubility parameters, and second order transition temperatures for several elastomers. The deviations of the square of the reported solubility parameters from the reported cohesive energy densities reflect the partial dependence of these values on the variables mentioned earlier (i.e., filler, density of crosslinking, etc.). Measurements of internal pressures of dimethyl- and phenylmethylsiloxane polymers suggest that the equation $CED = \delta^2$ may underestimate the intermolecular cohesion of a polymer (6). The very low values for the solubility parameter and cohesive energy density of poly(dimethyl-

TABLE XXIII

SOLUBILITY PARAMETERS OF SOLVENTS[a]

Solvent	δ
Linear poly(dimethylsiloxanes)[b]	4.97– 5.90
Fluorocarbons[c]	5.5 – 8.2
Aliphatic hydrocarbons	6.7 – 7.6
Aromatic hydrocarbons	8.5 – 9.5
Ethers	7.4 – 9.9
Chlorinated hydrocarbons	8.2 –10.0
Ketones	7.8 –11.0
Esters	7.8 –14.7
Alcohols	8.9 –16.5
Water	24.2

[a] References (437, 90).

[b] Two to eleven silicon atoms.

[c] Aliphatic and aromatic.

TABLE XXIV

COHESIVE ENERGY DENSITY, SOLUBILITY PARAMETERS, AND GLASS TEMPERATURES
FOR ELASTOMERS

Elastomer	Cohesive energy density (cal/cc)[a]	$\delta_p{}^b$	T_g (°C)[c]
Polytetrafluoroethylene	—	6.2	> +20
Poly(dimethylsiloxane)	54	7.3	−123
Polyisobutylene	60	7.8	−70
Polyethylene	62	7.9	∼−85
Natural rubber	64	8.1	−72
GRS[d]	65.5	8.1	—
Polystyrene	80	8.6	+100
Buna N[e]	88	8.9	—
Polyvinyl chloride	90	9.5	+82

[a] Reference (468).
[b] Polymer solubility parameter (437, p. 66).
[c] References (437, 486).
[d] 75% butadiene–25% styrene.
[e] 75% butadiene–25% acrylonitrile.

siloxanes) reflect the low interchain forces and the low solubility of these polymers in nonpolar solvents (468). Only Teflon exhibits a lower solubility parameter. The values in Table XXIV show that polymers with low solubility parameters generally have low second-order transition temperatures; the exceptional behavior of Teflon is attributed to restricted rotation about the carbon-carbon bond. The dependence of the glass temperature on solubility parameter, chain length and stiffness, and rotational freedom has been discussed elsewhere (437) (see Chapter 1). Thus, polymers containing polar groups such as $(F_3CCH_2CH_2MeSiO)_x$ and

TABLE XXV

SOLUBILITY OF GASES IN WATER AND POLY(DIMETHYLSILOXANES)

Gas	Soly. at 25°C (ml gas/ml liquid)	
	In water[a]	In silicone[b]
Nitrogen	0.0143	0.163–0.172
Carbon dioxide	0.759	1.00
Air	0.0171	0.168–0.190

[a] Reference (194).
[b] Reference (272).

(NCCH₂CH₂MeSiO)$_x$ would be expected to have larger solubility parameters than (Me₂SiO)$_x$, higher cohesive energy densities, higher interchain attractive forces, greater chain stiffness, more restricted rotation about the siloxane linkage, and higher second order transition temperatures.

The approximate solubilities of several gases in poly(dimethylsiloxanes) at 25°C are shown and compared with water in Table XXV. Nitrogen and air are about ten times as soluble in the silicone polymers as in water, while carbon dioxide has about the same solubility in both fluids.

4. Rheological Properties

Some of the most important and useful properties of polysiloxanes are manifested in their rheological behavior. Their low viscosities, small temperature coefficients of viscosity, high compressibility, and stability to shearing stress are unique among polymers of similar molecular weights. The reasons proposed for these unusual properties are those discussed previously, i.e., low intermolecular forces, coiled helix-type structures, and freedom of bond rotation (468).

The lower members of the cyclic and linear poly(dimethylsiloxanes) possess viscosities considerably lower than those of hydrocarbons of comparable molecular weight (201, 202). This is illustrated in Fig. 14. The viscosities of the dimethylsiloxane lower polymers may be related to their degrees of polymerization as expressed in the following equations (479):

for cyclics D$_n$ where $n = 4$ to 8 and T is °K,

$$\log \eta_c - -2.13 + \frac{214}{T} - \left[0.04 - \frac{866}{T}\right] \log n$$

for linears MD$_{n-2}$M where $n = 2$ to 11,

$$\log \eta_l = -2.04 + \frac{380}{T} + \left[0.37 + \frac{326}{T}\right] \log n$$

These equations are empirical and cannot be validly extrapolated much beyond the limits of n indicated.

For the higher polymers of the linear poly(dimethylsiloxanes), the following relationship between bulk viscosity and number-average molecular weight has been established (30):

$$\log \eta_{(cs/25°C)} = 1.00 + 0.0123 \sqrt{M}$$

This expression is valid for molecular weights greater than 2500 and conforms with the Flory equation relating melt viscosity to the square root of molecular weight, generally applicable to many polymer systems.

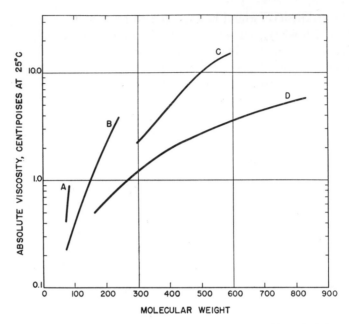

Fɪɢ. 14. Viscosity-molecular weight relationships of poly(dimethylsiloxanes) and hydrocarbons: (A) cyclic alkanes, (B) normal alkanes, (C) poly(dimethylsiloxane) cyclics D_n, (D) poly(dimethylsiloxane) linears MD_nM.

The activation energies for viscous flow of polysiloxanes have been extensively studied (*201–203*). For the linear and cyclic dimethylsiloxane polymers, the E_{visc} values were found to increase with molecular weight as shown in Fig. 15. Furthermore, their values are seen to be appreciably lower than those for hydrocarbons of corresponding molecular weights, plotted for comparison in the same figure. The low activation energies for viscous flow observed in polysiloxanes are due to the presence of the oxygen atoms in the polymer backbone (*402*); this is apparent when E_{visc} values for corresponding polysiloxanes and polysilmethylenes are compared in Table XXVI. The values of the activation energy for viscous flow of the polysiloxanes can also be changed by altering the nature of the substituent groups on the silicon atoms. The E_{visc}, fundamentally a measure of intermolecular forces in the polymer, is increased by the substitution of almost any group for methyl on silicon because of (i) steric or bulk effects of the larger group, (ii) dipole attractions and interactions of polar substituent groups, and (iii) the effect of a substituent metal atom upon the ease of rotation of the methyl groups (*389*). The effect of bulky groups upon increasing E_{visc} is apparent when $Me_3SiO(Ph_2SiO)SiMe_3$ (E_{visc} 4553 cal) is compared with $Me_3SiO(Me_2SiO)SiMe_3$ (E_{visc} 2446 cal) (*203*). The effects

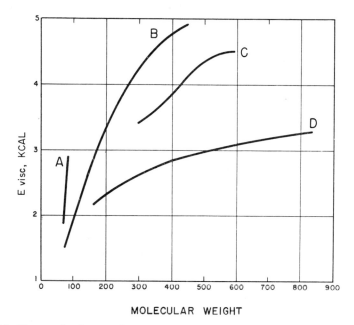

MOLECULAR WEIGHT

FIG. 15. E_{visc}-molecular weight relationships for poly(dimethylsiloxanes) and hydrocarbons: (A) cyclic alkanes, (B) normal alkanes, (C) cyclic poly(dimethylsiloxanes) D_n, (D) linear poly(dimethylsiloxanes) MD_nM.

of dipole and steric interactions upon increasing E_{visc} are found, for example, in ethoxy end-blocked poly(dimethysiloxanes) (*30*), carboalkoxyalkyl (*399, 407*), chlorophenyl (*93*), salicyloxymethyl (*286*), vinylethoxysiloxy (*9*), thiocyanomethyl (*117*), and chloromethyl groups (*409*). The position and concentration of the polar groups are of importance in determining their effect on E_{visc}. For example, E_{visc} for $Me_3SiO(MeSiCH_2ClO)_2$-

TABLE XXVI

ACTIVATION ENERGIES OF VISCOUS FLOW FOR $Me(Me_2SiX)_nSiMe_3$[a]

	E_{visc} (kcal)	
n	$X = -CH_2-$	$-O-$
1	2.32	2.17
2	3.13	2.45
3	3.83	2.67
4	4.42	2.78

[a] Reference (*402*).

SiMe$_3$ is larger than for ClCH$_2$Me$_2$SiO(Me$_2$SiO)$_2$SiMe$_2$CH$_2$Cl, while E_{visc} for ClCH$_2$Me$_2$SiO(MeSiCH$_2$ClO)$_2$SiMe$_2$CH$_2$Cl is still higher (*409*). In compounds of the series Me$_3$SiO(MeRSiO)SiMe$_3$, E_{visc} was found to vary with R in the order (*389*):

Me$_3$SiCH$_2$CH$_2$ > Me$_3$SnCH$_2$, Me$_3$GeCH$_2$ > Me$_3$CCH$_2$ > Me$_3$SiCH$_2$ > ClCH$_2$ > Me

It was concluded that in the series carbon-silicon-germanium-tin the effects of dipole and steric interactions and the ease of rotation about the metal tended to oppose each other and thus limit observed changes in activation energy.

Activation energies of viscous flow are reflected in the viscosity-temperature coefficients commonly used to characterize high polymer fluids and lubricants. Although not as precisely significant as E_{visc}, the viscosity-temperature coefficient (VTC), defined as:

$$\text{VTC} = 1 - \frac{\text{viscosity at } 210°\text{F}}{\text{viscosity at } 100°\text{F}}$$

has been more popularly used for practical comparisons. Poly(dimethylsiloxanes) are unique among fluid polymers in that their VTC values are extraordinarily small (*346, 347*). This is apparent in Fig. 16 showing the change of viscosity with temperature for dimethylsiloxane polymers of varying viscosities; one curve for a paraffin oil is included for comparison. The coefficients for several polysiloxane fluids are shown in Table XXVII.

TABLE XXVII

DEPENDENCE OF TEMPERATURE COEFFICIENT OF VISCOSITY OF POLYSILOXANES
UPON SUBSTITUENT GROUPS[a]

Substituents	Viscosity[b]	VTC[c]	Substituents	Viscosity[b]	VTC[c]
Me$_2$ (MM)	0.65	0.31	10% PhMe	42	0.61
Me$_2$ (MD$_3$M)	2.0	0.48	50% PhMe	115	0.78
Me$_2$	10	0.57	100% PhMe	482	0.88
Me$_2$	100	0.60	EtMe	1300	0.71
Me$_2$	1000	0.62	Et$_2$	800	0.90
Me$_2$	10,000	0.61	MeH	ca. 25	0.50
Me$_2$	100,000	0.61	p-(ClC$_6$H$_4$)Me	55[d]	0.84
Mineral oil	110[d]	0.91			

[a] References (*43, 93, 126, 283, 434*).
[b] Centistokes at 25°C.
[c] VTC $= (V_{100°\text{F}} - V_{210°\text{F}})/V_{100°\text{F}}$.
[d] Centistokes at 38°C.

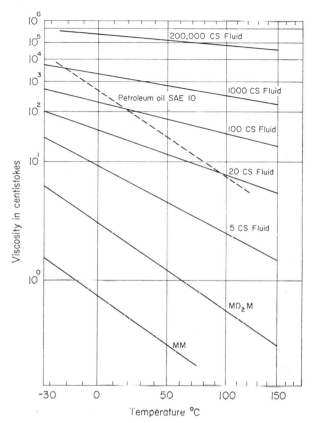

Fig. 16. Viscosity-temperature relationship for poly(dimethylsiloxanes), based on Dow Corning 200 Fluids.

As seen in the first column, the coefficient for the dimethylsiloxane polymers increases with molecular weight from 0.31 for the dimer to a maximum of about 0.62 for the highest polymers, approaching this limit asymptotically at about 1000-cs viscosity *(434)*. The larger coefficient for mineral oil illustrates its greater viscosity sensitivity to temperature change than the poly(dimethylsiloxanes).

The coefficient in polysiloxanes becomes smaller when methyl groups on silicon are replaced by hydrogen and larger when replaced by more bulky groups as seen in the right-hand column of Table XXVII. The increase effected by hydrocarbon moieties *in* the chain has been indicated by the E_{visc} data of Table XXVI. Polysiloxanes containing polar groups such as *p*-chlorophenyl (Table XXVII) increase the viscosity-temperature coefficient as do the other polar substituents discussed in connection with activation energies of viscous flow.

Solution viscosities of polysiloxanes have received more attention than bulk viscosities, especially for the purpose of molecular weight determination. Measurements of solution viscosities can be extended to polymers of extremely high molecular weight, so high that they might exhibit no measurable bulk flow rate. The number-average molecular weight of a poly-(dimethylsiloxane) may be determined from the intrinsic viscosity of its toluene solution by the relationship (*30*):

$$[\eta] = 2.00 \times 10^{-4} M_n^{0.66}$$

Several other equations of this general form, but varying in their constants, have been proposed for dimethylsiloxane polymers [(*59*), (*392*), (*157*), respectively]:

$$[\eta] = 2.15 \times 10^{-4} M_n^{0.65}$$

$$[\eta] = 3.0 \ \times 10^{-4} M_w^{0.62}$$

$$[\eta] = 8.0 \ \times 10^{-4} M_n^{0.5}$$

The first two of these were based upon toluene solutions; the last equation was critically determined for polymer fractions in the Θ solvent, 2-butanone.

The intrinsic viscosities of poly(methylphenylsiloxanes) have been reported:

in chlorobenzene (*392*), $[\eta] = 3.0 \times 10^{-4} M_w^{0.62}$

in toluene (*227*), $[\eta] = 3.66 \times 10^{-5} M^{0.78}$

Several attempts have been made to determine the molecular weights of resins (*342, 343*) and cross-linked fluids (*241*) as functions of their intrinsic viscosities.

The viscosities of polysiloxanes are greatly increased by increasing pressure (*83*). This will be discussed in connection with compressibility of polysiloxanes, in Section III,B,6.

Compared with other polymers, poly(dimethylsiloxanes) are relatively resistant to shearing stress. The polysiloxanes show transitory decrease of viscosity with shear; many other fluids show permanent decrease in viscosity or "shear breakdown" upon being passed through small orifices under pressure. Figure 17 shows the apparent viscosity with shear for poly(dimethylsiloxanes) of different molecular weight. It is apparent that the shear dependence of viscosity becomes greater with increasing molecular size. Polymers of less than 1000-cp (centipoise) viscosity show Newtonian behavior, but polymers of greater than 1000-cp viscosity show pseudoplastic flow, i.e., their curves of the logarithm of apparent viscosity versus shear rate deviate from linearity. The shear dependence of the higher polysiloxanes has been attributed to the decrease in viscosity caused

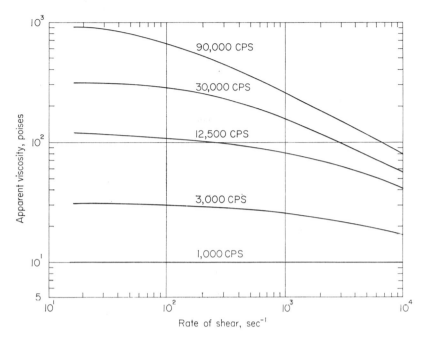

Fɪɢ. 17. Shear dependence of viscosity for poly(dimethylsiloxanes).

by the lining up of polymer molecules in an orderly fashion by high shear rates. Low shear rates are relatively ineffective in untangling the molecules and in lining them up (*127, 229*). The resistance to shear exhibited by the lower viscosity polymers (under 1000 cp) has also been confirmed in practical tests in hydraulic systems (*152*).

5. *Surface Properties*

The surface properties of polysiloxanes are manifested in their insolubility in water, high water repellency, and low surface tensions, and are responsible for their use as water-repellent coatings on textiles, glass, and leather (*311*), as release agents, and as "antifoams." Poly(dimethylsiloxane) coatings on glass surfaces give contact angles of 90 to 110° with liquid water compared with 105 to 111° shown by paraffin, ordinarily regarded as a very hydrophobic material (*158, 200, 418*). Silicone films on glass surfaces are more stable after short periods of heating, apparently because removal of adsorbed water from the glass permits orientation of the polymer chain so that the oxygen atoms are at the glass surface and the methyl groups directed outward. Similar orientation effects also occur on water; insoluble thin films of poly(dimethylsiloxanes) lie flat with the silicon and oxygen atoms in the water interface and the methyl groups in the air interface. Polymers possessing polar end groups such as hydroxyl groups acquire a resultant configuration due to two opposing forces: (i) the attraction of the OH dipole for water and its tendency to orient perpendicular to the surface, and (ii) the attraction of the silicon and oxygen atoms for the water (*299*). Increasing the length of the alkyl chain attached to silicon increases the water repellency somewhat (while decreasing thermal stability) and decreases the coefficient of friction. It is important to note that polysiloxane films are repellent to *liquid* water, not water vapor. Thus textiles and leather treated with silicones prevent passage of liquid water but allow "breathing" or passage of air and water vapor. For the same reason silicone films by themselves do not prevent rusting or corrosion of metal surfaces.

The unusually low surface tensions of poly(dimethylsiloxanes) indicate their high surface activity. The surface tensions for cyclics, D_{3-7}, lie between 17.3 and 18.3 dynes/cm at 25°C and increase slightly with increasing ring size (*201*). Those of the linear polymers vary from about 15 dynes/cm for hexamethyldisiloxane to about 21 to 22 for a fluid of 10^5-cs viscosity (Fig. 18) (*158, 202, 432, 434*). Extreme sensitivity of the surface tension to silanol end groups and trace amounts of impurities probably accounts

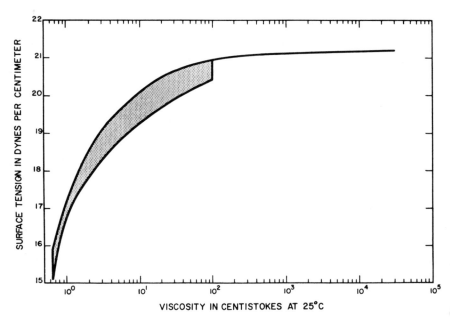

Fig. 18. Variation of surface tension with viscosity for linear poly(dimethylsiloxanes) at 25°C.

for the variation of values reported for organopolysiloxanes (shaded area, Fig. 18). The surface tensions are much lower than those for water (72.8), benzene (28.9), toluene (28.5), and the xylenes (28.4–30.1). Only a few of the lower alkanes, amines, and alcohols have surface tensions so low (*194*). Phenyl and ethyl substituents increase the surface tension somewhat (*158, 349*); ethoxy end-blocking groups alter the surface tension very little (*154*). As expected, the surface tension decreases with increasing temperature and for poly(dimethyl- and diethyl-siloxanes) the $d\gamma/dt$ is about -0.07 dyne/cm/°C, and for poly(methylphenylsiloxanes) about -0.08 to -0.12 dyne/cm/°C (*158*). Polymers of low surface tension such as the poly(dimethylsiloxanes) tend to creep on metal surfaces, while with poly(methylphenylsiloxanes) the tendency to creep is reduced (*349*).

6. Compressibility

Many of the organopolysiloxanes are characterized by a very high order of liquid compressibility. This is especially so for siloxanes containing hydrogen or methyl groups on the silicon atoms. Aside from the type of substituent group, the chain length of the molecule also plays a dominant role in this property. Comparison of compressibilities among several classes of liquids is afforded by the selected data of Table XXVIII (*83*).

In common with other polymer-homologous series, the compressibilities of the poly(dimethylsiloxanes) decrease with increasing molecular weight, starting with 10.04% for hexamethyldisiloxane and becoming asymptotic at about 7.3% for the high viscosity fluids. For comparison, heptane, the lowest member of the paraffin hydrocarbons in Table XXVIII, shows a compressibility of only 8.35% even though its molecular weight is lower

TABLE XXVIII

COMPRESSIBILITIES OF SELECTED FLUIDS AT 1000 KG/CM²

Poly(dimethylsiloxanes)	Vol %	Organic compound	Vol %
Me₃SiOSiMe₃	10.04	Heptane	8.35
Me₃SiO(Me₂SiO)SiMe₃	9.21	Octane	7.51
Me₃SiO(Me₂SiO)₂SiMe₃	8.64	Decane	6.83
Me₃SiO(Me₂SiO)₃SiMe₃	8.62	Dodecane	6.09
Me₃SiO(Me₂SiO)₄SiMe₃	8.00	Paraffin oil	4.45–4.85
Me₃SiO(Me₂SiO)₆SiMe₃	7.80	m-Xylene	6.02
Fluid, 100 cs	7.34	Chlorobenzene	5.43
Fluid, 350 cs	7.42	Chloroform	6.82
Fluid, 1000 cs	7.36	Amyl ether	6.81
Fluid, 12,500 cs	7.29	Ethyl acetate	7.39
		Fluorocarbon oil	4.93

than that of hexamethyldisiloxane; a value of 4.45 to 4.85% gathered from several sources represents the probable asymptote for the higher paraffins. The aromatic hydrocarbons exhibit rather low compressibilities despite the low molecular weights of some of them. An exception may be noted among the fluorocarbons, which approach a lower compressibility limit of about 4.9% for their oils yet show a remarkably high value of 10.7% for the "light" members, not otherwise characterized.

The compressibilities of the polysiloxanes are dramatically affected by the nature of the side groups, as the data in Table XXIX illustrate (*137*). If, in the methyl-containing polymers, one methyl group on each silicon atom is replaced by a hydrogen atom, the volume changes at 20,000 psi are increased from 11.9% for $Me_3SiOSiMe_3$ to 12.5% for $HMe_2SiOSiMe_2H$ and from 9.0% for the dimethylsiloxane polymer $(Me_2SiO)_n$ to 9.3% for the monomethylsiloxane polymer $(MeHSiO)_n$. If, on the other hand, methyl groups are displaced by larger alkyl groups, compressibility is decreased progressively with the size of the substituent.

The dimethylsiloxane polymers exhibit a surprisingly large viscosity dependence upon pressure (*83*). At 5000 kg/cm² pressure, their viscosities range between a hundredfold and a thousandfold their normal viscosities, whereas many organic substances, including isopentane, increase only about ten- or twentyfold in viscosity on imposition of that pressure. Contrariwise, the poly(dimethylsiloxanes) from the trimer through the 12,500-cs fluid remain liquid at pressures as high as 40,000 kg/cm²—well beyond the pressure at which the ordinarily liquid paraffins freeze.

The behavior of the poly(dimethylsiloxanes) under high pressures has led to their growing use in hydraulic springs since their first reported development in 1947 (*21*).

7. Sound Transmission

The velocity of sound in poly(dimethylsiloxanes) increases with increasing chain length from 873.2 meters/sec at 30°C for hexamethyl-

TABLE XXIX

COMPRESSIBILITIES OF SILOXANES AT 20,000 PSI

Polysiloxane fluid	Vol %	Disiloxanes	Vol %
$(MeHSiO)_n$	9.32	$(Me_2HSi)_2O$	12.5
$(Me_2SiO)_n$	9.05	$(Me_3Si)_2O$	11.9
$(MePrSiO)_n$	7.50		
$(MeBuSiO)_n$	6.80		
$(MePhSiO)_n$	5.45		

disiloxane to 987.3 meters/sec for 1000-cs viscosity fluid (*473*). These values are somewhat lower than those shown by most organic liquids. Phenyl substituents on silicon increase the speed of sound in the polymers to about 1054 to 1236 meters/sec, a value which lies in the range of those for organic liquids. Increasing temperature decreases the velocity of sound in the polymers, the temperature coefficient of sound transmission varying from −3.8 meters/sec/°C for hexamethyldisiloxane to −2.6 for 200- to 1000-cs viscosity fluid.

Molar sound velocity is an additive property, and bond increments have been calculated for Si—O bonds (61.5) and Si—C bonds (35.4) in MM through MD_3M using 95.2 as the value for the C—H bond (*473*). Equation (128), which relates the molecular weight M, of poly(dimethylsiloxanes)

$$M = \frac{48.10d}{v^{\frac{1}{3}} - 40.885[(n^2 - 1)/(n^2 + 2)]} \tag{128}$$

to their density d, refractive index n, and the velocity of sound in them v, is valid up to about molecular weight 15,000 (*473, 474*). The velocity of sound may also be related to thermal conductivity, heat capacity, and molar volume (*72*), and its use in connection with refraction, viscosity, and parachor has been suggested for characterizing polymers (*471*).

C. Uses of Silicone Polymers

The many uses of polysiloxanes are dictated by their desirable chemical and physical properties and are discussed at length elsewhere (*272, 283, 348*). Table XXX summarizes the most important applications together with the properties that make them possible. In addition to these uses silicones have shown great promise in various aspects of medicine and surgery (*89, 273, 363*).

IV. Modified Silicones

Silicones may be considered as one of the possible classes of polymers having the structure shown in XIII, for which M is Si, Z is O, and R and

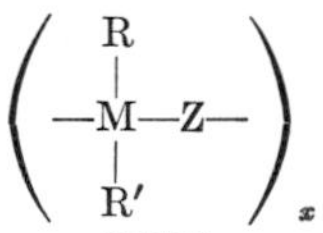

$$\left(\begin{array}{c} R \\ | \\ -M-Z- \\ | \\ R' \end{array} \right)_x$$

(XIII)

Generic structure for modified silicone

TABLE XXX

Uses of Polysiloxanes Related to Their Properties

Use	Heat stability	Low temperature performance	Resistance to O_2 and O_3	Chemical and hydrolytic stability	Initial solubility	Solvent resistance: Nonpolar	Solvent resistance: Polar	Water repellency	Flexibility	Rheological stability	Electrical properties	Surface properties	Viscosity-temperature coefficient
Resins													
Electrical insulation	X	X	X	X	X		X	X	X		X		
Metal coating	X	X	X	X	X		X	X	X				
Laminates	X	X	X	X	X		X	X			X		
Molding compounds	X	X	X	X	X		X		X		X		
Bread pan coatings	X			X		X						X	
Rubbers													
Regular	X	X	X	X			X	X	X		X		
Low swell	X	X	X	X		X		X	X		X		
Fluids													
Electrical	X	X	X	X						X	X		X
Lubricant	X	X	X	X						X		X	X
Hydraulic	X	X		X						X			X
Damping		X								X	X		X
Greases	X	X	X							X			
Textile finishes			X	X	X	X	X	X	X			X	
Release agents	X			X	X							X	
Antifoams				X								X	

R′ are alkyl or aryl groups; polymers of the same general formula, deviating in some respect from the composition of the silicones but still containing sufficient silicon to affect the properties measurably, may be called modified silicones. The modified silicones may be formed by alteration of the side groups or of either element of the backbone. Thus the pendant groups R and/or R′ could be functional groups such as H, vinyl, hydroxypropyl, cyanoethyl, etc., or nonfunctional groups such as trifluoropropyl. The structures might be graft copolymers in which the pendant groups themselves could be polymeric units. The backbone might consist of repeating units in which some of the M's are Si and the rest are other metals such as Al, Sn, or Ge. The Z units could be O, CH_2, NH, —NHNH—, arylene, alkylene, or disubstituted Si atoms, or any combination of such units. It is apparent that an extremely large number of different polymers is theoretically possible. A corresponding proliferation of properties might be anticipated, representing compromises among the characteristics of the structural components. For example, a polymer consisting of polyacrylonitrile units grafted onto a substrate of poly(dimethylsiloxane) would be expected to possess solvent resistance better than that of the pure silicone (but poorer than that of the pure polynitrile) and better thermal stability than that of pure polyacrylonitrile (but poorer than that of the pure

TABLE XXXI
Species of Modified Silicones

M	Z	Polymer formula	Polymer name
Si	O	$(Me_2SiO)_x$	Poly(dimethylsiloxane)[a]
Si	CH_2	$(Me_2SiCH_2)_x$	Poly(dimethylsilcarbane)
Si	$CH_2CH_2CH_2$	$(Me_2SiCH_2CH_2CH_2)_x$	Poly(dimethylsilmethylene, Poly(dimethylsiltricarbane) Poly(dimethylsilpropylene)
Si		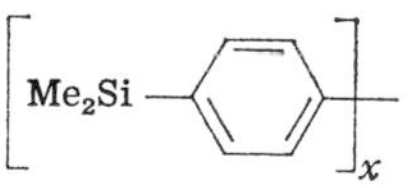	Poly(dimethylsilphenane) Poly(dimethylsilphenylene)
Si	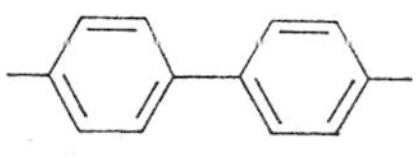	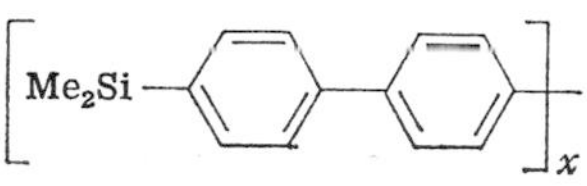	Poly(dimethylsilbiphenane) Poly(dimethylsilbiphenylene)
Si	NH	$(Me_2SiNH)_x$	Poly(dimethylsilazane)
Si	NHNH	$(Me_2SiNHNH)_x$	Poly(dimethylsildiazane)
Si	–	$(Me_2Si)_x$	Poly(dimethylsilane)
Si	S	$(Me_2SiS)_x$	Poly(dimethylsilthiane)
Al	O	$(MeAlO)_x$	Poly(methylaluminoxane)
Ge	O	$(Me_2GeO)_x$	Poly(dimethylgermanoxane)
Sn	O	$(Me_2SnO)_x$	Poly(dimethylstannoxane)

[a] The name poly(dimethyl)siloxamer is suggested by IUPAC rules of polymer nomenclature (*199*). However, these rules have been little accepted.

polysiloxane). Similarly, a poly(tetramethylsilphenylenesiloxane) (XIV), should possess more crystallinity than a poly(dimethylsiloxane) but less than poly(dimethylsilphenylene) (XV), at the same temperature.

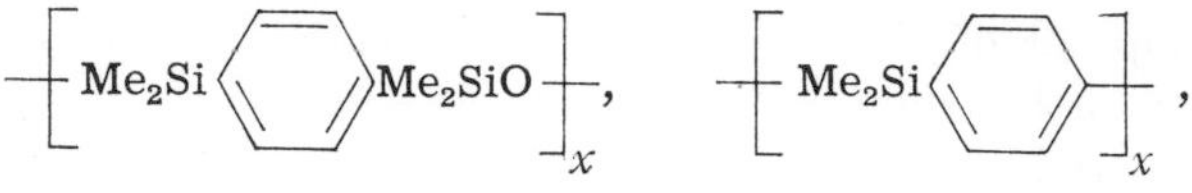

$$\left[\!\!\begin{array}{c} Me_2Si \end{array}\!\!\raisebox{-0.5ex}{\Large\hexagon}\!\!\begin{array}{c} Me_2SiO \end{array}\!\!\right]_x, \qquad \left[\!\!\begin{array}{c} Me_2Si \end{array}\!\!\raisebox{-0.5ex}{\Large\hexagon}\!\!\right]_x,$$

(XIV)   (XV)

The structure and nomenclature of the modified silicone polymers depend upon the nature of M and Z (Structure XIII). Generic names for several modified silicones and metal oxide polymers are shown in Table XXXI. The formulas assume a high molecular weight (i.e., x is large) so that the contribution of end blocking to the formula can be ignored. Modified copolymeric silicones are frequently named by combining the names of the individual units described above. Examples are:

$-(SiCH_2SiO-)_x$ Polysilmethylenesiloxane
$-(SiCH_2CH_2SiO-)_x$ Polysilethylenesiloxane

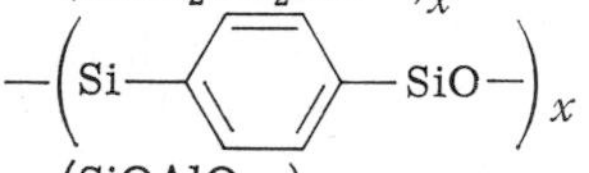

$-\left(Si\!\!\raisebox{-0.5ex}{\Large\hexagon}\!\!SiO-\right)_x$ Poly-p-silphenylenesiloxane

$-(SiOAlO-)_x$ Polysiloxanealuminoxane
$-(SiOPbO-)_x$ Polysiloxaneplumboxane

Many such copolymers can become so complex that it is more desirable to write their structural formulas rather than attempt to name them.

Obviously the possible number and variation of modified silicones appear to be limited only by one's imagination (*171*). Equally obvious is the fact that all such modifications might not result in useful materials. The following sections will attempt to outline only the more important and representative modified silicones.

A. Alteration of Pendant Groups

Silicones modified in the pendant groups, R and R′, of Structure XIII have so far enjoyed more widespread usage than those modified in the backbone. The most common modifications are through organofunctional groups, nonreactive pendant groups, and grafted polymeric units.

1. Variation in Types of Hydrocarbon Groups

In the polysiloxanes so far considered the substituents have been principally methyl and phenyl groups. Yet almost any aliphatic group could be substituted for them, preferably by the addition of the appropriate ≡SiH compound to an olefin. The utility of higher alkyl silicones is restricted by their lack of thermal and oxidative stability and by the effect of increasing C/Si ratios, which make their properties characteristic less of polysiloxane chains and more like hydrocarbons (e.g., viscosity-temperature slope, compressibility, etc.). Nevertheless, they nicely serve a number of special uses for which the question of stability can be waived. Thus, the fluid polymers of the poly(ethylmethylsiloxanes) are useful as thickeners and viscosity-index improvers in certain hydraulic fluids based on silicate esters because, while their viscosity-temperature slopes are nearly equivalent to those of the poly(dimethylsiloxanes), the ethyl-containing polymers are more soluble in the fluids, and formulations containing them therefore remain compatible over a wider range of temperatures (*36, 42, 43, 164*). The higher polymers in the ethylmethylsiloxane series afford rubbers that will not crystallize and whose second-order transition temperatures are among the lowest known (*332*). Thus, while they are impractically susceptible to oxidative embrittlement at temperatures near 200°C, they should be very useful in frigid climates. Polysiloxanes containing higher alkyl groups have outstanding water-repellent properties. Treatment of glass with a siloxane polymer containing octadecyl groups, either by treating the glass with octadecyltrichlorosilane or by transferring a hydrolyzate film by the Langmuir technique, affords a surface monolayer having a hydrophobic nature and very low coefficient of friction (*200*). Such surface films are used to advantage in protecting glass panes, fibers, and bottles against self abrasion.

The similar deposition of monofilms of vinyl, allyl, or other unsaturated silicon compounds in glass fabrics is employed to secure good resin-to-glass bonds in laminates made from them (*61–63, 421, 435, 491*); this affords improved mechanical properties, little affected by moisture. Another important application of vinyl substitution on silicon was discussed in connection with elastomers, where it was shown that a relatively few methylvinylsiloxane units copolymerized in a high polymer gum markedly increased the efficiency of the peroxide vulcanization process (*139*).

The use of tolyl, benzyl, cumyl, naphthyl, biphenylyl, terphenylyl, and other aromatic groups in place of phenyl has been extensively reported in the literature. Some of these on silicon are about as hydrolytically or thermally stable as phenyl, but over-all have shown no particular attributes that would justify their replacement of phenyl compounds for general purposes. In general, bulkier groups yield inferior polymer structures because (1) steric hindrance encourages formation of cyclics and short chains instead of long linear molecules and (2) the number of siloxane chains per unit volume of elastomer or resin is less.

2. Halogens on Side Groups

The haloorganosilicon compounds afford interesting and useful polymers. Chlorophenylchlorosilanes may be prepared by the reaction of chlorobenzene with trichlorosilane or methyldichlorosilane (*31, 35*). In the presence of boron chloride as a catalyst, relatively low temperature reaction yields the *m* and *p* isomers with little sacrifice of chlorine on the aromatic nucleus [Eqs. (129) and (130)]. Alternatively, phenyltrichloro-

$$C_6H_5Cl + HSiCl_3 \rightarrow ClC_6H_4SiCl_3 + H_2 \qquad (129)$$

$$C_6H_5Cl + MeHSiCl_2 \rightarrow ClC_6H_4SiMeCl_2 + H_2 \qquad (130)$$

silane may be chlorinated directly to produce the chlorophenyl, dichlorophenyl, and polychlorophenyl compounds (*153, 195, 351*). Hydrolysis and cocondensation of these with other organochlorosilanes yield a wide variety of copolymer fluids (*155, 197, 480*) useful in the field of special high temperature lubricants. Polymers containing chlorophenyl groups are better extreme pressure lubricants than are similar polymers without the chlorine substitution.

Among the halogenated derivatives the newest and probably the most important polymers are the fluoroalkylsilicones. The trifluoropropylmethylsiloxane polymers in particular are commercially important as the base material for special low swell silicone rubbers. They combine excellent resistance to nonpolar solvents with heat resistance, hydrolytic stability, and flexibility. Their preparation is straightforward; they are made by silicon hydride addition to the corresponding olefins followed by hydrolysis and polymerization as shown in Eq. (131), where *n* is 1 to 3 (*173, 226, 324*).

$$MeHSiCl_2 + CH_2{=}CH(CF_2)_nF \xrightarrow[\text{or } h\nu]{H_2PtCl_6} F(CF_2)_nCH_2CH_2MeSiCl_2 \xrightarrow{H_2O}$$

$$[F(CF_2)_nCH_2CH_2MeSiO]_x \xrightarrow{KOH} \text{cyclic trimer} \xrightarrow[150°]{NaOH} [F(CF_2)_nCH_2CH_2MeSiO]_{5-6000} \quad (131)$$

The polymerization of the cyclic trimer proceeds rapidly and irreversibly through linear high polymer to the cyclic tetramer [Eq. (132)]. At equi-

$$\text{Trimer} \rightarrow \text{linear high polymer} \rightleftharpoons \text{tetramer} \qquad (132)$$

librium, linear polymer is present to the extent of only a few per cent. Therefore, the polymerization is carried out in such a manner that the reaction may be stopped when high polymer is present in about 98 to 99%. Groups containing more fluorine than the trifluoropropyl group do not substantially change the swelling behavior. The lower polymer members of this family show promise as dielectric fluids.

Chloroalkylsilicon compounds may be prepared by direct chlorination under free radical conditions (*252, 411*), or by use of sulfuryl chloride

(269, 398, 408). The chlorination of methylchlorosilanes is illustrated in Eqs. (133) and (134). There is a marked tendency toward exhaustive

$$Me_3SiCl + Cl_2 \xrightarrow{h\nu} \underset{62\%}{ClCH_2Me_2SiCl} + \underset{23\%}{Cl_2CHMe_2SiCl} + \underset{9\%}{(ClCH_2)_2MeSiCl} \quad (133)$$

$$Me_2SiCl_2 + Cl_2 \xrightarrow{h\nu} \underset{37\%}{ClCH_2MeSiCl_2} + \underset{38\%}{Cl_2CHMeSiCl_2} + \underset{7\%}{Cl_3CMeSiCl_2} \quad (134)$$

chlorination of one methyl group, more apparent in Me_2SiCl_2 than in Me_3SiCl. The polysiloxanes formed by hydrolysis of chloromethylchlorosilanes are in themselves of limited value because of their hydrolytic and thermal instability but, because the halogen reacts in the classical organic manner, these compounds are strategic intermediates for making other special siloxane structures, to be considered in the next section.

3. Organofunctional Compounds

Organofunctional polysiloxanes are readily obtained by conventional hydrolysis and polymerization of organofunctional intermediates preferably obtained from the addition of the appropriate unsaturated organic compound to a silane containing at least one active hydrogen, as illustrated in Eq. (135). The group X might be OH, NH_2, CO_2H, CO_2R', Cl, CF_3, CN, $CONH_2$, RCO, RCOO, CHO, or any other functional group. Vulnerability of the group to reaction with halosilane in some cases may restrict choice of method to the lower path of Eq. (135). Appropriate

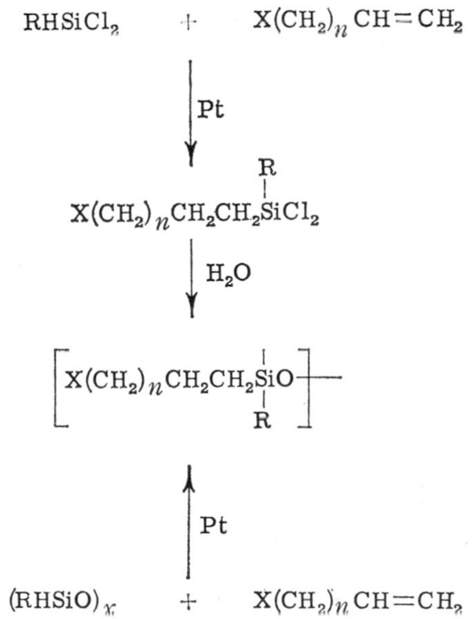

$$RHSiCl_2 \quad + \quad X(CH_2)_n CH{=}CH_2$$

$$\downarrow Pt$$

$$X(CH_2)_n CH_2CH_2\overset{\displaystyle R}{\underset{\displaystyle |}{Si}}Cl_2$$

$$\downarrow H_2O$$

$$\left[X(CH_2)_n CH_2CH_2\overset{\displaystyle |}{\underset{\displaystyle |}{Si}}O \right]$$
$$ R$$

$$\uparrow Pt$$

$$(RHSiO)_x \quad + \quad X(CH_2)_n CH{=}CH_2$$

$$(135)$$

molecular size may be achieved by including end-blocking species in the cohydrolysis or equilibration as illustrated in Eq. (136). Precautions must

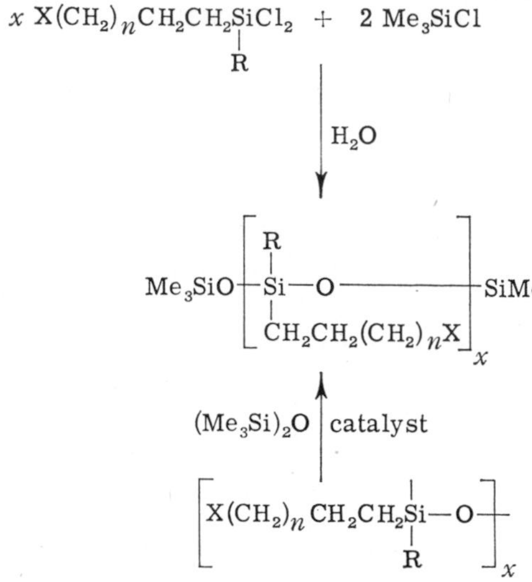

$$x\ X(CH_2)_n CH_2CH_2\underset{\underset{R}{|}}{Si}Cl_2\ +\ 2\ Me_3SiCl$$

$$\downarrow H_2O$$

$$Me_3SiO\left[\underset{\underset{CH_2CH_2(CH_2)_nX}{|}}{\overset{\overset{R}{|}}{Si}}-O-\right]_x SiMe_3$$

$$(Me_3Si)_2O\ \Big\uparrow\ catalyst$$

$$\left[X(CH_2)_n CH_2CH_2\underset{\underset{R}{|}}{\overset{|}{Si}}-O-\right]_x$$

$$(136)$$

be exercised in the choice of the equilibrium catalyst to prevent undesired reactions of certain functional (X) groups. Copolymers may be made in the usual manner by equilibration in the presence of other cyclics or cohydrolysis with other chlorosilanes. Analogous reactions starting with trichlorosilane afford organofunctional intermediates ultimately useful for resin preparation.

The importance of these organofunctional modifications of silicones merits special discussion of a few outstanding types which also illustrate the variety of syntheses available.

Ester-functional siloxanes may be derived from a variety of compounds obtained by salt-halide reactions of chloroalkylsilicon compounds, by silane addition reactions, and by alcoholysis of cyanoalkylsilicon compounds, as illustrated:

$$Me_3SiOSiMe_2CH_2Cl + CH_2{=}CHCOONa \rightarrow Me_3SiOSiMe_2CH_2OOCCH{=}CH_2 + NaCl$$
$$(137)$$

$$Me_3SiOSiMe_2CH_2Cl + NaCH(CO_2Et)_2 \rightarrow Me_3SiOSiMe_2CH_2CH(CO_2Et)_2 + NaCl \quad (138)$$

$$HSiCl_3 + H_2C{=}CHCH_2OAc \xrightarrow{\ Pt\ } Cl_3Si(CH_2)_3OAc \quad (139)$$

$$MeHSiCl_2 + H_2C{=}CMeCOOMe \xrightarrow{\ Pt\ } MeCl_2SiCH_2CHMeCOOMe \quad (140)$$

$$[N{\equiv}C(CH_2)_3MeSiO]_4 \xrightarrow[H_2O]{EtOH} [EtOOC(CH_2)_3MeSiO]_4 \quad (141)$$

The first reaction, Eq. (137), illustrates the preparation of an acryloxy-methylsiloxane from chloromethylpentamethyldisiloxane (*284, 285, 410*). The reaction of sodiomalonic ester with the same starting material gives the expected diester derivative (Eq. 138) (*401*). The silane addition reactions illustrated in Eqs. (139) and (140) and more fully discussed in Section II,A,3 afford two types of esters. The last reaction, Eq. (141) (*65*), is typical of the alcoholysis of organonitriles in general.

Carboxy-functional siloxanes may be prepared upon saponification [Eq. (142)] or acid hydrolysis of their corresponding esters [Eq. (143)] (*401*).

$$[EtOOC(CH_2)_3MeSiO]_4 \xrightarrow{H_2O} [HOOC(CH_2)_3MeSiO]_4 \tag{142}$$

$$Me_3SiOSiMe_2CH_2CH(CO_2Et)_2 \xrightarrow[HCl]{HOAc} (HO_2CCH_2CH_2Me_2Si)_2O + (Me_3Si)_2O + CH_3CO_2Et \tag{143}$$

In the latter case the expected decarboxylation yields a monobasic acid. The oxidation of tolyl silicon compounds results in siloxanes containing carboxylic acid groups [Eq. (144)] (*44, 263,* cf. *24*), as does the hydrolysis of cyanoalkylsiloxanes [Eq. (145)] (*64, 65*).

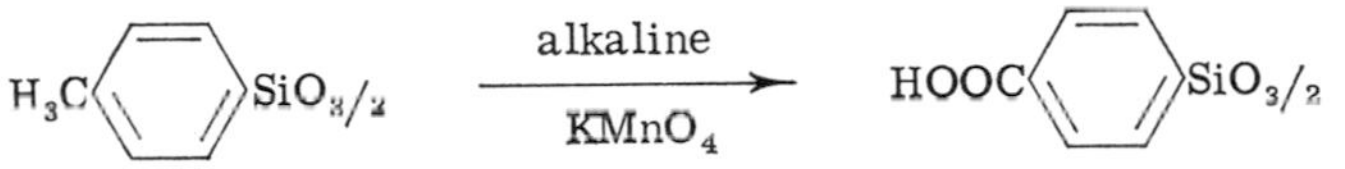

$$(144)$$

$$[N{\equiv}C(CH_2)_3MeSiO]_x \xrightarrow{H_2O} [HOOC(CH_2)_3MeSiO]_x \tag{145}$$

Hydroxyalkylsiloxanes are available by hydrolysis of the appropriate ester. For example, 1,3-bis(hydroxypropyl)tetramethyldisiloxane is obtained from 1,3-bis(acetoxypropyl)tetramethyldisiloxane:

$$(AcOCH_2CH_2CH_2Me_2Si)_2O \xrightarrow[KOH]{MeOH} (HOCH_2CH_2CH_2Me_2Si)_2O \tag{146}$$

Epoxy-functional siloxanes undergo the reactions typical of the epoxy group (*260*) and have found valuable application in resin formulations (*328*). They are readily prepared by the silicon hydride addition to unsaturated epoxy compounds such as allyl 2,3-epoxypropyl ether [Eq. (147)] (*328, 330*) or vinylcyclohexene monoepoxide. Epoxidation of

$$M'D_xM' + CH_2{=}CHCH_2OCH_2\overline{CHCH_2O} \xrightarrow{Pt} [\overline{OCH_2CHCH_2}OCH_2CH_2CH_2Me_2SiO]_2D_x \tag{147}$$

where M′ = HMe₂SiO₁/₂

$Vi(CH_2)_nSi$ compounds where $n > 1$ with peracetic acid may also be employed (*330*, cf. *54*). Curing in the presence of functional compounds such as 4,4'-methylenedianiline gives tough, flexible, heat-stable resins (*328*).

Cyanoalkylsiloxanes are of interest because they illustrate the effect of polar substituent groups on stiffness and the temperature coefficient of viscosity and in suppressing the polymer solubility in nonpolar solvents (*77*, *345*). Cyanomethylsiloxanes may be prepared by the reaction of cyanogen with Grignard reagents [Eq. (148)] (*344*, *345*). Cyanofunctional

$$Me_3SiOMe_2SiCH_2MgCl + (CN)_2 \rightarrow Me_3SiOMe_2SiCH_2CN \qquad (148)$$

silanols and siloxanes also may be obtained upon hydrolysis (*97*, *326*, *345*) of intermediates obtained from the catalyzed addition of trichlorosilane and methyldichlorosilane to acrylonitrile [Eq. (149)] (*68*, *69*, *120*, *304*, *326*,

$$MeHSiCl_2 + ViCN \xrightarrow{\text{catalyst}} Cl_2MeSiCH_2CH_2CN + Cl_2MeSiCHMeCN \qquad (149)$$

366). The particular ratio of isomeric products obtained in this reaction is strongly dependent upon the catalyst system used. For example, platinum catalysis generally gives a mixture of α and β adducts. The former, however, are of limited utility because of their hydrolytic instability especially toward alkali. The more stable β isomers are produced almost to exclusion of the α isomers in the presence of phosphines, amides, or basic catalysts such as amines. The preparation of β-cyanoethylmethyldichlorosilane by addition of trichlorosilane followed by methylation is preferred over the addition of methyldichlorosilane because of the greater reactivity of the former [Eq. (150)].

$$CH_2{=}CHCN + HSiCl_3 \xrightarrow{(n\text{-}Bu)_3N} NC(CH_2)_2SiCl_3 \xrightarrow{MeMgBr} NC(CH_2)_2MeSiCl_2 \xrightarrow{H_2O}$$
$$[NC(CH_2)_2MeSiO]_x \qquad (150)$$

Aminoalkylsiloxanes are conveniently prepared by amine-halide reactions (*170*, *223*, *301*). For example, the amination of chloromethylpentamethyl-disiloxane yields aminomethylpentamethyldisiloxane (Eq. 151). Reduction

$$Me_3SiOSiMe_2CH_2Cl + 2\ NH_3 \xrightarrow[75°C]{300\ psi} Me_3SiOSiMe_2CH_2NH_2 + NH_4Cl \qquad (151)$$

of cyanoalkylsilicon compounds by catalytic hydrogenation also serves to introduce the amino group [Eq. (152)] (*224*). The olefin addition reac-

$$N{\equiv}C(CH_2)_3Si(OEt)_3 \xrightarrow[H_2]{Raney\ Ni} H_2N(CH_2)_4Si(OEt)_3 \qquad (152)$$

tion serves as a synthetic method for aminoalkylsiloxanes when the amine moiety is rendered suitably inactive to prevent liberation of hydrogen (*365*). The deactivating group may be subsequently removed to yield the desired product [Eq. (153)].

$$(EtO)_3SiH + H_2C{=}CHCH_2NHSiMe_3 \xrightarrow[(2)\ EtOH]{(1)\ Pt} (EtO)_3SiCH_2CH_2CH_2NH_2 \quad (153)$$

A quite different class of reactive silicon compounds, the silylalkylboranes, may be prepared in a manner somewhat analogous to the silicon hydride additions discussed above. Thus, hydroboration (*85, 86, 207*) of vinyl and allyl silicon compounds yields oxygen-sensitive α and β isomers of tris-silylethyl- and propylboranes (*56, 388*) and trisdisiloxanylethylboranes [Eq. (154)] (*56*). Equilibration of such boranes with cyclics gives tris-polysiloxanylalkylboranes, [Eq. (155)] (*387*).

$$B_2H_6 + 6\ Me_3SiOSiMe_2CH{=}CH_2 \rightarrow 2\ [Me_3SiOSiMe_2CH_2CH_2]_3B \quad (154)$$

$$3x\ D_4 + (Me_3SiOSiMe_2CH_2)_3B \xrightarrow{OH^-} [Me_3SiO(Me_2SiO)_{4x}SiMe_2CH_2]_3B \quad (155)$$

4. Graft Copolymers

Graft copolymerization (*96, 101, 167, 221, 309*) offers another method of modifying polysiloxanes through the pendant groups. These polymers are different from those discussed so far in that the pendant groups are themselves polymers (Structure XVI). Thus A may represent a polymer side

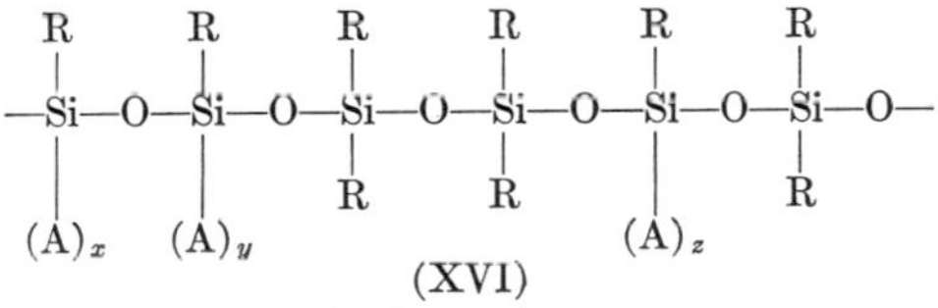

(XVI)
Graft copolymer

chain such as polyacrylonitrile or polystyrene. In contrast to the ionic mechanisms in the preparation of polysiloxanes, the formation of graft copolymers generally involves a free radical polymerization of an olefinic monomer initiated at an active site on a preformed polysiloxane. The properties of the grafted polymer will, of course, depend upon the nature of the grafted and substrate polymers and upon the length, concentration, and distribution of the grafted units. Homopolymer formed along with graft copolymer should be removed by suitable extraction.

Relatively few preparations of graft copolymers with polysiloxane backbones have been reported (*28, 104, 233, 466, 467, 475*), but with one exception the general methods applicable to other polymers can be used for polysiloxane grafts. In general, grafting may be accomplished by treatment with initiator of the substrate polymer (i) immersed in the monomer, (ii) swollen with the monomer, (iii) dissolved along with the monomer in a common solvent, and (iv) alone, and subsequently immersing it in the monomer, possibly with heating. Methods (i) to (iii) are illustrated by Eq. (156) for a poly(dimethylsiloxane) and acrylonitrile (*104, 466, 467*).

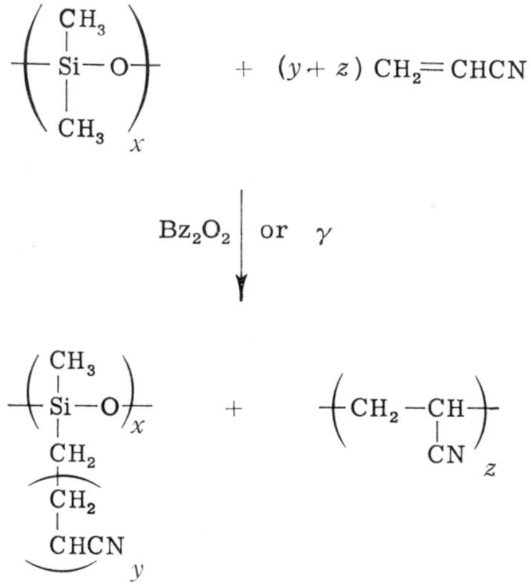

$$
\left(\begin{array}{c} CH_3 \\ | \\ -Si-O- \\ | \\ CH_3 \end{array}\right)_x \quad + \quad (y+z)\ CH_2\!=\!CHCN
$$

$$
Bz_2O_2 \left.\right| \ \text{or} \ \ \gamma \ \downarrow
$$

$$
\left(\begin{array}{c} CH_3 \\ | \\ -Si-O- \\ | \\ CH_2 \\ \overset{|}{\underset{|}{CH_2}} \\ CHCN \end{array}\right)_{x \atop y} \quad + \quad \left(\begin{array}{c} -CH_2-CH- \\ | \\ CN \end{array}\right)_z
$$

$$(156)$$

Initiation may be accomplished in these cases by suitable peroxides, hydroperoxides, and azo compounds, and by high energy radiation. Method (iv), often accomplished by gamma radiation or ozone for other polymer substrates, requires an active intermediate species of sufficient stability so that it may be transferred into monomer after activation and before decomposition or cross-linking occurs. Such species on poly(dimethylsiloxanes) (Eq. 157) appear to be stable only at extremely low tempera-

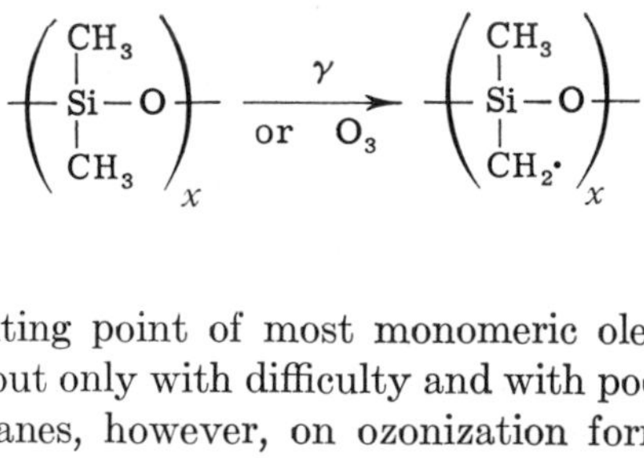

$$
\left(\begin{array}{c} CH_3 \\ | \\ -Si-O- \\ | \\ CH_3 \end{array}\right)_x \quad \xrightarrow[\text{or} \ \ O_3]{\gamma} \quad \left(\begin{array}{c} CH_3 \\ | \\ -Si-O- \\ | \\ CH_2\cdot \end{array}\right)_x
$$

$$(157)$$

tures below the melting point of most monomeric olefins; therefore this technique is carried out only with difficulty and with poor efficiency. Vinyl-containing polysiloxanes, however, on ozonization form relatively stable

active species; these will form graft copolymers when immersed in a variety
of olefins and heated [Eq. (158)] (*56*). Since methyl groups on silicon are

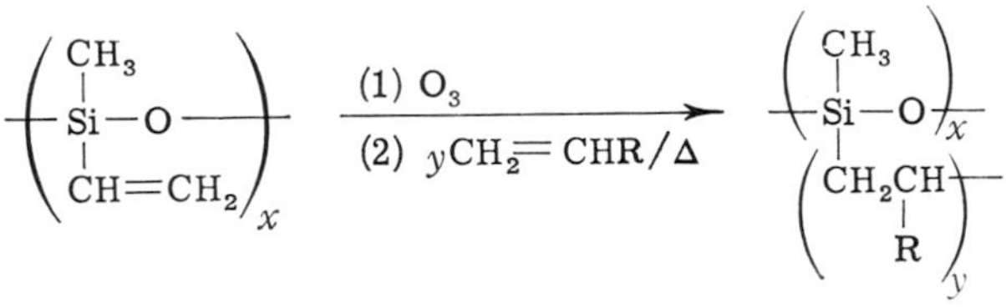

$$\left(\begin{array}{c} CH_3 \\ | \\ -Si-O- \\ | \\ CH=CH_2 \end{array}\right)_x \quad \xrightarrow[\text{(2) } yCH_2=CHR/\Delta]{\text{(1) } O_3} \quad \left(\begin{array}{c} CH_3 \\ | \\ -Si-O- \\ | \\ \left(\begin{array}{c} CH_2CH- \\ | \\ R \end{array}\right)_y \end{array}\right)_x$$

(158)

inert to ozone under ordinary conditions, grafts are attached only at the
positions originally occupied by vinyl groups.

5. Hydrosiloxanes

The polysiloxanes $(H_2SiO)_n$ and $(RHSiO)_n$ are unique because they dis-
play the smallest pendant unit, hydrogen, and thereby derive properties of
special interest. While prosiloxane, $(H_2SiO)_n$, can be made (*424*), it is very
sensitive to hydrogen cleavage by hydrolysis or air oxidation, even at
normal temperatures. Understandably, the interest in this polymer prototype is academic. On the other hand, the polymers of monomethylsiloxane,
$(MeHSiO)_n$, enjoy broad fundamental and practical attention. They are
made by hydrolysis of methylchlorosilanes containing hydrogen on silicon
(Section II,A,3), as indicated in Eq. (159). The sensitivity of the silicon-

$$x \text{ MeHSiCl}_2 + 2 \text{ HMe}_2\text{SiCl} + (x+1) \text{ H}_2\text{O} \rightarrow$$
$$\text{HMe}_2\text{SiO}—(—\text{MeHSiO}—)_x—\text{SiMe}_2\text{H} + (2x+2) \text{ HCl} \quad (159)$$

hydrogen bond to acid and especially to base requires that the hydrolysis
be carried out under essentially neutral conditions. Since the resulting
mixture of linears and cyclics cannot be equilibrated with either a base or a
strong acid, high polymers of the type shown are very difficult to obtain.
The low polymers $(MeHSiO)_n$ find extensive use in textile coatings where
the sensitivity of the Si—H bond makes possible the formation of involved
cross-linked polymer networks [Eq. (160)]. This envelops the fibers,

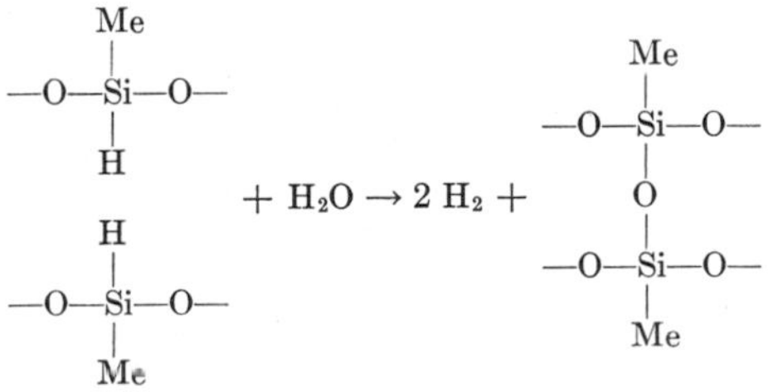

$$\begin{array}{ccc}
\begin{array}{c} Me \\ | \\ -O-Si-O- \\ | \\ H \\ | \\ H \\ | \\ -O-Si-O- \\ | \\ Me \end{array} & + H_2O \rightarrow 2 H_2 + & \begin{array}{c} Me \\ | \\ -O-Si-O- \\ | \\ O \\ | \\ -O-Si-O- \\ | \\ Me \end{array}
\end{array} \quad (160)$$

making the textile fabric hydrophobic and of good "hand." These polymers are unique in that they offer a means of preparing organofunctional polysiloxanes by olefin addition as shown in the lower path of Eq. (135) (*300*).

B. Modification of Polymer Backbone

Modifying polysiloxanes by changing the backbone units, M and Z in Structure XIII, yields new polymers whose properties are in general quite different from those of polysiloxanes. Previous discussion has indicated that the most desirable properties of polysiloxanes are a direct result of their unique backbone. It is reasonable to suppose that any structural deviation from this backbone will tend toward degeneration of these properties. As a result, it is not surprising that most of the polymers prepared by backbone modifications have not enjoyed the widespread utility of the unmodified polysiloxanes or those modified through the substituent groups on silicon.

1. Silazanes and Sildiazanes

Of those bonds capable of forming polymers with silicon the silicon-nitrogen bond is second only to the silicon-oxygen bond in thermal bond strength (Table XI). For this reason polysilazanes are often considered for use at high temperatures (*355*), but no linear polysilazanes of high molecular weight have been reported in the literature. Since silazanes form rings much more readily than do siloxanes (*82*), attempts to prepare them yield mainly cyclic trimers and tetramers [Eq. (161)] (*308*).

$$7 \text{ Me}_2\text{SiCl}_2 + 21 \text{ NH}_3 \xrightarrow{\text{PhH}} (\text{Me}_2\text{SiNH})_3 + (\text{Me}_2\text{SiNH})_4 + 14 \text{ NH}_4\text{Cl} \qquad (161)$$

In addition, polysilazanes suffer from extreme hydrolytic instability, being rapidly hydrolyzed to polysiloxanes. Hence, they could be useful only when employed under completely anhydrous conditions, or if some means could be found to inhibit hydrolysis. One approach to this objective takes advantage of the greater capacity of nitrogen than oxygen to donate electrons; this makes feasible the formation of coordination polymers with metal ions (*292*). Thus the coordination compound of beryllium with the polymer $-[\text{Me}_2\text{SiNHCH}_2\text{CH}_2\text{NH}-]_x-$ does not hydrolyze so rapidly

$$
\begin{array}{cc}
-\text{Me}_2\text{Si}-\text{N}-\text{Me}_2\text{Si}-\text{N}- \\
| \qquad\quad | \\
\text{CH}_2 \qquad \text{CH}_2 \\
| \qquad\quad | \\
\text{CH}_2 \qquad \text{CH}_2 \\
| \qquad\quad | \\
-\text{Me}_2\text{Si}-\text{N}-\text{Me}_2\text{Si}-\text{N}-
\end{array}
$$

(XVII)

as the polymer alone. Further, attempted coordination of the same polymer with copper results in rearrangement, presumably through a square-planar complex, to give a crosslinked "ladder-like" silazane polymer (XVII). This hydrolyzes only about one third as fast as the original polymer. Thus there is some possibility of producing hydrolytically stable polysilazanes, provided that the electron pairs on nitrogen are tied up in some manner.

Sildiazanes are prepared in a manner analogous to silazanes by using hydrazine or substituted hydrazines in place of ammonia or amines (*22, 169, 384, 385, 457, 458, 484*). In general only cyclic or linear dimers have been reported. A soluble gummy polymer of about 40 units has been reported in one instance [Eq. (162)] (*457*). In view of the ease of dimeric

$$x \text{ Me}_2\text{SiCl}_2 + 3x \text{ N}_2\text{H}_4 \rightarrow -[-\text{Me}_2\text{SiNHNH}-]_x- + 2x \text{ N}_2\text{H}_5\text{Cl} \qquad (162)$$

ring closure reported in some cases (*169, 451*), it is possible that this polymer is not a pure linear but consists of both linear and cyclic units. Polysildiazanes exhibit the extreme hydrolytic instability characteristic of the silazanes, but in addition are thermally unstable because of the relatively weak nitrogen-nitrogen bond.

2. *Silalkylenes**

Polysilalkylenes more nearly resemble hydrocarbons in their properties than they do polysiloxanes (*402, 441*); this tendency becomes more pronounced with increasing size of the alkylene unit. In general, they may be prepared by direct process methods (Section II,A,3) or by using alkali metals or Grignard reagents.

a. Silmethylenes. Low molecular weight silmethylene polymers containing $-(-\text{Cl}_2\text{SiCH}_2-)-$ groups may be prepared by passing methylene chloride over copper-silicon alloys in a direct process, but the yields are poor (*163, 297, 312, 440*). Methylchlorosilanes react with a complex of methylene chloride and aluminum or aluminum-copper alloy to give $\text{Me}_3\text{Si}(\text{CH}_2\text{SiMe}_2)_{2.3}\text{Me}$ (*107*). Alkali metals may also be used to prepare polysilmethylenes by the Wurtz-Fittig type of coupling reactions from chloromethylchlorosilanes [Eq. (163)] (*181, 182*). Grignard methods (Eq. 164) and also lithium couplings require stepwise syntheses (*400, 402,*

$$x \text{ ClCH}_2\text{Me}_2\text{SiCl} + 2x \text{ Na}° \rightarrow -(\text{CH}_2\text{Me}_2\text{Si}-)_x- + 2x \text{ NaCl} \qquad (163)$$

$$\text{Me}_3\text{SiCH}_2\text{Cl} \xrightarrow[\text{(2) ClCH}_2\text{Me}_2\text{SiCl}]{\text{(1) Mg}} \text{Me}_3\text{SiCH}_2\text{Me}_2\text{SiCH}_2\text{Cl} \xrightarrow[\text{(2) ClCH}_2\text{Me}_2\text{SiCl}]{\text{(1) Mg}}$$

$$\text{Me}_3\text{SiCH}_2(\text{Me}_2\text{SiCH}_2)_2\text{Cl} \xrightarrow{\text{etc.}} \text{Me}_3\text{SiCH}_2(\text{Me}_2\text{SiCH}_2)_x\text{SiMe}_3 \qquad (164)$$

---

* Cf. Chapter 0.

403). Thus the preparation of high molecular weight polymer becomes exceedingly tedious and results in low over-all yields.

b. Silethylenes. Pure polysilethylenes may be prepared by silicon hydride additions involving compounds which contain both vinyl and hydrogen on the same silicon atom [Eq. (165)] (*128*). A polysilethylene of

$$x \ RR'ViSiH \xrightarrow{Pt} -(-RR'SiCH_2CH_2-)_x- \tag{165}$$

about 20 units prepared in this manner from Me_2ViSiH showed a greater viscosity than the poly(dimethylsiloxane) of equivalent molecular weight; this is in accord with earlier observation of viscosity increase due to carbon in the polymer backbone (cf. Section III,B,4).

Most of the silethylene polymers that have been prepared contain siloxane linkages as well. Polymers containing $(SiCH_2CH_2SiCH_2CH_2SiO)$ and $(SiCH_2CH_2SiO)$ have been readily synthesized by platinum-catalyzed addition of HSi compounds to vinylsilanes (*320, 323, 339*). One of the most interesting of these involves the formation of a five-membered silethylenesiloxane cyclic that undergoes base-catalyzed polymerization to yield high molecular weight linear silethylenesiloxane polymers in a manner similar to siloxane cyclics, [Eq. (166)] (*287, 323*). Heats of polymeriza-

$$MePhSiHCl + ViPh_2SiCl \xrightarrow{H_2PtCl_6} ClPhMeSiCH_2CH_2Ph_2SiCl \xrightarrow[(2)\ LiOH]{(1)\ H_2O}$$

$$PhMeSiCH_2CH_2Ph_2SiO \xrightarrow{K(OSiMe_2)_nOK} [PhMeSiCH_2CH_2Ph_2SiO]_{250} \tag{166}$$

tion, infrared spectra, and polymerization rates suggest that the five-membered ring is highly strained.

c. Higher Silalkylenes. Polysilpropylene and silpropylenesiloxanes are prepared in a manner analogous to the silethylenes by silicon hydride addition to allyl silicon compounds [Eq. (167)] (*320, 339, 439*). Silbutyl-

$$(CH_2=CHCH_2)_2SiMe_2 + Me_2HSiCl \xrightarrow{Pt} Me_2Si(CH_2CH_2CH_2Me_2SiCl)_2 \xrightarrow{H_2O}$$

$$-[-Me_2Si(CH_2)_3Me_2Si(CH_2)_3Me_2SiO-]_x- \tag{167}$$

enesiloxanes may be prepared by Grignard and methyl cleavage reactions, [Eq. (168)] (*397*). Addition of Me_2HSiCl to butadiene followed by hy-

$$Br(CH_2)_4Br \xrightarrow[(2)\ Me_3SiCl]{(1)\ Mg} Me_3Si(CH_2)_4SiMe_3 \xrightarrow[(2)\ H_2O]{(1)\ H_2SO_4} [Me_2Si(CH_2)_4Me_2SiO]_n + CH_4 \tag{168}$$

drolysis should give a similar polymer. Polysilhexylenesiloxane polymers can be obtained from 1,5-hexadiene by silane addition [Eq. (169)] (*320*), and from 1,6-dihalobutanes by Grignard couplings [Eq. (170)] (*79, 427*).

$$Et_2HSiCl + Vi(CH_2)_2Vi \xrightarrow[(2)\ H_2O]{(1)\ Pt} —[—Et_2Si(CH_2)_6Et_2SiO—]_x— \quad (169)$$

$$X(CH_2)_6X \xrightarrow[(2)\ Me_2SiCl_2]{(1)\ Mg} ClMe_2Si(CH_2)_6SiMe_2Cl \xrightarrow{H_2O} —[—Me_2Si(CH_2)_6Me_2SiO—]_x— \quad (170)$$

*3. Silarylenes**

Many types and arrangements of arylene groups may be introduced into polysilarylene and polysilarylenesiloxane polymers such as:

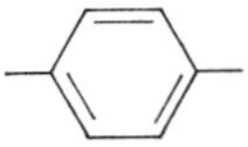 (*80,341*), 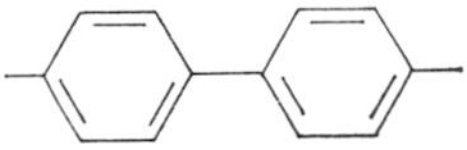 (*53*),

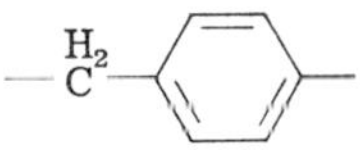 (*78*), 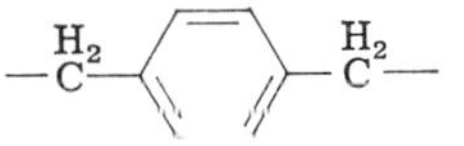 (*482*),

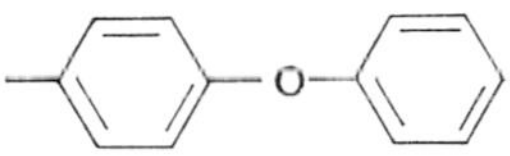 (*53, 77*), 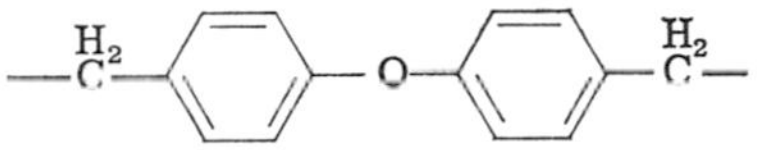 (*56*),

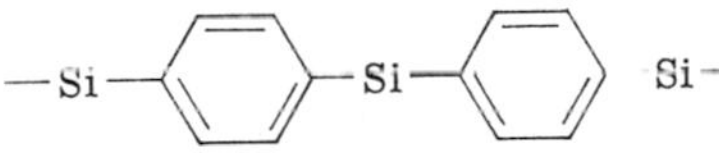 (*106*), 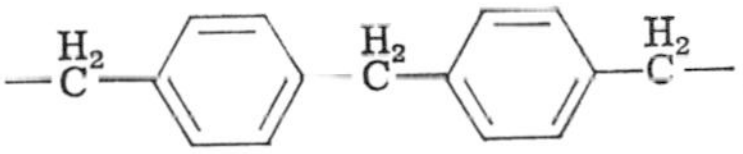 (*16*),

and 1,4-naphthalene (*56*).

Ortho, meta, and para isomers have been obtained, but the para isomers have received the greatest attention. Arylene groups favor crystallinity of the polymer (*341, 428*), induce greater viscosity (*184*) and viscosity-temperature coefficient (*77*), and are generally expected to promote thermal stability. Relative bond energies of the silicon-carbon and silicon-oxygen bonds (Table XI) lead one to believe that these materials should be somewhat less thermally stable than unmodified polysiloxanes, but the inability of the meta and para isomers to form volatile cyclics may lead to thermal stabilities somewhat better than might otherwise be expected.

Polysilphenylenes have been of little practical use. They have been obtained as by-products in the direct process (Section II,A,3,*b*, also *108, 175, 183, 352*) and have been prepared by Grignard reactions (Section

* See also Chapter 6, Section II,B.

II,A,2) [Eq. (171)] (*352*), and by alkali metal couplings [Eq. (172)] (*106, 113*).

$$2 \equiv\!SiCl \ + \ XMg\!\!\left\langle\!\!\bigcirc\!\!\right\rangle\!\!MgX \ \longrightarrow \ \equiv\!Si\!\!\left\langle\!\!\bigcirc\!\!\right\rangle\!\!Si\!\equiv \ + \ 2\ MgXCl$$

$$(171)$$

$$2\ Me_3SiC_6H_4Cl \ + \ 4\ Na \begin{cases} \xrightarrow{(ClMe_2Si)_2CH_2} (Me_3SiC_6H_4Me_2Si)_2CH_2 \ + \ 4\ NaCl \\[3em] \xrightarrow[R_2SiCl_2]{} (Me_3SiC_6H_4)_2R_2Si \ + \ 4\ NaCl \end{cases}$$

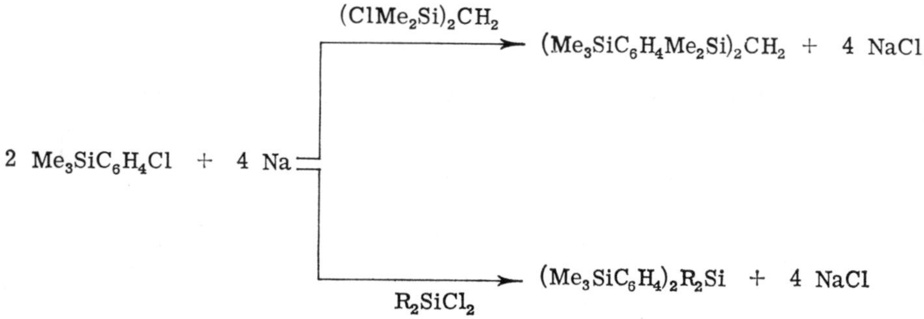

$$(172)$$

Polysilphenylenesiloxanes have received much more attention both as linear polymers and in resins. The intermediates are prepared by direct process methods, by Grignard reagents [Eq. (173)] (*10, 78, 80, 81, 105, 115, 166, 276, 427*), by organolithium reagents [Eq. (174)] (*53, 427*), and by sodium couplings [Eq. (175)] (*78, 114, 427*). Hydrolysis yields the

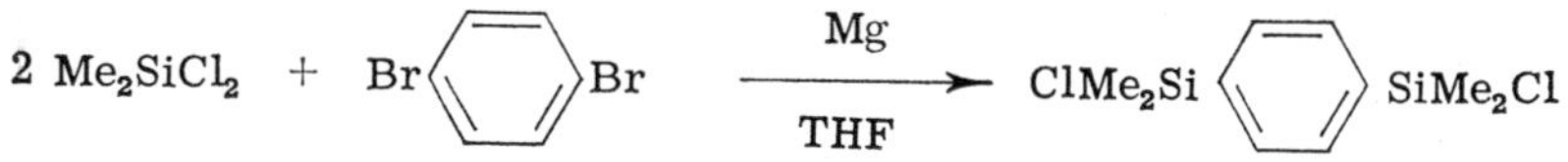

$$2\ Me_2SiCl_2 \ + \ Br\!\!\left\langle\!\!\bigcirc\!\!\right\rangle\!\!Br \ \xrightarrow[\text{THF}]{\text{Mg}} \ ClMe_2Si\!\!\left\langle\!\!\bigcirc\!\!\right\rangle\!\!SiMe_2Cl$$

$$(173)$$

$$Br\!\!\left\langle\!\!\bigcirc\!\!\right\rangle\!\!-O\!\!-\!\!\left\langle\!\!\bigcirc\!\!\right\rangle\!\!Br$$

$$\Big\downarrow \ \ \text{(1) 2 Li or 2 } n\text{-BuLi} \ \ | \ \ \text{(2) } Me_2SiCl_2$$

$$ClMe_2Si\!\!\left\langle\!\!\bigcirc\!\!\right\rangle\!\!-O\!\!-\!\!\left\langle\!\!\bigcirc\!\!\right\rangle\!\!SiMe_2Cl$$

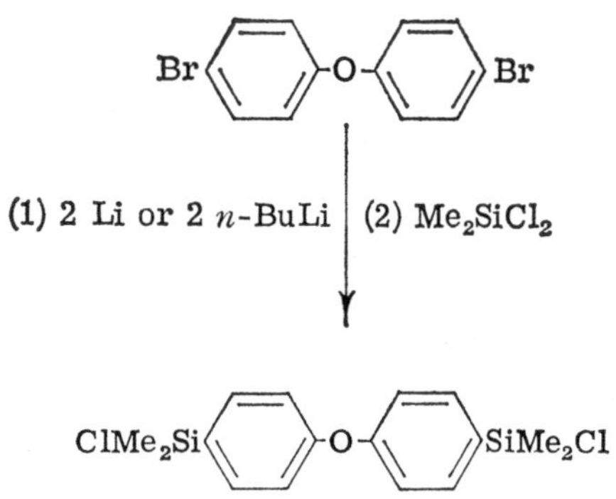

$$(174)$$

corresponding polysilphenylenesiloxanes (*10, 16, 79, 482*). Another method proceeds through condensation of the corresponding diols (Eq. 176), (*11,*

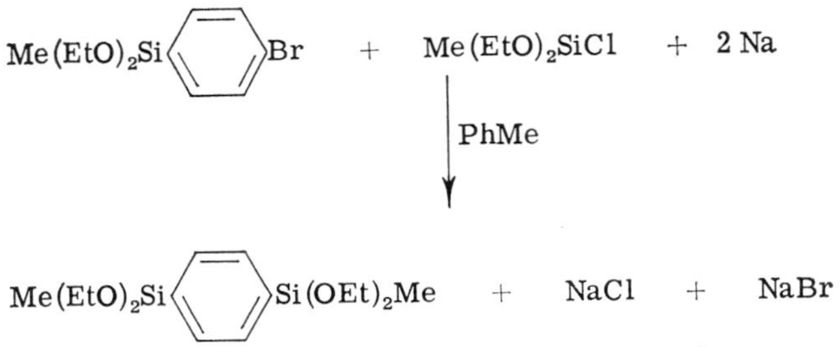

$$(175)$$

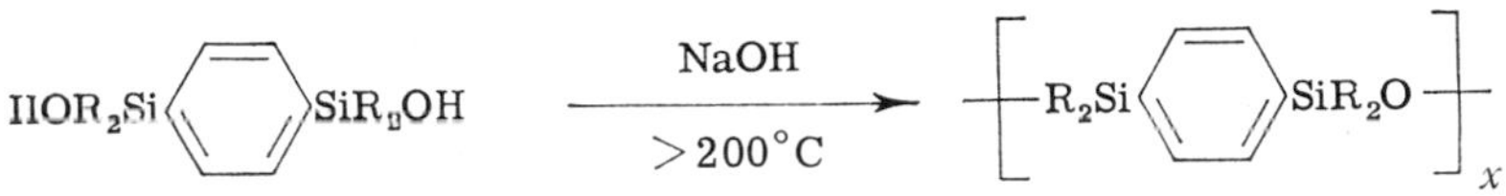

$$(176)$$

276, 428). Other methods involve sodium couplings of the chlorosilane monomers with silanols (*105*) or chlorosilanes (*184*).

4. Polysilanes*

Polysilanes may be considered as a type of modified silicone in which each oxygen atom of a polysiloxane has been replaced with a disubstituted silicon atom (Z, Structure XIII). The parent members of this family of polymers, (Si_nH_{2n+2}), may be prepared by the action of acidic materials such as HCl or NH_4Br in liquid ammonia upon metallic silicides in an inert atmosphere, but the yields are poor [Eq. (177)] (*124, 143, 145, 230, 231,*

$$Mg_2Si + HCl \xrightarrow{Si(OEt)_4} MgCl_2 + Si_nH_{2n+2} \qquad (177)$$

424). Poly(dichlorosilanes), $(Cl_2Si)_x$, have been obtained as minor by-products in the direct process (Section II,A,3,*a*), but are better prepared from simple chlorosilanes by rearrangements of silicon-silicon bonds catalyzed by amines, amine salts, and quaternary compounds [Eq. (178)]

$$5\,Si_2Cl_6 \xrightarrow{Me_3N} 4\,SiCl_4 + Si_6Cl_{14} \qquad (178)$$

(*66, 119, 174, 448, 481*). Wurtz-type coupling reactions using alkali metals in a hydrocarbon solvent and an inert atmosphere readily yield higher

---

* Cf. Chapter 6.

polysilanes (*92, 110, 133, 178, 222, 245, 483*). For example, linear poly(di-methylsilane) containing about 50 silicons per chain is obtained as an insoluble powder as shown in Eq. (179); some cyclic hexamer is apparently by-produced (*92*).

$$n \ Me_2SiCl_2 + 2n \ Na \xrightarrow{\text{PhH}} -(-Me_2Si-)_x- + 2n \ NaCl \qquad (179)$$

Most of the chemistry of polysilanes has been based upon studies of relatively low molecular weight linears and cyclics (*178, 245*, and previous papers), while relatively little attention has been devoted to the higher polymers. Compared with polysiloxanes, the polysilanes are composed of more rigid and less stable molecules with higher intermolecular forces. The relatively low bond strength (Table XI) of the silicon-silicon bond is re-sponsible for their lower thermal stability. They are relatively sensitive to oxygen, the sensitivity increasing markedly with increased hydrogen sub-stitution on silicon. The oxidation of the silicon-silicon bond to siloxane linkages releases, as one might anticipate, a considerable amount of energy. The silicon-silicon bond is readily cleaved by many reagents and is espe-cially sensitive to base; the consequent evolution of hydrogen is the basis of an analytical method for the determination of the number of Si—Si bonds present [Eq. (180)]:

$$\equiv Si-Si \equiv + H_2O \xrightarrow{OH^-} H_2 + \equiv Si-O-Si \equiv \qquad (180)$$

Polymers possessing silicon-silicon bonds in addition to silcarbane and siloxane linkages are prepared by alkali metal couplings with appropriate silicon polymers (*109*). Perhaps the most noteworthy of such compounds is "siloxene"; it is obtained as an insoluble high polymer when calcium silicide is digested with dilute hydrochloric acid (*237–240*). It appears to consist of planar molecules of very large surface area consisting of cyclo-hexasilane rings connected by siloxane bridges (XVIII). Consistent with this structure, "siloxene" is a powerful reducing agent.

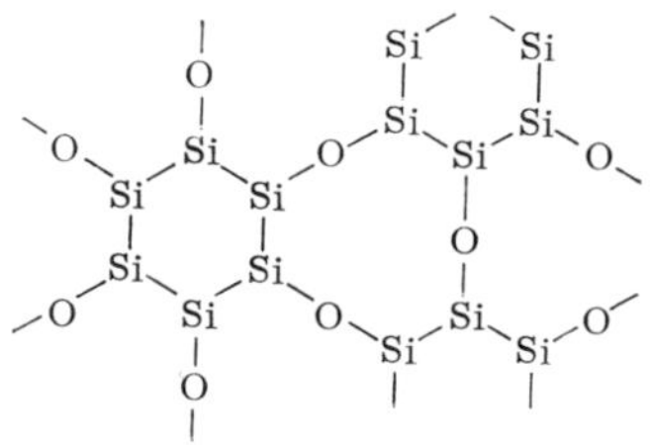

"Siloxene"

(XVIII)

5. Siloxane-Metalloxane Copolymers*

Another type of modified silicone results when some of the silicon atoms in a polysiloxane structure are replaced by atoms of other metals (Structure XIII, where Z is oxygen and M is a mixture of metals including silicon). The silicon-oxygen-metal bonds required in such structures have been produced by many methods as illustrated in Eqs. (181)–(192).

Cohydrolysis of chlorides and alkoxides   (8, 74, 100)   (181)

Cocondensation of hydroxy compounds   (447)   (182)

$SiOH + M° \rightarrow SiOM + H_2$ (8, 15, 405, 433)   (183)

$SiOH + RM \rightarrow SiOM + RH$ (198)   (184)

$SiH + MOH \rightarrow SiOM + H_2$ (136)   (185)

$SiOSi + MCl \rightarrow SiOM + SiCl$ (122, 215, 271, 478)   (186)

$SiOSi + MOH$ (or oxides) $\rightarrow SiOM + SiOH$ (378, 404, 451)   (187)

$M'OH + MCl \rightarrow M'OM + HCl$ (acceptor)   (1, 13, 144, 236, 495)   (188)

$MOR + M'OH$ (or oxides) $\rightarrow MOM' + ROH$ (3, 76, 79, 130, 313)   (189)

$MCl + NaOM' \rightarrow MOM' + NaCl$ (1, 15, 100, 198, 433)   (190)

$MOR + M'Cl \rightarrow MOM' + RCl$ (146, 249)   (191)

$MOAc + M'OR \rightarrow MOM' + ROAc$ (193)   (192)

About 20 elements have been investigated as replacements for part or all of the silicon in silicone-type structures (Table XXXII); the modifications involving aluminum have aroused special interest. To date, however, the work has resulted in no metalloxane polymers superior to conventional silicones. Generally the products are thermally and hydrolytically inferior and, especially in the case of aluminum copolymers, are glassy, brittle solids when heated to the point of being resistant to solvents.

An examination of the partial ionic character of the metal-oxygen bonds reported in SiOM polymers (Table XXXII) reveals that with a few exceptions the other metal-oxygen bonds are considerably more polar than Si—O and therefore more subject to nucleophilic attack at the metal atom. Thus even though zirconium-oxygen and aluminum-oxygen bonds are thermally more stable than a silicon-oxygen bond (from a bond energy consideration (121, 232), they are far less stable hydrolytically. Also, even though the boron-oxygen bond is somewhat stronger and less ionic than the silicon-oxygen bond, the catalytic effects of boron (as well as aluminum) in rearranging substituent groups at high temperatures are well known (Section

---

* Cf. Chapter 7.

TABLE XXXII

PARTIAL IONIC CHARACTER OF VARIOUS METAL-OXYGEN BONDS

Bond	$(X_O - X_M)^a$	Ionic character (%)	
		Pauling[b]	Hannay and Smyth[c]
C—O	1.0	22	19.5
S—O	1.0	22	19.5
P—O	1.4	39	29
As—O	1.5	43	32
B—O	1.5	43	32
Sb—O	1.6	47	34.5
Hg—O	1.6	47	34.5
Fe—O	1.7	51	37
Si—O	1.7	51	37
Pb—O	1.7	51	37
Co—O	1.7	51	37
Ge—O	1.7	51	37
Ni—O	1.7	51	37
Sn—O	1.7	51	37
Cd—O	1.8	55	40
Nb—O	1.9	59	43
Cr—O	1.9	59	43
V—O	1.9	59	43
Zn—O	1.9	59	43
Ti—O	2.0	63	46
Al—O	2.0	63	46
Zr—O	2.1	67	49

[a] $(X_O - X_M)$ is the electronegativity difference for oxygen and metal M.
[b] Pauling (*316*).
[c] Hannay and Smyth (*189*).

II,A,4). For example, tristrimethylsiloxyaluminum readily decomposes through scission of the Al—O bond at a relatively low temperature [Eq. (193)] (*270*, cf. *17*). These considerations plus the possibly unfavorable

$$(Me_3SiO)_3Al \xrightarrow{260-280°C} (Me_3Si)_2O \tag{193}$$

geometry provide an explanation for the deficiencies of the copolymer systems of this type so far investigated.

ACKNOWLEDGMENT

The authors wish to express their appreciation to many colleagues at Dow Corning Corporation for their kind criticism and helpful suggestions.

REFERENCES

The literature cited amply documents the text of this chapter but, because of space limitations, it cannot represent an exhaustive survey of the field. To avoid a too long bibliography, references were selected for their pertinence to the subject and their further citation of supporting literature. Moreover, the authors have made no responsible effort toward literature review beyond the year 1960.

1. Abel, E. W., and Singh, A., *J. Chem. Soc.* p. 690 (1959).
2. Aggarwal, E. W., and Bauer, S. H., *J. Chem. Phys.* **18**, 42 (1950).
3. Alfrey, T., Honn, F. J., and Mark, H., *J. Polymer Sci.* **1**, 102 (1946).
4. Allen, A. D., Charlton, J. C., Eaborn, C., and Modena, G., *J. Chem. Soc.* p. 3668 (1957).
5. Allen, A. D., and Modena, G., *J. Chem. Soc.* p. 3671 (1957).
6. Allen, G., Gee, G., Mangaraj, D., Sims, D., and Wilson, G. J., *Polymer* **1**, 467 (1960).
7. Andrianov, K. A., *J. Gen. Chem. U.S.S.R.* **8**, 1255 (1938); *Chem. Abstr.* **33**, 4193 (1939).
8. Andrianov, K. A., *Uspekhi Khim.* **26**, 895 (1957); *Chem. Abstr.* **52**, 2801 (1958).
9. Andrianov, K. A., and Kurasheva, N. A., *Izvest. Akad. Nauk S.S.S.R., Otdel Khim. Nauk* p. 950 (1957), *Chem. Abstr.* **52**, 4472 (1958).
10. Andrianov, K. A., Nikitenkov, V. E., Kukharchuk, L. A., and Sokolov, N. N., *Izvest. Akad. Nauk S.S.S.R., Otdel. Khim. Nauk* p. 1004 (1958); p. 974 Consultants Bureau translation.
11. Andrianov, K. A., Nikitenkov, V. E., and Sokolov, N. N., *Vysokomolekulyarnye Soedineniya* **2**, 158 (1960); *Chem. Abstr.* **54**, 19005d (1960).
12. Andrianov, K. A., and Shu-Meng, S., *Vysokomolekulyarnye Soedineniya* **2**, 554 (1960); Current Review of the Soviet Technical Press 60–21441–28, p. 3 (Nov. 18, 1960).
13. Andrianov, K. A., and Zhdanov, A. A., *Izvest. Akad. Nauk S.S.S.R. Otdel Khim. Nauk* p. 1590 (1959); *Chem. Abstr.* **54**, 8687f (1960).
14. Andrianov, K. A., Zhdanov, A. A., and Bogdanova, A. A., *Doklady Akad. Nauk S.S.S.R.* **94**, 697 (1954); *Chem. Abstr.* **49**, 6087 (1955).
15. Andrianov, K. A., Zhdanov, A. A., Kurasheva, N. A., and Dulova, V. G., *Doklady Akad. Nauk S.S.S.R.* **112**(6), 1050 (1957); p. 147 Consultants Bureau translation.
16. Andrianov, K. A., Zhdanov, A. A., and Odinets, V. A., *Doklady Akad. Nauk S.S.S.R.* **130**, 75 (1960); p. 1 Consultants Bureau translation.
17. Andrianov, K. A., Zhdanov, A. A., and Pavlov, S. A., *Doklady Akad. Nauk S.S.S.R.* **102**, 85 (1955); *Chem. Abstr.* **50**, 4771i (1956).
18. Angelotti, N. C., and Smith, A. L., *Toilet Goods Assoc. Methods Anal.*, No. 100 (Jan. 5, 1959).
19. Asai, K., *Sci. Repts. Research Insts. Tohoku Univ.* **2**, 205 (1950).
20. Atkins, D. C., Murphy, C. M., and Saunders, C. E., *Ind. Eng. Chem.* **39**, 1395 (1947).
21. *Automotive and Aviation Inds.* March 15, p. 192 (1947); June 1, p. 47 (1947).
22. Aylett, B. J., *J. Inorg. & Nuclear Chem.* **2**, 325 (1956).
23. Bailey, D. L., U. S. Patent 2,723,983 (Nov. 15, 1955); U. S. Patent 2,723,984 (Nov. 15, 1955); U. S. Patent 2,723,985 (Nov. 15, 1955); U. S. Patent 2,745,860 (May 15, 1956).
24. Bailey, D. L., Jex, V. B., and Black, W. T., French Patent 1,189,993 (Oct. 8, 1959)

25. Bailey, D. L., and Pines, A. N., *Ind. Eng. Chem.* **46**, 2363 (1954).
26. Bailey, P. S., *Chem. Revs.* **58**, 925 (1958).
27. Baker, E. B., Barry, A. J., and Hunter, M. J., *Ind. Eng. Chem.* **38**, 1117 (1946).
28. Ballantine, D. S., *Modern Plastics* **35**(1), 171 (1957).
29. Barnes, W., Dewhurst, H. A., Kilb, R. W., and St. Pierre, L. E., *J. Polymer Sci.* **36**, 525 (1959).
30. Barry, A. J., *J. Appl. Phys.* **17**, 1020 (1946).
31. Barry, A. J., U. S. Patent 2,499,561 (March 7, 1950).
32. Barry, A. J., U. S. Patent 2,499,561 (March 7, 1950); U. S. Patent 2,626,269 (Jan. 20, 1953).
33. Barry, A. J., U. S. Patent 2,557,931 (June 26, 1951); U. S. Patent 2,572,302 (Oct. 23, 1951); U. S. Patent 2,626,266 (Jan. 20, 1953).
34. Barry, A. J., U. S. Patent 2,626,267 (Jan. 20, 1953).
35. Barry, A. J., U. S. Patent 2,626,269 (Jan. 20, 1953).
36. Barry, A. J., U. S. Patent 2,746,926 (May 22, 1956).
37. Barry, A. J., Paper presented before Division of Inorganic Chemistry, 137th Meeting, American Chemical Society, Cleveland, Ohio, 1960.
38. Barry, A. J., Daudt, W. H., Domicone, J. J., and Gilkey, J. W., *J. Am. Chem. Soc.* **77**, 4248 (1955).
39. Barry, A. J., and De Pree, L., U. S. Patent 2,488,487 (Nov. 15, 1949).
40. Barry, A. J., De Pree, L., Gilkey, J. W., and Hook, D. E., *J. Am. Chem. Soc.* **69**, 2916 (1947).
41. Barry, A. J., and Gilkey, J. W., U. S. Patent 2,465,188 (March 22, 1949).
42. Barry, A. J., and Gilkey, J. W., U. S. Patent 2,495,362 (Jan. 24, 1950).
43. Barry, A. J., and Gilkey, J. W., U. S. Patent 2,495,363 (Jan. 24, 1950).
44. Barry, A. J., and Gilkey, J. W., U. S. Patent 2,601,237 (June 24, 1952); British Patent 669,790 (April 9, 1952).
45. Barry, A. J., and Gilkey, J. W., U. S. Patent 2,647,912 (Aug. 4, 1953); British Patent 642,630 (Dec. 18, 1950).
46. Barry, A. J., Gilkey, J. W., and Hook, D. E., *Advances in Chemistry Ser. No.* **23**, 246 (1959); *Ind. Eng. Chem.* **51**, 131 (1959).
47. Barry, A. J., Hook, D. E., and De Pree, L., U. S. Patent 2,510,853 (June 6, 1950); U. S. Patent 2,546,330 (March 27, 1951); U. S. Patent 2,591,668 (April 8, 1952); Belgian Patent 473,675 (July 31, 1947).
48. Barry, A. J., Hook, D. E., and De Pree, L., U. S. Patent 2,556,462 (June 12, 1951).
49. Barry, A. J., Hook, D. E., and De Pree, L., Belgian Patent 473,674 (July 31, 1947); Belgian Patent 473,675 (July 31, 1947); U. S. Patent 2,475,122 (July 5, 1949); British Patent 633,732 (Dec. 19, 1949); U. S. Patent 2,510,853 (June 6, 1950); U. S. Patent 2,626,268 (Jan. 20, 1953); U. S. Patent 2,626,271 (Jan. 20, 1953).
50. Bass, S. L., Hunter, M. J., and Kauppi, T. A., *Trans. Electrochem. Soc.* **90**, 255 (1946).
51. Bates, O. K., *Ind. Eng. Chem.* **41**, 1966 (1949).
52. Batschinski, A. J., *Z. physik. Chem.* **84**, 643 (1913).
53. Baum, G., *J. Org. Chem.* **23**, 480 (1958).
54. Bazant, V., and Matousek, V., *Collection Czechoslov. Chem. Communs.* **24**(11), 3758 (1959).
55. Beaman, R. G., *J. Polymer Sci.* **9**, 470 (1952).
56. Beck, H. N., Unpublished data.
57. Bellamy, L. J., "The Infra-red Spectra of Complex Molecules," 2nd ed. Methuen, London, 1958.

57a. Benkeser, R. A., Grossman, R. F., and Stanton, G. M., *J. Am. Chem. Soc.* **83**, 5029 (1961).

58. Berlin, A. A., and Dubinskaya, A. M., *J. Polymer Sci.* **44**, 284 (1960).

59. Berlin, A. A., and Dubinskaya, A. M., *Vysokomolekulyarnye Soedineniya* **1**, 1678 (1959); *Chem. Abstr.* **54**, 17942i (1960).

60. Berridge, C. A., U. S. Patent 2,843,555 (July 15, 1958).

61. Biefeld, L. P., U. S. Patent 2,683,097 (July 6, 1944); U. S. Patent 2,723,210 (Nov. 8, 1955)

62. Biefeld, L. P., and Philipps, T. E., U. S. Patent 2,799,598 (July 16, 1957).

63. Bjorksten, J., 7th Annual Technical Session, Society of the Plastics Industry, 1952.

64. Black, W. T., French Patent 1,189,992 (Oct. 8, 1959).

65. Black, W. T., Bailey, D. L., and Jex, V. B., French Patent 1,189,989 (Oct. 8, 1959); French Patent 1,189,990 (Oct. 8, 1959).

66. Bluestein, B. A., U. S. Patent 2,709,176 (May 24, 1955).

67. Bluestein, B. A., U. S. Patent 2,717,257 (Sept. 6, 1955).

68. Bluestein, B. A., German Patent 1,092,917 (Nov. 17, 1960).

69. Bluestein, B. A., *J. Am. Chem. Soc.* **83**, 1000 (1961).

70. Bluestein, B. A., and McEntee, H. R., *Advances in Chem. Ser. No.* **23**, 233 (1959).

71. Boggs, J. H., and Sibbett, W. L., *Ind. Eng. Chem.* **47**, 289 (1955).

72. Bondi, A., *J. Chem. Phys.* **19**, 128 (1951).

73. Bovey, F. A., "The Effects of Ionizing Radiation on Natural and Synthetic High Polymers," Interscience, New York, 1958.

74. Boyd, T., U. S. Patent 2,716,656 (Aug. 30, 1955).

75. Boyer, R. F., and Spencer, R. S., *Advances in Colloid Sci.* **2**, 1 (1946).

76. Bradley, D. C., and Thomas, I. M., *Chem. & Ind. (London)* p. 17 (1958).

77. Braun, D. B., Paper presented at American Chemical Society, Division of Rubber Chemistry, Spring Meeting, Buffalo, New York, May, 1960.

78. Breed, L. W., *J. Org. Chem.* **25**, 1198 (1960).

79. Breed, L. W., Haggerty, W. J., Jr., and Baiocchi, F., *WADC (Wright Air Develop. Center) Tech. Rept.* **57–143**, Part III, ASTIA Document No. 212268, April 1959.

80. Breed, L. W., Haggerty, W. J., Jr., and Baiocchi, F., 137th Meeting, American Chemical Society, Cleveland, Ohio, 1960.

81. Breed, L. W., Haggerty, W. J., Jr., and Baiocchi, F., *J. Org. Chem.* **25**, 1633 (1960).

82. Brewer, S. D., and Haber, C. P., *J. Am. Chem. Soc.* **70**, 3888 (1948).

83. Bridgman, P. W., *Proc. Am. Acad. Arts Sci.* **77**, 115 (1949).

84. Bridgman, P. W., *J. Chem. Phys.* **19**, 203 (1951).

85. Brokaw, R. S., and Pease, R. N., *J. Am. Chem. Soc.* **72**, 3237 (1950).

86. Brown, H. C., and Subba Rao, B. C., *J. Am. Chem. Soc.* **78**, 5694 (1956); *J. Org. Chem.* **22**, 1135, 1136 (1957).

87. Brown, J. F., Jr., Vogt, L. H., Jr., Katchman, A., Eustance, J. W., Kiser, K. M., and Krantz, K. W., *J. Am. Chem. Soc.* **82**, 6194 (1960).

88. Bueche, A. M., *J. Polymer Sci.* **19**, 297 (1956).

89. The Bulletin, Dow Corning Center for Aid to Medical Research, Quarterly, Oct. 1959 to present.

90. Burell, H., *Interchem. Rev.* **14**, 31 (1955).

91. Burkhard, C. A., *J. Am. Chem. Soc.* **67**, 2173 (1945).

92. Burkhard, C. A., *J. Am. Chem. Soc.* **71**, 963 (1949); U. S. Patent 2,554,976 (May 29, 1951).

93. Burkhard, C. A., *J. Am. Chem. Soc.* **74**, 6275 (1952).

94. Burkhard, C. A., and Krieble, R. H., *J. Am. Chem. Soc.* **69**, 2687 (1947).

95. Burkhard, C. A., and Winslow, E. H., *J. Am. Chem. Soc.* **72**, 3276 (1950).
96. Burlant, W. J., and Hoffman, A. S., "Block and Graft Polymers." Reinhold, New York, 1960.
97. Cahoy, R. P., Meals, R. N., Ashby, B. A., and Silva, P. F., *J. Org. Chem.* **26**, 2008 (1961).
98. Calingaert, G., *et al.*, *J. Am. Chem. Soc.* **61**, 2748–2760, 3300 (1939); **62**, 1099–1110 (1940).
99. Cerato, C. C., Lauer, J. L., and Beachell, H. C., *J. Chem. Phys.* **22**, 1 (1954).
100. Chamberland, B. L., and MacDiarmid, A. G., *J. Am. Chem. Soc.* **83**, 549 (1961).
101. Chapiro, A., *Ind. plastiques mod. (Paris)* **9**, 34 (1957).
102. Charlesby, A., *J. Polymer Sci.* **17**, 379 (1955).
103. Charlesby, A., *Proc. Roy. Soc.* **A230**, 120 (1955).
104. Chen, W. K. W., Mesrobian, R. B., Ballantine, D. S., Metz, D. J., and Glines, A., *J. Polymer Sci.* **23**(104), 903 (1957).
105. Chugunov, V. S., *Izvest. Akad. Nauk S.S.S.R., Otdel. Khim. Nauk* p. 942 (1960); *Chem. Abstr.* **54**, 24482 (1960).
106. Clark, H. A., U. S. Patent 2,507,515 (May 16, 1950).
107. Clark, H. A., U. S. Patent 2,507,521 (May 16, 1950).
108. Clark, H. A., U. S. Patent 2,557,782 (June 19, 1951).
109. Clark, H. A., U. S. Patent 2,563,004 (Aug. 7, 1951); U. S. Patent 2,672,104 (March 16, 1954); U. S. Patent 2,672,105 (March 16, 1954).
110. Clark, H. A., U. S. Patent 2,563,005 (Aug. 7, 1951); U. S. Patent 2,606,879 (Aug. 12, 1952).
111. Clark, H. A., British Patent 663,810 (Dec. 27, 1951).
112. Clark, H. A., British Patent 663,690 (Dec. 27, 1951); British Patent 663,691 (Dec. 27, 1951).
113. Clark, H. A., British Patent 669,178 (March 26, 1952); British Patent 669,179 (March 26, 1952).
114. Clark, H. A., U. S. Patent 2,628,242 (Feb. 10, 1953); British Patent 671,553 (May 7, 1952).
115. Clark, H. A., Gordon, A. F., Young, C. W., and Hunter, M. J., *J. Am. Chem. Soc.* **73**, 3798 (1951).
116. Coleman, A. M., Ph.D. Thesis, Univ. of Pittsburgh, Pittsburgh, Pennsylvania, 1958.
117. Cooper, G. D., *J. Am. Chem. Soc.* **76**, 2499 (1954).
118. Cooper, G. D., *J. Am. Chem. Soc.* **76**, 3713 (1954).
119. Cooper, G. D., and Gilbert, A. R., *J. Am. Chem. Soc.* **82**, 5042 (1960).
120. Cooper, G. D., and Prober, M., French Patent 1,116,726 (May 11, 1956).
121. Cottrell, T. L., "The Strengths of Chemical Bonds," 2nd ed. Butterworths, London, 1958.
122. Cowley, A. H., Fairbrother, F., and Scott, N., *J. Chem. Soc.* p. 717 (1959).
123. Crane, E. J., *Chem. Eng. News* **24**, 1233 (1946); *Compt. rend. union intern. chim. pure et appl. 15th Conf., Amsterdam*, 1949, pp. 127–132; *Chem. Eng. News* **30**, 4517 (1952).
124. Culbertson, J. B., U. S. Patent 2,551,571 (May 8, 1951).
125. Curl, R. F., Jr., and Pitzer, K. S., *J. Am. Chem. Soc.* **80**, 2371 (1958).
126. Currie, C. C., and Hommel, M. C., *Ind. Eng. Chem.* **42**, 2452 (1950).
127. Currie, C. C., and Smith, B. F., *Ind. Eng. Chem.* **42**, 2457 (1950).
128. Curry, J. W., *J. Am. Chem. Soc.* **78**, 1686 (1956); *J. Org. Chem.* **26**, 1308 (1961).
129. Dakin, T. W., and Works, C. N., *J. Appl. Phys.* **18**, 789 (1947).

130. Danforth, J. D., *J. Am. Chem. Soc.* **80**, 2585 (1958).
131. Daudt, W. H., and Hyde, J. F., *J. Am. Chem. Soc.* **74**, 386 (1952).
132. Denbigh, K. G., *Trans. Faraday Soc.* **36**, 936 (1940).
133. Denk, H., Ph.D. Thesis, Ludwig-Maximilians-Universität, Munich, 1960.
134. Dewhurst, H. A., and St. Pierre, L. E., *J. Phys. Chem.* **64**, 1063 (1960).
135. Dibeler, V. H., Mohler, F. L., and Reese, R. M., *J. Chem. Phys.* **21**, 180 (1953).
136. Dolgov, B. N., Khudobin, Iu. I., and Kharitonov, N. B., *Doklady Akad. Nauk S.S.S.R.* **122**, 607 (1958); p. 717 Consultants Bureau translation.
137. Dow Corning Corporation, Unpublished data.
138. Doyle, C. D., *J. Polymer Sci.* **31**, 95 (1958).
139. Dunham, M. L., Bailey, D. L., and Mixer, R. Y., *Ind. Eng. Chem.* **49**, 1373 (1957).
140. Eaborn, C., *J. Chem. Soc.* p. 3077 (1950).
141. Eaborn, C., "Organosilicon Compounds." Butterworths, London, 1960.
142. El-Abbady, A. M., and Anderson, L. C., *J. Am. Chem. Soc.* **80**, 1737 (1958).
143. Emeleus, H. J., and Maddock, A. G., *J. Chem. Soc.* p. 1131 (1946).
144. English, W. D., and Sommer, L. H., *J. Am. Chem. Soc.* **77**, 170 (1955).
145. Feher, F., Kuhlborsch, G., and Luhleigh, H., *Z. anorg. u. allgem. Chem.* **303**, 283 (1960).
146. Fertig, J., Gerrard, W., and Herbst, H., *J. Chem. Soc.* p. 1488 (1957).
147. Fessenden, R., and Fessenden, J. S., *Chem. Revs.* **61**, 361 (1961).
148. Fischer, D. J., Chaffee, R. G., and Flegel, V., *Rubber Age (N. Y.)* **87**(1), 59 (1960).
149. Fischer, D. J., Chaffee, R. G., and Warrick, E. L., *Rubber Age (N. Y.)* **88**(1), 77 (1960).
150. Fischer, D. J., and Flegel, V., *Rubber Age (N. Y.)* **88**(5), 816 (1961).
151. Fischer, D. J., Zack, J. F., and Warrick, E. L., *Lubrication Eng.*, p. 407 (1959).
152. Fitzsimmons, V. G., Pickett, D. L., Militz, R. O., and Zisman, W. A., *Trans. Am. Soc. Mech. Engrs.* **68**(4), 361 (1946).
153. Fletcher, H. J., and Dingman, H. D., British Patent 673,322 (June 4, 1952).
154. Fletcher, H. J., and Hunter, M. J., *J. Am. Chem. Soc.* **71**, 2918 (1949).
155. Fletcher, H. J., and Hunter, M. J., U. S. Patent 2,599,984 (June 10, 1952).
156. Flood, E. A., *J. Am. Chem. Soc.* **55**, 1735 (1933).
157. Flory, P. J., Mandelkern, L., Kinsinger, J. B., and Shultz, W. B., *J. Am. Chem. Soc.* **74**, 3364 (1952).
158. Fox, H. W., Taylor, P. W., and Zisman, W. A., *Ind. Eng. Chem.* **39**, 1401 (1947).
159. Frevel, L. K., and Hunter, M. J., *J. Am. Chem. Soc.* **67**, 2275 (1945).
160. Friedel, C., and Crafts, J. M., *Ann. Chem. Justus Liebigs* **127**, 28 (1863).
161. Friedlina, R. K., *Izvest. Akad. Nauk S.S.S.R. Otdel. Khim. Nauk* p. 1333 (1957); *Chem. Abstr.* **52**, 7217 (1958).
162. Frieser, H., Eagle, M. V., and Speier, J. L., *J. Am. Chem. Soc.* **75**, 2824 (1953).
163. Fritz, G., and Thielking, H., *Z. anorg. u. allgem. Chem.* **306**, 39 (1960).
164. Furby, N. W., and Newnan, C. D., U. S. Patent 2,960,474 (Nov. 15, 1960)
165. Gadsby, G. N., *Research (London)* **3**, 338 (1950); *Chem. Abstr.* **44**, 8881 (1950).
166. Gainer, G. C., U. S. Patent 2,709,692 (May 31, 1955).
167. Gaylord, N. G., *Interchem. Rev.* **15**(4), 91 (1956–1957).
168. Gehman, S. D., and Gregson, T. C., *Rubber Chem. and Technol.* **33**, 1375 (1960).
169. George, M. V., Wittenberg, D., and Gilman, H., *J. Am. Chem. Soc.* **81**, 361 (1959).
170. George, P. D., and Elliott, J. R., *J. Am. Chem. Soc.* **77**, 3493 (1955).
171. George, P. D., Prober, M., and Elliott, J. R., *Chem. Revs.* **56**, 1065 (1956).
172. George, P. D., Sommer, L. H., and Whitmore, F. C., *J. Am. Chem. Soc.* **75**, 1585 (1953).

173. Geyer, A. M., Haszeldine, R. N., Leedham, K., and Marklow, R. J., *J. Chem. Soc.* p. 4472 (1957).
174. Gilbert, A. R., and Cooper, G. D., U. S. Patent 2,842,580 (July 8, 1958).
175. Gilkey, J. W., British Patent 749,938 (June 6, 1956).
176. Gillespie, R. J., *J. Am. Chem. Soc.* **82**, 5978 (1960).
177. Gilliam, W. F., Meals, R. N., and Sauer, R. O., *J. Am. Chem. Soc.* **68**, 1161 (1946).
178. Gilman, H., Peterson, D. J., Jarvie, A. W., and Winkler, H. J. S., *J. Am. Chem. Soc.* **82**, 2076 (1960).
179. Gemlins Handbuch der Anorganischen Chemie, 8th Ed., "Silicium, Teil C, Organische Siliciumverbindungen," Weinheim/Bergstrasse, Verlag Chemie, G.m.b.H., 1958.
180. Goddard, A. E., and Goddard, D., "Textbook of Inorganic Chemistry" (J. N. Friend, ed.), Vol. XI, Pt. I, p. 246. Lippincott, Philadelphia, Pennsylvania, 1928.
181. Goodwin, J. T., Jr., British Patent 624,551 (June 10, 1949); U. S. Patent 2,483,972 (Oct. 4, 1949); British Patent 631,619 (Nov. 7, 1949); British Patent 667,435 (Feb. 27, 1952).
182. Goodwin, J. T., Jr., Baldwin, W. E., and McGregor, R. R., *J. Am. Chem. Soc.* **69**, 2247 (1947).
183. Gordon, A. F., U. S. Patent 2,755,295 (July 17, 1956).
184. Gordon, A. F., and Clark, H. A., U. S. Patent 2,696,480 (Dec. 7, 1954).
185. Grubb, W. T., *J. Am. Chem. Soc.* **76**, 3408 (1954).
186. Grubb, W. T., and Osthoff, R. C., *J. Am. Chem. Soc.* **77**, 1405 (1955).
187. Gundyrev, A. A., Nametkin, N. S., and Topchiev, A. V., *Doklady Akad. Nauk S.S.S.R.* **121**, 1031 (1958); *Chem. Abstr.* **52**, 19307d (1958).
188. Hall, R. A., British Patent 791,169 (Feb. 26, 1958).
189. Hannay, N. B., and Smyth, C. P., *J. Am. Chem. Soc.* **68**, 171 (1946).
190. Harrington, R., *Rubber Age* (*N. Y.*) **81**, 971 (1957); **82**, 461 (1957); **83**, 472 (1958); **85**, 963 (1959); **88**, 475 (1960).
191. Hartshorn, L., Parry, T. V. L., and Rushton, E., *Proc. Inst. Elec. Engrs.* (*London*). *Pt.* 2A **100**, 23 (1953).
192. Harvey, M. C., Nebergall, W. H., and Peake, J. S., *J. Am. Chem. Soc.* **79**, 1437 (1957).
193. Henglein, F. A., Lang, R., and Schmack, L., *Makromol. Chem.* **22**, 103 (1957).
194. Hodgman, C. D., ed., "Handbook of Chemistry and Physics," 34th ed. Chemical Rubber Publ. Co., Cleveland, Ohio, 1952.
195. Holdstock, N. G., French Patent 1,137,470 (May 29, 1957); U. S. Patent 2,803,638 (Aug. 20, 1957); British Patent 784,260 (Oct. 9, 1957).
196. Holland, R. S., and Smyth, C. P., *J. Am. Chem. Soc.* **77**, 268 (1955).
197. Hommel, M. C., U. S. Patent 2,599,917 (June 10, 1952).
198. Hornbaker, E. D., and Conrad, F., *J. Org. Chem.* **24**, 1858 (1959).
199. Huggins, M. L., and Hermans, J. J., *J. Polymer Sci.* **8**, 257 (1952).
200. Hunter, M. J., Gordon, M. S., Barry, A. J., Hyde, J. F., and Heidenreich, R. D., *Ind. Eng. Chem.* **39**, 1389 (1947).
201. Hunter, M. J., Hyde, J. F., Warrick, E. L., and Fletcher, H. J., *J. Am. Chem.Soc.* **68**, 667 (1946).
202. Hunter, M. J., Warrick, E. L., Hyde, J. F., and Currie, C. C., *J. Am. Chem. Soc.* **68**, 2284 (1946).
203. Hurd, C. B., *J. Am. Chem. Soc.* **68**, 364 (1946).
204. Hurd, D. T., *J. Am. Chem. Soc.* **67**, 1545 (1945).

205. Hurd, D. T., *J. Am. Chem. Soc.* **67**, 1813 (1945).
206. Hurd, D. T., U. S. Patent 2,403,370 (July 2, 1946).
207. Hurd, D. T., *J. Am. Chem. Soc.* **70**, 2053 (1948).
208. Hurd, D. T., *J. Am. Chem. Soc.* **77**, 2998 (1955).
209. Hurd, D. T., Osthoff, R. C., and Corrin, M. L., *J. Am. Chem. Soc.* **76**, 249 (1954).
210. Hurd, D. T., and Rochow, E. G., *J. Am. Chem. Soc.* **67**, 1057 (1945).
211. Hyde, J. F., Unpublished data.
212. Hyde, J. F., U. S. Patent 2,438,478 (March 23, 1948).
213. Hyde, J. F., U. S. Patent 2,490,357 (Dec. 6, 1949).
214. Hyde, J. F., U. S. Patent 2,634,284 (April 7, 1953).
215. Hyde, J. F., British Patent 685,183 (Dec. 31, 1952); U. S. Patent 2,645,654 (July 14, 1953).
216. Hyde, J. F., *J. Am. Chem. Soc.* **75**, 2166 (1953).
217. Hyde, J. F., Brown, P. L., and Smith, A. L., *J. Am. Chem. Soc.* **82**, 5854 (1960).
218. Hyde, J. F., and Daudt, W. H., U. S. Patent 2,443,353 (June 15, 1948).
219. Hyde, J. F., and De Long, R. C., *J. Am. Chem. Soc.* **63**, 1194 (1941).
220. Hyde, J. F., and Johannson, O. K., U. S. Patent 2,453,092 (Nov. 2, 1948).
221. Immergut, E. H., and Mark, H., *Makromol. Chem.* **18**, 322 (1956).
222. Jarvie, A. W. P., Winkler, H. J. S., Peterson, D. J., and Gilman, H., *J. Am. Chem. Soc.* **83**, 1921 (1961).
223. Jex, V. B., and Bailey, D. L., French Patent 1,140,301 (July 19, 1957); U. S. Patent 2,832,754 (April 29, 1958); U. S. Patent 2,920,095 (Jan. 5, 1960); U. S. Patent 2,930,809 (March 29, 1960); U. S. Patent 2,943,103 (June 28, 1960).
224. Jex, V. B., and Bailey, D. L., French Patent 1,189,988 (Oct. 8, 1959); U. S. Patent 2,930,809 (March 29, 1960).
225. Johannson, O. K., U. S. Patent 2,994,684 (Aug. 1, 1961).
226. Johannson, O. K., U. S. Patent 3,002,951 (Oct. 3, 1961).
227. Johannson, O. K., Pollnow, G. F., and Saylor, J. C., 135th Meeting, American Chemical Society, Boston, Massachusetts, 1959; and private communication.
228. Johnson, D. H., McLaughlin, J. R., and Tobolsky, A. V., *J. Phys. Chem.* **58**, 1073 (1954).
229. Johnson, G. C., *J. Chem. Eng. Data* **6**(2), 275 (1961).
230. Johnson, W. C., and Hogness, T. R., *J. Am. Chem. Soc.* **56**, 1252 (1934).
231. Johnson, W. C., and Isenberg, S., *J. Am. Chem. Soc.* **57**, 1349 (1935).
232. "JANAF Interim Thermochemical Tables," Joint Army-Navy-Air Force Thermochemical Panel, W. H. Jones, Chairman, Thermal Laboratory, The Dow Chemical Company, Midland, Michigan, 1960, Vol. 1 and 2.
233. Kanner, B., and Reid, W. G., Paper, Division of Polymer Chemistry, 139th American Chemical Society Meeting, St. Louis, Missouri, 1961.
234. Kantor, S. W., *J. Am. Chem Soc.* **75**, 2712 (1953).
235. Kantor, S. W., Grubb, W. T., and Osthoff, R. C., *J. Am. Chem. Soc.* **76**, 5190 (1954).
236. Kary, R. M., and Frisch, K. C., *J. Am. Chem. Soc.* **79**, 2140 (1957).
237. Kautsky, H., *Z. anorg. u. allgem. Chem.* **117**, 209 (1921); *Z. Elektrochem.* **32**, 349 (1926).
238. Kautsky, H., and Bartocha, B., *Z. Naturforsch.* **10b**, 422 (1955).
239. Kautsky, H., and Herzberg, G., *Ber. deut. chem. Ges.* **57**, 1665 (1924).
240. Kautsky, H., Vogell, W., and Oeters, F., *Z. Naturforsch.* **10b**, 597 (1955).
241. Kilb, R. W., *J. Phys. Chem.* **63**, 1838 (1959).
242. Kipping, F. S., *Proc. Chem. Soc.* **20**, 15 (1904); **21**, 65 (1905).

243. Kipping, F. S., *J. Chem. Soc.* **101**, 2108, 2125 (1912).
244. Kipping, F. S., and Lloyd, L. L., *J. Chem. Soc.* **79**, 449 (1901).
245. Kipping, F. S., and Sands, J. E., *J. Chem. Soc.* **119**, 830 (1921).
246. Koch, R. J., U. S. Patent 2,833,742 (May 6, 1958).
247. Koike, M., and Danno, A., *J. Phys. Soc. Japan* **15**, 1501 (1960).
248. Konkle, G. M., Selfridge, R. R., and Servais, P. C., *Ind. Eng. Chem.* **39**, 1410 (1947).
249. Kreshkov, A. P., and Karateev, D. A., *Zhur. Obshchei Khim.* **27**(10), 2715 (1957); p. 2755 Consultants Bureau translation.
250. Kreshkov, A. P., Mikhailenko, Y. Y., and Yakimovich, G. F., *Zhur. Fiz. Khim.* **28**, 537 (1954); *Chem. Abstr.* **48**, 13427 (1954); *Zhur. Anal. Khim.* **9**, 208 (1954); *Chem. Abstr.* **48**, 13542 (1954); *J. Anal. Chem. U.S.S.R.* (*English Transl.*) **9**, 231 (1954); *Chem. Abstr.* **49**, 6782 (1955).
251. Krieble, R. H., U. S. Patent 2,524,529 (Oct. 3, 1950).
252. Krieble, R. H., and Elliott, J. R., *J. Am. Chem. Soc.* **67**, 1810 (1945).
253. Kriegsman, H., *Z. Elektrochem.* **61**, 1088 (1957).
254. Kucera, M., *Collection Czechoslov. Chem. Communs.* **25**(2), 547 (1960).
255. Kurita, Y., and Kondo, M., *Bull. Chem. Soc. Japan* **27**, 160 (1954).
256. Lady, J. H., Bower, G. M., Adams, R. E., and Byrne, F. P., *Anal. Chem.* **31**, 1100 (1959).
257. Lagemann, R., *J. Polymer Sci.* **3**, 663 (1948).
258. Lawton, E. J., Balwit, J. S., and Powell, R. S., *J. Polymer Sci.* **32**, 257 (1958).
259. Lawton, E. J., Bueche, A. M., and Balwit, J. S., *Nature* **172**, 76 (1953).
260. Lee, H., and Neville, K., "Epoxy Resins." McGraw-Hill, New York, 1957.
261. Lewis, C. W., *J. Polymer Sci.* **33**, 153 (1958).
262. Lewis, C. W., *J. Polymer Sci.* **37**, 425 (1959).
263. Lewis, D. W., and Gainer, G. C., *J. Am. Chem. Soc.* **74**, 2931 (1952).
264. Lipscomb, R. V., U. S. Patent 2,570,462 (Oct. 9, 1951).
265. Long, L., Jr., *Chem. Revs.* **27**, 437 (1940).
266. Lord, R. C., Robinson, D. W., and Schumb, W. C., *J. Am. Chem. Soc.* **78**, 1327 (1956).
267. Lucas, G. R., and Martin, R. W., *J. Am. Chem. Soc.* **74**, 5225 (1952).
268. Lufcy, C. W., Palubinskas, F. J., and Maxwell, L. R., *J. Chem. Phys.* **19**, 217 (1951).
269. McBride, J. J., Jr., and Beachell, H. C., *J. Am. Chem. Soc.* **70**, 2532 (1948).
270. McCloskey, A. L., *et al.*, *WADC* (*Wright Air Develop. Center*) *Tech. Rept.* **59–761** (1960).
271. McCusker, P. A., and Ostdick, T., *J. Am. Chem. Soc.* **80**, 1103 (1958).
272. McGregor, R. R., "Silicones and Their Uses," 1st ed. McGraw-Hill, New York, 1954.
273. McGregor, R. R., "Silicones in Medicine and Surgery." Dow Corning Corporation, Midland, Michigan, 1957.
274. McGregor, R. R., and Warrick, E. L., U. S. Patent 2,380,057 (July 10, 1945); U. S. Patent 2,384,384 (Sept. 4, 1945).
275. McGregor, R. R., and Warrick, E. L., U. S. Patent 2,389,802 (Nov. 27, 1945); U. S. Patent 2,389,807 (Nov. 27, 1945).
276. MacKay, F. P., Ph.D. Thesis, Pennsylvania State Univ., State College, Pennsylvania, 1956.
277. McKean, D. C., *Spectrochim. Acta* **13**, 38 (1958).
278. Marsden, J., U. S. Patent 2,445,794 (July 27, 1948).

279. Marsden, H., and Kipping, F. S., *J. Chem. Soc.* **93**, 198 (1908).
280. Mathur, R. M., *Chem. & Ind. (London)* p. 1125 (1957).
281. Mathur, R. M., *Trans. Faraday Soc.* **54**, 1477 (1958).
282. Mathur, R. M., and Kanekar, C. R., *Chem. & Ind. (London)* p. 767 (1956).
283. Meals, R. N., and Lewis, F. M., "Silicones." Reinhold, New York, 1959.
284. Merker, R. L., U. S. Patent 2,793,223 (May 21, 1957).
285. Merker, R. L., and Noll, J. E., *J. Org. Chem.* **21**, 1537 (1956).
286. Merker, R. L., and Scott, M. J., *J. Polymer Sci.* **24**, 1 (1957).
287. Merker, R. L., and Scott, M. J., *J. Polymer Sci.* **43**, 297 (1960).
288. Miller, A. A., *J. Am. Chem. Soc.* **82**, 3519 (1960).
289. Miller, A. A., *J. Am. Chem. Soc.* **83**, 31 (1961).
290. Miller, A. A., Lawton, E. J., and Balwit, J. S., *J. Phys. Chem.* **60**, 599 (1956).
291. Mills, A. P., and MacKenzie, C. A., *J. Am. Chem. Soc.* **76**, 2672 (1954).
292. Minne, R., and Rochow, E. G., *J. Am. Chem. Soc.* **82**, 5625, 5628 (1960).
293. Moeller, T., "Inorganic Chemistry," Wiley, New York, 1952.
294. Murata, H., *J. Chem. Phys.* **19**, 649 (1951).
295. Murata, H., and Kumada, M., *J. Chem. Phys.* **21**, 945 (1953).
296. Murphy, C. M., Saunders, C. E., and Smith, D. C., *Ind. Eng. Chem.* **42**, 2462 (1950).
297. Nametkin, N. S., Topchiev, A. V., and Sokolova, O. P., *Doklady Akad. Nauk S.S.S.R.* **93**, 285 (1953); *Chem. Abstr.* **48**, 12671 (1954).
298. Newing, M. J., *Trans. Faraday Soc.* **46**, 613 (1950).
299. Newing, M. J., *Trans. Faraday Soc.* **46**, 755 (1950).
300. Nitzsche, S., *Makromol. Chem.* **34**, 231 (1959).
301. Noll, J. E., Speier, J. L., and Daubert, B. F., *J. Am. Chem. Soc.* **73**, 3867 (1951).
302. Noll, W. German Patent 825,087 (Dec. 17, 1951).
303. Nozakura, S., *Bull. Chem. Soc. Japan* **29**, 784 (1956).
304. Nozakura, S., and Konotsune, S., *Bull. Chem. Soc. Japan* **29**, 322, 326 (1956).
305. Ohlberg, S. M., Alexander, L. E., and Warrick, E. L., *J. Polymer Sci.* **27**, 1 (1958).
306. Orlov, N. F., *Doklady Akad. Nauk S.S.S.R.* **114**, 1033 (1957); *Chem. Abstr.* **52**, 2742 (1958).
307. Osthoff, R. C., Bueche, A. M., and Grubb, W. T., *J. Am. Chem. Soc.* **76**, 4659 (1954).
308. Osthoff, R. C., and Kantor, S. W., *Inorg. Syntheses* **5**, 55 (1957).
309. Overberger, C. G., and Katchman, A., *Chem. Eng. News* **36**, 80 (1958).
310. Pacault, A., *Compt. rend. acad. sci.* **232**, 1352 (1951).
311. Patnode, W. I., U. S. Patent 2,306,222 (Dec. 22, 1942).
312. Patnode, W. I., and Scheisler, R. W., U. S. Patent 2,381,000 (Aug. 7, 1945); U. S. Patent 2,381,002 (Aug. 7, 1945).
313. Patnode, W. I., and Schmidt, F. C., *J. Am. Chem. Soc.* **67**, 2272 (1945).
314. Patnode, W., and Wilcock, D. F., *J. Am. Chem. Soc.* **68**, 358 (1946).
315. Pauling, L., "General Chemistry," 1st ed. W. H. Freeman, San Francisco, California, 1947.
316. Pauling, L., "The Nature of the Chemical Bond," 3rd ed. Cornell Univ. Press, Ithaca, New York, 1960.
317. Pauling, L., and Branson, H. R., *Proc. Natl. Acad. Sci. U. S.* **37**, 205 (1951).
318. Petrov, A. D., Chernyshev, E. A., Dolgaya, M. E., Egorov, Y. P., and Leites, L. A., *Zhur. Obshchei Khim.* **30**(2), 376 (1960); p. 400 Consultants Bureau translation.
319. Petrov, A., and Vdovin, V. M., *Izvest. Akad. Nauk S.S.S.R. Otdel Khim. Nauk* p. 1490 (1957); *Chem. Abstr.* **52**, 7135 (1958).

320. Petrov, A. D., and Vdovin, V. M., *Izvest. Akad. Nauk S.S.S.R. Otdel Khim. Nauk* p. 1139 (1959); *Chem. Abstr.* **54,** 1270e (1960).
321. Philippoff, W., *Trans. Soc. Rheol.* **4,** 169 (1960).
322. Philippoff, W., *Rheol. Acta* **1,** 371 (1961).
323. Piccoli, W. A., Haberland, G. G., and Merker, R. L., *J. Am. Chem. Soc.* **82,** 1883 (1960).
324. Pierce, O. R., Holbrook, G. W., Johannson, O. K., Saylor, J. C., and Brown, E. D., *Ind. Eng. Chem.* **52,** 783 (1960).
325. Pietrusza, E. W., Sommer, L. H., and Whitmore, F. C., *J. Am. Chem. Soc.* **70,** 484 (1948).
326. Pike, R. A., McMahon, J. E., Jex, V. B., Black, W. T., and Bailey, D. L., *J. Org. Chem.* **24,** 1939 (1959).
327. Pimentel, G. C., and McClellan, A. L., "The Hydrogen Bond," W. H. Freeman, New York, 1960.
328. Plueddemann, E. P., *J. Chem. Eng. Data* **4,** 59 (1959).
329. Plueddemann, E. P., U. S. Patent 2,963,501 (Dec. 6, 1960).
330. Plueddemann, E. P., and Fanger, G., *J. Am. Chem. Soc.* **81,** 2632 (1959).
331. Polis, A., *Ber. deut. chem. Ges.* **18,** 1540 (1885); **19,** 1012 (1886).
332. Polmanteer, K. E., Private communication.
333. Polmanteer, K. E., British Patent 798,667 (July 23, 1958); French Patent 1,172,177 (Feb. 6, 1959).
334. Polmanteer, K. E., U. S. Patent 2,927,907 (March 8, 1960).
335. Polmanteer, K. E., and Hunter, M. J., *J. Appl. Polymer Sci.* **1,** 1 (1959).
336. Polmanteer, K. E., and Koch, R. J., *Ind. Eng. Chem.* **49,** 49 (1957); U. S. Patent 2,842,520 (July 8, 1958).
337. Polmanteer, K. E., Servais, P. C., and Konkle, G. M., *Ind. Eng. Chem.* **44,** 1576 (1952).
338. Polmanteer, K. E., and Weyenberg, D. R., French Patent 1,100,170 (Sept. 16 1955); British Patent 750,534 (June 20, 1956).
339. Polyakova, A. M., and Chumaevskii, N. A., *Doklady Akad. Nauk S.S.S.R.* **130,** 1037 (1960); p. 161 Consultants Bureau translation.
340. Price, F. P., *J. Am. Chem. Soc.* **70,** 871 (1948).
341. Price, F. P., *J. Polymer Sci.* **37,** 71 (1959).
342. Price, F. P., Martin, S. G., and Bianchi, J. P., *J. Polymer Sci.* **22,** 41 (1956).
343. Price, F. P., Martin, S. G., and Bianchi, J. P., *J. Polymer Sci.* **22,** 49 (1956).
344. Prober, M., *J. Am. Chem. Soc.* **77,** 3224 (1955).
345. Prober, M., and Cooper, G. D., French Patent 1,116,725 (May 11, 1956).
346. Reuther, H., *Chem. Tech. (Berlin)* **4,** 451 (1952); *Chem. Abstr.* **47,** 10934h (1953).
347. Reuther, H., *Chem. Tech. (Berlin)* **5,** 268 (1953); *Chem. Abstr.* **48,** 9774h (1954).
348. Reuther, H., "Silikone, Ihre Eigenschaften und ihre Anwendungsmoglichkeiten." Steinkopff, Dresden, 1959.
349. Reuther, H., and Reichel, G., *Plaste u. Kautschuk* **7,** 171 (1960); *Chem. Abstr.* **54,** 25734a (1960).
350. Richards, R. E., and Thompson, H. W., *J. Chem. Soc.* p. 124 (1949).
351. Rochow, E. G., U. S. Patent 2,258,219 (Oct. 7, 1941).
352. Rochow, E. G., U. S. Patent 2,352,974 (July 4, 1944).
353. Rochow, E. G., *J. Am. Chem. Soc.* **67,** 963 (1945); U. S. Patent 2,380,995 (Aug. 7, 1945).

354. Rochow, E. G., "An Introduction to the Chemistry of the Silicones," 2nd ed. Wiley, New York, 1951.

355. Rochow, E. G., *Chem. Eng. News* **38**, 51 (1960).

356. Rochow, E. G., and Gilliam, W. F., *J. Am. Chem. Soc.* **63**, 798 (1941).

357. Rochow, E. G., and Gilliam, W. F., *J. Am. Chem. Soc.* **67**, 1772 (1945).

358. Rochow, E. G., and Le Clair, H. G., *J. Inorg. & Nuclear Chem.* **1**, 92 (1955).

359. Rochow, E. G., and Patnode, W. I., U. S. Patent 2,380,996 (Aug. 7, 1945).

360. Roth, W. L., *J. Am. Chem. Soc.* **69**, 474 (1947).

361. Roth, W. L., *Ann. Rev. Phys. Chem.* **2**, 217 (1951).

362. Roth, W. L., and Harker, D., *Acta Cryst.* **1**, 34 (1948).

363. Rowe, V. K., Spencer, H. C., and Bass, S. L., *Arch. Ind. Hyg. Occupational Med.* **1**, 539 (1950); *J. Ind. Hyg. Toxicol.* **30**(6), 322 (1948).

364. Saam, J. C., and Speier, J. L., *J. Am. Chem. Soc.* **80**, 4104 (1958).

365. Saam, J. C., and Speier, J. L., *J. Org. Chem.* **24**, 119 (1959).

366. Saam, J. C., and Speier, J. L., *J. Org. Chem.* **24**, 427 (1959).

367. Saam, J., and Speier, J., *J. Am. Chem. Soc.* **83**, 1351 (1961).

368. St. Pierre, L. E., Dewhurst, H. A., and Bueche, A. M., *J. Polymer Sci.* **36**, 105 (1959).

369. Sasin, M., and Cermak, J., *Chem. listy* **51**, 1766 (1957); *Chem. Abstr.* **52**, 4534 (1958).

370. Sauer, R. O., *J. Am. Chem. Soc.* **66**, 1707 (1944).

371. Sauer, R. O., *J. Am. Chem. Soc.* **68**, 954 (1946).

372. Sauer, R. O., U. S. Patent 2,647,136 (July 28, 1953).

373. Sauer, R. O., U. S. Patent 2,730,540 (Jan. 10, 1956).

374. Sauer, R. O., and Hadsell, E. M., *J. Am. Chem. Soc.* **70**, 3590 (1948).

375. Sauer, R. O., and Hadsell, E. M., *J. Am. Chem. Soc.* **70**, 4258 (1948).

376. Sauer, R. O., and Mead, D. J., *J. Am. Chem. Soc.* **68**, 1794 (1946).

377. Savidan, L., *Bull. soc. chim. France* p. 411 (1953).

378. Schmidt, M., and Schmidbaur, H., *Angew. Chem.* **70**, 704 (1958).

379. Schomaker, V., and Stevenson, D. P., *J. Am. Chem. Soc.* **63**, 37 (1941).

380. Schumb, W. C., and Stevens, A. J., *J. Am. Chem. Soc.* **72**, 3178 (1950).

381. Schuyten, H. A., Weaver, J. W., and Reid, J. D., *J. Am. Chem. Soc.* **69**, 2110 (1947).

382. Scott, D. W., *J. Am. Chem. Soc.* **68**, 356 (1946).

383. Scott, D. W., *J. Am. Chem. Soc.* **68**, 2294 (1946).

384. Sergeeva, Z. I., Dolgov, B. N., and Tsitovich, D. D., *Khim. i Prakt. Primenenie Kremneorg. Soedineniĭ Trudy Konf., Leningrad No.* **1**, 235 (1958); *Chem. Abstr.* **53**, 11199b (1959).

385. Sergeeva, Z. I., Tszyan, S., and Tsitovich, D. D., *Zhur. Obshcheĭ Khim.* **30**, 694 (1960); *Chem. Abstr.* **54**, 24349c (1960).

386. Servais, P. C., U. S. Patent 2,485,928 (Oct. 25, 1949).

387. Seyferth, D., U. S. Patent 2,831,009 (April 15, 1958).

388. Seyferth, D., *J. Am. Chem. Soc.* **81**, 1844 (1959).

389. Seyferth, D., and Rochow, E. G., *J. Polymer Sci.* **18**, 543 (1955).

390. Shaffer, L. H., and Flanigen, E. M., *J. Phys. Chem.* **61**, 1591,1595 (1957).

391. Shaw, R. A., *J. Chem. Soc.* p. 2831 (1957).

392. Shazka, V. S., and Shaltyko, L. G., *Vysokomolekulyarnye Soedineniya* **2**, 572 (1960); *Chem. Abstr.* **55**, 4104a (1961).

393. Shostakovskii, M. F., Shikhiev, I. A., Kochkin, D. A., and Belyaev, V. I., *Zhur. Obshcheĭ Khim.* **24**, 2202 (1954); *Chem. Abstr.* **50**, 162 (1956).

394. Slobodin, Ya. M., Shmulyakovskii, Ya. E., and Rzhedzinskaya, K. A., *Doklady Akad. Nauk S.S.S.R.* **105**, 958 (1955).

395. Smith, A. L., and McHard, J. A., *Anal. Chem.* **31**, 1174 (1959).

396. Societe Des Usines Chimiques Rhone-Poulenc, French Patent 1,198,749 (Dec. 9, 1959).

397. Sommer, L. H., and Ansul, G. R., *J. Am. Chem. Soc.* **77**, 2482 (1955).

398. Sommer, L. H., Dorfman, E., Goldberg, G. M., and Whitmore, F. C., *J. Am. Chem. Soc.* **68**, 488 (1946).

399. Sommer, L. H., English, W. D., Ansul, G. R., and Vivona, D. N., *J. Am. Chem. Soc.* **77**, 2485 (1955).

400. Sommer, L. H., Goldberg, G. M., Gold, J., and Whitmore, F. C., *J. Am. Chem. Soc.* **69**, 980 (1947).

401. Sommer, L. H., Masterson, J. M., Steward, O. W., and Leitheiser, R. H., *J. Am. Chem. Soc.* **78**, 2010 (1956).

402. Sommer, L. H., Mitch, F. A., and Goldberg, G. M., *J. Am. Chem. Soc.* **71**, 2746 (1949).

403. Sommer, L. H., Murch, R. M., and Mitch, F. A., *J. Am. Chem. Soc.* **76**, 1619 (1954).

404. Sommer, L. H., Pietrusza, E. W., Kerr, G. T., and Whitmore, F. C., *J. Am. Chem. Soc.* **68**, 156 (1946).

405. Sommer, L. H., Pietrusza, E. W., and Whitmore, F. C., *J. Am. Chem. Soc.* **68**, 2282 (1946).

406. Sommer, L. H., Pietrusza, E. W., and Whitmore, F. C., *J. Am. Chem. Soc.* **69**, 188 (1947).

407. Sommer, L. H., and Pioch, R. P., *J. Am. Chem. Soc.* **75**, 6337 (1953).

408. Sommer, L. H., and Whitmore, F. C., *J. Am. Chem. Soc.* **68**, 485 (1946).

409. Speier, J. L., *J. Am. Chem. Soc.* **71**, 273 (1949).

410. Speier, J. L., U. S. Patent 2,550,205 (April 24, 1951).

411. Speier, J. L., *J. Am. Chem. Soc.* **73**, 824 (1951).

412. Speier, J. L., Jr., U. S. Patent 2,723,987 (Nov. 15, 1955); British Patent 769,496 (March 6, 1957).

413. Speier, J. L., Address on "Organofunctional Silicon Compounds," Organometallic Symposium, Pennsylvania State University, State College, Pennsylvania, 1960.

414. Speier, J. L., and Hook, D. E., U. S. Patent 2,823,218 (Feb. 11, 1958).

415. Speier, J. L., and Webster, J. A., *J. Org. Chem.* **21**, 1044 (1956).

416. Speier, J. L., Webster, J. A., and Barnes, G. H., *J. Am. Chem. Soc.* **79**, 974 (1957).

417. Speier, J. L., Zimmerman, R., and Webster, J., *J. Am. Chem. Soc.* **78**, 2278 (1956).

418. Spitze, L. A., and Richards, D. O., *J. Appl. Phys.* **18**, 904 (1947).

419. Sprung, M. M., and Guenther, F. O., *J. Polymer Sci.* **28**, 17 (1958).

420. Steinfink, H., Post, B., and Fankuchen, I., *Acta Cryst.* **8**, 420 (1955).

421. Steinman, R., U. S. Patent 2,563,288 (Aug. 7, 1951); U. S. Patent 2,688,006 (Aug 31, 1954); U. S. Patent 2,688,007 (Aug. 31, 1954).

422. Steward, O. W., and Pierce, O. R., *J. Am. Chem. Soc.* **81**, 1983 (1959).

423. Steward, O. W., and Pierce, O. R., *J. Am. Chem. Soc.* **83**, 1916 (1961).

424. Stock, A., "Hydrides of Boron and Silicon," Cornell Univ. Press, Ithaca, New York, 1933.

425. Sun, K. H., *Modern Plastics* **32**, 141 (1954).

426. Sutton, L. E., *et al.*, *Chem. Soc.* (*London*) *Spec. Publ. No.* **11**, (1958).

427. Sveda, M., U. S. Patent 2,561,429 (July 24, 1951).

428. Sveda, M., U. S. Patent 2,562,000 (July 24, 1951).

429. Swiss, J., U. S. Patent 2,465,296 (Mar. 22, 1949).
430. "Tables of Dielectric Materials," Vol. II, p. 139. Laboratory for Insulation Research, Mass. Inst. Technol., Cambridge, Massachusetts (1945).
431. Takiguchi, T., *J. Am. Chem. Soc.* **81,** 2359 (1959).
432. Tarkow, H., *J. Polymer Sci.* **28,** 35 (1958).
433. Tatlock, W. S., and Rochow, E. G., *J. Org. Chem.* **17,** 1555 (1952).
434. Technical Bulletin, "Dow Corning 200 Fluids," Dow Corning Corp., Midland. Michigan, 1952.
435. Te Grotenhuis, T. A., U. S. Patent 2,742,378 (April 17, 1956); U. S. Patent 2,841,566 (July 1, 1958).
436. Thomson, H. W., *J. Chem. Soc.* p. 289 (1947).
437. Tobolsky, A. V., "Properties and Structure of Polymers." Wiley, New York, 1960.
438. Topchiev, A. V., Nametkin, N. S., and Durgar'yan, S. G., *Zhur. Obshchei Khim.* **30,** 927 (1960); p. 941 Consultants Bureau translation.
439. Topchiev, A. V., Nametkin, N. S., and Durgar'yan, S. G., *Doklady Akad. Nauk S.S.S.R.* **130,** 105 (1960); p. 39 Consultants Bureau translation.
440. Topchiev, A. V., Nametkin, N. S., and Zetkin, V. I., *Doklady Akad. Nauk S.S.S.R.* **82,** 927 (1952); *Chem. Abstr.* **47,** 4281 (1953).
441. Topchiev, A. V., Nametkin, N. S., and Zetkin, V. I., *Doklady Akad. Nauk S.S.S.R* **99,** 551 (1954); *Chem. Abstr.* **49,** 5271 (1955).
442. Tsvetkov, Yu. D., Bubnov, N. N., Makul'skii, M. A., Lazurkin, S., and Voevodskii, V. V., *Doklady Akad. Nauk S.S.S.R.* **122,** 1053 (1958); *Chem. Abstr.* **54,** 23786c, (1960).
443. Tsvetkov, Yu. D., Molin, Yu. N., and Voevodskii, V. V., *Vysokomolekulyarnye Soedineniya* **1,** 1805 (1959); *Chem. Abstr.* **54,** 19171f (1960).
444. Tyler, L. J., U. S. Patent 2,605,274 (July 29, 1952).
445. Tyler, L. J., *J. Am. Chem. Soc.* **77,** 770 (1955).
446. Ulbrich, R., *Z. Naturforsch.* **9b,** 380 (1954).
447. Upson, R. W., U. S. Patent 2,517,945 (Aug. 8, 1950).
448. Urry, G., and Kaczmarczyk, A., *J. Am. Chem. Soc.* **82,** 751 (1960).
449. Vdovin, V. M., and Petrov, A. D., *Zhur. Obshchei Khim.* **30,** 838 (1960); p. 852 Consultants Bureau translation.
450. Vogel, A. I., Cresswell, W. T., and Leicester, J., *J. Phys. Chem.* **58,** 174 (1954).
451. Voronkov, M. G., *Zhur. Obshchei Khim.* **25,** 469 (1955); *Chem. Abstr.* **50,** 2418 (1956).
452. Voronkov, M. G., Dolgov, B. N., and Dmitrieva, N. A., *Doklady Akad. Nauk S.S.S.R.* **84,** 959 (1952); *Chem. Abstr.* **47,** 3228 (1953).
453. Wacker-Chemie G.m.b.H., British Patent 841,825 (July 20, 1960).
454. Wagner, G. H., U. S. Patent 2,632,013 (March 17, 1953); U. S. Patent 2,637,738 (May 5, 1953).
455. Wagner, G. H., and Burnham, M. M., British Patent 738,541 (Oct. 12, 1955); U. S. Patent 2,746,981 (May 22, 1956).
456. Wagner, G. H., and Strother, C. O., British Patent 670,617 (April 23, 1952).
457. Wannagat, U., and Liehr, W., *Angew. Chem.* **69,** 783 (1957); *Z. anorg. u. allgem. Chem.* **297,** 129 (1958); **299,** 341 (1959).
458. Wannagat, U., and Niederprum, H., *Angew. Chem.* **70,** 745 (1958); **71,** 574 (1959).
459. Warren, B. E., and Biscoe, J., *J. Am. Ceram. Soc.* **21,** 259 (1938).
460. Warrick, E. L., *J. Am. Chem. Soc.* **68,** 2455 (1946).
461. Warrick, E. L., U. S. Patent 2,460,795 (Feb. 1, 1949).
462. Warrick, E. L., U. S. Patent 2,541,137 (Feb. 13, 1951).

463. Warrick, E. L., U. S. Patent 2,634,252 (April 7, 1953).
464. Warrick, E. L., *Ind. Eng. Chem.* **47,** 2388 (1955).
465. Warrick, E. L., *J. Polymer Sci.* **27,** 19 (1958).
466. Warrick, E. L., U. S. Patent 2,958,707 (Nov. 1, 1960).
467. Warrick, E. L., U. S. Patent 2,959,569 (Nov. 8, 1960).
468. Warrick, E. L., Hunter, M. J., and Barry, A. J., *Ind. Eng. Chem.* **44,** 2196 (1952).
469. Warrick, E. L., and Lauterbur, P. C., *Ind. Eng. Chem.* **47,** 486 (1955).
470. Watanabe, M., *J. Ceram. Assoc. Japan* p. 135 (1951).
471. Waterman, H. I., van Herwijnen, W. E. R., and den Hartog, H. W., *J. Appl. Chem.* **8,** 625 (1958).
472. Weir, C. E., Leser, W. H., and Wood, L. A., Research Paper 2084, *J. Research Natl. Bur. Standards* **44,** 367 (1950); *Rubber Chem. and Technol.* **24,** 366 (1951).
473. Weissler, A., *J. Am. Chem. Soc.* **71,** 93 (1949).
474. Weissler, A., Fitzgerald, J. W., and Resnick, I., *J. Appl. Phys.* **18,** 434 (1947).
475. West, J. P., U. S. Patent 2,716,128 (Aug. 23, 1955).
476. West, R., and Baney, R. H., *J. Am. Chem. Soc.* **81,** 6145 (1959).
477. West, R., Baney, R. H., and Powell, D. L., *J. Am. Chem. Soc.* **82,** 6269 (1960).
478. Wiberg, E., and Kruerke, U., *Z. Naturforsch.* **8b,** 610 (1953).
479. Wilcock, D. F., *J. Am. Chem. Soc.* **68,** 691 (1946).
480. Wilcock, D. F., U. S. Patent 2,716,129 (Aug. 23, 1955).
481. Wilkins, C. J., *J. Chem. Soc.* p. 3409 (1953).
482. Wilson, G. R., Paper, Conference on High Temperature Polymer and Fluid Research, Session II, Dayton, Ohio, May 26–28, 1959.
483. Wilson, G. R., and Smith, A. G., *J. Org. Chem.* **26,** 557 (1961).
484. Wittenberg, D., George, M. V., Wu, T. C., Miles, D. H., and Gilman, H., *J. Am. Chem. Soc.* **80,** 4532 (1958).
485. Wood, L. A., *Advances in Colloid Sci.* **2,** 57 (1946).
486. Wood, L. A., *J. Polymer Sci.* **28,** 319 (1958).
487. Wormuth, W. J., and Savage, R. M., British Patent 781,488 (Aug. 21, 1957).
488. Wright, J. G. E., and Oliver, C. S., U. S. Patent 2,448,565 (Sept. 7, 1948).
489. Wright, N., and Hunter, M. J., *J. Am. Chem. Soc.* **69,** 803 (1947).
490. Yamasaki, K., Kotera, A., Yokoi, M., and Ueda, Y., *J. Chem. Phys.* **18,** 1414 (1950).
491. Yeager, L. L., 6th Annual Technical Session, Society of the Plastics Industry, 1951.
492. Young, C. W., Servais, P. C., Currie, C. C., and Hunter, M. J., *J. Am. Chem. Soc.* **70,** 3758 (1948).
493. Young, O. B., and Dickerman, C. E., *Ind. Eng. Chem.* **46,** 364 (1954).
494. Zack, J. F., Jr., Warrick, E. L., and Knoll, G., *J. Chem. and Eng. Data* **6,** 279 (1961).
495. Zeitler, V. A., and Brown, C. A., *J. Am. Chem. Soc.* **79,** 4616 (1957).
496. Zemany, P. D., and Price, F. P., *J. Am. Chem. Soc.* **70,** 4222 (1948).

—6—

Organopolymers of Silicon, Germanium, Tin, and Lead

ROBERT K. INGHAM

Ohio University, Athens, Ohio

and

HENRY GILMAN

Iowa State University, Ames, Iowa

TABLE OF CONTENTS

I. Introduction

Organosilicon polymers may be divided into the following general types
(*378*): (a) silicon-silicon chains, (b) silicon-carbon chains, (c) siloxane
chains, and (d) siloxane networks. Although the dividing line between

these various polymer types is not always well-defined, we shall consider the first two types in this chapter; polymers containing Si—S—Si and Si—N—Si bonding are more closely related to the silicones and, therefore, will not be given any detailed coverage here. The germanium, tin, and lead analogs of all four of the above polymer types will be included in our discussion.

Commercial applications of the organopolymers of Group IVB elements have been mentioned when appropriate but have not been stressed for two reasons. First, most of the research in this area is quite recent and commercial applications have not yet been developed. Second, it is felt desirable at this stage to give lesser emphasis to the patent literature.

An attempt has been made to include all important references appearing in the literature through 1960; several 1961 references have also been given. There has been an uncommon development in the last few years of the area covered by this chapter. Partly for this reason, the authors have felt that it would prove more helpful to the reader to aim for the inclusion of all significant descriptive material. This has made unavoidable a highly succinct style of presentation which has involved the condensation of some papers to one sentence or less. However, the liberal use of structural formulas and of equations should prove helpful in obtaining a satisfactory picture of the tremendous volume of published work which has appeared recently.

II. Organosilicon Polymers

The chemistry of the organopolysiloxanes has been discussed in the preceding chapter. This section will, therefore, be limited to substances containing only silicon-silicon and/or silicon-carbon bonding. Although one normally thinks first of the silicones when organosilicon polymers are mentioned, considerable attention has been given to other types of organosilicon polymers (*102, 128, 186, 378*).

A. Polysilmethylenes

Polysilmethylenes are analogs of silicones with oxygen atoms replaced by CH_2 groups. These compounds are of particular interest because of the increased stability of the silmethylene linkage over siloxane bonding. However, most reported methods give relatively short chain materials.

Silmethylene compounds have been prepared by reacting the Grignard reagent of a chloromethyl silicon derivative with a silicon halide (*38, 365, 420, 421*):

$$(CH_3)_4Si + Cl_2 \rightarrow (CH_3)_3SiCH_2Cl + HCl \tag{1}$$

$$(CH_3)_3SiCH_2Cl + Mg \rightarrow (CH_3)_3SiCH_2MgCl \tag{2}$$

$$(CH_3)_3SiCH_2MgCl + ClSi(CH_3)_3 \rightarrow (CH_3)_3SiCH_2Si(CH_3)_3 \tag{3}$$

$$2 (CH_3)_3SiCH_2MgCl + Cl_2Si(CH_3)_2 \rightarrow (CH_3)_3SiCH_2Si(CH_3)_2CH_2Si(CH_3)_3 \tag{4}$$

The corresponding organolithium compound may replace the Grignard reagent with, at least in some cases, improved yields (*365, 417, 421, 422*):

$$(CH_3)_3SiCH_2Cl + 2 Li \rightarrow (CH_3)_3SiCH_2Li + LiCl \tag{5}$$

$$(CH_3)_3SiCl + Cl_2 \rightarrow ClCH_2Si(CH_3)_2Cl + HCl \tag{6}$$

$$(CH_3)_3SiCH_2Li + ClCH_2Si(CH_3)_2Cl \rightarrow (CH_3)_3SiCH_2Si(CH_3)_2CH_2Cl \tag{7}$$

$$(CH_3)_3SiCH_2Si(CH_3)_2CH_2Li + ClCH_2Si(CH_3)_2Cl \rightarrow (CH_3)_3Si[CH_2Si(CH_3)_2]_2CH_2Cl \tag{8}$$

$$(CH_3)_3Si[CH_2Si(CH_3)_2]_2CH_2Li + (CH_3)_3SiCl \rightarrow (CH_3)_3Si[CH_2Si(CH_3)_2]_2CH_2Si(CH_3)_3 \tag{9}$$

By this method, polysilmethylenes containing from two to five silicon atoms have been synthesized. Similarly, tetrakis(trimethylsilylmethyl)-silane has been prepared from trimethylsilylmethyllithium and silicon tetrachloride (*415, 417, 422*):

$$4 (CH_3)_3SiCH_2Li + SiCl_4 \rightarrow [(CH_3)_3SiCH_2]_4Si + 4 LiCl \tag{10}$$

Recently, the reactions of triphenylsilyllithium with haloforms and with methylene halides have been reported (*130*); small amounts of bis(tri-phenylsilyl)methane are obtained but the reactions appear to be complex and may involve carbene intermediates.

A closely related process for the preparation of polysilmethylenes involves sodium coupling of chloromethyl silicon derivatives with chloro-silanes (*75, 91–94, 150–153, 155–157, 159*):

$$C_6H_5(CH_3)_2SiCH_2Cl + C_6H_5Si(CH_3)Cl_2 + 4 Na \rightarrow$$
$$C_6H_5(CH_3)_2SiCH_2Si(C_6H_5)(CH_3)CH_2Si(CH_3)_2C_6H_5 + 4 NaCl \tag{11}$$

$$(CH_3)_3SiCl + ClCH_2Si(CH_3)_2OC_2H_5 + 2 Na \rightarrow (CH_3)_3SiCH_2Si(CH_3)_2OC_2H_5 + 2 NaCl \tag{12}$$

$$(CH_3)_3SiCH_2Si(CH_3)_2OC_2H_5 + CH_3COCl \rightarrow (CH_3)_3SiCH_2Si(CH_3)_2Cl + CH_3COOC_2H_5 \tag{13}$$

$$(CH_3)_3SiCH_2Si(CH_3)_2Cl + ClCH_2Si(CH_3)_2OC_2H_5 + 2 Na \rightarrow$$
$$(CH_3)_3Si[CH_2Si(CH_3)_2]_2OC_2H_5 + 2 NaCl \tag{14}$$

$$(CH_3)_2Si(OC_2H_5)_2 + ClCH_2Si(CH_3)_2OC_2H_5 + 2 Na \rightarrow$$
$$C_2H_5OSi(CH_3)_2CH_2Si(CH_3)_2OC_2H_5 + NaCl + NaOC_2H_5 \tag{15}$$

Compounds containing as many as five silicon atoms have been prepared by this method. The ethoxyl group is necessary for a controlled reaction; $ClCH_2SiR_2Cl$ compounds undergo self-condensation very readily in the presence of sodium. Treatment with acetyl chloride or with a methyl Grignard reagent achieves replacement of the ethoxyl group by a chlorine atom or a methyl group; the compounds also can be hydrolyzed to the corresponding silicones (154). Both the chloromethyl group and the chlorosilane moiety may be incorporated into the same molecule; for example, $ClCH_2SiR_2Cl$ and $(ClCH_2)_2SiRCl$ compounds give polymers of the type $(-CH_2SiR_2-)_n$ and $[(-CH_2)_2SiR-]_n$ when treated with an alkali metal (95, 99, 110, 149, 159, 236). The reaction is very rapid and only high molecular weight products are isolated. A cyclic trimer, $(-CH_2SiR_2-)_3$, and higher polymers are produced when $(ClCH_2)_2SiR_2$ or $R_2ClSiCH_2SiR_2Cl$ compounds are reacted with sodium (89, 97, 158).

When methylene chloride is passed over silicon-copper at 300 to 400°, $Cl_3SiCH_2SiCl_3$, $Cl_3SiCH_2SiHCl_2$, $(-SiCl_2CH_2-)_3$, as well as higher polymers are obtained (103, 318, 320, 336, 337, 444); the yield of any single compound is usually quite low, even after long recycling periods. Recently, it was shown that $Cl_3SiCH_2SiCl_2CH_2SiHCl_2$ and $Cl_3SiCH_2SiCl_2CH_2SiH_2Cl$ also are products of this reaction (121, 124). Similar reactions with chloroform (313), 1,1-dichloroethane (103, 356), and 2,2-dichloropropane (356) give various silmethylene derivatives. Redistribution reactions of $ClCH_2$-$SiCl_3$, $Cl_2CHSiCl_3$, $CH_3SiCl_2CH_2Cl$, $CH_3CHClSiCl_3$, $CH_3SiCl_2CHCl_2$, and $ClCH_2CH_2SiCl_3$ over silicon-copper at 300 to 400° lead to the formation of silmethylenes (312, 353, 382). Compounds of this type also are obtained in side reactions which accompany the redistribution of methylchlorosilanes at 400° with aluminum chloride (72, 384, 385):

$$2\ CH_3SiCl_3 \rightarrow CH_4 + Cl_3SiCH_2SiCl_3 \qquad (16)$$

A related reaction is that of trimethylchlorosilane with the complex prepared from methylene chloride and aluminum-copper; products from this reaction include hexamethyldisilane, $(CH_3)_3Si[CH_2Si(CH_3)_2]_2CH_3$, and $(CH_3)_3Si[CH_2Si(CH_3)_2]_3CH_3$ as well as higher polymers (68). By-products from the reaction of benzene with trichlorosilane include $Cl_3SiCH(CH_3)$-$SiCl_3$ and $Cl_3SiCH_2CH_2SiCl_3$ (28). The chlorine atoms of the various chloro-substituted silmethylenes mentioned above are readily replaced with organic groups by reaction with the appropriate Grignard reagent (70, 72, 117a, 117b, 182, 313, 315–319, 440–443).

Other reactions giving silmethylenes include the thermal rearrangement of hexamethyldisilane (399):

$$(CH_3)_3SiSi(CH_3)_3 \xrightarrow{\ 600°\ } (CH_3)_3SiCH_2Si(CH_3)_2H \qquad (17)$$

A low yield of bis(trimethylsilyl)methane was obtained from the coupling reaction of methylene bromide and trimethylchlorosilane with lithium (*456*); when some of the higher polymethylene dibromides were used, greatly increased yields of the corresponding bis(trimethylsilyl) derivatives were achieved. Polysilmethylenes are formed when ethyltrimethylsilane and related compounds are passed through a silent discharge (*8*).

The cyclic polysilmethylenes are especially interesting. It has already been mentioned that a cyclic trimer, $(-CH_2SiR_2-)_3$ (I), is formed when $(ClCH_2)_2SiR_2$ or $R_2ClSiCH_2SiR_2Cl$ compounds are reacted with sodium

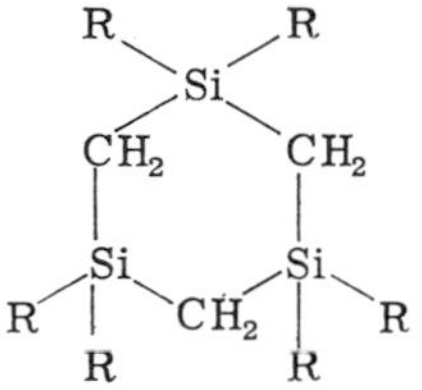

(I) 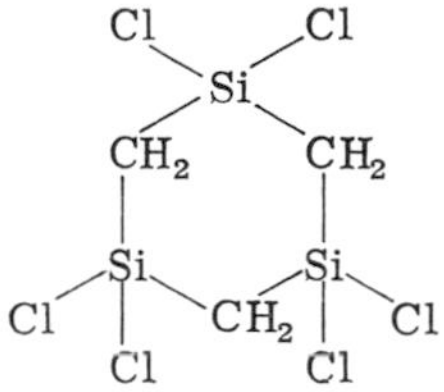   (II)

(*97*) while $(-SiCl_2CH_2-)_3$ (II) is one of the products of the reaction of methylene chloride with silicon-copper at 300° to 400° (*121, 319, 336, 337, 351*). Recently, the thermal decomposition of tetramethylsilane at 600 to 700° was reported to give the following products (*114–119*): $(CH_3)_3-SiCH_2SiH(CH_3)_2$, $(CH_3)_3SiCH_2Si(CH_3)_3$, $Si_3C_8H_{22}$ (III), $Si_3C_9H_{24}$ (IV), $Si_4C_{10}H_{26}$, $Si_4C_{11}H_{28}$ (V), $Si_5C_{13}H_{34}$ (VI), $Si_6C_{14}H_{36}$ (VII), $Si_7C_{18}H_{46}$ (VIII), $Si_8C_{20}H_{50}$ (IX), $Si_8C_{24}H_{66}$, and $Si_9C_{27}H_{74}$. Evidence has been presented favoring the accompanying cyclic polysilmethylene structures (III–IX) for some of the more complex of these compounds.

In a later article, Fritz and Grobe (*117c*) reported that investigation of the products of the pyrolysis of tetramethylsilane led to the isolation of a compound, $Si_2C_6H_{16}$; an unusual structure containing a carbon-silicon double bond, $(CH_3)_2Si=CHSi(CH_3)_3$, was proposed for this substance. However, it seems likely that this compound is the previously reported 1,1,3,3-tetramethyl-1,3-disilacyclobutane (*223a*).

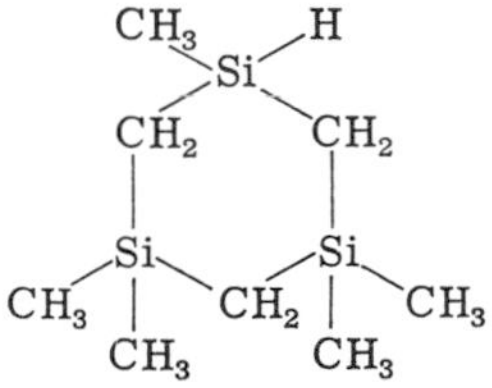

(III) 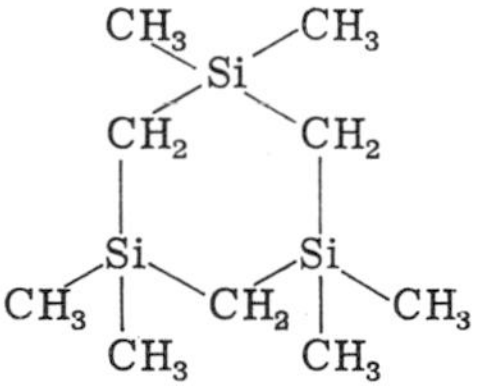   (IV)

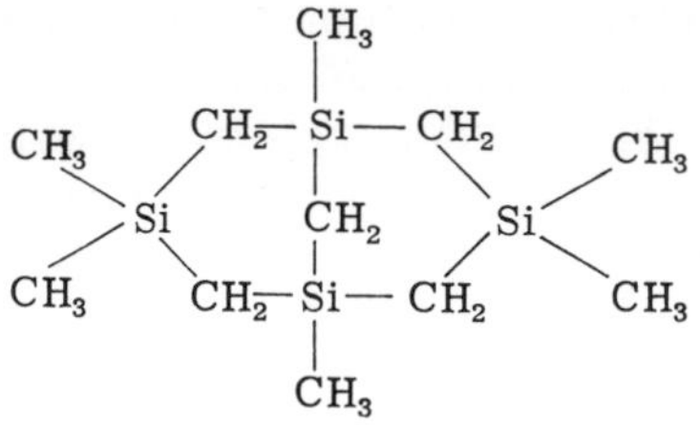

(V)

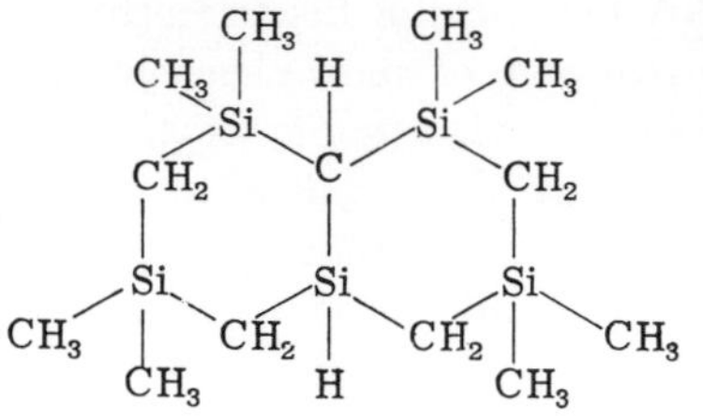

(VI)

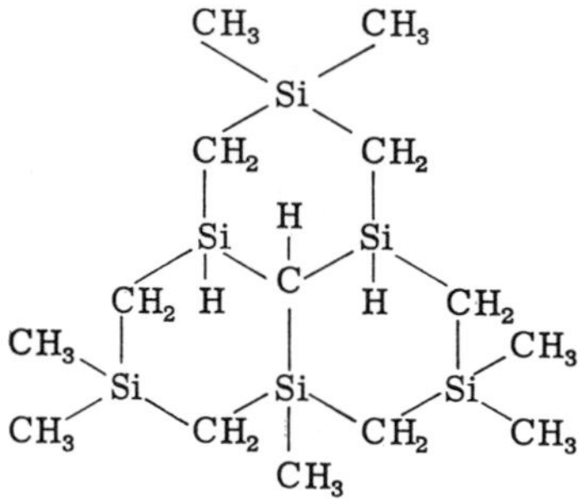

(VII)

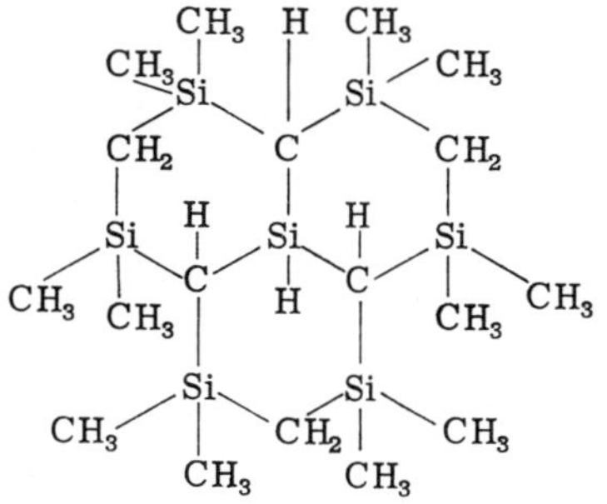

(VIII)

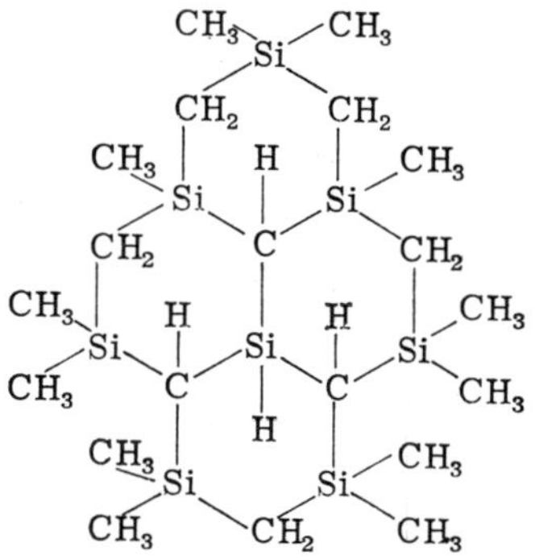

(IX)

Similarly, thermal decomposition of methyltrichlorosilane at 700 to 800° gives $Si_2Cl_6CH_2$, $Si_3Cl_6C_3H_6$ (liquid), $Si_3Cl_6C_3H_6$ (crystalline) (structure II), $Si_4Cl_4C_9H_{20}$ (X), and $Si_8Cl_{13}C_8H_{13}$ (XI) (*112, 113, 120, 122*).

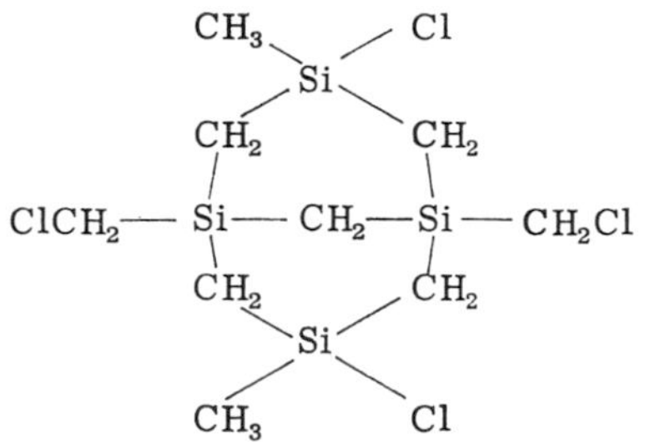

(X) 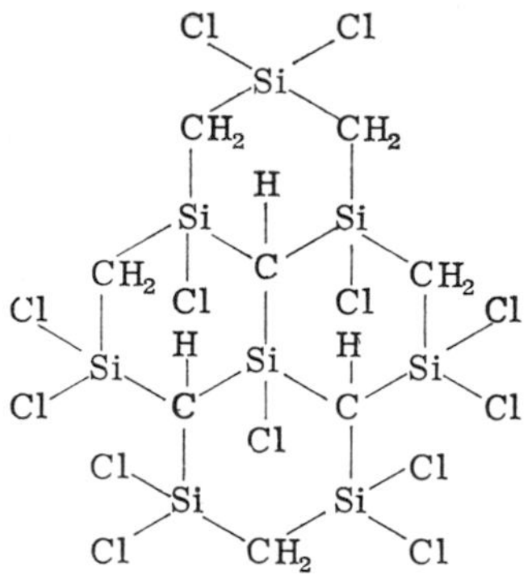   (XI)

Related cyclic compounds having a skeleton of alternate silicon and carbon atoms are obtained from the thermal decomposition of dimethyl dichlorosilane and trimethylchlorosilane (*122, 123*). Most of these cyclic polysilmethylenes are yellow but compound (XI) is a deep red (*120*). Polysilmethylene derivatives also are obtained from the thermal decomposition of methylsilane (*462*):

$$CH_3SiH_3 \xrightarrow{400°} (CH_3SiH)_n \xrightarrow{600°} (CH_3Si)_n \qquad (18)$$

Several compounds of the type $(R_3SiCH_2)_3M$, where $M = P$, As, Sb, or Bi, have been reported (*394a*).

A number of polysilicon compounds in which groups larger than methylene separate the silicon atoms has been prepared. Compounds containing two silicon atoms bridged by a chain of two or more carbon atoms have been reviewed and tabulated (*128*). α,ω-Polymethylene chlorides react with silicon-copper at elevated temperatures to give $Cl_3Si(CH_2)_nSiCl_3$ derivatives (*103, 445*). Similarly, halosilanes undergo redistribution reactions when heated to 300 to 400° over silicon-copper; for example, $CH_3Cl_2SiCH_2CH_2CH_2SiHCl_2$, $CH_3Cl_2SiCH_2CH_2CH_2SiCl_3$, $(CH_3Cl_2SiCH_2-CH_2CH_2-)_2$, and $(CH_3Cl_2SiCH_2CH_2CH_2)_2SiCl_2$ are formed from $CH_3Cl_2-SiCH_2CH_2CH_2Cl$ (*355*). Various chlorosilanes and α,ω-polymethylene chlorides can be coupled by using magnesium (*41, 427*):

$$Cl(CH_2)_6Cl + 2\ (CH_3)_2SiCl_2 + 2\ Mg \rightarrow Cl(CH_3)_2Si(CH_2)_6Si(CH_3)_2Cl + 2\ MgCl_2 \quad (19)$$

$$BrMg(CH_2)_6MgBr + 2\ ClSi(OC_2H_5)_2CH_3 \rightarrow$$

$$CH_3Si(OC_2H_5)_2(CH_2)_6Si(OC_2H_5)_2CH_3 + MgBr_2 + MgCl_2 \quad (20)$$

Acetylenic silicohydrocarbons and chlorosilanes can be prepared by treating acetylenic Grignard compounds with chlorosilanes in the presence of copper(I) chloride (*111, 260a*).

$$2 \ (CH_3)_2SiCl_2 + BrMgC\equiv CMgBr \rightarrow Cl(CH_3)_2SiC\equiv CSi(CH_3)_2Cl \tag{21}$$

A polymer of the type $[(C_2H_5)_4Si_2(C\equiv CH)_2]_n$ is reported to be formed in the reaction of diethyldifluorosilane and sodium acetylide (*204a*). The dimagnesium derivatives of 1,5-dichloropentane and *p*-dibromobenzene react with silicon tetrachloride to form resinous products (*375*). Silicon hydrides, in the presence of peroxide or platinum, add readily to acetylenes, polyolefins, and unsaturated alkylsilanes (*2, 21, 29, 55, 101a, 147, 171, 176, 302a, 313d, 437, 438, 449, 451, 461*):

$$HC\equiv CH + 2 \ HSiCl_3 \rightarrow Cl_3SiCH_2CH_2SiCl_3 \tag{22}$$

$$CH_2{=}CHCH{=}CH_2 + 2 \ HSiCl_3 \rightarrow Cl_3Si(CH_2)_4SiCl_3 \tag{23}$$

$$CH_2{=}CHSiH_3 + SiH_4 \rightarrow H_3SiCH_2CH_2SiH_3 \tag{24}$$

$$(CH_3)_2Si(CH_2CH{=}CH_2)_2 + 2 \ HSiCl_3 \rightarrow (CH_3)_2Si(CH_2CH_2CH_2SiCl_3)_2 \tag{25}$$

Related resinous products are obtained when trichlorosilane is added to the unsaturated linkages in natural or synthetic rubber (*24, 27, 30*).

Recently, it was reported that polymers are formed from the reaction of diphenylsilane with various difunctional unsaturated silanes (*228, 229*):

$$\underset{\underset{C_6H_5}{|}}{\overset{\overset{C_6H_5}{|}}{H{-}Si{-}H}} + CH_2{=}CH{-}R{-}CH{=}CH_2 \rightarrow \left[\underset{\underset{C_6H_5}{|}}{\overset{\overset{C_6H_5}{|}}{-Si{-}CH_2CH_2{-}R{-}CH_2CH_2{-}}} \right]_n \tag{26}$$

Polymeric products are obtained from diallyl phthalate, divinyltetramethyldisiloxane, diallyl adipate, divinyl adipate, tetramethylene dimethacrylate, divinylbenzene, and hexadiene; these polymers are resinous solids or viscous liquids.

Poly(chlorosilylalkyl)-substituted aromatic derivatives are obtained from the reaction of (chloroalkyl)chlorosilanes with aromatic hydrocarbons in the presence of aluminum chloride (*172–174*):

$$ClCH_2CH_2SiCl_3 + C_6H_6 \xrightarrow{AlCl_3} C_6H_4(CH_2CH_2SiCl_3)_2 \tag{27}$$

Naphthalene reacts with (1,2-dichloroethyl)trichlorosilane to form a resinous mass which may have structure (XII). All of the above poly-(chlorosilane) derivatives may be hydrolyzed to give polymers by formation of siloxane linkages.

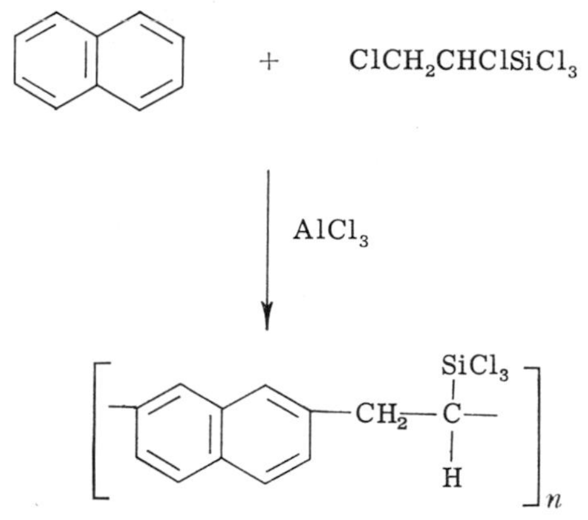

$$+ \quad ClCH_2CHClSiCl_3$$

$$\downarrow AlCl_3$$

$$\left[\text{naphthalene}-CH_2-\underset{\underset{H}{|}}{\overset{\overset{SiCl_3}{|}}{C}}- \right]_n \tag{28}$$

(XII)

A similar group of polymers has been prepared by a different route (*418*):

$$BrMg(CH_2)_4MgBr + 2 \ (CH_3)_3SiCl \rightarrow (CH_3)_3Si(CH_2)_4Si(CH_3)_3 \tag{29}$$

$$(CH_3)_3Si(CH_2)_4Si(CH_3)_3 \xrightarrow[\text{2. H}_2\text{O}]{\text{1. H}_2\text{SO}_4} \left[\underset{\underset{CH_3}{|}}{\overset{\overset{CH_3}{|}}{Si}}-(CH_2)_4\underset{\underset{CH_3}{|}}{\overset{\overset{CH_3}{|}}{Si}}-O- \right]_n \tag{30}$$

$$\left[-\underset{\underset{CH_3}{|}}{\overset{\overset{CH_3}{|}}{Si}}-(CH_2)_4\underset{\underset{CH_3}{|}}{\overset{\overset{CH_3}{|}}{Si}}-O- \right]_n + (CH_3)_3SiOSi(CH_3)_3 \xrightarrow[\text{2. H}_2\text{O}]{\text{1. H}_2\text{SO}_4}$$

$$CH_3-\underset{\underset{CH_3}{|}}{\overset{\overset{CH_3}{|}}{Si}}-O-\left[-\underset{\underset{CH_3}{|}}{\overset{\overset{CH_3}{|}}{Si}}-(CH_2)_4\underset{\underset{CH_3}{|}}{\overset{\overset{CH_3}{|}}{Si}}-O- \right]_n -\underset{\underset{CH_3}{|}}{\overset{\overset{CH_3}{|}}{Si}}-CH_3 \tag{31}$$

(XIII)

A methyl group is cleaved with concentrated sulfuric acid from each silicon atom of 1,4-bis(trimethylsilyl)butane; following hydrolysis, the resulting siloxane mixture is equilibrated with hexamethyldisiloxane in the presence of a small amount of concentrated sulfuric acid to give liquid, linear polymers of structure (XIII), with $n = 1$–4 (*418*).

The reaction between bis(iodomethyl)dimethylsilane and magnesium in ether results in the formation of polymeric products which presumably consist of cyclic compounds $[-CH_2-Si(CH_3)_2CH_2-]_n$ and linear polymers having structure (XIV) (*374*). Polymeric products of type (XV) are obtained by reaction of $CH_3(C_2H_5)Si(CH_2CH_2CH_2Cl)Cl$ with metallic sodium (*236*). It has been reported (*449a, 449b*) that 1,1-dimethylsilacyclopentane and 1,4-bis(trimethylsilyl)butane yield polymers when treated

$$
I-\left[-CH_2-\underset{\underset{CH_3}{|}}{\overset{\overset{CH_3}{|}}{Si}}-CH_2-\right]_n-I
\qquad
\left[-\underset{\underset{C_2H_5}{|}}{\overset{\overset{CH_3}{|}}{Si}}-CH_2CH_2CH_2-\right]_n
$$

(XIV)   (XV)

with aluminum halides:

$$
\underset{CH_3}{\overset{CH_3}{\diagdown}}\underset{CH_2-CH_2}{\overset{CH_2-CH_2}{\diagup}}
\!\!\!\!\!Si\!\!\!\!\!\qquad\xrightarrow{Al_2X_6}\quad [-Si(CH_3)_2CH_2CH_2CH_2CH_2-]_n \tag{32}
$$

$$
(CH_3)_3SiCH_2CH_2CH_2CH_2Si(CH_3)_3 \xrightarrow{Al_2Br_6}
$$

$$
\left[-\underset{|}{\overset{|}{Si}}CH_2CH_2CH_2CH_2-\right]_n + (CH_3)_4Si \tag{33}
$$

Similarly, when 1,2-bis(trimethylsilyl)ethane is heated with aluminum bromide, a dimer, $[-(CH_3)_2SiCH_2CH_2-]_2$, and a trimer, $[-(CH_3)_2-SiCH_2CH_2-]_3$, are among the products isolated (*449c*).

B. Polysilphenylenes

Polymers containing silicon atoms linked through phenylene groups are also known. A variety of alkylated or arylated derivatives of *p*-phenylene-disilane is described in the literature (*128*). The first such compound, $p\text{-}(C_2H_5)_3SiC_6H_4SiCl_3$, was obtained by Grüttner and Cauer from the reaction of $(C_2H_5)_3SiC_6H_4MgBr$ with dimethyldichlorosilane (*14*, *165*); several disilphenylene derivatives were similarly prepared by Sanin (*383*). Sveda (*427*) and Chugunov (*63a*), using a modification of this reaction, coupled *p*-dibromobenzene and dimethyldichlorosilane:

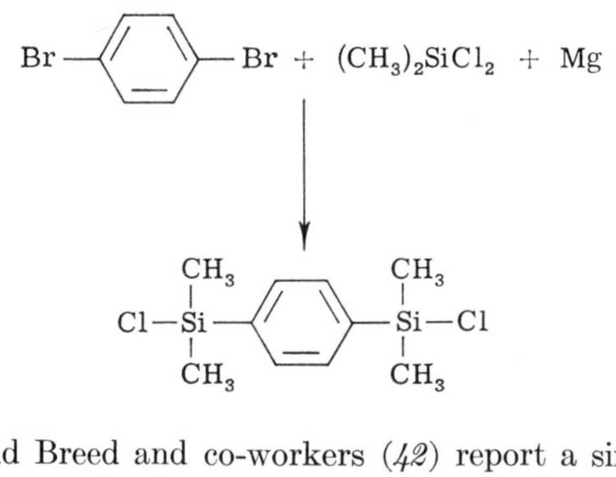

$$
Br-\!\!\!\left\langle\!\!\bigcirc\!\!\right\rangle\!\!-Br + (CH_3)_2SiCl_2 + Mg
$$

$$
\downarrow
$$

$$
Cl-\underset{\underset{CH_3}{|}}{\overset{\overset{CH_3}{|}}{Si}}-\!\!\!\left\langle\!\!\bigcirc\!\!\right\rangle\!\!-\underset{\underset{CH_3}{|}}{\overset{\overset{CH_3}{|}}{Si}}-Cl \tag{34}
$$

Gainer (*126*) and Breed and co-workers (*42*) report a similar coupling of *p*-dibromobenzene and triethoxymethylsilane with magnesium to give $p\text{-}BrC_6H_4Si(OC_2H_5)_2CH_3$ and $p\text{-}C_6H_4[Si(OC_2H_5)_2CH_3]_2$. Rochow (*375*, *378*) has described the reaction of the di-Grignard reagent of *p*-dibromobenzene with silicon tetrachloride to give a resinous polymer:

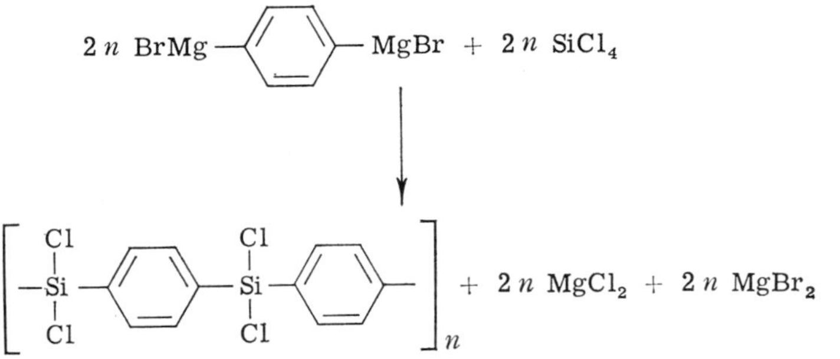

$$2n \ \mathrm{BrMg}{-}\!\!\bigcirc\!\!{-}\mathrm{MgBr} \ + \ 2n \ \mathrm{SiCl_4}$$

$$\downarrow$$

$$\left[{-}\underset{\underset{\textstyle \mathrm{Cl}}{|}}{\overset{\overset{\textstyle \mathrm{Cl}}{|}}{\mathrm{Si}}}\!\!-\!\!\bigcirc\!\!-\!\!\underset{\underset{\textstyle \mathrm{Cl}}{|}}{\overset{\overset{\textstyle \mathrm{Cl}}{|}}{\mathrm{Si}}}\!\!-\!\!\bigcirc\!\!- \right]_n \ + \ 2n \ \mathrm{MgCl_2} \ + \ 2n \ \mathrm{MgBr_2} \qquad (35)$$

Fluorescent organosilicon polymers have been prepared by allowing a mono-Grignard derivative of a dihalogen-substituted aryl compound to react with a silicon halide in the presence of a free radical forming catalyst (*128a*). For example, magnesium is reacted with an excess of *p*-dibromobenzene in ether; subsequent treatment with dimethyldichlorosilane in the presence of cobalt(II) chloride gives a yellow solid which is highly fluorescent under ultraviolet light.

$R_3SiC_6H_4Li$ compounds also readily couple with chlorosilanes (*136, 424*):

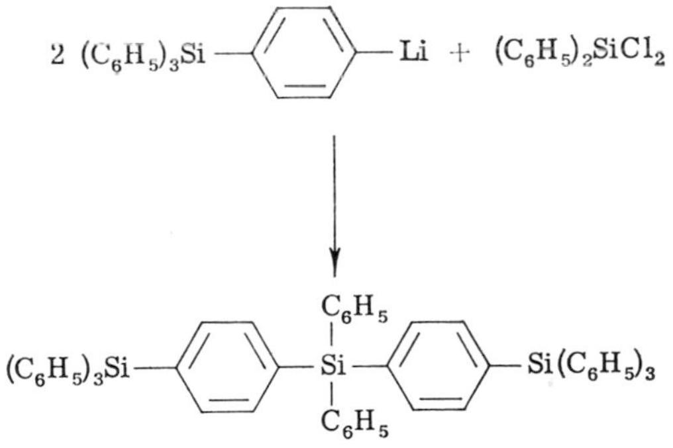

$$2 \ (C_6H_5)_3Si{-}\!\!\bigcirc\!\!{-}Li \ + \ (C_6H_5)_2SiCl_2$$

$$\downarrow$$

$$(C_6H_5)_3Si{-}\!\!\bigcirc\!\!-\underset{\underset{\textstyle C_6H_5}{|}}{\overset{\overset{\textstyle C_6H_5}{|}}{Si}}\!\!-\!\!\bigcirc\!\!-Si(C_6H_5)_3 \qquad (36)$$

$$(C_6H_5CH_2)_3Si{-}\!\!\bigcirc\!\!{-}Li \ + \ SiCl_4$$

$$\downarrow$$

$$\left[(C_6H_5CH_2)_3Si{-}\!\!\bigcirc\!\!- \right]_4 Si \qquad (37)$$

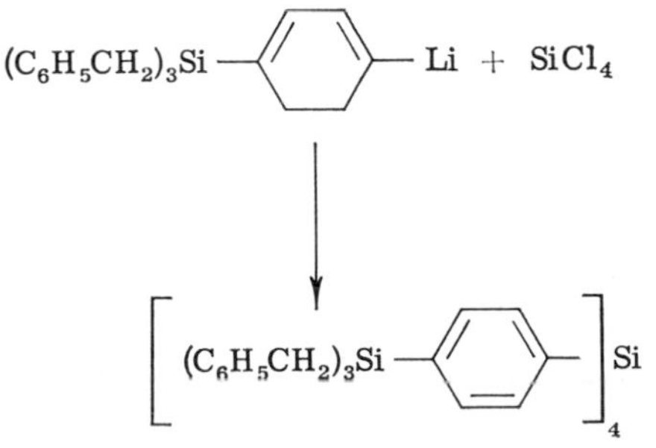

Dihydrosilanthrene derivatives are obtained from the reaction of *o*-phenyl-enedilithium and R_2SiCl_2 compounds (*143, 144*):

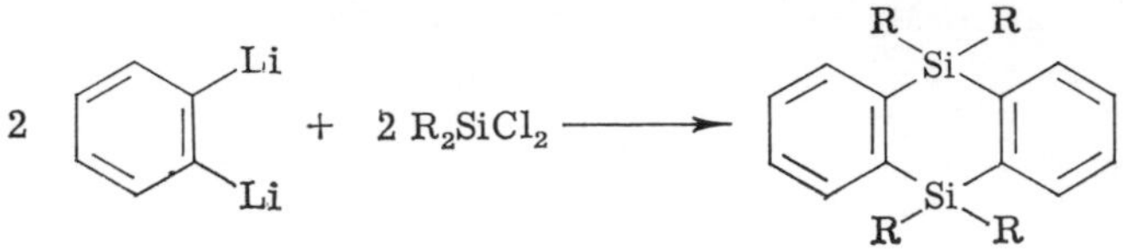

$$2 \quad \text{[o-phenylenedilithium]} \quad + \quad 2\ R_2SiCl_2 \quad \longrightarrow \quad \text{[dihydrosilanthrene]} \qquad (38)$$

Using dilithium intermediates, Baum (*34*) obtained 4,4′-bis(chlorodimethylsilyl)biphenyl and bis[*p*-(chlorodimethylsilyl)phenyl]ether. Anthracene and other aromatic hydrocarbons react with lithium metal followed by R_3SiCl to give disubstituted derivatives (*342, 343*):

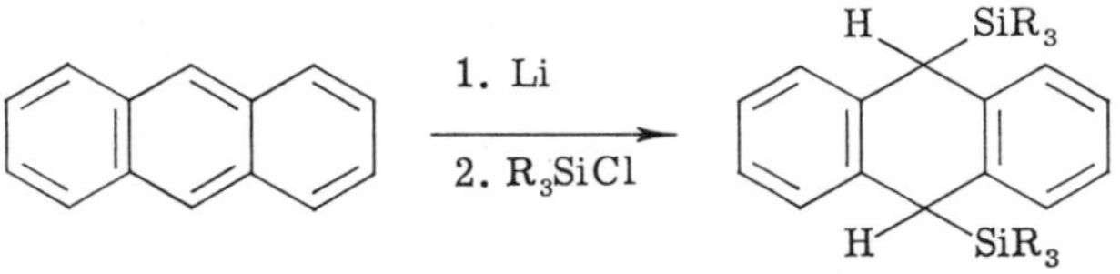

$$\text{[anthracene]} \quad \xrightarrow[\text{2. } R_3SiCl]{\text{1. Li}} \quad \text{[9,10-disubstituted product]} \qquad (39)$$

Clark and co-workers (*67, 73, 78*) have reported the sodium coupling of silyl-substituted aromatic halides with chlorosilanes:

$$R_3SiC_6H_4Cl + R'_3SiCl + 2\ Na \rightarrow R_3SiC_6H_4SiR'_3 + 2\ NaCl \qquad (40)$$

$$2\ R_3SiC_6H_4Cl + R'_2SiCl_2 + 4\ Na \rightarrow (R_3SiC_6H_4)_2SiR'_2 + 4\ NaCl \qquad (41)$$

However, attempts to couple *o*- or *p*-dichlorobenzene and chlorotrimethyl-silane using sodium were unsuccessful. Similar sodium coupling reactions of aromatic halides and chlorodiethoxymethylsilane have been described by Breed and associates (*41, 42*):

$$BrC_6H_4\text{—}O\text{—}C_6H_4Br + 2\ ClSi(OC_2H_5)_2CH_3 + 4\ Na\rightarrow$$
$$[CH_3Si(OC_2H_5)_2\text{—}C_6H_4\text{—}]_2O + 2\ NaCl + 2\ NaBr \qquad (42)$$

A mixed silmethylene-silphenylene, $[(CH_3)_3SiC_6H_4Si(CH_3)_2]_2$, is obtained when $ClC_6H_4Si(CH_3)_3$ and $[Cl(CH_3)_2Si]_2CH_2$ are added to molten sodium in refluxing toluene (*66*). A polymer, presumably of type (**XVI**), is formed when (*p*-chlorophenyl)dimethylchlorosilane is treated with sodium (*236*).

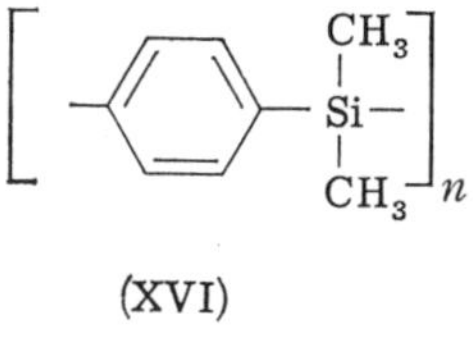

$$\left[\begin{array}{c} \\ \end{array} \text{—} \underset{\underset{CH_3}{|}}{\overset{\overset{CH_3}{|}}{Si}} \text{—} \right]_n$$

(**XVI**)

Many of the chloro- and ethoxy-substituted silanes described above, as well as those which will follow, have been hydrolyzed in aqueous media to yield hybrid arylenesiloxane polymers. Moreover, polymers containing Si—Si, Si—C$_6$H$_4$—Si, and Si—O—Si bonding can be prepared by reacting a siloxane having polymeric units of [ClC$_6$H$_4$(CH$_3$)SiO]$_n$ and an organo-halosilane, such as C$_6$H$_5$(CH$_3$)SiCl$_2$ or (CH$_3$)$_2$SiCl$_2$, with molten sodium or potassium (*161*); the phenylene linkages increase the viscosity of the liquid polysiloxanes.

Poly(trimethylsilyl)phenols undergo an interesting thermal rearrangement (*81a*):

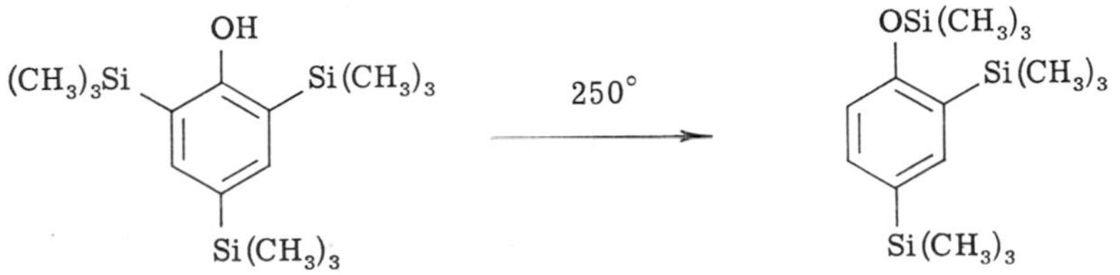

(42a)

It is suggested that *ortho* rearrangement occurs predominantly by an intra-molecular process while *meta* and *para* rearrangements involve a series of intermolecular desilylation reactions.

Aromatic chlorosilanes are obtained from the reaction of chlorosilanes with aromatic hydrocarbons; almost invariably, silphenylene derivatives are obtained as by-products. For example, benzene reacts with trichlorosilane in the presence of a boron trihalide and at elevated temperatures to give trichlorophenylsilane; C$_6$H$_5$SiCl$_2$C$_6$H$_4$SiCl$_3$ and C$_6$H$_4$(SiCl$_3$)$_2$ are by-products in this reaction (*28, 160, 296*). Similar silphenylenes are obtained as by-products when other chlorosilanes, such as CH$_3$SiHCl$_2$ (*88*), and various chloro-substituted benzenes (*11b, 26, 62, 86, 90, 107a, 147a*) are employed in this reaction; often (*62, 86, 90*) no catalyst is required. The chlorophenyl and silane groupings may be in the same molecule; for example, a polymeric material may be prepared by the thermal condensation of (chlorophenyl)methylphenylsilane at 400 to 700° (*409a*). Polymeric chlorosilanes containing Si—C$_6$H$_4$—Si linkages are formed when a mixture of methyl- and phenylchlorosilanes is heated in the presence of boron trichloride (*25*). Dichlorodiphenylsilane when heated at 210 to 300° in the presence of small amounts of aluminum chloride yields polymers of the type C$_6$H$_5$Cl$_2$Si(C$_6$H$_4$SiCl$_2$)$_n$C$_6$H$_5$ (*69*). Since redistribution of the phenyl groups and chlorine atoms occurs readily in the presence of aluminum chloride, a mixture of the various phenylchlorosilanes also may be used; polymers having the general formula Y$_3$Si(C$_6$H$_4$SiYCl)$_n$Y, where Y is either a chlorine atom or a phenyl group, are obtained.

When hexachlorodisilane and benzene are heated at 225 to 260° in the presence of aluminum chloride, $C_6H_5SiCl_3$, $Cl_3SiC_6H_4SiCl_3$, $C_6H_5SiCl_2C_6H_4$-$SiCl_3$, and a residue containing polymeric chlorophenylsilanes linked by phenylene groups are formed (*76*). It has recently been reported that bis(silyl)benzene, $H_3SiC_6H_4SiH_3$, readily adds to various monomeric and polymeric substances containing multiple olefinic bonds; this reaction proceeds at relatively low temperatures and in the presence or absence of peroxide catalysts (*390*). This compound may prove to be a useful cross-linking agent for various linear, unsaturated polymers. 1,3-Bis(silyl)-benzene is obtained in good yield by the reduction of 1,3-bis(trichloro-silyl)benzene with lithium aluminum hydride (*37a*).

Wilson and co-workers (*464–466*) have reported attempts to prepare polymers having structure (XVII). Although unsuccessful, they were able

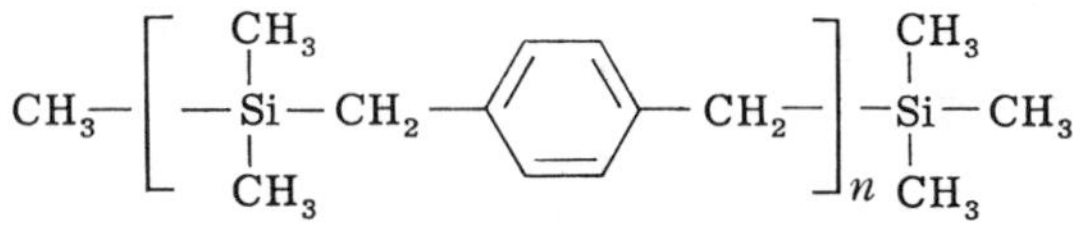

$$CH_3\!-\!\left[\begin{array}{c} CH_3 \\ | \\ -Si-CH_2- \\ | \\ CH_3 \end{array}\!-\!-CH_2-\right]_n\!\!\begin{array}{c} CH_3 \\ | \\ -Si-CH_3 \\ | \\ CH_3 \end{array}$$

(XVII)

to obtain several interesting silxylylene derivatives. These compounds were synthesized by coupling the xylylene dihalide and the appropriate chlorosilane with magnesium [Eqs. (43) and (44)]. The product in the second of these reactions [Eq. (44)], bis(dimethylchlorosilyl)-*p*-xylene, was polymerized to the corresponding polysiloxane. A related compound, bis(methyldichlorosilyl)xylylene, has been reported by Chernyshev and co-workers (*63*).

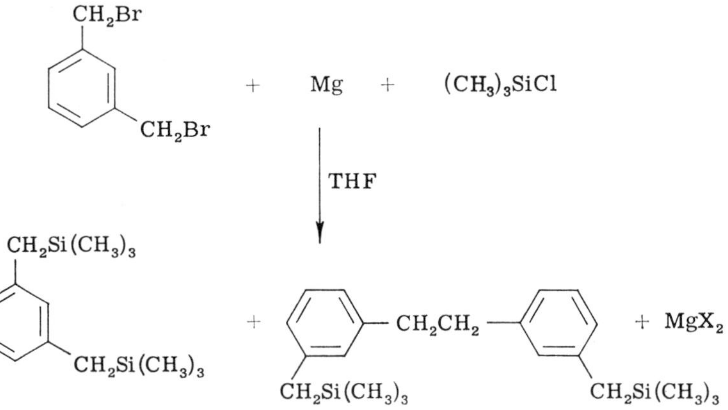

$$(43)$$

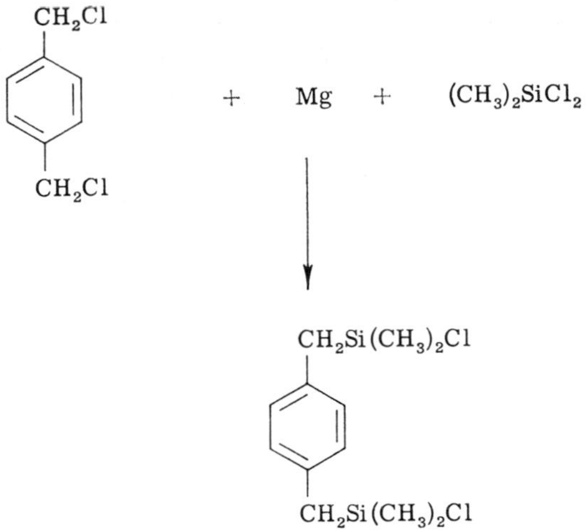

$$
\underset{\substack{\\ \text{CH}_2\text{Cl} \\ \\ \\ \\ \text{CH}_2\text{Cl}}}{\bigcirc} \quad + \quad \text{Mg} \quad + \quad (\text{CH}_3)_2\text{SiCl}_2
$$

$$
\downarrow
$$

$$
\underset{\substack{\\ \text{CH}_2\text{Si}(\text{CH}_3)_2\text{Cl} \\ \\ \\ \\ \text{CH}_2\text{Si}(\text{CH}_3)_2\text{Cl}}}{\bigcirc}
\tag{44}
$$

C. Organosilicon Polymers from Unsaturated Silanes

Another method of obtaining organosilicon polymers is via unsaturated silanes with subsequent polymerization of the unsaturated function. Polymerization studies of olefinic silicon compounds have concerned primarily vinyl and allyl derivatives. Methods of preparation of the vinyl and allyl monomers have been adequately reviewed (*102, 128, 204, 244, 324, 330, 346, 347, 403, 405*) and, therefore, will not be discussed further here.

1. Vinyl-Substituted Silanes

Vinylsilane polymerizes to form a white solid when treated with ultraviolet light (*461*):

$$
n\ \text{CH}_2{=}\text{CHSiH}_3 \rightarrow \left[-\text{CH}_2\text{CH}_2{-}\underset{\underset{\text{H}}{|}}{\overset{\overset{\text{H}}{|}}{\text{Si}}}{-} \right]_n
\tag{45}
$$

Various organosilanes containing a vinyl group and a hydrogen atom joined to the same silicon atom can be polymerized to linear polysilethylenes at atmospheric pressure, using platinum suspended on finely divided carbon as the catalyst (*83, 297, 450*):

$$
n\ \text{CH}_2{=}\text{CH}{-}\underset{\underset{\text{R}'}{|}}{\overset{\overset{\text{R}}{|}}{\text{Si}}}{-}\text{H} \rightarrow \left[-\text{CH}_2\text{CH}_2{-}\underset{\underset{\text{R}'}{|}}{\overset{\overset{\text{R}}{|}}{\text{Si}}}{-} \right]_n
\tag{46}
$$

The resulting polymers vary greatly in viscosity according to the nature of the R groups; those in which both groups are alkyl are rather fluid substances, but the introduction of phenyl groups results in materials which are considerably more viscous. In addition to the polymeric products, small amounts of 1,4-disilacyclohexane derivatives can be isolated (*83*). Later work indicates the cyclic dimer to be a mixture of the 1,4-disilacyclohexane and the 1,3-disilacyclopentane (*84a*):

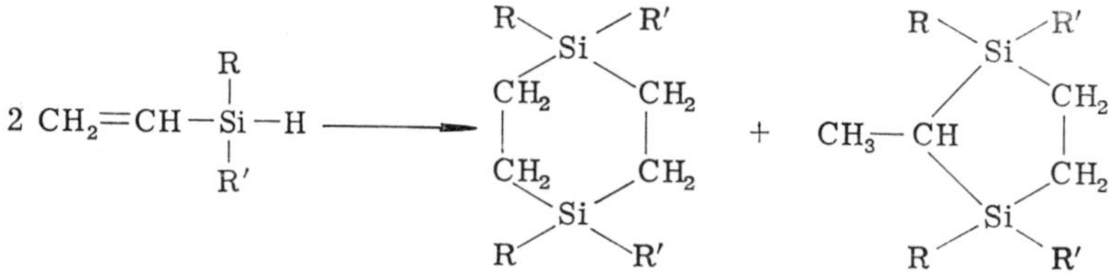

(46a)

Unsaturated hydrocarbons may be added to form copolymers (*450*). If these vinyl- and hydrogen-substituted silanes are polymerized by heating in the presence of an alkali metal alkoxide under anhydrous conditions, polymers retaining the silicon-hydrogen bond are formed (*84*):

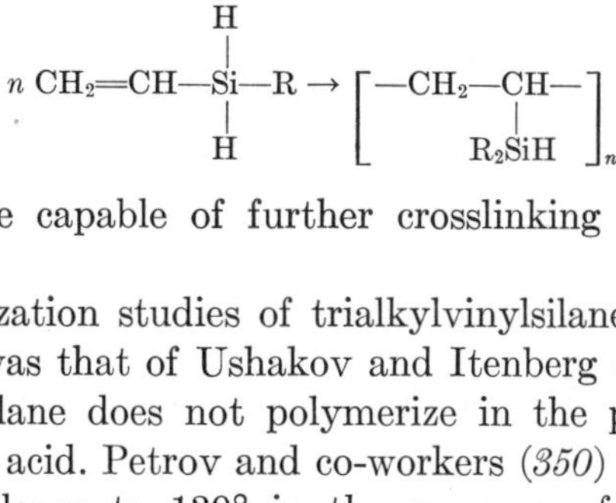

$$n \ CH_2{=}CH{-}\underset{\underset{H}{|}}{\overset{\overset{H}{|}}{Si}}{-}R \rightarrow \left[{-}CH_2{-}\underset{\underset{R_2SiH}{|}}{CH}{-} \right]_n$$
(47)

These polymers are capable of further crosslinking by reaction of the silane hydrogen.

Several polymerization studies of trialkylvinylsilanes have been made. The earlier study was that of Ushakov and Itenberg (*448*), who reported that triethylvinylsilane does not polymerize in the presence of benzoyl peroxide or sulfuric acid. Petrov and co-workers (*350*) heated a number of vinyl-substituted silanes to 130° in the presence of *tert*-butyl peroxide under 5500-atm pressure. Under these conditions, triethylvinylsilane gave a colorless, octameric polymer and trimethylisopropenylsilane formed a viscous dimer; trimethylpropenylsilane and trimethyl(2-methylpropenyl)-silane failed to polymerize. Later, Polyakova and co-workers (*362*) extended this study and found viscous liquid polymers could be obtained with triethylpropenylsilane and triethyl(2-methylpropenyl)silane although the corresponding methyl analogs as well as trimethyl(2-chlorovinyl)silane, triethyl(2-chlorovinyl)silane, and dimethyldivinylsilane could not be polymerized. Tetravinylsilane gave a solid polymer when subjected to these conditions (*362*). Triethylvinylsilane formed a tetramer when heated in the presence of *tert*-butyl peroxide at atmospheric pressure (*350*).

Korshak and associates (*239*) have continued this polymerization study of trialkylvinylsilanes. Using *tert*-butyl peroxide as an initiator, at 6000-atm pressure and 120°, triethylvinylsilane polymerized more readily than trimethylvinylsilane or tripropylvinylsilane. Highly hindered compounds such as ethyldimethyl(2-methylpropenyl)silane, ethyldimethylpropenylsilane, trimethyl(1-methyl-2-butenyl)silane, and trimethyl(1-cyclohexenyl)silane were not polymerized under these conditions.

Natta and co-workers (*323*) have reported that trimethylvinylsilane does not form solid polymers between 60 and 120° with either $(C_2H_5)_3Al\text{-}TiCl_4$ or $(C_2H_5)_3Al\text{-}TiCl_3$ catalysts; the latter catalyst gives high polymers with allylsilanes (see below). Korshak and associates (*233*) have found that trimethylvinylsilane gives a liquid polymer of low molecular weight when heated at 120° and 6000-atm pressure in the presence of *tert*-butyl peroxide. Similarly, Kanazashi (*205*) obtained a low molecular weight polymer by heating trimethylvinylsilane at 150° in a sealed tube and in the presence of acetyl and benzoyl peroxide.

Polymers may be obtained by the polyaddition of polysilmethylene dihydrides to divinylpolysilmethylene derivatives; both starting materials may be obtained from the same dichloropolysilmethylene (*161a*).

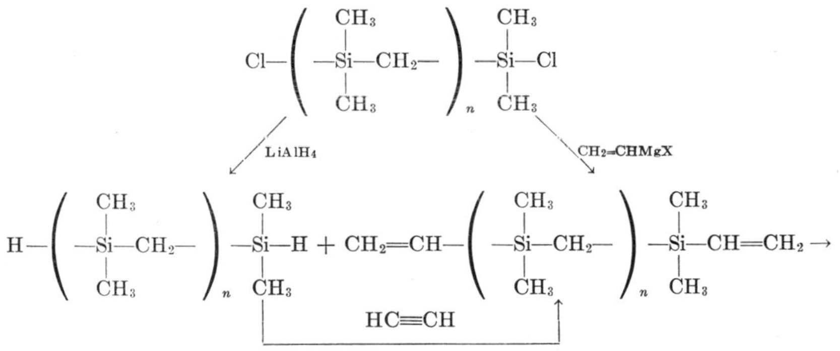

$$Cl-\left(\begin{array}{c} CH_3 \\ | \\ -Si-CH_2- \\ | \\ CH_3 \end{array}\right)_n \begin{array}{c} CH_3 \\ | \\ -Si-Cl \\ | \\ CH_3 \end{array}$$

polymer (47a)

An interesting polymerization of trimethyl(3,4,4-trifluorobuta-1,3-dienyl)silane has been reported (*129*):

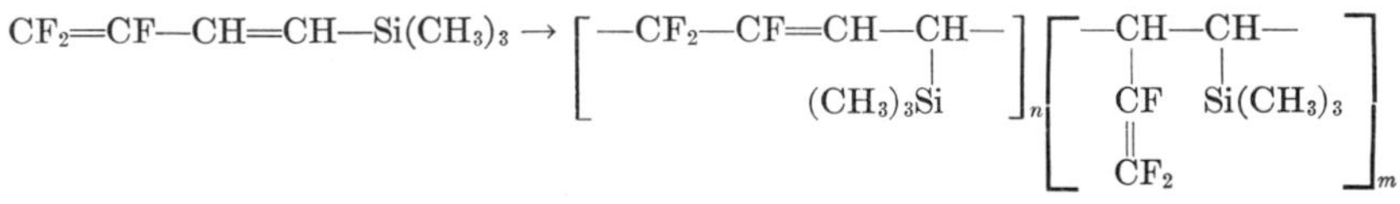

$$CF_2{=}CF{-}CH{=}CH{-}Si(CH_3)_3 \rightarrow \left[\begin{array}{c} -CF_2-CF{=}CH-CH- \\ | \\ (CH_3)_3Si \end{array}\right]_n \left[\begin{array}{cc} -CH-CH- \\ | \quad | \\ CF \quad Si(CH_3)_3 \\ \| \\ CF_2 \end{array}\right]_m \quad (48)$$

This compound when heated to 100° in a sealed tube with a small amount of acetyl peroxide forms a white, stable solid; infrared absorption data indicate —$CF_2CF{=}CHCH$— and $CF_2{=}CF$— units but no band was obtained in the —CH=CH— region. A brief report of the polymerization of trialkyl(1-chlorovinyl)silanes has appeared in the patent literature (416).

The polymerization of vinyltrichlorosilane by heating in the presence of a peroxide has been reported (447); however, later work failed to substantiate this claim (452). Vinyltrichlorosilane can be polymerized at moderate pressures and without a catalyst by heating from 250 to 290°:

$$n \; CH_2\!\!=\!\!CHSiCl_3 \rightarrow \left[\begin{array}{c} -CH_2-CH- \\ | \\ SiCl_3 \end{array} \right]_n \tag{49}$$

Low molecular weight polymers (mainly tetramer) are obtained (452). (1-Chlorovinyl)trichlorosilane polymerizes with surprising ease; irradiation of this monomer with ultraviolet light produces a solid polymer within 32 hours (419). This behavior is not characteristic of (1-chlorovinyl)trimethylsilane or vinyltrichlorosilane. Vinyltriethoxysilane, in contrast to vinyltrichlorosilane, very readily polymerizes in the presence of a peroxide (452). The polymerization of this monomer has been studied in some detail (306). A clear, colorless, viscous liquid of low molecular weight is obtained; the low molecular weight is the result of chain transfer with polymer and monomer.

Presumably, the above polymers can be crosslinked by hydrolysis and formation of siloxane bonding. Polymers of this type also have been prepared by the reverse procedure. Vinylchlorosilanes and vinylalkoxysilanes have been hydrolyzed to yield vinylpolysiloxanes; these products are capable of further polymerization through their unsaturated linkages (13a, 20a, 45, 50b, 77, 164a, 187, 188, 206, 297a, 452). Vinylmagnesium halides react with ω,ω'-dichloropolysiloxanes to form divinylpolysiloxanes; these, in turn, may be polymerized with tert-butyl peroxide to form crosslinked insoluble products (162, 164). Vinyl groups, usually less than 1%, are also found in many present-day silicones; the purpose of these groups is to aid in curing and in controlling the cure of the silicone rubber (105c, 290 424a). Silicone rubber with high vinyl content can be vulcanized with sulfur, as organic rubbers are; the vinyl silicones also are important as sizing materials for glass fibers (290, 448a).

Disiloxanes of the type $(R_2SiH)_2O$ react with unsaturated silanes such as $R_2Si(CH\!\!=\!\!CH_2)_2$ in the presence of a chloroplatinic acid catalyst to form polymeric products (243, 361, 372e). It is suggested that the divinyl monomers react with equimolar amounts of the disiloxane to yield cyclic products while diallylic monomers tend to form linear polymers. Siloxanes and polysiloxanes of the type $(R_2SiH)_2O$ also can be made to react with acetylene and its derivatives; polymers containing vinyl groupings are formed and are capable of further polymerization in the presence of a peroxide initiator to give solid, insoluble products (163, 363). An earlier patent describes the reaction of a silane containing one or more Si—H bond with unsaturated hydrocarbons in the presence of a platinum catalyst (*450*); vinyldichlorosilane, for example, when heated at 250° and 160 atm forms a liquid polymer containing no reactive hydrogen atoms.

Vinyl silicon compounds copolymerize with various vinyl monomers. Compounds such as tetravinylsilane and divinyldimethylsilane may be copolymerized with styrene, methyl methacrylate, or vinyl acetate to give cross-linked polymers (*46*). Substances of the type $CH_2{=}CClSiR_3$ may be copolymerized with styrene or vinyl chloride (*416*). An early patent (*447*) mentions the copolymerization of vinyltrichlorosilane with various vinyl monomers. A later paper suggests that vinyltrichlorosilane copolymerizes to a limited extent with various olefins, such as styrene or isobutylene, in the presence of an acid catalyst and with vinyl monomers, such as vinyl acetate and methyl methacrylate, in the presence of peroxide catalysts (*452*). Vinylmethyldichlorosilane and vinylethyldichlorosilane do not readily form copolymers with vinyl monomers when heated in the presence of 2,2'-azobis[2-methylpropionitrile]; however, a small yield of copolymer is formed when vinylmethyldichlorosilane and vinylpyrrolidine are subjected to these conditions (*402*). In contrast to the corresponding chlorosilanes, vinyltriethoxysilane copolymerizes extensively with ethyl maleate and maleic anhydride, forming hard, brittle resins with molecular weights up to 3000 (*452*):

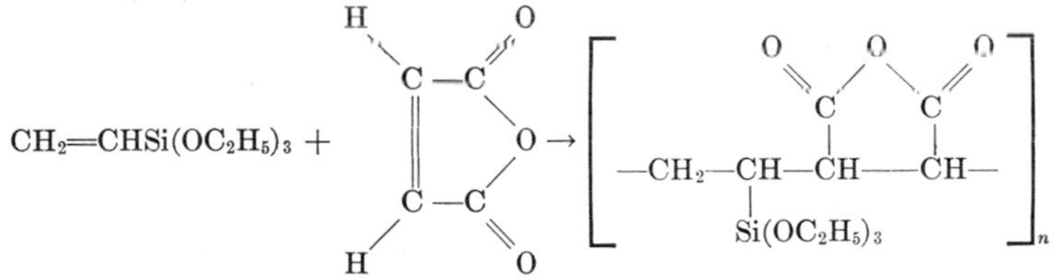

$$\tag{50}$$

A brief investigation has been made of the copolymerization of various vinylalkoxysilanes with vinyl chloride and acrylonitrile (*435*). The copolymerization of methylvinylpolysiloxane with methyl methacrylate in the presence of a peroxide has been reported (*81, 188, 380*); thermally stable, water-soluble substances are obtained from the copolymerization of vinyl-substituted siloxanes with olefinic pyrrolidinones (*20, 359*).

Vinyl- and allyltriorganosilanes dimerize when heated at 200° with small amounts of triisobutylaluminum; the structures of the dimers were established by conversion to saturated products (*200a*):

$$2\,(C_6H_5)_3SiCH{=}CH_2 \rightarrow (C_6H_5)_3SiCH{=}CHCH_2CH_2Si(C_6H_5)_3 \tag{50a}$$

$$2\,(C_6H_5)_3SiCH_2CH{=}CH_2 \rightarrow CH_2{=}CCH_2CH_2CH_2Si(C_6H_5)_3 \tag{50b}$$

$$\overset{\displaystyle |}{\underset{\displaystyle \overset{|}{Si(C_6H_5)_3}}{CH_2}}$$

2. Allyl-Substituted Silanes

The polymerization of allyl-substituted silanes has attracted even more attention than that of the vinyl analogs. Most workers in this field agree that allyl-silicon compounds can be polymerized much more easily than vinyl-silicon derivatives. Korshak and co-workers (*239*) have, however, found that alkylvinylsilanes polymerize far more easily than alkylallylsilanes.

An early patent concerns the polymerization of tetraallylsilane by heating in the presence of an organic peroxide or other catalyst such as cobalt linoleate, tin(IV) chloride, or boron trifluoride (*261*). Somewhat later, it was suggested that alkali metal carbonates and oxidizing agents accelerate the thermal polymerization of tetraallylsilane (*44, 377*). In 1948, Sommer and co-workers reported that allyltrimethylsilane readily forms low molecular weight polymers in the presence of aluminum chloride (*423*). Yakovlev, in 1949, indicated that diallyldiethylsilane is capable of polymerization in the presence of benzoyl peroxide and other catalysts (*475*).

Petrov and co-workers (*350*) studied the polymerization of a number of allyl-substituted silanes using *tert*-butyl peroxide as a catalyst at 5500-atm pressure and 130°. Under these conditions allyltrialkylsilanes gave low molecular weight polymers (trimers to pentamers) while diallyldialkyl(or aryl)silanes formed yellow, solid, tridimensional polymers. Hard, colorless, tridimensional materials also were obtained from triallylmethylsilane, tetraallylsilane, and tetramethallylsilane. This study was continued by Polyakova and associates (*362*); a wide variety of allyl-substituted silanes was found to polymerize under the above conditions. A number of diallyl, triallyl, and tetraallyl derivatives gave solid polymers (*362*). Later, Korshak and co-workers (*232, 239*) extended this study to additional allyl-silicon compounds. Methallylsilanes were found to polymerize less readily than allylsilanes; allyltributylsilane, dimethallyldimethylsilane, tetramethallylsilane, and diallylmethylsilane failed to form high molecular weight materials, either when heated in the presence of benzoyl peroxide or under the influence of ionic catalysts such as aluminum chloride or boron trifluoride.

The polymerization of allyltrimethylsilane, diallyldimethylsilane, triallylmethylsilane, and tetraallylsilane has been studied by Mikulášová and Hrivík (*184, 298, 299*); a *tert*-butyl peroxide initiator and temperatures of 110 to 150° were employed. Allyltrimethylsilane was especially difficult to polymerize; low molecular weight materials were obtained with all of these monomers. Peroxide-initiated polymerization of diallyldimethylsilane as well as diallyldiphenylsilane also has been reported by Butler (*56*); solid polymers were formed. The patent literature (*22*) contains a reference to the polymerization of tetraallylsilane, triallylmethylsilane, or allyldimethylsilane by heating at 200 to 300° in an oxygen-containing atmosphere.

Mironov and Petrov (*302*) obtained a paraffin-like polymer from allyldichlorosilane by refluxing the monomer in the presence of platinized carbon; similarly, allyldiethylsilane and allyldiphenylsilane gave viscous liquid polymers. Although Mironov and Petrov were unable to cause the polymerization of allyldimethylsilane under their conditions, Curry and Harrison (*85*) report that this monomer polymerizes smoothly to yield a colorless viscous liquid when refluxed with a platinum-on-carbon catalyst. Nuclear magnetic resonance data have confirmed the linear structure (XVIII) for this liquid polymer. However, when the reaction was conducted in the presence of toluene as a solvent, in addition to the linear polymer a small amount of the crystalline, cyclic dimer (XIX) was obtained (*85*).

$$
\left[\begin{array}{c} \mathrm{CH_3} \\ | \\ -\mathrm{Si-CH_2CH_2CH_2-} \\ | \\ \mathrm{CH_3} \end{array} \right]_n
$$

(XVIII)

$$
\begin{array}{ccc}
\mathrm{CH_3} & \mathrm{CH_2-CH_2-CH_2} & \mathrm{CH_3} \\
& \diagdown \; \diagup & \diagdown \; \diagup \\
& \mathrm{Si} & \mathrm{Si} \\
& \diagup \; \diagdown & \diagup \; \diagdown \\
\mathrm{CH_3} & \mathrm{CH_2-CH_2-CH_2} & \mathrm{CH_3}
\end{array}
$$

(XIX)

Korshak and associates (*234*) have reported that compounds of the type $R_2HSiCH_2CH{=}CH_2$ gave polymers with repeating units $-SiR_2CH_2CH_2{-}CH_2-$ when heated in the presence of platinized carbon; however, when polymers were prepared from these monomers with an organic peroxide catalyst, the Si—H bonds were retained and presumably the repeating unit was $-CH(CH_2SiR_2H)CH_2-$.

In the past three years, Ziegler-type catalysts have been receiving increased attention for the polymerization of allyl-substituted silanes. Natta and co-workers (*322, 323*) reported that good yields of low molecular weight liquids were formed when allylsilane, $CH_2{=}CHCH_2SiH_3$, was heated to 70° in the presence of $Al(C_2H_5)_3\text{-}TiCl_4$; if titanium trichloride was substituted for titanium tetrachloride, a crystalline poly(allylsilane) was obtained. This polymer, owing to the presence of Si—H bonds, could be easily cross-linked. Allyltrimethylsilane gave crystalline polymers in the presence of either of the above catalysts (*323*). Several other recent reports of the polymerization of trialkylallylsilanes in the presence of Ziegler-type catalysts have appeared (*57a, 307a, 307b, 313a, 313e*). Topchiev and associates (*313c, 313e, 439*) have studied the polymerization of diallyldimethylsilane and diallyldiethylsilane using a triethylaluminum-titanium tetrachloride complex catalyst. These authors reported that both liquid and solid polymers were obtained; from the liquids, trimers, tetramers, and pentamers could be isolated. Bogomol'yni̇ (*40*) has described the polymerization of diallyldimethylsilane and diallylmethylphenylsilane with a $(C_2H_5)_3Al\text{-}TiCl_4$ catalyst; white, solid polymers were formed from the former monomer while the latter gave gum-like products. A cyclic structure (XX) for these polymers has been suggested by this author and others (*57, 231, 286*):

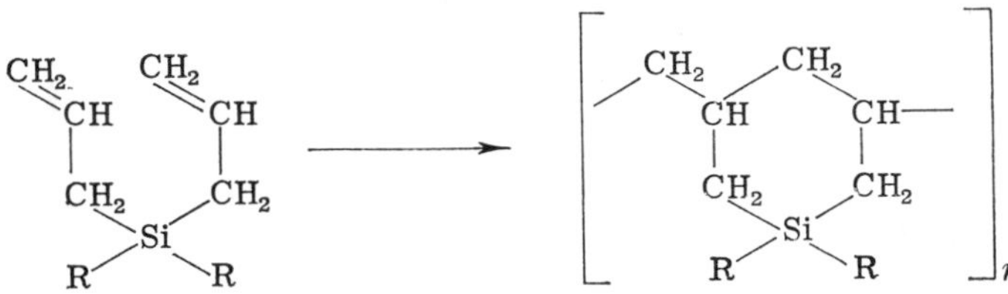

$$(51)$$

(XX)

Kolesnikov and co-workers (*231*) were unable to polymerize diallyldimethylsilane and diallyldiethylsilane in the presence of benzoyl peroxide but were able to isolate polymers of low molecular weight using a $(C_2H_5)_3Al\text{-}TiCl_4$ catalyst. Using similar conditions, Butler and Stackman (*56, 57*) obtained benzene-soluble polymers from diallyldimethylsilane and diallyldiphenylsilane; attempts to polymerize dimethallyldimethylsilane with a Ziegler catalyst were not successful. Marvel and Woolford (*286*) also have reported the polymerization of diallyldimethylsilane with Ziegler-type catalysts.

Various allylalkoxy silicon derivatives, such as methallyltriethoxysilane, can be easily polymerized to hard transparent films by heating with an organic peroxide catalyst (*428, 457, 459*); diallyldichlorosilane undergoes similar polymerization (*447*). Presumably, these polymers can be crosslinked by hydrolysis and subsequent formation of siloxane bonding. Crosslinked polymers also may be obtained by hydrolyzing allylalkoxy silicon compounds, such as diallyldiethoxysilane, with subsequent polymerization of the unsaturated linkages (*429, 430, 431, 458, 460*). Polymers of this type can be obtained by a similar treatment of allylchloro silicon derivatives such as diallyldichlorosilane (*1, 187, 188, 331*). Cross-linked products are obtained from the polyaddition of polysiloxane dihydrides to diallylpolysiloxanes (*163*) and from the addition of tetraalkyldisiloxane to diallyldialkylsilanes (*357*).

Allyl silicon compounds readily form copolymers with a variety of vinyl monomers. An early patent (*261*) described the peroxide-catalyzed copolymerization of tetraallylsilane with alkyd resins, vinyl acetate, styrene, esters of acrylic acid, and other related monomers. The copolymerization of tetraallylsilane with vinyl acetate and methyl or butyl methacrylate was the subject of another early patent (*277*). Somewhat later, patents were issued concerning the copolymerization of tetraallylsilane, triallylmethylsilane, or diallyldimethylsilane with styrene, vinyl chloride, vinyl acetate, or methyl methacrylate in the presence of a peroxide (*46*, *366*). Korshak and co-workers (*232*, *362*) have studied the peroxide-initiated copolymerization of a number of allyl-substituted silanes with methyl methacrylate and with styrene; the products are usually hard solids. The copolymerization of tetraallylsilane and triallylmethylsilane with methyl methacrylate in the presence of benzoyl peroxide was recently reported by Mikulášová and co-workers (*300*); using similar conditions, Zhivukhin and Sobolevskaya (*478*) have obtained copolymers of diallyldimethylsilane and allyltrimethylsilane with styrene, methyl methacrylate, acrylonitrile, and vinyl acetate. Zhivukhin (*478*) reported that the organosilicon monomers did not retard the polymerization of the vinyl monomers while Kolesnikov (*231a*) and Mikulášová (*300*) found the opposite to be true.

Nametkin and associates (*314*) have studied the copolymerization of diallyldimethylsilane and diallylmethylphenylsilane with propylene in the presence of a Ziegler-type catalyst. The copolymerization of various allylalkoxysilanes with allyl phthalate or allyl carbonate in the presence of a peroxide catalyst has been patented (*457*, *459*); allylchloro silicon compounds also form copolymers with vinyl monomers (*447*, *457*). Methallyltriethoxysilane and similar compounds form glass-like copolymers with maleic and fumaric esters (*51*, *175*, *260*) while diallyldiethoxysilane and related derivatives form copolymers with fluorinated olefins (*125*). Tetraallyl orthosilicate is capable of copolymerization with methyl methacrylate and acrylonitrile (*477*). Various organosilyl acrylate and methacrylate esters have been shown to be capable of polymerization (*8a*, *292a*). A number of substances containing silicon and sulfur has been prepared by both emulsion and solution polymerization of the products resulting from the addition of hydrogen polysulfide to various allyl-substituted silanes (*321*). Addition polymers also have been obtained by reacting diphenylsilane, or other diorganosilanes, with diallyl sulfide or sulfone (*323c*) or with diallyl phthalate and other diallyl esters (*229a*).

3. Silylstyrene Derivatives

Organosilicon derivatives of styrene have been reported by several authors. The earlier methods of synthesis involve dehydration (*341*, *472*) or dehydrochlorination (*52*, *268*, *280*, *281*) of the appropriate organosilanes. More recently, the availability of *p*-vinylphenylmagnesium chloride has made the reaction of this Grignard reagent with a halosilane the choice method of synthesis (*101*, *227*, *282*, *329*, *358*, *391*).

Bunnell and Hatcher (*52*) reported the first polymerization of an organo-silicon derivative of styrene; *p*-trichlorosilylstyrene was polymerized by warming with a peroxide initiator. The polymerization of *p*-trimethylsilyl-styrene, *p*-triethylsilylstyrene, and *p*-trimethylsilyl-*α*-methylstyrene has been the subject of several studies (*22, 237, 238, 329, 358, 472*).

(52)

These monomers polymerize readily at 70 to 90° in the presence of radical initiators, preferably 2,2'-azobis[2-methylpropionitrile], to give clear, colorless solids; thermal polymerization is also possible but this requires prolonged heating (*329*). High pressure conditions are advocated by some authors (*237, 238*). The polymerization of *p*-trimethylsilylstyrene using a $(C_2H_5)_3Al$-$TiCl_4$ catalyst has been reported (*313b*); various *p*-(methoxy-methylsilyl)styrenes also readily form polymers and copolymers (*268a*). A brief report has been made of the reaction of *p*-vinylphenylmagnesium bromide with silicon tetrachloride to give polymerizable products (*101*); no details were given. *p*-Trialkylsilylstyrene derivatives readily copolymerize with styrene and methyl methacrylate to form glass-like materials (*52, 237, 267, 283*).

A different approach to the preparation of poly(*p*-trimethylsilylstyrene) has been reported by Houel and Jaćović (*183a*). This silicon-containing polymer was prepared either by reacting poly(*p*-bromosytrene) and chlorotrimethylsilane with lithium or by reacting poly(*p*-styrenyllithium) with chlorotrimethylsilane.

In addition to the vinyl and allyl silicon derivatives discussed above, a number of longer chained alkenyl-substituted silanes also are readily polymerized in the presence of a peroxide initiator (*13, 350, 362, 397*). 5-Trimethylsilyl-1-pentene forms a crystalline polymer with Ziegler-type catalysts (*323*). Many organosilanes containing conjugated multiple bonds polymerize readily on standing at room temperature (*232, 344, 352, 354, 400, 400c*).

D. Organopolysilanes

In concluding this section it is not inappropriate for us to focus our attention on the organopolysilanes. The silicon-silicon bond is in general much less stable than the carbon-carbon bond [Si—Si, 45 kcal/mole; C—C, 80 kcal/mole *(360)*]. While the length of the carbon-carbon chain is almost unlimited, the silicon-silicon chains known at the present time are relatively short. A considerable amount of work has been reported on the polysilanes, Si_xH_{2x+2}, and the poly(silicon chlorides), Si_xCl_{2x+2}; however, these are not organosilicon compounds and are not, therefore, within the scope of this review.

Almost all of our modern organosilicon chemistry has been built upon the foundation laid by Frederick S. Kipping and his co-workers; this is especially true in the organopolysilane area. A summary of the Kipping researches has been published *(364)*; in the following paragraphs, the work that concerns organopolysilanes will be discussed. Only the trisilanes and the higher polysilanes will be considered; the disilanes are less pertinent and have been reviewed elsewhere *(102, 324)*.

In 1911, Kipping first reported studies of the reaction of R_2SiCl_2 compounds with sodium; in this paper *(210)* he reported the isolation of 1,2-diethyl-1,2-diphenylsilene, $C_2H_5(C_6H_5)Si≡Si(C_6H_5)C_2H_5$. However, Ladenburg *(262)* had reported earlier that no $(C_6H_5)_2Si≡Si(C_6H_5)_2$ was formed from the reaction of dichlorodiphenylsilane with sodium. After more extensive studies, Kipping also concluded that no compounds containing a silicon-silicon double bond are formed in the reaction of sodium with R_2SiCl_2 types *(216, 220, 221)*.

One of the reactions examined by Kipping and co-workers in their extensive series was that of dichlorodiphenylsilane with sodium *(211–216, 219, 221, 222, 426)*. When the reaction was carried out above the melting point of sodium without solvent, a complex mixture of chlorine-free organosilicon substances resulted. This mixture was resolved into six components after a painstaking series of operations. Of the six components, two substances designated as Compound (A) and Compound (B) have been the most thoroughly studied.

$$
\begin{array}{cccc}
C_6H_5 & C_6H_5 & C_6H_5 & C_6H_5 \\
| & | & | & | \\
\!-\!\!-\!Si\!\!-\!\!-\!Si\!\!-\!\!-\!Si\!\!-\!\!-\!Si\!\!-\!\!- \\
| & | & | & | \\
C_6H_5 & C_6H_5 & C_6H_5 & C_6H_5
\end{array}
$$

(XXI)

To Compound (A), Kipping assigned structure (XXI) *(211–213, 215, 216, 221)*. This structure provided a reasonable explanation for the high reactivity of the compound in the free radical type of reaction. For example, Compound (A) reacted with one equivalent of iodine to give 1,4-diiodooctaphenyltetrasilane *(221)*, with atmospheric oxygen or nitrobenzene to give siloxanes *(211, 212)*, and with certain halogenated solvents to give

1,4-dihalooctaphenyltetrasilanes. The analytical results showed that the compound was composed of diphenylsilylene units and molecular weight determinations indicated that four such units were present. Two reactions of the diiodo derivative confirmed the presence of four diphenylsilylene units (*212, 221*):

$$
\begin{array}{ccccc}
& C_6H_5 & C_6H_5 & C_6H_5 & C_6H_5 \\
& | & | & | & | \\
I\!\!-\!\!-\!\!Si\!\!-\!\!-\!\!Si\!\!-\!\!-\!\!Si\!\!-\!\!-\!\!Si\!\!-\!\!-\!\!I + Na \xrightarrow{\;[xylene]\;} [(C_6H_5)_2Si]_4 \\
& | & | & | & | \\
& C_6H_5 & C_6H_5 & C_6H_5 & C_6H_5
\end{array}
\tag{53}
$$

$$
\begin{array}{ccccccccc}
C_6H_5 & C_6H_5 & C_6H_5 & C_6H_5 & & C_6H_5 & C_6H_5 & C_6H_5 & C_6H_5 \\
| & | & | & | & & | & | & | & | \\
I\!\!-\!\!Si\!\!-\!\!Si\!\!-\!\!Si\!\!-\!\!Si\!\!-\!\!I + 2\,C_2H_5MgBr \rightarrow C_2H_5\!\!-\!\!Si\!\!-\!\!Si\!\!-\!\!Si\!\!-\!\!Si\!\!-\!\!C_2H_5 \\
| & | & | & | & & | & | & | & | \\
C_6H_5 & C_6H_5 & C_6H_5 & C_6H_5 & & C_6H_5 & C_6H_5 & C_6H_5 & C_6H_5
\end{array}
$$

$$
\tag{54}
$$

Analytical data and molecular weight determinations agreed with the structure shown for the 1,4-diiodo- and the 1,4-diethyloctaphenyltetrasilane. Compound (A) was also obtained from the reaction of chlorophenoxydiphenylsilane and sodium (*215*).

Compound (B) was markedly less reactive than Compound (A). Thus, Compound (B) did not react with either iodine or oxygen (*221*); it reacted with aluminum chloride in chloroform to give an insoluble product whose low hydrogen value indicated that many Si—Si bonds had been broken (*105*). The analytical data suggested that the compound was composed of diphenylsilylene units. Kipping assigned structure (XXII) to Compound

$$
\begin{array}{cc}
C_6H_5 & C_6H_5 \\
| & | \\
C_6H_5\!\!-\!\!-\!\!Si\!\!-\!\!-\!\!-\!\!-\!\!Si\!\!-\!\!-\!\!C_6H_5 \\
| & | \\
| & | \\
C_6H_5\!\!-\!\!-\!\!Si\!\!-\!\!-\!\!-\!\!-\!\!Si\!\!-\!\!-\!\!C_6H_5 \\
| & | \\
C_6H_5 & C_6H_5
\end{array}
$$

(XXII)

(B) (*214, 215, 221, 222*). Reported cryoscopic molecular weight determinations agree with the octaphenylcyclotetrasilane structure (*221*). The other four substances isolated from the reaction of dichlorodiphenylsilane with sodium were presumably higher polymers but their constitution was not established (*216*). Compound (B), when destructively distilled, formed tetraphenylsilane and triphenylsilane; the distillation residue contained polymeric products with molecular weights as high as 4000 (*219*). Compound (A), when similarly distilled, gave tetraphenylsilane and triphenylsilane; no cyclic products were obtained (*219*).

Two isomers very similar in behavior to Compound (A) and Compound (B) were obtained from the reaction of dichlorodi-*p*-tolylsilane with sodium in dry toluene under nitrogen (*426*). Analytical data indicated these isomeric products to be $[(p\text{-}CH_3C_6H_4)_2Si]_4$; linear and cyclic structures similar to those of Compounds (A) and (B) were assigned to these two compounds (*216, 426*). The reaction of dibenzyldichlorosilane did not afford similar products; instead, the main product was $[Si(CH_2C_6H_5)_2]_4O$, accompanied by small amounts of hexabenzyldisiloxane and tetrabenzylsilane (*216, 218*). When dichlorodiphenoxysilane was treated with sodium, phenyl orthosilicate and materials rich in silicon but of undetermined structure were formed (*216, 436*). The reaction of sodium with phenyltrichlorosilane produced unidentified, polymeric material; these polymers contain oxygen and have molecular weights of about 5000 (*217, 220, 223*).

Dimethyldichlorosilane reacts with molten sodium to give a major quantity of hydrocarbon-insoluble material together with a minor amount of hydrocarbon-soluble product; the reaction is best carried out in an autoclave with benzene as a solvent (*53, 54*). The hydrocarbon-insoluble product has been shown to be a polymer, $[(CH_3)_2Si]_n$, with an average degree of polymerization of approximately 55. The hydrocarbon-soluble material has been reported to give the cyclic hexamer, dodecamethylcyclohexasilane (XXIII), and a substance which appears to be a copolymer of $[(CH_3)_2Si]$

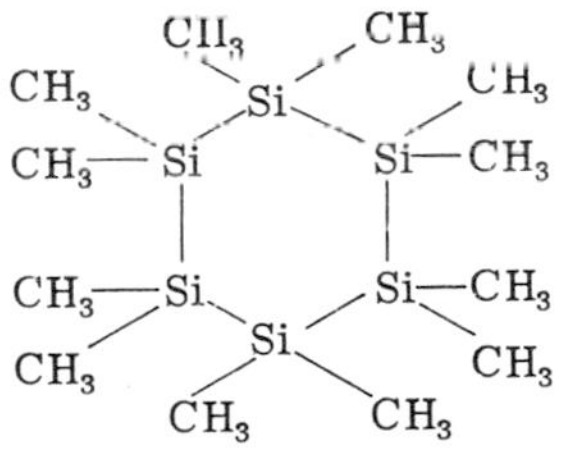

XXIII

and $[(CH_3)_2SiO]$ units (*53*). Similarly, wax-like polymers of the type $CH_3[(CH_3)_2Si]_nCH_3$ are obtained from the reaction of a mixture of trimethylchlorosilane and dimethyldichlorosilane with sodium in refluxing xylene (*185*). Diethyldichlorosilane, on treatment with molten sodium in xylene gives a high polymeric, white grease, $[(C_2H_5)_2Si]_n$ (*98*). Polymers containing both Si—Si and Si—C bonding in the backbone are formed when a $CH_2(SiR_2Cl)_2$ compound is treated with molten sodium (*71, 74*); for example, $CH_2[Si(CH_3)_2Cl]_2$ reacts with sodium to give a polymer (XXIV).

(XXIV)

Hydrocarbon-insoluble polymers which contain both Si—Si and Si—O—Si linkages have been prepared by reaction of methylmagnesium iodide with hexachlorodisilane and subsequent hydrolysis of the remaining silicon-halogen bonds (284, 285); similar polymers are obtained by partial hydrolysis of various organochlorosilanes and subsequent reaction of these products with sodium (96, 100).

Various silicon hydrides on treatment with sodium-potassium alloy in ethyl ether or with lithium in tetrahydrofuran yield the corresponding silyl alkali metal compounds; a polymeric material, $(R_2Si)_n$, often is a by-product of these reactions and its formation may be explained by Eqs. (55)–(60) (473, 474):

$$R_3SiH + 2 Li \rightarrow R_2SiHLi + RLi \tag{55}$$

$$R_2SiHLi + 2 Li \rightarrow RSiHLi_2 + RLi \tag{56}$$

$$RLi + R_3SiH \rightarrow R_4Si \tag{57}$$

$$R_4Si + 2 Li \rightarrow R_3SiLi + RLi \tag{58}$$

$$n\ R_2SiHLi \rightarrow n\ LiH + (R_2Si)_n \tag{59}$$

$$n\ RSiHLi_2 \rightarrow n\ LiH + (RSiLi)_n \tag{60}$$

The reduction of silicon tetrabromide with silicon at 1200° gives a brown, translucent, rosin-like polymer, $(SiBr_2)_n$. This polymer reacts readily with Grignard reagents to form viscous oils of the type $(R_2Si)_n$, where R is methyl, ethyl, propyl, or butyl (386). A similar polymeric material is obtained from the reaction of phenylmagnesium bromide with hexachloro-disilane and may be accounted for as follows (135):

$$Cl_3SiSiCl_3 + C_6H_5MgBr \rightarrow Cl_3SiSiCl_2C_6H_5 + MgBrCl \tag{61}$$

$$Cl_3SiSiCl_2C_6H_5 + C_6H_5MgBr \rightarrow (C_6H_5)_2SiCl_2 + BrMgSiCl_3 \tag{62}$$

$$BrMgSiCl_3 \rightarrow [:SiCl_2] + MgBrCl \tag{63}$$

$$n\ [:SiCl_2] \rightarrow [—SiCl_2—]_n \tag{64}$$

Polymeric resins also have been reported in some related studies (133, 473).

Although hexaaryldisilanes and hexaaryldisiloxanes may be prepared in good yields from the corresponding silicon chlorides, the reaction cannot be extended to the preparation of compounds containing the Si—Si—Si structure; thus, the reaction of octachlorotrisilane and phenylmagnesium bromide gives tetraphenylsilane and hexaphenyldisilane but no octaphenyltrisilane (387). However, octaphenyltrisilane is obtained from the reaction of two moles of triphenylsilylpotassium with one mole of diphenyl-dichlorosilane (142):

$$2\ (C_6H_5)_3SiK + (C_6H_5)_2SiCl_2 \rightarrow (C_6H_5)_3SiSi(C_6H_5)_2Si(C_6H_5)_3 \tag{65}$$

Lithium cleavage of octaphenyltrisilane in tetrahydrofuran gives a mixture of triphenylsilyllithium and pentaphenyldisilanyllithium. The latter reagent, along with triphenylsilyllithium and heptaphenyltrisilanyllithium, is also obtained when decaphenyltetrasilane is similarly cleaved with lithium:

$$(C_6H_5)_3SiSi(C_6H_5)_2Si(C_6H_5)_2Si(C_6H_5)_3 \xrightarrow{Li} (C_6H_5)_3SiSi(C_6H_5)_2Li +$$

$$(C_6H_5)_3SiSi(C_6H_5)_2Si(C_6H_5)_2Li + (C_6H_5)_3SiLi \quad (66)$$

Subsequent hydrolysis gives triphenylsilane, pentaphenyldisilane, and heptaphenyltrisilane (*473*). A small yield of tris(triphenylsilyl)silane is formed in the reaction of trichlorosilane with triphenylsilyllithium (*473*):

$$(C_6H_5)_3SiLi + Cl_3SiH \rightarrow [(C_6H_5)_3Si]_3SiH \quad (67)$$

The syntheses of octamethyltrisilane and of decamethyltetrasilane have been reported (*466a*). The former was obtained by reacting a mixture of trimethylchlorosilane and pentamethylchlorodisilane with sodium-potassium alloy in benzene; decamethyltetrasilane was similarly prepared by treating pentamethylchlorodisilane with sodium-potassium alloy.

Recently, a new study has been made of the products obtained from the reaction of dichlorodiphenylsilane with alkali metals. Compound (A), to which Kipping assigned structure (XXI), has now been shown to be octaphenylcyclotetrasilane (XXII) (*138*, *196*). Although Compound (A) can be obtained by the reaction of dichlorodiphenylsilane with sodium in toluene or xylene as described by Kipping, improved yields are obtained when lithium in tetrahydrofuran is employed (*196*). Octaphenylcyclotetrasilane is cleaved by lithium to form 1,4-dilithiooctaphenyltetrasilane; subsequent treatment of this product with trimethyl phosphate gives 1,4-dimethyloctaphenyltetrasilane:

$$\begin{array}{c} (C_6H_5)_2Si-Si(C_6H_5)_2 \\ | \qquad\qquad | \\ (C_6H_5)_2Si-Si(C_6H_5)_2 \end{array} \xrightarrow{THF,Li} LiSi(C_6H_5)_2[Si(C_6H_5)_2]_2Si(C_6H_5)_2Li \quad (68)$$

with $Cl_2CHCHCl_2$ and $(CH_3)_3PO_4$ / CH_3Li pathways:

$$ClSi(C_6H_5)_2[Si(C_6H_5)_2]_2Si(C_6H_5)_2Cl \xrightarrow{CH_3Li}$$

$$CH_3Si(C_6H_5)_2[Si(C_6H_5)_2]_2Si(C_6H_5)_2CH_3 \quad (69)$$

$$CH_3Si(C_6H_5)_2Li + ClSi(C_6H_5)_2Si(C_6H_5)_2Cl \quad (70)$$

The 1,4-dimethyl derivative also is obtained from the reaction of methyllithium with 1,4-dichlorooctaphenyltetrasilane. An independent synthesis

of 1,4-dimethyloctaphenyltetrasilane by the coupling of *sym*-dichloro-
tetraphenyldisilane with methyldiphenylsilyllithium, using a 1:2 ratio,
confirmed the structure (*138, 196*). Similarly, phenyllithium reacted with
1,4-dichlorooctaphenyltetrasilane to give the known decaphenyltetrasilane (*142, 196*):

$$2\ C_6H_5Li + ClSi(C_6H_5)_2[Si(C_6H_5)_2]_2Si(C_6H_5)_2Cl \rightarrow$$

$$(C_6H_5)_3Si[Si(C_6H_5)_2]_2Si(C_6H_5)_3 \tag{71}$$

$$\uparrow \ \text{Na, xylene}$$

$$2\ (C_6H_5)_3SiK + 2\ (C_6H_5)_2SiCl_2 \rightarrow 2\ (C_6H_5)_3SiSi(C_6H_5)_2Cl \tag{72}$$

Compound (B), to which Kipping assigned structure (XXII), has now
been shown to be decaphenylcyclopentasilane (XXV) (*130a, 139, 471*).

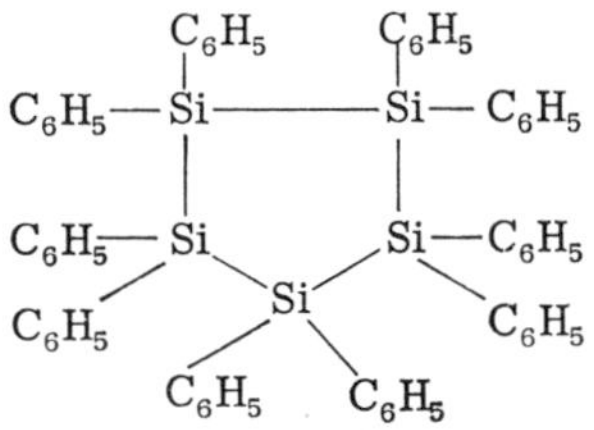

(XXV)

The chemical evidence for the structure of Compound (B) was obtained
by two different reactions. First, the cleavage of Compound (B) by lithium
in tetrahydrofuran gave a dilithio derivative which with tri-*n*-butyl phosphate gave an 83% yield of 1,5-di-*n*-butyldecaphenylpentasilane whose
structure was confirmed by NMR measurements. Second, the reaction of
Compound (B) with bromine gave a 94% yield of 1,5-dibromodecaphenyl-
pentasilane which, on treatment with methylmagnesium iodide, gave a
97% yield of 1,5-dimethyldecaphenylpentasilane. The structure of this
compound was also confirmed by NMR measurements (*130a*).

$$\text{Compound (B)} \xrightarrow[\text{2. } (n\text{-}C_4H_9O)_3PO]{\text{1. Li}} n\text{-}C_4H_9[Si(C_6H_5)_2]_5C_4H_{9}\text{-}n \tag{73}$$

$$\text{Compound (B)} \xrightarrow{\text{Br}_2} Br[Si(C_6H_5)_2]_5Br \xrightarrow{\text{CH}_3\text{MgI}} CH_3[Si(C_6H_5)_2]_5CH_3 \tag{74}$$

The reaction of *sym*-dichlorotetraphenyldisilane with sodium gives an
octaphenylcyclotetrasilane and decaphenylcyclopentasilane mixture of
approximately the same composition as that obtained from dichlorodiphenylsilane and sodium (*468*). Octaphenylcyclotetrasilane has also been

isolated from the reaction of azobenzene-, stilbene-, and tetraphenylethyl-ene-dilithium adducts with *sym*-dichlorotetraphenyldisilane (*195*). Octa-phenylcyclotetrasilane may be converted to decaphenylcyclopentasilane by the action of catalytic amounts of lithium or sodium; this has led to a markedly improved method of preparation of decaphenylcyclopenta-silane from dichlorodiphenylsilane and a slight excess of lithium (*469*).

Inorganic halides such as mercury(II) halides, tin(IV) chloride, and copper(II) chloride react with octaphenylcyclotetrasilane to form the corresponding 1,4-dihalooctaphenyltetrasilane (*134, 193*):

$$[(C_6H_5)_2Si]_4 + 2 HgCl_2 \rightarrow ClSi(C_6H_5)_2[Si(C_6H_5)_2]_2Si(C_6H_5)_2Cl + Hg_2Cl_2 \qquad (75)$$

Palladium chloride, silver chloride, and cadmium chloride fail to react (*193*). Octaphenylcyclotetrasilane is cleaved by lithium in tetrahydrofuran; hydrolysis of the resulting 1,4-dilithio derivative gives 1,1,2,2,3,3,4,4-octaphenyltetrasilane (*467*). This tetrasilane also has been isolated from the reaction of dichlorodiphenylsilane with sodium dispersion in ether (*467*). In a similar manner, cleavage of decaphenylcyclopentasilane with lithium in tetrahydrofuran, followed by acid hydrolysis, gives a linear pentasilane with Si—H groups in the terminal positions [Eq. (77)]. An independent synthesis of this compound has been effected by reduction of the 1,5-dibromodecaphenylpentasilane [Eq. (78)].

$$[(C_6H_5)_2Si]_4 \xrightarrow[\text{2. } H^+]{\text{1. Li, THF}} H[Si(C_6H_5)_2]_4H \qquad (76)$$

$$[(C_6H_5)_2Si]_5 \xrightarrow[\text{2. } H^+]{\text{1. Li, THF}} H[Si(C_6H_5)_2]_5H \qquad (77)$$

$$Br[Si(C_6H_5)_2]_5Br \xrightarrow{\text{LiAlH}_4} H[Si(C_6H_5)_2]_5H \qquad (78)$$

1,1,1,2,2,3,3-Heptaphenyltrisilane was obtained when triphenylsilyl-lithium was reacted with one equivalent of *sym*-dichlorotetraphenyldi-silane followed by reduction of the resulting product with lithium aluminum hydride (*467*). A study has been made of the reactions of octaphenylcyclo-tetrasilane and of decaphenylcyclopentasilane with phenyllithium, phenyl-magnesium bromide, and triphenylsilyllithium; it was found that deca-phenylcyclopentasilane was more resistant to Si—Si bond cleavage by these reagents than was octaphenylcyclotetrasilane (*192*). An article by Andrianov (*11a*) contains a number of structures which would indicate the preparation of various cyclotrisilanes and cyclotetrasilanes; however, these are intended to represent cyclopolysiloxane compounds.

The hydrolysis of 1,4-dihalooctaphenyltetrasilanes leads to the forma-tion of octaphenylcyclotetrasilanoxide (XXVI); even under mild hydrolysis conditions attempts to isolate a 1,4-disilanol have failed (*191, 194*):

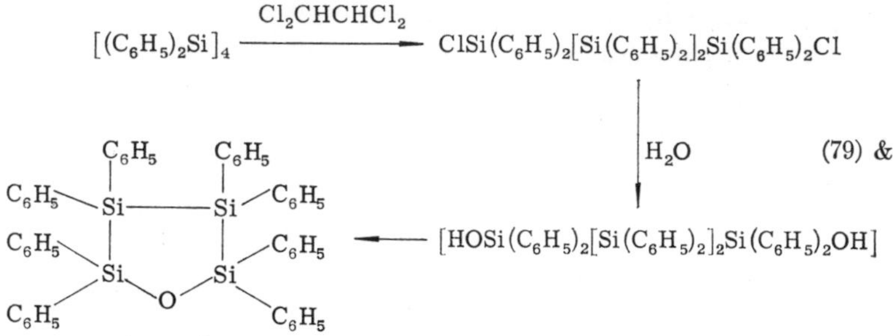

$$[(C_6H_5)_2Si]_4 \xrightarrow{\;Cl_2CHCHCl_2\;} ClSi(C_6H_5)_2[Si(C_6H_5)_2]_2Si(C_6H_5)_2Cl$$

(XXVI)

$$\xleftarrow{} [HOSi(C_6H_5)_2[Si(C_6H_5)_2]_2Si(C_6H_5)_2OH] \xleftarrow{\;H_2O\;} \qquad (79)\ \&\ (80)$$

The structure of one of the two isomeric cyclic siloxanes isolated by Kipping (*221*) has been identified as 2,2,3,3,5,5,6,6-octaphenyl-1,4-dioxa-2,3,5,6-tetrasilacyclohexane (XXVII) (*194, 470*):

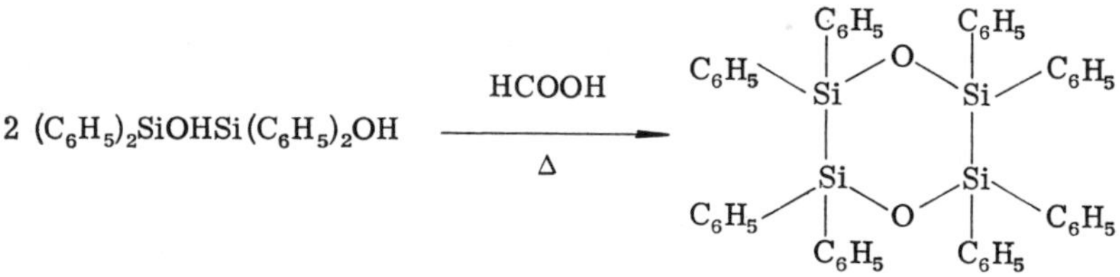

$$2\ (C_6H_5)_2SiOHSi(C_6H_5)_2OH \xrightarrow[\Delta]{\;HCOOH\;} \qquad (81)$$

(XXVII)

In contrast to the behavior of 1,4-dihalooctaphenyltetrasilanes, 1,5-di-bromodecaphenylpentasilane readily yields 1,5-dihydroxydecaphenylpenta-silane on hydrolysis (*191, 194*):

$$[(C_6H_5)_2Si]_5 \xrightarrow{\;Br_2\;} BrSi(C_6H_5)_2[Si(C_6H_5)_2]_3Si(C_6H_5)Br \qquad (82)$$

$$\downarrow H_2O$$

$$HOSi(C_6H_5)_2[Si(C_6H_5)_2]_3Si(C_6H_5)_2OH \qquad (83)$$

Piękoś and Radecki (*357b*) have reinvestigated the reactions between phenoxyhalosilanes and metallic sodium and have obtained somewhat different results from those reported by Thompson and Kipping (*436*). In addition to tetraphenoxysilane, sodium halide, and free silicon, sodium phenolate was found among the products in each case; substances having Si—Si bonding also were obtained in some reactions (*357b*).

III. Organogermanium Polymers

During the past 10 years, the organic chemistry of germanium has been the subject of several review articles (*40a*, *127*, *146*, *199*, *332*). These reviews reveal that, until quite recently, only a few studies of organogermanium polymers have been made.

A. Organogermanium Oxides

The organogermanium oxides have not received the attention given their silicon counterparts. Organogermanium oxides, some of which are polymeric, are usually obtained by hydrolysis of the appropriate halogermanes. Although several examples of germanols are known, compounds of this type are difficult to prepare unless special precautions are taken to avoid intermolecular dehydration with concomitant formation of digermoxanes. While similar in this respect to the silanols, the germanols lose water much more easily. The only trialkylgermanols which are known [triisopropylgermanol (*6*) and tricyclohexylgermanol (*33*)] contain bulky groups which offer steric hindrance to dehydration. The trisubstituted silanols do not lose water spontaneously; usually, they can be dehydrated over phosphorus pentoxide. The triarylgermanols are more resistant to dehydration, but this may be due to steric factors also. Although hexaphenyldigermoxane is usually obtained from the hydrolysis of triphenylhalogermanes, with special precautions triphenylgermanol can be isolated (*48*). The hydrolysis of bromotri-1-naphthylgermane and bromotri-*o*-tolylgermane yields tri-1-naphthylgermanol (*455*) and tri-*o*-tolylgermanol (*406*); the less-hindered bromotri-*m*-tolylgermane and bromotri-*p*-tolylgermane form the corresponding digermoxanes under similar hydrolysis conditions (*406*).

No dialkyl- or diarylgermanediols have been isolated and characterized; the diols immediately lose water to form either low molecular weight cyclic trimers and tetramers or higher molecular weight linear polymers:

$$R_2GeX_2 + 2\ H_2O \rightarrow R_2Ge(OH)_2 + 2\ HX \tag{84}$$

$$x\ R_2Ge(OH)_2 \rightarrow (R_2GeO)_x + x\ H_2O \tag{85}$$

Attempts to prepare dimethylgermanium oxide by hydrolysis of dichlorodimethylgermane were unsuccessful (*376*). Rochow attributed this failure to obtain the oxide to a reversibility of the reaction accompanied by an unfavorable equilibrium:

$$(CH_3)_2GeCl_2 + 2\ H_2O \rightleftharpoons (CH_3)_2Ge(OH)_2 + 2\ HCl \tag{86}$$

Although dichlorodimethylsilane is readily hydrolyzed to form a water-insoluble film, the germanium analog was found to be completely soluble in 100 volumes of water. Later, Rochow and Allred (*379*) reported that dichlorodimethylgermane is completely hydrolyzed to dimethylgermanediol in aqueous solution. The oxide was obtained, however, by hydrolysis of dimethylgermanium sulfide with sulfuric acid; cryoscopic measurements indicate a tetramer, $[(CH_3)_2GeO]_4$ (*47, 376*).

In a recent paper, Brown and Rochow (*50*) found that dimethylgermanium oxide is conveniently prepared by hydrolysis of dichlorodimethylgermane with aqueous sodium hydroxide, followed by extraction with petroleum ether and subsequent crystallization. The colorless crystals obtained in this manner were identified as tetrameric $[(CH_3)_2GeO]_4$ by cryoscopic measurements. The tetramer is very soluble in water, although the rate of solution is slow; presumably, dimethylgermanediol is formed.

$$n \; (CH_3)_2Ge(OH)_2 \rightleftharpoons [(CH_3)_2GeO]_n + n \; H_2O \qquad (87)$$

If an aqueous solution of dimethylgermanium oxide is allowed to evaporate, a white, fibrous material is obtained; the properties of this substance are in accord with a high polymeric structure (*50*). Tensimetric experiments show that, at temperatures of about 160 to 250° and in the vapor phase at pressures of about 100 mm, dimethylgermanium oxide exists as the trimer $[(CH_3)_2GeO]_3$. Crystalline dimethylgermanium sulfide can be obtained by hydrolysis of dichlorodimethylgermane and subsequent treatment with hydrogen sulfide; dimethylgermanium sulfide appears to be trimeric either in the solid or in the vapor phase (*50*).

Flood (*108*) has reported the hydrolysis of diethyldihalogermanes to give two polymeric forms of diethylgermanium oxide. At room temperature, the stable form is a white, amorphous solid which is insoluble in organic solvents and in water; an unstable liquid form, soluble in the common organic solvents, also may be obtained. Cryoscopic measurements indicate that the unstable form is a trimer, $[(C_2H_5)_2GeO]_3$. Trautman and Ambrose (*446*) also report obtaining the liquid trimeric form by heating the stable form near its melting point (175°). Anderson (*3, 4*), using similar hydrolytic methods followed by vacuum distillation, obtained a third polymeric form which melted from 27 to 29°; cryoscopic measurements in camphor indicated a tetramer, $[(C_2H_5)_2GeO]_4$. Liquid, trimeric dimethyl- and diethylgermanium oxides have been suggested as antifoaming agents for lubricating oils (*446*).

Basic hydrolysis of difluorodipropylgermane produces a trimeric form of dipropylgermanium oxide, $[(n\text{-}C_3H_7)_2GeO]_3$, which melts at 5.8° (*5*). This low melting form slowly changes into another form melting at about 153°; on heating at its melting point, the high melting form reverts to the less stable, low melting form. A tetrameric form of dipropylgermanium oxide, $[(n\text{-}C_3H_7)_2GeO]_4$, is reported to be obtained from the hydrolysis of dichlorodipropylgermane (*201*). Hydrolysis of difluorodiisopropylgermane produces only a single trimeric form of diisopropylgermanium oxide (*6*).

Studies concerning diphenylgermanium oxide are especially interesting. On hydrolysis with silver nitrate of dibromodiphenylgermane, prepared by reacting phenylmagnesium bromide with germanium tetrabromide, Morgan and Drew (*311*) obtained two crystalline modifications of diphenylgermanium oxide. The first of these, m.p. 149°, was formulated as a linear tetramer (XXVIII), while for the second form, m.p. 218°, a cyclic tetrameric structure (XXIX) was proposed. A third amorphous, insoluble oxide, m.p. 260°, was also reported.

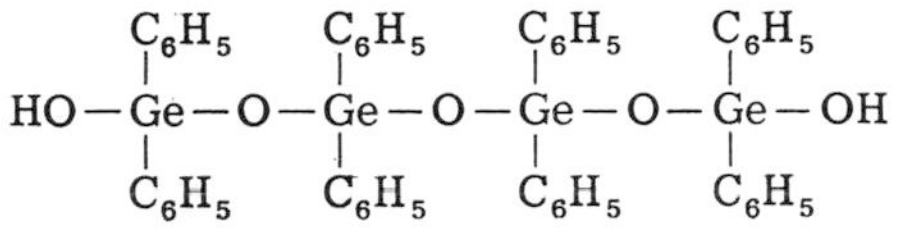

$$HO-\underset{\underset{C_6H_5}{|}}{\overset{\overset{C_6H_5}{|}}{Ge}}-O-\underset{\underset{C_6H_5}{|}}{\overset{\overset{C_6H_5}{|}}{Ge}}-O-\underset{\underset{C_6H_5}{|}}{\overset{\overset{C_6H_5}{|}}{Ge}}-O-\underset{\underset{C_6H_5}{|}}{\overset{\overset{C_6H_5}{|}}{Ge}}-OH$$

(XXVIII)

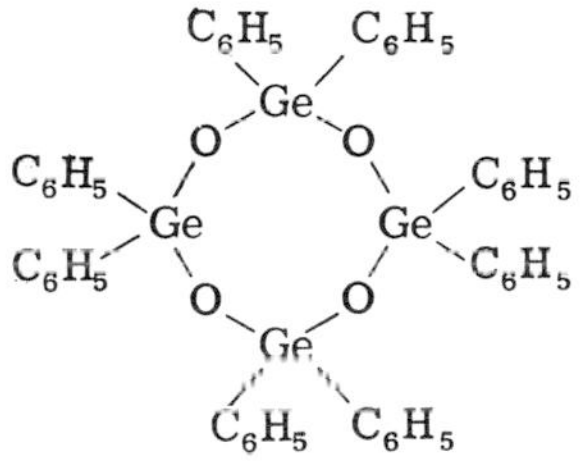

(XXIX)

Orndorff and co-workers (*333*) prepared impure dibromodiphenylgermane by reacting bromine with tetraphenylgermane. Hydrolysis of the bromination mixture gives, in addition to hexaphenyldigermoxane, two substances, m.p. 147 and 210°, which appeared to be the same tetramers isolated by Morgan and Drew.

The above hydrolysis reactions were run with mixtures of bromides containing dibromodiphenylgermane. Kraus and Brown (*252*) repeated this hydrolysis reaction using the pure dichloride and obtained samples of the oxide melting over the ranges 133–150, 140–185, and 149–300°. A similar mixture of the oxides was obtained by hydrolysis of diphenylgermanium imine. Later, Johnson and Harris (*200*) hydrolyzed dibromodiphenylgermane with aqueous ammonia and obtained, subsequent to several recrystallizations from nitromethane, a crystalline diphenylgermanium oxide which sintered at 145° and melted from 180 to 210°.

Recently, Metlesics and Zeiss (*295*) reinvestigated the diphenylgermanium oxide research. Cleavage of tetraphenylgermane with bromine and subsequent hydrolysis gave a crude insoluble oxide, m.p. 230–295°, similar to that reported by Morgan and Drew. When refluxed with acetic acid for a prolonged period, this material can be dissolved and then crystallized in almost quantitative yield as the soluble oxide, m.p. 219–221°. The infrared spectrum of this form contains characteristic germanium-oxygen absorption bands while hydroxyl absorption bands are absent; these data indicate the tetrameric structure (**XXIX**) proposed by Morgan and Drew. When pure dibromodiphenylgermane is hydrolyzed, under either acidic or alkaline conditions, a microcrystalline diphenylgermanium oxide, m.p. 290–295°, is formed; this oxide can be converted to diiododiphenylgermane with hydriodic acid and subsequently hydrolyzed to the crystalline oxide, m.p. 147–149°. This lower melting oxide is presumably the same as that described by Morgan and Drew in terms of structure (**XXVIII**). However, Metlesics and Zeiss report that the 149°-melting oxide is a pure trimeric form of diphenylgermanium oxide; based chiefly on molecular weight information and the absence of hydroxyl infrared absorption bands, structure (**XXX**) has been assigned to this form. The trimeric

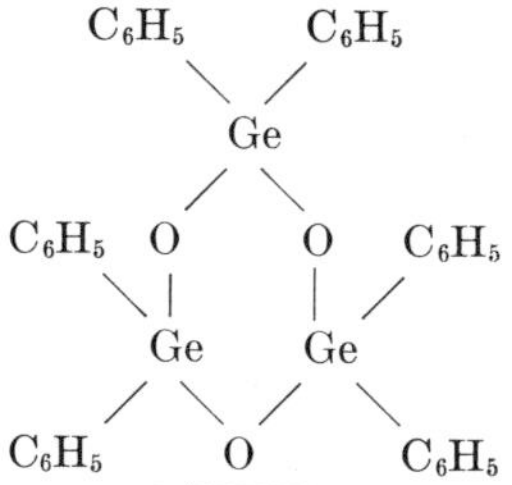

$$
\begin{array}{ccc}
C_6H_5 & & C_6H_5 \\
& \diagdown \quad \diagup & \\
& Ge & \\
& \diagup \quad \diagdown & \\
C_6H_5 \;\; O & & O \;\; C_6H_5 \\
\diagdown \;\; | & & | \;\; \diagup \\
Ge & & Ge \\
\diagup \quad \diagdown & \diagup \quad \diagdown \\
C_6H_5 & O & C_6H_5
\end{array}
$$

(**XXX**)

form also may be obtained [Eq. (88)] by distillation of either the 218°

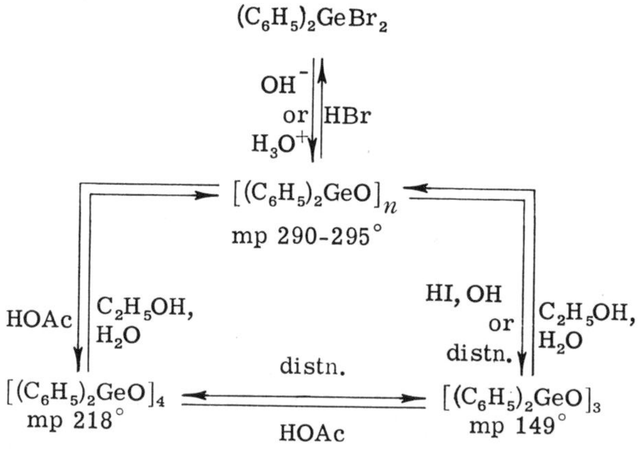

$$(C_6H_5)_2GeBr_2$$

$$
\begin{array}{c}
OH^- \\
or \quad\Big\| HBr \\
H_3O^+ \quad\downarrow
\end{array}
$$

$$[(C_6H_5)_2GeO]_n$$
mp 290-295°

$$[(C_6H_5)_2GeO]_4 \qquad\qquad [(C_6H_5)_2GeO]_3$$
mp 218°   mp 149°

HOAc $\Big\|$ $C_2H_5OH,\; H_2O$ HI, OH or distn. $\Big\downarrow$ $C_2H_5OH,\; H_2O$

distn.   HOAc

(88)

melting oxide or the 295°-melting oxide. The trimer may be transformed into the 218°-melting oxide by refluxing in acetic acid and into the 295°-melting oxide by refluxing in dilute ethanol. Data available did not permit any structural conclusion for the 295°-melting oxide.

The organogermanetriols, from the hydrolysis of the corresponding trihalides, are not stable but dehydrate immediately to form polymeric solids.

$$RGeX_3 + 3 H_2O \rightarrow RGe(OH)_3 + 3 HX \tag{89}$$

$$RGe(OH)_3 \rightarrow RGeOOH + H_2O \tag{90}$$

$$2n \ RGeOOH \rightarrow [(RGeO)_2O]_n + n \ H_2O \tag{91}$$

These polymers are insoluble in water and in the common organic solvents but may be dissolved in both acids and alkalies; they are reprecipitated from the latter solutions by carbon dioxide. The composition of the polymers usually corresponds to that of the anhydride, $[(RGeO)_2O]$; compounds of this type in which R = ethyl, butyl, phenyl, or various aryl groups are all polymeric with no definite melting point (*7, 79, 199*). The hydrolysis of bis(trichlorogermyl)methane gives a compound whose structure has been reported (*433, 434*) as $CH_2(GeOOH)_2$; this material is probably a polymeric anhydride.

The hydrolysis and condensation of trichloromethylgermane is stated to be reversible and, although methylgermanetriol has not been isolated, it is reported that there is strong evidence favoring the existence of this triol (*264*). A highly polymeric methylgermanium oxide can be obtained from this hydrolysis reaction; this polymer undergoes no change when heated in air to 480° (*264*).

Diethylgermanium oxide reacts with 100% sulfuric acid to form crystalline, dimeric diethylgermanium sulfate, $[(C_2H_5)_2Ge(SO_4)]_2$ (*3*). Structure (XXXI), an eight-membered ring similar to structure (XXIX) for tetrameric diorganogermanium oxides, has been proposed for this dimer.

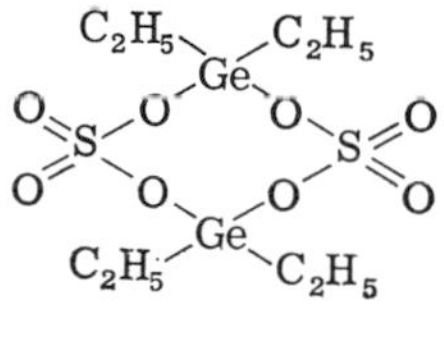

(XXXI)

Other reported polymeric organogermanium compounds include the imines, $(R_2GeNH)_n$, and the nitrides, $(RGeN)_n$; these substances are obtained by reacting the corresponding halides with liquid ammonia:

$$n \ R_2GeX_2 + 3n \ NH_3 \rightarrow (R_2GeNH)_n + 2n \ NH_4X \qquad (92a)$$

$$n \ RGeX_3 + 4n \ NH_3 \rightarrow (RGeN)_n + 3n \ NH_4X \qquad (92b)$$

Molecular weight measurements for diethylgermanium imine indicated a trimer (*108*); diphenylgermanium imine is described (*252*) as an extremely viscous, colorless liquid. Both of these imines are very easily hydrolyzed to the corresponding $(R_2GeO)_n$ derivatives. Ethylgermanium nitride is formed as a white precipitate in the reaction of ethyltriiodogermane with liquid ammonia (*109*); it is very easily hydrolyzed to $(C_2H_5GeO)_2O$. Triphenylgermylamine, $(C_6H_5)_3GeNH_2$, easily loses ammonia to form bis(triphenylgermyl)amine, $[(C_6H_5)_3Ge]_2NH$; the bisamine is a viscous liquid which on heating *in vacuo* to 200° again loses ammonia to give tris(triphenylgermyl)amine, $[(C_6H_5)_3Ge]_3N$ (*258*).

Schmidt and Schmidbaur (*386b, 386c, 386d, 386h*) have prepared various compounds of the type $R_3GeOSiR_3$ as well as dimethylbis(trimethyl-siloxy)germane:

$$2 \ (CH_3)_3SiOLi + (CH_3)_2GeCl_2 \rightarrow [(CH_3)_3SiO]_2Ge(CH_3)_2 \qquad (92c)$$

Trimethyl(trimethylsiloxy)germane reacts with sulfur trioxide or chromic acid to give trimethylgermyl trimethylsilyl sulfate or chromate (*386d*):

$$(CH_3)_3SiOGe(CH_3)_3 + SO_3 \rightarrow (CH_3)_3SiOSO_2OGe(CH_3)_3 \qquad (92d)$$

Silver arsenate reacts with chlorotrimethylgermane to form tris(trimethyl-germyl) arsenate (*386g*); a similar reaction occurs with chlorotrimethyl-germane and silver vanadate (*386f*):

$$3 \ (CH_3)_3GeCl + Ag_3VO_4 \rightarrow [(CH_3)_3GeO]_3VO + 3 \ AgCl \qquad (92e)$$

$$x \ [(CH_3)_3GeO]_3VO \rightarrow x \ (CH_3)_3GeOGe(CH_3)_3 + [(CH_3)_3GeOVO_2]_x \qquad (92f)$$

Recently reported is the interesting compound $[(CH_3)_4N^+][(C_6H_5)_3GeB-(C_6H_5)_3^-]$ (*396a*).

B. Organopolygermanes

A number of hexaalkyl- and hexaaryldigermanes have been reported; the synthesis of these types and their properties have been thoroughly reviewed (*49, 146, 199, 332*) and, therefore, will not be discussed in this chapter. Of interest here, however, are the higher polygermane derivatives.

The reaction of triphenylgermylsodium with dichlorodiphenylgermane in benzene results in the formation of octaphenyltrigermane (*252, 253*):

$$2\ (C_6H_5)_3GeNa + (C_6H_5)_2GeCl_2 \rightarrow C_6H_5\text{—}\underset{\underset{C_6H_5}{|}}{\overset{\overset{C_6H_5}{|}}{Ge}}\text{——}\underset{\underset{C_6H_5}{|}}{\overset{\overset{C_6H_5}{|}}{Ge}}\text{——}\underset{\underset{C_6H_5}{|}}{\overset{\overset{C_6H_5}{|}}{Ge}}\text{——}C_6H_5 + 2\ NaCl \quad (93)$$

Octaphenyltrigermane is a white crystalline substance, m.p. 247–248°, which is readily soluble in warm benzene and chloroform; it is stable toward air and moisture.

Divalent, inorganic germanium compounds are not uncommon. In an attempt to prepare a divalent organogermanium compound, Kraus and Brown (*253*) reacted dichlorodiphenylgermane with sodium in refluxing xylene; a white crystalline material, m.p. 294–295°, was obtained. From analytical data and molecular weight studies, this product was indicated to be a tetramer having the formula $[(C_6H_5)_2Ge]_4$. A cyclic structure (**XXXII**) has been considered possible for this derivative (*199*) but sub-

$$\begin{array}{ccc} (C_6H_5)_2Ge & \text{——} & Ge(C_6H_5)_2 \\ | & & | \\ (C_6H_5)_2Ge & \text{——} & Ge(C_6H_5)_2 \end{array}$$

(**XXXII**)

stantiating evidence is lacking. Kipping and Sands (*221*) similarly reacted dichlorodiphenylsilane with sodium and obtained two isomeric substances having the formula $[(C_6H_5)_2Si]_4$; this reaction has been reinvestigated and a compound whose properties agree with an octaphenylcyclotetrasilane was obtained (*138*) (see Section II, D). In liquid ammonia, sodium reacts with the polymeric diphenylgermanium to give a red solution previously reported as characteristic of diphenylgermylsodium (*253*).

More recently, Jacobs (*190*) has reported the reaction of diethylmercury and of dibutylmercury with germanium diiodide; the corresponding dialkyl-germanium (R_2Ge) compounds were not isolated but speculation concerning their existence was presented.

Schwarz and co-workers (*388, 389*) have reported the reaction of tri-chlorophenylgermane with either sodium or potassium in boiling xylene to give an amorphous polymeric solid; analyses and molecular weight studies indicated a hexamer, $(C_6H_5Ge)_6$, and these authors speculated that the structure might be either (**XXXIII**) or, more probably, (**XXXIV**). Recently, this reaction was reinvestigated by Metlesics and Zeiss (*294*). When the conditions reported by Schwarz and co-workers were used, satisfactory yields of polymeric material were not obtained. However, by using a 50% excess of potassium in toluene and dispersing the molten potassium under nitrogen with very vigorous agitation, these workers obtained an intractable, dark brown powder containing 28% germanium;

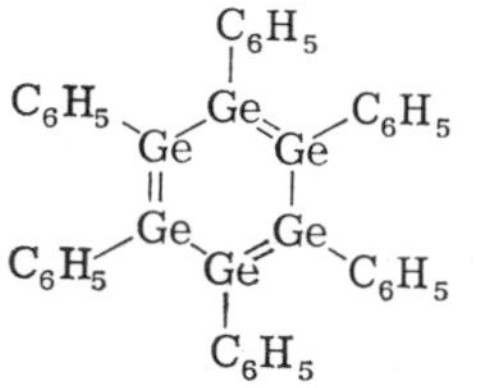

(XXXIII)

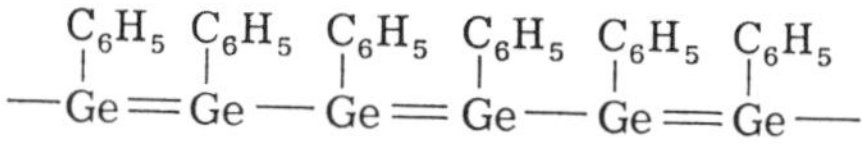

(XXXIV)

further studies of this material were not reported. A similar material has been reported (*36*) from the reaction of trichlorophenylsilane with a large excess of alkali metal.

Metlesics and Zeiss (*294*), in order to avoid excessive as well as incomplete reaction, interrupted the above dehalogenation reaction at a stage at which the solution did not undergo color change when exposed to air, and obtained a yellow solid similar to that reported by Schwarz. This material had a phenyl/germanium ratio of 1:1 but analysis and infrared data indicated an oxygen content of 5 to 10%. The amorphous substance had a softening point of about 240° and molecular weight values ranging from 805 to 1280, corresponding to 5 to 8 phenylgermanium units, were obtained. This phenylgermanium polymer also was obtained from the reaction of trichlorophenylgermane with lithium amalgam. Brominative degradation studies indicate the polymeric material to be composed of phenylgermanium, diphenylgermanium, phenylgermanium-oxygen, and germanium-oxygen units but an exact formulation of the structure was not possible (*294*). Kipping and co-workers (*220*) similarly obtained a polymeric organosilicon material with a phenyl/silicon ratio of 1:1 but which contained considerable amounts of oxygen.

Dichlorodipropylgermane and trichloropropylgermane may be prepared by the reaction of propyllithium with germanium tetrachloride (*201*). A colorless, liquid by-product usually is also obtained in this reaction, especially if temperatures above 85° are employed. This liquid has not been identified but, based on analytical data, the formula $(C_3H_7Ge)_n$ has been proposed.

Several organogermanium compounds containing two germanium atoms per molecule, excluding the digermanes, have been reported. In 1932, Kraus and Nutting (*257*) described the reaction of triphenylgermylsodium with dichloromethane in liquid ammonia; the principal reaction product is

bis(triphenylgermyl)methane, accompanied by methyltriphenylgermane
and hexaphenyldigermoxane:

$$2 \ (C_6H_5)_3GeNa + CH_2Cl_2 \xrightarrow{NH_3} (C_6H_5)_3GeCH_2Ge(C_6H_5)_3 + 2 \ NaCl \qquad (94)$$

The same products are obtained from the reaction of triphenylgermylsodium with chloroform in liquid ammonia *(257)*; in ethyl ether, these
reactants give hexaphenyldigermane and a small yield of bis(triphenylgermyl)methane *(407)*. In liquid ammonia, triphenylgermylsodium reacts
with carbon tetrachloride to form hexaphenyldigermoxane plus a number
of unidentified lower melting substances *(257)*; with ethyl ether as a
solvent, hexaphenyldigermane and a small amount of hexaphenyldigermoxane are obtained *(407)*.

1,3-Dibromopropane and 1,5-dibromopentane react with triphenylgermylsodium in liquid ammonia to form 1,3-bis(triphenylgermyl)propane
and 1,5-bis(triphenylgermyl)pentane *(407)*:

$$(C_6H_5)_3GeNa + Br(CH_2)_nBr \xrightarrow{NH_3} (C_6H_5)_3Ge(CH_2)_nGe(C_6H_5)_3 \qquad (95)$$

Acetylenebis(magnesium bromide) in chloroform or sodium acetylide in
tetrahydrofuran react with R_3GeBr (R = ethyl, cyclohexyl, or phenyl)
compounds to form the corresponding bis(triorganogermyl)acetylene
derivatives *(169)*:

$$2 \ R_3GeBr + BrMgC{\equiv}CMgBr \to R_3GeC{\equiv}CGeR_3 + 2 \ MgBr_2 \qquad (96)$$

$$R_3GeBr + HC{\equiv}CNa \to R_3GeC{\equiv}CH + NaBr \qquad (97)$$

$$2 \ R_3GeC{\equiv}CH \to R_3GeC{\equiv}CGeR_3 + HC{\equiv}CH \qquad (98)$$

The trialkylethynylgermanes initially formed with the sodium acetylide
apparently disproportionate readily to the bis-substituted derivatives.
However, trialkylethynylgermanes can be prepared *(287, 288)* either by
dehydrohalogenation of trialkyl(1,2-dibromoethyl)germane or directly
from the trialkylbromogermane and ethynylmagnesium bromide:

$$R_3GeCH{=}CH_2 + Br_2 \to R_3GeCHBrCH_2Br \qquad (99)$$

$$R_3GeCHBrCH_2Br + (C_2H_5)_2NH \to R_3GeCBr{=}CH_2 + (C_2H_5)_2NH{\cdot}HBr \qquad (100)$$

$$R_3GeCBr{=}CH_2 + NaNH_2 \to R_3GeC{\equiv}CH + NaBr + NH_3 \qquad (101)$$

$$HC{\equiv}CH + C_2H_5MgBr \xrightarrow{THF} HC{\equiv}CMgBr + C_2H_6 \qquad (102)$$

$$R_3GeBr + HC{\equiv}CMgBr \to MgBr_2 + R_3GeC{\equiv}CH \qquad (103)$$

Bis(triphenylgermyl)butadiyne has been prepared from triphenylgermyl-sodium and diiodobutadiyne (*170a*):

$$2 \ (C_6H_5)_3GeNa + I—C≡C—C≡C—I \rightarrow (C_6H_5)_3Ge—C≡C—C≡C—Ge(C_6H_5)_3 \qquad (103a)$$

The preparation of organosilicon compounds by the free radical addition of silanes to olefins has been reported in a number of publications. The extension of this work to germanes has been made by Fisher *et al.* (*107*), who described the addition of trichlorogermane to 1-hexene. Later, it was found that triphenylgermane adds, with peroxide catalysis, to the olefinic linkage in a normal manner to give terminally substituted alkylgermanes (*132*). Thus, triphenylgermane reacts with allyltriphenylgermane to give 1,3-bis(triphenylgermyl)propane:

$$(C_6H_5)_3GeCH_2CH=CH_2 + (C_6H_5)_3GeH \rightarrow (C_6H_5)_3Ge(CH_2)_3Ge(C_6H_5)_3 \qquad (104)$$

Similarly, two equivalents of triethylgermane react with acetylene to form 1,2-bis(triethylgermyl)ethane while tributylgermane reacts with tributyl-germylacetylene to give 1,2-bis(tributylgermyl)ethene (*266, 383a*):

$$2 \ (C_2H_5)_3GeH + HC≡CH \rightarrow (C_2H_5)_3GeCH_2CH_2Ge(C_2H_5)_3 \qquad (105a)$$

$$(C_4H_9)_3GeC≡CH + (C_4H_9)_3GeH \rightarrow (C_4H_9)_3GeCH=CHGe(C_4H_9)_3 \qquad (105b)$$

β-Substituted styrene derivatives are obtained from the reaction of tri-chlorogermane or triphenylgermane with phenylacetylene (*101b, 177a*):

$$R_3GeH + H—C≡C—C_6H_5 \rightarrow R_3Ge—CH=CH—C_6H_5 \qquad (106)$$

C. Organogermanium Polymers from Unsaturated Germanes

Although the syntheses of a number of potentially polymerizable allyl and vinyl germanium derivatives have been published (*132, 178, 289, 303, 304, 345, 348, 392*), reports of actual polymerization studies are rather limited. The allyl compounds usually are prepared by reacting allylmag-nesium bromide with germanium tetrachloride or with an organogermanium halide (*132, 178, 289*) while the vinyl compounds are prepared similarly, using the vinyl Grignard reagent in tetrahydrofuran (*178, 204, 289, 303, 345, 392*). Allyltrichlorogermane has been prepared directly by heating allyl chloride with a germanium-copper mixture in a sealed tube at 340° (*348*). Trichlorovinylgermane has been synthesized by the chlorination of trichloroethylgermane with sulfuryl chloride; the trichloro(2-chloro-

ethyl)germane formed in this reaction is dehydrochlorinated to trichlorovinylgermane by distilling from quinoline (*304, 348*):

$$CH_3CH_2GeCl_3 \xrightarrow{SO_2Cl_2} CH_3CHClGeCl_3 + ClCH_2CH_2GeCl_3 \qquad (107)$$

$$CH_2{=}CHCl + HGeCl_3 \rightarrow ClCH_2CH_2GeCl_3 \qquad (108)$$

$$ClCH_2CH_2GeCl_3 \xrightarrow[\text{quinoline}]{\Delta} CH_2{=}CHGeCl_3 \qquad (109)$$

Trichloro(2-chloroethyl)germane also is obtained from the reaction of
vinyl chloride and trichlorogermane (*305, 349*). The reaction of divinyl-
mercury with germanium tetrachloride (*43*) affords a more direct route to
trichlorovinylgermane.

$$GeCl_4 + (CH_2{=}CH)_2Hg \rightarrow CH_2{=}CHGeCl_3 + CH_2{=}CHHgCl \qquad (110)$$

Tetrakis(2-phenylvinyl)germane has been prepared from the reaction of
β-bromostyrene and germanium(IV) chloride with sodium while tetrakis-
(phenylethynyl)germane has been obtained by reacting lithium phenyl-
acetylide with germanium(IV) chloride (*376*):

$$4\ C_6H_5CH{=}CHBr + GeCl_4 + 8\ Na \rightarrow (C_6H_5CH{=}CH{-})_4Ge + 4\ NaCl + 4\ NaBr \qquad (110a)$$

$$4\ C_6H_5C{\equiv}CLi + GeCl_4 \rightarrow (C_6H_5C{\equiv}C{-})_4Ge + 4\ LiCl \qquad (110b)$$

The first polymerization report was that of Korshak and co-workers
(*235*). In this study, various allylalkylgermanes were subjected to polymerization at 6000-atm pressure and 120° in the presence of *tert*-butyl
peroxide. The trialkylallylgermanes ($R_3GeCH_2CH{=}CH_2$), where R is
methyl or ethyl, form oily polymers; diallyldimethylgermane and triallyl-
methylgermane polymerize to transparent glasses having the molecular
weight of a trimer. 2-Isobutenyltrimethylgermane showed practically no
tendency to polymerize. All of these allylalkylgermanes formed copolymers
with methyl methacrylate; the introduction of alkenylgermanium units
into the methyl methacrylate polymer lowers the viscosity and, therefore,
the molecular weight. Copolymerization of the monoalkenylgermanium
derivatives with methyl methacrylate gave linear polymers; at definite
temperatures they changed from a glass to a highly elastic state and then
to a viscous, flowable state (*235*).

Later, Korshak and co-workers (*233*) reported the copolymerization of
allyltrimethylgermane with styrene as well as with methyl methacrylate.
This paper also contains a report that diethyldivinylgermane can be
polymerized to form a colorless glass having a cross-linked structure.

Recently, Kolesnikov and associates (*231*) reported the polymerization of diallyldimethylgermane in the presence of triethylaluminum and titanium tetrachloride. A low molecular weight substance was formed for which structure (**XXXV**) was proposed. Kolesnikov and Davydova (*230*)

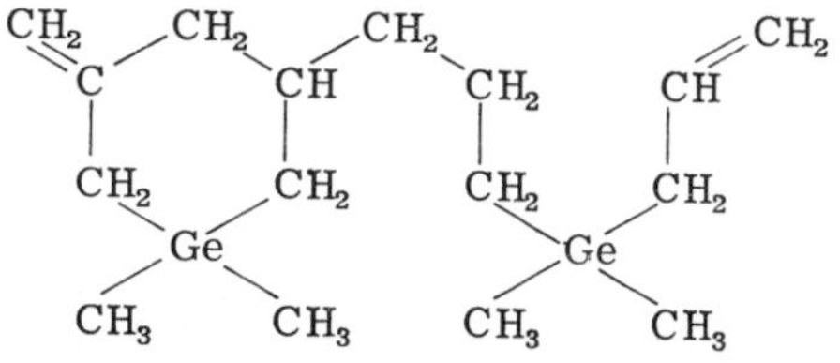

(**XXXV**)

also have discussed the synthesis and attempted polymerization of *p*-(triethylgermyl)styrene; although a number of initiators and catalysts were tried, no significant yield of polymerized product was obtained. The *p*-(triethylgermyl)styrene was prepared from *p*-(triethylgermyl)phenyl-magnesium bromide and vinyl bromide in the presence of cobalt(II) chloride; this compound also has been obtained by reacting chlorotriethyl-germane and *p*-chlorostyrene with magnesium in tetrahydrofuran (*357a*). Recently, *p*-(triphenylgermyl)styrene and diphenylbis(*p*-vinylphenyl)ger-mane were obtained from bromotriphenylgermane or dibromodiphenyl-germane and *p*-vinylphenylmagnesium bromide in tetrahydrofuran (*326*). *p*-(Trimethylgermyl)styrene and *p*-(trimethylgermyl)-α-methylstyrene are reported to polymerize at 70 to 90° in the presence of free radical initiators, such as 2,2'-azobis[2-methylpropionitrile], to give clear, colorless solids (*327*). Kolesnikov and co-workers (*231b*, *231c*, *231d*) have studied the peroxide-initiated polymerization of triethylgermyl methacrylate and its copolymerization with methyl methacrylate and styrene; the copolymeriza-tion of diallyl derivatives of germanium with styrene and with methyl methacrylate also were investigated (*231a*, *231c*, *231d*).

Reduction of trichlorovinylgermane with lithium aluminum hydride yields vinylgermane:

$$4\ CH_2\text{==}CHGeCl_3 + 3\ LiAlH_4 \rightarrow 4\ CH_2\text{==}CHGeH_3 + 3\ LiCl + 3\ AlCl_3 \qquad (111)$$

This compound polymerized, in daylight and especially in the presence of mercury, to form a white solid, $(C_2H_6Ge)_n$ (*43*). Polymeric vinylgermane commences measurable decomposition above 275°, giving hydrogen with lesser amounts of ethylene and germane. Like polymeric vinylsilane, poly-vinylgermane is insoluble in a variety of solvents. Vinyltin trihydride, prepared in a similar manner, is much less stable than vinylgermane and must be stored at low temperatures to avoid decomposition.

Similarly, dibutyl(2-phenylvinyl)germane and allyldibutylgermane have been found to polymerize readily (*383a*):

$$(C_4H_9)_2GeHCH{=}CHC_6H_5 \rightarrow \left[\begin{array}{c} C_4H_9 \\ | \\ {-}Ge{-}CH_2{-}CH{-} \\ | \qquad\qquad | \\ C_4H_9 \qquad C_6H_5 \end{array} \right]_n \qquad (111a)$$

$$(C_4H_9)_2GeHCH_2CH{=}CH_2 \rightarrow \left[\begin{array}{c} C_4H_9 \\ | \\ {-}CH_2CH_2CH_2{-}Ge{-} \\ | \\ C_4H_9 \end{array} \right]_n \qquad (111b)$$

Polymers of allyltrimethylgermane and related compounds are reported in the patent literature (*307a, 307b*).

D. Polymers Containing Germanium and Other Group IV Elements

Henry and Noltes (*179, 180, 325*) have reported several organo-Group IVB compounds which contain both germanium and tin; these derivatives were obtained by reacting an organotin hydride with a vinyl-substituted organogermanium compound. For example, triphenyltin hydride adds to triphenylvinylgermane or diphenyldivinylgermane to form triphenyl-2-(triphenylstannyl)ethylgermane or diphenylbis[2-triphenylstannyl)-ethyl]-germane, respectively (*179, 325*):

$$(C_6H_5)_3SnH + (C_6H_5)_3GeCH{=}CH_2 \rightarrow (C_6H_5)_3SnCH_2CH_2Ge(C_6H_5)_3 \qquad (112)$$

$$2\,(C_6H_5)_3SnH + (C_6H_5)_2Ge(CH{=}CH_2)_2 \rightarrow$$

$$\begin{array}{c} C_6H_5 \\ | \\ (C_6H_5)_3SnCH_2CH_2GeCH_2CH_2Sn(C_6H_5)_3 \\ | \\ C_6H_5 \end{array} \qquad (113)$$

However, the reaction of diphenyltin dihydride and triphenylvinylgermane produces triphenyl-2-(triphenylstannyl)ethylgermane; presumably, diphenyltin dihydride undergoes disproportionation and the triphenyltin hydride thus formed adds to the vinyl grouping. When equimolecular amounts of diphenyltin dihydride and diphenyldivinylgermane are heated together, the principal product is 1,1,4,4-tetraphenyl-1-stanna-4-germa-cyclohexane; also isolated is an insoluble, nonmelting material which, although not studied, may have been the corresponding linear polymer (*180, 325*):

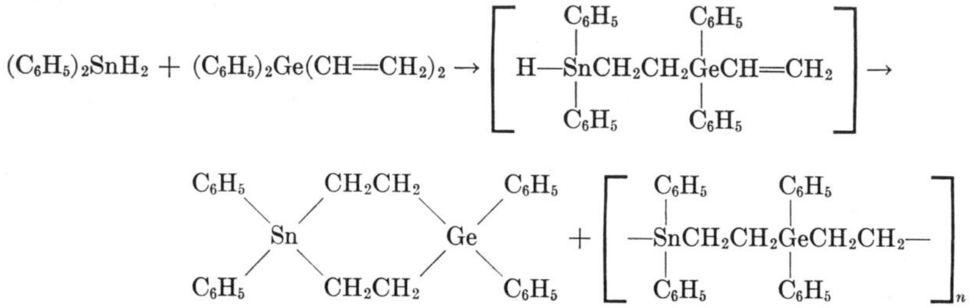

$$(C_6H_5)_2SnH_2 + (C_6H_5)_2Ge(CH=CH_2)_2 \rightarrow \left[\begin{array}{cc} C_6H_5 & C_6H_5 \\ | & | \\ H-Sn CH_2CH_2 Ge CH=CH_2 \\ | & | \\ C_6H_5 & C_6H_5 \end{array} \right] \rightarrow$$

$$\begin{array}{c} C_6H_5 \quad CH_2CH_2 \quad C_6H_5 \\ \diagdown \quad \diagup \quad \diagdown \quad \diagup \\ Sn \qquad\qquad Ge \\ \diagup \quad \diagdown \quad \diagup \quad \diagdown \\ C_6H_5 \quad CH_2CH_2 \quad C_6H_5 \end{array} + \left[\begin{array}{cc} C_6H_5 & C_6H_5 \\ | & | \\ -Sn CH_2CH_2 Ge CH_2CH_2- \\ | & | \\ C_6H_5 & C_6H_5 \end{array} \right]_n \qquad (114)$$

Diphenyltin dihydride reacts with diphenylbis(*p*-vinylphenyl)germane to give a glass-like polymer having a molecular weight of 27,000 (*327*):

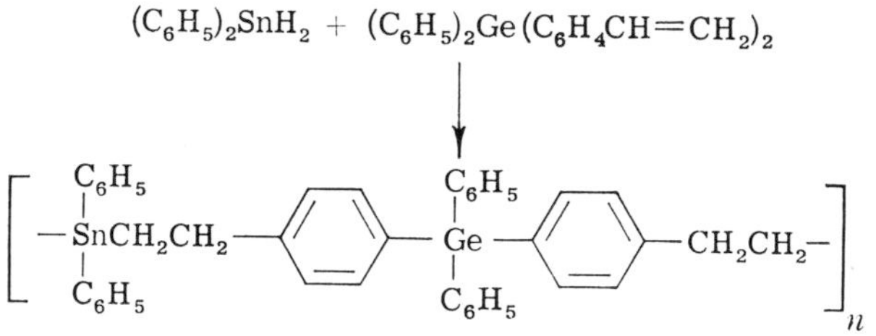

$$(C_6H_5)_2SnH_2 + (C_6H_5)_2Ge(C_6H_4CH=CH_2)_2$$

$$\downarrow$$

$$\left[\begin{array}{c} C_6H_5 \\ | \\ -Sn CH_2CH_2 - \bigcirc - \overset{\displaystyle C_6H_5}{\underset{\displaystyle C_6H_5}{|\atop|}} Ge - \bigcirc - CH_2CH_2- \\ | \\ C_6H_5 \end{array} \right]_n \qquad (115)$$

In recent years, a number of reports of organo-Group IVB derivatives containing both germanium and silicon have appeared. *p*-Trimethylsilylphenyllithium reacts with germanium tetrachloride to form tetrakis(*p*-trimethylsilylphenyl)germane (*291*):

$$4\ (CH_3)_3SiC_6H_4Li + GeCl_4 \rightarrow [(CH_3)_3SiC_6H_4]_4Ge + 4\ LiCl \qquad (116)$$

Similarly, the reaction of sodium triphenylsilanolate with germanium tetrachloride gives tetrakis(triphenylsiloxy)germane (*168*). The reaction of trimethylgermylmethylmagnesium chloride with trimethoxymethylsilane produces dimethoxymethyl(trimethylgermylmethyl)silane (*395*):

$$(CH_3)_3GeCH_2MgCl + CH_3Si(OCH_3)_3 \rightarrow$$

$$\begin{array}{c} OCH_3 \\ | \\ (CH_3)_3GeCH_2 SiCH_3 + CH_3OMgCl \\ | \\ OCH_3 \end{array} \qquad (117)$$

The hydrolysis and subsequent equilibration of this compound with hexamethyldisiloxane gives a polysiloxane (**XXXVI**) which contains an organogermanium side chain (*396*). Petrov and co-workers (*349*) have synthesized 2-(trichlorogermyl)ethyltrichlorosilane and [2-chloro-2-(trichlorogermyl)-

$$CH_3-\underset{\underset{CH_3}{|}}{\overset{\overset{CH_3}{|}}{Si}}-O-\left[-\underset{\underset{CH_2Ge(CH_3)_3}{|}}{\overset{\overset{CH_3}{|}}{Si}}-O-\right]_n-\underset{\underset{CH_3}{|}}{\overset{\overset{CH_3}{|}}{Si}}-CH_3$$

(XXXVI)

ethyl]trichlorosilane by reacting trichlorogermane with the appropriate vinyl-substituted silane:

$$HGeCl_3 + CH_2{=}CHSiCl_3 \rightarrow Cl_3GeCH_2CH_2SiCl_3 \tag{118}$$

$$HGeCl_3 + ClCH{=}CHSiCl_3 \rightarrow Cl_3GeCH(Cl)CH_2SiCl_3 \tag{119}$$

Hydrolysis products from these compounds should be interesting but were not reported.

Triphenylgermylsodium and trichlorosilane react in ether solution to form tris(triphenylgermyl)silane (*301*); tris(triphenylgermyl)silane, in turn, reacts with lithium in ethylamine to give tris(triphenylgermyl)silyl-lithium. This intermediate reacts with bromoethane (*301*) and with triphenyltin chloride (*148*):

$$3 \ (C_6H_5)_3GeNa + SiHCl_3 \rightarrow 3 \ NaCl + [(C_6H_5)_3Ge]_3SiH \tag{120}$$

$$[(C_6H_5)_3Ge]_3SiH + 2 \ Li \rightarrow [(C_6H_5)_3Ge]_3SiLi + LiH \tag{121}$$

$$[(C_6H_5)_3Ge]_3SiLi + C_2H_5Br \rightarrow [(C_6H_5)_3Ge]_3SiC_2H_5 + LiBr \tag{122}$$

$$[(C_6H_5)_3Ge]_3SiLi + (C_6H_5)_3SnCl \rightarrow [(C_6H_5)_3Ge]_3SiSn(C_6H_5)_3 + LiCl \tag{123}$$

Korshak and co-workers (*243*) report that diethyldimethyldihydrosiloxanes add to organogermanium compounds containing two unsaturated groups to give polymeric products; the reaction is carried out by heating the mixture at 120° for 6 hours in a sealed tube and in the presence of a trace of chloroplatinic acid:

$$H-\underset{\underset{C_2H_5}{|}}{\overset{\overset{CH_3}{|}}{Si}}-O-\underset{\underset{C_2H_5}{|}}{\overset{\overset{CH_3}{|}}{Si}}-H + (C_2H_5)_2Ge(CH{=}CH_2)_2 \rightarrow \left[-\underset{\underset{C_2H_5}{|}}{\overset{\overset{CH_3}{|}}{Si}}-O-\underset{\underset{C_2H_5}{|}}{\overset{\overset{CH_3}{|}}{Si}}CH_2CH_2\underset{\underset{C_2H_5}{|}}{\overset{\overset{C_2H_5}{|}}{Ge}}CH_2CH_2-\right]_n \tag{124}$$

$$H-\underset{\underset{C_2H_5}{|}}{\overset{\overset{CH_3}{|}}{Si}}-O-\underset{\underset{C_2H_5}{|}}{\overset{\overset{CH_3}{|}}{Si}}-H + (CH_3)_2Ge(CH_2CH{=}CH_2)_2 \rightarrow \left[-\underset{\underset{C_2H_5}{|}}{\overset{\overset{CH_3}{|}}{Si}}-O-\underset{\underset{C_2H_5}{|}}{\overset{\overset{CH_3}{|}}{Si}}(CH_2)_3\underset{\underset{CH_3}{|}}{\overset{\overset{CH_3}{|}}{Ge}}(CH_2)_3-\right]_n \tag{125}$$

With diethyldivinylgermane, n is reported to be approximately 15, while with diallyldimethylgermane a value of 13 is reported for n. A later report *(361)* lists a value of 6 for n with the latter polymer.

The effect of incorporating germanium atoms into a polysiloxane structure has been investigated by Stavitskiĭ and co-workers *(425)*. The joint hydrolysis of dichlorodimethylsilane and dibromodimethylgermane results in the formation of cyclic germanosiloxanes of low molecular weight. Polymerization of these germanosiloxanes with concentrated sulfuric acid gives polydimethylgermanosiloxanes of high molecular weight; their properties are much the same as those of polydimethylsiloxane rubber. It was found that with an increase in the ratio of germanium/silicon the relative length of the chain decreases; thermal stability of the polymer is not affected by the presence of germanium in the siloxane structure.

In closing this section, it might be well to mention briefly a recent patent *(398)* for the polymerization of olefins with catalyst mixtures containing trialkyl- or triarylgermanes and halides of titanium, vanadium, chromium, or molybdenum. These catalysts are claimed to be superior to Ziegler catalysts with respect to the crystallinity of the polymers produced.

IV. Organotin Polymers

A. Organotin Oxides and Related Compounds

A recent review *(189)* of organotin chemistry reveals that, while a number of polymeric or polymerizable organotin compounds have been reported, few extensive investigations of organotin polymers have been made. The organotin dihalides, by analogy to the organodihalosilanes, might be expected to be suitable starting materials for preparing organotin polymers *(189, 325)*. The R_2SnX_2 compounds hydrolyze readily to form the corresponding organotin oxides. These organotin oxides, R_2SnO, are white, amorphous powders which do not melt but decompose at high temperatures; usually, they are insoluble in the common organic solvents and in water. Although these substances are represented by the formula $[-R_2SnO-]_n$, their physical properties resemble those of metallic oxides and are quite different from those of the structurally similar silicones *(372d)*. The partial hydrolysis of dialkyltin dihalides produces an addition complex of the cyclic tristannoxane and the dialkyltin dihalide, $[R_2SnO]_3 \cdot 3R_2SnX_2$ *(2a)*.

Smith and Kipping *(409)* have studied the properties of a dibenzyltin oxide derivative, $HOSn(CH_2C_6H_5)_2[OSn(CH_2C_6H_5)_2]_nOSn(CH_2C_6H_5)_2OH$; molecular weight determinations indicated n to be 6 or 7. In a few cases it has been noted that freshly prepared oxides are soluble in alkali but, after standing, they become insoluble. Solerio (*414*) has reported that R_2SnO compounds are monomeric if the R group is large, e.g., $C_{12}H_{25}$, but polymeric if R is small. Another group of compounds, the organostannonic acids, recently has received some study (*105b, 207, 325*). The alkylstannonic acids, $[RSnOOH]_n$, are polymeric solids which do not melt but decompose, usually at temperatures above 300°; they are insoluble in water and in most organic solvents but are readily soluble in the lower aliphatic alcohols. Probably organotin esters are formed with these alcohols; evaporation of the solvent from the alcoholic solutions and subsequent heating yields a transparent polymeric material for which structure (**XXXVII**) is probable.

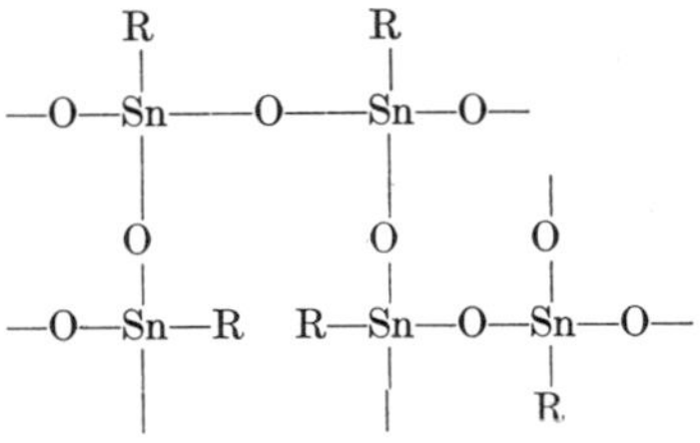

(XXXVII)

The action of diazomethane on tin(II) chloride, in benzene solution, produces high molecular weight products of the type (**XXXVIII**); these substances presumably result from the polymerization of the initial addition product (**XXXIX**) (*476*).

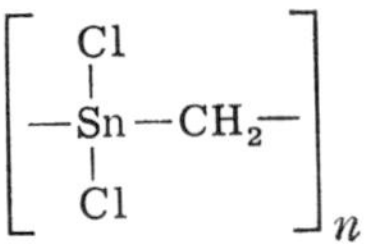

(XXXVIII) 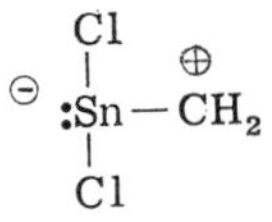   (XXXIX)

Although polymeric organotin compounds have not yet achieved large scale commercial application, the use of organotin compounds as polymer stabilizers, especially with polyvinyl chloride, has been of industrial importance for several years (*408*). A number of the organotin stabilizers mentioned in the patent literature have been polymeric substances containing tin-oxygen bonding.

In 1942 (*367*), Quattlebaum and Noffsinger obtained a patent covering a number of organotin salts of organic acids, including dibutyltin maleate, $[-(C_4H_9)_2SnOOCCH=CHCOO-]_n$. Dibutyltin maleate is subject to polymerization at room temperature, passing from a sticky material to a lumpy product of unknown molecular weight. By deliberate peroxide catalysis of the newly formed material in a suspension system, it is possible to achieve some molecular weight control and to produce a free-flowing powder. The low molecular weight material is a good polyvinyl stabilizer but it is a powerful lachrymator; the high molecular weight material is less lachrymatory but also is less effective as a stabilizer.

More recently (9), the reaction of dibutyltin oxide or dibutyltin diacetate with a number of dicarboxylic acids or anhydrides has been reported to yield polymeric derivatives, $[-(C_4H_9)_2SnOOC-R_x-COO-]_n$. Aliphatic acids such as succinic and adipic acids formed soluble cyclic derivatives of low molecular weight; oxalic acid yielded an insoluble, infusible product with the characteristics of a salt; and terephthalic acid and the long chain sebacic acid gave linear polymers of considerable molecular weight. Sulfur-containing dicarboxylic acids such as thiomalic acid (410, 412) and S-acylthiomalic acid (411) similarly have been reported to give polymeric products with dibutyltin salts; these are probably polymers of the type (XL). Dibutyltin oxide reacts with diethyleneglycol dithioglycolate (58) to produce a polymer of type (XLI). Other sulfur-containing organotin polymers have been prepared (86a).

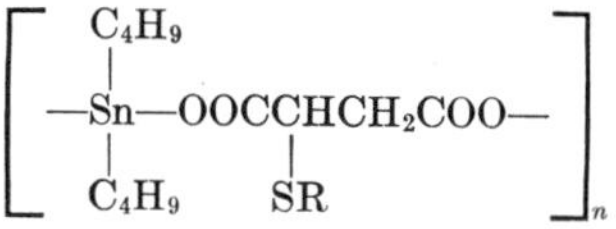

$$\left[\begin{array}{c} C_4H_9 \\ | \\ -Sn-OOCCHCH_2COO- \\ | \quad\quad | \\ C_4H_9 \quad\quad SR \end{array}\right]_n$$

(XL)

$$\left[\begin{array}{c} C_4H_9 \\ | \\ -Sn-S-CH_2COOCH_2CH_2OCH_2CH_2OOCCH_2S- \\ | \\ C_4H_9 \end{array}\right]_n$$

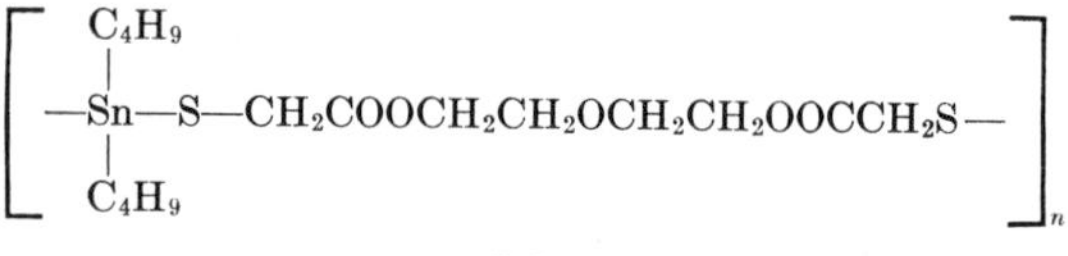

(XLI)

Dialkyltin oxides and other organotin salts can be reacted with alcohols to form low molecular weight polymers of the general type (XLII). Several

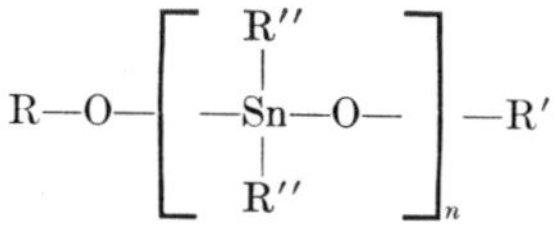

$$R-O-\left[\begin{array}{c} R'' \\ | \\ -Sn-O- \\ | \\ R'' \end{array}\right]_n -R'$$

(XLII)

polymeric organotin alkoxides of this type have been reported (273, 372, 381) for polyvinyl stabilization. Many monomeric organotin alkoxides tend to polymerize on standing or with heating, the tendency rising with

increasing molecular weight (*275*). Polymers having structure (XLIII) are
obtained when the monomeric $R_2Sn(OOCR')_2$ compounds are subjected to

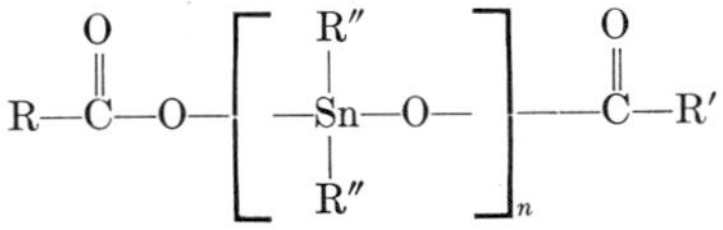

$$R-\overset{O}{\overset{\|}{C}}-O-\left[\;-\overset{R''}{\underset{R''}{\overset{|}{\underset{|}{Sn}}}}-O-\;\right]_n-\overset{O}{\overset{\|}{C}}-R'$$

(XLIII)

steam distillation; higher polymers are obtained by blowing moist air
through the mixture at 140° (*274*). Polymers of the type (XLIV) have
been reported (*307*).

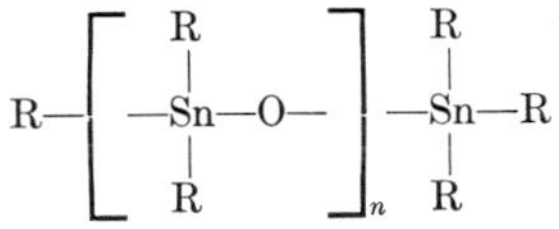

$$R-\left[\;-\overset{R}{\underset{R}{\overset{|}{\underset{|}{Sn}}}}-O-\;\right]_n-\overset{R}{\underset{R}{\overset{|}{\underset{|}{Sn}}}}-R$$

(XLIV)

Polyorganostannoxanes also may be obtained by heating a mixture of a
tin tetraalkoxide with a dialkyltin diacetate (*246*):

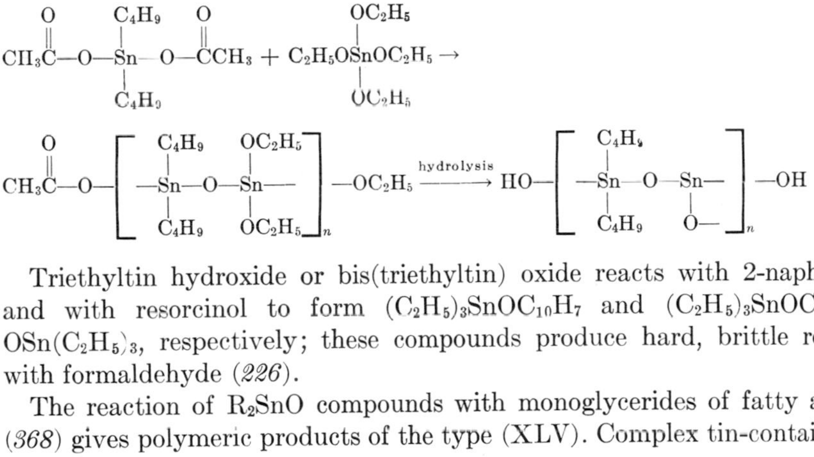

$$CH_3\overset{O}{\overset{\|}{C}}-O-\overset{C_4H_9}{\underset{C_4H_9}{\overset{|}{\underset{|}{Sn}}}}-O-\overset{O}{\overset{\|}{C}}CH_3 + C_2H_5O\overset{OC_2H_5}{\underset{OC_2H_5}{\overset{|}{\underset{|}{Sn}}}}OC_2H_5 \rightarrow$$

$$CH_3\overset{O}{\overset{\|}{C}}-O-\left[\;-\overset{C_4H_9}{\underset{C_4H_9}{\overset{|}{\underset{|}{Sn}}}}-O-\overset{OC_2H_5}{\underset{OC_2H_5}{\overset{|}{\underset{|}{Sn}}}}-\;\right]_n-OC_2H_5 \xrightarrow{\text{hydrolysis}} HO-\left[\;-\overset{C_4H_9}{\underset{C_4H_9}{\overset{|}{\underset{|}{Sn}}}}-O-\overset{}{\underset{O}{\overset{}{\underset{|}{Sn}}}}-\;\right]_n-OH \quad (126)$$

Triethyltin hydroxide or bis(triethyltin) oxide reacts with 2-naphthol
and with resorcinol to form $(C_2H_5)_3SnOC_{10}H_7$ and $(C_2H_5)_3SnOC_6H_4$-
$OSn(C_2H_5)_3$, respectively; these compounds produce hard, brittle resins
with formaldehyde (*226*).

The reaction of R_2SnO compounds with monoglycerides of fatty acids
(*368*) gives polymeric products of the type (XLV). Complex tin-containing

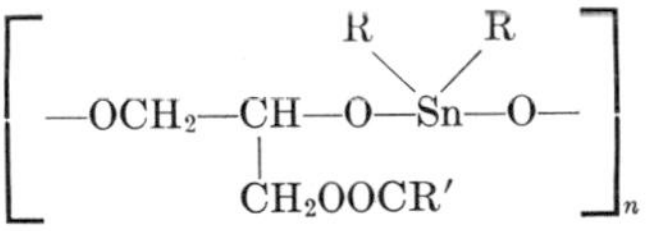

$$\left[\;-OCH_2-\underset{CH_2OOCR'}{\overset{}{\underset{|}{CH}}}-O-\overset{R\quad R}{\underset{}{\overset{\diagdown\diagup}{Sn}}}-O-\;\right]_n$$

(XLV)

alkyd resins have been prepared by the reaction of a polycarboxylic acid
or anhydride with a polyhydric alcohol in the presence of a dialkyl- or
diaryltin oxide (*453*). Similarly, organotin resins have been prepared by the

interaction of bis(triethyltin) oxide or diethyltin oxide with glycidic alcohols as well as by the interaction of β-naphthol esters or resorcinol and triethyltin hydroxide with formaldehyde (*400b*).

Also recently reported (*276*) as polyvinyl chloride stabilizers are polymeric organotin compounds of the type (XLVI). Other related polymeric

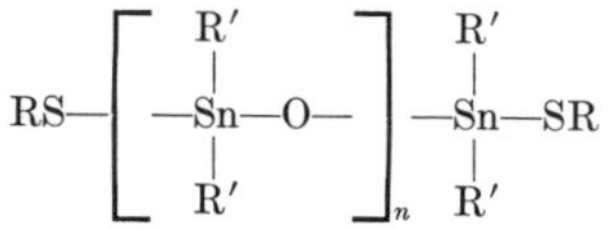

$$RS-\left[\begin{array}{c} R' \\ | \\ -Sn-O- \\ | \\ R' \end{array}\right]_n \begin{array}{c} R' \\ | \\ -Sn-SR \\ | \\ R' \end{array}$$

(XLVI)

stabilizers are obtained from the condensation of organotin compounds with mercaptoalkyl or mercaptoaryl borates (*369, 370*).

Dialkyltin oxides react with aldehydes and ketones to form polymeric addition complexes having the following general formulas (*64, 65, 408*):

$$(R_2SnO)_x(R'_2C{=}O)_y$$

(XLVII)

$$[(R_2SnO)_x(R'CHO)_y]_n$$

(XLVIII)

where $x = 1\text{--}10$, $y = 1\text{--}6$, and $n = 1\text{--}7$. Similarly, dialkyltin oxides and esters of carboxylic acids are reported (*59, 198*) to form polymers with repeating units of structure (XLIX).

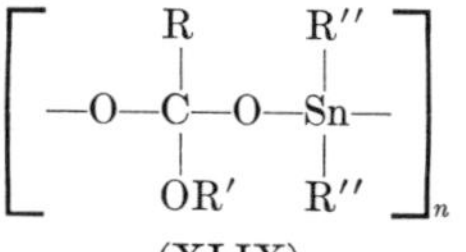

$$\left[\begin{array}{cc} R & R'' \\ | & | \\ -O-C-O-Sn- \\ | & | \\ OR' & R'' \end{array}\right]_n$$

(XLIX)

Many other organotin complex compounds have been reported (*189*); it is probable that a number of these have polymeric structures (*82*).

B. Organopolytin Substances

Catenation is most important with carbon; although this property becomes decreasingly important as one departs from carbon either within the group or within the period, organic derivatives containing from two to five tin-tin bonds per molecule have been reported. The most widely studied of these derivatives are those conforming to the general formula R_3SnSnR_3, and much of the information reported on the structure of the higher homologs is of a speculative nature. The hexaorganoditin compounds recently have been reviewed (*189*).

Diphenyltin, when refluxed with an excess of phenylmagnesium bromide, deposits metallic tin and hexaphenylditin (*259*). Boeseken and Rutgers

(39) repeated this experiment and isolated not only hexaphenylditin but also tetraphenyltin and a compound specified as dodecaphenylpentatin. These authors proposed two structures (L and LI) for their pentatin de-

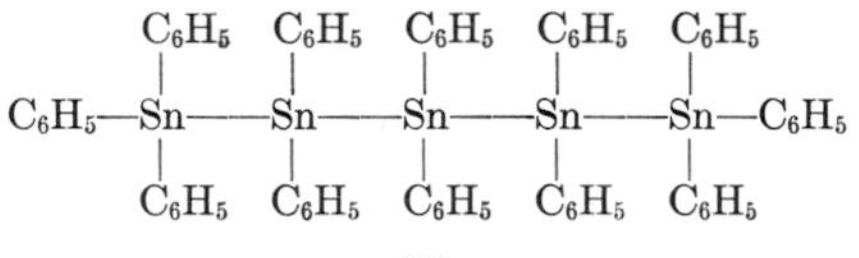

$$
\begin{array}{ccccc}
C_6H_5 & C_6H_5 & C_6H_5 & C_6H_5 & C_6H_5 \\
| & | & | & | & | \\
C_6H_5-Sn- & Sn- & Sn- & Sn- & Sn-C_6H_5 \\
| & | & | & | & | \\
C_6H_5 & C_6H_5 & C_6H_5 & C_6H_5 & C_6H_5
\end{array}
$$

(L)

$$
\begin{array}{c}
C_6H_5 \\
| \\
C_6H_5-Sn-C_6H_5 \\
\end{array}
$$

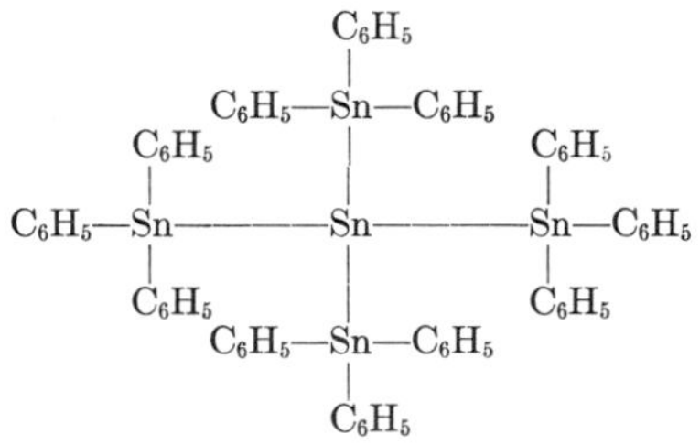

(LI)

rivative. Of these, structure (LI) was preferred because of the stability of the compound. The dodecaphenylpentatin is reported to be a solid which does not melt but begins to decompose at 280°.

Kraus and Neal *(256)* have reported the preparation of decamethyltetratin by reacting dimethyltin dibromide with sodium in liquid ammonia, with the subsequent addition of trimethyltin bromide:

$$2\,(CH_3)_2SnBr_2 + 6\,Na \rightarrow 4\,NaBr + Na(CH_3)_2SnSn(CH_3)_2Na \tag{127}$$

$$Na(CH_3)_2SnSn(CH_3)_2Na + 2\,(CH_3)_3SnBr \rightarrow$$

$$2\,NaBr + (CH_3)_3SnSn(CH_3)_2Sn(CH_3)_2Sn(CH_3)_3 \tag{128}$$

The decamethyltetratin is reported as a colorless liquid which is somewhat viscous and which oxidizes readily with the formation of a white solid.

Similar reactions in liquid ammonia have been used to prepare 1,3-diethyl-1,1,2,2,3,3-hexamethyltritin and dodecamethylpentatin *(254)*:

$$(CH_3)_2SnBr_2 + 4\,Na \rightarrow 4\,NaBr + (CH_3)_2SnNa_2 \tag{129}$$

$$2\,(CH_3)_2SnNa_2 + (CH_3)_2SnBr_2 \rightarrow 2\,NaBr + NaSn(CH_3)_2Sn(CH_3)_2Sn(CH_3)_2Na \tag{130}$$

$$NaSn(CH_3)_2Sn(CH_3)_2Sn(CH_3)_2Na + 2\,C_2H_5Br \rightarrow$$

$$C_2H_5Sn(CH_3)_2Sn(CH_3)_2Sn(CH_3)_2C_2H_5 + 2\,NaBr \tag{131}$$

$$NaSn(CH_3)_2Sn(CH_3)_2Sn(CH_3)_2Na + 2\,(CH_3)_3SnBr \rightarrow$$

$$(CH_3)_3SnSn(CH_3)_2Sn(CH_3)_2Sn(CH_3)_2Sn(CH_3)_3 + 2\,NaBr \tag{132}$$

1,3-Diethyl-1,1,2,2,3,3-hexamethyltritin and dodecamethylpentatin are both reported to be oily liquids which are slowly oxidized in air. Polymers of the type $(C_2H_5)_3Sn—[—Sn(C_2H_5)_2—]_n—Sn(C_2H_5)_3$ have been proposed as intermediates in disproportionation reactions of hexaethylditin (*372a*, *372b*).

The first report of an R_2Sn compound was that of Löwig (*272*), who treated a sodium-tin alloy with ethyl iodide and obtained diethyltin as well as triethyltin iodide and hexaethylditin. A number of R_2Sn compounds has now been reported (*189*); the most used method of preparation being the reaction of a Grignard reagent with tin(II) chloride. These compounds are usually polymeric substances; in a few cases, monomeric compounds which slowly polymerize on standing have been obtained. The careful measurements of Jensen and Clauson-Kass (*197*) on diphenyltin are especially illuminating. When freshly prepared, diphenyltin is monomeric; it readily polymerizes to reach the molecular weight of a pentamer or greater, and it is diamagnetic at all stages. The dipole moment is about 1.0 debye unit at all stages of polymerization. A possible interpretation for the polymerization of diphenyltin might be pictured as follows:

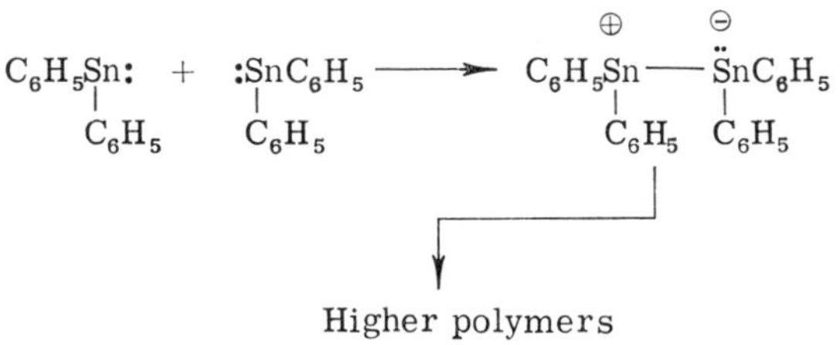

$$
\underset{\underset{C_6H_5}{|}}{C_6H_5Sn:} + \underset{\underset{C_6H_5}{|}}{:SnC_6H_5} \longrightarrow \underset{\underset{C_6H_5}{|}}{C_6H_5\overset{\oplus}{Sn}}\!—\!\underset{\underset{C_6H_5}{|}}{\overset{\ominus}{Sn}C_6H_5}
$$

(133)

Higher polymers

R_2Sn compounds usually melt between 100 and 200°; the melting point may increase considerably as the compound ages (*18*, *255*). At higher temperatures, usually 200–300°, the compounds decompose with the deposition of metallic tin; di-9-phenanthryltin possesses unusual thermal stability, with no tin depositing even when heated to 360° (*18*).

Recently, some new modifications of diphenyltin were reported; one yellow and two colorless forms were obtained (*261b*). X-ray powder patterns show that the structures of these forms are different. Another recent paper describes the disproportionation of hexamethylditin in the presence of Lewis acids; white-to-yellow polymeric dimethyltin and tetramethyltin are formed (*52a*):

$$(CH_3)_6Sn_2 \rightarrow (CH_3)_4Sn + [Sn(CH_3)_2]_n$$

(133a)

When a benzene solution of equimolar amounts of diphenyltin and benzoquinone is allowed to stand for 24 hours, a 93% yield of an insoluble, pale buff-colored polymer is formed; its analysis corresponds to a one-to-one adduct of the reactants (*261a*):

$$(C_6H_5)_2Sn + C_6H_4O_2 \rightarrow \left[\begin{array}{c} C_6H_5 \\ | \\ -Sn-O-C_6H_4-O- \\ | \\ C_6H_5 \end{array}\right]_n \tag{133b}$$

C. Organotin-Methylene Polymers

A number of monomers containing carbon-to-tin bonding and having two or more tin atoms per molecule have been reported (*189, 203a*). Polymeric "stannoethylene" having the general formula $[R_2SnCH_2]_n$ have been prepared according to Eq. (134), using either liquid ammonia or polyethers as a solvent (*104, 254*):

$$n\ R_2SnNa_2 + n\ CH_2Cl_2 \rightarrow \lceil R_2SnCH_2 \rceil_n + 2n\ NaCl \tag{134}$$

Dimethyl(methylene)tin, $[(CH_3)_2SnCH_2]_n$, when freshly prepared is an oily liquid which slowly solidifies on standing. The molecular weight of the freshly prepared material, determined cryoscopically in benzene, suggests a polymerization number of 6; determinations have not been made on aged products.

Dibutyl(methylene)tin, $[(C_4H_9)_2SnCH_2]_n$, is obtained as a very viscous oil which gradually solidifies to a glassy solid on standing. (Methylene)diphenyltin, $[(C_6H_5)_2SnCH_2]_n$, has been prepared using tetrahydrofuran as a solvent; a clear, resinous product is obtained. Diphenyl(diphenylmethylene)tin, $[(C_6H_5)_2SnC(C_6H_5)_2]_n$, the product of the reaction of diphenyltindisodium with dichlorodiphenylmethane in 1,2-dimethoxyethane, is a gummy solid. Other polymeric materials have been reported from the reaction of diphenyltindisodium with phosgene, dichlorodimethylsilane, or sulfuryl chloride (*104*).

An elastomeric polymer has been obtained from the reaction of diphenyltindisodium with 1,4-dibromobutane (*82*):

$$(C_6H_5)_2SnNa_2 + Br(CH_2)_4Br \rightarrow \left[\begin{array}{c} C_6H_5 \\ | \\ -Sn(CH_2)_4- \\ | \\ C_6H_5 \end{array}\right]_n \tag{135}$$

The reaction of diphenyltindisodium with *p*-dibromobenzene also has been investigated (*82*); a reaction does occur but conclusive results have not been reported.

D. Polymers from Organotin Hydrides and Unsaturated Compounds

Noltes and van der Kerk (*207–209, 325, 326*) have made extensive studies of reactions of organotin hydrides with unsaturated organic derivatives; in the course of these studies, several interesting organotin polymers were obtained. Triphenyltin hydride adds to acrylic acid but the addition compound is not stable, losing benzene to give an infusible, polymeric solid (*16, 209*):

$$(C_6H_5)_3SnH + CH_2{=}CHCOOH \rightarrow$$

$$[(C_6H_5)_3SnCH_2CH_2COOH] \xrightarrow{-C_6H_6} [-(C_6H_5)_2SnCH_2CH_2COO-]_n \quad (136)$$

Similarly, but less readily, tributyl-2-carboxyethyltin loses a molecule of butane with the formation of a polymeric product:

$$(C_4H_9)_3SnCH_2CH_2COOH \xrightarrow{-C_4H_{10}} [-(C_4H_9)_2SnCH_2CH_2COO-]_n \quad (137)$$

This addition reaction also can be used to prepare unsaturated organotin derivatives. For example, triphenyltin hydride and phenylacetylene quantitatively yield triphenyl(β-styryl)tin; with an excess of the organotin hydride, the di-addition product is obtained (*208*):

$$(C_6H_5)_3SnH + HC{\equiv}CC_6H_5 \rightarrow (C_6H_5)_3SnCH{=}CHC_6H_5 \quad (138)$$

$$(C_6H_5)_3SnCH{=}CHC_6H_5 + (C_6H_5)_3SnH \rightarrow (C_6H_5)_3SnCH_2CH(C_6H_5)Sn(C_6H_5)_3 \quad (139)$$

In contrast to the corresponding reactions of triphenylsilane and triphenylgermane, addition reactions of triphenyltin hydride proceed without a catalyst and are best carried out in the absence of a solvent.

The reaction of organotin dihydrides with dienic compounds offers a direct method for the preparation of polymeric organotin compounds containing tin-carbon bonds. In general, aliphatic organotin hydrides react only with activated olefinic double bonds; simple dienes such as butadiene or hexadiene are not suitable. When a mixture of dipropyltin dihydride and glycol diacrylate is heated under nitrogen at 80° for 5 hours, a rubber-like polyaddition product is formed (*325*):

$$(C_3H_7)_2SnH_2 + CH_2{=}CHCOOCH_2CH_2OOCCH{=}CH_2 \rightarrow$$

$$[-(C_3H_7)_2SnCH_2CH_2COOCH_2CH_2OOCCH_2CH_2-]_n \quad (140)$$

Physical measurements of this polymer have not been reported and it is, therefore, not known whether a straight chain or a cyclic structure is present. Similarly, the heating of equimolar amounts of *p*-divinylbenzene and dipropyltin dihydride at 100° for 6 hours and subsequently at 130° for 3 hours gives a colorless, transparent, rubbery solid (*325*):

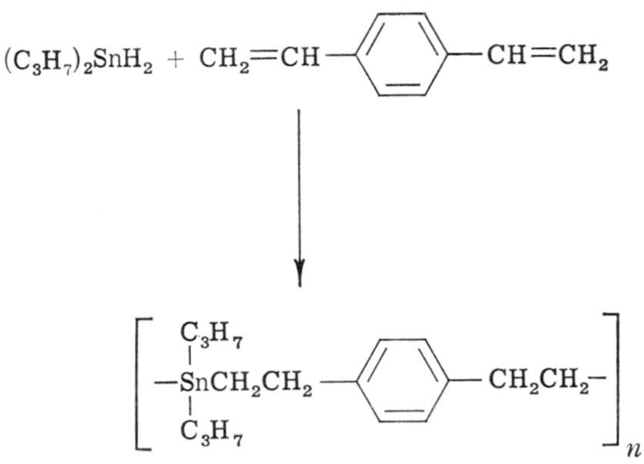

$$(C_3H_7)_2SnH_2 + CH_2{=}CH{-}\text{⟨C}_6H_4\text{⟩}{-}CH{=}CH_2$$

$$\left[\begin{array}{c} C_3H_7 \\ | \\ -SnCH_2CH_2{-}\text{⟨C}_6H_4\text{⟩}{-}CH_2CH_2{-} \\ | \\ C_3H_7 \end{array}\right]_n \tag{141}$$

Again, no physical measurements have been reported but, with the *p*-vinyl groups in relatively fixed positions, a linear structure seems probable. Similar polymers are obtained from the reaction of a diorganotin dihydride and *p*-diisopropenylbenzene (*1a*).

The reaction of diphenyltin dihydride with divinyl sulfone, carried out under nitrogen at 60° for 4 hours, produces a yellow polymeric solid which has a molecular weight of approximately 6500 (*339*). Elemental analysis indicates that the ratio of tin to sulfur in the polymer is greater than one; structure (LII), containing tin-tin bonds, has been proposed.

$$\left[\left(\begin{array}{c} C_6H_5 \\ | \\ -Sn- \\ | \\ C_6H_5 \end{array}\right)_x CH_2CH_2SO_2CH_2CH_2{-}\right]_y$$

(LII)

Dipropyltin dihydride reacts with phenylacetylene to give a viscous polymeric oil (*207*):

$$(C_3H_7)_2SnH_2 + HC{\equiv}CC_6H_5 \rightarrow H{-}\underset{\underset{C_3H_7}{|}}{\overset{\overset{C_3H_7}{|}}{Sn}}{-}CH{=}CHC_6H_5 \rightarrow \left[\begin{array}{c} C_3H_7 \\ | \\ -Sn-CH_2-CH- \\ | \qquad | \\ C_3H_7 \qquad C_6H_5 \end{array}\right]_n \tag{142}$$

When equimolar amounts of diphenyltin dihydride and phenylacetylene are heated in pentane solution, 1,1,2,4,4,5-hexaphenyl-1,4-distannacyclohexane is obtained rather than the expected polymer (*180, 325*):

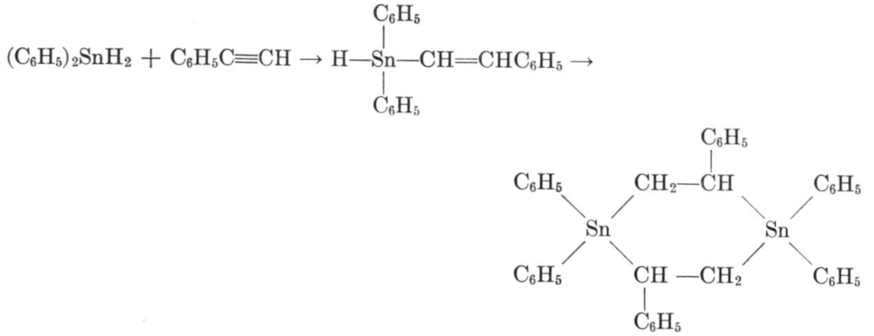

$$(C_6H_5)_2SnH_2 + C_6H_5C\equiv CH \rightarrow H-\overset{\underset{|}{C_6H_5}}{\underset{|}{\underset{C_6H_5}{Sn}}}-CH=CHC_6H_5 \rightarrow$$

$$(143)$$

An equimolar mixture of diphenyltin dihydride and diphenyldivinyl-silane, when heated at 65–80° for 13 hours, produces 1,1,4,4-tetraphenyl-1-stanna-4-silacyclohexane accompanied by a small amount of insoluble, un-meltable, polymeric material (*180*):

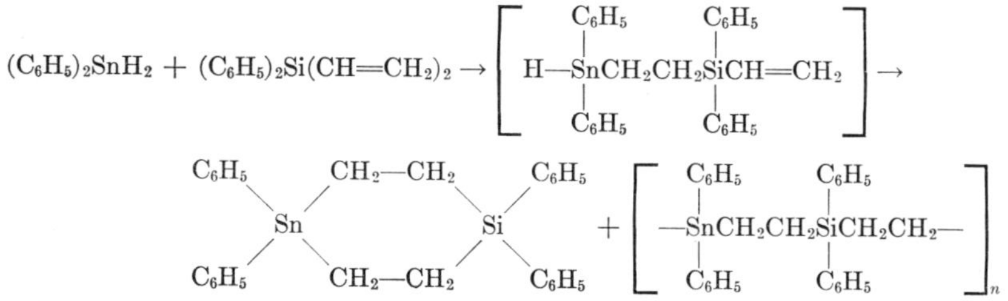

$$(C_6H_5)_2SnH_2 + (C_6H_5)_2Si(CH=CH_2)_2 \rightarrow \left[H-\overset{\underset{|}{C_6H_5}}{\underset{C_6H_5}{Sn}}CH_2CH_2\overset{\underset{|}{C_6H_5}}{\underset{C_6H_5}{Si}}CH=CH_2 \right] \rightarrow$$

$$(144)$$

An attempted synthesis of the corresponding 1,4-distannacyclohexane compound by reaction of diphenyltin dihydride with diphenyldivinyltin was unsuccessful, only low melting products and an insoluble, infusible material being obtained (*180*).

Other compounds containing two or more different Group IVB elements have been prepared by the addition of organotin hydrides to various un-saturated organo-Group IVB compounds (*179*):

$$(C_6H_5)_3SnH + (C_6H_5)_3MCH=CH_2 \rightarrow (C_6H_5)_3SnCH_2CH_2M(C_6H_5)_3 \quad (145)$$

$$M = Si, Ge, or Sn$$

$$2\,(C_6H_5)_3SnH + (C_6H_5)_2M(CH=CH_2)_2 \rightarrow (C_6H_5)_3SnCH_2CH_2\overset{\underset{|}{C_6H_5}}{\underset{C_6H_5}{M}}CH_2CH_2Sn(C_6H_5)_3$$

$$M=Si\ or\ Ge \qquad\qquad (146)$$

$$(C_6H_5)_2SnH_2 + 2\,(C_6H_5)_3MCH=CH_2 \rightarrow (C_6H_5)_3SnCH_2CH_2M(C_6H_5)_3 \quad (147)$$

$$M = Si, Ge, or Sn$$

In the last of the above reactions, triphenyltin hydride must be formed from the starting diphenyltin dihydride either by phenyl-hydrogen exchange or by disproportionation (*179*); a similar abnormal addition product is obtained from the reaction of dimethyltin dihydride with various olefins (*87*). Additional compounds containing two or more Group IVB elements have been reported by Noltes and van der Kerk (*327, 327a*):

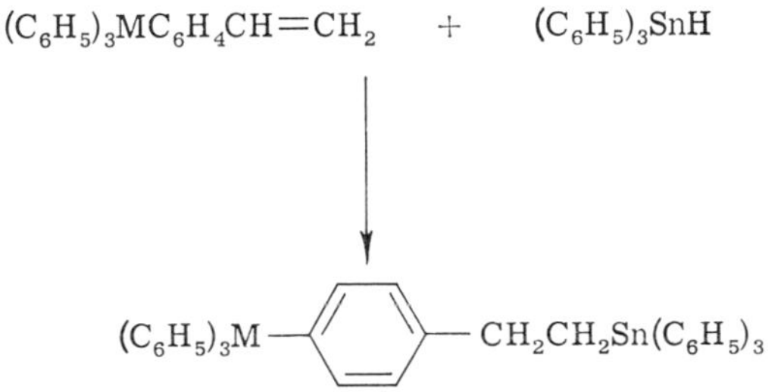

$$(C_6H_5)_3MC_6H_4CH{=}CH_2 \quad + \quad (C_6H_5)_3SnH$$

$$(C_6H_5)_3M \underset{}{-\!\!\!\bigcirc\!\!\!-} CH_2CH_2Sn(C_6H_5)_3 \qquad (148)$$

M = Ge, Sn, Pb

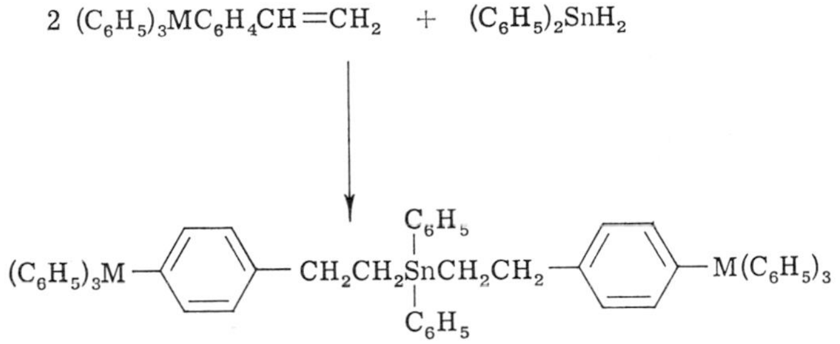

$$2\ (C_6H_5)_3MC_6H_4CH{=}CH_2 \quad + \quad (C_6H_5)_2SnH_2$$

$$(C_6H_5)_3M\underset{}{-\!\!\!\bigcirc\!\!\!-}CH_2CH_2\overset{\displaystyle C_6H_5}{\underset{\displaystyle C_6H_5}{Sn}}CH_2CH_2\underset{}{-\!\!\!\bigcirc\!\!\!-}M(C_6H_5)_3 \qquad (149)$$

M = Ge, Sn, or Pb

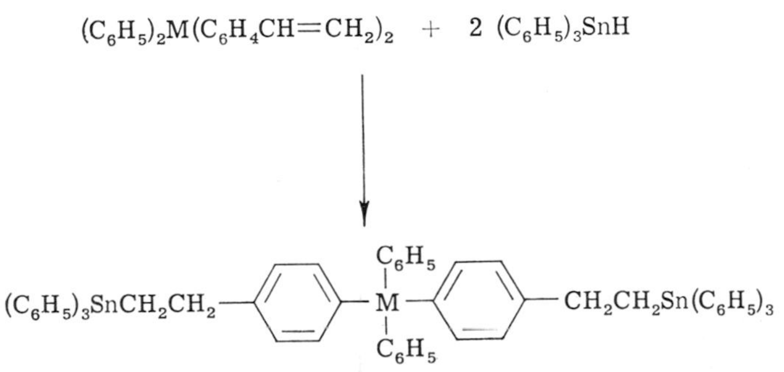

$$(C_6H_5)_2M(C_6H_4CH{=}CH_2)_2 \quad + \quad 2\ (C_6H_5)_3SnH$$

$$(C_6H_5)_3SnCH_2CH_2\underset{}{-\!\!\!\bigcirc\!\!\!-}\overset{\displaystyle C_6H_5}{\underset{\displaystyle C_6H_5}{M}}\underset{}{-\!\!\!\bigcirc\!\!\!-}CH_2CH_2Sn(C_6H_5)_3 \qquad (150)$$

M = Ge, Sn, or Pb

The reaction of diphenyltin dihydride with diphenylbis(*p*-vinylphenyl)tin gives a glass-like polymer with a molecular weight of 48,000. Similarly, both 1,4-divinylbenzene and 3,9-divinyl-2,4,8,10-tetraoxaspiro[5.5]-undecane yield solid, glass-like products when treated with diphenyltin dihydride (*327*):

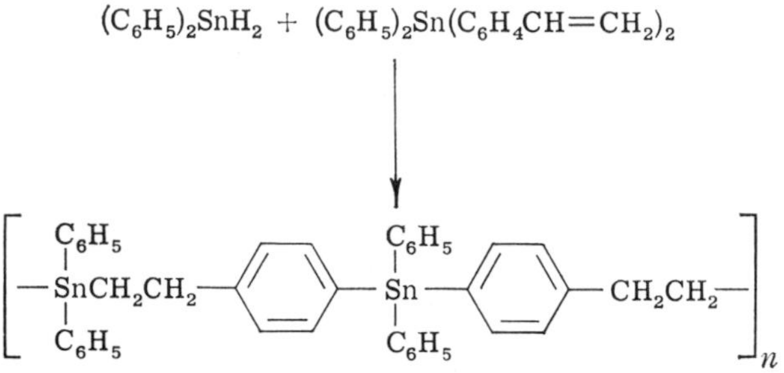
(C6H5)2SnH2 + (C6H5)2Sn(C6H4CH=CH2)2
C6H5
SnCH2CH2
C6H5
C6H5
Sn
C6H5
CH2CH2
n

(151)

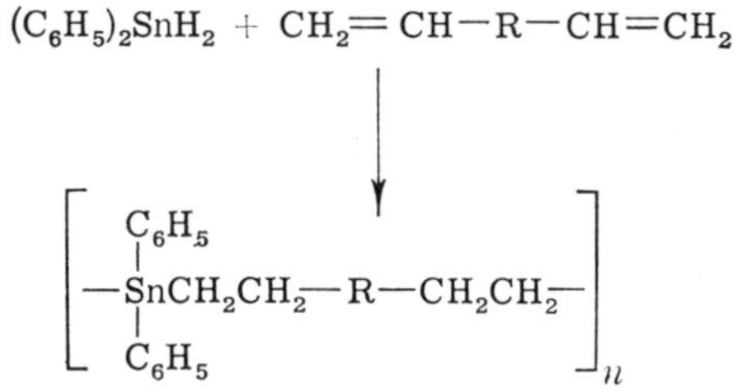
(C6H5)2SnH2 + CH2=CH—R—CH=CH2
C6H5
SnCH2CH2—R—CH2CH2
C6H5
n

(152)

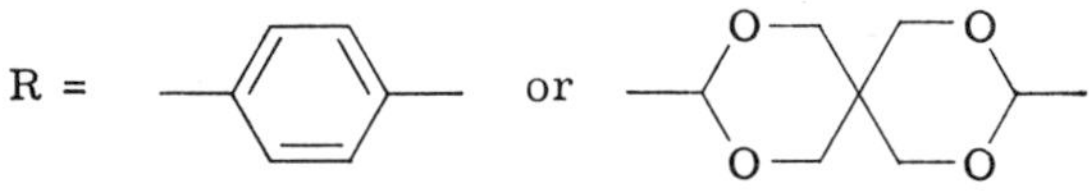
R =
or
O
O
O
O

A polymeric material containing phosphorus and tin is obtained from the reaction of phenyldivinylphosphine and diethyltin dihydride (*323a*).

E. Stannosiloxanes

Grüttner and Krause (*166*) prepared the first organic compound containing both silicon and tin by reacting *p*-triethylsilylphenylmagnesium bromide with triethyltin bromide to form triethyl(*p*-triethylsilylphenyl)tin. In addition to the reports mentioned above, several recent papers concerning mixed silicon-tin compounds have appeared. Papetti and Post (*334*) and Seyferth (*393*) have reported the preparation of several compounds of the general formula $[(CH_3)_3SiCH_2]_xSnR_{4-x}$, while $(CH_3)_2(C_2H_5)Si(CH_2)_3$-$OSn(C_2H_5)_3$ is reported by Shostakovskiĭ and co-workers (*404*). (β-Trichlorosilylethyl)triethyltin is obtained by the addition of trichlorosilane to triethylvinyltin (*394*); compounds of this type should, upon hydrolysis, produce tin-containing polysiloxanes:

$$(C_2H_5)_3SnCH=CH_2 + Cl_3SiH \rightarrow (C_2H_5)_3SnCH_2CH_2SiCl_3 \tag{153}$$

Reactions of this type also have been reported by Merker (*292*):

$$(C_4H_9)_3SnCH_2SiH(CH_3)_2 + CH_2=CHSi(CH_3)_2Cl \rightarrow$$

$$Cl(CH_3)_2Si(CH_2)_2Si(CH_3)_2CH_2Sn(C_4H_9)_3 \xrightarrow{H_2O}$$

$$O[Si(CH_3)_2CH_2CH_2Si(CH_3)_2CH_2Sn(C_4H_9)_3]_2 \tag{154}$$

Tetrakis(triphenylsiloxy)tin has been prepared by the reaction of sodium triphenylsilanolate and tin(IV) chloride (*168*); dimethylbis(trimethylsiloxy)tin and methyltris(trimethylsiloxy)tin have been prepared in a similar manner (*261b*).

In the past few years there has been a considerable effort directed toward polymers which not only have good mechanical properties but are also thermally stable. The polysiloxanes have many of the desired properties and improvements in their thermal stability can be made by adding small amounts of other metallic compounds as cross-linking agents (*82*). This discovery has led to several studies of various organometallosiloxanes, including the stannosiloxanes.

Compounds having the general formula (LIII) have been reported by Andrianov and co-workers (*10–12*). For example, the hydrolysis of a mixture of 0.6 mole of dichlorodiethylsilane, 0.3 mole of trichlorophenyl-

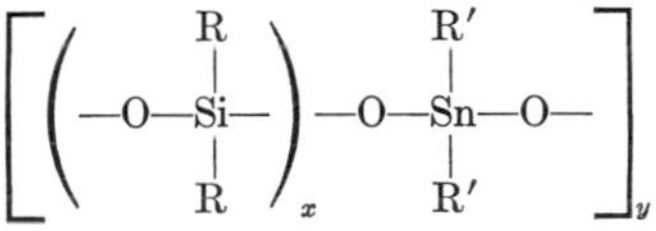

$$\left[\left(-O-\underset{\underset{R}{\overset{\overset{R}{|}}{|}}{Si}-\right)_x -O-\underset{\underset{R'}{\overset{\overset{R'}{|}}{|}}{Sn}-O-\right]_y$$

(LIII)

silane, and 0.1 mole of diethyltin dichloride gives a polymeric product which can be fractionated according to solubility in ethanol, toluene, and acetone. The polymeric products are glassy substances in which the ratio of Si/Sn varies from 4 to 11 (*12*). Polymers of this type also have been prepared by the following reactions (*11, 105a, 177*):

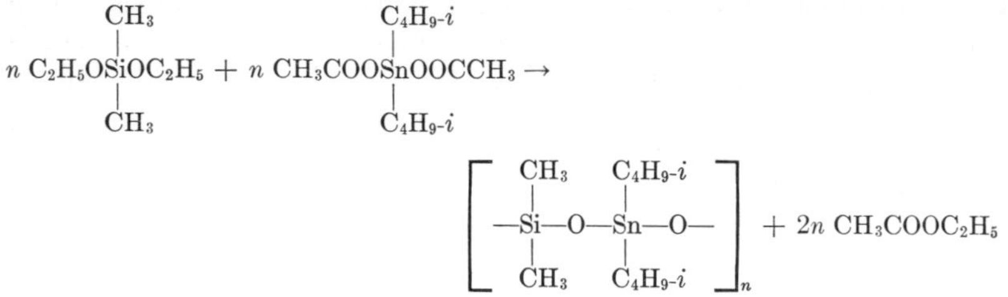

$$n\ C_2H_5OSi(CH_3)_2OC_2H_5 + n\ CH_3COOSn(C_4H_9\text{-}i)_2OOCCH_3 \rightarrow$$

$$\left[\begin{array}{c} CH_3 \quad C_4H_9\text{-}i \\ -Si-O-Sn-O- \\ CH_3 \quad C_4H_9\text{-}i \end{array}\right]_n + 2n\ CH_3COOC_2H_5 \quad (155)$$

$$n\ C_2H_5OSi(CH_3)_2OC_2H_5 + n\ CH_3COOSnOOCCH_3 \rightarrow$$

$$\left[\begin{array}{c} CH_3 \\ -Si-O-Sn-O- \\ CH_3 \end{array}\right]_n + 2n\ CH_3COOC_2H_5 \quad (156)$$

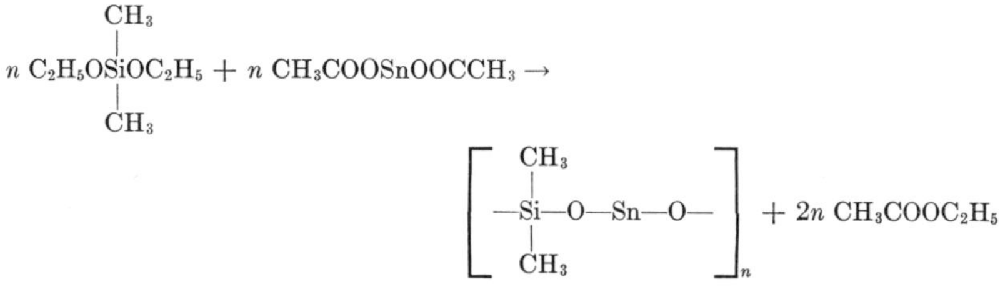

Related stannosiloxane polymers are obtained from the reaction of poly-siloxanes with organotin oxides (*400a*). The reaction of disodium diphenyl-silanediolate with anhydrous tin(II) chloride produces a yellow resin (*183*):

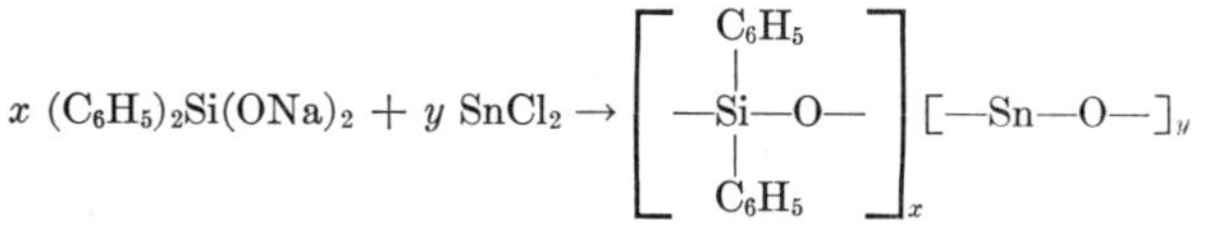

$$x\ (C_6H_5)_2Si(ONa)_2 + y\ SnCl_2 \rightarrow \left[\begin{array}{c} C_6H_5 \\ -Si-O- \\ C_6H_5 \end{array}\right]_x [-Sn-O-]_y \quad (157)$$

This stannosiloxane polymer was stable for 1 hour up to 175° when it darkened somewhat; this darkening also occurred at lower temperatures upon longer heating.

Crain and Koenig have reported the preparation and study of a number of stannosiloxanes (*16, 82*); the reactions leading to these stannosiloxanes are illustrated by the following equations:

$$R_2SnO + R'_2Si(OH)_2 \rightarrow (-R_2Sn-O-)_x(-R'_2Si-O-)_y \quad (158)$$

$$R_2SnCl_2 + R'_2Si(ONa)_2 \rightarrow (-R_2Sn-O-)_x(-R'_2Si-O-)_y \quad (159)$$

$$R_2SnCl_2 + R'_2SiCl_2 \xrightarrow{OH^-} (-R_2Sn-O-)_x(-R'_2Si-O-)_y \quad (160)$$

$$R_2SnO + R'_3SiOH \rightarrow R'_3SiO-(-R_2Sn-O-)_n-SiR'_3 \quad (161)$$

The molecular weights of these benzene-soluble polymers ranged from 1000 to 5000. None of the polymers tested was as stable as poly(diphenyl-siloxane); however, the stannosiloxane polymers were less affected by prolonged heating than were poly(methylsiloxane) and poly(vinylsiloxane). The stannosiloxanes containing phenylsilicon moieties were more stable than the methylsilicon analogs. The polymers appeared to become more stable as the relative amount of tin decreased (*82*).

Tin-containing polysiloxanes as well as cyclic stannosiloxanes have been reported by Merker and Scott (*292b*, *293*); the following reactions were employed:

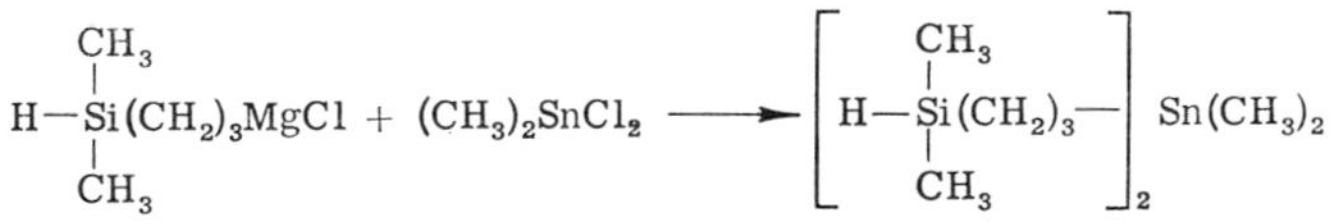

$$
\text{H}-\underset{\underset{\text{CH}_3}{|}}{\overset{\overset{\text{CH}_3}{|}}{\text{Si}}}(\text{CH}_2)_3\text{MgCl} + (\text{CH}_3)_2\text{SnCl}_2 \longrightarrow \left[\text{H}-\underset{\underset{\text{CH}_3}{|}}{\overset{\overset{\text{CH}_3}{|}}{\text{Si}}}(\text{CH}_2)_3-\right]_2 \text{Sn}(\text{CH}_3)_2 \tag{162}
$$

$$
\left[\text{H}-\underset{\underset{\text{CH}_3}{|}}{\overset{\overset{\text{CH}_3}{|}}{\text{Si}}}(\text{CH}_2)_3\right]_2 \text{Sn}(\text{CH}_3)_2 + \text{H}_2\text{O} \xrightarrow{\text{NaOH}} \left[-\underset{\underset{\text{CH}_3}{|}}{\overset{\overset{\text{CH}_3}{|}}{\text{Si}}}(\text{CH}_2)_3\underset{\underset{\text{CH}_3}{|}}{\overset{\overset{\text{CH}_3}{|}}{\text{Sn}}}(\text{CH}_2)_3\underset{\underset{\text{CH}_3}{|}}{\overset{\overset{\text{CH}_3}{|}}{\text{Si}}}-\text{O}-\right]_n \tag{163}
$$

$$
\left[-\underset{\underset{\text{CH}_3}{|}}{\overset{\overset{\text{CH}_3}{|}}{\text{Si}}}(\text{CH}_2)_3\underset{\underset{\text{CH}_3}{|}}{\overset{\overset{\text{CH}_3}{|}}{\text{Sn}}}(\text{CH}_2)_3\underset{\underset{\text{CH}_3}{|}}{\overset{\overset{\text{CH}_3}{|}}{\text{Si}}}-\text{O}-\right]_n \xrightarrow[\Delta]{\text{KOH}} \tag{164}
$$

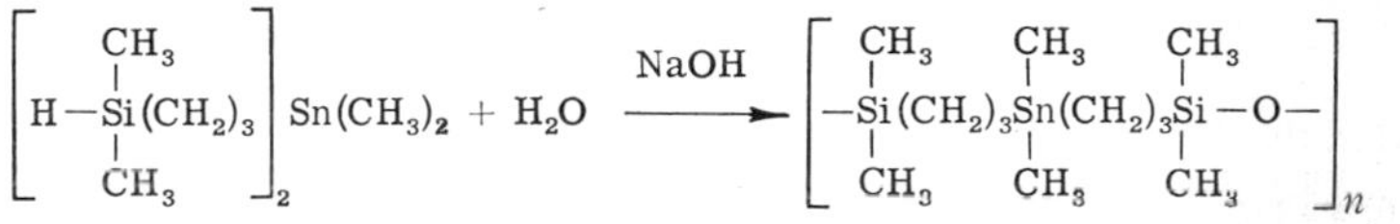

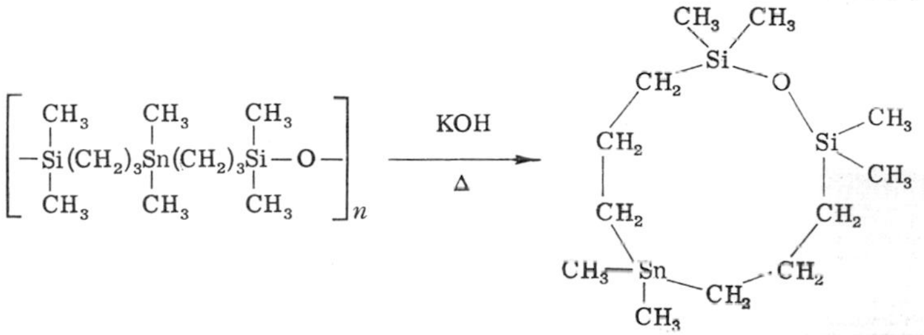

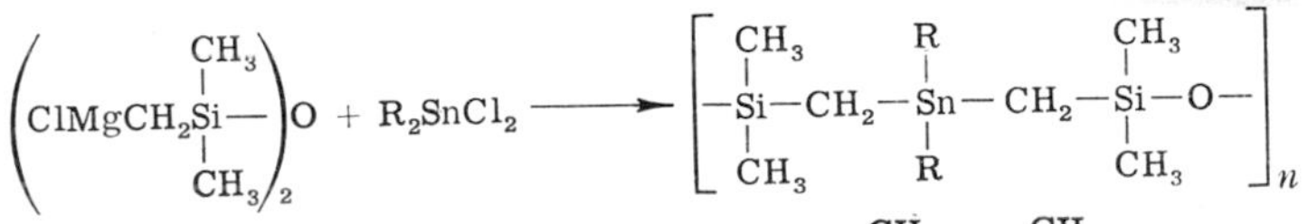

$$
\left(\text{ClMgCH}_2\underset{\underset{\text{CH}_3}{|}}{\overset{\overset{\text{CH}_3}{|}}{\text{Si}}}-\right)_2\text{O} + \text{R}_2\text{SnCl}_2 \longrightarrow \left[-\underset{\underset{\text{CH}_3}{|}}{\overset{\overset{\text{CH}_3}{|}}{\text{Si}}}-\text{CH}_2-\underset{\underset{\text{R}}{|}}{\overset{\overset{\text{R}}{|}}{\text{Sn}}}-\text{CH}_2-\underset{\underset{\text{CH}_3}{|}}{\overset{\overset{\text{CH}_3}{|}}{\text{Si}}}-\text{O}-\right]_n \tag{165}
$$

$$
\left[-\underset{\underset{\text{CH}_3}{|}}{\overset{\overset{\text{CH}_3}{|}}{\text{Si}}}-\text{CH}_2-\underset{\underset{\text{R}}{|}}{\overset{\overset{\text{R}}{|}}{\text{Sn}}}-\text{CH}_2-\underset{\underset{\text{CH}_3}{|}}{\overset{\overset{\text{CH}_3}{|}}{\text{Si}}}-\text{O}-\right]_n \xrightarrow[\Delta]{\text{KOH}} \tag{166}
$$

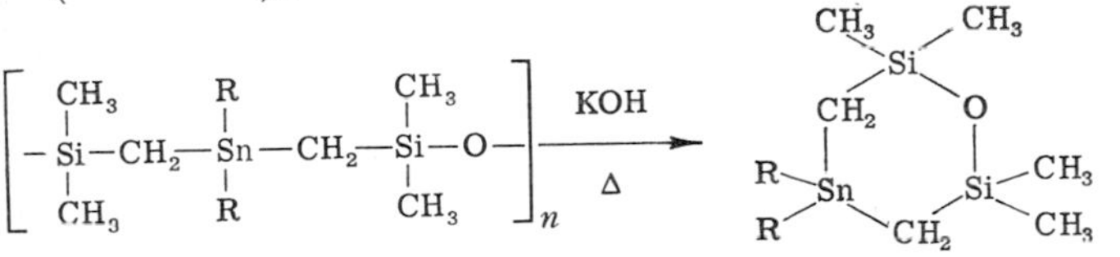

Recently, Okawara and co-workers (*332a*, *332b*, *332c*) have reported the cohydrolysis of trimethylchlorosilane with a dialkyltin dichloride; disiloxytin compounds are formed initially but are unstable and slowly change into the stable distannoxanes:

$$4\,\text{R}_3\text{SiCl} + 2\,\text{R}'_2\text{SnCl}_2 + 2\,\text{H}_2\text{O} \rightarrow 2\,\text{R}_3\text{SiO}-\text{SnR}'_2-\text{OSiR}_3 \rightarrow$$

$$\text{R}_3\text{SiO}-[-\text{SnR}'_2\text{O}-]_2-\text{SiR}_3 + (\text{R}_3\text{Si})_2\text{O} \tag{166a}$$

Tetramethyl-1,3-bis(trimethylsiloxy)distannoxane appears to be dimeric in benzene and in cyclohexane; X-ray analysis indicates structure (LIIIa)

$$
\begin{array}{c}
\text{R}\ \ \text{X}\ \ \text{R} \\
\diagdown\ \ |\ \ \diagup \\
\text{Sn} \\
\text{R}\diagdown\ \ \diagup\ \ \diagdown\ \ \diagup\text{R} \\
\text{X—Sn—O}\ \ \ \ \ \text{O—Sn—X}\qquad \text{R} = \text{CH}_3,\ \text{X} = (\text{CH}_3)_3\text{Si} \\
\text{R}\diagup\ \ \diagdown\ \ \diagup\ \ \diagdown\text{R} \\
\text{Sn} \\
\diagup\ \ |\ \ \diagdown \\
\text{R}\ \ \text{X}\ \ \text{R}
\end{array}
$$

(LIIIa)

for this dimer. A polymeric stannosiloxane has been prepared by reacting tetramethyl-1,3-divinyldisiloxane with diethyltin dihydride (*323b*):

$$
\underset{\overset{|}{\text{CH}_3}}{\overset{\overset{\text{CH}_3}{|}}{\text{CH}_2\!=\!\text{CH—Si—O—Si—CH}\!=\!\text{CH}_2}}\ +\ (\text{C}_2\text{H}_5)_2\text{SnH}_2 \to \text{polymer} \qquad (166b)
$$

Seyferth and Rochow (*395*) have prepared compounds of the type $\text{R}_3\text{SnCH}_2\text{SiR}'_3$; in a number of these compounds R' represents halogen or a methoxyl group and, therefore, the compounds can be hydrolyzed to give tin-containing polysiloxanes. The properties of polysiloxane (LIV),

$$
\text{CH}_3\!-\!\underset{\overset{|}{\text{CH}_3}}{\overset{\overset{\text{CH}_3}{|}}{\text{Si}}}\!-\!\text{O}\!-\!\left[\ -\underset{\overset{|}{\text{CH}_2\text{Sn}(\text{CH}_3)_3}}{\overset{\overset{\text{CH}_3}{|}}{\text{Si}}}\!-\!\text{O}\!-\!-\!-\ \right]_n\!-\!\underset{\overset{|}{\text{CH}_3}}{\overset{\overset{\text{CH}_3}{|}}{\text{Si}}}\!-\!\text{CH}_3
$$

(LIV)

prepared in this manner and possessing an organotin substituent in the side chain, have been reported (*396*). The hardening of organosilicon polymers by vulcanizing with organotin compounds is mentioned in the Russian patent literature (*23*). Chamberland and MacDiarmid (*60, 61*) recently have announced the preparation of several compounds containing tin-oxygen-arsenic bonds; substances of the type $[\text{OSnR}_2\text{OAs}(\text{O})\text{R}']_n$ and $[\text{OAs}(\text{OSnR}_2\text{O})_3\text{AsO}]_n$ were obtained by reacting an organotin dichloride with an arsenic-containing acid or its salt. Tetrakis(triphenylstannoxy)-titanium, $[(\text{C}_6\text{H}_5)_3\text{SnO}]_4\text{Ti}$ (*80*), bis(trimethylsiloxy)dimethyltin, $(\text{CH}_3)_2\text{Sn}[(\text{CH}_3)_3\text{SiO}]_2$ (*432*), and tris(trimethylstannyl)phosphine, $[(\text{CH}_3)_3\text{Sn}]_3\text{P}$ (*50a*) have also been prepared. Tetramethyl(trimethylsiloxy)antimony is cleaved by trimethyltin chloride to form trimethyl(trimethylsiloxy)tin (*386a*).

F. Polymers from Unsaturated Organotin Compounds

Many organotin compounds containing polymerizable unsaturated groupings have been reported in recent years (*189*). Reports of polymerization studies of the compounds are now beginning to appear. Several Russian chemists have been especially active in this area (*181*).

The first compound of this type to receive attention was triethyl(*p*-isopropenylphenyl)tin; Bachman and co-workers prepared this compound in low yield by reaction of *p*-isopropenylphenyllithium with triethyltin chloride in ethyl ether (*17*):

$$CH_2{=}C(CH_3)C_6H_4Li + (C_2H_5)_3SnCl \rightarrow CH_2{=}C(CH_3)C_6H_4Sn(C_2H_5)_3 \qquad (167)$$

This styrene derivative was then copolymerized with butadiene in a typical emulsion system to give a high yield of a crumbly rubber; the polymerization was rather slow (*17*). Later, Korshak and co-workers (*241*) reported an improved synthesis of triethyl(*p*-isopropenylphenyl)tin by reaction of triethyltin chloride with the corresponding Grignard reagent, formed *in situ*, in tetrahydrofuran:

$$p\text{-}BrC_6H_4C(CH_3){=}CH_2 + (C_2H_5)_3SnCl \xrightarrow{Mg} p\text{-}(C_2H_5)_3SnC_6H_4C(CH_3){=}CH_2 \qquad (168)$$

This monomer was then polymerized by heating at 80–130° for 6 hours under 6000-atm pressure with benzoyl peroxide, *tert*-butyl peroxide, or 2,2'-azobis[2-methylpropionitrile]. The last of these three initiators appeared to be the most effective (*241*).

Other tin-containing styrene derivatives for which polymerization reports have appeared include triethyl(*p*-vinylphenyl)tin (*230*) and triphenyl(*p*-vinylphenyl)tin (*247*, *248*, *251a*). The former of these derivatives showed considerable resistance to polymerization with various catalysts, titanium tetrachloride being the most effective. The latter, triphenyl(*p*-vinylphenyl)tin, is reported to polymerize readily and to copolymerize with styrene or methyl methacrylate to yield transparent and plastic films. A very brief mention of the preparation and polymerization of tetrakis(*p*-vinylphenyl)tin was recently published (*101*). Trimethyl(*p*-vinylphenyl)tin and (*p*-isopropenylphenyl)trimethyltin can be polymerized at 70 to 90° in the presence of free radical initiators to form clear, colorless solids (*329*); trimethyl(*p*-vinylphenyl)tin also readily copolymerizes with styrene or with methyl methacrylate to give glass-like substances.

Many reports appear in the recent literature of the synthesis of various vinyl and allyl derivatives of tin; although most of these compounds obviously were prepared for polymerization studies, brief reports of only a few of these studies have been published to date.

Koton and Kiseleva (*245, 251, 251a*) have reported polymerization studies of allyltriphenyltin, diallyldiphenyltin, and tetraallyltin. It was found that these derivatives did not block polymerize in the presence or absence of initiators. The effect of the addition of the allyl derivatives of tin on the polymerization of styrene, methyl methacrylate, and vinyl acetate at 120° was studied; copolymers were obtained but with methyl methacrylate and vinyl acetate a considerable slowing of the polymerization and a fall in polymer yield were observed. This latter effect increased as the number of allyl groups in the molecule increased; indeed, tetraallyltin was found to be an effective inhibitor of methyl methacrylate and of vinyl acetate polymerizations (*231a, 245, 251*).

Korshak and co-workers (*233*) have reported polymerization studies of triethylvinyltin, allyltrimethyltin, and allyltriethyltin. Triethylvinyltin, when heated in the presence of *tert*-butyl peroxide for 6 hours at 120° and under 6000-atm pressure, forms a low molecular weight polymeric oil. Under similar conditions, allyltrimethyltin and allyltriethyltin failed to polymerize; the former did, however, form a copolymer with methyl methacrylate. The polymerization of vinyl chloride in the presence of small amounts of vinyl-substituted organotin compounds, $R_3SnCH{=}CH_2$, leads to copolymers which are reported to be stable to light and heat (*413*). Koton and co-workers (*251*) report that prolonged heating of tetravinyltin and diphenyldivinyltin in the presence of 2,2′-azobis[2-methylpropionitrile] and in a nitrogen atmosphere leads to the formation of a small amount of insoluble, infusible material; these substances do not undergo change on heating to 300 to 400° and apparently are polymeric compounds of tin. Allyltrimethyltin and related compounds are reported to give solid, linear polymers when treated with Ziegler-type catalysts (*307a, 307b*); these unsaturated organotin derivatives also can be copolymerized with propylene.

Some of the more promising polymeric substances are those obtained from organotin-acrylate esters. In 1958, Montermoso and co-workers (*308, 309*) reported that tributyltin acrylate and tributyltin methacrylate can be polymerized by both solution and emulsion polymerizations to form elastomeric products:

$$(C_4H_9)_3SnOOCC(CH_3){=}CH_2 \rightarrow \begin{bmatrix} & CH_3 & \\ & | & \\ -C & \!\!\!\!\!- CH_2 & \!\!\!\!\!- \\ & | & \\ & COOSn(C_4H_9)_3 & \end{bmatrix}_n \qquad (169)$$

These materials are typical vinyl chain polymerization products with carbon-to-carbon bonding forming the connecting links in the chain. The monomer is readily obtained by reacting bis(tributyltin) oxide with the appropriate unsaturated acid in one-to-one ratio. Also in 1958, Shostakovskiĭ and co-workers (*404*) reported the polymerization of triethyltin methacrylate and its copolymerization with methyl methacrylate.

Later, Koton and co-workers (*249, 250, 251a*) reported the preparation and polymerization of several acrylate and methacrylate esters of the type $R_3SnOOCC(CH_3)=CH_2$ (R = methyl, ethyl, butyl, or phenyl). These esters were found to polymerize either in the absence of added catalysts or upon addition of peroxides or azo compounds. Several trialkyl- and triaryltin methacrylates and related compounds give strong transparent polymers and copolymers which are effective barriers to X-rays (*181, 400b*). Kochkin, Shostakovskiĭ, and co-workers (*225, 226, 400d, 401*) have published a more detailed description of the products obtained from triethyltin acrylate and methacrylate by polymerization or by copolymerization with methyl methacrylate, methacrylic acid, styrene, acrylonitrile, cyclopentadiene, and divinylbenzene. These authors also discuss the polymerization of the diacrylate and dimethacrylate esters of dialkyl- and diaryltin oxides; the polymers of these diesters have a linear, vinyl-like structure (*400b*). Similar studies have been reported by Ling (*271*).

Recently, Montermoso (*310*) reported additional studies concerning the organotin methacrylate polymers. Tributyltin methacrylate polymerizes to give a tough, rubbery material but, when copolymerized with dibutyltin methacrylate, a clear, very elastic material is formed. This raw material has a tensile strength of approximately 125 lb/sq in. and an elongation of 400%. Vulcanization is difficult; zinc oxide causes decomposition but may be replaced by dibutyltin oxide, with sulfur and dibutyltin dihydride serving as vulcanizing agents. Cures at 250° for 45 min and at 290° for 30 min result in tensile strengths of 400 and 300 lb/sq in. and elongations of 370 and 250%, respectively; the volume changes in isoöctane at 25° for 24 hours are 125 and 32.4% (*310*). The alkyltin methacrylate polymers show promise for applications for which flame retardance, resistance to exotic fuels, and dependable performance at high temperatures are needed; at present, they are inferior to conventional rubbers in tensile strength and ultimate elongation (*15*).

V. Organolead Polymers

Although organolead chemistry has attracted considerable attention (*265*), there have been few reports of studies of organolead polymers. Undoubtedly, this is partially because of the lower stability of organolead compounds; organolead derivatives are more readily decomposed by heat or light and are more reactive toward acids and oxidizing agents than the other organo-Group IVB compounds.

Diphenyllead sulfide has been found to be trimeric in solution (270). Diphenyllead dihydroxide has not been isolated since it very readily loses water to form diphenyllead oxide (11, 265); although detailed studies are lacking, it is probable that diphenyllead oxide is polymeric:

$$n\ (C_6H_5)_2Pb(OH)_2 \rightarrow \left[\begin{array}{c} C_6H_5 \\ | \\ -Pb-O- \\ | \\ C_6H_5 \end{array} \right]_n + n\ H_2O \qquad (170)$$

Other organolead oxides have been reported (265) but molecular weight and structural information have not been given.

A number of hexaalkyl- and hexaaryldilead compounds have been prepared (19, 265). These are decidedly less stable than their tin analogs; most of the R_6Pb_2 derivatives decompose between 100° and 200°:

$$2\ R_6Pb_2 \rightarrow 3\ R_4Pb + Pb \qquad (171)$$

This instability of the lead-lead bond explains the absence of any reports of polylead compounds having three or more lead atoms per molecule. Polymers of the type $(C_2H_5)_3Pb-[-Pb(C_2H_5)_2-]_n-Pb(C_2H_5)_3$ have been proposed as intermediates in disproportionation reactions of hexaethyldilead (372b, 372c).

In contrast to the great stability of inorganic lead(II) compounds, R_2Pb derivatives are unstable and difficult to prepare. Krause and Reissaus (260) obtained diphenyllead and di-o-tolyllead in very low yields by the reaction of lead(II) chloride with the Grignard reagent at 2°. These compounds were obtained as deep red solids. This difficult work was painstakingly carried out, and the diphenyllead was characterized by analyses for lead, carbon, and hydrogen and by cryoscopic measurements which indicated the compound to be monomeric. Attempts to duplicate the preparation have never been successful (265); Krause and Reissaus themselves experienced difficulty in duplicating the synthesis and presented some probable reasons. The reaction of phenyllithium with lead(II) chloride at −10° proceeds in two distinguishable stages, corresponding to Eqs. (172) and (173):

$$2\ C_6H_5Li + PbCl_2 \rightarrow (C_6H_5)_2Pb + 2\ LiCl \qquad (172)$$

$$(C_6H_5)_2Pb + C_6H_5Li \rightleftharpoons (C_6H_5)_3PbLi \qquad (173)$$

The first reaction is irreversible and produces an intermediate which is believed to be diphenyllead (141, 265); this intermediate has not been isolated and identified and it is yellow rather than the deep red described by Krause and Reissaus.

Several dialkyllead compounds have been reported but not definitely identified (*265*). More recently, Fischer and Grubert (*106*) synthesized dicyclopentadienyllead from cyclopentadienylsodium and lead(II) nitrate in dimethylformamide. This compound is a solid with no definite melting point; apparently, it is not a "sandwich" molecule but contains normal homopolar bonds (*106, 454*).

Several reports of organic polymers containing lead-oxygen-carbon or lead-oxygen-silicon bonding have appeared. Lead salts of acrylic acid have been polymerized (*125a, 263, 373*) and polymeric substances are obtained from the interaction of lead(II) oxide and glycerol (*37*). Patnode and Schmidt (*338*) reported the reaction of trimethylsilanol and lead(II) oxide:

$$2 \ (CH_3)_3SiOH + PbO \rightarrow [(CH_3)_3SiO]_2Pb + H_2O \tag{174}$$

From the reaction of disodiumdiphenylsilanediolate and lead(II) chloride a mixture of polymers having either structure (LV) or structure (LVI) was obtained (*183*). Andrianov and co-workers (*11*) have reported polymers of types (LVII) and (LVIII).

$$[-(C_6H_5)_2Si-O-Pb-O-]_n$$
(LV)

$$[-(C_6H_5)_2Si-O-]_n$$
(LVI)

$$\begin{bmatrix} \overset{R}{\underset{O-}{\overset{|}{Si}}}-O-Pb-O-\overset{R}{\underset{O-}{\overset{|}{Si}}}-O- \end{bmatrix}_n$$
(LVII)

$$\begin{bmatrix} \overset{CH_3}{\underset{OM'}{\overset{|}{Si}}}-O- \end{bmatrix}_n \begin{bmatrix} \overset{OM}{\underset{OM'}{\overset{|}{Si}}}-O- \end{bmatrix} \overset{OM}{\underset{OM'}{\overset{|}{Pb}}}-O-$$
(LVIII)

Tetrakis(trimethylsilylmethyl)lead has been prepared by the reaction of lead(IV) chloride with the appropriate Grignard reagent (*394b*):

$$4 \ (CH_3)_3SiCH_2MgX + PbCl_4 \rightarrow [(CH_3)_3SiCH_2]_4Pb \tag{174a}$$

A plumbosiloxane derivative, trimethyl(trimethylsiloxy)lead, is obtained from sodium trimethylsilanolate and trimethyllead chloride (*386e*).

In addition to the hexaalkyl- and hexaaryldilead compounds (see Ref. *265* for a review of R_3PbPbR_3 derivatives), several compounds have been prepared which contain two lead atoms per molecule. Grüttner and co-workers (*167*) prepared pentamethylenebis(trimethyllead) as well as pentamethylene(trimethyllead)(trimethyltin) from trimethyllead bromide and the required Grignard reagent. Wiczer (*463*) reported the synthesis of compounds of the type $R_3PbCH_2PbR_3$ and $R_3PbCH_2CH_2PbR_3$; these were obtained by heating a mixture of a tetraalkyllead and the appropriate dibromoalkane in the presence of aluminum trichloride. Trimethylenebis-

(triphenyllead) and tetramethylenebis(triphenyllead) can be obtained from the reaction of triphenylleadlithium and the dihaloalkane (*140*), while *p*-phenylenebis(triphenyllead) is prepared from *p*-phenylenedilithium and triphenyllead chloride (*137*). Hartmann and associates (*35, 170, 170a*) have prepared a number of $R_3PbC{\equiv}CPbR_3$ compounds from the Grignard reagent [Eq. (175)] or the sodium salt [Eq. (176)] of acetylene:

$$2\ R_3PbX + BrMgC{\equiv}CMgBr \rightarrow R_3PbC{\equiv}CPbR_3 + 2\ MgBrX \tag{175}$$

$$R_3PbX + NaC{\equiv}CH \xrightarrow{NH_3} R_3PbC{\equiv}CH + NaX \tag{176}$$

$$2\ R_3PbC{\equiv}CH \rightarrow R_3PbC{\equiv}CPbR_3 + HC{\equiv}CH \tag{177}$$

A number of allyl-, 3-butenyl, and β-styryl-substituted lead derivatives have been prepared (*31, 131, 265, 340, 357a*) from the appropriate Grignard reagent and an organolead halide. The synthesis of triethyl(2-methyl-1-propenyl)lead from triethyllead chloride and 2-methyl-1-propenyllithium has been reported (*145*). The discovery that good yields of vinylmagnesium bromide can be otained in tetrahydrofuran has been followed by a number of reports of vinyl-substituted lead compounds (*32, 178, 202–204, 278, 279, 371*). Although some of these derivatives undoubtedly were prepared for polymerization studies, no such studies are mentioned in the above references. Recently, the polymerization of triphenyllead acrylate and methacrylate was reported (*249, 251a*); also newly published are studies of the polymerization of diphenyllead dimethacrylate and its copolymerization with methyl methacrylate (*224, 224a*).

Korshak and co-workers (*240*), by reacting vinylmagnesium bromide with triethyllead chloride or diethyllead dichloride, have prepared triethylvinyllead and diethyldivinyllead. In addition, polymerization studies of these compounds have been reported. The two compounds were found to be very unstable and to decompose under the action of peroxides at 120 to 130° with the liberation of metallic lead. Copolymerization products of triethylvinyllead with styrene and α-methylstyrene were obtained. Diethyldivinyllead copolymerized with diethyldimethylsiloxane:

$$H{-}\underset{C_2H_5}{\overset{CH_3}{Si}}{-}O{-}\underset{C_2H_5}{\overset{CH_3}{Si}}{-}H + CH_2{=}CH\underset{C_2H_5}{\overset{C_2H_5}{Pb}}CH{=}CH_2 \rightarrow \left[{-}\underset{C_2H_5}{\overset{CH_3}{Si}}{-}O{-}\underset{C_2H_5}{\overset{CH_3}{Si}}CH_2CH_2\underset{C_2H_5}{\overset{C_2H_5}{Pb}}CH_2CH_2{-} \right]_n \tag{178}$$

The use of tetrahydrofuran as a convenient solvent for the preparation of *p*-vinylphenylmagnesium bromide has led to the synthesis of several *p*-styrenyllead derivatives. Koton and co-workers (*247*) reacted this

Grignard reagent with triphenyllead chloride to obtain triphenyl(p-vinylphenyl)lead:

$$(C_6H_5)_3PbCl + CH_2{=}CH-\langle\!\!\langle\bigcirc\rangle\!\!\rangle-MgBr$$

$$\downarrow THF$$

$$(C_6H_5)_3Pb-\langle\!\!\langle\bigcirc\rangle\!\!\rangle-CH{=}CH_2 \qquad (179)$$

These authors state that this monomer readily polymerizes and copolymerizes with styrene or methyl methacrylate to form transparent plastics; details were not included in the initial report (*247–249, 251a*). Noltes and co-workers (*328*) similarly prepared triphenyl(p-vinylphenyl)lead and diphenylbis(p-vinylphenyl)lead; no polymerization data were included in this paper. Later, Noltes and van der Kerk reported the reaction of diphenyltin dihydride with diphenylbis(p-vinylphenyl)lead to form a solid, glass-like polymer; this product has a low softening point and a molecular weight of 14,000 (*329*):

$$(C_6H_5)_2SnH_2 + (C_6H_5)_2Pb(C_6H_4CH{=}CH_2)_2$$

$$\downarrow$$

$$\left[\begin{array}{c} C_6H_5 \\ | \\ -SnCH_2CH_2-\langle\!\!\langle\bigcirc\rangle\!\!\rangle- \end{array}\begin{array}{c} C_6H_5 \\ | \\ Pb-\langle\!\!\langle\bigcirc\rangle\!\!\rangle-CH_2CH_2- \\ | \\ C_6H_5 \end{array}\right]_n \qquad (180)$$

Pars and associates (*335*) also have employed p-vinylphenylmagnesium bromide to synthesize triphenyl(p-vinylphenyl)lead and triethyl(p-vinylphenyl)lead. Polymerization of triphenyl(p-vinylphenyl)lead was accomplished with *tert*-butyl hydroperoxide. Triethyl(p-vinylphenyl)lead is a liquid at room temperature; it can be polymerized by exposure to ultraviolet light to give a hard, transparent polymer. Recently, the preparation of p-styrenyllead compounds, presumably including tetrakis(p-vinylphenyl)lead, was reported by Drefahl and co-workers (*101*); polymerization studies were mentioned but no details were given. Korshak and co-workers (*242*) have reported the synthesis and polymerization of triethyl(*p*-iso-propenylphenyl)lead:

$$BrC_6H_4C(CH_3)\!=\!CH_2 \xrightarrow{\text{Mg, } (C_2H_5)_3PbCl, \text{ THF}} (C_2H_5)_3PbC_6H_4C(CH_3)\!=\!CH_2 \qquad (181)$$

Koton and co-workers have reported that allyltriphenyllead does not polymerize under conditions of radical polymerization and that this compound inhibits the polymerization of vinyl monomers such as styrene or methyl methacrylate (*251, 251a*). The polymerization of allyl-substituted organolead compounds in the presence of Ziegler-type catalysts has been mentioned in the patent literature but details are not given (*307a, 307b*). Recently, the polymerization of trimethyl(*p*-vinylphenyl)lead and (*p*-iso-propenylphenyl)trimethyllead was reported; in the presence of 2,2′-azobis-[2-methylpropionitrile] at 70 to 90°, clear, colorless, solid polymers are formed (*329*). Trimethyl(*p*-vinylphenyl)lead also easily forms glass-like copolymers with styrene or methyl methacrylate.

ACKNOWLEDGMENTS

The authors are grateful for assistance from Dr. Hans-Georg Glide, Oren L. Marrs, and William H. Atwell.

REFERENCES

1. Adelson, D. E., and Larsen, R. G., *British Patent* 596,668; *Chem. Abstr.* **42,** 3997 (1948).
1a. Adrova, N. A., Koton, M. M., and Klages, V. A., *Vysokomolekulyarnye Soedineniya* **3,** 1041 (1961).
2. Agre, C. L., *J. Am. Chem. Soc.* **71,** 300 (1949).
2a. Alleston, D. L., Davies, A. G., and Figgis, B. N., *Angew. Chem.* **73,** 683 (1961).
3. Anderson, H. H., *J. Am. Chem. Soc.* **72,** 194 (1950).
4. Anderson, H. H., *J. Am. Chem. Soc.* **72,** 2089 (1950).
5. Anderson, H. H., *J. Am. Chem. Soc.* **74,** 2370 (1952).
6. Anderson, H. H., *J. Am. Chem. Soc.* **75,** 814 (1953).
7. Anderson, H. H., *J. Am. Chem. Soc.* **82,** 3016 (1960).
8. Andreev, D. N., and Kukharskaya, E. V., *Doklady Akad. Nauk S.S.S.R.* **134,** 89 (1960); *Chem. Abstr.* **55,** 359 (1961).
8a. Andreev, D. N., and Kukharskaya, E. V., *Zhur. Obshcheĭ Khim.* **30,** 2782 (1960); *Chem. Abstr.* **55,** 15332 (1961).
9. Andrews, T. M., Bower, F. A., LaLiberte, B. R., and Montermoso, J. C., *J. Am. Chem. Soc.* **80,** 4102 (1958).
10. Andrianov, K. A., *Uspekhi Khim.* **26,** 895 (1957); *Chem. Abstr.* **52,** 2801 (1958).
11. Andrianov, K. A., *Uspekhi Khim.* **27,** 1257 (1958); *Chem. Abstr.* **53,** 4802 (1959).
11a. Andrianov, K. A., *J. Polymer Sci.* **52,** 257 (1961).
11b. Andrianov, K. A., and Nikitenkov, V. E., *Vysokomolekulyarnye Soedineniya* **2,** 1099 (1960).

12. Andrianov, K. A., Ganina, T. N., and Krustaleva, E. N., *Izvest. Akad. Nauk S.S.S.R. Otdel. Khim. Nauk* p. 798 (1956); *Chem. Abstr.* **51**, 3487 (1957).
13. Andrianov, K. A., Leznov, N. S., and Dabagova, A. K., *Izvest. Akad. Nauk S.S.S.R. Otdel. Khim. Nauk* p. 459 (1957); *Chem. Abstr.* **51**, 15457 (1957).
13a. Andrianov, K. A., Khananashvili, L. M., and Konopchenko, Yu. F., *Vysokomole-kulyarnye Soedineniya* **2**, 719 (1960).
14. Andrianov, K. A., Nikitenkov, V. E., and Sokolov, N. N., *Izvest. Akad. Nauk S.S.S.R. Otdel. Khim. Nauk* p. 1224 (1960); *Chem. Abstr.* **55**, 429 (1961).
15. Anonymous, *Ind. Eng. Chem.* **52**, (1), 21A (1960).
16. Atlas, S. M., and Mark, H. F., *Angew. Chem.* **72**, 249 (1960).
17. Bachman, G. B., Carlson, C. L., and Robinson, M., *J. Am. Chem. Soc.* **73**, 1964 (1951).
18. Bähr, G., and Gelius, R., *Chem. Ber.* **91**, 829 (1958).
19. Bähr, G., and Zoche, G., *Chem. Ber.* **88**, 542 (1955).
20. Bailey, D. L., and Pike, R. M., *U. S. Patent* 2,820,798; *Chem. Abstr.* **52**, 7777 (1958).
20a. Bailey, D. L., and Pike, R. M., *U. S. Patent* 2,928,806; *Chem. Zentr.* p. 5273 (1961).
21. Bailey, D. L., and Pines, A. N., *Ind. Eng. Chem.* **46**, 2363 (1954).
22. Baker, W. O., Grisdale, R. O., and Winslow, F. H., *U. S. Patent* 2,697,029; *Chem. Abstr.* **49**, 5883 (1955).
23. Baranovskaya, N. B., Berlin, A. A., Zakharova, M. Z., Mizikin, A. I., and Zil'berman, E. N., *U.S.S.R. Patent* 126,115; *Chem. Abstr.* **54**, 16008 (1960).
24. Barry, A. J., *U. S. Patent* 2,557,778; *Chem. Abstr.* **45**, 8288 (1951).
25. Barry, A. J., *U. S. Patent* 2,557,931; *Chem. Abstr.* **45**, 8816 (1951).
26. Barry, A. J., *British Patent* 671,710; *Chem. Abstr.* **47**, 4909 (1953).
27. Barry, A. J., *British Patent* 671,747; *Chem. Abstr.* **46**, 9338 (1952).
28. Barry, A. J., *U. S. Patent* 2,626,266; *Chem. Abstr.* **48**, 7636 (1954).
29. Barry, A. J., DePree, L., and Hook, D. E., *British Patent* 633,732; *Chem. Abstr.* **45**, 3409 (1951).
30. Barry, A. J., Hook, D. E., and DePree, L., *U. S. Patent* 2,475,122; *Chem. Abstr.* **43**, 8194 (1949).
31. Bartocha, B., Douglas, C. M., and Gray, M. Y., *Z. Naturforsch.* **14b**, 809 (1959).
32. Bartocha, B., and Gray, M. Y., *Z. Naturforsch.* **14b**, 350 (1959).
33. Bauer, H., and Burschkies, K., *Ber. deut. chem. Ges.* **65**, 956 (1932).
34. Baum, G., *J. Org. Chem.* **23**, 480 (1958).
35. Beerman, C., and Hartmann, H., *Z. anorg. u. allgem. Chem.* **276**, 20 (1954).
36. Benkeser, R. A., and Foster, D. J., *J. Am. Chem. Soc.* **74**, 5314 (1952).
37. Berlin, A. A., and Parini, V. P., *Uspekhi Khim.* **18**, 546 (1949); *Chem. Abstr.* **45**, 5957 (1951).
37a. Bilow, N., Brady, J. L., and Segal, C. L., *J. Org. Chem.* **26**, 929 (1961).
37b. Birr, K. H., and Kräft, D., *Z. anorg. u. allgem. Chem.* **311**, 235 (1961).
38. Bluestein, B. A., *J. Am. Chem. Soc.* **70**, 3068 (1948).
39. Boeseken, J., and Rutgers, J. J., *Rec. trav. chim.* **42**, 1017 (1923).
40. Bogomol'nyĭ, V. Ya., *Vysokomolekulyarnye Soedineniya* **1**, 1469 (1959); *Chem. Abstr.* **54**, 14753 (1960).
40a. Braun, D., *Angew. Chem.* **73**, 197 (1961).
41. Breed, L. W., *J. Org. Chem.* **25**, 1198 (1960).
42. Breed, L. W., Haggerty, W. J., Jr., and Baiocchi, F., *J. Org. Chem.* **25**, 1633 (1960).
43. Brinckman, F. E., and Stone, F. G. A., *J. Inorg. & Nuclear Chem.* **11**, 24 (1959).

44. British Thomson-Houston Co. Ltd., *British Patent* 616,320; *Chem. Abstr.* **43**, 5637 (1949).
45. British Thomson-Houston Co. Ltd., *British Patent* 618,451; *Chem. Abstr.* **43**, 5625 (1949).
46. British Thomson-Houston Co. Ltd., *British Patent* 641,268; *Chem. Abstr.* **45**, 391 (1951).
47. British Thomson-Houston Co. Ltd., *British Patent* 654,571; *Chem. Abstr.* **46**, 4561 (1952).
48. Brook, A. G., and Gilman, H., *J. Am. Chem. Soc.* **76**, 77 (1954).
49. Brown, M. P., and Fowles, G. W. A., *J. Am. Chem. Soc.* p. 2811 (1958).
50. Brown, M. P., and Rochow, E. G., *J. Am. Chem. Soc.* **82**, 4166 (1960).
50a. Bruker, A. B., Balashova, L. D., and Soborovskiǐ, L. Z., *Doklady Akad. Nauk S.S.S.R.* **135**, 843 (1960); *Chem. Abstr.* **55**, 13301 (1961).
50b. Bulatov, M. A., and Spasskiǐ, S. S., *Vysokomolekulyarnye Soedineniya* **2**, 658 (1960).
51. Bunnell, R. H., *U. S. Patent* 2,632,755; *Chem. Abstr.* **47**, 6442 (1953).
52. Bunnell, R. H., and Hatcher, D. B., *U. S. Patent* 2,469,154; *Chem. Abstr.* **43**, 5635 (1949).
52a. Burg, A. B., and Spielman, J. R., *J. Am. Chem. Soc.* **83**, 2667 (1961).
53. Burkhard, C. A., *J. Am. Chem. Soc.* **71**, 963 (1949).
54. Burkhard, C. A., *U. S. Patent* 2,554,976; *Chem. Abstr.* **45**, 8809 (1951).
55. Burkhard, C. A., and Krieble, R. H., *J. Am. Chem. Soc.* **69**, 2687 (1947).
56. Butler, G. B., Paper presented at WADC Materials Laboratory Conference on High Polymer and Fluid Research, Dayton, Ohio, May 26–28, 1959.
57. Butler, G. B., and Stackman, R. W., *J. Org. Chem.* **25**, 1643 (1960).
57a. Campbell, T. W., *U. S. Patent* 2,958,681; *Chem. Abstr.* **55**, 6028 (1961).
58. Carlisle Chemical Works, Inc., *Japanese Patent* 4,992 (1958); *Chem. Zentr.* p. 13210 (1960).
59. Carroll, R. T., *U. S. Patent* 2,597,920; *Chem. Abstr.* **46**, 7824 (1952).
60. Chamberland, B. L., and MacDiarmid, A. G., *Abstr. Papers Presented 138th Meeting Am. Chem. Soc. N.Y. 1960* p. 20N.
61. Chamberland, B. L., and MacDiarmid, A. G., *J. Chem. Soc.* p. 445 (1961).
62. Chernyshev, E. A., *Collection Czechoslov. Chem. Communs.* **25**, 2161 (1960).
63. Chernyshev, E. A., Dolgaya, M. E., and Egorov, Yu. P., *Zhur. Obshcheǐ Khim.* **27**, 2676 (1957); *Chem. Abstr.* **52**, 7187 (1958).
63a. Chugunov, V. S., *Izvest. Akad. Nauk S.S.S.R. Otdel. Khim. Nauk* p. 942 (1960).
64. Church, J. M., Johnson, E. W., and Ramsden, H. E., *U. S. Patent* 2,591,675; *Chem. Abstr.* **48**, 5207 (1954).
65. Church, J. M., Johnson, E. W., and Ramsden, H. E., *U. S. Patent* 2,593,267; *Chem. Abstr.* **48**, 6460 (1954).
66. Clark, H. A., *U. S. Patent* 2,507,514; *Chem. Abstr.* **45**, 2197 (1951).
67. Clark, H. A., *U. S. Patent* 2,507,515; *Chem. Abstr.* **45**, 2197 (1951).
68. Clark, H. A., *U. S. Patent* 2,507,521; *Chem. Abstr.* **45**, 2265 (1951).
69. Clark, H. A., *U. S. Patent* 2,557,782; *Chem. Abstr.* **46**, 529 (1952).
70. Clark, H. A., *U. S. Patent* 2,557,942; *Chem. Abstr.* **46**, 1027 (1952).
71. Clark, H. A., *U. S. Patent* 2,563,004; *Chem. Abstr.* **45**, 10676 (1951).
72. Clark, H. A., *U. S. Patent* 2,590,937; *Chem. Abstr.* **46**, 7360 (1952).
73. Clark, H. A., *British Patent* 671,553; *Chem. Abstr.* **47**, 4909 (1953).
74. Clark, H. A., *British Patent* 671,773; *Chem. Abstr.* **46**, 8146 (1952).
75. Clark, H. A., *British Patent* 672,825; *Chem. Abstr.* **47**, 3869 (1953).

76. Clark, H. A., *British Patent* 674,591; *Chem. Abstr.* **47**, 3875 (1953).

77. Clark, H. A., *U. S. Patent* 2,762,717; *Chem. Abstr.* **51**, 3955 (1957).

78. Clark, H. A., Gordon, A. F., Young, C. W., and Hunter, M. J., *J. Am. Chem. Soc.* **73**, 3798 (1951).

79. Coates, G. E., "Organo-Metallic Compounds," 2nd ed., pp. 164–213. Methuen, London, 1960.

80. Cohen, H. J., and Dessy, R. E., *Abstr. Papers Presented 138th Meeting Am. Chem. Soc. N.Y. 1960* p. 20N.

81. Cohen, M., and Ladd, J. R., *U. S. Patent* 2,716,638; *Chem. Abstr.* **50**, 7502 (1956).

81a. Cooper, G. D., *J. Org. Chem.* **26**, 925 (1961).

82. Crain, R. D., and Koenig, P. E., Paper presented at WADC Materials Laboratory Conference on High Temperature Polymer and Fluid Research, Dayton, Ohio, May 26–28, 1959.

83. Curry, J. W., *J. Am. Chem. Soc.* **78**, 1686 (1956).

84. Curry, J. W., *U. S. Patent* 2,811,541; *Chem. Abstr.* **52**, 10639 (1958).

84a. Curry, J. W., *J. Org. Chem.* **26**, 1308 (1961).

85. Curry, J. W., and Harrison, G. W., Jr., *J. Org. Chem.* **23**, 1219 (1958).

86. DePree, L., Barry, A. J., and Hook, D. E., *U. S. Patent* 2,580,159; *Chem. Abstr.* **46**, 6670 (1952).

86a. Deutsche Advance Produktion G.m.b.H., *German Patent* 1,080,555; *Chem. Zentr.* p.2457 (1961).

87. Dillard, C. R., *Abstr. Papers Presented 138th Meeting Am. Chem. Soc. N.Y. 1960* p. 50N.

88. Dow Corning Corp., *British Patent* 646,629; *Chem. Abstr.* **45**, 5184 (1951).

89. Dow Corning Corp., *German Patent* 855,401; *Chem. Zentr.* p. 7928 (1953).

90. Dow Corning Corp., Barry, A. J., DePree, L., and Hook, D. E., *British Patent* 635,645; *Chem. Abstr.* **44**, 6882 (1950).

91. Dow Corning Corp. and Goodwin, J. T., Jr., *British Patent* 624,551; *Chem. Abstr.* **44**, 4924 (1950).

92. Dow Corning Corp. and Goodwin, J. T., Jr., *British Patent* 624,814; *Chem. Abstr.* **44**, 2010 (1950).

93. Dow Corning Corp. and Goodwin, J. T., Jr., *British Patent* 631,619; *Chem. Abstr.* **44**, 4491 (1950).

94. Dow Corning Corp. and Goodwin, J. T., Jr., *British Patent* 632,563; *Chem. Abstr.* **44**, 6425 (1950).

95. Dow Corning Corp. and Goodwin, J. T., Jr., *German Patent* 847,594; *Chem. Zentr.* p. 7927 (1953).

96. Dow Corning Ltd., *British Patent* 657,912; *Chem. Zentr.* p. 3347 (1955).

97. Dow Corning Ltd., *British Patent* 667,435; *Chem. Abstr.* **46**, 6429 (1952).

98. Dow Corning Ltd., *British Patent* 671,774; *Chem. Abstr.* **46**, 8895 (1952).

99. Dow Corning Ltd., *British Patent* 688,799; *Chem. Abstr.* **47**, 7700 (1953).

100. Dow Corning Ltd., *British Patent* 689,648; *Chem. Zentr.* p. 3020 (1955).

101. Drefahl, G., Plötner, G., and Lorenz, D., *Angew. Chem.* **72**, 454 (1960).

101a. Durgar'yan, S. G., Egorov, Yu. P., Nametkin, N. S., and Topchiev, A. V., *Zhur. Obshcheĭ Khim.* **30**, 2600 (1960).

101b. Dzhurinskaia, N. G., Mironov, V. F., and Petrov, A. D., *Doklady Akad. Nauk S.S.S.R.* **138**, 1107 (1961).

102. Eaborn, D., "Organosilicon Compounds," Chapters 12, 14, and 15. Butterworths, London, 1960.

103. English, W. D., Taurins, A., and Nicholls, R. V. V., *Can. J. Chem.* **30**, 646 (1952).

104. Evers, E. C., Paper presented at WADC Materials Laboratory Conference on High Temperature Polymer and Fluid Research, Dayton, Ohio, May 26–28, 1959.
105. Evison, W. E., and Kipping, F. S., *J. Chem. Soc.* p. 2774 (1931).
105a. Farbenfabriken Bayer Akt.-Ges., *German Patent* 1,099,743; *Chem. Zentr.* p. 10,000 (1961).
105b. Farbwerke Hoechst Akt.-Ges., *German Patent* 1,078,772; *Chem. Abstr.* **55,** 13927 (1961).
105c. Fekete, F., *U. S. Patent* 2,954,357; *Chem. Abstr.* **55,** 4027 (1961).
106. Fischer, E. O., and Grubert, H., *Z. anorg. u. allgem. Chem.* **286,** 237 (1956).
107. Fisher, A. K., West, R. C., and Rochow, E. G., *J. Am. Chem. Soc.* **76,** 5878 (1954).
107a. Fisher, E., and Petrov, A. D., *Doklady Akad. Nauk S.S.S.R.* **138,** 136 (1961); *Chem. Abstr.* **55,** 21010 (1961).
108. Flood, E. A., *J. Am. Chem. Soc.* **54,** 1663 (1932).
109. Flood, E. A., *J. Am. Chem. Soc.* **55,** 4935 (1933).
110. Francis, J. D., *U. S. Patent* 2,573,426; *Chem. Abstr.* **46,** 1300 (1952).
111. Frisch, K. C., and Young, R. B., *J. Am. Chem. Soc.* **74,** 4853 (1952).
112. Fritz, G., *Z. Naturforsch.* **12b,** 66 (1957).
113. Fritz, G., *Z. Naturforsch.* **12b,** 123 (1957).
114. Fritz, G., *Angew. Chem.* **70,** 402 (1958).
115. Fritz, G., *Angew. Chem.* **70,** 701 (1958).
116. Fritz, G., and Grobe, J., *Angew. Chem.* **70,** 701 (1958).
117. Fritz, G., and Grobe, J., *Z. anorg. u. allgem. Chem.* **299,** 302 (1959).
117a. Fritz, G., and Grobe, J., *Z. anorg. u. allgem. Chem.* **309,** 77 (1961).
117b. Fritz, G., and Grobe, J., *Z. anorg. u. allgem. Chem.* **309,** 98 (1961).
117c. Fritz, G., and Grobe, J., *Z. anorg. u. allgem. Chem.* **311,** 325 (1961).
118. Fritz, G., and Raab, B., *Z. anorg. u. allgem. Chem.* **286,** 149 (1956).
119. Fritz, G., and Raab, B., *Z. anorg. u. allgem. Chem.* **299,** 232 (1959).
120. Fritz, G., and Teichmann, G., *Angew. Chem.* **70,** 701 (1958).
121. Fritz, G., and Thielking, H., *Z. anorg. u. allgem. Chem.* **306,** 39 (1960).
122. Fritz, G., Habel, D., Kummer, D., and Teichmann, G., *Z. anorg. u. allgem. Chem.* **302,** 60 (1959).
123. Fritz, G., Habel, D., and Teichmann, G., *Z. anorg. u. allgem. Chem.* **303,** 85 (1960).
124. Fritz, G., Teichmann, G., and Thielking, H., *Angew. Chem.* **72,** 209 (1960).
125. Frost, L. W., *U. S. Patent* 2,596,967; *Chem. Abstr.* **47,** 4365 (1953).
125a. Fuji Chemical Co., *Japanese Patent* 2,360 (1960); *Chem. Abstr.* **55,** 5186 (1961).
126. Gainer, G. C., *U. S. Patent* 2,709,692; *Chem. Abstr.* **49,** 12875 (1955).
127. Gastinger, E., *Fortschr. chem. Forsch.* **3,** 633 (1955).
128. George, P. D., Prober, M., and Elliott, J. R., *Chem. Revs.* **56,** 1065 (1956).
128a. George, P. J., *U. S. Patent* 2,910,495; *Chem. Abstr.* **54,** 7225 (1960).
129. Geyer, A. M., Haszeldine, R. N., Leedham, K., and Marklow, R. J., *J. Chem. Soc.* p. 4472 (1957).
130. Gilman, H., and Aoki, D., *Chem. & Ind.* (*London*) p. 1165 (1960).
130a. Gilman, H., and co-workers, unpublished studies.
131. Gilman, H., and Eisch, J., *J. Org. Chem.* **20,** 763 (1955).
132. Gilman, H., and Gerow, C. W., *J. Am. Chem. Soc.* **79,** 342 (1957).
133. Gilman, H., and Gorsich, R. D., *J. Am. Chem. Soc.* **80,** 3243 (1958).
134. Gilman, H., and Jarvie, A. W. P., *Chem. & Ind.* (*London*) p. 965 (1960).
135. Gilman, H., and Lichtenwalter, G. D., *J. Org. Chem.* **24,** 1588 (1959).
136. Gilman, H., and Marrs, O. L., *J. Org. Chem.* **25,** 1194 (1960).

137. Gilman, H., and Melstrom, D. S., *J. Am. Chem. Soc.* **72**, 2953 (1950).
138. Gilman, H., Peterson, D. J., Jarvie, A. W., and Winkler, H. J. S., *J. Am. Chem. Soc.* **82**, 2076 (1960).
139. Gilman, H., Peterson, D. J., Jarvie, A. W., and Winkler, H. J. S., *Tetrahedron Letters No.* **23**, 5 (1960).
140. Gilman, H., and Summers, L., *J. Am. Chem. Soc.* **74**, 5924 (1952).
141. Gilman, H., Summers, L., and Leeper, R. W., *J. Org. Chem.* **17**, 630 (1952).
142. Gilman, H., Wu, T. C., Hartzfeld, H. A., Guter, G. A., Smith, A. G., Goodman, J. J., and Eidt, S. H., *J. Am. Chem. Soc.* **74**, 561 (1952).
143. Gilman, H., and Zuech, E. A., *Chem. & Ind. (London)* p. 120 (1960).
144. Gilman, H., and Zuech, E. A., *J. Am. Chem. Soc.* **82**, 3605 (1960).
145. Glockling, F., *J. Chem. Soc.* p. 716 (1955).
146. "Gmelins Handbuch der Anorganischen Chemie," System No. 45, 8th ed., Suppl. pp. 547–557. Verlag Chemie, Weinheim, 1958.
147. Goldblatt, L. O., and Oldroyd, D. M., *U. S. Patent* 2,533,240; *Chem. Abstr.* **45**, 2262 (1951).
147a. Golubtsov, S. A., Popeleva, G. S., and Andrianov, K. A., *U.S.S.R. Patent* 134,688; *Chem. Abstr.* **55**, 15418 (1961).
148. Goodman, J. J., and Gilman, H., Unpublished studies; see Zeiss, H., "Organometallic Chemistry," p. 274. Reinhold, New York, 1960.
149. Goodwin, J. T., Jr., *U. S. Patent* 2,483,972; *Chem. Abstr.* **44**, 2011 (1950).
150. Goodwin, J. T., Jr., *U. S. Patent* 2,507,512; *Chem. Abstr.* **45**, 3410 (1951).
151. Goodwin, J. T., Jr., *U. S. Patent* 2,507,513; *Chem. Abstr.* **45**, 3410 (1951).
152. Goodwin, J. T., Jr., *U. S. Patent* 2,511,056; *Chem. Abstr.* **44**, 8362 (1950).
153. Goodwin, J. T., Jr., *U. S. Patent* 2,511,812; *Chem. Abstr.* **44**, 8362 (1950).
154. Goodwin, J. T., Jr., *U. S. Patent* 2,527,808; *Chem. Abstr.* **45**, 2016 (1951).
155. Goodwin, J. T., Jr., *U. S. Patent* 2,544,079; *Chem. Abstr.* **45**, 6654 (1951).
156. Goodwin, J. T., Jr., *U. S. Patent* 2,592,681; *Chem. Abstr.* **46**, 6141 (1952).
157. Goodwin, J. T., Jr., *U. S. Patent* 2,592,682; *Chem. Abstr.* **46**, 6141 (1952).
158. Goodwin, J. T., Jr., *U. S. Patent* 2,607,791; *Chem. Abstr.* **48**, 13732 (1954).
159. Goodwin, J. T., Jr., Baldwin, W. E., and McGregor, R. R., *J. Am. Chem. Soc.* **69**, 2247 (1947).
160. Gordon, A. F., *U. S. Patent* 2,755,295; *Chem. Abstr.* **51**, 2033 (1957).
161. Gordon, A. F., and Clark, H. A., *U.S. Patent* 2,696,480; *Chem. Abstr.* **49**, 9324 (1955).
161a. Greber, G., and Degler, G., *Angew. Chem.* **73**, 243 (1961).
162. Greber, G., and Metzinger, L., *Makromol. Chem.* **39**, 167 (1960).
163. Greber, G., and Metzinger, L., *Makromol. Chem.* **39**, 189 (1960).
164. Greber, G., and Metzinger, L., *Makromol. Chem.* **39**, 217 (1960).
164a. Greber, G., and Reese, E., *Makromol. Chem.* **47**, 228 (1961).
165. Grüttner, G., and Cauer, M., *Ber. deut. chem. Ges.* **51**, 1283 (1918).
166. Grüttner, G., and Krause, E., *Ber. deut. chem. Ges.* **50**, 1559 (1917).
167. Grüttner, G., Krause, E., and Wiernik, M., *Ber. deut. chem. Ges.* **50**, 1549 (1917).
168. Gutmann, V., and Meller, A., *Monatsh. Chem.* **91**, 519 (1960).
169. Hartmann, H., and Ahrens, J. U., *Angew. Chem.* **70**, 75 (1958).
170. Hartmann, H., and Eschenbach, W., *Naturwissenschaften* **46**, 321 (1959).
170a. Hartmann, H., Dietz, E., Komorniczyk, K., and Reiss, W., *Naturwissenschaften* **48**, 570 (1961).
171. Hatcher, D. B., and Bunnell, R. H., *U. S. Patent* 2,545,780; *Chem. Abstr.* **45**, 7590 (1951).

172. Hatcher, D. B., and Bunnell, R. H., *U. S. Patent* 2,570,551; *Chem. Abstr.* **46,** 4568 (1952).

173. Hatcher, D. B., and Bunnell, R. H., *U. S. Patent* 2,612,510; *Chem. Abstr.* **47,** 11243 (1953).

174. Hatcher, D. B., and Bunnell, R. H., *U. S. Patent* 2,618,646; *Chem. Abstr.* **47,** 8088 (1953).

175. Hatcher, D. B., and Bunnell, R. H., *U. S. Patent* 2,624,720; *Chem. Abstr.* **47,** 3614 (1953).

176. Hatcher, D. B., and Bunnell, R. H., *U. S. Patent* 2,624,721; *Chem. Abstr.* **47,** 3613 (1953).

177. Henglein, F. A., Land, R., and Schmack, L., *Makromol. Chem.* **22,** 103 (1957).

177a. Henry, M. C., and Downey, M. F., *J. Org. Chem.* **26,** 2299 (1961).

178. Henry, M. C., and Noltes, J. G., *J. Am. Chem. Soc.* **82,** 555 (1960)

179. Henry, M. C., and Noltes, J. G., *J. Am. Chem. Soc.* **82,** 558 (1960).

180. Henry, M. C., and Noltes, J. G., *J. Am. Chem. Soc.* **82,** 561 (1960.)

181. Hester, A. S., *Chem. Eng. News* **38**(26), 21 (1960).

182. Hizawa, K., and Nojimoto, E., *Japanese Patent* 3,767 (1952); *Chem. Abstr.* **48,** 3992 (1954).

183. Hornbaker, E. D., and Conrad, F., *J. Org. Chem.* **24,** 1858 (1959).

183a. Houel, B., and Jácović, M. S., *Compt. rend. acad. sci.* **251,** 2523 (1960).

184. Hrivík, A., and Mikulášová, D., *Chem. zvesti* **12,** 32 (1958); *Chem. Abstr.* **52,** 13616 (1958).

185. Hunter, M. J., *U. S. Patent* 2,554,193; *Chem. Abstr.* **46,** 1027 (1952).

186. Hunyar, A., "Chemie der Silicone," 2nd ed., Chap. 4. VEB Verlag Technik, Berlin, 1959.

187. Hurd, D. T., *J. Am. Chem. Soc.* **67,** 1813 (1945).

188. Hurd, D. T., and Roedel, G. F., *Ind. Eng. Chem.* **40,** 2078 (1948).

189. Ingham, R. K., Rosenberg, S. D., and Gilman, H., *Chem. Revs.* **60,** 459 (1960).

190. Jacobs, G., *Compt. rend. acad. sci.* **238,** 1825 (1954).

191. Jarvie, A. W. P., and Gilman, H., *Chem. & Ind. (London)* p. 1271 (1960).

192. Jarvie, A. W. P., and Gilman, H., *J. Org. Chem.* **26,** 1999 (1961).

193. Jarvie, A. W. P., and Gilman, H., *J. Org. Chem.* in press.

194. Jarvie, A. W. P., Winkler, H. J. S., and Gilman, H., *J. Org. Chem.* **27,** 614 (1962).

195. Jarvie, A. W. P., Winkler, H. J. S., and Gilman, H., unpublished studies.

196. Jarvie, A. W. P., Winkler, H. J. S., Peterson, D. J., and Gilman, H., *J. Am. Chem. Soc.* **83,** 1921 (1961).

197. Jensen, K. A., and Clauson-Kaas, N., *Z. anorg. u. allgem. Chem.* **250,** 277 (1943).

198. Johnson, E. W., *British Patent* 737,033; *Chem. Abstr.* **50,** 13992 (1956).

199. Johnson, O. H., *Chem. Revs.* **48,** 259 (1951).

200. Johnson, O. H., and Harris, D. M., *J. Am. Chem. Soc.* **72,** 5564 (1950).

200a. Johnson, W. K., and Pollart, K. A., *J. Org. Chem.* **26,** 4092 (1961).

201. Johnson, O. H., and Jones, L. V., *J. Org. Chem.* **17,** 1172 (1952).

202. Juenge, E. C., and Cook, S. E., *J. Am. Chem. Soc.* **81,** 3578 (1959).

203. Juenge, E. C., and Seyferth, D., *Abstr. Papers Presented 128th Meeting Am. Chem. Soc. N.Y. 1960* p. 51P.

203a. Kaesz, H. D., *J. Am. Chem. Soc.* **83,** 1514 (1961).

204. Kaesz, H. D., and Stone, F. G. A., *in* "Organometallic Chemistry" (H. Zeiss, ed.), pp. 115–128. Reinhold, New York, 1960.

204a. Kali-Chemie Akt.-Ges., *German Patent* 1,089,552; *Chem. Zentr.* p. 4907 (1961).

205. Kanazashi, M., *Bull. Chem. Soc. Japan* **28,** 44 (1955).

206. Kantor, S. W., Osthoff, R. C., and Hurd, D. T., *J. Am. Chem. Soc.* **77,** 1685 (1955).
207. Kerk, G. J. M. van der, Luijten, J. G. A., and Noltes, J. G., *Angew. Chem.* **70,** 298 (1958).
208. Kerk, G. J. M. van der, and Noltes, J. G., *J. Appl. Chem.* **9,** 106 (1959).
209. Kerk, G. J. M. van der, and Noltes, J. G., *J. Appl. Chem.* **9,** 113 (1959).
210. Kipping, F. S., *Proc. Chem. Soc.* **27,** 143 (1911).
211. Kipping, F. S., *J. Chem. Soc.* **123,** 2590 (1923).
212. Kipping, F. S., *J. Chem. Soc.* **123,** 2598 (1923).
213. Kipping, F. S., *J. Chem. Soc.* **125,** 2291 (1924).
214. Kipping, F. S., *J. Chem. Soc.* p. 2719 (1927).
215. Kipping, F. S., *J. Chem. Soc.* p. 2728 (1927).
216. Kipping, F. S., *Proc. Roy. Soc.* **A159,** 139 (1937).
217. Kipping, F. S., Blackburn, J. C., and Short, J. F., *J. Chem. Soc.* p. 1290 (1931).
218. Kipping, F. S., and Murray, A. G., *J. Chem. Soc.* p. 1431 (1928).
219. Kipping, F. S., and Murray, A. G., *J. Chem. Soc.* p. 360 (1929).
220. Kipping, F. S., Murray, A. G., and Maltby, J. G., *J. Chem. Soc.* p. 1180 (1929).
221. Kipping, F. S., and Sands, J. E., *J. Chem. Soc.* **119,** 830 (1921).
222. Kipping, F. S., and Sands, J. E., *J. Chem. Soc.* **119,** 848 (1921).
223. Kipping, F. S., and Short, J. F., *J. Chem. Soc.* p. 1029 (1930).
223a. Knoth, W. H., Jr., and Lindsey, R. V., Jr., *J. Org. Chem.* **23,** 1392 (1958).
224. Kochkin, D. A., *Doklady Akad. Nauk S.S.S.R.* **135,** 857 (1960).
224a. Kochkin, D. A., Novichenko, Yu. P., Kuznetsova, G. I., and Laĭne, L. V., *U.S.S.R. Patent* 133,224; *Chem. Abstr.* **55,** 11923 (1961).
225. Kochkin, D. A., Kotrelev, V. N., Kalinina, S. P., Kuznetsova, G. I., Laĭne, L. V., Chervova, L. V., Borisova, A. I., and Borisenko, V. V., *Vysokomolekulyarnye Soedineniya* **1,** 1507 (1959); *Chem. Abstr.* **54,** 14107 (1960).
226. Kochkin, D. A., Kotrelev, V. N., Shostakovskiĭ, M. R., Kalinina, S. P., Kuznetsova, G. I., and Borisenko, V. V., *Vysokomolekulyarnye Soedineniya* **1,** 482 (1959); *Chem. Abstr.* **54,** 5150 (1960).
227. Kohama, S., *J. Chem. Soc. Japan* **80,** 284 (1959).
228. Kojima, K., *Bull. Chem. Soc. Japan* **31,** 663 (1958).
229. Kojima, K., *Bull. Chem. Soc. Japan* **33,** 1400 (1960).
229a. Kojima, K., *Bull. Chem. Soc. Japan* **34,** 18 (1961).
230. Kolesnikov, G. S., and Davydova, S. L., *Zhur. Obshcheĭ Khim.* **29,** 2042 (1959); *Chem. Abstr.* **54,** 8687 (1960).
231. Kolesnikov, G. S., Davydova, S. L., and Ermolaeva, T. I., *Vysokomolekulyarnye Soedineniya* **1,** 1493 (1959); *Chem. Abstr.* **54,** 17940 (1960).
231a. Kolesnikov, G. S., Davydova, S. L., Ermolaeva, T. I., Shilova, N. D., and Bykhovksya, M. B., *Vysokomolekulyarnye Soedineniya* **2,** 567 (1960); *Chem. Abstr.* **55,** 4039 (1961).
231b. Kolesnikov, G. S., Davydova, S. L., and Klimentova, N. V., *Vysokomolekulyarnye Soedineniya* **2,** 563 (1960); *Chem. Abstr.* **55,** 4039 (1961).
231c. Kolesnikov, G. S., Davydova, S. L., and Klimentova, N. V., *Mezhdunarod. Simpozium po Makromol. Khim. Doklady Moscow Sektsiya* **1,** p. 159 (1960); *Chem. Abstr.* **55,** 6907 (1961).
231d. Kolesnikov, G. S., Davydova, S. L., and Klimentova, N. V., *J. Polymer Sci.* **52,** 55 (1961).
232. Korshak, V. V., Petrov, A. D., Matveeva, N. G., Mironov, V. F., Nikitin, G. I., and Sadykh-Zade, S. I., *Zhur. Obshcheĭ Khim.* **26,** 1209 (1956); *Chem. Abstr.* **50,** 16705 (1956).

233. Korshak, V. V., Polyakova, A. M., Mironov, V. F., and Petrov, A. D., *Izvest. Akad. Nauk S.S.S.R. Otdel. Khim. Nauk* p. 178 (1959); *Chem. Abstr.* **53,** 15959 (1959).
234. Korshak, V. V., Polyakova, A. M., Mironov, V. F., Petrov, A. D., and Tambovtseva, V. S., *Izvest. Akad. Nauk S.S.S.R. Otdel. Khim. Nauk* p. 1116 (1959); *Chem. Abstr.* **54,** 1271 (1960).
235. Korshak, V. V., Polyakova, A. M., Petrov, A. D., and Mironov, V. F., *Doklady Akad. Nauk S.S.S.R.* **112,** 436 (1957); *Chem. Abstr.* **51,** 13815 (1957).
236. Korshak, V. V., Polyakova, A. M., Sakharova, A. A., Mironov, V. F., and Chernyshev, E. A., *Vysokomolekulyarnye Soedineniya* **2,** 1370 (1960).
237. Korshak, V. V., Polyakova, A. M., Sakharova, A. A., Petrov, A. D., and Chernyshev, E. A., *Doklady Akad. Nauk S.S.S.R.* **119,** 282 (1958); *Chem. Abstr.* **52,** 14556 (1958).
238. Korshak, V. V., Polyakova, A. M., Sakharova, A. A., Petrov, A. D., and Chernyshev, E. A., *Doklady Akad. Nauk S.S.S.R.* **126,** 791 (1959); *Chem. Abstr.* **53,** 21747 (1959).
239. Korshak, V. V., Polyakova, A. M., Sakharova, A. A., Petrov, A. D., Mironov, V. F., Glukhovtsev, V. G., and Nikishin, G. I., *Zhur. Obshchei Khim.* **27,** 2445 (1957); *Chem. Abstr.* **52,** 7133 (1958).
240. Korshak, V. V., Polyakova, A. M., and Suchkova, M. D., *Vysokomolekulyarnye Soedinenya* **2,** 13 (1960); *Chem. Abstr.* **55,** 361 (1961).
241. Korshak, V. V., Polyakova, A. M., and Tambovtseva, E. S., *Izvest. Akad. Nauk S.S.S.R. Otdel. Khim. Nauk* p. 742 (1959); *Chem. Abstr.* **54,** 359 (1960).
242. Korshak, V. V., Polyakova, A. M., and Tambovtseva, E. S., *Vysokomolekulyarnye Soedineniya* **1,** 1021 (1959); *Chem. Abstr.* **54,** 22438 (1960).
243. Korshak, V. V., Polyakova, A. M., Vdovin, V. M., Mironov, V. F., and Petrov, A. D., *Doklady Akad. Nauk S.S.S.R.* **128,** 960 (1959); *Chem. Abstr.* **54,** 7536 (1960).
244. Koton, M. M., *Uspekhi Khim.* **26,** 1125 (1957); *Chem. Abstr.* **52,** 6267 (1958).
245. Koton, M. M., and Kiseleva, T. M., *Zhur. Obshchei Khim.* **27,** 2553 (1957); *Chem. Abstr.* **52,** 7136 (1958).
246. Koton, M. M., and Kiseleva, T. M., *Doklady Akad. Nauk S.S.S.R.* **130,** 86 (1960); *Chem. Abstr.* **54,** 10839 (1960).
247. Koton, M. M., Kiseleva, T. M., and Florinskiĭ, F. S., *Izvest. Akad. Nauk S.S.S.R. Otdel. Khim. Nauk* p. 948 (1959); *Chem. Abstr.* **54,** 1378 (1960).
248. Koton, M. M., Kiseleva, T. M., and Florinskiĭ, F. S., *Angew. Chem.* **72,** 712 (1960).
249. Koton, M. M., Kiseleva, T. M., and Florinskiĭ, F. S., *Vysokomolekulyarnye Soedineniya* **2,** 1639 (1960).
250. Koton, M. M., Kiseleva, T. M., and Paribok, V. A., *Doklady Akad. Nauk S.S.S.R.* **125,** 1263 (1959); *Chem. Abstr.* **53,** 17563 (1959).
251. Koton, M. M., Kiseleva, T. M., and Zapevalova, N. P., *Zhur. Obshchei Khim.* **30,** 186 (1960).
251a. Koton, M. M., Kiseleva, T. M., and Florinskiĭ, F. S., *J. Polymer Sci.* **52,** 237 (1961).
252. Kraus, C. A., and Brown, C. L., *J. Am. Chem. Soc.* **52,** 3690 (1930).
253. Kraus, C. A., and Brown, C. L., *J. Am. Chem. Soc.* **52,** 4031 (1930).
254. Kraus, C. A., and Greer, W. N., *J. Am. Chem. Soc.* **47,** 2568 (1925).
255. Kraus, C. A., and Johnson, E. G., *J. Am. Chem. Soc.* **55,** 3542 (1933).
256. Kraus, C. A., and Neal, A. M., *J. Am. Chem. Soc.* **51,** 2403 (1929).
257. Kraus, C. A., and Nutting, H. S., *J. Am. Chem. Soc.* **54,** 1622 (1932).

258. Kraus, C. A., and Wooster, C. B., *J. Am. Chem. Soc.* **52**, 372 (1930).

259. Krause, E., and Becker, R., *Ber. deut. chem. Ges.* **53**, 173 (1920).

260. Krause, E., and Reissaus, G., *Ber. deut. chem. Ges.* **55**, 888 (1922).

260a. Kriegsmann, H., and Beyer, H., *Z. anorg. u. allgem. Chem.* **311**, 180 (1961).

261. Kropa, E. L., *U. S. Patent* 2,388,161; *Chem. Abstr.* **40**, 592 (1946).

261a. Kuivila, H. G., and Jakusik, E. R., *J. Org. Chem.* **26**, 1430 (1961).

261b. Kuivila, H. G., Sawyer, A. K., and Armour, A. G., *J. Org. Chem.* **26**, 1426 (1961).

262. Ladenburg, A., *Ber. deut. chem. Ges.* **40**, 2274 (1907).

263. Langkammerer, C. M., *U. S. Patent* 2,253,128; *Chem. Abstr.* **35**, 8151 (1941).

264. Laubengayer, A. W., and Allen, B., *Abstr. Papers Presented 117th Meeting Am. Chem. Soc. Detroit, Michigan 1950* p. 16–0.

265. Leeper, R. W., Summers, L., and Gilman, H., *Chem. Revs.* **54**, 101 (1954).

266. Lesbre, M., and Satgé, J., *Compt. rend. acad. sci.* **250**, 2220 (1960).

267. Lewis, C. W., and Lewis, D. W., *J. Polymer Sci.* **36**, 325 (1959).

268. Lewis, D. W., *J. Org. Chem.* **23**, 1893 (1958).

268a. Lewis, D. W., *U. S. Patent* 2,982,757; *Chem. Abstr.* **55**, 19327 (1961).

269. Libbey-Owens-Ford Glass Co., *British Patent* 663,770; *Chem. Abstr.* **46**, 11228 (1952).

270. Lile, W. J., and Menzies, R. C., *J. Chem. Soc.* p. 617 (1950).

271. Ling, Y.-C., *K'o Hsüeh T'ung Pao No.* **3**, p. 89 (1959); *Chem. Abstr.* **54**, 20286 (1960).

272. Löwig, C., *Ann. Chem. Liebigs* **84**, 308 (1852).

273. Mack, G. P., and Parker, E., *U. S. Patent* 2,592,926; *Chem. Abstr.* **46**, 11767 (1952).

274. Mack, G. P., and Parker, E., *U. S. Patent* 2,628,211; *Chem. Abstr.* **47**, 5165 (1953).

275. Mack, G. P., and Parker, E., *U. S. Patent* 2,700,675; *Chem. Abstr.* **50**, 397 (1956).

276. Mack, G. P., and Parker, E., *U. S. Patent* 2,809,956; *Chem. Abstr.* **52**, 3863 (1958).

277. MacKenzie, C. A., and Rust, J. B., *U. S. Patent* 2,438,612; *Chem. Abstr.* **42**, 4795 (1948).

278. Maier, L., *Angew. Chem.* **71**, 161 (1959).

279. Maier, L., *Tetrahedron Letters No.* **6**, 1 (1959).

280. Manami, H., *J. Chem. Soc. Japan Ind. Chem. Sect.* **62**, 529 (1959).

281. Manami, H., and Nishizaki, S., *J. Chem. Soc. Japan Ind. Chem. Sect.* **61**, 1344 (1958).

282. Manami, H., and Nishizaki, S., *J. Chem. Soc. Japan Ind. Chem. Sect.* **62**, 1262 (1959).

283. Manami, H., and Nishizaki, S., *J. Chem. Soc. Japan Ind. Chem. Sect.* **62**, 1791 (1959).

284. Martin, G., *Ber. deut. chem. Ges.* **46**, 2442 (1913).

285. Martin, G., *Ber. deut. chem. Ges.* **46**, 3289 (1913).

286. Marvel, C. S., and Woolford, R. G., *J. Org. Chem.* **25**, 1641 (1960).

287. Mazerolles, P., *Bull. soc. chim. France* p. 856 (1960).

288. Mazerolles, P., *Compt. rend. acad. sci.* **251**, 2041 (1960).

289. Mazerolles, P., and Lesbre, M., *Compt. rend. acad. sci.* **248**, 2018 (1959).

290. Meals, R. N., and Lewis, F. M., "Silicones," pp. 96, 106, 119. Reinhold, New York, 1959.

291. Meen, R. H., and Gilman, H., *J. Org. Chem.* **22**, 564 (1957).

292. Merker, R. L., *U. S. Patent* 2,920,060; *Chem. Abstr.* **54**, 16386 (1960).

292a. Merker, R. L., *U. S. Patent* 2,956,044; *Chem. Abstr.* **55**, 6028 (1961).

292b. Merker, R. L., *U. S. Patent* 2,956,045; *Chem. Abstr.* **55**, 5552 (1961).

293. Merker, R. L., and Scott, M. J., *J. Am. Chem. Soc.* **81**, 975 (1959).

294. Metlesics, W., and Zeiss, H., *J. Am. Chem. Soc.* **82**, 3321 (1960).
295. Metlesics, W., and Zeiss, H., *J. Am. Chem. Soc.* **82**, 3324 (1960).
296. Midland Silicones Ltd., *British Patent* 749,938; *Chem. Abstr.* **51**, 2033 (1957).
297. Midland Silicones Ltd., *British Patent* 786,259; *Chem. Abstr.* **52**, 19236 (1958).
297a. Midland Silicones Ltd., *British Patent* 846,978; *Chem. Abstr.* **55**, 12922 (1961).
298. Mikulášová, D., and Hrivík, A., *Chem. zvesti* **11**, 641 (1957); *Chem. Abstr.* **52**, 9028 (1958).
299. Mikulášová, D., and Hrivík, A., *Chem. zvesti* **11**, 708 (1957); *Chem. Abstr.* **52**, 9950 (1958).
300. Mikulášová, D., Pavlinec, J., Šimek, I., and Hrivík, A., *Chem. zvesti* **13**, 228 (1959); *Chem. Abstr.* **53**, 21621 (1959).
301. Milligan, J. G., and Kraus, C. A., *J. Am. Chem. Soc.* **72**, 5297 (1950).
302. Mironov, V. F., and Petrov, A. D., *Izvest. Akad. Nauk S.S.S.R. Otdel. Khim. Nauk* p. 383 (1957); *Chem. Abstr.* **51**, 15457 (1957).
302a. Mironov., V. F., and Shchukovskaya, L. L., *Izvest. Akad. Nauk S.S.S.R. Otdel. Khim. Nauk* p. 760 (1960).
303. Mironov, V. F., Petrov, A. D., and Maksimova, N. G., *Izvest. Akad. Nauk S.S.S.R. Otdel. Khim. Nauk* p. 1954 (1959); *Chem. Abstr.* **54**, 9731 (1960).
304. Mironov, V. F., Egorov, Yu. P., and Petrov, A. D., *Izvest. Akad. Nauk S.S.S.R. Otdel. Khim. Nauk* p. 1400 (1959); *Chem. Abstr.* **54**, 1266 (1960).
305. Mironov, V. F., Dzhurinskaya, N. G., and Petrov, A. D., *Doklady Akad. Nauk S.S.S.R.* **131**, 98 (1960); *Chem. Abstr.* **54**, 11977 (1960).
306. Mixer, R. Y., and Bailey, D. L., *J. Polymer Sci.* **18**, 573 (1955).
307. Montecatini Società general per l'industria mineraria e chemica, *Italian Patent* 519,728; *Chem. Abstr.* **51**, 16001 (1957).
307a. Montecatini Società generale per l'industria mineraria e chimica, *French Patent* 1,217,343; *Chem. Zentr.* p. 8499 (1961).
307b. Montecatini Società generale per l'industria mineraria e chimica, *Italian Patent* 589,299; *Chem. Abstr.* **55**, 5034 (1961).
308. Montermoso, J. C., Andrews, T. M., and Marinelli, L. P., *Abstr. Papers Presented 133rd Meeting Am. Chem. Soc. San Francisco, Calif. 1958* p. 3R.
309. Montermoso, J. C., Andrews, T. M., and Marinelli, L. P., *J. Polymer Sci.* **32**, 523 (1958).
310. Montermoso, J. C., Andrews, T. M., Marinelli, L. P., and LaLiberte, B. R., *Proc. Intern. Rubber Conf. Washington, D. C. 1959*, p. 526.
311. Morgan, G. T., and Drew, H. D. K., *J. Chem. Soc.* **127**, 1760 (1925).
312. Müller, R., and Schnurrbusch, K., *Chem. Ber.* **91**, 1805 (1958).
313. Müller, R., and Seitz, G., *Chem. Ber.* **91**, 22 (1958).
313a. Murahashi, S., Nozakura, S., and Sumi, M., *Bull. Chem. Soc. Japan* **32**, 670 (1959).
313b. Murahashi, S., Nozakura, S., and Tadokoro, H., *Bull. Chem. Soc. Japan* **32**, 534 (1959).
313c. Nametkin, N. S., Topchiev, A. V., and Durgar'yan, S. G., *J. Polymer Sci.* **52**, 51 (1961).
313d. Nametkin, N. S., Topchiev, A. V., Durgar'yan, S. G., and Kuz'mina, N. A., *Zhur. Obshchei Khim.* **30**, 2594 (1960); *Chem. Abstr.* **55**, 14345 (1961).
313e. Nametkin, N. S., Topchiev, A. V., and Durgar'yan, S. G., *Mezhdunarod. Simpozium po Makromol. Khim. Doklady Moscow Sektsiya* 1, p. 152 (1960); *Chem. Abstr.* **55**, 7329 (1961).
314. Nametkin, N. S., Topchiev, A. V., Durgar'yan, S. G., and Tolchinskiǐ, I. M., *Vysokomolekulyarnye Soedineniya* **1**, 1739 (1959); *Chem. Abstr.* **54**, 14767 (1960).

315. Nametkin, N. S., Topchiev, A. V., and Machus, F. F., *Doklady Akad. Nauk S.S.S.R.* **96**, 1003 (1954); *Chem. Abstr.* **49**, 8791 (1955).
316. Nametkin, N. S., Topchiev, A. V., and Povarov, L. S., *Doklady Akad. Nauk S.S.S.R.* **99**, 403 (1954); *Chem. Abstr.* **49**, 15727 (1955).
317. Nametkin, N. S., Topchiev, A. V., and Povarov, L. S., *Doklady Akad. Nauk S.S.S.R.* **117**, 245 (1957); *Chem. Abstr.* **52**, 8943 (1958).
318. Nametkin, N. S., Topchiev, A. V., and Solovova, O. P., *Doklady Akad. Nauk S.S.S.R.* **93**, 285 (1953); *Chem. Abstr.* **48**, 12671 (1954).
319. Nametkin, N. S., Topchiev, A. V., and Zetkin, V. I., *Doklady Akad. Nauk S.S.S.R.* **93**, 1045 (1953); *Chem. Abstr.* **49**, 842 (1955).
320. Nametkin, N. S., Topchiev, A. V., and Zetkin, V. I., *Trudy Moskov. Neft. Inst. im. I. M. Gubkina No.* **13**, 152 (1953); *Chem. Abstr.* **50**, 9996 (1956).
321. Nasiak, L. D., and Post, H. W., *J. Org. Chem.* **24**, 492 (1959).
322. Natta, G., Mazzanti, G., Longi, P., and Bernardini, F., *J. Polymer Sci.* **31**, 181 (1958).
323. Natta, G., Mazzanti, G., Longi, P., and Bernardini, F., *Chim. e ind. (Milan)* **40**, 813 (1958); *Chem. Abstr.* **53**, 6673 (1959).
323a. Niebergall, H., *German Patent* 1,086,896; *Chem. Abstr.* **55**, 16016 (1961).
323b. Niebergall, H., *German Patent* 1,087,810; *Chem. Abstr.* **55**, 15998 (1961).
323c. Niebergall, H., *German Patent* 1,093,994; *Chem. Abstr.* **55**, 20503 (1961).
324. Noll, W., "Chemie und Technologie der Silicone," Chapts. 4 and 7. Verlag Chemie, Weinheim, 1960.
325. Noltes, J. G., Paper Presented at WADC Materials Laboratory Conference on High Temperature Polymer and Fluid Research, Dayton, Ohio, May 26–28, 1959.
326. Noltes, J. G., and Kerk, G. J. M. van der, "Functionally Substituted Organotin Compounds." Tin Research Institute, Greenford, Middlesex, England, 1958.
327. Noltes, J. G., and Kerk, G. J. M. van der, Technical Note No. 3, Contract No. AF 61(052)–218, United States Air Force, Air Research and Development Command, European Office, Brussels, Belgium, November 30, 1960.
327a. Noltes, J. G., and Kerk, G. J. M. van der, *Rec. trav. chim.* **80**, 623 (1961).
328. Noltes, J. G., Budding, H. A., and Kerk, G. J. M. van der, *Rec. trav. chim.* **79**, 408 (1960).
329. Noltes, J. G., Budding, H. A., and Kerk, G. J. M. van der, *Rec. trav. chim.* **79**, 1076 (1960).
330. Normant, H., "Advances in Organic Chemistry, Methods and Results," Vol. 2, Chapt. 1. Interscience New York, 1960.
331. N. V. de Bataafsche Petroleum Maatschappij, *Dutch Patent* 68,393; *Chem. Abstr.* **46**, 6436 (1952).
332. Oikawa, H., and Shiota, M., *Yûki Gôsei Kagaku Kyôkai Shi* **15**, 411 (1957); *Chem. Abstr.* **51**, 16284 (1957).
332a. Okawara, R., *Angew. Chem.* **73**, 683 (1961).
332b. Okawara, R., *Proc. Chem. Soc. (London)* p. 383 (1961).
332c. Okawara, R., White, D. G., Fujitani, K., and Sata, H., *J. Am. Chem. Soc.* **83**, 1342 (1961).
333. Orndorff, W. R., Tabern, D. L., and Dennis, L. M., *J. Am. Chem. Soc.* **49**, 2512 (1927).
334. Papetti, S., and Post, H. W., *J. Org. Chem.* **22**, 526 (1957).
335. Pars, H. G., Graham, W. A. G., Atkinson, E. R., and Morgan, C. R., *Chem. & Ind. (London)* p. 693 (1960).

336. Patnode, W. I., and Schiessler, R. W., *U. S. Patent* 2,381,000; *Chem. Abstr.* **39**, 4889 (1945).
337. Patnode, W. I., and Schiessler, R. W., *U. S. Patent* 2,381,002; *Chem. Abstr.* **39**, 4888 (1945).
338. Patnode, W., and Schmidt, F. C., *J. Am. Chem. Soc.* **67**, 2273 (1945).
339. Pearce, E. M., *J. Polymer Sci.* **40**, 273 (1959).
340. Petrov, A. A., and Zavgorodniĭ, V. S., *Zhur. Obshcheĭ Khim.* **30**, 1055 (1960).
341. Petrov, A. D., Chernyshev, E. A., and Tolstikova, N. G., *Doklady Akad. Nauk S.S.S.R.* **118**, 957 (1958); *Chem. Abstr.* **52**, 12787 (1958).
342. Petrov, A. D., and Chernysheva, T. I., *Doklady Akad. Nauk S.S.S.R.* **84**, 515 (1952); *Chem. Abstr.* **47**, 3288 (1953).
343. Petrov, A. D., and Chernysheva, T. I., *Doklady Akad. Nauk S.S.S.R.* **89**, 73 (1953); *Chem. Abstr.* **50**, 9361 (1956).
344. Petrov, A. D., Gverdtsiteli, I. M., and Cherkezishvili, K. I., *Doklady Akad. Nauk S.S.S.R.* **129**, 805 (1959); *Chem. Abstr.* **54**, 7533 (1960).
345. Petrov, A. D., and Mironov, V. F., *Izvest. Akad. Nauk S.S.S.R. Otdel. Khim. Nauk* p. 1491 (1957); *Chem. Abstr.* **52**, 7136 (1958).
346. Petrov, A. D., and Mironov, V. F., *Angew. Chem.* **73**, 59 (1961).
347. Petrov, A. D., Mironov, V. F., and Chernyshev, E. A., *Uspekhi Khim.* **26**, 292 (1957); *Chem. Abstr.* **51**, 11988 (1957).
348. Petrov, A. D., Mironov, V. F., and Dolgiĭ, I. E., *Izvest. Akad. Nauk S.S.S.R. Otdel. Khim. Nauk* p. 1146 (1956); *Chem. Abstr.* **51**, 4938 (1957).
349. Petrov, A. D., Mironov, V. F., and Dzhurinskaya, N. G., *Doklady Akad. Nauk S.S.S.R.* **128**, 302 (1959); *Chem. Abstr.* **54**, 7546 (1960).
350. Petrov, A. D., Polyakova, A. M., Sakharova, A. A., Korshak, V. V., Mironov, V. F., and Nikishin, G. I., *Doklady Akad. Nauk S.S.S.R.* **99**, 785 (1954); *Chem. Abstr.* **49**, 15727 (1955).
351. Petrov, A. D., and Ponomarenko, V. A., *Doklady Akad. Nauk S.S.S.R.* **90**, 387 (1953); *Chem. Abstr.* **48**, 5080 (1954).
352. Petrov, A. D., and Sadykh-Zade, S. I., *Doklady Akad. Nauk S.S.S.R.* **85**, 1297 (1952); *Chem. Abstr.* **47**, 4281 (1953).
353. Petrov, A. D., Sadykh-Zade, S. I., Chernyshev, E. A., and Mironov, V. F., *Zhur. Obshcheĭ Khim.* **26**, 1248 (1956); *Chem. Abstr.* **50**, 14516 (1956).
354. Petrov, A. D., Sadykh-Zade, S. I., and Egorov, Yu. P., *Izvest. Akad. Nauk S.S.S.R. Otdel. Khim. Nauk* p. 722 (1954); *Chem. Abstr.* **49**, 10835 (1955).
355. Petrov, A. D., Sadykh-Zade, S. I., Ponomarenko, V. A., Sokolov, B. A., and Egorov, Yu. P., *Zhur. Obshcheĭ Khim.* **27**, 2479 (1957); *Chem. Abstr.* **52**, 7135 (1958).
356. Petrov, A. D., Sadykh-Zade, S. I., and Tsetlin, I. L., *Doklady Akad. Nauk S.S.S.R.* **107**, 99 (1956); *Chem. Abstr.* **50**, 13728 (1956).
357. Petrov, A. D., and Vdovin, V. M., *Izvest. Akad. Nauk S.S.S.R. Otdel. Khim. Nauk* p. 939 (1959); *Chem. Abstr.* **54**, 265 (1960).
357a. Petrov, A. D., Chernyshev, E. A., and Krasnova, T. L., *Doklady Akad. Nauk S.S.S.R.* **140**, 837 (1961).
357b. Piękoś, R., and Radecki, A., *Z. anorg. u. allgem. Chem.* **309**, 258 (1961).
358. Pike, R. M., *J. Polymer Sci.* **40**, 577 (1959).
359. Pike, R. M., and Bailey, D. L., *J. Polymer Sci.* **22**, 55 (1956).
360. Pitzer, K. S., *J. Am. Chem. Soc.* **70**, 2140 (1948).
361. Polyakova, A. M., and Chumaevskiĭ, N. A., *Doklady Akad. Nauk S.S.S.R.* **130**, 1037 (1960); *Chem. Abstr.* **54**, 11977 (1960).

362. Polyakova, A. M., Korshak, V. V., Sakharova, A. A., Petrov, A. D., Mironov, V. F., and Nikishin, G. I., *Izvest. Akad. Nauk S.S.S.R. Otdel. Khim. Nauk* p. 979 (1956); *Chem. Abstr.* **51**, 4979 (1957).

363. Polyakova, A. M., Korshak, V. V., Suchkova, M. D., Vdovin, V. M., and Chumaevskiĭ, N. A., *Vysokomolekulyarnye Soedineniya* **2**, 1360 (1960).

364. Post, H. W., "Silicones and Other Organic Silicon Compounds," Chap. 3. Reinhold, New York, 1949.

365. Post, H. W., and Daniels, B. F., *J. Org. Chem.* **22**, 748 (1957).

366. Pyle, J. J., *U. S. Patent* 2,448,391; *Chem. Abstr.* **43**, 1223 (1949).

367. Quattlebaum, W. M., Jr., and Noffsinger, C. A., *U. S. Patent* 2,307,157; *Chem. Abstr.* **37**, 3533 (1943).

368. Ramsden, H. E., *U. S. Patent* 2,744,876; *Chem. Abstr.* **51**, 459 (1957).

369. Ramsden, H. E., *U. S. Patent* 2,904,569; *Chem. Abstr.* **54**, 2175 (1960).

370. Ramsden, H. E., *U. S. Patent* 2,904,570; *Chem. Abstr.* **54**, 2175 (1960).

371. Ramsden, H. E., *British Patent* 824,944; *Chem. Abstr.* **54**, 17238 (1960).

372. Ramsden, H. E., and Banks, C. K., *U. S. Patent* 2,789,994; *Chem. Abstr.* **51**, 14786 (1957).

372a. Razuvaev, G. A., Shchepetkova, O. A., and Vyazankin, N. S., *Zhur. Obshchei Khim.* **31**, 1401 (1961); *Chem. Abstr.* **55**, 23321 (1961).

372b. Razuvaev, G. A., Vyazankin, N. S., and Dergunov, Yu. I., *Doklady Akad. Nauk S.S.S.R.* **132**, 364 (1960); *Chem. Abstr.* **54**, 20937 (1960).

372c. Razuvaev, G. A., Vyazankin, N. S., and Dergunov, Yu. I., *Zhur. Obshchei Khim.* **30**, 1310 (1960).

372d. Reichle, W. T., *J. Polymer Sci.* **49**, 521 (1961).

372e. Reikhsfeld, V. O., and Bondarenko, A. I., *Vysokomolekulyarnye Soedineniya* **3**, 1487 (1961).

373. Restaino, A. J., *Nucleonics* **15**(9), 189 (1957).

374. Roberts, J. D., and Dev, S., *J. Am. Chem. Soc.* **73**, 1879 (1951).

375. Rochow, E. G., *U. S. Patent* 2,352,974; *Chem. Abstr.* **39**, 225 (1945).

376. Rochow, E. G., *J. Am. Chem. Soc.* **70**, 1801 (1948).

377. Rochow, E. G., *U. S. Patent* 2,538,657; *Chem. Abstr.* **45**, 4485 (1951).

378. Rochow, E. G., "An Introduction to the Chemistry of the Silicones," 2nd ed., Chapt. 5. Wiley, New York, 1951.

379. Rochow, E. G., and Allred, A. L., *J. Am. Chem. Soc.* **77**, 4489 (1955).

380. Roedel, G. F., *U. S. Patent* 2,420,911; *Chem. Abstr.* **41**, 4965 (1947).

381. Rybakova, N. A., Taĭkova, N. K., and Zil'berman, E. N., *Trudy Khim. i Khim. Tekhnol.* **2**, 183 (1959); *Chem. Abstr.* **54**, 10838 (1960).

382. Sadykh-Zade, S. I., Chernyshev, E. A., and Mironov, V. F., *Doklady Akad. Nauk S.S.S.R.* **105**, 496 (1955); *Chem. Abstr.* **50**, 11233 (1956).

383. Sanin, P. S., *Zhur. Obshchei Khim.* **23**, 986 (1953); *Chem. Abstr.* **48**, 8765 (1954).

383a. Satgé, J., *Ann. chim. (Paris)* [13] **6**, 519 (1961).

384. Sauer, R. O., *U. S. Patent* 2,491,833; *Chem. Abstr.* **44**, 2547 (1950).

385. Sauer, R. O., and Hadsell, E. M., *J. Am. Chem. Soc.* **70**, 3590 (1948).

386. Schmeisser, M., and Schwarzmann, M., *Z. Naturforsch.* **11b**, 278 (1956).

386a. Schmidbaur, H., and Schmidt, M., *Angew. Chem.* **73**, 655 (1961).

386b. Schmidbaur, H., and Schmidt, M., *Chem. Ber.* **94**, 1138 (1961).

386c. Schmidbaur, H., and Schmidt, M., *Chem. Ber.* **94**, 1349 (1961).

386d. Schmidbaur, H., and Schmidt, M., *Chem. Ber.* **94**, 2137 (1961).

386e. Schmidbaur, H., and Schmidt, M., *J. Am. Chem. Soc.* **83**, 2963 (1961).

386f. Schmidt, M., and Ruidisch, I., *Angew. Chem.* **73**, 408 (1961).

386g. Schmidt, M., Ruidisch, I., and Schmidbaur, H., *Chem. Ber.* **94**, 2451 (1961).

386h. Schmidt, M., Schmidbaur, H., and Ruidisch, I., *Angew. Chem.* **73**, 408 (1961).

387. Schumb, W. C., and Saffer, C. M., Jr., *J. Am. Chem. Soc.* **61**, 363 (1939).

388. Schwarz, R., and Lewinsohn, M., *Ber. deut. chem. Ges.* **64**, 2352 (1931).

389. Schwarz, R., and Schmeisser, M., *Ber. deut. chem. Ges.* **69**, 579 (1936).

390. Segal, C. L., and Rust, J. B., *Abstr. Papers Presented 137th Meeting Am. Chem. Soc. Cleveland, Ohio 1960* p. 37–M.

391. Senear, A. E., Wirth, J., and Neville, R. G., *J. Org. Chem.* **25**, 807 (1960).

392. Seyferth, D., *J. Am. Chem. Soc.* **79**, 2738 (1957).

393. Seyferth, D., *J. Am. Chem. Soc.* **79**, 5881 (1957).

394. Seyferth, D., *J. Org. Chem.* **22**, 1252 (1957).

394a. Seyferth, D., *U. S. Patent* 2,964,550; *Chem. Abstr.* **55**, 6439 (1961).

394b. Seyferth, D., and Freyer, W., *J. Org. Chem.* **26**, 2604 (1961).

395. Seyferth, D., and Rochow, E. G., *J. Org. Chem.* **20**, 250 (1955).

396. Seyferth, D., and Rochow, E. G., *J. Polymer Sci.* **18**, 543 (1955).

396a. Seyferth, D., Raab, G., and Grim, S. O., *J. Org. Chem.* **26**, 3034 (1961).

397. Shchukovskaya, L. L., Petrov, A. D., and Egorov, Yu. P., *Zhur. Obshcheĭ Khim.* **26**, 3338 (1956); *Chem. Abstr.* **51**, 9474 (1957).

398. Shearer, N. H., Jr., and Coover, H. W., *U. S. Patent* 2,925,409; *Chem. Abstr.* **54**, 13732 (1960).

399. Shiina, K., and Kumada, M., *J. Org. Chem.* **23**, 139 (1958).

400. Shikhiev, I. A., Shostakovskiĭ, M. F., and Kayutenko, L. A., *Doklady Akad. Nauk Azerbaĭdzhan. S.S.R.* **14**, 687 (1958); *Chem. Abstr.* **53**, 6993 (1959).

400a. Shin-Etsu Chemical Industry Co., Ltd., *Japanese Patent* 13,245 (1960); *Chem. Abstr.* **55**, 11301 (1961).

400b. Shostakovskiĭ, M. F., Kalinina, S. P., Kotrelev, V. N., Kochkin, D. A., Kuznetsova, G. I., Laĭne, L. V., Borisova, A. I., and Borisenko, V. V., *J. Polymer Sci.* **52**, 223 (1961).

400c. Shostakovskiĭ, M. F., Khomutov, A. M., Baikova, R. I., and Kayutenko, L. A., *Izvest. Akad. Nauk S.S.S.R. Otdel. Khim. Nauk* p. 488 (1961).

400d. Shostakovskiĭ, M. F., Kotrelev, V. N., Kalinina, S. P., Kuznetsova, G. I., Laĭne, L. V., and Borisova, A. I., *Vysokomolekulyarnye Soedineniya* **3**, 1128, 1131 (1961).

401. Shostakovskiĭ, M. F., Kalinina, S. P., Kotrelev, V. N., Kochkin, D. A., Kuznetsova, G. I., Laĭne, L. V., Borisova, A. Ch., and Borisenko, V. V., *Angew. Chem.* **72**, 711 (1960).

402. Shostakovskiĭ, M. F., Kochkin, D. A., Neterman, V. A., and Sidel'kovskaya, F. P., *Zhur. Obshcheĭ Khim.* **28**, 2710 (1958); *Chem. Abstr.* **53**, 9037 (1959).

403. Shostakovskiĭ, M. F., Kochkin, D. A., and Vinogradov, V. L., *Uspekhi Khim.* **27**, 1221 (1958); *Chem. Abstr.* **53**, 5121 (1959).

404. Shostakovskiĭ, M. F., Kotrelev, V. N., Kochkin, D. A., Kuznetsova, G. I., Kalinina, S. P., and Borisenko, V. V., *Zhur. Priklad. Khim.* **31**, 1434 (1958); *Chem. Abstr.* **53**, 3040 (1959).

405. Šimek, I., *Chem. zvesti* **14**, 388 (1960).

406. Simons, J. K., Wagner, E. C., and Müller, J. H., *J. Am. Chem. Soc.* **55**, 3705 (1933).

407. Smith, F. B., and Kraus, C. A., *J. Am. Chem. Soc.* **74**, 1418 (1952).

408. Smith, H. V., "The Development of the Organotin Stabilizers." Tin Research Institute, Greenford, Middlesex, England, 1959.

409. Smith, T. A., and Kipping, F. S., *J. Chem. Soc.* **103**, 2034 (1913).

409a. Sobolevskiĭ, M. V., Belyakova, Z. V., Pomerantseva, M. G., and Golubtsov, S. A., *U.S.S.R. Patent* 132,637; *Chem. Abstr.* **55**, 8930 (1961).

410. Société anon. des manufactures des glaces et produits chimiques de Saint-gobain, Chauny & Cirey, *British Patent* 773,434; *Chem. Abstr.* **52,** 1686 (1958).

411. Société anon. des manufactures des glaces et produits chimiques de Saint-Gobain, Chauny & Cirey, *British Patent* 775,242; *Chem. Abstr.* **52,** 6398 (1958).

412. Société anon. des manufactures des glaces et produits chimiques de Saint-Gobain, Chauny & Cirey, *Dutch Patent* 91,801; *Chem. Zentr.* p. 5991 (1960).

413. Société des usines chimiques Rhône-Poulenc, *French Patent* 1,166,281; *Chem. Zentr.* p. 13209 (1960).

414. Solerio, A., *Gazz. chim. ital.* **81,** 664 (1951).

415. Sommer, L. H., *U. S. Patent* 2,507,551; *Chem. Abstr.* **45,** 790 (1951).

416. Sommer, L. H., *U. S. Patent* 2,512,390; *Chem. Abstr.* **44,** 8698 (1950).

417. Sommer, L. H., *British Patent* 668,234; *Chem. Abstr.* **47,** 2766 (1953).

418. Sommer, L. H., and Ansul, G. R., *J. Am. Chem. Soc.* **77,** 2482 (1955).

419. Sommer, L. H., Bailey, D. L., Goldberg, G. M., Buck, C. E., Bye, T. S., Evans, F. J., and Whitmore, F. C., *J. Am. Chem. Soc.* **76,** 1613 (1954).

420. Sommer, L. H., Goldberg, G. M., Gold, J., and Whitmore, F. C., *J. Am. Chem. Soc.* **69,** 980 (1947).

421. Sommer, L. H., Mitch, F. A., and Goldberg, G. M., *J. Am. Chem. Soc.* **71,** 2746 (1949).

422. Sommer, L. H., Murch, R. M., and Mitch, F. A., *J. Am. Chem. Soc.* **76,** 1619 (1954).

423. Sommer, L. H., Tyler, L. J., and Whitmore, F. C., *J. Am. Chem. Soc.* **70,** 2872 (1948).

424. Spialter, L., and Harris, C. W., *Abstr. Papers Presented 126th Meeting Am. Chem. Soc. N. Y. 1954* p. 86–0.

424a. Stavitskiǐ, I. K., and Svetozarova, V. M., *Kauchuk i Rezina* **19**(5), 6 (1960); *Chem. Abstr.* **55,** 18157 (1961).

425. Stavitskiǐ, I. K., Borisov, S. N., Ponomarenko, V. A., Sviridova, N. G., and Zueva, G. Ya., *Vysokomolekulyarnye Soedineniya* **1,** 1502 (1959); *Chem. Abstr.* **54,** 14106 (1960).

426. Steele, A. R., and Kipping, F. S., *J. Chem. Soc.* p. 2545 (1929).

427. Sveda, M., *U. S. Patent* 2,561,429; *Chem. Abstr.* **46,** 1814 (1952).

428. Swiss, J., and Arntzen, C. E., *U. S. Patent* 2,595,727; *Chem. Abstr.* **46,** 7362 (1952).

429. Swiss, J., and Arntzen, C. E., *U. S. Patent* 2,595,728; *Chem. Abstr.* **46,** 7820 (1952).

430. Swiss, J., and Arntzen, C. E., *U. S. Patent* 2,595,729; *Chem. Abstr.* **46,** 7821 (1952).

431. Swiss, J., and Arntzen, C. E., *U. S. Patent* 2,595,730; *Chem. Abstr.* **46,** 7821 (1952).

432. Tatlock, W. S., and Rochow, E. G., *J. Org. Chem.* **17,** 1555 (1952).

433. Tchakirian, A., *Ann. chim. (Paris)* **12,** 415 (1939).

434. Tchakirian, A., and Lewinsohn, M., *Compt. rend. acad. sci.* **201,** 835 (1935).

435. Thompson, B. R., *J. Polymer Sci.* **19,** 373 (1956).

436. Thompson, R. A., and Kipping, F. S., *J. Chem. Soc.* p. 1176 (1929).

437. Topchiev, A. V., Nametkin, N. S., and Durgar'yan, S. G., *Doklady Akad. Nauk S.S.S.R.* **130,** 105 (1960); *Chem. Abstr.* **54,** 10833 (1960).

438. Topchiev, A. V., Nametkin, N. S., and Durgar'yan, S. G., *Zhur. Obshcheǐ Khim.* **30,** 927 (1960); *Chem. Abstr.* **55,** 430 (1961).

439. Topchiev, A. V., Nametkin, N. S., Durgar'yan, S. G., and Dyankov, S. S., *Khim. i Prakt. Primenenie Kremneorg. Soedineniǐ Trudy Konf., Leningrad No.* **2,** 118 (1958); *Chem. Abstr.* **53,** 8686 (1959).

440. Topchiev, A. V., Nametkin, N. S., and Machus, F. F., *Doklady Akad. Nauk S.S.S.R.* **116,** 248 (1957); *Chem. Abstr.* **52,** 6162 (1958).

441. Topchiev, A. V., Nametkin, N. S., and Povarov, L. S., *Doklady Akad. Nauk S.S.S.R.* **97,** 99 (1954); *Chem. Abstr.* **49,** 8792 (1955).

442. Topchiev, A. V., Nametkin, N. S., and Povarov, L. S., *Doklady Akad. Nauk S.S.S.R.* **109,** 332 (1956); *Chem. Abstr.* **51,** 1826 (1957).

443. Topchiev, A. V., Nametkin, N. S., and Shcherbakova, A. A., *Doklady Akad. Nauk S.S.S.R.* **86,** 559 (1952); *Chem. Abstr.* **47,** 12223 (1953).

444. Topchiev, A. V., Nametkin, N. S., and Zetkin, V. I., *Doklady Akad. Nauk S.S.S.R.* **82,** 927 (1952); *Chem. Abstr.* **47,** 4281 (1953).

445. Topchiev, A. V., Nametkin, N. S., and Zetkin, V. I., *Doklady Akad. Nauk S.S.S.R.* **82,** 981 (1952); *Chem. Abstr.* **47,** 3228 (1953).

446. Trautman, C. E., and Ambrose, H. A., *U. S. Patent* 2,416,360; *Chem. Abstr.* **42,** 2760 (1948).

447. Tyran, L. W., *U. S. Patent* 2,532,583; *Chem. Abstr.* **45,** 2264 (1951).

448. Ushakov, S. N., and Itenberg, A. M., *Zhur. Obshcheĭ Khim.* **7,** 2495 (1937); *Chem. Abstr.* **32,** 2083 (1938).

448a. Vanderbilt, B. M., and Simko, J. P., Jr., *Modern Plastics* **38**(4), 135 (1960).

449. Vdovin, V. M., and Petrov, A. D., *Zhur. Obshcheĭ Khim.* **30,** 838 (1960); *Chem. Abstr.* **55,** 356 (1961).

449a. Vdovin, V. M., and Pushchevaya, K. S., *U.S.S.R. Patent* 135,314; *Chem. Abstr.* **55,** 23344 (1961).

449b. Vdovin, V. M., Pushchevaya, K. S., Belikova, N. A., Sultanov, R., Plate, A. F., and Petrov, A. D., *Doklady Akad. Nauk S.S.S.R.* **136,** 96 (1961).

449c. Vdovin, V. M., Pushchevaya, K. S., and Petrov, A. D., *Izvest. Akad. Nauk S.S.S.R. Otdel. Khim. Nauk* p. 281 (1961); *Chem. Abstr.* **55,** 19763 (1961).

450. Wagner, G. H., *U. S. Patent* 2,632,013; *Chem. Abstr.* **48,** 2760 (1954).

451. Wagner, G. H., *U. S. Patent* 2,637,738; *Chem. Abstr.* **48,** 8254 (1954).

452. Wagner, G. H., Bailey, D. L., Pines, A. N., Dunham, M. L., and McIntire, D. B., *Ind. Eng. Chem.* **45,** 367 (1953).

453. Weinberg, E. L., *U. S. Patent* 2,715,111; *Chem. Abstr.* **49,** 16521 (1955).

454. Weiss, E., *Z. anorg. u. allgem. Chem.* **287,** 236 (1956).

455. West, R., *J. Am. Chem. Soc.* **74,** 4364 (1952).

456. West, R., and Rochow, E. G., *J. Org. Chem.* **18,** 1739 (1953).

457. Westinghouse Electric International Co., *British Patent* 624,361; *Chem. Abstr.* **44,** 2287 (1950).

458. Westinghouse Electric International Co., *British Patent* 624,362; *Chem. Abstr.* **44,** 2287 (1950).

459. Westinghouse Electric International Co., *British Patent* 624,363; *Chem. Abstr.* **44,** 2287 (1950).

460. Westinghouse Electric International Co., *British Patent* 624,364; *Chem. Abstr.* **44,** 2287 (1950).

461. White, D. G., and Rochow, E. G., *J. Am. Chem. Soc.* **76,** 3897 (1954).

462. Wiberg, E., and Simmler, W., *Angew. Chem.* **69,** 98 (1957).

463. Wiczer, S. B., *U. S. Patent* 2,447,926; *Chem. Abstr.* **42,** 7975 (1948).

464. Wilson, G. R., Paper Presented at WADC Materials Laboratory Conference on High Temperature Polymer and Fluid Research, Dayton, Ohio, May 26–28, 1959.

465. Wilson, G. R., and Hutzel, G. M., *J. Org. Chem.* **24,** 1791 (1959).

466. Wilson, G. R., Hutzel, G. M., and Smith, A. G., *J. Org. Chem.* **24,** 381 (1959).

466a. Wilson, G. R., and Smith, A. G., *J. Org. Chem.* **26,** 557 (1961).

467. Winkler, H. J. S., and Gilman, H., *J. Org. Chem.* **27,** 254 (1962).

468. Winkler, H. J. S., and Gilman, H., *J. Org. Chem.* in press.

469. Winkler, H. J. S., and Gilman, H., unpublished studies.
470. Winkler, H. J. S., and Gilman, H., *J. Org. Chem.* **26**, 1265 (1961).
471. Winkler, H. J. S., Jarvie, A. W. P., Peterson, D. J., and Gilman, H., *J. Am. Chem. Soc.* **83**, 4089 (1961).
472. Winslow, F. H., *U. S. Patent* 2,642,415; *Chem. Abstr.* **47**, 9058 (1953).
473. Wittenberg, D., George, M. V., and Gilman, H., *J. Am. Chem. Soc.* **81**, 4812 (1959).
474. Wittenberg, D., and Gilman, H., *Quart. Revs.* **13**, 116 (1959).
475. Yakovlev, B. I., *Zhur. Obshcheǐ Khim.* **19**, 1969 (1949); *Chem. Abstr.* **44**, 1016 (1950).
476. Yakubovich, A. Ya., Makarov, S. K., Ginsburg, V. A., Gavrilov, G. I., and Merkulova, E. N., *Doklady Akad. Nauk S.S.S.R.* **72**, 69 (1950); *Chem. Abstr.* **45**, 2856 (1951).
477. Zhivukhin, S. M., Barkova, M. V., and Losev, I. P., *Zhur. Obshcheǐ Khim.* **26**, 2247 (1956); *Chem. Abstr.* **51**, 4045 (1957).
478. Zhivukhin, S. M., and Sobolevskaya, L. V., *Trudy Moskov. Khim-Tekhnol. Inst. im. D. I. Mendeleeva No.* **25**, 94 (1957); *Chem. Abstr.* **52**, 14215 (1958).

—7—

Polymeric Metal Alkoxides, Organometalloxanes, and Organometalloxanosiloxanes

D. C. BRADLEY

Department of Chemistry, The University of Western Ontario, London, Ontario, Canada

TABLE OF CONTENTS

I. Introduction

This chapter is primarily concerned with polymers containing metal-oxygen bonds. In some respects it is appropriate to consider many of the metal oxides as giant covalent macromolecules containing metalloxane chains ·M·O·M·O·M·O crosslinked into a three-dimensional rigid structure. Some of the bonds will be coordinate bonds and the structure as a whole will be, so to speak, a coordination-condensation polymer. We shall be concerned not with metal oxides but with polymeric compounds containing metal-oxygen bonds together with organic groupings. The purpose of the organic groups is to reduce the functionality of the monomer units from which the polymer may be considered to be derived and thus to prevent the formation of a rigid three-dimensional lattice.

This concept is well illustrated by the nature of the silicone polymers. By attaching two alkyl groups to each silicon atom the siloxane polymerization is confined to the formation of chains as in (I).

$$\begin{array}{ccccc}
& R & & R & & R \\
& | & & | & & | \\
-& Si & -O- & Si & -O- & Si & -O- \\
& | & & | & & | \\
& R & & R & & R
\end{array}$$

(I)

The length of the chain can be controlled by the introduction of trialkylsilyloxy groups to act as chain stoppers while crosslinking may be achieved by introducing trifunctional groups.

$$\begin{array}{c}
\qquad\qquad O \\
\qquad\qquad \diagup \\
R-Si-O \\
\qquad\qquad \diagdown \\
\qquad\qquad O
\end{array}$$

By limiting the functionality of silicon in this manner the valuable silicone fluids and resins are obtained in contrast to the rigid three-dimensional structure of silicon dioxide, which is built up from SiO_4 tetrahedra.

Accordingly, it seems reasonable to suppose that by limiting the functionality of the metals it should be possible to produce metalloxane polymers with more useful thermomechanical properties than those exhibited by the metal oxides. In the metal alkoxides $M(OR)_x$ we have examples in which the functionality is so restricted that polymerization must involve metal-oxygen coordinate bonds alone and we shall see that this results in very low degrees of polymerization. In the polyorganometalloxanes the introduction of $M \cdot O \cdot M \cdot O \cdot M \cdot$ chains leads to the higher degrees of polymerization exhibited by the metal oxide alkoxides. In general the metal-oxygen bonds in metal alkoxy groups are rather labile and susceptible to hydrolysis; hence the metal oxide alkoxides are of limited use as polymers. However, the replacement of alkoxide groups by trialkyl silyl oxide groups appears to confer added stability and attempts have been made to produce polymers containing metalloxane chains with R_3SiO groups attached to the metal atoms. These compounds are called the polyorganosiloxanometalloxanes. Another approach, which has received considerable attention in recent years, is to break down the rigid structure of the mineral silicates by judicious introduction of organic groups. These compounds are generally referred to as polyorganometalloxanosiloxanes since they contain chains involving metal, oxygen, and silicon atoms as in $M \cdot O \cdot Si \cdot O \cdot Si \cdot O \cdot M \cdot O \cdot Si \cdot O \cdot$, etc. Another way of considering these compounds is to think of them as modifications of the silicone polymers by the introduction of metal atoms into the siloxane chains. It is evident that polymers involving other nonmetals or metalloids in the metalloxane chain are feasible; in this context recent work on the polyorganometalloxanophosphonanes (containing $M \cdot O \cdot P \cdot O \cdot M \cdot O$ chains) will also be mentioned.

II. Polymeric Metal Alkoxides

A. General Considerations

A striking contrast between the aliphatic orthoesters [e.g., $B(OR)_3$, $C(OR)_4$, $Si(OR)_4$] and the metal alkoxides $M(OR)_x$ is caused by the fact that the orthoesters are simple monomeric compounds, whereas the lower aliphatic alkoxides of the metals are polymeric. The polymeric nature of the metal alkoxides is believed to be due to intermolecular coordination between the metal and the oxygen of a neighboring alkoxide group (II). By this means the metal is able to increase its coordination number. The chemistry of boron suggests that this element will also increase its covalency to four but by intramolecular coordination involving overlap of the p_π electrons of the oxygen with the vacant p_π orbital of the boron (III).

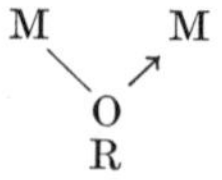

(II) 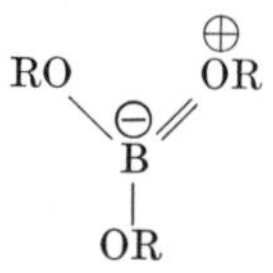 (III)

Similarly it is probable that the orthosilicate esters are stabilized by π electron drift from oxygen to silicon. Accordingly it follows that the polymeric nature of metal alkoxides arises from the preference of the metal to expand its coordination number by σ bonding. Such compounds are in fact coordination polymers $[M(OR)_x]_n$ and it is of interest to inquire whether there is any relationship between the degree of polymerization n, the primary valency of the metal x, and the higher coordination number and stereochemistry of the metal. It is evident from (II) that an increase in coordination number by unity could suffice to cause the formation of an infinite linear polymer. In fact the data in Table I for the degrees of polymerization in boiling benzene show that most metal alkoxides form relatively low polymers. These values are of course number-average degrees of polymerization and the presence of nonintegral values suggests that in some cases more than one molecular species is present. Unfortunately, the subject is handicapped by a dearth of definitely known structures, although some valuable deductions have been made in recent years and there are signs of activity by X-ray crystallographers.

TABLE I

DEGREES OF POLYMERIZATION OF METAL NORMAL ALKOXIDES

Metal alkoxide	Degree of polymerization	Reference
TlOR	4	(48)
Al(OR)$_3$	4	(42)
Fe(OR)$_3$	3	(35)
Ti(OR)$_4$	2–3	(29)
Zr(OR)$_4$	3–4	(29)
Ce(OR)$_4$	4–5	(33)
Th(OR)$_4$	6–7	(33)
V^{IV}(OR)$_4$	2–3	(25)
Nb(OR)$_5$	2	(32)
Ta(OR)$_5$	2	(30)
U(OR)$_5$	2–3	(23)

B. Structural Aspects of Metal Alkoxides

One of the first structural predictions in this field was that made by Sidgwick and Sutton (48) for tetrameric thallous alkoxides (Fig. 1). Preliminary reports on the X-ray diffraction of thallous methoxide (39) are essentially in agreement with this structure. It seems probable that the orbitals used by oxygen and thallium are directed tetrahedrally (sp^3 hybrids) with the fourth orbital of each thallium occupied by a lone pair of electrons.

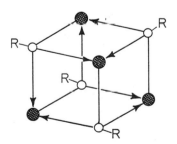

FIG. 1. Tetrameric thallous alkoxide.

KEY: Cross-hatched circle = Tl

Clear circle = oxygen in alkoxide

Robinson and Peak (*47*) suggested a structure for the aluminum alkoxides (Fig. 2) based on the tetrahedral coordination of the aluminum. However, it is not at all clear why a cyclic tetramer should be a preferred structure; an alternative possibility has been put forward (*21*) and this will be discussed later.

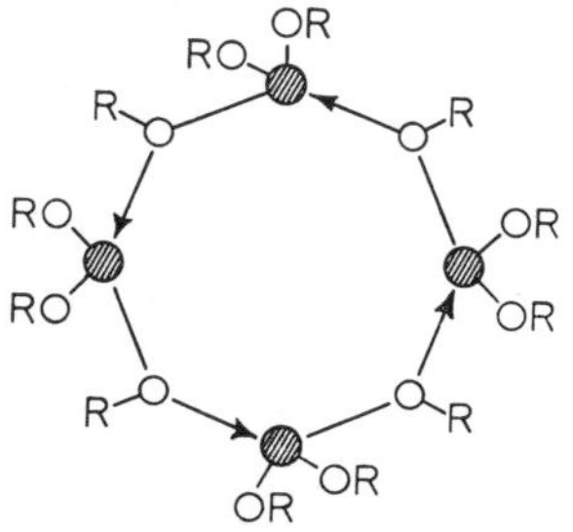

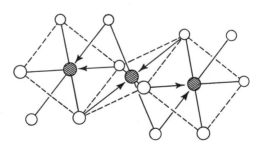

FIG. 2. Tetrameric aluminum alkoxide.

KEY: Striped circle = Al

Clear circle = O in alkoxide

In 1951, Caughlan and co-workers (*37*) reported on the cryoscopically determined molecular weights of $Ti(OEt)_4$, $Ti(OPr^n)_4$, $Ti(OBu^n)_4$, and $TiCl(OEt)_3$ in benzene. In each case the number-average degree of polymerization increased with increasing concentration and reached a maximum of trimeric at a mole fraction of about 0.01. It was therefore suggested that the trimeric unit $Ti_3(OR)_{12}$ was of structural significance and two possible structures were proposed (Fig. 3) based on the octahedral 6-coordination of titanium following the example of rutile (TiO_2). An interesting feature of the trimer unit for titanium tetraalkoxides is that it is the *smallest* possible polymer in which each titanium can achieve octahedral 6-coordination. This is a consequence of the fact that the maximum num-

FIG. 3. Trimeric titanium alkoxide.

KEY: Striped circle = Ti

Clear circle = O in alkoxide (R groups omitted)

TABLE II

PREDICTED MINIMUM DEGREES OF POLYMERIZATION

Metal alkoxide	Group valency of metal	Coordination no. of the metal	Stereochemistry of the metal	Min. degree of polymerization	Example
$M(OR)_6$	6	8	Cube or square antiprism	2	Possibly in $U_2(OMe)_{12}$
$M(OR)_5$	5	8	Cube or square antiprism	4	—
$M(OR)_5$	5	6	Octahedron	2	$Nb_2(OR)_{10}$, $Ta_2(OR)_{10}$, $U_2(OR)_{10}$
$M(OR)_4$	4	8	Cube	8	Possibly in $Th(OR)_4$
$M(OR)_4$	4	8	Square antiprism	8	—
$M(OR)_4$	4	6	Octahedron	3	$Ti(OR)_4$, $V(OR)_4$
$M(OR)_4$	4	6	Trigonal prism	2	—
$M(OR)_4$	4	5	Trigonal bipyramid	2	—
$M(OR)_3$	3	6	Octahedron	8	Possibly in $Al(OR)_3$
$M(OR)_3$	3	6	Trigonal prism	4	—
$M(OR)_3$	3	5	Trigonal bipyramid	3	—
$M(OR)_3$	3	5	Tetragonal pyramid	2	—
$M(OR)_3$	3	4	Tetrahedron	2	Possibly in $Al_2(OBu^t)_6$
$M(OR)_3$	3	4	Square plane	2	—
$M(OR)_2$	2	6	Octahedron	Infinite 3-dimensional polymer	—
$M(OR)_2$	2	6	Trigonal prism	Infinite linear polymer	—
$M(OR)_2$	2	5	Trigonal bipyramid	Infinite linear polymer	—
$M(OR)_2$	2	5	Tetragonal pyramid	Infinite linear polymer	—
$M(OR)_2$	2	4	Square plane	4	—
$M(OR)_2$	2	4	Tetrahedron	3	—
$M(OR)_2$	2	3	Trigonal plane	3	—
MOR	1	4	Tetrahedron	Infinite polymer	LiOMe
MOR	1	3	Trigonal pyramid or incomplete tetrahedron	4	$[TlOR]_4$
MOR	1	2	Trigonal plane	3	—

ber of bridging groups common to two octahedra is three, whereas to form a dimer with 6-coordinated titanium would require four common alkoxide groups shared between the two metal atoms. On the other hand, higher polymers could easily be formed by the sharing of edges of adjacent octahedra instead of faces. Thus the trimer is unique in being the smallest polymer for octahedrally 6-coordinated titanium in the tetraalkoxides. Another interesting feature of the trimer unit was its application to the problem of the low degrees of polymerization found for the titanium oxide ethoxides $[TiO_h(OEt)_{4-2h}]_n$. As we shall see later a rational explanation was given to the characteristic variation of number-average degree of polymerization as a function of degree of hydrolysis in terms of structures based on a trimeric repeating unit (*31*). Each of these structures also appeared to exemplify the smallest polymer consistent with octahedrally 6-coordinated titanium and it was accordingly proposed by Bradley (*20*) that the structures formed by the metal alkoxides in solution are determined by the principle of the minimum degree of polymerization. In other words, the metal alkoxide forms the smallest unit in which all of the metal atoms attain their maximum coordination number. With this restriction in mind and a knowledge of the stereochemical configuration of the metal in its state of maximum coordination, it is then possible to deduce the size of the polymer. In Table II are shown the predicted minimum degrees of polymerization for the metal alkoxides as a function of primary valency and maximum coordination number of the metal.

Inspection of Table II reveals the many gaps in our knowledge of the structures of metal alkoxides and points the way to further research. However, it is noteworthy that the dimeric pentaalkoxides (Fig. 4) of niobium, tantalum, and uranium(V) agree exactly with the requirements of the 6-coordinated metals. Moreover, the dimeric alcoholates of the Group IV metal isopropoxides $M_2(OPr^i)_8,(Pr^iOH)_2$, where M = Zr, Hf, Ce, or Sn, are structurally analogous with the $M_2(OR)_{10}$ compounds.

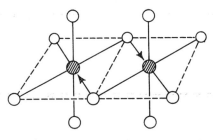

FIG. 4. Dimeric niobium, tantalum, or uranium alkoxide.
KEY: Striped circle = Nb(Ta)(U)
      Clear circle = O in alkoxide (R groups omitted)

The trimeric tetraalkoxides of titanium and vanadium(IV) also agree exactly with the theoretical requirements of the octahedrally 6-coordinated metals. A coordination maximum of six for titanium and vanadium is in keeping with the chemistry of these elements but for zirconium coordination numbers of seven and eight are also known. Similarly, with cerium(IV) and thorium a maximum coordination number of eight appears to be the rule. It is interesting to note that the data in Table I show a steady increase in the degree of polymerization of $M(OR)_4$ as M increases in size from Ti, Zr, Ce, to Th. In fact for thorium the values are near to the predicted octameric value for cubic 8-coordination, as shown in Fig. 5. The

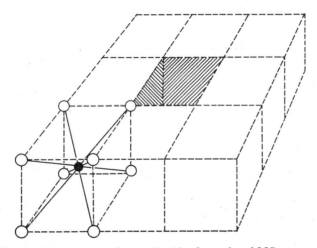

FIG. 5. Octameric metal tetraalkoxide. One cube of MO_8 exposed.

KEY: Black circle = M

       Clear circle = O in alkoxide (R groups omitted)

degrees of polymerization for zirconium alkoxides are a little higher than predicted for 6-coordinated zirconium but much too low for 8-coordination. The zirconium oxide alkoxides (see later) appear to favor 6-coordinated zirconium also. The behavior of cerium(IV) is rather interesting. Thus the alcoholate $Ce_2(OPr^i)_8(Pr^iOH)_2$ and the oxide isopropoxides suggest that cerium is 6-coordinated, whereas the normal alkoxides (Table I) have degrees of polymerization intermediate between the predicted values for 6- and 8-coordination. Of course it is feasible that the steric effect of the isopropoxide groups prevents the cerium from attaining 8-coordination but that some 8-coordination is attained in the normal alkoxides. It is conceivable that a pentamer is formed (Fig. 6) in which the central cerium is 8-coordinated (square antiprism) and the four outer ceriums are 6-coordinated.

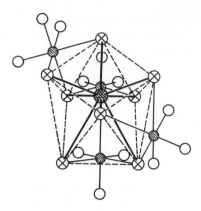

FIG. 6. Pentameric ceric alkoxide.

KEY: Cross-hatched circle = Ce in 8-coordination (square antiprism)
Striped circle = Ce in 6-coordination (octahedron)
Circle with × = Oxygens common to antiprism and octahedron
Clear circle = Oxygens in octahedra only
--- = Ce—O bonds in antiprism
— = Ce—O bond in octahedron

In the case of tervalent metals the theory predicts either dimers or octamers depending on whether the metal is 4-coordinated (tetrahedral) or 6-coordinated (octahedral). Unfortunately, from the predictive viewpoint these metals may be either 4- or 6-coordinated. However, it is possible

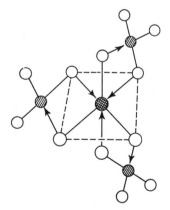

FIG. 7. Tetrameric aluminum alkoxide.
Cross-hatched circle = 6-coordinated (octahedral) Al
Striped circle = 4-coordinated (tetrahedral) Al
Clear circle = O in alkoxide (R groups omitted)

that steric effects may force the lower coordination in certain alkoxides and it is noteworthy that aluminum *tert*-butoxide is dimeric and the metal therein presumably 4-coordinated. Nevertheless, the aluminum normal alkoxides are tetrameric; this suggests that some 6-coordinated aluminum is present. There is the possibility that a tetramer could be formed as shown in Fig. 7 in which the central aluminum is octahedrally 6-coordinated and the other aluminums tetrahedrally 4-coordinated. Another unique structure is the hexamer shown in Fig. 8, in which one third of the aluminum is 6-coordinated (*21*).

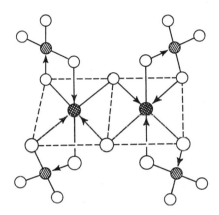

FIG. 8. Hexameric aluminum alkoxide.
KEY: Cross-hatched circle = 6-coordinated (octahedral) Al
Striped circle = 4-coordinated (tetrahedral) Al
Clear circle = O in alkoxide (R groups omitted)

There is very little information of structural significance available on the alkoxides of bivalent metals; of the Group II elements beryllium is the most likely to form covalent alkoxides. Recent work by Turova *et al.* (*50*) showed that beryllium ethoxide is insoluble and hence is probably highly polymeric.

Similarly there is not much information on alkoxides of univalent metals. The behavior of thallium, which has already been mentioned, is of special interest insofar as the structure may well be determined by the presence of the nonbonding valence electrons. Recently the structure of lithium methoxide was determined by Wheatley (*53*) by X-ray diffraction. An interesting layer structure is formed in which the lithium atoms are in approximately tetrahedral 4-coordination. A section through the two-dimensional infinite polymer is shown in Fig. 9. The theory predicts an infinite polymer for the alkoxide of a tetrahedrally 4-coordinated metal but it must be remembered that the lithium methoxide structure might be ionic.

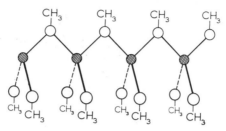

FIG. 9. Lithium methoxide (sectional structure).

KEY: Striped circle = Li

　　　 Clear circle = O in methoxide

While it is too early to judge the proposition of the minimum degree of polymerization for metal alkoxide polymers, it does appear to rationalize the known degrees of polymerization in terms of a fundamental structural theory. A point to be borne in mind is that the structures of metal alkoxides in solution in hydrocarbon solvents may well be different from structures in the crystalline state and it would not be surprising to find more highly polymeric structures in the solid state.

Martin and Winter (41a) have determined the variation of molecular weight with concentration for titanium tetrabutoxide in benzene by precise cryoscopic measurements. Their results not only confirmed the tendency toward trimerization as the limiting degree of polymerization but they also revealed that a monomer-trimer equilibrium occurred with a negligible concentration of dimeric species. These authors have also proposed an alternative structure for the trimeric titanium alkoxides based on 6-coordinated titanium with a trigonal prismatic configuration. This gives rise to a symmetrical cyclic molecule in which the three titanium atoms are in a trigonal plane.

C. Nature of the Intermolecular Bonds in Polymeric Metal Alkoxides

Since the polymeric metal alkoxides are bound together by means of intermolecular coordinate bonds it is of interest to consider the strength and nature of these intermolecular bonds.

Measurements on titanium and zirconium alkoxides showed that, in these compounds, the intermolecular bonds are rather weak. For example, Bradley et al. (29) deduced from vapor pressure determinations the entropies of vaporization at 5 mm pressure ($\Delta S_{5.0}$ cal/deg/mole) shown in

Table III. Since the *tert*-butoxide is monomeric it was assumed that the abnormally high values of $\Delta S_{5.0}$ for the ethoxide and isopropoxide were caused by the change in structure involved in the depolymerization of these alkoxides prior to vaporization. Vapor densities suggested that the ethoxide and isopropoxide were monomeric in the vapor under the conditions of the vapor pressure determinations.

TABLE III

VAPOR PRESSURE DATA ON ZIRCONIUM ALKOXIDES

Compound	$T_{5.0}$	ΔH_v	$\Delta S_{5.0}$
$Zr(OEt)_4$	234.8	30.2	59.4
$Zr(OPr^i)_4$	203.8	31.5	66.0
$Zr(OBu^t)_4$	89.1	15.2	42.0

It seemed reasonable, therefore, to assume that the latent heats of vaporization (ΔH_v, kcal/mole) of the polymeric alkoxides contained the energies of depolymerization and this in turn explained the high boiling points ($T_{5.0}$ = b.p. in °C under 5.0 mm pressure) of the polymers. By an extrapolation procedure based on the boiling points of the monomeric tertiary alkoxides, estimates were made of the hypothetical boiling points of "monomeric" zirconium ethoxide and isopropoxide. Then assuming that these "monomeric" species would have the same $\Delta S_{5.0}$ as the monomeric *tert* butoxide, estimates of the hypothetical latent heats of vaporization of "monomeric" ethoxide and isopropoxide $(\Delta H_v)_{mon.}$ were made. The energy of depolymerization, $\Delta E = \Delta H_v - (\Delta H_v)_{mon.}$, was thus obtained: $Zr(OEt)_4$, 17.6; $Zr(OPr^i)_4$, 17.7 kcal/mole. For $Ti(OEt)_4$ a value of 10 kcal/mole for ΔE was obtained. If the metal is entirely 6-coordinated in the polymers then the average energy per intermolecular bond will be $\Delta E/2$. Nesmeyanov *et al.* (*46*) estimated the activation energy of dissociation of polymeric titanium alkoxide from the variation of molecular weights in benzene with temperature over the range 10–35°C. The following values were obtained: $Ti(OEt)_4$, 8.0; $TiO(OEt)_2$, 8.1; $Ti(OPr^n)_4$, 7.7 kcal/mole. Another estimate of depolymerization energies for titanium alkoxides was obtained by Bradley *et al.* (*36*) from viscosity studies. The activation energies for viscous flow for the polymeric titanium alkoxides were much higher than for the monomeric alkoxides and it was concluded that viscous flow in the polymeric compounds involved prior depolymerization. The following values of the depolymerization energy were thus obtained: $Ti(OEt)_4$, 5.7; $Ti(OPr^n)_4$, 5.2; $Ti(OBu^n)_4$, 3.0 kcal/mole. Thus for titanium tetraethoxide we have the following estimates for ΔE: 10, 8.1, and 5.7

kcal/mole, and although the spread in values is rather wide, and this is not surprising in view of all the assumptions made, it is quite clear that ΔE is not very large.

A determination of the heat of depolymerization ΔE for titanium tetrabutoxide was also made by Martin and Winter (*41a*) by precise calorimetric measurements of the heat of solution of $Ti(OBu^n)_4$ in benzene as a function of concentration. A value of $\Delta E = 9.8$ kcal/mole was thus obtained leading to a value of 4.9 kcal for the energy per intermolecular bond. Their calorimetric results also provided a value (4×10^{-6}) for the equilibrium constant of the monomer-trimer system at 30°C which, applied with the value (1×10^{-4}) at 5.5°C obtained cryoscopically to the van't Hoff Reaction Isochore, yielded an independent value for $\Delta E \sim 8$ kcal/mole.

An intriguing feature of the polymeric metal alkoxides is the tendency of the metal to expand its coordination number by the polymerization process rather than by coordination with another ligand. Moreover, a common feature of all of the structures mentioned in the previous section is the presence of four-membered rings (IV) involving two metals

$$
\begin{array}{c}
\text{R} \\
\text{O} \\
\diagup \quad \diagdown \\
\text{M} \qquad \text{M} \\
\diagdown \quad \diagup \\
\text{O}
\end{array}
$$

(IV)

and two oxygens. Evidently the bridge structures have enhanced stability, which must presumably involve an entropy effect. Thus the coordination polymerization mechanism may be likened to chelation in that dissociation of the bridge (IV) requires the disruption of two coordinate bonds, whereas in a complex involving a ligand attached to the metal only one bond needs to be dissociated. In fact the tendency of metal alkoxides to form the minimum polymer consistent with all of the metal being in its highest coordination number may be a consequence of the stability of the four-membered bridges. For example, in a tetraalkoxide $M(OR)_4$ involving an octahedrally 6-coordinated metal M, the trimer (Fig. 3) is the smallest polymer because it involves the sharing of faces of octahedra. However, the metals could still achieve 6-coordination if the octahedra shared edges instead of faces, but an infinite linear polymer would result. Of course steric factors will be involved, and these would probably favor the infinite polymer structure, but the observed results suggest that the trimer is the favored structure. To detach a monomer unit from a trimer requires the dissociation of three intermolecular bonds between two metals, whereas the infinite polymer can be split by dissociating only two intermolecular bonds between two metals. We may rationalize the concept of the minimum degree of polymerization by suggesting that the alkoxide tends to adopt that polymeric structure which contains the maximum number of alkoxide bridges between adjacent metal atoms. In this manner the handicap of relatively weak intermolecular bonds (enthalpy effect) is offset by an entropy effect.

III. Polymeric Metal Oxide Alkoxides

Metal alkoxides are very readily hydrolyzed to the metal hydroxides or oxides. Nevertheless under carefully controlled conditions it is possible to isolate soluble polymeric intermediates called the metal oxide alkoxides.

Boyd (*19*) and Winter (*51*) studied the hydrolysis of titanium tetra-*n*-butoxide and concluded that linear polymers [$(BuO)_3Ti \cdot O \cdot Ti(OBu)_3$, $(BuO)_3Ti \cdot O[Ti(OBu)_2O \cdot]_xTi(OBu)_3$, etc.] were formed. It was observed by these authors that the titanium oxide butoxides were less readily hydrolyzed than the original tetrabutoxide. Cullinane and co-workers (*38*) also investigated the hydrolysis of titanium alkoxides and isolated solids corresponding in analysis to $TiO(OH)(OR)$. Minami and Ishino (*43*) carried out a detailed study on the hydrolysis of titanium tetrabutoxide. They found that the addition of water to butanolic solutions of $Ti(OBu)_4$ at various temperatures from 20–80°C caused a rapid change in viscosity at first; this was followed by a slow subsequent change until a steady value was finally reached in about 7 to 8 hr. These results were interpreted in terms of a rapid hydrolysis step: $Ti—OR + H_2O \rightarrow Ti—OH + ROH$, followed by a slower condensation: $Ti—OH + HO—Ti \rightarrow Ti \cdot O \cdot Ti + H_2O$. It was further suggested that an equilibrium is set up because of the reversibility of the hydrolysis step and that the equilibrium position is temperature dependent. Boyd (*19*) had previously shown that the hydrolysis of $Ti(OBu)_4$ is incomplete when the ratio of water molecules added per atom of titanium exceeded about 1.2. Minami and Ishino isolated some of the titanium oxide butoxides and carried out molecular weight determinations (cryoscopic in benzene). The following polymers were thus formulated on the basis of chemical analysis and the extrapolation of molecular weights to infinite dilution: $[Ti_2O(OBu)_6]_{1.5}$, $[TiO(OBu)_2]_{2.2}$, and $[TiO_{1.44}(OBu)_{1.22}(OH)_{0.07}]_7$. It is noteworthy that even the highly hydrolyzed compounds exhibited low degrees of polymerization and it seems unlikely that these could be linear polymers. The hydrolysis of titanium tetraethoxide was investigated by Nesmeyanov *et al.* (*45*), who discovered that the addition of 1 gm mole of water to 2 gm moles of Ti(OEt)$_4$ gave, not (EtO)$_3$TiOTi(OEt)$_3$, but instead the crystalline compound Ti$_3$O$_2$(OEt)$_8$, whose molecular weight was determined cryoscopically in benzene. Polymeric titanium oxide alkoxides were also produced by thermolysis of the titanium tetraalkoxides (*38, 45, 52*).

The interest in polymeric metal oxide alkoxides is twofold since they are potentially both condensation and coordination polymers. The condensation polymerization arises from the formation of M·O·M bridges following the hydrolysis of the metal alkoxide. In addition, there may be coordination polymerization involving either the alkoxide oxygen or the oxo oxygen or both. Moreover, the metal oxide alkoxides may be regarded as the intermediate stages in the transition from the three-dimensional macromolecular metal oxides to the relatively low polymeric metal alkoxides.

With this view in mind Bradley and co-workers have investigated the structural aspects of a number of metal oxide alkoxides. In their work on the hydrolysis of titanium ethoxide, Bradley and associates (*31*) were unaware of the results of Nesmeyanov *et al.* (*45*) and independently showed that a crystalline derivative was readily obtained in the early stages of the hydrolysis. While their analysis agreed with the empirical formula proposed by the Russian workers, their molecular weight determinations suggested that the compound is the hexamer Ti$_6$O$_4$(OEt)$_{16}$. In view of its degree of hydrolysis, this compound has a remarkably low degree of polymerization, but ebulliometric studies (*31*) revealed that all of the soluble titanium oxide ethoxides were characterized by low degrees of polymerization. However, these authors showed that the characteristic variation of number-average degree of polymerization n as a function of the degree of hydrolysis h [the ratio of H$_2$O:Ti(OEt)$_4$] could be explained in terms of a series of structural models for the titanium oxide ethoxides. The polymers were

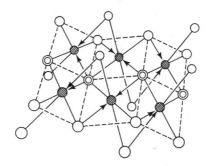

FIG. 10. Ti$_6$O$_4$(OEt)$_{16}$.

KEY: Striped circle = 6-coordinated (octahedral) Ti

Double circle = O in Ti·O·Ti bridges

Clear circle = O in ethoxide (Et groups omitted)

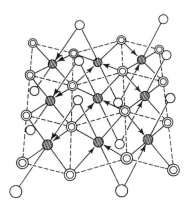

FIG. 11. [$Ti_3O_4(OEt)_4$].

KEY: Striped circle = 6-coordinated (octahedral) Ti
Double circle = O in Ti·O·Ti bridges
Clear circle = O in ethoxide (Et groups omitted)

imagined to be formed by a condensation process involving hydrolyzed trimer units based on the postulated structure (Fig. 3) for titanium tetraethoxide. It follows directly that the first structurally significant titanium oxide ethoxide is the hexamer, shown in Fig. 10, which has the same formula as the crystalline $Ti_6O_4(OEt)_{16}$. The next member of the polymer series would be $Ti_9O_8(OEt)_{20}$ and this would be succeeded by $Ti_{12}O_{12}(OEt)_{24}$. The compound of composition $TiO(OEt)_2$ was crystallized with difficulty from petroleum and its molecular weight was reasonably close to the requirements of $Ti_{12}O_{12}(OEt)_{24}$. The polymer series can be represented as $Ti_{3(x+1)}O_{4x}(OEt)_{4(x+3)}$, where $x = 0, 1, 2, 3, \cdots \infty$. Moreover, it is easily shown that, for such a system, the variation of n with h is, simply, $n = 12/(4 - 3h)$. According to the predictions of this expression, low values of n will occur in the early stages of hydrolysis but, as h approaches 1.33, there will be a very rapid rise in n. At $h = 1.33$ the infinite polymer $[Ti_3O_4(OEt)_4]_\infty$ (see Fig. 11) should be formed; it was significant that in the ebulliometric experiments a precipitate was eventually formed whose analysis was fairly near to that for the infinite polymer. Insoluble nonvolatile products of similar composition were also obtained by thermal disproportionation of other titanium oxide ethoxides. That is:

$$Ti_6O_4(OEt)_{16} \rightarrow [Ti_3O_4(OEt)_4]_\infty + 3Ti(OEt)_4 \uparrow$$

Inspection of the structures in Figs. 10 and 11 shows that these molecules are indeed condensation-coordination polymers and that the sharing of faces of octahedra is a common feature. Evidently the formation of low polymers by the titanium oxide ethoxides is controlled by the same fundamental processes that cause the metal alkoxides to form low polymers. In the ebulliometric studies of the hydrolysis of Ti(OEt)$_4$ in ethanol the agreement between theory and experiment was good for $h = 0$ to ~ 1.2, but for $h > 1.2$ the experimental values of n were significantly less than calculated. The discrepancies were most marked in the experiment involving the lowest initial concentration of titanium ethoxide. Thus it appeared that some alternative process must be competing with polymerization to allow the titanium to achieve 6-coordination. Solvation was proposed to explain this phenomenon since the original Ti(OEt)$_4$ was a little less than trimeric. A small proportion of the solvated dimer Ti$_2$(OEt)$_8$,(EtOH)$_2$ (Fig. 12) would explain the initial degree of polymerization of Ti(OEt)$_4$.

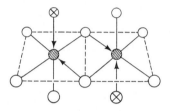

FIG. 12. Solvated dimer Ti$_2$(OEt)$_8$, (EtOH)$_2$.
KEY: Striped circle = 6-coordinated (octahedral) Ti
Clear circle = O in ethoxide group (Et group omitted)
Circle with $\times$ = O in ethanol molecule (Et and H omitted)

The solvated dimer could then be the building block from which a series of solvated titanium oxide ethoxides could be derived, as shown for example in Fig. 13. The general formula for this polymer series is Ti$_{2(x+1)}$O$_{3x}$

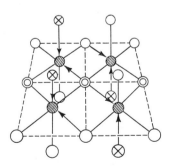

FIG. 13. Ti$_4$O$_3$(OEt)$_{10}$,(EtOH)$_4$.
KEY: Striped circle = 6-coordinated (octahedral) Ti
Double circle = Oxygen in Ti·O·Ti bridges
Clear circle = Oxygen in ethoxide (Et groups omitted)
Circle with $\times$ = Oxygen in ethanol (Et and H omitted).

$(OEt)_{2(x+4)}, (EtOH)_{2(x+1)}$ and the variation of n with h is $n = 6/(3 - 2h)$. For a given degree of hydrolysis it is evident that the solvated dimer series gives much smaller polymers than the trimer series, especially at $h > 1.0$. For example, at $h = 1.25$ the trimer series has $n = 48$ and the solvated dimer series has $n = 12$. Allowance for the solvated dimer present in the initial solution of $Ti(OEt)_4$ then gave improved agreement between theory and experiment on the assumption that the proportions of titanium in the trimer and solvated dimer series remains constant. Later work (*34*) showed that the same structural principles could be applied to other titanium oxide alkoxides. It was necessary to postulate a third polymer series this time based on a disolvated monomer $Ti(OR)_4, (ROH)_2$. Only two species were predicted, as shown in Fig. 14, and the general equation was: $n = 3/(3 - h)$.

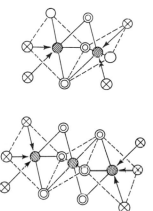

Fig. 14. $Ti_2O_3(OR)_2, (ROH)_4$ and $Ti_3O_6, (ROH)_6$.

KEY: Striped circle = 6-coordinated (octahedral) Ti
Double circle = Oxygen in Ti·O·Ti bridges
Clear circle = Oxygen in alkoxide (R groups omitted)
Circle with × = Oxygen in alcohol (R and H omitted).

Recently, Martin and Winter (*41a*, *41b*) have pointed out that the structures for the titanium oxide ethoxides proposed by Bradley *et al.* (*31*) are not unique and they have made some interesting suggestions for alternative structures based on the trigonal prism stereochemistry involving the cyclic trimer. These views have been criticized by Bradley and Westlake (*36a*) and it is generally agreed that direct structural measurements are needed to solve this problem.

Bradley and Carter (*22*) have studied the hydrolysis of zirconium alkoxides. In view of the fact that zirconium may attain a maximum coordination number of 8 it was not expected that the zirconium oxide alkoxides would show the same variation of degree of polymerization with degree of hydrolysis as found for the titanium compounds. However, it was found that the initial degree of polymerization of $Zr(OEt)_4$ was lower than for $Ti(OEt)_4$, suggesting that in the former a greater proportion of solvated dimer was present. In the early stages of hydrolysis the proportion of polymers based on the trimer rapidly increased until it became predominant. The reason for the odd behavior of $Zr(OEt)_4$ in boiling ethanol has not yet been explained but it may be that the system was not in true thermodynamic equilibrium and that the presence of zirconium oxide ethoxides catalyzed the approach to equilibrium. An insoluble product, which deposited when h reached 1.43, had a composition fairly near to that for the infinite polymer of the trimer system $[Zr_3O_4(OEt)_4]_\infty$. The behavior of some other zirconium oxide alkoxides was also interpreted in terms of the same polymer series as used to explain the variation of n with h for titanium oxide alkoxides. It was particularly interesting to find that the variation of n with h for zirconium oxide isopropoxides and zirconium oxide *sec*-butoxides was close to the requirements of the polymer series based on the solvated dimer. Both zirconium isopropoxide and zirconium *sec*-butoxide form solvated dimers $Zr_2(OR)_8,(ROH)_2$ and this constitutes authentic evidence for the solvation theory. From these results it appears that zirconium oxide alkoxides are condensation-coordination polymers based on octahedrally 6-coordinated zirconium. The hydrolysis products of zirconium *tert*-amyl oxide presented a special problem. Thus the tetra *tert*-amyl oxide is monomeric both in benzene and *tert*-amyl alcohol. The monomeric nature in benzene is undoubtedly due to the steric effect of the branched alkyl groups preventing close enough approach of neighboring molecules to form stable intermolecular bonds. Nevertheless, the steric effect might not prevent the approach of alcohol molecules to form the solvated monomer $Zr(OR)_4,(ROH)_2$, and so it is not known whether a 4-coordinated or 6-coordinated zirconium is originally present in *tert*-amyl alcohol. As hydrolysis proceeds and the *tert*-alkoxide groups are removed, the steric hindrance to polymerization will be relieved and there might be a transition from a polymer series involving less coordination polymerization to one involving more. The experimental results could indeed be interpreted in terms of a trend from the disolvated monomer series to the solvated dimer series. On the other hand, the results are in quite good agreement with a new polymer series based on the disolvated monomer $Zr(OR)_4,(ROH)_2$. The new polymer series involves octahedra sharing edges, as illustrated by the structure for $Zr_4O_6(OR)_8$ in Fig. 15, and the variation of n with h is given by: $n = 2/(2 - h)$. Recent work by Bradley and Holloway (*24*) has demonstrated that the structural theory for the

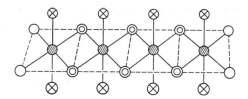

FIG. 15. $Zr_4O_6(OR)_4,(ROH)_8$.

KEY: Cross-hatched circle = 6-coordinated (octahedral) Zr
Double circle = Oxygen in $Zr \cdot O \cdot Zr$ bridges
Clear circle = Oxygen in alkoxide (R groups omitted)
Circle with $\times$ = Oxygen in alcohol (R and H omitted).

titanium and zirconium oxide alkoxides is of fundamental significance since it is applicable to other 6-coordinated metals in valence states other than four. Molecular weights in benzene of tantalum oxide ethoxides $TaO_h(OEt)_{5-2h}$ over the hydrolysis range $h = 0$ to 0.75 were in reasonable agreement with the requirements of the expression $n = 6/(3 - 2h)$. This is the equation calculated for a polymer series $Ta_{2(x+1)}O_{3x}(OR)_{2(2x+5)}$ based on the dimer $Ta_2(OR)_{10}$ (Fig. 4) and structurally analogous to the solvated dimer series $M_2(OR)_8,(ROH)_2$ (Figs. 12 and 13) postulated for quadrivalent metals. In boiling ethanol, tantalum pentaethoxide has a degree of polymerization of 1.85, which indicates that some solvated monomers $Ta(OEt)_5,EtOH$ must be present; ebulliometric experiments showed that the number-average degrees of polymerization of tantalum oxide ethoxides were a little lower than predicted by the equation for the polymer series based on the dimer. However, excellent agreement was obtained by assuming that 90% of the tantalum was present in the series based on the dimer and 10% was present in the polymer series $[n = 3/(3 - h)]$ based on the solvated monomer. The results were of sufficient accuracy to show that the alternative monomer series $[n = 2/(2 - h)]$ was not present in this system. Bradley and Holloway (24) have proposed a convenient nomenclature for describing the different polymer systems in terms of their fundamental structural characteristics. They noted that, in general, the variation of degree of polymerization with degree of hydrolysis could be arranged in the linear form:

$$n^{-1} = a - bh$$

where a and b are constants. For the polymer series $M_{3(x+1)}O_{4x}(OR)_{4(x+3)}$ based on the trimeric repeating unit, the characteristic equation is $n^{-1} = 0.333 - 0.25h$. For the series $M_{2(x+1)}O_{3x}(OR)_{2(x+4)},(ROH)_{2(x+1)}$, based on the dimer (solvated) repeating unit, the characteristic equation is $n^{-1} = $

$0.5 - 0.333h$. It follows that, for a system containing both the dimer and trimer polymer series, the values of a and b in the general equation will be between 0.333–0.5 and 0.25–0.333, respectively. The two polymer series referred to are called Regular Polymer Series because they are each made up of regular repeating units that were originally based on the degree of polymerization of the metal alkoxide. It is easily shown that the numerical values of a and b are related to the structural parameters of the Regular Polymer Series and are independent of the nature of the metal. For example, a Regular Polymer Series is completely defined by two parameters p and q, where p is the degree of polymerization of the repeating unit and q is the number of metal-oxygen-metal bridges between adjacent repeating units. The characteristic equation is simply: $n^{-1} = p^{-1} - q^{-1}h$. Thus the trimer polymer series is termed the (p_3,q_4) Regular Polymer Series, since for this example $p = 3$ and $q = 4$. Another Regular Polymer Series based on the trimer repeating unit but with only three $M \cdot O \cdot M$ bridges between adjacent units would be the (p_3,q_3) series with $n^{-1} = 0.333 - 0.333h$; a section of this polymer is illustrated in Fig. 16. It should be pointed out that the

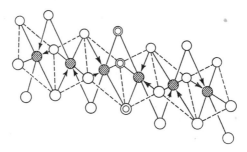

FIG. 16. $M_6O_3(OR)_{18}$ a (p_3,q_3) polymer.

KEY: Striped circle = 6-coordinated quadrivalent metal M

Double circle = Oxygen in $M \cdot O \cdot M$ bridges

Clear circle = Oxygen in alkoxide (R groups omitted).

Regular Polymer Series are not restricted to octahedral structures but will apply to any geometrical arrangements that conform with the principles of Regular Polymers. A very simple example would be the linear polydimethylsiloxanes, in which the repeating unit is the monomer based on tetrahedral silicon in, say, $Me_2Si(OR)_2$. In this case there is one $Si \cdot O \cdot Si$ bridge between adjacent units, and a (p_1,q_1) series results for which $n^{-1} = 1 - h$. To return to the metal alkoxides, we note that the two alternative polymer series based on 6-coordinated monomers [i.e., $n = 3/(3 - h)$ and $n = 2/(2 - h)$] are in fact the Regular Polymer Series (p_1,q_3) and (p_1,q_2). In principle a third series (p_1,q_1) is also possible in which adjacent octahedral units are jointed by only one $M \cdot O \cdot M$ bridge. It can also be shown that, if a given metal oxide alkoxide system involves more than one Regular Polymer Series, a linear relationship between n^{-1} and h can still be obtained. In fact for systems containing up to three simultaneous Regular Polymer Series the proportions of metal in each series may be evaluated from the constants a and b in the general equation. Let the three Regular Polymer Series be (p_a,q_r), (p_b,q_s), and (p_c,q_t), respectively. Further, let it be assumed that the proportion of metal atoms conforming to (p_a,q_r) be α_a, the proportion conforming to (p_b,q_s) be α_b, then the proportion in (p_c,q_t) will be $(1 - \alpha_a - \alpha_b)$. It follows that the number-average degree of polymerization $\bar{n}$ is given by: $(\bar{n})^{-1} = [\alpha_a p_a^{-1} + \alpha_b p_b^{-1} + (1 - \alpha_a - \alpha_b) p_c^{-1}] - [\alpha_a q_r^{-1} + \alpha_b q_s^{-1} + (1 - \alpha_a - \alpha_b) q_t^{-1}]h$. Thus the values of α_a, α_b, and $(1 - \alpha_a - \alpha_b)$ may be calculated from the values of the intercept $(\bar{n})_0^{-1}$ (at $h = 0$) and the slope $d[(\bar{n})^{-1}]/dh$.

The hydrolysis products of some other tantalum alkoxides were found to conform to the theory of Regular Polymer Series. Thus the tantalum oxide methoxides behaved as though 85.6% of the tantalum was in the (p_2,q_3) series and 14.4% in the (p_1,q_2) series. Similarly, the tantalum oxide n-propoxides had degrees of polymerization consistent with the (p_2,q_3) and (p_1,q_2) series but with a lower proportion (72.4%) of the (p_2q_3) series. The case of the tantalum oxide sec-butoxides was particularly interesting since $Ta(OBu^s)_5$ is practically monomeric in either boiling benzene or boiling sec-butanol. Clearly the steric effect of the branched alkoxide groups prevents polymerization in benzene and thus the tantalum is 5-coordinated in that solvent. However, it is still possible that a 6-coordinated tantalum could be present in sec-butanol as the solvate $Ta(OBu^s)_5 Bu^s OH$ since the steric hindrance to coordination of an alcohol molecule will be less than toward polymerization. In any case the steric effects in the tantalum oxide sec-butoxides will diminish as the degree of hydrolysis and removal of alkoxide groups increases. This might lead to a change from one Regular Polymer Series to another more polymeric series as h increases. In fact the plot of n^{-1}/h showed curvature in the region $h = 0 - 0.35$, followed by a linear portion from $h = 0.35 - 1.3$. Calculations showed that the linear portion was consistent with the presence of Regular Polymer Series (p_2,q_3) 28.6% and (p_1,q_2) 71.4%. Furthermore, it appears that in the region $h = 0 - 0.35$, the amount of the (p_2,q_3) series rises rapidly from 13.1 to 28.6%; this is exactly the type of behavior predicted if strong steric effects were opposing polymerization of the tantalum sec-butoxide.

So far we have dealt only with the alkoxides of transition metals, but experiments show that the stannic oxide isopropoxides also conform to the theory of Regular Polymers (*24*). Stannic isopropoxide is interesting in that it forms a crystalline dimeric solvate $Sn_2(OPr^i)_8,(Pr^iOH)_2$. It was not surprising to find, therefore, that the stannic oxide isopropoxides appeared to adopt Regular Polymer Series (p_2,q_3) 88.9% and (p_1,q_2) 11.1%. The chemistry of cerium(IV) shows that a coordination number of eight is sometimes exhibited and the degrees of polymerization of the soluble normal alkoxides suggested that some 8-coordinated cerium might be present. However, ceric isopropoxide forms a dimeric crystalline solvate $Ce_2(OPr^i)_8$, $(Pr^iOH)_2$ in which the cerium is presumably 6-coordinated. In fact the degrees of polymerization of cerium oxide isopropoxides agree very well with the presence of the Regular Polymer Series (p_2,q_3) 92.8% and (p_1,q_2) 7.2%, and it appears that octahedral 6-coordination is the rule. Experiments have also been carried out on the hydrolysis of uranium(V) pentaethoxide. Because the compound is practically dimeric in benzene it is suggested that the uranium is 6-coordinated. The low degree of polymerization in boiling ethanol $(n)_0 = 1.48$ suggested that an appreciable proportion of solvated monomer must also be present (more so than in the case of tantalum pentaethoxide). In the tantalum oxide ethoxides the large percentage of (p_2,q_3) species made it difficult to decide between (p_1,q_2) and (p_1,q_3) for the monomer series, but in the case of the uranium oxide ethoxides the greater percentage of monomer species should make a decision easier. The results showed unambiguously that in the uranium oxide ethoxides the species present were (p_2,q_3) 64.9% and (p_1,q_2) 35.1%. Some preliminary experiments on the hydrolysis of aluminum isopropoxide show that the aluminum oxide isopropoxides conform extremely well to a linear equation relating n^{-1} and h; we have thus shown that the theory of Regular Polymers appears to be valid for tervalent, quadrivalent, or quinquevalent metals. The body of data that supports the theory is now quite substantial and gives cause for cautious optimism in predicting degrees of polymerization of metal oxide alkoxides. An important feature of the theory is that it provides a rational explanation of the rather low polymers formed by these metal condensation-coordination polymers in the early stages of hydrolysis. At the higher degrees of polymerization there is a tendency for a rapid growth in polymer size leading to precipitation of insoluble products or alternatively the hydrolysis becomes incomplete. For example, in the hydrolysis of titanium alkoxides there is evidence that alkoxide groups in, say, $[Ti_2O_3(OR)_2]_x$ are considerably less readily hydrolyzed than those in the original $Ti(OR)_4$ (*18, 34, 43*). It is evident that many interesting problems in this field still await solution.

IV. Polyorganosiloxanometalloxanes, Polyorganometalloxanosiloxanes, and Related Compounds

A. General Considerations

The concept of using organic groups to break down the three-dimensional structures of macromolecular metal oxides and form more tractable polymers has also been applied to the mineral silicates. Important contributions in this field have been made in recent years by K. A. Andrianov (*2*) and his school, who have prepared a number of so-called polyorganometallosiloxanes, some of which appear to have potentialities as useful polymers. Another reason for investigating the metallosiloxane field was the knowledge of the valuable properties of the silicones (polyorganosiloxanes) and the possibility of improving these properties by introducing $M \cdot O \cdot M$ bridges into the silicone polymers. This work has undoubtedly received considerable stimulation by the need to produce new materials with enhanced chemical and thermal stabilities over conventional organic polymers in order to meet the special requirements of missiles and space vehicles.

It is convenient to classify these compounds under two headings, depending on the nature of the polymer chains. When the backbone of the polymer consists of $\cdot M \cdot O \cdot M \cdot O \cdot M \cdot O$ chains with the metals also bonded to organosilyloxy groups ($R_3SiO \cdot$), the compounds are called polyorganosiloxanometalloxanes. When the polymer backbone consists of $\cdot MO \cdot Si \cdot O \cdot M \cdot O \cdot Si \cdot$ chains, the compounds are referred to as polyorganometalloxanosiloxanes.

B. Polyorganosiloxanometalloxanes and Related Compounds

Just as the polymeric metal oxide alkoxides were obtained by hydrolysis of the metal alkoxides, so the polyorganosiloxanometalloxanes may be derived from the organosilyloxy derivatives of the metals $M(OSiR_3)_x$. Thus it is logical to begin this section with a consideration of the organosilyloxy derivatives. Although English and Sommer (*40*) first prepared tetrakistrimethylsilyloxytitanium, it remained for the work of Bradley and Thomas (*27*) to establish that the trimethylsilyloxy derivatives of transition metals were slightly polymeric. In particular it was shown that $Zr(OSiMe_3)_4$ had a number-average degree of polymerization of $2 \cdot$, and this had a profound effect on the volatility of this compound. It was concluded that the steric effect of the $Me_3SiO \cdot$ group was less than that of a *tert*-butoxide group because of the greater size of the silicon atom compared with carbon. Thus the methyl groups in Me_3SiO are slightly farther away from the metal than are the methyl groups in Me₃CO groups and the shielding of the metal is less. Another notable feature of the $M(OSiR_3)_x$ compounds was their greater resistance to hydrolysis and to thermolysis. This was particularly striking in the case of tetrakistriphenylsilyloxytitanium, which was shown by Zeitler and Brown (*56*) to resist attack by strong hydrochloric acid. Tristrialkylsilyloxy derivatives of aluminum were prepared by Andrianov and Zhdanov (*9*), who reported that the rate of hydrolytic cleavage of $Al \cdot O \cdot Si$ groups in $Al(OSiEt_3)_3$ by hydrochloric acid was significantly less than in the aluminosilicate mineral kaolin. Molecular weight studies showed that tristriethylsilyloxyaluminum was dimeric (*28*); hence the trialkylsilyloxy derivatives of aluminum are coordination polymers. This being the case, it would be predicted that polyorganosiloxanoaluminoxanes should be condensation-coordination polymers. Organosilyloxy derivatives of tin have also been prepared. For example, Tatlock and Rochow (*49*) showed that $Sn(OSiMe_3)_2$ and $Me_2Sn(OSiMe_3)_2$ were solids that were slowly hydrolyzed by water and more rapidly by acids. The tetrakistriethylsilyloxytin(IV) was obtained by Andrianov and Zhdanov (*8*).

The preparation of polyorganosiloxanoaluminoxanes and polyorganosiloxanotitanoxanes has been described by Andrianov and co-workers (*14*). The aluminum compounds were produced by the hydrolysis of $Al(OSiEt_3)_3$ either in acetone solution with controlled quantities of water at 20°C or by passing moist air through the molten compound at 165–170°C. The course of the hydrolysis in solution at h values from 2.33–3.73 was followed by viscosity measurements. The rate of increase of viscosity with time was markedly dependent on the value of h. As h was increased the rate of increase in viscosity rose sharply and the time required for gelation to occur decreased dramatically (Table IV). It was deduced from these results that in the initial stages linear or cyclic polymers are formed that are soluble in organic solvents. In the final stages crosslinking occurs, with the formation of three-dimensional insoluble polymers.

TABLE IV

VISCOSIMETRIC STUDIES ON THE HYDROLYSIS OF TRIETHYLSILOXYALUMINUM

h	Time prior to gelation (min)
2.32	12,960
2.80	320
3.27	100
3.73	6

When molten $Al(OSiEt_3)_3$ was aspirated with moist air condensation and polymerization were found to increase with time, as shown by viscosity measurements on the polymer and the detection of triethylsilanol and hexaethyldisiloxane in the volatile products. A polymer with a degree of polymerization of 23 was obtained and its analysis (Al 13.15%, Si 19.65%) was fairly near to that for the compound $AlO(OSiEt_3)$ (requires Al 15.48%, Si 16.10%). The following sequence of reactions was suggested to account for the formation of the polytriethylsiloxanoaluminoxane:

$$Al(OSiEt_3)_3 + H_2O \rightarrow Al(OH)(OSiEt_3)_2 + Et_3SiOH$$

$$2\ Al(OH)(OSiEt_3)_2 \rightarrow (Et_3SiO)_2AlOAl(OSiEt_3)_2 + H_2O$$

$$(Et_3SiO)_2AlOAl(OSiEt_3)_2 + H_2O \rightarrow (Et_3SiO)_2AlOAl(OH)(OSiEt_3) + Et_3SiOH$$

$$2\ Et_3SiOH \rightarrow Et_3SiOSiEt_3 + H_2O, \text{ etc.}$$

The polytriethylsiloxanoaluminoxanes were described as colorless or pale brown glassy substances that were soluble in benzene, alcohol, and acetone. It was also claimed that heat-stable films could be obtained by allowing the polymer solution to evaporate on a hard surface.

The same authors studied the hydrolysis of $Ti(OSiMe_3)_4$ in solution in acetone. They reported that for $h = 0.5$ there was no reaction during 3 hr at 50°C and most of the $Ti(OSiMe_3)_4$ was recovered by distillation. For $h > 1$ and in the presence of acid catalysts they reported that hydrolysis occurred with the formation of polytrimethylsiloxanotitanoxanes. Hexamethyldisiloxane and trimethylsilanol were isolated as products of the reaction. The polymers obtained by this method were soluble in benzene, toluene, chlorobenzene, and mixtures of these solvents with alcohols. Hard films were obtained when solutions of the polytrimethylsiloxanotitanoxanes were allowed to evaporate on metallic surfaces. It is interesting to note that we have found that in dioxane solution $Ti(OSiMe_3)_4$ is hydrolyzed at $h = 0.5$ but that the $(Me_3SiO)_3TiOTi(OSiMe_3)_3$ so formed is unstable due to disproportionation (*26*). Distillation resulted in recovery of the major proportion of $Ti(OSiMe_3)_4$ but a solid polytrimethylsiloxanotitanoxane remained as a soluble nonvolatile residue. Similar results were obtained at higher values of h; the presence of an acid catalyst appears to be unnecessary.

A recent paper by Andrianov and Novikov (*5*) described the preparation of polyorganophosphonoaluminoxanes. Thus in attempting to obtain butylmethylphosphonoaluminum dibutoxide from the reaction involving butylmethyl phosphonochloridate with aluminum tributoxide:

$$\underset{BuO}{\overset{Me}{\diagdown}} \underset{Cl}{\overset{O}{\diagup}} P + Al(OBu)_3 \rightarrow (BuO)MeP(O)Al(OBu)_2 + BuCl$$

they obtained the partial hydrolysis product 1,3-dibutoxybis(butylmethyl-phosphonoaluminoxane) (V).

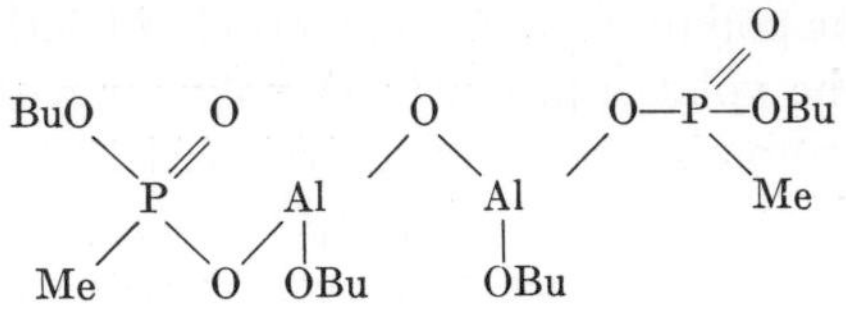

(V)

Solutions of (V) in xylene were hydrolyzed at various h values from 0.5 to 2.5 by the addition of aqueous butanol followed by heating to 210°C and distillation of volatile products. The polymers thus obtained were pale yellow solids that were soluble in benzene and xylene and gave brittle solid films when the solutions were allowed to evaporate on solid surfaces. Thermomechanical measurements showed that the glass temperatures of the polymers were in the region 50–150° and increased with the degree of hydrolysis, but the polymers failed to flow even up to a temperature of 650°C. The polymer formed when $h = 1.0$ had a degree of polymerization of 12 while the product for $h = 1.5$ had $n = 24$. In the hydrolysis it was suggested that the butoxide groups attached to aluminum were replaced by hydroxyl groups, which led to condensation polymerization with the formation of a linear aluminoxane (VI).

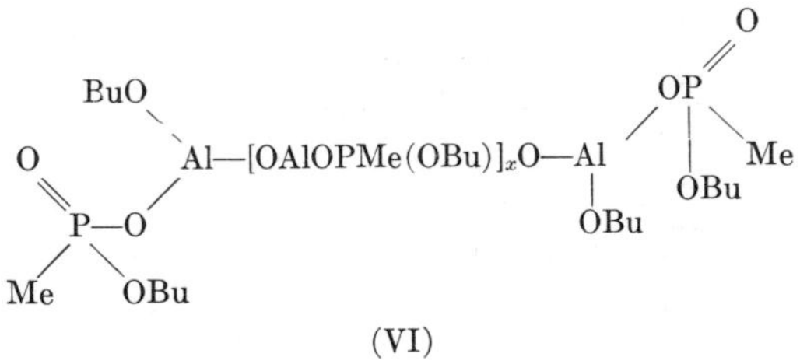

(VI)

It is quite clear that much work is being done and much more needs to be done in the field of polyorganometalloxanes.

C. Polyorganometalloxanosiloxanes and Related Compounds

In 1947, Andrianov (1) showed that organosilicon compounds containing the Si—OH group would react with metals from Groups II and III to produce polymers containing chains of metal, oxygen, and silicon atoms called polyorganometallosiloxanes. The nature of the products depended on the functionality and the reactivity of the silanol. For example a reactive diol would tend to condense to a polysiloxane in competition with the reaction with the metal. In recent years Andrianov and co-workers (*4, 6, 7, 10, 12, 13, 15*) developed other methods for preparing polyorganometal-losiloxanes. For example, dimethyldichlorosilane, phenyltrichlorosilane, and aluminum chloride were caused to hydrolyze in an alkaline (NaOH) solution with the formation of polyaluminoxanetetra(dimethylphenyl disiloxane) (*4, 12*):

$$\text{Me}_2\text{SiCl}_2 + \text{C}_6\text{H}_5\text{SiCl}_3 + \text{AlCl}_3 \xrightarrow[\text{NaOH}]{\text{H}_2\text{O}} -[\text{OSiMe}_2\text{—O—SiC}_6\text{H}_5]_4\text{—O—}\overset{\overset{\displaystyle O}{|}}{\underset{\underset{\displaystyle O}{|}}{\text{Al}}}\text{—O} \quad \text{etc.}$$

Brittle, glassy solids, soluble in organic solvents, were also obtained from the double decomposition reactions involving the sodium salts of alkyl- or arylsilanetriols and either aluminum chloride or aluminum sulfate (*6, 7, 10*):

$$3 \text{ C}_6\text{H}_5\text{Si}(\text{OH})_2\text{ONa} + \text{AlCl}_3 \rightarrow [\text{C}_6\text{H}_5\text{Si}(\text{OH})_2\text{O}]_3\text{Al} + 3 \text{ NaCl}$$

$$n \text{ [C}_6\text{H}_5\text{Si}(\text{OH})_2\text{O}]_3\text{Al} \rightarrow \{[\text{C}_6\text{H}_5\text{Si}(\text{O})\text{O}]_3\text{Al}\}_n + n \text{ H}_2\text{O}$$

The cohydrolysis of diethyldichlorosilane, phenyltrichlorosilane, and diethyltin dichloride by 10% hydroxylamine solution gave liquid products that condensed at 105–150°C to give hard glasses (*13*). The polydiethyl-stannoxane organosiloxanes had silicon to tin ratios varying from 4 to 11. The same authors obtained vitreous soluble polymers by the cohydrolysis of organochlorosilanes with titanium tetrabutoxide followed by condensation at 200°C. The proportion of silicon to titanium atoms in the poly-titanoxane organosiloxanes depended on the alkyl groups attached to silicon. When a mixture of Me_2SiCl_2 (2 moles), $\text{C}_6\text{H}_5\text{SiCl}_3$ (1 mole), and $\text{Ti}(\text{OBu})_4$ (0.3 mole) was used the polymer produced was fractionated into substances having Si:Ti ratios of 25:1, 30:1, and 40:1. From the reaction involving Et_2SiCl_2 (2 moles), $\text{C}_6\text{H}_5\text{SiCl}_3$ (1 mole), and $\text{Ti}(\text{OBu})_4$ (0.3 mole) the product was fractionated into substances having Si:Ti ratios of 18:1, 22:1, and 24:1. Nesmeyanov and Nogina (*44*) investigated condensation reactions involving titanium oxide alkoxides $\text{TiO}(\text{OR})_2$ and silicon tetraalkoxides $\text{Si}(\text{OR}^1)_4$. Although compounds of the type $(\text{RO})_3\text{TiOSi}(\text{OR}^1)_3$ and $(\text{R}^1\text{O})_2\text{Si}[\text{OTi}(\text{OR})_3]_2$ were obtained, they proved to be thermally unstable because disproportionation occurred with volatilization of $\text{Ti}(\text{OR})_4$. This result is not very surprising since work on the titanium oxide alkoxides showed that these compounds underwent thermal disproportionation.

The polyorganophosphonoaluminoxanes prepared by Andrianov and Novikov (*5*) are believed to contain an aluminoxane backbone with organo-phosphorus groups attached to each aluminum. A recent paper by Andrianov and associates (*16*) describes the preparation of polymers containing the $\cdot O \cdot Al \cdot O \cdot P \cdot O \cdot$ chain. Two methods were employed. In one method a mixture of equimolecular proportions of $Al(OSiEt_3)_3$ and triethylsilyl-phosphoric acid $Et_3SiOP(O)(OH)_2$ were caused to react first at 160–170°C for 7 hr and then at 230–250°C for 20 hr. The volatile product consisted of hexaethyldisiloxane. Samples of the polymer were taken at various times and the viscosity of a 10% solution in toluene was measured. A slow rise in viscosity was observed; this was considered indicative of a stepwise condensation process. From the analytical data for Si, P, and Al, and the molecular weight of 2336 (cryoscopic in benzene) it was concluded that the polytriethylsilyloxyaluminoxane triethylsilylphosphonane had the linear structure (VII).

$$Et_3SiO-\left[Al\underset{\overset{|}{OSiEt_3}}{\text{------}}O\text{------}\overset{\overset{O}{\parallel}}{\underset{\overset{|}{OSiEt_3}}{P}}\text{------}O\right]_6 H$$

(VII)

In the second method $Al(OSiEt_3)_3$ and tristriethylsilyl phosphate $(Et_3SiO)_3PO$ were heated at 160–180°C and the mixture aspirated with moist air during a period of 34 hr. The process of condensation was followed by periodic checks on the viscosity of the polymer in toluene. The final product was a pale yellow, glassy solid, soluble in benzene and toluene. From the molecular weight of 3566 (cryoscopic in benzene) and analytical data (Si, P, Al) the structure of the polytriethylsilyloxyaluminoxane triethylsilylphosphonane was deduced to be as shown in (VIII).

$$Et_3SiO-\left[Al\underset{\overset{|}{OSiEt_3}}{\text{------}}O\text{------}\overset{\overset{O}{\parallel}}{\underset{\overset{|}{OSiEt_3}}{P}}\text{------}O\text{------}\right]_9 SiEt_3$$

(VIII)

Following their success in producing polyorganoaluminoxane organosiloxanes by the reactions involving aluminum chloride and the sodium salts of alkyl silanols (7), Andrianov and Zhdanov (11) attempted to apply this method to the formation of polycobaltoxane organosiloxanes and polynickeloxane organosiloxanes but without success. For example, the addition of the sodium salt of phenylsilanetriol or ethylsilanetriol to either cobalt or nickel chlorides in aqueous alcohol led to the precipitation of metal oxide or hydroxide and the formation of a metal-free organosiloxane polymer. It was deduced that the precipitation of the metal oxide was caused by the alkali liberated by hydrolysis of the sodium salt of the silanol. Thus it was necessary to minimize the concentration of alkali in order to incorporate any cobalt or nickel in the polymer. This objective was achieved by adding aluminum chloride together with the cobalt chloride and sodium silanolate. According to Andrianov and Zhdanov the alkali liberated by the hydrolysis of the sodium silanolate reacts with the aluminum to form $Al(OH)_3$, which condenses with the alkyl silanetriol to form polyaluminoxane alkylsiloxanes. During the reaction some of the cobalt chloride is able to combine with silanolate and become incorporated into the polymeric siloxane. As is strikingly shown in Fig. 17 the optimum ratio of $CoCl_2 : AlCl_3$ is about equimolar. At higher $CoCl_2 : AlCl_3$ ratios there appears to be insufficient aluminum chloride to keep down the $[OH]^-$ and hence the cobalt is precipitated. At lower $CoCl_2 : AlCl_3$ ratios it is presumable that the concentration of $CoCl_2$ is so low that it cannot compete effectively with the

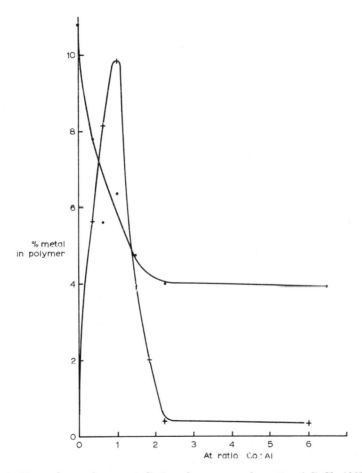

FIG. 17. Dependence of per cent Co in polymer on molar ratio of $CoCl_2 : AlCl_3$ in the reactants: (●) % Al in polymer; (+) % Co in polymer.

$AlCl_3$ in the reaction with silanolate. The sequence of reactions (1) to (5) were proposed to account for the phenomenon.

$$x \, RSi(OH)_2ONa + MCl_x \rightarrow [RSi(OH)_2O]_xM + x \, NaCl \qquad (1)$$

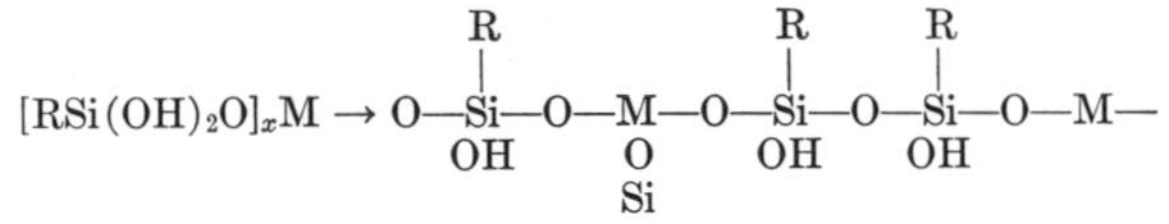

$$[RSi(OH)_2O]_xM \rightarrow \underset{\underset{OH}{|}}{O-\underset{\underset{O}{|}}{Si}-O-M-O-\underset{\underset{OH}{|}}{\overset{\overset{R}{|}}{Si}}-O-\underset{\underset{OH}{|}}{\overset{\overset{R}{|}}{Si}}-O-M- \qquad (2)$$

$$RSi(OH)_2Na + H_2O \rightleftharpoons RSi(OH)_3 + NaOH \qquad (3)$$

$$CoCl_2 + 2 \, NaOH \rightarrow Co(OH)_2 \downarrow \; + 2 \, NaCl \qquad (4)$$

$$RSi(OH)_3 + Al(OH)_3 \rightarrow [RSi(OH)_2O]_3Al + 3 \, H_2O \qquad (5)$$

To explain the failure to incorporate cobalt into the polymer in the absence of $AlCl_3$ it was suggested that reaction (4) must be considerable faster than (1). The polymer obtained from the reaction involving the sodium salt of phenylsilanetriol (1 mole), cobalt chloride (2 moles), and aluminum chloride (2 moles) was dissolved in benzene and fractionated by the addition of petroleum ether, which caused precipitation of the less soluble fraction. The results are shown in Table V. It is evident that in contrast to the aluminum and silicon, whose percentages remain sensibly constant throughout each fraction, the cobalt is predominantly present in the less soluble fractions.

TABLE V

FRACTIONAL PRECIPITATION OF CO-AL-SILOXANE POLYMER

(12.75 gm in 150 cm³ benzene)

Sample	Total vol. of precipitant, (cm³ petroleum ether)	Fraction wt. (gm)	Analysis of fraction (%)				
			C	H	Si	Al	Co
Original polymer	—	12.75	44.23	4.02	18.86	3.82	6.72
Fraction I	125	1.69	34.80	3.52	15.17	4.43	14.28
Fraction II	195	2.26	43.48	3.69	19.57	4.64	6.90
Fraction III	265	1.88	44.22	3.85	19.42	4.02	6.44
Fraction IV	335	1.40	43.97	3.70	18.35	2.76	4.39
Fraction V	475	1.43	44.06	3.73	19.51	3.28	3.20
Fraction VI	620	1.10	46.63	3.85	19.06	2.51	3.06

Further work on the polyaluminoxane organosiloxanes was reported by Andrianov *et al.* (*17*). The polyaluminoxane phenylsiloxanes and poly-aluminoxane ethylsiloxanes were obtained by the double decomposition involving the monosodium salt of the appropriate organosilanetriol and aluminum sulfate. Both polymers were infusible up to 500°C but they were soluble in the common organic solvents. The "phenyl" polymer approximating in composition to $[(C_6H_5)_8Si_8(OH)_4O_{10}Al_2O_3]_5$ was made the subject of detailed studies. The substance was found to retain its solubility in toluene, ethanol, acetone, and chlorobenzene notwithstanding the action of heat at 150°C for 10 hr. At higher temperatures the polymer was changed to a less soluble product, which had a lower hydroxyl content than the original material, and it is evident that heating causes further condensation polymerization of the starting material. Because the action of heat at 150°C lowered the hydroxyl content but did not lower the solubility of the product, it was argued that condensation at 150°C does not lead to the formation of a three-dimensional polymer. The decrease in solubility caused by heating from 200–500°C was ascribed to crosslinking, which becomes important between 400–500°C. A sample of the original polymer was fractionated by a precipitation procedure involving the addition of petroleum ether to a carbon tetrachloride solution of the polymer. In this manner the most soluble fraction (lowest molecular weight) was isolated. The precipitated polymer was redissolved in carbon tetrachloride and the second most soluble fraction obtained by adding a smaller proportion of petroleum ether than in the first stage. Four fractions were thus obtained and analyzed. The data are shown in Table VI. Evidently the polymer is chemically homogeneous since the composition of each fraction is substantially the same as in the original polymer. However, it is obvious that there is a distribution of polymer sizes because the molecular weight of Fraction I is about one half, and Fraction IV about twice, that of the original polymer. An odd feature of these results is the fact that the molecular weights determined cryoscopically in benzene are considerably lower than those determined ebullioscopically on the same compounds. This feature is not commented on in the paper but the authors appear to favor the ebullioscopic results since these alone are mentioned in the text. Thus they observe that the "polycondensation coefficient" (presumably number-average degree of polymerization) for the original polymer is 10, while for Fractions I and IV it is 5 and 20, respectively. Moreover they suggest that polymer probably has a cyclic structure and not a three-dimensional structure. However, in an attempt to explain the infusible nature of the polymers they claim that the introduction of aluminum in the molecular chains imposes rigidity, although there is no obvious reason why this should be so. It would seem to be more probable, in view of loss of solubility and decrease in hydroxyl content when the polymer is heated, that raising the temperature causes further condensation and crosslinking and that the substance is converted into a three-dimensional infusible polymer. This would also explain their

TABLE VI

FRACTIONATION OF POLYALUMINOXANEPHENYLSILOXANE

Sample	Yield (%)	M.W. in benzene		Analysis (%)					Ratio Si:Al
		Ebullioscopic	Cryoscopic	C	H	Si	Al	OH	
Original polymer	—	5990	2415	49.30	4.45	18.29	4.31	4.29	4.0
Fraction I	21.5	2770	1241	49.27	4.62	18.14	3.93	5.15	4.4
Fraction II	13.4	4330	3114	49.60	4.58	18.19	4.24	4.95	4.1
Fraction III	19.2	7880	3385	49.20	4.40	18.51	4.26	5.53	4.1
Fraction IV	17.95	11800	4193	48.98	4.32	17.28	4.73	5.04	3.5

failure to achieve compression moulding at 210°C and 400 kgm/cm² pressure. It is noteworthy that the polyaluminoxane ethylsiloxane prepared by a similar method to the "phenyl" polymer had an average Si:Al ratio of 5:1 and a number-average degree of polymerization of 84.

In a recent communication, Andrianov and Asnovich (*3*) have attempted to assign structures to polytitanoxane methylsiloxanes and polytitanoxane ethylsiloxanes. The compounds $[(CH_3)_4Si_4TiO_8]_n$ and $[(C_2H_5)_4Si_4-(OH)_2TiO_7]_{22}$, prepared by the double decomposition involving the sodium salt of the alkylsilanetriol and titanium tetrachloride, were both pale yellow, brittle, glassy solids that were soluble in common organic solvents. However, attempts to melt the compounds revealed that they were infusible up to 500°C. In addition, the action of heat at above 150–209°C rendered the polymers no longer soluble in organic solvents. Thermomechanical tests showed that the polymers were devoid of regions of high elasticity or viscous flow and suggested that they might have three dimensional structures. Nevertheless, it was held that the solubility in organic solvents was inconsistent with a three-dimensional structure. Some experiments with plasticizers proved of interest. The addition of 30% pentachlorodiphenyl to the polytitanoxane methylsiloxane imparted no flow characteristics, but with 50% plasticizer flow occurred at 20°C. A high boiling (320°C) hydrocarbon was used as plasticizer for the polytitanoxane ethylsiloxane. With 30% plastizer the polymer had a glass-transition temperature at 20°C and a flow temperature at 67°C with a region of elasticity between 20–65°C. With 50% plasticizer the polymer had a flow temperature of 25°C.

Infrared spectra on the original polymers were determined in the 900–1300 cm⁻¹ region. Bands at 917 and 914 cm⁻¹ were assigned to the Ti—O bond in the TiOSi grouping in the "methyl" and "ethyl" polymers, respectively. Strong bands at 1100 and 1109 cm⁻¹ and weak bands at 1030 cm and 1036 cm⁻¹, respectively, were assigned to the Si—O bonds. The high vibration frequencies of the Si—O bonds were considered to be indicative of cyclic tetrasiloxane rings (1080–1090 cm⁻¹; refs. (*54*) and (*55*) and on this basis the polymers were assigned to linear-cyclic structures (IX) and (X).

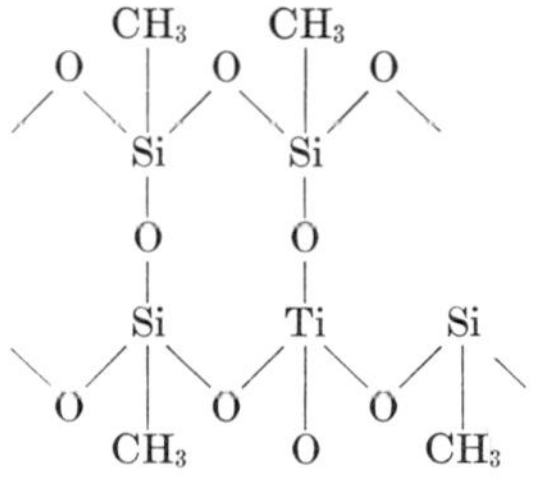

(IX) 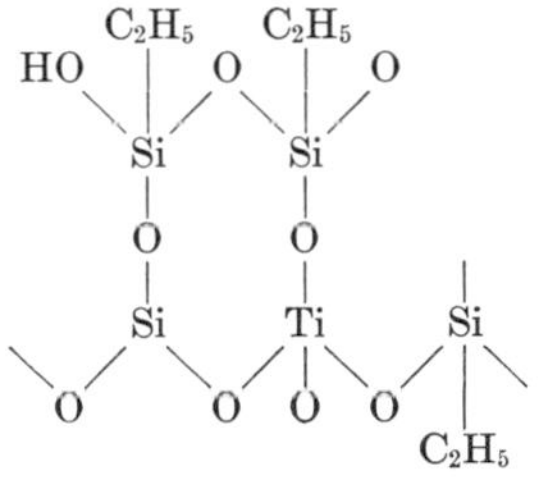 (X)

It seems worthy of comment at this stage that, in assigning possible structures to the polyorganosiloxanometalloxanes or the polyorganometallosiloxanes, Andrianov and his colleagues appear to adopt the view that the metals are present in the coordination numbers characteristic of their Group valencies (e.g., Al 3 and Ti 4). This seems surprising in the light of the well-known tendencies of these metals to expand their coordination numbers whenever possible. Therefore it would seem reasonable to bear in mind such a possibility when working out structures for these polymers. This was one of the key factors used by Bradley and colleagues (*22, 24, 31, 34*) in interpreting the number-average degrees of polymerization of metal oxide alkoxides, which are in fact examples of polyalkoxymetalloxanes.

To bring this section on polymetallosiloxanes to a close we now mention the work of Hornbaker and Conrad (*41*) in which attempts were made to prepare polymetallodiphenylsiloxanes containing the metals tin(II), lead(II), magnesium, copper(II), zinc, or mercury. Two synthetic approaches were explored, one involving the reaction of disodium diphenylsilanediolate with the metal chloride and the other the addition of diphenylsilanediol to the metal alkyl. A polystannoxane diphenylsiloxane of approximately the composition $[(C_6H_5)_{10}Si_5Sn_4O_9]_n$ was obtained as a brittle yellow resin soluble in benzene but insoluble in petroleum ether. Fractions precipitated by addition of the petroleum ether to the benzene solution were all shown to contain silicon and tin. The determination of the molecular weight was precluded by the rapid deposition of a pale yellow precipitate, but it was inferred from the resinous nature of the substance and the viscosity of its solutions that it was polymeric. With the other metals there was evidence for the formation of polymetallosiloxanes as unstable intermediates, but the ultimate products were metal oxides (except in the case of Hg) and cyclic polydiphenylsiloxanes or hexaphenyltrisiloxane-1,5-diol. The polymetallosiloxanes produced from the reactions involving $(C_6H_5)_2Si(OH)_2$ and either diethylmagnesium or diethylzinc were similarly unstable. The possibility that the instability of these metallosiloxanes was caused by hydrolysis or trace impurities was considered but regarded as improbable, and the authors inclined to the view that a low thermal stability of the Si—O—M bonding system was the cause. This seems a little surprising in comparison with the high thermal stability of the trialkylsilyoxy derivatives $M(OSiR_3)_x$ of aluminum, titanium, zirconium, and tantalum (*27*).

V. Summary

To summarize this chapter it is well to bear in mind that a number of interesting new compounds have been made in a rapidly developing field of polymer chemistry. However, it is all too apparent that many major problems remain to be solved, especially in the structural field, and there is no doubt that these problems will be very difficult to solve. Perhaps we may be permitted to close with the following note of warning. In his classical researches in the organic chemistry of silicon Kipping failed to realize the potential applications for some of the polymers that nature thrust upon him because he was chiefly preoccupied with an academic problem, namely, the resolution of an optically active quadrivalent silicon compound. In the last 10 to 15 years, conscious efforts have been made to produce polymers superior in chemical resistance and thermal stability to the "silicones" by introducing metal atoms into the polymer chains. It would indeed be ironic if a preoccupation with applied chemistry in this new field resulted in a failure to recognize some new discovery of a more fundamental nature.

REFERENCES

1. Andrianov, K. A., Certificate of Authorship No. 71, 115 (1947).
2. Andrianov, K. A., *Upsekhi Khim.* **26,** 895 (1957).
3. Andrianov, K. A., and Asnovitch, E. Z., *Vysokomolekulyarnye Soedineniya* **2,** 136 (1960).
4. Andrianov, K. A., and Ganina, T., *Izvest. Akad. Nauk S.S.S.R. Otdel. Khim. Nauk* p. 74 (1956).
5. Andrianov, K. A., and Novikov, V. M., *Vysokomolekulyarnye Soedineniya* **1,** 1390 (1959).
6. Andrianov, K. A., and Zhdanov, A. A., *Tekh. Otchet. Inst. Elementoorg. Soedineniĭ, Akad. Nauk S.S.S.R.* (1955).
7. Andrianov, K. A., and Zhdanov, A. A., *Doklady Akad. Nauk S.S.S.R.* **114,** 1105 (1957)·
8. Andrianov, K. A., and Zhdanov, A. A., *Izvest. Akad. Nauk S.S.S.R. Otdel. Khim. Nauk* p. 779 (1958).
9. Andrianov, K. A., and Zhdanov, A. A., *J. Polymer Sci.* **30,** 513 (1958); see also, Andrianov, K. A., Zhdanov, A. A., and Pavlov, S. A., *Doklady Akad. Nauk S.S.S.R.* **102,** 85 (1958).
10. Andrianov, K. A., and Zhdanov, A. A., *Khim. i Prakt. Primenenie Kremneorg. Soedineniĭ Trudy Konf. Leningrad 1958 No.* **2,** 100 (1958).
11. Andrianov, K. A., and Zhdanov, A. A., *Izvest. Akad. Nauk S.S.S.R. Otdel. Khim. Nauk* p. 1590 (1959).
12. Andrianov, K. A., Zhdanov, A. A., and Ganina, T., *Byull. Vsesoyuz. Khim. Obshchestva im Mendeleeva No.* **3,** 2 (1955).
13. Andrianov, K. A., Ganina, T., and Khrustaleva, E., *Izvest. Akad. Nauk S.S.S.R. Otdel. Khim. Nauk* p. 798 (1956).
14. Andrianov, K. A., Zhdanov, A. A., Kurasheva, N. A., and Dulova, V. G., *Doklady Akad. Nauk S.S.S.R.* **112,** 1050 (1957).
15. Andrianov, K. A., Zhdanov, A. A., and Asnovitch, E. Z., *Doklady Akad. Nauk S.S.S.R.* **118,** 1124 (1958).
16. Andrianov, K. A., Zhdanov, A. A., Kazakova, A. A., *Izvest. Akad. Nauk S.S.S.R. Otdel. Khim. Nauk* p. 466 (1959).
17. Andrianov, K. A., Zhdanov, A. A., and Asnovitch, E. Z., *Izvest. Akad. Nauk S.S.S.R. Otdel. Khim. Nauk* p. 1760 (1959).

18. Bistan, E., and Gomory, I., *Chem. zvesti* **10**, 91 (1956).
19. Boyd, T., *J. Polymer Sci.* **7**, 591 (1951).
20. Bradley, D. C., *Nature* **182**, 1211 (1958).
21. Bradley, D. C., *Advances in Chem. Ser. No.* **23**, 10 (1959).
22. Bradley, D. C., and Carter, D. G., *Can. J. Chem.* **39**, 1434 (1961); **40**, 15 (1962).
23. Bradley, D. C., and Chatterjee, A. K., *J. Inorg. & Nuclear Chem.* **4**, 279 (1957).
24. Bradley, D. C., and Holloway, H., *Can. J. Chem.* **39**, 1818 (1961); **40**, 62 (1962).
25. Bradley, D. C., and Mehta, M. L., Unpublished results.
26. Bradley, D. C., and Prevedorou, C. C. A., Unpublished results.
27. Bradley, D. C., and Thomas, I. M., *J. Chem. Soc.* p. 3404 (1959).
28. Bradley, D. C., and Thomas, I. M., Unpublished results.
29. Bradley, D. C., Mehrotra, R. C., Swanick, J. D., and Wardlaw, W., *J. Chem. Soc.* p. 2025 (1953).
30. Bradley, D. C., Wardlaw, W., and Whitley, A., *J. Chem. Soc.* p. 726 (1955).
31. Bradley, D. C., Gaze, R., and Wardlaw, W., *J. Chem. Soc.* p. 721 (1955); p. 3977 (1955).
32. Bradley, D. C., Chakravarti, B. N., and Wardlaw, W., *J. Chem. Soc.* p. 2381 (1956).
33. Bradley, D. C., Chatterjee, A. K., and Wardlaw, W., *J. Chem. Soc.* p. 2260 (1956).
34. Bradley, D. C., Gaze, R., and Wardlaw, W., *J. Chem. Soc.* p. 469 (1957).
35. Bradley, D. C., Multani, R. K., and Wardlaw, W., *J. Chem. Soc.* p. 126 (1958).
36. Bradley, D. C., Prevedorou, C. C. A., and Wardlaw, W., *Can. J. Chem.* **39**, 1619 (1961).
36a. Bradley, D. C., and Westlake, A. H., *Nature* **191**, 273 (1961).
37. Caughlan, C. N., Smith, H. S., Katz, W., Hodgson, W., and Crowe, R. W., *J. Am. Chem. Soc.* **73**, 5652 (1951).
38. Cullinane, N. M., Chard, S. J., Price, G. F., Millward, B. B., and Langlois, G., *J. Appl. Chem.* **1**, 400 (1951).
39. Dahl, L. F., Personal communication.
40. English, W. D., and Sommer, L. H., *J. Am. Chem. Soc.* **77**, 170 (1955).
41. Hornbaker, E. D., and Conrad, F., *J. Org. Chem.* **24**, 1858 (1959).
41a. Martin, R. L., and Winter, G., *J. Chem. Soc.* p. 2947 (1961).
41b. Martin, R. L., and Winter, G., *Nature* **188**, 313 (1960) and **191**, 274 (1961).
42. Mehrotra, R. C., *J. Indian Chem. Soc.* **30**, 585 (1953); **31**, 85 (1954).
43. Minami, S., and Ishino, T., *Technol. Repts. Osaka Univ.* **3**, 357 (1953).
44. Nesmeyanov, A. N., and Nogina, O. V., *Doklady Akad. Nauk S.S.S.R.* **117**, 249 (1957).
45. Nesmeyanov, A. N., Brainina, E. M., and Freidlina, R. Kh., *Doklady Akad. Nauk S.S.S.R.* **85**, 571 (1952).
46. Nesmeyanov, A. N., Nogina, O. V., and Dubovitskii, V. A., *Doklady Akad. Nauk S.S.S.R.* **128**, 964 (1959).
47. Robinson, R. A., and Peak, D. A., *J. Phys. Chem.* **39**, 1125 (1935).
48. Sidgwick, N. V., and Sutton, L. E., *J. Chem. Soc.* p. 1461 (1930).
49. Tatlock, W. S., and Rochow, E. G., *J. Org. Chem.* **17**, 1555 (1952).
50. Turova, N. Ya., Novoselova, A. V., and Semenenko, K. N., *Russ. J. Inorg. Chem.* (*Engl. Transl.*) **4**, 453 (1959).
51. Winter, G., *Australian Dept. Supply, Paint Notes No.* **5**, 285 (1950).
52. Winter, G., *J. Oil & Colour Chemists' Assoc.* **34**, 30 (1951).
53. Wheatley, P. J., *J. Chem. Soc.* p. 4270 (1960).
54. Wright, N., and Hunter, M. J., *J. Am. Chem. Soc.* **69**, 803 (1947).
55. Young, C. W., Servais, P. C., Currie, C. C., and Hunter, M. J., *J. Am. Chem. Soc.* **70**, 3758 (1948).
56. Zeitler, V. A., and Brown, C. A., *J. Am. Chem. Soc.* **79**, 4616 (1957).

—8—

Coordination Polymers

B. P. BLOCK

Pennsalt Chemicals Corporation, Wyndmoor, Pennsylvania

TABLE OF CONTENTS

I. Introduction

The term "coordination polymer" has been used to describe a great many relatively unrelated materials. In its broadest sense it can be applied to any macromolecular entity which contains coordinate covalent bonds.

447

For the purposes of this discussion no attempt will be made to restrict the concept of coordination polymer except the limitation that a metallic element must be involved in the coordinate covalent bond. Although coordination polymers are generally classified as inorganic polymers, it should be recognized that a large fraction of the ligands employed are, perforce, organic and that, consequently, many of the materials involved are really semiorganic, or in some cases almost completely organic, in nature. In accordance with current usage such systems will be considered to be inorganic polymers.

Two categories of coordination polymers are easily recognized, one in which the coordinated metallic element is an integral part of the backbone and a second in which the metallic element is coordinated to a polymer repeating unit containing donor groups. Most of the known coordination polymers fall in the first group, and a majority of them can be considered "natural coordination polymers" insofar as they were not deliberately made as polymers but, rather, are substances found to be polymeric in the course of their characterization. It is only recently that any substantial effort has been devoted to deliberate attempts to synthesize coordination polymers, both classes being sought.

Perhaps one of the most striking aspects about the field of coordination chemistry is the relatively large variety of geometrical configurations encountered among the various coordination numbers. This is carried over into coordination polymers, of course, and gives rise to possibilities unknown to organic polymers. This aspect will be emphasized in the first part of the discussion, which is devoted to natural coordination polymers. Various systems that have been explored in attempts to synthesize coordination polymers involving monomeric ligands will be reviewed next, followed by a discussion of coordination compounds with polymeric ligands. As with any classification there has to be a certain amount of arbitrariness. In some cases it is not clear whether the object of a given piece of work was preparation of a polymer or study of a reaction. For the most part such research is included in the section emphasizing syntheses. Furthermore, when earlier work is clearly not polymer oriented but has been followed by related specific polymer work, all the material is kept together in Section IV, Synthetic Coordination Polymers.

II. Natural Coordination Polymers

A. General Discussion

In the solid state there are relatively few inorganic substances with molecular lattices. The great majority are polymers, although not in the sense of consisting of infinite molecular arrays of one sort or another. Thus sodium chloride can be considered a type of polymer, but the forces holding the atoms together are largely nondirectional in nature and are frequently termed ionic (*236*, p. 6). At the other extreme lie substances such as diamond that also have polymeric structures, but the atoms of which are held together by covalent, directional bonds. Among the coordination polymers to be discussed first (natural coordination polymers) it is sometimes quite arbitrary as to whether the bonding is considered to be of the former or the latter type. For the purposes of this discussion sufficient covalent character in the bonding to impart direction to the bonds will be considered necessary for the substance in question to be classed as a polymer.

The criterion most used, although not unambiguous, is comparison of the bond length involved with the sum of the ionic radii of the bond partners. In this connection it is useful to employ Pauling's equation for interatomic distances of fractional bonds (*236*, p. 255) in order to calculate bond numbers for the longer interatomic distances in a structure. There may well be some question about the significance of this equation, but, in the absence of any other criterion, it is certainly preferable to use an empirical relationship of this sort to interpret bonding in terms of bond lengths rather than to rely on intuition, as has frequently been done. A good criterion in conjunction with a short interatomic distance is the presence of an unusual packing relationship not expected from normal radius-ratio relationships. This, of course, indicates that directional bonding, typical of covalent character, is involved.

Where complete structural data are lacking, the proof that a coordination compound is polymeric is generally even more tenuous. In very few cases has a molecular weight been established comparable to the normal procedure with organic polymers, for in most cases there is not a suitable solvent for molecular weight determination. Because it is rather difficult to establish polymeric character for many inorganic substances, there has been a marked tendency to describe any insoluble and inert or tacky and resinous-appearing product as a polymer, i.e., the substance has physical properties typical of some organic polymers so it is a polymer. A related approach for assigning polymeric structure is based on chemical analysis. If the composition of a substance is such that there are not sufficient donor groups sterically available to a coordination center to permit it to have its usual coordination pattern, polymerization is assumed to occur in order to enable the center to attain its normal coordination number. These procedures do not constitute proof of structure although, taken together, they may be indicative of a polymeric structure.

As was mentioned earlier, the different coordination numbers possible can lead to coordination polymers with a multiplicity of geometrical pat-

terns. By and large current polymer knowledge is limited to systems in
which the coordination number is two, four, or six, but it is clear that
other possibilities exist, e.g., the substances involving coordination numbers of three, seven, and nine to be considered later. Natural coordination
polymers will be divided into one-, two-, and three-dimensional types and
then considered by coordination number.

B. One-Dimensional Polymers

1. Coordination Number Two

The least complicated polymer imaginable would be a simple linear
chain of atoms, and such systems do exist for coordination compounds of
metals exhibiting a coordination number of two. The geometry about the
coordination center in this case is quite simple, the two bonds, presumably
of the sigma type involving *sp* hybridization, being at an angle of 180°
from one another (*312*, p. 48). Gold(I) iodide is one of the simplest substances known to be a linear coordination polymer (*308*). It consists of the
zigzag chain, formula (I), with an interatomic distance of 2.60 A, an
I—Au—I angle of 180°, and an Au—I—Au angle pictured to be obtuse by
the investigators although no value is reported. The interatomic distance
calculated for an ionic, coordination number two array of gold(I) and
iodide ions is about 3.2 A when using Pauling's method of correcting
standard crystal radii (*236*, p. 537). The markedly shorter distance observed is a good indication that this structure is covalent in nature.

(I)   (II)

A very simple chain has also been found in the substance $2HgO \cdot Hg_2Cl_2$
(*264*). The crystal consists of mercury(I) chloride molecules associated
with zigzag chains of composition HgO, formula (II). The observed mer-
cury-to-oxygen distance of 2.03 A is less than the calculated ionic distance
with coordination number two and also less than the sum of the tetrahedral
covalent radii of mercury and oxygen. The O—Hg—O angle at every other
mercury is 168°, indicating that there is relatively strong interaction between the mercury(I) chloride molecules and the chain.

A geometrically less complicated chain is found in silver(I) cyanide
(*31, 313*) and gold(I) cyanide (*325*) even though there are three different

atoms present. The reason for this is that the cyanide ion, when acting as a bridge, has electrons available for coordination only at either end of the ion in a linear 180° relationship because of the rigid triple bond between the carbon and nitrogen. Since silver(I) and gold(I) have the same 180° relationship between their two coordination positions, the resulting chains are rigid rods of the form $(—C≡N—M—C≡N—M—)_x$. On the basis of the metal-to-metal distances in these substances, 5.26 and 5.09 Å for silver(I) cyanide and gold(I) cyanide, respectively, the bonding along the chains is considered to be primarily covalent in nature. The exact metal-to-carbon and -nitrogen distances are not known because of the difficulty in locating light atoms in the presence of heavy atoms.

The addition of one more atom to this system results again in a zigzag chain. Although silver(I) thiocyanate also is a linear chain of atoms (*175*), the stereochemistry of the thiocyanate anion is such that the pairs of electrons available for coordination at either end of it are not directed at an angle of 180° from one another, and the structure found is (III), in

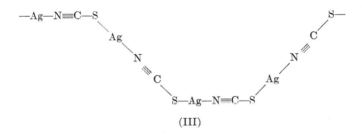

(III)

which the C—S—Ag angle is 103.79°. This follows from the electronic structure of the thiocyanate anion, —S—C≡N or S=C=N— or a resonance hybrid, in which the unshared pairs will be directed at an angle from the SCN axis. The interatomic distances support covalent bonding. The structure of copper(I) azide (*315*) is a zigzag chain for the same reason. The azide ion also has an electronic configuration such that the unshared electron pairs are directed at an angle from the NNN axis.

So far the only systems considered have been those in which all the atoms present in the polymer are found in the backbone of the polymer. There are also numerous examples in which various atoms form side chains. When the coordination center has a linear, coordination number two pattern, such side chains have to be developed in the ligand portion of the polymer. The structural investigations of $HgN(COCH_3)N(COCH_3)$ (*49*) and $Hg_2N(COCH_3)N(COCH_3)$ (*48*) indicate that both compounds are of this type with —Hg—N—N— or —Hg—Hg—N—N— units in the backbone and one side chain acetyl group bonded to each nitrogen. The experimental data do not offer definitive proof but are in agreement with these polymers having the zigzag configurations (IV) and (V).

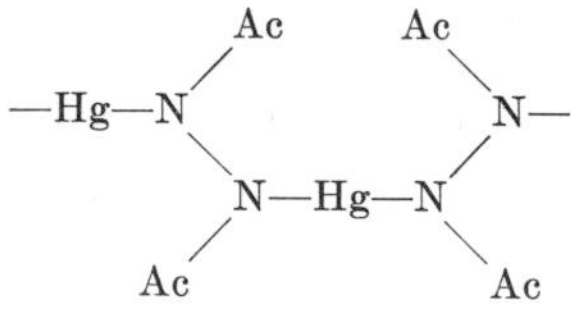

(IV) 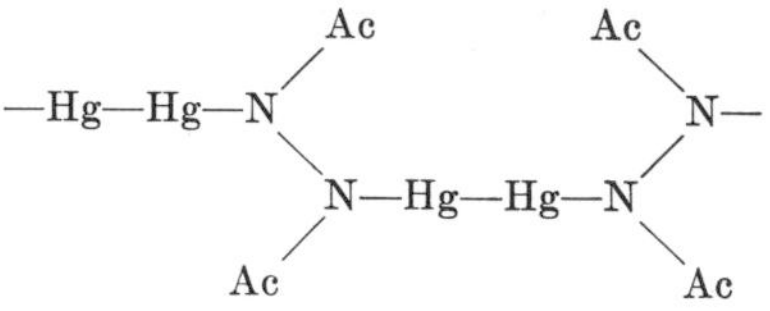   (V)

A somewhat more complex bonding situation is encountered in the insoluble ethynyl compounds $RC{\equiv}CCu$ and $RC{\equiv}CAg$ (*25*), for in them the association of monomer units into a polymer is via d_π, p_π bonding, as in (VI). There appears to be substantial back coordination from the filled

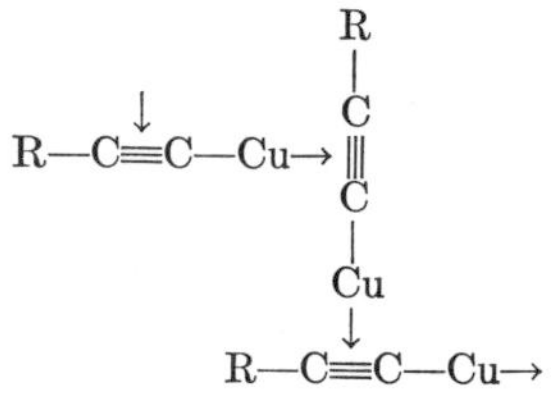

(VI)

metal d orbitals to the antibonding orbitals of at least two acetylene groups, the antibonding orbitals presenting a π aspect to the metal whether end-on or sideways. Although the structures of these interesting materials are not proved, the good bonding strength involved in the polymers is shown by the fact that, in general, they are unaffected by solvents such as pyridine and triethylamine, whereas a strong donor with back coordinating properties such as triethylphosphine will break down their structure. It is suggested that there may be additional bonding if the polymer chains are so oriented that acetylene groups lie next to copper atoms.

Very closely related to the neutral linear polymers just considered are a family of polymeric cations formed by elements with a coordination number of two. The reported examples of this class are of two types, a few mercury(II)-containing compounds and a pair of unusual silver compounds. The mercury compounds are of the type $Hg(NH_2)X$ (*75, 178, 227, 252*) and $Hg(en)Cl_2$ (*47*), compositions which would probably not be expected to exhibit the structures found. In both types the mercury has a coordination number of two which is satisfied by two mercury-to-nitrogen bonds, and the halide ions are present as ions in the lattice along with the resulting polymeric cations, which have the linear, zigzag configurations (VII) and (VIIa). It thus appears that the bonding between mercury and nitrogen is so much stronger than mercury-to-halide bonding that polymers are formed even though there is a possibility of forming monomers if all the potential ligands present are used in coordination. Deductions from

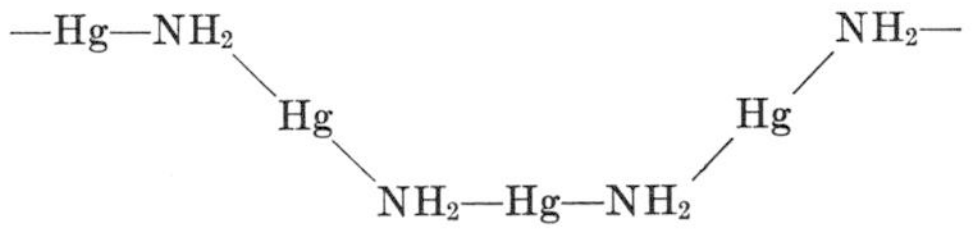

$$
\begin{array}{ccc}
-\text{Hg}-\text{NH}_2 & & \text{NH}_2- \\
& \searrow \text{Hg} \quad\quad \text{Hg} \swarrow & \\
& \text{NH}_2-\text{Hg}-\text{NH}_2 &
\end{array}
$$

(VII)

$$
\begin{array}{ccc}
-\text{Hg}-\text{NH}_2 & & \text{NH}_2- \\
& \searrow \text{CH}_2-\text{CH}_2 \quad\quad \text{CH}_2-\text{CH}_2 \swarrow & \\
& \text{NH}_2-\text{Hg}-\text{NH}_2 &
\end{array}
$$

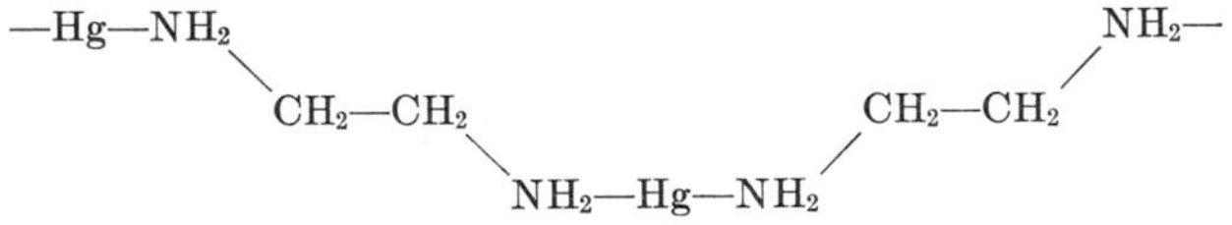

(VIIa)

interatomic distances for the $Hg(NH_2)X$ type indicate that the bonding in the polymer chain is covalent, but it should be noted that the distances reported are based on reasonable interpretations due to the difficulty of locating the light atoms in the presence of mercury. The bond order for the mercury-to-X bonds seem to be about one-sixth, a rather low order suggesting little true bonding. The structure for $Hg(en)Cl_2$ was not worked out in as great detail, being based on X-ray powder patterns and infrared spectra. It is interesting that ethylenediamine acts as a catenating group rather than a chelating ligand in this compound. This is a direct consequence of the stereochemistry of coordination number two, it being impossible for the bidentate ligand to bond to one mercury atom in two positions at an angle of 180°.

The silver polymers in this class are the polymeric cations found in the substances $AgClO_4 \cdot C_6H_6$ (*258, 287*) and $AgNO_3 \cdot C_8H_8$ (*204*). The significant feature of each structure is the infinite chain of silver atoms bonded to the double bond system of the benzene or 1,3,5,7-cyclooctatetraene. Actually the silver atoms are not equally spaced between the organic rings, so that the bonding into infinite chains is weak. The evidence for silver-to-oxygen bonding is not strong, the distances being about equal to the adjusted sum of the ionic radii.

2. Coordination Number Three

There are relatively few well-established instances of the existence of coordination compounds based on a coordination number of three (*229*). Unexpectedly, such a structure has been found for $KCu(CN)_2$ (*71*). Although the corresponding gold and silver compounds contain monomeric anions of linearly coordinated metal atoms, the copper compound contains a polymeric spiral chain anion in which the copper(I) has a coordination number of three (Fig. 1a). There is single bridging from copper to copper with cyanide ions and in addition there is a pendant cyanide on each copper atom. The geometrical arrangement about each copper atom

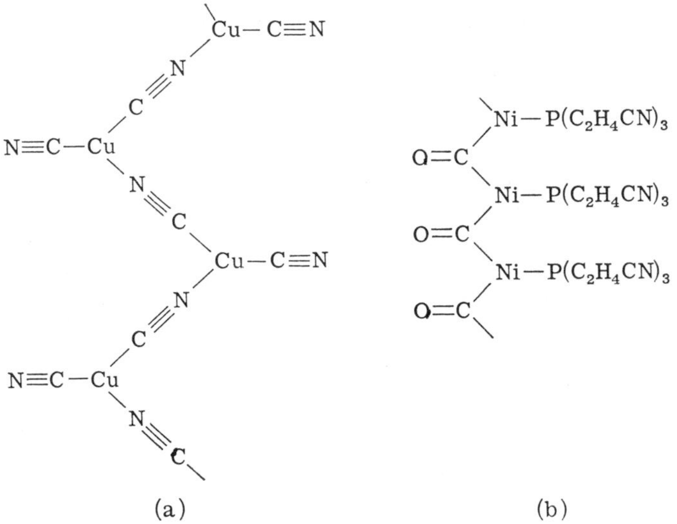

FIG. 1. One-dimensional polymers based on coordination number three: (a) $Cu(CN)_2^-$; (b) $(NCC_2H_4)_3PNiCO$.

is almost planar and probably involves sp^2 hybridization. In view of the rarity of this kind of structure the interatomic distances have little meaning insofar as bond types are concerned.

On the basis of the evidence at hand it appears that $(NCC_2H_4)_3PNiCO$ may be of this type also (*207*), with carbonyl bridging between nickel atoms and pendant triscyanoethylphosphine groups on the nickel atoms (Fig. 1b). Although there are more than enough donor groups present to permit the nickel(0) to assume its normal coordination number of four, the infrared spectrum shows all the nitrile groups to be equivalent and the carbonyl group to be of the bridging type. Because of this superfluity of donor groups if all are used, it has been suggested that none of the nitrile groups is coordinated.

3. Planar Coordination Number Four

a. Double bridged chains. Some coordination compounds are known in which the central element is quadricoordinate with a square planar distribution of coordinated groups (*26*). With such a basic structure symmetrical repeating units are possible with either single or double bridging between centers (Fig. 2).

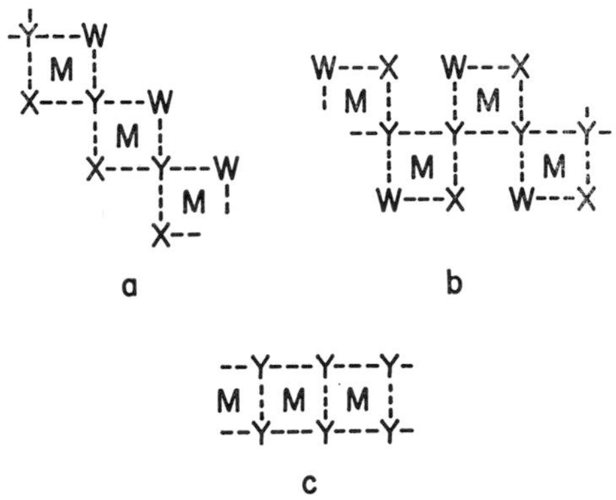

FIG. 2. General formulas for one-dimensional polymers based on square planar coordination: (a) *trans* single bridging; (b) *cis* single bridging; (c) double bridging.

There have been relatively few polymeric systems found in which all four of the coordination positions of a planar element are involved in the backbone of the polymer. Perhaps the best known of these is palladium(II) chloride, which consists of infinite chains formed by double chloride bridging between palladium atoms (Fig. 2c, M = Pd and Y = Cl) (*309*). It is interesting that the packing in this substance resembles that of a long chain hydrocarbon. The same structure has been reported for platinum(II) chloride (*89*). Closely related are the structures of copper(II) chloride (*311*) and bromide (*120*). Their predominant feature is also a chain of metal atoms joined by double halide bridging. There is a difference in the packing of the chains, however, which results in there being two longer copper-to-halogen distances. This can be interpreted as completing a distorted octahedral configuration about the copper, resulting in an association of the chains to sheets. This difference is due to the fact that the palladium(II) chloride chains pack with palladium next to palladium, whereas the copper(II) halide chains pack with copper next to halogen.

These two structures illustrate the use of bond lengths to aid in the interpretation of structures. In palladium(II) chloride there are four palladium-to-chlorine distances of 2.31 A with four next nearest chlorines at 3.85 A. On the other hand, in copper(II) chloride, in addition to the four nearest chlorine atoms at 2.3 A, there are only two next nearest chlorines at 2.95 A. The next nearest neighbors in palladium(II) chloride are at such a distance that the calculated bond order is 0.003, and there is clearly no question of appreciable bonding between them and palladium.

Since the steric relationship is quite different for copper(II) chloride, a real question arises as to how strong an interaction there is between the copper and its next nearest chlorine neighbors. For this interaction the calculated bond order is 0.08, from which it can be concluded that these fifth and sixth bonds are very weak, suggesting that the square planar environment is the predominant factor in the structure. In the analogous copper(II) bromide the bond order is even lower, 0.05, showing still weaker interaction.

Jensen has proposed that a number of mercaptides of nickel(II) belong to the doubly bridged planar class of coordination polymers (*136*). The magnetic moments of $Ni(SR)_2$ where R is C_2H_5, C_6H_5, p-$CH_3C_6H_4$, furfuryl, or 2-methyl-4-quinolyl are zero, indicating a planar dsp^2 configuration, and the other physical properties of the products are in accord with a polymeric nature. This suggestion seems quite reasonable.

There is an incorrect interpretation that has crept into some of the literature, however, with respect to the nature of nickel(II) cyanide. It has been stated that nickel(II) cyanide is a linear double cyanide bridged polymer of the palladium(II) chloride type (*142*), with Long's work (*179*) cited as support for this statement. The exchange experiments cited show nothing of the sort, but rather indicate that there are two kinds of nickel atoms in nickel(II) cyanide. The same conclusion has been reached on the basis of polarographic (*131*) and magnetic moment (*246*) studies; thus the consensus is that the nickel(II) cyanide structure contains planar $Ni(CN)_4^{--}$ units held together by nickel(II) ions bonded to the nitrogens of these units in some fashion. This structure, which has not yet been determined, is probably closely related to that of $Ni(CN)_2(NH_3)$, which will be discussed later.

Earwicker (*84*) has suggested that in solid $K_2Pd(SO_3)_2$ and $Na_2Pd(SO_3)_2 \cdot H_2O$ there are polymeric anions of composition $Pd(SO_3)_2^{--}$ formed by sulfite bridging between palladium atoms (Fig. 2c, M = Pd and Y = SO_3). The two bonds in each bridge are assumed to be different, palladium-to-sulfur on one side and palladium-to-oxygen on the other. The latter is much weaker than the former, so that the polymer is easily attacked to break the chain and form monomeric coordination compounds of palladium(II).

b. Single bridged chains. Polymeric coordination compounds built up by linking planar species through only two corners are rare. It is possible that a series of aromatic nitriles of gold(III) are of this sort (*145*). The stability of $Cl_2AuC_6H_4CN$ and related compounds with other aromatic nitriles suggested to Kharasch and Beck that these substances were polymerized through a nitrile to gold covalent bond (Fig. 2a, M = Au, W = X = Cl, Y = $C_6H_3(CH_3)CN$). Unfortunately molecular weights could not be determined, so that these compounds may be cyclic rather than linear polymers. It is also possible that the one-to-one hydrazine derivatives of platinum(II) chloride and bromide are of this type (*107*). The structure of hydrazine is such that it is very unlikely that it can function as a chelate as in (VIII). Consequently it has to be a catenating agent in order that the

$$
\begin{array}{c}
\text{Cl} \qquad \text{NH}_2 \\
\diagdown \diagup \\
\text{Pt} \quad | \\
\diagup \diagdown \\
\text{Cl} \qquad \text{NH}_2
\end{array}
$$

(VIII)

platinum(II) or palladium(II) achieve a coordination number of four (Fig. 2a, M = Pt or Pd, W = X = Cl or Br, Y = —NH_2NH_2—).

Hendra and Powell have investigated the infrared spectra of the one-to-one compounds formed by dioxane with copper(II) chloride and by its analog *p*-dithiane with copper(II) chloride, platinum(II) chloride, and gold(III) chloride (*120a*). They conclude that the most probable structure for these compounds is a polymeric chain in which the dioxane or *p*-dithiane serves as a catenating group between the metal atoms (Fig. 2a, Y = $O(C_2H_4)_2O$ or $S(C_2H_4)_2S$). The platinum(II) and gold(III) almost certainly are planar, and the copper(II) structure will at least approximate a planar configuration.

Wells has found that in $CsCuCl_3$ there is a polymeric anion formed by bridging one pair of adjacent corners with chloride ions (*310*). The resulting chain (Fig. 2b, M — Cu and W — X — Y — Cl) is arranged in a spiral in the crystal lattice. As with the copper(II) halides, there is a pair of next nearest chlorides, but in this case at the relatively close distance of 2.65 A from the copper atom, giving a bond number of 0.4. Such bonding, although weaker than that in the spiral chains, is strong enough in this case to pose a serious problem as to whether the copper should be classed as planar or octahedral. In accordance with the usual treatment of this compound it has been considered here to exhibit planar coordination. An alternate classification would be as a member of the one-dimensional class of polymers formed from octahedrally coordinated elements by triple bridging between coordination centers. See $CsPbI_3$, Section II,B,5,*a*.

4. Tetrahedral Coordination Number Four

a. Double bridged chains. As with the planar configuration it is possible also to have either single or double bridging between tetrahedral units (Fig. 3). In this case, however, there is only one steric possibility for the single bridged system because one corner of the tetrahedron has the same steric relationship to all three remaining corners.

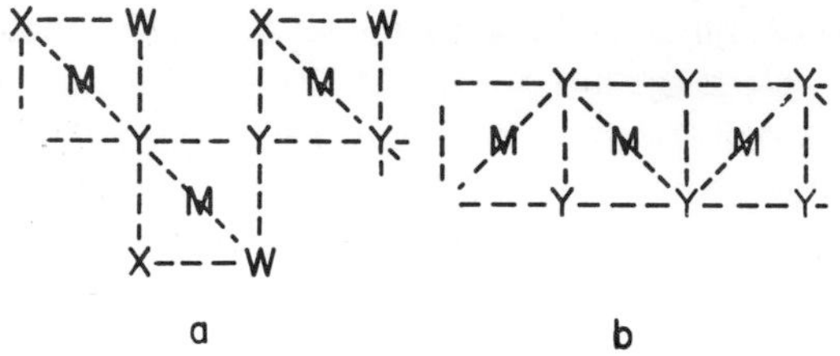

Fig. 3. General formulas for one-dimensional polymers based on tetrahedral co-ordination: (a) single bridging; (b) double bridging.

There have been no structures determined in which a tetrahedral co-ordination center has been found to have all four of its bonds incorporated into the backbone of a neutral, linear polymer. A few compounds have been suggested to have such a configuration: $Mo(OOCR)_2$, where R may

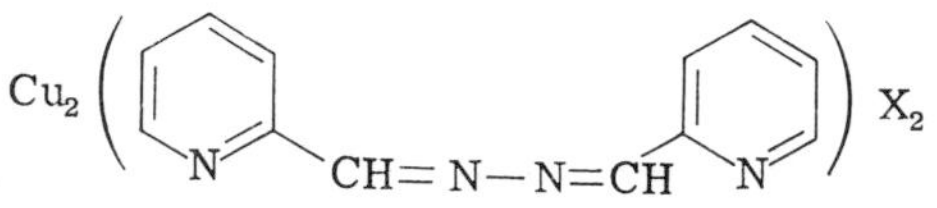

(IX)

be C_6H_5, CH_3, or C_2H_5 (17); (IX), where X = Cl or Br (291); $Fe(OOCCH_2-OH)_2$ (223); and $Zn(SCH_2CH(S)CH_2OH)$ (173). The suggested structures for the second and fourth of these compounds are in accord with usual coordination patterns, whereas the first and third, if substantiated, will be rather unusual.

Such a polymer pattern has been found for the anion in $KFeS_2$ (28). The iron(III) atoms are clearly tetrahedral and joined into a linear chain by double sulfide bridges with the interatomic distances shorter than those expected for ionic bonding (Fig. 3b, M = Fe and Y = S). This is an interesting material propertywise and, perhaps, offers a starting point for a practical, high temperature polymer. It is not a good candidate itself because it is readily oxidized and is too crystalline in nature, but it appears to possess marked thermal stability, for it is prepared at red heat in an inert atmosphere (183).

Similarly this type of polymer has been found to exist in the cation of $[Cu(NCC_2H_4CN)_2]NO_3$ (148). The two nitrile groups in succinonitrile can each act as a donor in coordination compounds, but the two unshared pairs of electrons are at such an angle to one another that succinonitrile cannot act as a chelating group. In this compound the succinonitrile molecules act as double bridging groups between tetrahedral copper(I) ions, giving the polymeric cation $Cu(NCC_2H_4CN)_2{}^+$ with the structure shown in Fig. 3b with M = Cu and Y = NCC_2H_4CN. The observed bond distances are a little shorter than the sum of the tetrahedral covalent radii of copper and carbon or nitrogen, indicating that the bonding is substantially covalent in this structure. It has been suggested that some hydrazine coordination compounds are similar with hydrazine acting as a double bridging group between zinc or nickel ions (*280*).

b. Single bridged chains. No structural evidence has been reported for the existence of neutral polymeric chains built up by the linking of two corners of a central element with a tetrahedral configuration. Burg and Mahler (*57*) have suggested that the product obtained from the reaction of nickel tetracarbonyl with $(CF_3P)_4$ is a mixture containing among other things chains of the composition $(CF_3P)_4Ni(CO)_2$ in which the four-membered phosphorus ring in $(CF_3P)_4$ remains intact and bridges between $Ni(CO)_2$ units, (X).

$$
\begin{array}{c}
CF_3 \\
| \\
P \quad CF_3 \\
\diagup \quad \diagup \quad | \\
-P \qquad P-Ni(CO)_2- \\
| \quad \diagdown \quad \diagup \\
\quad \quad P \\
CF_3 \; | \\
\quad CF_3
\end{array}
$$

(X)

Although Prasad and Srivastava suggest that in the one-to-one complexes formed by beryllium chloride with aryl-substituted thioureas the beryllium is coordinatively satisfied by back coordination with one of the chloride ions (*242*), it seems more likely that the compounds are polymers in which there is chloride bridging between beryllium atoms (Fig. 3a, M = Be, W = $ArNHCSNH_2$ or $(ArNH)_2CS$, and X = Y = Cl). This is the same kind of structure that has been suggested for $Zn(NH_3)Cl_2$ (*213, 284*). Some effort has been devoted to a study of the latter because it is completely inorganic and has some properties suggestive of a polymeric structure, in particular fiber-forming character (*284*) and a rubbery relaxation at room temperature accompanied by low extensibility (*296*). Use of this compound as a polymer per se is not likely because it has a very low softening point and it is quite sensitive to water. There is also the possibility that the material has a glassy structure rather than a polymer structure, but such a distinction seems to be one of bonding type, or perhaps definition.

Dioxane apparently also serves as a catenating group between tetrahedral central atoms. Its one-to-one adduct with beryllium chloride is suggested to be a linear polymer (*296a*). The infrared spectra of its one-to-one adducts with the chlorides of mercury(II) and cadmium(II) indicate that they too are chain polymers, and similar polymers appear to be formed with the analagous catenating groups *p*-dithiane and piperazine (*120a*). Rather surprisingly the infrared spectra of $M(NH_2C_2H_4NH_2)Cl_2$ with M = Hg, Cd, and Zn also indicate that the most probable structure for these compounds is a polymeric chain instead of the expected chelate configuration (*225a*). It is desirable that a detailed structural study be made to confirm this unusual role for ethylenediamine.

An interesting series of organoaluminum compounds has been reported with the composition $R_2Al(CH_2)_nY$ in which *n* has the values 3, 4, and 5 and Y is the donor group OC_2H_5 or $N(C_2H_5)_2$ (*323*). When *n* is 3 or 4, the donor group coordinates back to the same aluminum, i.e., there is chelation. When *n* is 5, however, the coordination is to a neighboring aluminum atom (intermolecular complex formation), and polymerization results (Fig. 3a, M = Al, W = X = R, Y = $—(CH_2)_5N(C_2H_5)_2$ or $—(CH_2)_5-$ OC_2H_5). The structure of the product was not completely elucidated, but this demonstrates the fact that steric differences can make a profound change in over-all structure. In this case the five- and six-membered chelate rings are more stable than a polymer, but the polymeric structure is more stable than the seven-membered ring.

Brink and her co-workers have shown that there are chains of tetrahedral copper(I) or silver(I) atoms linked by single halide bridges in a number of compounds with the general composition M'_2MX_3 where M' represents a cation such as K^+ or NH_4^+, M represents Cu or Ag, and X represents Cl, Br, or I (*40–42*). In addition to the two bonds to bridged halide ions, there are also two bonds to unshared halide ions from each M atom in these polymeric anions. The result is a zigzag chain with the tetrahedral M atoms lying one above another and sharing single halogen atoms with each

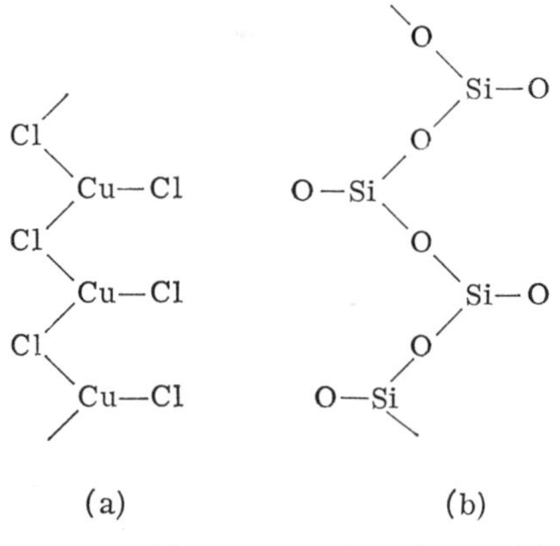

(a)   (b)

FIG. 4. Two different single-bridged tetrahedral chains: (a) $CuCl_3^{--}$; (b) SiO_3^{--}. One atom bonded to each central atom is not shown. There is a Cl or an O bonded to each Cu or Si in the direction perpendicular to the paper.

neighboring metal atom (Fig. 3a). This structure is different from the SiO_3^{--} chain in pyroxene although one might expect the two to be the same. In the pyroxene chain (*312*, p. 578) the structure is more open because the silicon atoms are not lined up as are the metal atoms in these M'_2MX_3 structures (Fig. 4). The interatomic distances are all just about exactly equal to the sum of the tetrahedral covalent radii, indicating that the bonding is primarily covalent in these structures.

For some time $Cu(SC(NH_2)_2)_3Cl$ was considered to be a typical coordination number three monomer because the chloride had been shown to be ionic (*155*). This has not proved to be the configuration, however, for a detailed structure determination shows that the compound consists of a polymeric cation in addition to the chloride ions present (*151*). One of the three thiourea sulfur atoms bridges between adjacent tetrahedral copper(I) atoms while the other two coordinate in normal unidentate fashion [Fig. 3a, $W = X = Y = SC(NH_2)_2$]. The result is the presence of a spiral polymeric cation and the associated stoichiometric number of chloride ions. This is a good example of the general tendency for the coordination requirements of a central atom to be satisfied and suggests that compounds in which there apparently are unusual coordination numbers should be examined carefully for evidence of polymerization by sharing of ligands. In this particular case it is quite striking that polymerization by sharing of sulfur occurs even though there are uncoordinated chloride ions and NH_2 groups present. The copper(I) evidently has a strong preference for sulfur. The copper-to-sulfur distances for the unshared ligands are less than the sum of the covalent tetrahedral radii, and for the shared ligands, just less and just greater. The bonding is undoubtedly covalent within the polymeric cation.

5. Coordination Number Six

a. Triple bridged chains. As with the tetrahedral elements there is little structural proof that there are linear polymers based on octahedral coordination centers with all the bonds involved in the backbone of the polymer. Whereas planar or tetrahedral polymers of this type involve the sharing of edges between centers, the octahedral pattern requires that faces be shared. A preliminary report of the X-ray investigation of molybdenum(III) iodide and bromide indicates that both substances are of this type, i.e., chain polymers (XI) formed by the sharing of faces between

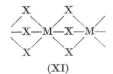

(XI)

MX_6 octahedra (*174*). The magnetic susceptibility of these compounds shows that there is probably some metal-to-metal interaction along the chain. These materials have rather unusual properties that are in accord with a polymeric nature. They occur as black, elongated fibrous crystals that felt readily, they are insoluble in both polar and nonpolar solvents, and they are air stable. Natta and co-workers have reported that the β-modification of $TiCl_3$ also is a linear polymer with the structure (XI) (*224a*).

Several other compounds have been suggested as being based on a linear octahedral pattern with the sharing of faces. Most of these are compounds prepared by Schmitz-DuMont and his students. In studying the analogies between hydroxides and amides they have prepared many cobalt and chromium compounds and postulated that a number of these, such as $Co(NH_2)_3$ (*277*), $Cr(NH_2)_3$ (*278*), $Ti(NH_2)_3$ (*276*), $Co(NH_2)_2(OH)$ (*271*), and $Cr(NH_2)(OR)_2$ (*269, 274*), are polymers in which the three anions may be bridged between pairs of metal atoms in such a fashion that a linear polymer results. They also believe that $TiO(NH_2)_2$ (*270*) and $Co(PH_2)_3$ (*279*) are similarly constituted. It is, of course, quite possible that all three anions are not shared between the same two metal atoms and that a quite different polymeric structure is present. It is desirable that at least one of these structures be studied in detail to learn whether a two- or three-dimensional polymerization is involved rather than the one-dimensional polymers pictured, particularly in view of the rarity of this type of polymer. Bandyopadhayay has proposed a quite similar structure for $Ni_2(NH_2C_2H_4NH_2)_2(NO_2)_3OH$ in which all six coordinated groups function as bridging units (*16*). This proposal, too, should be viewed with some reservation, especially in view of the unnatural use of ethylene-diamine as a bridging group instead of a bidentate ligand.

There is structural evidence that an anion of this pattern exists. In his investigation of the structure of the complex lead halides $CsPbX_3$, Møller has found the iodide to consist of polynuclear complex ions in chains with six iodides arranged octahedrally about each lead atom (*212*). This configuration results from the sharing of faces between neighboring octahedra in the chain. Schmitz-DuMont and Kron have suggested that $Co_2(NH_2)_3(NHK)_3$ has a somewhat similar structure (*272*). The six groups about an individual cobalt atom, of course, are not all the same in this case but are three amide ions and three imide ions. The same comments apply to this formulation as to the other structures proposed by Schmitz-DuMont's group.

b. Double bridged chains. The linear polymers built from octahedrally coordinated central atoms may involve from two to five bonds in the backbone and yet have at least one bond to a noncatenating group. A simple repeating unit is possible only for the cases in which two or four bonds are involved in the backbone, and indeed these two types account for the majority of this class of polymer.

The simplest substance for which a polymeric structure based on octahedra sharing two edges has been shown is niobium(IV) iodide (*73*). Pairs of iodide ions form double bridges between the niobium atoms to yield the chain backbone and in addition there are two unshared iodide atoms bonded to each niobium atom (Fig. 5, M = Nb, W = X = Y = I). The diamagnetic character of the substance, even though niobium(IV) should contain one unpaired electron, is explained by the shifting of the niobium atoms toward each other in pairs, presumably with metal-metal interaction. Preliminary indications are that tantalum(IV) iodide has the same structure.

Perhaps the first compound shown to have a polymeric chain structure based on double bridging between octahedra was $Cd(NH_3)_2Cl_2$ (Fig. 5, M = Cd, W = X = NH_3, Y = Cl) (*185*). In it and the corresponding bromide the cadmium-to-halogen distance is approximately the same as in the simple halides, which will be discussed later. The bonds probably have substantial covalent character.

Although there is some question about their covalent nature, several hydrated halides at least physically exhibit the steric relationships of this pattern. They include $CoCl_2 \cdot 2H_2O$ (*299*), $NiCl_2 \cdot 2H_2O$ (*301*), $MnCl_2 \cdot 2H_2O$ (*300*), and $CuF_2 \cdot 2H_2O$ (*102*). In each (Fig. 5, M = Ni, Mn, or Cu, W = X − H_2O, Y − Cl or F) the catenation is through double bridging halide ions. Perhaps the most questionable of these is the latter, in which the copper-to-fluorine bonds occur in two *trans* pairs with interatomic distances of 1.89 and 2.47 A. There is apparently quite some difference in the strength of interaction in the two cases, and perhaps the structure should be interpreted as monomeric planar units rather than a polymer. If Pauling's bond order equation can be used in this case, the longer bonds have an order of 0.1 assuming the shorter have an order of 1. In the remaining cases, however, all metal-to-halogen bonds are of about the same length, and the bonding is consequently the same for all.

This type of polymerization was employed by Mellor and Coryell (*206*) to explain the two forms of $Co(C_5H_5N)_2Cl_2$, which had been considered to be *cis* and *trans* isomers of a planar configuration. Their magnetic data were incompatible with a planar configuration, so they suggested that the blue form was a tetrahedrally coordinated monomer and that the violet form was an octahedrally coordinated polymer in which there was double chloride bridging between cobalt atoms (Fig. 5, M = Co, W = X = py, Y = Cl). Subsequent structure determinations (*82, 95*) have shown Mellor and Coryell to be correct in their surmises. It is interesting to note that the polymeric form is the stable form at room temperature but that it is converted to the tetrahedral form by heating. When cooled, the tetrahedral monomer then slowly reverts to the polymer. The analogous manganese compound was also presumed to be a polymer (*206*). Dunitz has determined the structure of the corresponding copper compound (*82*) and finds that it is made of square coplanar units aggregated into chains by weaker copper-to-chlorine bonds (Fig. 5, M = Cu, W = X = py, Y = Cl). The interatomic distances in this case are 2.28 A within the planar unit and 3.05 A between units, leading to a bond number of 0.05 for the longer one. The copper structure, however, is virtually identical with the cobalt structure when the two are viewed down the *c* axis in spite of the quite weak association between units.

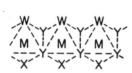

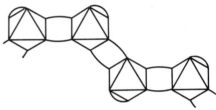

Fɪɢ. 5. General formula for one-dimensional polymer based on octahedral coordination with *trans* double bridging.

Fɪɢ. 6. General formula for one-dimensional polymer based on octahedral coordination with *cis* double bridging.

The formation of neutral polymeric chains by double chloride bridging between octahedrally coordinated metal atoms in the preceding fashion is quite common. Nardelli, Cavalca, and co-workers have found this structure for a number of cadmium chloride complexes, $CdCl_2 \cdot 2A$ (Fig. 5, M = Cd, W = X = A, Y = Cl), where A may be acetamide (*59*), thioacetamide (*215*), urea (*220*), or biuret (*61*). In all cases the cadmium-to-chlorine distances indicate covalent bonding. They have also found thiocyanate to function in a similar fashion in $Cd(NHCH_2CH_2NHCS)_2(SCN)_2$ (*60*).

Although the similar nickel compound, $Ni(SC(NH_2)_2)_2(SCN)_2$, is also polymeric (*219*), it polymerizes in a different fashion. The double bridging in this case is through the thiourea by the sharing of sulfur atoms, reminiscent of the bridging in $Cu(SC(NH_2)_2)_3Cl$.

The double bridging of octahedra to form polymeric chains has also been suggested to explain the solubility behavior of $Ru(CO)_2I_2$ (*135*), (XII),

$$RuX_2$$

(XII)

where X is Cl or Br (*1*), and $CH_2CH_2CH_2PtCl_2$ (*3*). The bidentate ligands in the latter two would force a *cis* pattern on the polymer and cause an as yet unestablished configuration (Fig. 6) to result. Abel *et al.* suggest that $Ru(CO)_2I_2$ also has such a *cis* structure. In their study of complexes of 2-pyridinaldoxime (*165*) Krause and Busch have suggested that the paramagnetic nickel(II) derivatives are polymeric with bridging 2-pyridinaldoxime or 2-pyridinaldoximate groups. Formally the suggested structures can be considered to belong to the same class as the preceding polymers because there are double bridges between nickel atoms, but there are differences in detail due to the nature of the bridging group.

In addition to the neutral linear polymers there are also polymeric anions formed by the sharing of edges between octahedra, although polymeric cations of this type do not seem to be known. The structure found for $K_2HgCl_4 \cdot H_2O$ (*186*) can be interpreted to consist of octahedral $HgCl_6$ units sharing edges to yield an infinite chain (Fig. 5, M = Hg, W = X = Y = Cl). This is another instance, however, where the interatomic distances have values indicating that the structure may not be truly polymeric. The two unshared chlorine atoms are 2.4 A from the mercury atom, whereas the bridged pairs are 2.8 and 3.15 A away. The bond orders for the latter two are 0.2 and 0.04, respectively.

Closely related to this structure is that of $K_2SnCl_4 \cdot H_2O$. Although a preliminary report indicated that the tin had a planar configuration in this compound (*70*), the detailed structural study of Brasseur and de Rassenfosse (*36*) showed that the material contains $SnCl_4^{--}$ anions polymerized through double chloride bridging to give octahedral coordination for the tin. The interatomic distances reported, 2.95 A for the bridge chlorine and 3.15 A for the unshared chlorines, are nearly the same, suggesting that all bonds are the same. The tin(II) radius, however, is not included in the usual listings, so there is nothing by which to judge the nature of these bonds. In the light of the unusual structure they have found for $SnCl_2 \cdot 2H_2O$, i.e., a coordination number of three for the tin(II) in a pyramidal molecule with a tin-to-chlorine distance of 2.59 A (*110*), Grdenić and Kamenar have reexamined the structure of $K_2SnCl_4 \cdot H_2O$ (*110a*) and conclude that it is not a polymer at all. Instead they report that the compound should be considered to be $KCl \cdot KSnCl_3 \cdot H_2O$ in which there are discrete $SnCl_3^-$ anions containing pyramidal coordination number three tin(II). Their tin-to-chlorine distances of 2.54 and 2.63 A are substantially shorter than the distances reported earlier. Some doubt is thus raised about what has been considered to be a bona fide example of a linear polymeric anion formed by double bridging an octahedral central element.

c. Single bridged chains. The second major class of linear polymers involving octahedrally coordinated elements is that in which the chain is formed by the sharing of two corners between octahedra, thus leaving four unshared ligands bonded to each central atom (Fig. 7). There appear to be several examples of this structure consisting of neutral chains, but relatively few have been completely studied by structural techniques. The interesting compound with the composition $Pt(NH_3)_2Br_3$ is of this type (*53*). In its structure there are formally alternating platinum(II) and platinum(IV) atoms with a planar *trans* configuration of two ammonia molecules and two bromine atoms about the former and an octahedral *trans* configuration of two ammonia molecules and four bromine atoms about the latter. Two of the bromine atoms in the octahedra are oriented so that they lie above and below platinum(II) atoms, thus forming a chain (Fig. 7, M = Pt, W = V = NH_3, U = X = Y = Br). The platinum(II)-to-bromine distance in the backbone is relatively long at 3.10 A compared to the other platinum(II)-to-bromine distance of 2.62 A and to the platinum(IV)-to-bromine distances of 2.45 A. If the 2.62 A distance is assumed to represent a covalent platinum(II)-to-bromine bond, the bond order of the longer bond is about one-sixth. Once more the nature of the bonding in the backbone is suspect. Although detailed structural analyses have not appeared, the suggestions that $Pd(NH_3)_2Cl_3$ (*67*), $Pd(NH_3)_2Cl_2 \cdot Pt(NH_3)_2Cl_4$ (*67*), and $Pt(NH_2C_2H_4NH_2)X_3$ where X is Cl, Br, or I (*305*) have this same structure are quite plausible. Indeed Ryan and Rundle subsequently found that the structure of $Pt(NH_2C_2H_4NH_2)Br_3$ is of this type, containing a chain of alternating platinum(II) and platinum(IV) atoms (*259a*).

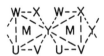

FIG. 7. General formula for one-dimensional polymer based on octahedral coordination with *trans* single bridging.

FIG. 8. Structure of SbF_5. The octahedron on the right shows the three kinds of F atoms: bridging (F'), *cis* unshared (F°), and *trans* unshared (F).

A nuclear magnetic resonance study of antimony pentafluoride showed it to have three nonequivalent sets of fluorine atoms in the ratio one-to-two-to-two (*124*). This was interpreted to mean that liquid antimony pentafluoride is a mixture of long chains of octahedral antimony pentafluoride groups sharing two fluorine atoms with neighboring octahedra. The three sets of fluorine atoms are one bridging fluorine, two unshared fluorine atoms *cis* to one another, and two unshared fluorine atoms *trans* to one another (Fig. 8). The bonding is assumed to be principally ionic with some fractional covalent character.

Porai-Koshits has determined the structure of $Ni(NH_3)_3(NCS)_2$ (*239*) and finds that it is a neutral polymeric chain in which there is bridging between nickel atoms by thiocyanate ions and in which there are three ammonia molecules and one thiocyanate ion coordinated to each nickel atom to complete the octahedral pattern (Fig. 7, M = Ni, Y = NCS, W = X = U = NH_3, V = NCS). The interatomic distances correspond to covalent bonding.

There have also been a number of compounds prepared which are suggested to be of this type. They include: (a) several one-to-one compounds formed between various tetrafluorides and coordinating groups such as tertiary amines and nitriles, e.g., $TiF_4 \cdot C_5H_5N$ (*214*) and $VF_4 \cdot NH_3$ (*62*); (b) polysulfide derivatives of cobalt and rhodium dimethylglyoxime complexes (*189, 191*); (c) the triammine complexes of cobalt(II) $Co(C_5H_5N)_3X_2$ and $Co(N_2H_4)_3X_2$ (*10*); (d) $Ni(Et_2PC_2H_4PEt_2)Br_3$ (*321*); and (e) $Cr(NH_3)_2(OPh)_3$ (*273*). In some of these cases the solubilities are low, so that molecular weight determinations have not been successful; in others it is merely suggested that the compound must be a polymer in order for the coordination pattern to be normal.

Established linear polymeric anions of this corner-sharing type all involve fluorides, in which there is some question about the nature of the bonding. In $(NH_4)_2MnF_5$, for example, the structure of the anion MnF_5^{--} is a *trans* bridged chain (Fig. 7; M = Mn, W = X = U = V = Y = F) (*282*). The manganese-to-fluorine distances are 1.84 and 1.85 A to the unshared fluorine atoms, but 2.12 A to the shared fluorine. It is thus apparent that the bonding along the backbone is substantially different from that between the manganese and the unshared fluorines. A very similar structure has been observed for Tl_2AlF_5, in which the aluminum-to-fluorine distance is about equal to the sum of the ionic radii (*51*).

Kolditz and co-workers in their investigations of some fluorine-containing compounds of fifth group elements have prepared $MSbOF_4$ with M representing Na or K (*157*) and $KAsOF_4$ (*156*). They consider that these compounds contain polymeric anions formulated as in Fig. 7 with M = Sb or As, Y = O, and W = X = U = V = F, but they have not been able to determine molecular weights because they could find no suitable solvents.

During their study of metal amides Schmitz-DuMont and his students isolated a number of compounds which they believe contain polymeric cations of this type (*267, 275*). These include $[Cr(NH_3)_3(NH_2)Br]_nBr_n$ and $[Co(NH_3)_3(NH_2)_2]_n(NO_3)_n$, in which there is presumed to be NH_2 bridging between central atoms. The recent X-ray examination of

$[Pt(C_2H_5NH_2)_4Cl_2][Pt(C_2H_5NH_2)_4]Cl_4 \cdot 4H_2O$, Wolffram's Red Salt *(70a)*, shows that it contains chains of alternating platinum(II) and platinum(IV) atoms bridged by single chloride ions (Fig. 7; M = Pt, W = X = U = V = $C_2H_5NH_2$, Y = Cl), although the investigators report that there is no long range order because of occasional slips in packing. Thus a polymeric cation similar to the neutral polymeric chain in $Pt(NH_3)_2Br_3$ has been found.

6. Coordination Number Seven

A detailed examination of the two-to-one thiourea adduct of lead(II) chloride *(216)* has shown that it does not have the double chloride bridged structure first suggested *(217)*. Instead each lead atom is surrounded by seven groups, one unshared chlorine, two bridging chlorines, and four bridging sulfur atoms (Fig. 9). The structure is based on trigonal prisms sharing bases to form a chain with a chlorine atom near the center of one lateral face of each prism. There is, of course, no reference to which to compare coordination number seven bond lengths, but the bonding must be substantially covalent for such a configuration to be found.

7. Miscellaneous

a. Single chain structures. A few coordination compounds not falling into the preceding categories have one-dimensional polymeric structures. In one of these compounds, $[Cu(NH_2C_2H_4NH_2)_2][Hg(SCN)_4]$, the backbone of the polymer consists of alternating copper and mercury atoms linked together by thiocyanate groups *(281)*. There are four sulfur atoms bonded

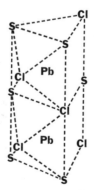

FIG. 9. Structure of $PbCl_2 \cdot 2(NH_2)_2CS$ showing a one-dimensional polymer based on coordination number seven with triple bridging.

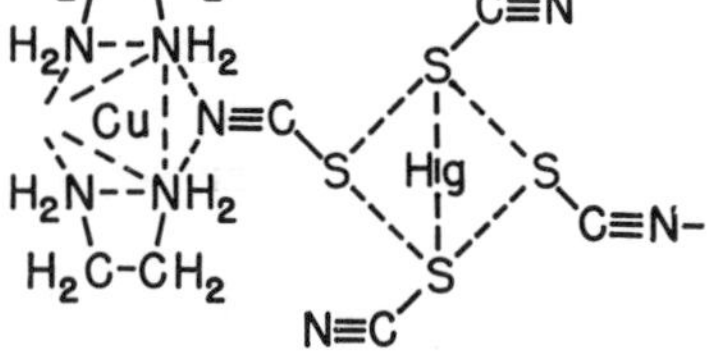

FIG. 10. Structure of $[Cu(NH_2C_2H_4NH_2)_2][Hg(SCN)_4]$.

to each mercury in a tetrahedral pattern with bond lengths corresponding to covalent bonds. The bonding about the copper is again of the typical four strong bond, two weak bond distorted octahedral relationship so common for copper (Fig. 10). In this case the two weak bonds are to the thiocyanate groups shared with the mercury atoms. The bond order for these bonds is about one seventh, indicating that the backbone is very weak and that perhaps the structure should be considered an association of planar and tetrahedral ions rather than a polymer.

An unusual structure is indicated for R_2NCS_2Au. It is soluble in nonpolar solvents to give solutions containing a dimer. An X-ray structure investigation, however, is reported to show that the compound in the solid state (XIII) is a high polymer with chains of gold atoms (*122*). In these chains the gold-to-gold distance is said to be about that found in metallic gold. The interdimer forces, nevertheless, cannot be very strong because of the ease with which solvents break the solid structure down to a dimer.

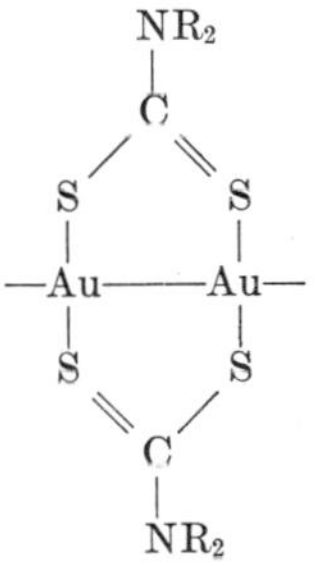

(XIII) 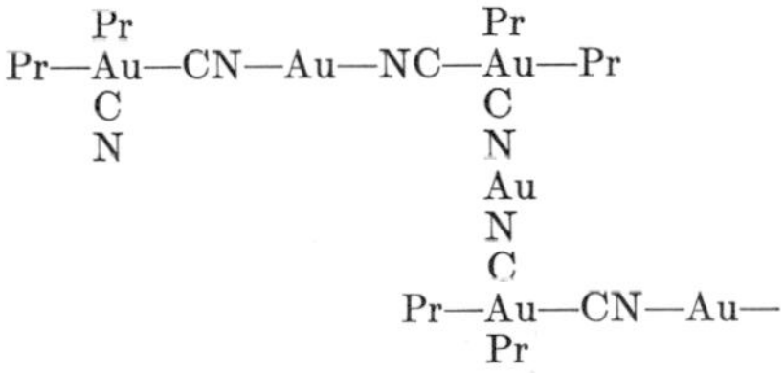   (XIV)

It has also been suggested that certain other kinds of linear polymers occur. Gibson has proposed, based on its insolubility, that the composition PrAuCN made by the thermal decomposition of Pr_2AuCN consists of a zigzag chain of alternate gold(III) and gold(I) atoms bridged by cyanide groups (XIV) (*103*). The diamagnetic nature of $Re_2Cl_4(bipy)$ and $Re_2Cl_4(o\text{-phen})$ along with the physical properties of these materials has led Colton et al. to propose a related, two oxidation state polymeric structure for them based on tetrahedral rhenium(III) and octahedral rhenium(I) (*69*). It is clear that every chloride must be shared between rhenium atoms to satisfy these requirements because there are only four chlorine atoms available to fill the eight positions left after two are occupied by the bidentate ligand. The structure pictured in the paper does not make this clear and implies that there are some unshared chlorine atoms. If the compound is polymeric, it would seem that a simple chain of alternating rhenium(I) and (III) atoms with double chloride bridging between them would be probable, although a structure similar to that proposed with all chlorine atoms shared and involving considerable branching is conceivable.

The magnetic and thermal stability data for the dioxane adduct of copper(II) formate have led Martin and Waterman to suggest an unusual polymeric chain structure for it (*194*). There are two copper atoms per dioxane, so that a simple bridging between copper atoms with dioxane does not lead to a polymer. The chain proposed (Fig. 11) has a unit containing two copper atoms held together by a copper-to-copper bond and by four formate ions shared in such a way that there are four oxygen atoms about each copper in a square planar array and a dioxane molecule that acts as the catenating group between these units.

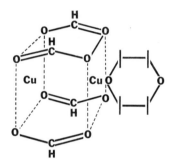

Fig. 11. Structure proposed for $Cu(OOCH)_2 \cdot \frac{1}{2}C_4H_8O_2$.

b. Double chain structures. A more complicated structure is found for some linear polymeric coordination compounds. Instead of a single chain backbone these polymers have a multiple chain or ladder-type backbone. Such a structure has been observed for central elements with coordination numbers of four (tetrahedral), six, and seven. In the compound $CuI \cdot CH_3NC$ there are two kinds of tetrahedral copper atoms, those coordinated to four iodide ions and those coordinated to two methyl isonitrile molecules (*96*). All the iodide ions are shared by three copper atoms while the methyl isonitrile molecules are unshared ligands. The resulting polymer is shown in Fig. 12a. This structure is built up of pairs of tetrahedra in an alternating pattern as indicated. The copper-to-iodine distance for the isonitrile-bonded copper atoms corresponds to a bond number of two thirds, assuming the distances in the CuI_4 tetrahedron correspond to one.

The double chains found in the polymeric anions of $CsCu_2Cl_3$ and $CsAg_2I_3$ (*43*) are built from pairs of tetrahedra sharing edges, but in these structures the pairs are joined together so that both tetrahedra share edges along the backbone as well as with each other. The staggered pattern of the $CuI \cdot CH_3CN$ structure is thus not present in this polymer pattern (Fig. 12b). All the bonds are substantially the same in the iodide, but the

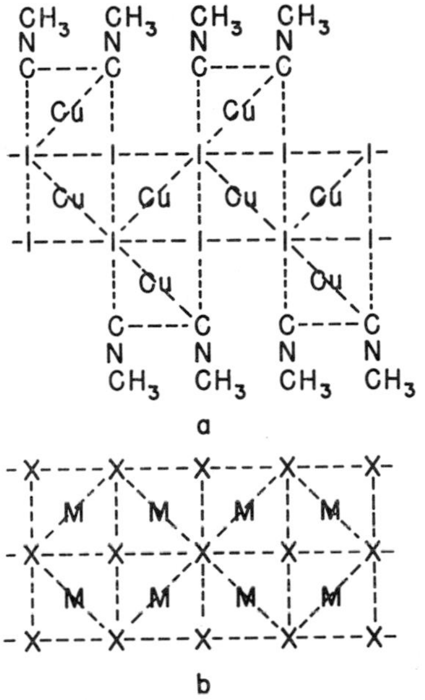

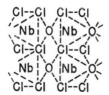

FIG. 12. Double chain polymers based on tetrahedral coordination: (a) $CuI \cdot CH_3CN$; (b) $M_2X_3^-$ with M representing Cu or Ag and X representing Cl or I.

quadruply shared chlorine atoms have a bond number of one fourth compared to the doubly shared ones in the chloride.

Double chains of octahedrally coordinated elements occur in $NbOCl_3$ (*263*), $CdCl_2(CH_3NHCONH_2)$ (*221*), and NH_4CdCl_3 (*35*, *187*). The linking between chains in $NbOCl_3$ is via double chloride bridging between niobium atoms so that a ladder polymer is present (Fig. 13). The bond number for the bridging chlorine to niobium bond is about one third. The other two

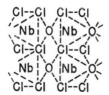

FIG. 13. Double chain polymer based on octahedral coordination in $NbOCl_3$.

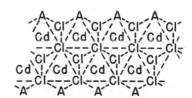

FIG. 14. Double chain polymer based on octahedral coordination in $CdCl_2 \cdot OC-(NHMe)NH_2$ and $CdCl_3^-$.

structures have closer association between the two chains with three co-ordination positions of each octahedron bridged to octahedra in the parallel chain (Fig. 14, A = $OC(NHCH_3)NH_2$ or Cl). In the two structures all the cadmium-to-chlorine distances are about the same, indicating similar bonding throughout. The basic double chain structure shown in Fig. 14 is also observed for $NaHgCl_3$ (*307*) and $KCuCl_3$ (*83*). Again the structure of a copper(II) compound is open to more than one interpretation. The bond distance between each copper atom and the chlorine atoms above and below the plane of the pair of copper atoms and their bridging chlorine atoms is longer than the other copper-to-chlorine distances, so that the bonding holding the chains together is weak. An alternative description of the structure, then, is a stepwise packing of planar $Cu_2Cl_6^{--}$ dimers.

Another thiourea complex, the one-to-one adduct with lead(II) acetate, has also been found in which the lead(II) exhibits a coordination number of seven, but in this instance the geometrical arrangement is that of a distorted pentagonal bipyramid (*218, 222*). The basic feature of the structure is a double chain formed by lead atoms and thiourea molecules. Each lead atom shares three sulfur atoms in the double chain and completes its coordination shell by bonds to four oxygen atoms in such a fashion that three oxygen atoms and two sulfur atoms are equatorial and one sulfur atom and one oxygen atom are apical. This is said to be the only compound in which the sulfur atom of a thiourea molecule is shared by three atoms.

C. Two-Dimensional Polymers

1. Coordination Number Two

It might be expected that any polymers derived from an element exhibiting a coordination number of two would consist of infinite chains. Such an assumption, however, tacitly assumes that the links between the coordination centers are acting as simple catenating groups. This, of course, is not necessarily true, and both two- and three-dimensional networks are known in which bicoordinated atoms serve as links between ligands. Brodersen has found this to be the case in both $Hg_2(NH)Br_2$ (*45, 50*) and $Hg_2(N_2H_2)Cl_2$ (*46*). The imide group in the former and the hydrazide group in the latter effectively serve as centers for the growth of sheets by coordinating with three mercury atoms and four mercury atoms, respectively. In both cases there are two nitrogen atoms bonded to each mercury atom in linear fashion at an angle of 180°. The two compounds in question thus contain polymeric cations in sheet form (Fig. 15). The bond distances are not known accurately enough to permit definite conclusions about the covalent nature of the bonds, but they are of about the right value for covalency.

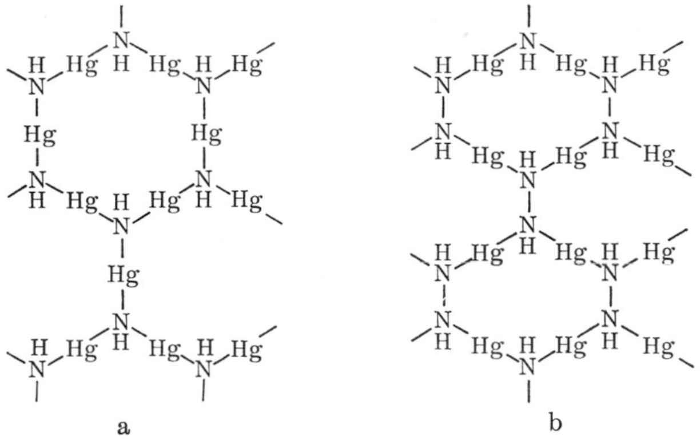

FIG. 15. Two-dimensional polymers based on coordination number two: (a) Hg_2NH^{++}; (b) $Hg_2(N_2H_2)^{++}$.

2. Coordination Number Three

In order to form a two-dimensional polymer with the coordination center serving as the nucleus of propagation it is necessary to have three bonds to each center. The smallest coordination number for which this is possible is three, and indeed one structure has been found in which a sheet polymer is formed from copper(I) with a coordination number of three (72). In $KCu_2(CN)_3 \cdot H_2O$ there are sheets made up of puckered hexagons of the composition $(CuCN)_6$ with each copper atom having three cyanide ions bonded to it in planar, presumably sp^2, fashion (Fig. 16). The water molecules are present in order to fill voids in the lattice.

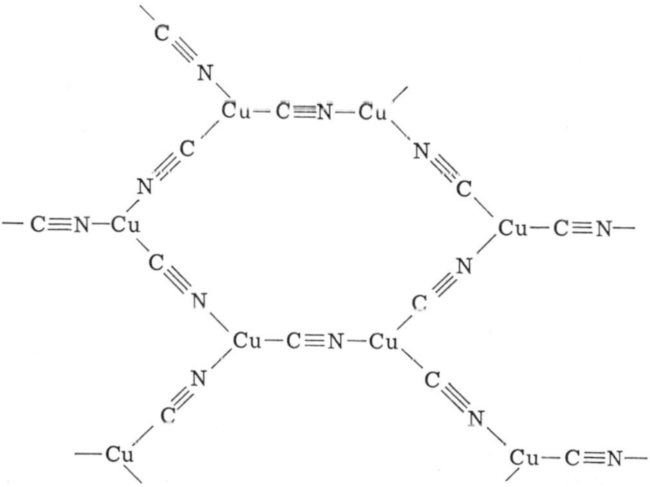

FIG. 16. Two-dimensional polymer based on coordination number three in $Cu_2(CN)_3^-$.

3. Planar Coordination Number Four

In the structure reported for $Ni(NH_3)(CN)_2$ (Fig. 17) (*248*) there are square planar coordinated atoms in a two-dimensional polymer. Actually only one-half the nickel atoms in this substance have planar coordination, the other half being octahedrally coordinated so that the sheets consist of alternating planar and octahedral units. The bond lengths suggest covalent bonding within both kinds of units. This arrangement leaves channels in the gross structure because the sheets do not pack tightly together and makes it possible for numerous clathrate compounds such as $Ni(CN)_2$-$(NH_3)(C_6H_6)$ to exist (*241, 247*). Perhaps the structure of anhydrous nickel(II) cyanide discussed earlier is related to this structure because in $Ni(CN)_2(NH_3)$ there are also two kinds of nickel atoms, as shown by the structure determination and by magnetic studies (*76, 159*). There do not appear to be sufficient donor groups in anhydrous $Ni(CN)_2$ to permit one-half the nickel atoms to be octahedral, however, so it is difficult to imagine the paramagnetic nickel atoms to be other than planar or tetrahedral.

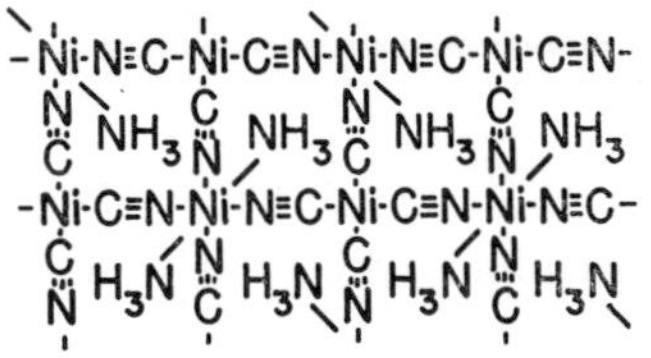

Fig. 17. Two-dimensional polymeric structure of $Ni(NH_3)(CN)_2$.

The basic copper(II) compound $Cu_2Br(OH)_3$ has a typical layer structure with hydroxyl groups and bromine atoms on both sides of the copper atoms (*4*). Each copper atom has four oxygen atoms around it in a square planar fashion at the covalent distance. In addition there are either two bromine atoms, bond number about one seventh, or one bromine atom, bond number about one sixth, and one oxygen, bond number about one third, completing the usual distorted octahedron about the copper atoms. The two different kinds of copper occur in chains that are bound together into sheets by copper-hydroxyl bridges (Fig. 18).

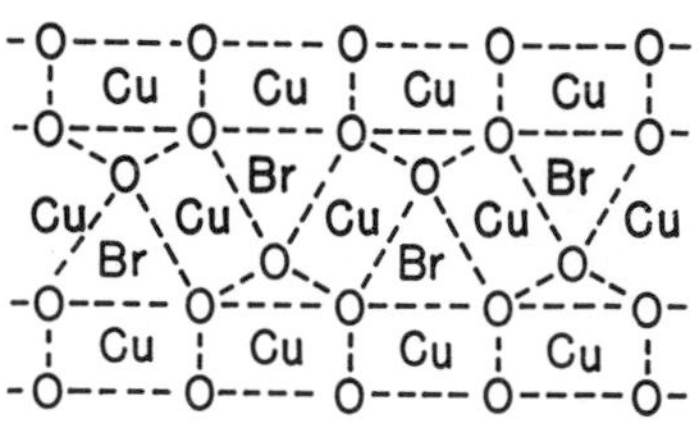

Fig. 18. Two-dimensional polymeric structure of $Cu_2Br(OH)_3$. The H atoms are not shown; each O represents a hydroxyl group.

4. Tetrahedral Coordination Number Four

Two fundamentally different types of sheet polymers have been observed for tetrahedrally coordinated mercury(II). In red mercury(II) iodide (*24, 130*) the sheets are composed of two layers of iodide atoms with the mercury atoms so placed between them that two iodine atoms from the layer above and two from the layer below occupy the four tetrahedral positions of the mercury (Fig. 19a). The bond distance corresponds to the sum of the covalent tetrahedral radii. The sheets in $2HgO \cdot HgCl_2$ (*265*), on the other hand, are formed by the linking together of oxygen and mercury. Each mercury atom in the sheet is surrounded tetrahedrally by three oxygen atoms at the tetrahedral covalent distance and by one chlorine atom at a distance intermediate between the sums of the covalent and ionic radii. Each oxygen atom in the sheet is bonded to three mercury atoms (Fig. 19b). The chlorine is not intrinsically involved in the layer structure but just completes the coordination sphere of the mercury. In addition to the mercury in this polymeric $HgOCl^-$ anion there are also mercury atoms present in special positions in the structure with octahedral coordination.

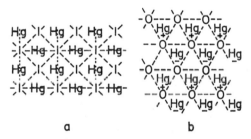

a   b

Fɪɢ. 19. Two-dimensional polymers based on tetrahedral coordination: (a) HgI_2; (b) polymeric portion of $2HgO \cdot HgCl_2$. The Hg atoms marked plus lie above the plane of the paper and are also bonded to single Cl atoms lying above them; those marked minus lie below the plane of the paper and are also bonded to single Cl atoms lying below them.

The structure found for the glutaronitrile complex of copper(I) in $Cu(NC(CH_2)_3CN)_2NO_3$ consists of a two-dimensional polymeric cation based on tetrahedral copper(I) atoms and discrete nitrate anions (*149*). All the copper atoms in planes perpendicular to the *c* axis are linked together by bridging glutaronitrile groups with the copper-to-nitrogen bond distances slightly less than the sum of the tetrahedral covalent radii. The addition of one carbon atom to the chain between the nitrile groups thus leads to an entirely different stereochemistry, for with a two carbon atom chain the resulting cation has a linear configuration (Section II,B,4,*a*).

Azomethane coordinates with copper(I) chloride to yield a one-to-two adduct ($Cu_2Cl_2 \cdot CH_3N_2CH_3$), which Brown and Dunitz have found to be a polymer (*55*). There are double chains with the composition CuCl joined together into sheets by azomethane molecules so as to give each copper atom a distorted tetrahedral arrangement of three chlorine atoms and one nitrogen atom (Fig. 20). All the bond distances indicate covalent bonding, but the copper-to-chlorine bonds holding the double chains together have a bond number of only one-half.

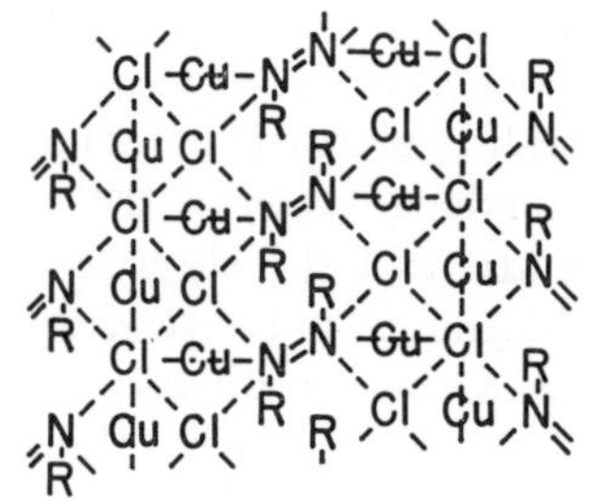

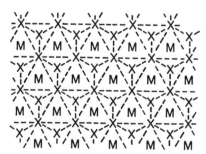

Fig. 20. Two-dimensional polymeric structure of $Cu_2Cl_2 \cdot CH_3N_2CH_3$. R represents CH_3.

5. *Coordination Number Six*

There are a number of sheet polymers known based on octahedral centers. Many binary compounds of transition elements are of this sort, the major problem being the kind of bonding involved. It would seem that there must be a certain amount of covalent character involved in the bonding in these sheets or the metallic atoms would not be distributed as they are. This follows from the unsymmetrical environment of the halogen atom, contrasted to the symmetrical arrangement in essentially ionic structures. Because of the number of compounds involved, it is necessary to limit the discussion to an outline of the typical structures.

Fig. 21. Two-dimensional polymer based on octahedral coordination in MX_2.

A large number of dihalides possess a layer structure with octahedral coordination of the metallic atom. Representative structures are those of cadmium iodide (*30*, *286*) and cadmium chloride (*237*). Actually the coordination pattern is the same in both, and the major difference between the two structures is the manner in which one layer is packed on top of the next. This is a result of the packing of the halogen atoms, which is hexagonal close-packing for the cadmium iodide structure and cubic close-packing for the cadmium chloride. A typical polymeric sheet, however, has the same geometrical pattern in both structures with cadmium atoms occupying completely the octahedral sites between two layers of close-packed halogen atoms (Fig. 21). Pauling (*235*) and Wells (*312*, p. 278) list a number of compounds having each of these structures, but their lists are not completely accurate. In most of the cases cited complete structure determinations have not been made, and it has been found recently, for example, that zinc chloride does not have the cadmium chloride structure (*38*, *232*). One compound not on the lists that has clearly been shown to have the cadmium iodide structure is germanium(II) iodide (*240*). Related to these structures is the structure of mercury(II) bromide (*302*) which is also exhibited by yellow mercury(II) iodide (*109*). Two of the six bromine atoms about the mercury atom are at a distance of 2.48 A, whereas the other four are at 3.23 A, leading to a bond number of 0.06 for the latter. It is more reasonable to consider the mercury(II) bromide structure to be molecular rather than polymeric.

Three different structures have been reported for trihalides, two of which are closely related in the same fashion as the cadmium iodide and cadmium chloride structures. These are the chromium(III) chloride (*318*) and bismuth(III) iodide (*33*) structures. In the former the halogens are cubic close-packed, in the latter hexagonal close-packed. Again the polymeric sheets consist of two layers of halogen atoms with metal atoms occupying octahedral sites between the layers. In the trihalides, however, only two-thirds of the sites are occupied (Fig. 22). Other compounds with the chro-

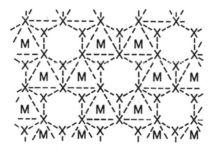

FIG. 22. Two-dimensional polymer based on octahedral coordination in MX_3.

mium(III) chloride structure are ruthenium(III) chloride (*293*), chromium(III) iodide (*114*), and various mixed halides of chromium such as CrBrCl₂ (*114*). Chromium(III) bromide (*32*) and iron(III) chloride (*319*) have the bismuth(III) iodide structure.

A novel structure has been reported for gallium(III) iodide (*5*). It differs fundamentally from the preceding two trihalide structures in that all the halogen atoms are not shared between gallium atoms. The sheet polymer is a square array of alternate gallium and iodine atoms with unshared iodine atoms located directly above and below each gallium atom (Fig. 23). The unusual packing of the iodide atoms is very strong evidence for directed covalent bonding in this structure.

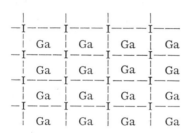

FIG. 23. Two-dimensional polymeric structure of GaI₃. Not shown are single unshared I atoms above and below each Ga atom completing the octahedral coordination.

FIG. 24. Two-dimensional polymeric structure of FeOCl. The Fe atoms marked minus lie a little below the plane of the O atoms, the unmarked Fe atoms a little above. There are single Cl atoms below the O atoms marked minus and above those marked plus, completing the octahedral coordination about the Fe atoms.

A number of basic halides also have a structure consisting of two-dimensional neutral polymeric sheets. Best known is the FeOCl structure (*106*), also exhibited by InOX where X may be chlorine or bromine (*98*). The layers are made up of sheets containing the metal atoms coordinated to four oxygen atoms in such a way that the halide ions on the outside of the layer complete a *cis* octahedral pattern about the metal atoms (Fig. 24). In Cd(OH)Cl the structure is not the same, but instead consists of alternating layers of hydroxyl groups, cadmium atoms, and chlorine atoms so packed that each cadmium is octahedrally coordinated with three hydroxyl groups on one side of it and three chloride groups on the other (*123*). This is very similar to the cadmium chloride structures (Fig. 21) with one-half of the chlorine atoms replaced with hydroxyl groups. The cadmium-to-chlorine distance is about the same in this structure as in cadmium chloride, so that the bonding apparently is of the same type in each structure.

Three different kinds of neutral polymeric sheets involving octahedral atoms remain to be mentioned. An examination of the structure of

$Cd(OOCCH_2NH_2)_2 \cdot H_2O$ *(180)* shows that the two glycinate ions are chelated in planar fashion about the cadmium atom but that these planar units are then linked together into an infinite sheet by a network of coordination bonds and hydrogen bonds. "Free" oxygens of two neighboring carboxyl groups are coordinated to the cadmium to give each cadmium a coordination number of six. The difference between the 2.3 A cadmium-to-oxygen distance within the planar unit and the 2.5 A distance from cadmium to neighboring "free" oxygens is in a region in which the bond number is very sensitive to the value. Because the distances are not reported accurately enough, it is not possible to compare the bonding types.

Their study of the reaction of pyrazine and its *N*-methyl derivatives with nickel(II) and cobalt(II) halides has led Lever *et al.* to the isolation of a number of one-to-one derivatives which they propose are an interesting type of two-dimensional polymer *(173a)*. The sheet structure suggested consists of *trans* double-halide-bridged octahedra (as in Fig. 5) linked together by pyrazine molecules, so that there is double bridging in one direction in the sheet and single bridging in the other.

Malatesta has proposed that the stable, diamagnetic, insoluble isonitrile complexes of palladium with the formula $Pd(CNR)_2$ where R may be phenyl, *p*-tolyl, or *p*-anisyl are polymers *(190)*. He suggests that each palladium atom is bonded to four neighboring palladium atoms in a square planar relationship with the aromatic isonitriles coordinated to the palladium from above and below to give an octahedral environment. An alternative suggestion that each palladium is coordinatively unsaturated and forms only two linear bonds with the two isonitrole molecules seems less likely in view of the insolubility of the products.

Polymeric sheet anions based on octahedral coordination are also known. Various tetrafluoroaluminates form sheets in which octahedral AlF_6^{3-} units share the four equatorial corners (Fig. 25) *(51, 52, 203)*. The same

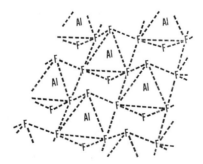

FIG. 25. Two-dimensional polymeric structure of AlF_4^- based on octahedral coordination with single bridging.

arrangement is found for the polymeric, anionic tetrafluoro complexes of nickel(II) (*15*, *254*, *257*), copper(II) (*154*), and zinc(II) (*268*). Since K_2MgF_4 has the same structure (*39*), it may well be that these substances are all ionic aggregates rather than systems containing any appreciable covalent bonding. The nickel-to-fluorine distance in K_2NiF_4 and also in Li_2NiF_4 is slightly less than the sum of the covalent radii, however, suggesting that in NiF_4 the bonds are covalent. It is interesting to note in this respect that the copper-to-fluorine distance to the unshared atoms above and below the sheet, 1.95 A, is somewhat less than the 2.08 A distance within the sheet. This unusual relationship for copper, i.e., an octahedral environment with two near and four far neighbors rather than vice versa, is interpreted as a Jahn-Teller effect in a substantially ionic system. It should be noted that here, also, the bond distances are all less than the sum of the covalent radii (2.12 A).

The structure of NH_4HgCl_3 (*116*) is a modification in which the halogen atoms within the polymeric sheet are shared by four rather than by two metallic atoms. Again there are unshared halogen atoms above and below the metal atom giving the polymeric anion the same structure found in gallium(III) iodide sheets (Fig. 23), and again there is some question as to whether the structure is a lattice of mercury(II) chloride molecules containing also ammonium and chloride ions or a true polymeric structure. The mercury-to-chlorine distance within the sheets is 2.96 A, whereas it is 2.34 A perpendicular to the sheet. This difference leads to a bond order of 0.09 for the bonds within the sheet, supporting a basically molecular structure.

Kolditz and Haage (*156*) have prepared samples of $KAsO_2F_2$ by heating $KAsF_4(OH)_2$ and concluded that the product is a sheet polymer with a structure similar to that of $KAlF_4$ (Fig. 25) with oxygen bridges between the octahedra. The analytical results suggest a molecular weight of about 7.6×10^3 if a regular structure with F and OH end groups is assumed. The authors believe that this molecular weight is a reasonable estimate because the two most likely factors leading to error, an irregular structure and holes in the structure, will have opposite effects on the apparent molecular weight.

In addition to the halide-based two-dimensional polymers of this type $NaCrS_2$ also contains a polymeric sheet anion (*28*, *255*). It differs markedly from the linear chain in $KFeS_2$. There are hexagonal layers of atoms of chromium, sulfur, sodium, and sulfur repeated in that order through the crystal. The structure is thus one in which the sheet anions consist of two layers of sulfur atoms with the chromium atoms located in octahedral sites between them, the sheets being held together by sodium ions. The structure of the polymeric sheet is similar to that of cadmium chloride

(Fig. 21), but the gross structure obviously has differences because the sheet is an anion. The structure of $NaCrSe_2$ is similar (*256*).

Although there are numerous examples of polymeric sheets based on octahedral coordination in which the sheet is neutral or an anion, no structure has yet been found in which the sheet is a cation. The reaction of chromium(III) chloride with the aliphatic diamines $NH_2(CH_2)_nNH_2$ with $n = 4$ to 7 is reported to lead to polymers with the composition $[Cr(diamine)_2Cl_2]Cl$ that may be of this type (*265a*).

D. Three-Dimensional Polymers

1. Coordination Number Two

Three-dimensional coordination networks have been established for several different patterns. Although a coordination center with a linear, coordination number two pattern cannot sustain such a network itself, several compounds contain the polymeric cation with the composition Hg_2N^+, in which there is linear sp coordination for the mercury(II) (*8, 177, 228, 253*). This cation has an inverse tridymite structure with mercury replacing oxygen and nitrogen replacing silicon. In this case, then, the tetrahedral ligand, the nitride ion, is really the key to the three-dimensional polymer, and the metal coordination center is acting as the catenating group. The bond lengths are longer than the sum of the covalent radii but appreciably less than the sum of the ionic radii. Covalent bonding dominates. Much the same situation is found in the structure of Ag_3SNO_3 (*19*). This substance, too, contains a polymeric cation in which the metallic ion has linear sp coordination. There is a difference, however, in that there are six silver atoms bonded to each sulfur in a distorted octahedral pattern. The silver-to-sulfur distances are close to the covalent radii sum.

2. Coordination Number Four

The remaining natural three-dimensional polymers are based on either tetrahedral or octahedral central elements. In many cases it is difficult to decide whether the bonding is covalent or ionic, and whether the substance in question should be considered a polymer in the sense of a network structure with directed bonding or merely an assemblage of ions, since most ionic materials would be expected to pack in tetrahedral or octahedral relationships (*312*, p. 64). The zinc blende and the wurtzite structures are, perhaps, the basic polymer structures for tetrahedral elements in one-to-one binary compounds. In both structures the cation is tetrahedrally surrounded by anions and vice versa. The difference between the two structures is again based on packing as with the cadmium chloride and iodide structures. In the zinc blende structure the anions are in cubic close-packing, in the wurtzite structure hexagonal close-packing (*312*, p. 154). Ordinary silver iodide has the zinc blende structure (*74, 292, 316, 317*) while its low temperature form has the wurtzite structure (*158*). The copper(I) halides similarly have forms with both structures (*74, 128, 166, 320*). The compounds Ag_2HgI_4 and Cu_2HgI_4 have related structures in that the three cations occupy the four cation sites on a statistical basis (*144*).

Zinc chloride represents another type of tetrahedral polymer in which now the anions bridge only two cations instead of four, as in the preceding structures (*38, 232*). In all three forms of zinc chloride there is tetrahedral coordination, and in all three the zinc-to-chlorine distance is about 2.30 A, which is only slightly less than the sum of the tetrahedral ionic radii 2.35 A. Both zinc bromide and zinc iodide present much the same picture (*231*). It thus appears that there is little covalent bonding in these structures. It will be recalled that both Wells and Pauling have indicated that zinc chloride has the cadmium chloride structure. These recent structure determinations show that it does not.

The structure of zinc cyanide is also of the three-dimensional network type based on tetrahedral coordination (*324*). In it the linear cyanide groups bridge between zinc atoms to give a fairly open structure. Zinc cyanide is a very stable substance in spite of this, reflecting the strength of its bonding. This is underlined by the weakness of the coordination compounds formed by zinc cyanide with ligands such as ammonia, pyridine, and 2,2'-iminodipyridine (*285*). The difficulty of preparing anhydrous nickel cyanide, and the ease with which it forms coordination compounds with neutral ligands, are in striking contrast and can be traced directly to the differences in structure between the two compounds. Cadmium cyanide has the same kind of structure as zinc cyanide (*283*).

The two-to-one adiponitrile complex of copper(I) nitrate completes the picture for dinitrile complexes. The complex cation in this substance is a three-dimensional four-connected network of copper atoms held together by dinitrile molecules (*147*). Thus the nature of the polymerization varies again as another carbon is added to the chain between the nitrile groups. The copper-to-nitrogen distance in the three-dimensional complex is also less than the sum of the tetrahedral covalent radii.

3. Coordination Number Six

Octahedral coordination is present in a number of different compositions. The simplest of these is the one-to-one binary composition which has the sodium chloride structure. Perhaps the best example of this structure is silver chloride (*74, 316, 317*) in which the interatomic distance of 2.77 A is substantially less than the sum of the ionic radii 3.07 A. Indeed a careful study of the physical properties of pure silver chloride (*210*) shows that it is not very similar to typical ionic materials but is quite plastic in nature. Silver bromide has this same structure in which the anion effectively bridges six cations (*74, 316, 317*).

Another simple composition having a polymeric octahedral configuration is the rhenium trioxide structure in which each anion is shared between two cations in such a fashion as to give octahedral coordination to each cation (*205*). Such a structure, which is relatively open, is found for $TiOF_2$ (*304*), NbO_2F (*101*), TaO_2F (*101*), MoF_3 (*113*), and TaF_3 (*113*). The interatomic distances in all these substances are less than the sum of the ionic radii, supporting covalent character in the bonding.

Another trifluoride, that of vanadium (*135a*), along with iron(III) fluoride and cobalt(III) fluoride (*121*), has a more compact structure based on alternate, regularly spaced metal atom and fluorine atom layers. This structure also consists of octahedra sharing corners but the octahedra are turned so that three fluorine atoms lie above and three below each metal atom. This structure does not contain the voids present in the preceding structure. The interatomic distances in these compounds also indicate covalent bonding.

Closely related to the rhenium trioxide structure is the perovskite structure, which is found for a number of substances with the composition $M'MX_3$ (*312*, p. 300). The polymeric anion has the same structure as has rhenium trioxide, but the uncoordinated cation in the compound occupies the hole in the center of the unit cell, giving a more compact structure. Since the early studies showing that $CsHgCl_3$ (*224*) and $CsCdCl_3$ (*94*) have this structure, there have been various other compounds also found to be so constituted. Among them are $CsNiCl_3$ (*295*), $CsPbX_3$ where X is chlorine or bromine (*211, 212*), and some complex fluorides with the composition $M'MF_3$ (*44, 85, 127, 181, 257*). It is interesting that, where available, the interatomic distances are close to the sum of the covalent radii and that in $KCuF_3$ the Jahn-Teller shortening of two copper-to-fluorine bonds is noted.

A number of complex cyanides have a polymeric three-dimensional structure (*23, 58, 250, 251, 306*). These are all related to the Prussian blue structure reported by Keggin and Miles (*141*) which is based on a cubic framework with octahedrally coordinated metal atoms at the corners of the cube and cyanide groups along the edges of the cube. The stereochemistry of the cyanide ion, as previously mentioned, is such that its available electron pairs are on either end of the ion, leading to a relatively rigid, open framework. The open spaces are generally occupied by cations such as K^+, leading to a structure quite similar to the perovskite structure. After they have been dried, the precipitated ferrocyanides are very stable toward acids, showing the good stability of the structure.

An example of a polymeric cation of this cubic type based on octahedral coordination is found in the dioxane complex of silver perchlorate, $AgClO_4 \cdot 3C_4H_8O_2$ (*243*). The tetrahedral perchlorate anion occupies the center of a cube that has silver atoms at its corners and dioxane molecules along the edges in such a manner that each silver atom is surrounded by six oxygen atoms. The silver-to-oxygen distance of 2.46 A is said to indicate negligible covalent character in the bonding. There is little or no hindrance to rotation of either the dioxane molecules or the perchlorate ion.

4. Coordination Number Nine

Although the interatomic distances are not all equivalent, the structure of lead(II) chloride is apparently based on a coordination number of nine for the lead (*34*). Each lead atom is surrounded by nine chlorine atoms in the form of two distorted octahedra with one face in common on which the lead atom is located. An idealized drawing showing the relationships is given in Fig. 26. Lead(II) bromide has the same kind of structure (*226*).

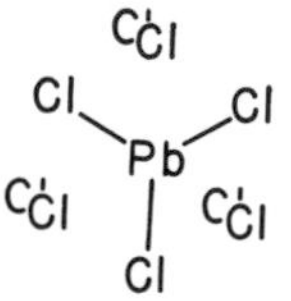

Fig. 26. The coordination pattern in $PbCl_2$. The three Cl atoms joined to the Pb atom are in the same plane with it. The others are in pairs lying above and below that plane.

The same coordination pattern is also present in uranium(III) chloride and the numerous trihalides which have the uranium(III) chloride structure (*322*). The over-all structures of the latter differ from the lead(II) chloride structure in much the same way that the chromium(III) chloride structure differs from the cadmium chloride structure, i.e., one third of the cation sites in the lead(II) chloride structure are not occupied in the uranium(III) chloride structure. The bonding in these substances is generally considered predominantly ionic.

III. Reactions Leading to Coordination Polymers

It is apparent from the foregoing that a great variety of coordination polymers has been found during the study of inorganic systems. This variety indicates the large number of possibilities confronting the investigator deliberately setting out to synthesize coordination polymers. The usual goal of such a program, the preparation of a thermally stable polymer for use in applications where known organic polymers break down, only serves to complicate the problem more, because there are very few data in the literature on the thermal stability of coordination compounds. The programs aimed at coordination polymers have thus taken several directions, depending on the way the individual investigator has assessed the many possibilities involved.

Before the specific systems investigated are discussed, it is appropriate to consider some general aspects of the synthesis of coordination polymers. Broadly speaking, the mechanism of organic polymerizations involves the building up of polymers from smaller units by addition or by condensation reactions. The former process involves unsaturation in the organic monomers. Since it is rare to find unsaturation of a comparable type in inorganic coordination compounds, such addition polymerization mechanisms are not expected to play an important part in the formation of coordination polymer backbones involving metals. On the other hand, polymerization of the condensation type should be strictly analogous to organic condensation polymerizations, and, indeed, most investigators have attempted to prepare coordination polymers by such techniques. Because there are no double bonds in coordination chemistry giving rise to unsaturation analogous to that in organic chemistry, coordinative unsaturation and the tendency to satisfy it by polymerization can be considered to be the basis for an addition-type class of polymerization in the formation of coordination-compound polymers.

From this point of view it is possible to conceive of a number of different routes by which coordination polymers can be built from monomeric units. A suggested classification follows (*26a*):

1. Condensation polymerization
   a. Homocondensation
   b. Heterocondensation
2. Addition-type polymerization
   a. Elimination-addition
   b. Substitution-addition
   c. Oxidation-addition
   d. Redistribution-addition
   e. Rearrangement-addition

The condensation types require little comment, for they are strictly analogous to some organic polymerizations and merely require the existence of the appropriate monomers from which small molecules can be split without affecting the coordination sphere. Hypothetical examples of 1a and 1b, respectively, would be the loss of water from $[Pt(NH_3)_2(Cl)_2(OH)_2]$ to yield polymeric $(—Pt(NH_3)_2(Cl)_2O—)_x$ and the splitting out of

HCl between $[Pt(NH_3)_2(Cl)_2(OH)_2]$ and $(CH_3)_2SiCl_2$ to form polymeric $(-Pt(NH_3)_2(Cl)_2OSi(CH_3)_2O-)_x$.

The number of addition-type polymerization classes reflects the fact that coordinative unsaturation can arise in two ways, first by loss of a ligand from a fully coordinated atom and second by a change in oxidation number of an atom with a concomitant change in coordination number. The latter is a novel procedure not yet attained in practice. Type 2a, of the former kind, involves the removal of a neutral ligand from a co-ordinated species, leaving a coordinatively unsaturated species, which then polymerizes so that the central atom may maintain its coordination number. An example of this mechanism would be the formation of $(-Cr(CH_3COCHCOCH_3)_2OP(C_6H_5)_2O-)_x$ from $[Cr(CH_3COCHCOCH_3)_2-(OP(C_6H_5)_2O)(NH_3)]$ by the loss of ammonia. This can be pictured to occur as shown in Fig. 27 with the postulated intermediate an unstable species with a coordination number of five.

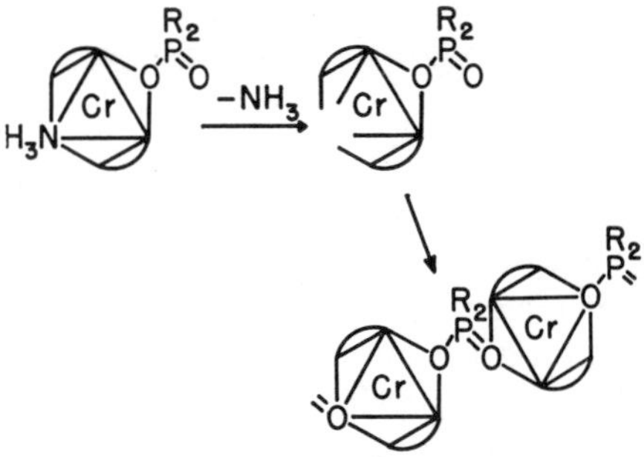

FIG. 27. A hypothetical elimination-addition polymerization.

The second type, 2b, involves much the same change. In it, however, a polydentate ligand or a combination of unidentate ligands is displaced by reaction with a catenating group that cannot function as a polydentate ligand. The exact mechanism of such a reaction could be quite compli-cated, but for the purposes of classification the net result is all that will be considered. Many of the systems that have been studied are of this type and detailed study of some of their mechanisms would be of interest. A simple example of this class is afforded by the reaction of chromium(III) acetylacetonate with diphenylphosphinic acid to displace acetylacetone and yield $(-Cr(CH_3COCHCOCH_3)_2OP(C_6H_5)_2O-)_x$. This is the same polymer used to illustrate type 2a, and the same intermediate could be involved although the reaction suggested could also proceed by other paths.

Type 2c is unique to inorganic systems. An example of this kind of polymerization is furnished by the hypothetical reaction (Fig. 28) in which bivalent, tetracoordinated platinum is oxidized to quadrivalent, hexaco-ordinated platinum by an oxidizing agent that can function as a catenating group when reduced. The same kind of polymerization could also be achieved by starting with a higher oxidation state with a lower coordination number, such as chromium(VI) with tetrahedral coordination, and reducing the element to a lower oxidation state with a higher coordination number, in this instance hexacoordinated chromium(III). Such a polymerization will also be classed as an oxidation-addition.

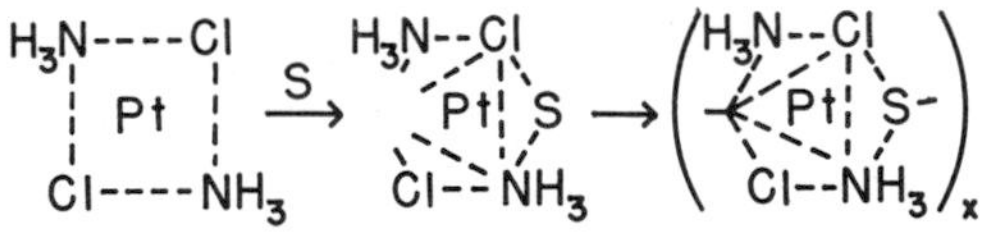

FIG. 28. A hypothetical oxidation-addition polymerization.

Type 2d is more complex. The kind of reaction under consideration is the opposite of a disproportionation. Thus, one mole of chromium(III) diphenylphosphinate could react with two moles of chromium(III) acetyl-acetonate to yield $(-Cr(CH_3COCHCOCH_3)_2OP(C_6H_5)_2O-)_x$. Such a reaction could again conceivably go through the same intermediate penta-coordinated species, $Cr(CH_3COCHCOCH_3)_2OP(C_6H_5)_2O$, suggested in 2a and 2b; the mechanism, however, could clearly be quite complicated.

The last class, 2e, represents a type of reaction that has been used or attempted rather frequently in the study of inorganic polymers. It is the formation of a linear polymer from a cyclic compound by a process in which the ring is opened, followed by recombination of the resulting radicals to a polymer. Some beryllium bis-β-diketone polymers, which will be discussed later, were prepared by this procedure *(150)*.

A type of reaction which differs in kind from the preceding classes is:

3. Degradation polymerization

By degradation polymerization is meant the process by which a natural two- or three-dimensional polymer is converted to a linear, or possibly a two-dimensional, polymer by reaction with appropriate coordinating agents. For example, it is conceivable that the three-dimensional network in zinc cyanide could be broken down by the reaction of zinc cyanide with acetylacetone in a one-to-one ratio, leading to the formation of the linear polymer $(-Zn(CH_3COCHCOCH_3)CN-)_x$.

Since the distinction between classes is quite fine in some instances, the differences merit further discussion. Obviously all homocondensations as well as those heterocondensations in which the coordination sphere of the metal is disturbed must involve coordinately unsaturated intermediates, but in deference to established usage these classes will be arbitrarily maintained for reactions obviously analogous to organic condensations. Homocondensation and elimination-addition differ in that the small molecule eliminated comes from *one* parent monomer molecule in the latter, whereas it comes from *two* parent molecules in the former. Accordingly, there are elimination-addition reactions that do not fit the homocondensation picture. An example would be the loss of pyridine from $[Zn(CH_3COCHCOCH_3)(CN)(C_5H_5N)]$ to form polymeric $(—Zn(CH_3COCHCOCH_3)CN—)_x$. It is very unlikely that polymerization reactions will be found in which the elements of pyridine are split out between molecules.

Likewise, heterocondensation and substitution-addition polymerizations resemble one another. The example given to illustrate substitution-addition differs from a typical heterocondensation in that the reaction is unsymmetrical, whereas heterocondensations are symmetrical, i.e., one covalent and one coordinate covalent bond are involved in the substitution-addition as opposed to two covalent bonds in the heterocondensation. The specific criterion to be used for distinguishing between the two will be that a coordinate-covalent bond is formed in the backbone during substitution-addition.

Although degradation polymerization is a special case of substitution-addition, the fact that an existing polymeric structure is being attacked seems worthy of emphasis because polymers are generally prepared by a building process. Rearrangement-addition and redistribution-addition polymerizations are similar to one another; however, they are clearly quite different in concept and should be classified separately.

IV. Synthetic Coordination Polymers

A. General Discussion

Very few of the programs directed toward the synthesis of coordination polymers involve strictly inorganic backbones, and, even if the backbone is inorganic there is generally organic material involved in the other ligands. This, of course, raises a serious question about the ultimate thermal stability of these systems as compared to strictly organic polymers, since carbon-to-carbon bonds are also involved in the coordination polymers. The statement that coordination increases the thermal stability of the ligand (*142, 288*) is not borne out by a careful study of the pyrolysis of acetylacetone and coordination compounds derived from it (*64, 65, 303*). The results show that acetylacetone undergoes very little decomposition in four hours at 266°C, whereas its metal derivatives decompose to a significant extent under the same conditions. It is thus necessary to investigate thermal stabilities in each system to establish the effect of coordination. Furthermore, Marvel and his students have found that simple Schiff base complexes are more stable thermally than more highly polymerized analogs (*199, 201*), suggesting that a coordination polymer may well be less stable thermally than its monomeric prototype. A study of some polymeric phthalocyanines leads to the same conclusion (*98*).

B. Quilon and Related Products

A commercially exploited system of what appear to be coordination polymers is that of the chromium complexes of carboxylic acids typified by Quilon and Volan (*119*). Although the structures of the compounds involved have not been explicitly proved, those postulated appear quite reasonable. A typical process involves the reduction of chromyl chloride by an alcohol in the presence of a carboxylic acid to give a solution presumed to contain a dimeric complex such as (XV). Dilution of the resulting

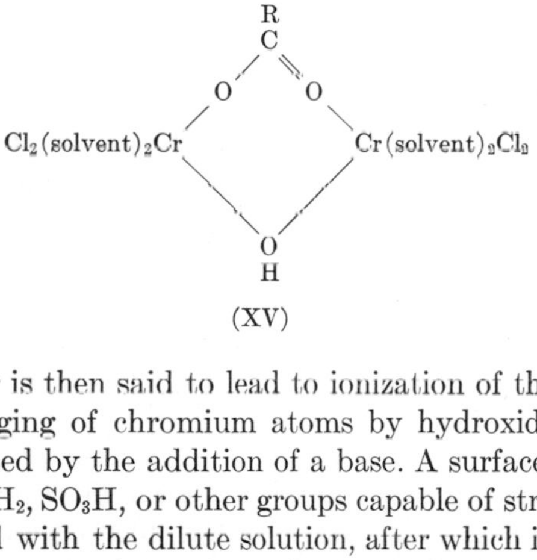

$$
\begin{array}{c}
R \\
C \\
O \diagup \quad \diagdown O \\
Cl_2(\text{solvent})_2Cr \diagdown \qquad \diagup Cr(\text{solvent})_2Cl_2 \\
O \\
H
\end{array}
$$

(XV)

solution with water is then said to lead to ionization of the chlorine atoms and a further bridging of chromium atoms by hydroxide ions (olation). This step is expedited by the addition of a base. A surface containing OH, NH_2, COOH, $CONH_2$, SO_3H, or other groups capable of strong bond formation is then treated with the dilute solution, after which it is heated. This heat treatment leads to further polymerization, giving an insoluble coating firmly attached to the surface. A typical picture of a treated surface is that suggested for the bond between Volan and glass (Fig. 29). This structure puts the organo group of the methacrylic acid away from the treated surface and imparts its properties to the substrate. In the example pictured it is then possible to treat the surface further using the Volan as a coupling agent for reinforced plastic laminates, the chromium bonding to the reinforcing material and the methacrylic acid with the laminating resin. By variation of the organic group (*105, 133, 134*) a number of different properties can be imparted to a surface. Quilon involves chromium

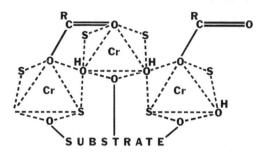

FIG. 29. Bonding between Volan and glass (substrate furnishing O atoms). S represents solvent molecules. See text for R.

complexes of stearic or myristic acid and gives water-repellent, nonadhesive surfaces. Another of the more exploited of these systems is that of fluorocarbon acids, which results in an oil- and water-repellent surface, the basis for one Scotchgard system (*54, 230, 249*). Tentatively the polymerization reaction involved here can be classed as a homocondensation.

C. Aluminum-Oxygen Backbones

The preparation of coordination polymers based on an aluminum-oxygen backbone has met with some success in the hands of Kugler. The treatment of $Al(OC_2H_5)_3$ with $CH_3COCH_2COOC_2H_5$ yielded $Al(OC_2H_5)_2$-($CH_3COCHCOOC_2H_5$), which was hydrolyzed with water in xylene and heated to yield a resin containing aluminum-oxygen chains (*167*). The reaction involved appears to be a homocondensation. The product presumably has the composition $Al(CH_3COCHCOOC_2H_5)O$ and could consist of linear chains with single oxygen bridges between aluminum atoms if the coordination number of the aluminum is four, but there is also the possibility that the aluminum has a coordination number of six, which would lead to more complicated multiple bridging of aluminum atoms. Very closely related to this composition is the copolymer Kugler has prepared by the controlled hydrolysis of the product from the reaction between $Al(OC_2H_5)_2(CH_3COCHCOOC_2H_5)$ and $(CH_3)_2Si(OC_2H_5)_2$ (*168*). Here too the bright yellow resin obtained might be linear (—Al(CH_3COCHCOOC$_2$H$_5$)OSi(CH$_3$)$_2$O—)$_x$ or a more complex structure depending on the coordination number of the aluminum. Breed and Haggerty have reported that a very similar reaction, that of $Al(O-i-C_3H_7)_2(CH_3COCHCOCH_3)$ with $(CH_3)_2Si(OOCCH_3)_2$, yields brittle, benzene-insoluble products analyzing approximately as $Al(CH_3COCHCOCH_3)OSi(CH_3)_2O$ when carried out without a solvent at elevated temperatures (*37*). In cyclohexane, however, only 40% of the theoretical amount of $CH_3COOC_3H_7$ is evolved, and the product has a molecular weight of 400.

In a study of polymers containing chelated aluminum Frank and co-workers (*100, 234*) have prepared some water-sensitive, glassy solids which are low polymers of the same type as the products reported by Kugler. Their polymers were made by the controlled hydrolysis of $[(i\text{-}C_3H_7O)_2\text{-}Al(C_2H_5OCOCHCOR)]$, with R representing CH_3 or OC_2H_5, to $(—OAl(C_2\text{-}H_5OCOCHCOR)—)_x$, reactions that can be classified as homocondensations or heterocondensations depending on the exact mechanism. The same reaction with $[(i\text{-}C_3H_7)_2Al(CH_3COCHCOCH_3)]$ produced $[Al(CH_3\text{-}COCHCOCH_3)_3]$ and an aluminum-containing precipitate. Apparently there was disproportionation in this case.

McCloskey and co-workers at U. S. Borax Research Corporation recently initiated a fundamental investigation of polymers based on aluminum-oxygen backbones (*184*). They have not reported any successful polymerizations yet, for their efforts have been directed mainly toward the study of monomers, but it would appear that some of the intermediates they have prepared, such as $Al(C_9H_6NO)(OC_2H_5)_2$, will soon lead to polymers.

D. Titanium-Oxygen Backbones

There has, perhaps, been more effort devoted to the study of systems involving the titanium-oxygen backbone than the aluminum-oxygen backbone. With these compounds there is also a question about the coordination number of the metal, both four and six being conceivable although the latter is certainly the more probable. A number of the compounds made have been written as containing four-coordinate titanium. Many of the systems involved here are alkoxides and as such are discussed in Chapter 7. The conversion of titanium tetrachloride or titanium tetraalkoxides to titanium carboxylates by reaction with RCOONa or RCOOH leads to $Ti(OH)_x(OOCR)_{4-x}$ with the value of x dependent on the reaction conditions (*14, 117, 118, 169*). On storage the materials become insoluble, presumably by homocondensation, although they are initially very soluble in nonpolar solvents. It has been suggested that the products after aging are linear polymers with tetracoordinate titanium in a titanium-oxygen backbone (*117*).

A related sequence involves the reaction of titanium tetraisopropoxide with acetylacetone to give $Ti(CH_3COCHCOCH_3)_2(OC_3H_7)_2$, which, after hydrolysis and drying, yields, via homocondensation, insoluble $Ti(CH_3\text{-}COCHCOCH_3)_2O$ formulated as a linear polymer with hexacoordinate titanium in a titanium-oxygen backbone (*117*). Frank and co-workers have prepared similar Ti(chelate)$_2$(OR)$_2$ monomers and converted them to Ti(chelate)$_2$O compositions in which the chelating group is 8-quinolinol or dibenzoylmethane (*100*). The product containing the former is stable to 400°C, infusible, and sparingly soluble. In addition to the homocondensation of these monomers they have investigated the heterocondensation with dihydroxy compounds, which will be considered in Section IV,K. Rust and co-workers have also prepared (Ti(C$_9$H$_6$NO)$_2$O)$_x$ and confirm its high melting point and solubility characteristics (*259, 294*). So far molecular weights have not been determined with assurance for these products. Related copolymers have been reported. The reaction of Ti(C$_9$H$_6$NO)$_2$(O-*i*-Pr)$_2$ with (C$_6$H$_5$)$_2$Si(OH)$_2$ carried out in distilling benzene yielded an insoluble yellow powder analyzing to be [Ti(C$_9$H$_6$NO)$_2$OSi-(C$_6$H$_5$)$_2$O]$_x$ (*37a*). It decomposed above 275°C. Cohydrolysis of a mixture of Ti(CH$_3$COCHCOCH$_3$)$_2$Cl$_2$ and R$_2$SiCl$_2$ is reported to yield polymeric bis(acetylacetonato)titaniumorganosiloxanes (*6b*).

E. Phthalocyanines

One of the most thermally stable systems of coordination compounds known is the phthalocyanine family. Various attempts have been made to build polymeric phthalocyanines in order to take advantage of this stability. These attempts have been of two kinds; first, polymerization through the phthalocyanine units, maintaining the phthalocyanine coordination pattern around the metal; second, polymerization through the metal by expanding its coordination number without changing the nature of the phthalocyanine (Fig. 30). Considerably greater effort has been devoted to the first approach.

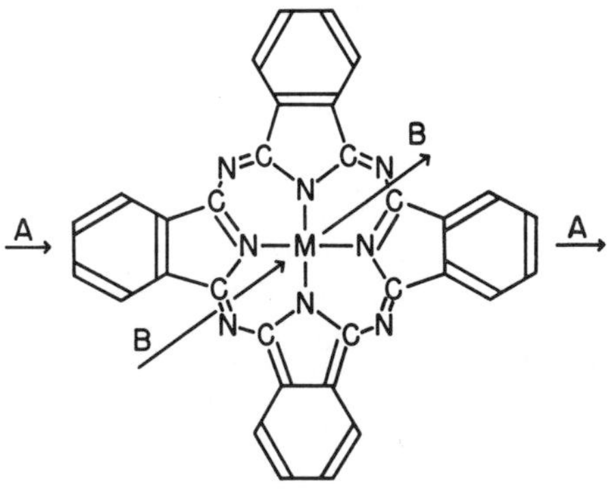

Fig. 30. Polymers based on phthalocyanine. A represents linking through the ligand, B through the metal.

Perhaps the first report of a reaction capable of yielding a polymeric phthalocyanine appears in the patent literature. The way in which it and analogous reactions have been carried out does not permit them to be unambiguously classified although heterocondensation appears most suitable. Bucher (*56*) reports that a dimer is isolated from the reaction of 3,3′,4,4′-tetracyanodiphenyl ketone or 4-cyanodiphenylsulfone-3,3′,4′-tricarboxylic acid (plus urea) and *o*-phthalonitrile with copper(I) chloride, although one might expect more complex products polymerized through the phthalocyanine. Marvel and his students have investigated the analogous reaction of 3,3′,4,4′-tetracyanodiphenyl ether (*197, 198*) and find that with the mixture of nitriles the reaction appears to go no further than a dimer or trimer. On the other hand if the phthalonitrile is omitted and the reaction is simply one between copper and 3,3′,4,4′-tetracyanodiphenyl ether, a product is obtained which is insoluble in sulfuric acid and is reported to be the first high molecular weight (presumably crosslinked) phthalocyanine. The characterization rests on analysis of the products and their physical properties because molecular weights could not be determined. They also found that the soluble products formed from the mixed nitriles were converted to insoluble crosslinked polyimides by fusion with m-$C_6H_4(NH_2)_2$. The path for this heterocondensation is via the reaction of the diamine with the anhydride and imide groups on the edges of the low molecular weight polymers. Somewhat before Marvel's studies the reaction of copper with 3,3′,4,4′-tetracyanodiphenyl was investigated in a search for high temperature stable dielectric films (*289*). Although the products were not fully characterized, they were soluble in sulfuric acid, suggesting their molecular weights were not very high.

A more rigid system should result if the polymer is based on 1,2,4,5-tetracyanobenzene. First studies again, however, were with mixed nitriles or with acid anhydrides in the presence of urea in an attempt to get linear polymers (*171, 172*). The products obtained have not been well characterized due to analytical difficulties and solubility problems, but the thermal stability of the products has proved to be less than that of simple phthalocyanines. With only the tetranitrile or pyromellitic anhydride as a reactant, rather than a mixture of nitriles or acid anhydrides, the reaction runs smoothly to give a polymer of relatively low degree of polymerization (*78*). Drinkard and Bailar report molecular weights up to 4000, i.e., degrees of polymerization up to six, on the basis of end group analysis, assuming the peripheral groups to be carboxylic acid groups. The molecular weight may be varied within limits by suitable control of reaction conditions, but a maximum is reached at a degree of polymerization of six. Epstein and Wildi have examined the electrical properties of this type of polymeric phthalocyanine (*88*) and suggest that *p*-type conductivity is involved in its electrical behavior. In a study of the conductivity of phthalocyanines which included products made from pyromellitic acid, urea, and copper(I) chloride (*90*) it was concluded that a higher molecular weight product was obtained when the reaction was run at 250° than when it was run at 350°C.

Although the product is not strictly speaking a phthalocyanine, it is appropriate at this point to consider the polymer prepared by the reaction of $Cu(CH_3COCHCOCH_3)_2$ with $C_2(CN)_4$ (*22*). Again the exact nature of the infusible, insoluble black product is not certain, but the suggestion of

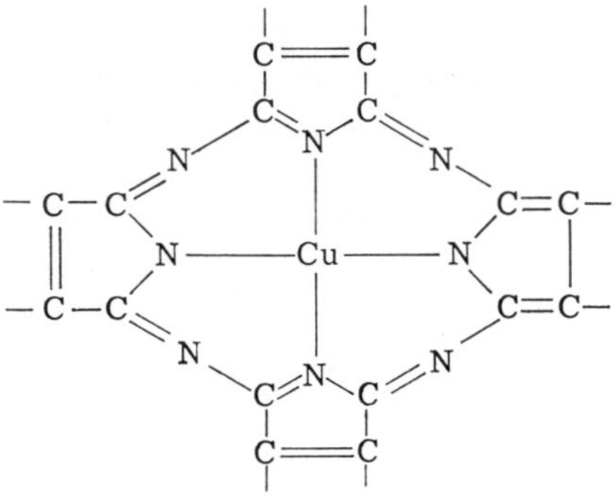

(XVI)

the authors that the basic unit of the structure is (XVI) is reasonable. The reported analyses are not in complete accord with such a structure. In particular the nitrogen content is quite low, and there is an appreciable

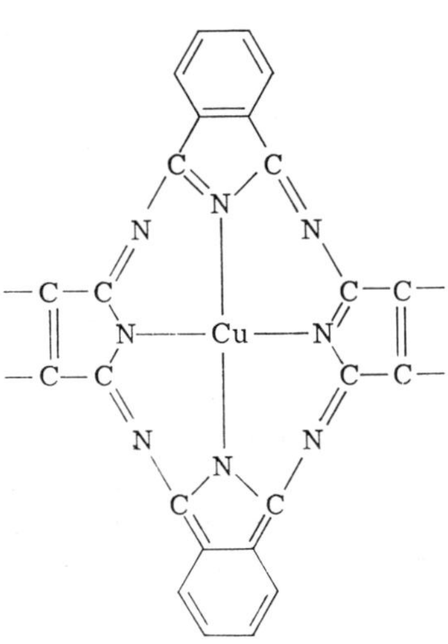

(XVII)

quantity of hydrogen present. This suggests that there is still CH_3-$COCHCOCH_3$ present in the structure. With phthalonitrile or *o*-phenylene-diamine also present during the reaction it is suggested that linear polymers with the structure (XVII) are formed. Apparently the same polymer can be formed as a film on the surface of iron, copper, or nickel plates by direct reaction with $C_2(CN)_4$ vapors (*22a*). The electrical resistance and capacity of such a film on iron show it to be a *p*-type conductor.

The second approach to phthalocyanine-containing polymers, in which the polymerization is through the metal, has not been exhaustively studied. In fact, the polymers seem to have been made incidentally as part of the study of phthalocyanines rather than by deliberate design. Elvidge and Lever have found that in pyridine there is first association of molecular oxygen with manganese(II) phthalocyanine followed by a series of equilibria leading to the formation of $(C_5H_5N)Mn(C_{32}H_{16}N_8)O$ (*87*):

$$MnC_{32}H_{16}N_8 + C_5H_5N + O_2 \rightleftharpoons Mn(C_{32}H_{16}N_8)(C_5H_5N)O_2 \rightleftharpoons$$

$$(C_5H_5N)Mn(C_{32}H_{16}N_8)O_2Mn(C_{32}H_{16}N_8)(C_5H_5N) \rightleftharpoons (C_5H_5N)Mn(C_{32}H_{16}N_8)O$$

The latter loses pyridine when heated under reduced pressure to form polymeric $(—Mn(C_{32}H_{16}N_8)O—)_x$, which is thermally stable but dissolves readily in pyridine, giving a solution that readily precipitates manganese(II) phthalocyanine when heated. It thus appears that the manganese(IV) in the polymer is not extremely stable. The formation of this polymer is an excellent example of an elimination-addition polymerization.

Joyner and Kenney have reported experiments involving germanium phthalocyanine that suggest that a similar polymer is formed with germanium (*137*). The germanium is introduced into the phthalocyanine ring by the direct action of germanium tetrachloride on phthalocyanine in quinoline to yield $Ge(C_{32}H_{16}N_8)Cl_2$. The latter is then converted to $Ge(C_{32}H_{16}N_8)(OH)_2$ either by heating with a pyridine-ammonium hydroxide mixture or by adding a sulfuric acid solution to water. After the hydroxide has been heated, there is no longer a hydroxyl band in the infrared spectrum, indicating that the polymer $(—Ge(C_{32}H_{16}N_8)O—)_x$ has been formed by a homocondensation with loss of water. A similar result has been found starting with silicon tetrachloride (*233*).

In their investigation of the chromium phthalocyanine system Elvidge and Lever prepared $Cr(C_{32}H_{16}N_8)OOCCH_3$ which they suggest is a similar type of polymer with acetate bridges between the chromium atoms (*87a*). The central element in this case is tervalent, meaning that the catenating group must be uninegative in order to give a neutral chain as opposed to the quadrivalent central atoms and binegative catenating groups just discussed. Very little was reported about the properties of this substance.

F. Beryllium Basic Carboxylates

Another classical stable coordination compound that has been used as a model for the synthesis of coordination polymers is $Be_4O(OOCCH_3)_6$. Marvel and Martin *(196)* have investigated the replacement of part of the monocarboxylate anions in basic beryllium acetate, propionate, and benzoate with dibasic acid groups by the reaction of equimolar quantities of the appropriate beryllium compound with the acid chlorides of adipic, sebacic, β-ethyladipic, terephthalic, and isophthalic acids in a hydrocarbon solvent. The polymerization reaction is of the substitution-addition type. Viscosity data for the products indicate a low degree of polymerization, in agreement with the analytical values, which show the presence of substantial quantities of end groups. Degrees of polymerization appear to be of the order of five, so short polymers containing the catenating link (XVIII) have been made. Even at room temperature the polymers con-

(XVIII)

taining aliphatic acids disproportionate within a few days to a monomeric basic beryllium carboxylate and an insoluble product assumed to be a cross-linked polymer with composition $Be_4O(OOCR'COO)_3$. The products containing aromatic acids are somewhat more stable, but at 340°C they also disproportionate quite readily. Melt polymerization techniques apparently led to insoluble polymeric products similar to the insoluble disproportionation products. The insoluble materials were not further characterized although they are undoubtedly coordination polymers.

Study of the behavior of $Be_4O(OOCCH_3)_6$ in boiling alcohols *(115)* has shown that products with variable composition, apparently linear or sheet polymers, are formed. Conductivity experiments suggest that $Be_4O_2^{4+}$ ions are present in the alcohol. It is postulated that the products formed are based on $Be_4O_2^{4+}$ chains and $Be_4O_3^{++}$ sheets with bridging acetate ions completing the coordination sphere. The reaction actually involves the loss of acetic anhydride from the $Be_4O(OOCCH_3)_6$ to yield Be_4O_{1+m}-$(OOCCH_3)_{6-2m}$ and is thus a homocondensation. It goes to a lesser extent with the higher alcohols. A similar behavior is noted with other solvents such as pyridine, chloroform, and benzene. It should be noted that another investigation of this same reaction in alcohols *(111)* has led to the report that $Be(OR)(OOCCH_3)$ is first formed, followed by formation of a soluble, polymeric product formulated as $3Be(OH)(OOCCH_3) \cdot Be(OC_4H_9)$-$(OOCCH_3)$ in the case of C_4H_9OH.

G. Polymeric Cyclopentadienyl Complexes

The thermal stability of the recently discovered ferrocene has led to attempts to incorporate its structure into polymeric backbones. Lüttring-haus and Kullick (*182*) have reported the synthesis of α,ω-biscyclopenta-dienyl alkanes by the reaction of the corresponding dibromo compound with sodium cyclopentadienide and the subsequent heterocondensation of this compound to a mixture containing predominantly polymeric ferro-cenes through reaction with iron(III) chloride. The polymer is presum-ably $(-C_5H_4(CH_2)_nC_5H_4Fe-)_x$ with $n = 3$, 4, or 5, although with $FeCl_3$ there is always a deficiency of iron in the polymer, suggesting that some strictly organic units are also incorporated into the polymer. Insolubility of the polymeric fractions prevented full characterization.

Knobloch has taken another approach to the introduction of ferrocene into the backbone (*152*). Instead of making the polymer by a coordination heterocondensation process, he has employed essentially normal organic heterocondensation reactions. A number of reactions were surveyed be-tween $ClCOC_5H_4FeC_5H_4COCl$ and diamine and dihydroxy compounds. The products formed using interfacial techniques have some physical properties like organic polymers of fairly low molecular weight. By and large after fusion the products were brittle. A transesterification between $CH_3OOCC_5H_4FeC_5H_4COOCH_3$ and ethylene glycol gave similar results.

Still a third approach to the linking of ferrocene nuclei through the ferrocene part of the molecule, again by a typical organic polymerization technique, has been reported by Korshak (*160*). The treatment of ferro-cene or its derivatives with free radicals has resulted in the formation of linear polymers of the form $(-C_5H_4FeC_5H_4-)_x$ along with some three-dimensional polymers. The molecular weight of the polymers formed is in the range 8–10,000.

A fundamentally different kind of polymer has been investigated by Gorsich (*108*). Although the cyclopentadienyl group is also involved in this type, the backbone of the polymer is formed between the metal and other groups, so that the cyclopentadienyl group is merely bonded to the backbone instead of being a part of it. Treatment of $Ti(C_5H_5)_2Cl_2$ with titanium tetrachloride in xylene or chlorine in carbon tetrachloride yields $Ti(C_5H_5)Cl_3$, which can then be hydrolyzed to a product with the com-position $Ti(C_5H_5)(Cl)O$, which melts at 258° to 260°C. The reaction is either a heterocondensation or a homocondensation. Attempts to deter-mine a molecular weight in organic solvents have not been successful because of the limited solubility of the product, so it has not been possible to decide whether the substance is cyclic or is a linear polymer. The hetero-condensation of $Ti(C_5H_5)_2Cl_2$ with $(C_6H_5)_2Si(OH)_2$ (*103a*) or with $(CH_3)_2$-

SiCl$_2$ (*6a*), on the other hand, yielded products that no longer contained cyclopentadienyl groups bonded to the titanium but were instead poly(organotitanosiloxanes).

H. Dithiooxamides

There are a number of organic molecules which can conceivably form coordination polymers by acting as bischelating agents, i.e., with one part of the molecule chelating to one metal atom and with another part of the molecule chelating to another metal atom. In the systems that have just been discussed the dicarboxylic acids function in this way between beryllium atoms (Section IV,F) and the biscyclopentadienyl compounds between iron atoms (Section IV,G). Much effort has been devoted to the synthesis and study of such compounds with the goal the preparation of the polymer type shown in Fig. 31. It is extremely likely that a number of polymers of this type have been made and reported in the literature as simple compounds. No attempt has been made to cover all such possibilities for this review.

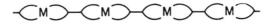

Fig. 31. General representation of polymers based on bischelating agents.

The metal derivatives of rubeanic acid have been known for some time (*245*) and were considered to be inner complexes until Jensen suggested from steric considerations that they must be linear polymers (*136*). His formulation was based on: (1) the magnetic moment of the nickel derivative, which indicated a planar configuration about the nickel; (2) the

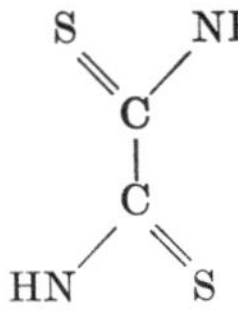

$$
\begin{array}{ccc}
S & & NH \\
\diagdown & & \diagup \\
& C & \\
& | & \\
& C & \\
\diagup & & \diagdown \\
HN & & S
\end{array}
$$

(XIX)

nature of the rubeanate anion, (XIX), which seemed to him such that all four of the planar positions of one nickel atom could not be satisfied by one anion; and (3) the physical properties of the rubeanates. The infrared spectra of several rubeanates are consistent with the structure proposed by Jensen (*18*). An interesting use of the copper and nickel derivatives has been patented involving their incorporation into organic polymers to give polarizing materials (*6*). In view of the publication dates it appears that Amon and Kane were not aware of Jensen's suggestions and considered the rubeanates to be chelates affecting the substrate due to some adsorption phenomenon. The later interpretation (*11*) that during the stretching of the substrate polymer the linear rubeanate polymer is oriented in the sheet accounts for the effect more clearly.

Hurd and co-workers have examined the nickel derivatives of a number of N,N'-disubstituted dithiooxamides prepared by the heterocondensation reactions of nickel salts with substituted dithiooxamides in aqueous alcohol (*132*). The analyses indicate the compositions to be approximately $Ni(RNCSCSNR)$, where R represents $C_6H_5CH_2$, $C_{18}H_{37}$, HOC_2H_4, CH_3-$COOC_2H_4$, or $(CH_3)_2NC_3H_6$. A more detailed examination of the N,N'-dimethyl compound suggests that it is a low polymer, the size and terminal structure of which depend on both the manner of preparation and purification. The preparation in the absence of base appears to yield a short polymer containing about six dithiooxamide nuclei and five nickel atoms, whereas in the presence of two equivalents of sodium hydroxide there is apparently sodium present in the end groups of the product with analytical results indicating the formula to be $(CH_3NCSCSNCH_3Ni)_{6-8}(CH_3-NHCSCSNCH_3Na)$ or $(NaCH_3NCSCSNHCH_3)(CH_3NCSCSNCH_3Ni)_{16}-(CH_3NHCSCSNCH_3Na)$. Although all the products are solids, there is some change in physical properties as the organic group in the substituted dithiooxamide becomes larger. In particular the melting points decrease, and the solubility in organic solvents increases. The N,N'-dimethyl products are stable at 198°C for two days *in vacuo*.

I. Hydroxyquinone Bischelates

Frequently cited examples of coordination polymers of similar type are the metal derivatives of 2,5-dihydroxy-*p*-benzoquinone (XX) studied by Frank and co-workers (*99*). Actually the authors do not claim to have

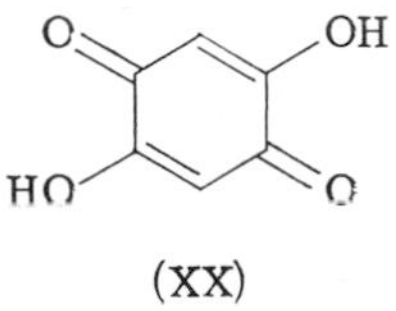

(XX)

made any polymers. In fact they believe that they made simple combinations rather than polymeric structures, and they specifically point out that solvation renders interpretation of the structures difficult. Kanda and Saito, on the other hand, report the preparation of one-to-one complexes of 2,5-dihydroxy-*p*-benzoquinone with copper(II), nickel(II), and cadmium(II) which they believe are polymers (*139*). The behavior of a polyvinyl alcohol film containing the copper derivative when stretched resembles that of a similar film containing nickel or copper rubeanate (Section IV,H) and is taken as supporting evidence for a linear polymeric structure. This property suggests the use of the compound for polarization (*262*). Light scattering, streaming birefringence, and electron microscopy indicate that colloidal particles of the copper(II) derivative of 2,5-dihydroxy-*p*-benzoquinone are rigid rods 1000 to 2000 A long (*138a*). Jain and Singhal have suggested that the compound formed between zirconium(IV) and 2,5-dihydroxy-*p*-benzoquinone is a three-dimensional polymer (*135b*).

Naphthazarin (XXI) and quinizarin (XXII) are other hydroxyquinones that have been studied. A comparison with (XX) shows the major difference between them and 2,5-dihydroxy-*p*-benzoquinone to be that the latter forms five-membered chelate rings, whereas both (XXI) and (XXII)

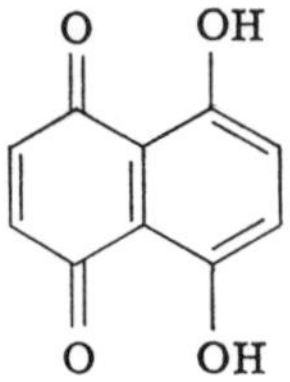

(XXI) 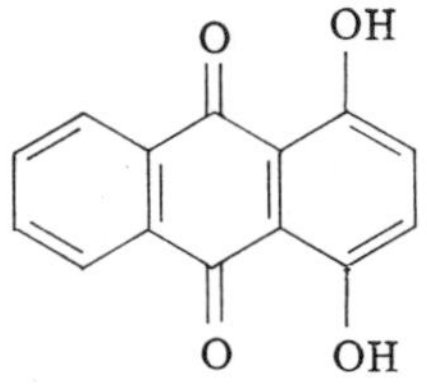   (XXII) 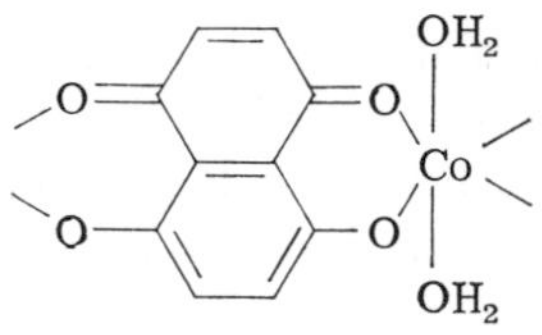   (XXIII)

give six-membered rings. It is quite possible that the one-to-one metal derivatives of both naphthazarin and quinizarin prepared sometime ago (*97, 112, 192*) were polymers although not recognized as such. Bailes and Calvin suggested that the cobalt(II) derivative of naphthazarin which they isolated as a dihydrate was a polymer of octahedrally coordinated cobalt (*13*) (XXIII). The bulk of the water could be removed by heating the yellow powder, but it was slowly reabsorbed from the air. Underwood and co-workers in their study of the nature of beryllium-naphthazarin complexes (*298*) decided on the basis of physical measurements that a one-to-one polymer existed, although they were not successful in preparing a pure sample. Drinkard and Chakravarty have reported the preparation of the copper derivative of naphthazarin by its heterocondensation reaction with copper(II) chloride in the presence of triethylamine (*79*). Analytical data indicate a degree of polymerization of about five, and the compound is reported to be thermally stable above 450°C. The copper(II), cobalt(II), zinc, nickel, and beryllium derivatives of naphthazarin were prepared by heterocondensation of an alcoholic solution of the ligand with an aqueous solution of the appropriate metal ion (*29*). The products were all deliquescent powders considered to be polymers on the basis of elemental analysis and infrared spectra, but no information about end groups was obtained from the latter. Structures postulated for the dihydrates of the cobalt, nickel, and zinc derivatives are analogous to (XXIII); those for the anhydrous copper and beryllium derivatives are of the type shown in Fig. 31. On the basis of thermogravimetric analyses the order of decreasing stability was found to be beryllium > nickel > zinc > copper > cobalt. (The work with copper has been reported in detail separately in reference *62a*.)

Knobloch and Rauscher have investigated the use of various techniques to prepare coordination polymers (*152*, *153*). Interfacial polymerization proved possible for the preparation of the one-to-one copper derivative of quinizarin when the copper was present as $Cu(NH_3)_4^{++}$ in an aqueous phase and quinizarin was present in a benzene solution, a polymer being readily produced by heterocondensation at room temperature in a few minutes. The copper analysis was a little low for an infinite chain polymer. A substitution-addition melt polymerization between beryllium acetylacetonate and quinizarin gave a polymer with a degree of polymerization of about five. In similar melt polymerizations between quinizarin and a number of metal derivatives of acetylacetone (*163*) Korshak and co-workers have found the degree of polymerization of the insoluble black products to be mostly under 10. X-ray diffraction showed the nickel, zinc, cadmium, and copper derivatives to be crystalline and the cobalt derivative to be amorphous. The order of decreasing thermal stability was found to be nickel > zinc > manganese > cadmium > copper > cobalt with the nickel compound stable at 400° and the cobalt derivative starting to decompose at 318°C. Similar results were obtained by solution polymerization of metal acetates with quinizarin.

J. 8-Quinolinol-Type Bischelates

The metallic derivatives of 8-quinolinol are, in general, among the more stable coordination compounds involving organic ligands. This, of course, has led to some effort to prepare polymers with the 8-quinolinolate chelate ring in the system. There are some quadridentate heterocyclic ring systems

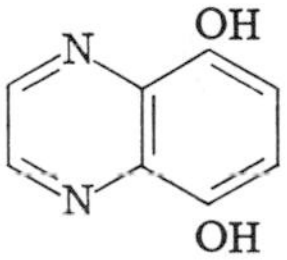

(XXIV)

that have this function on both sides of the ring. In general these have not been studied for other than analytical purposes, and for the most part the metallic derivatives have not been characterized. [See for example the studies on 5,8-dihydroxyquinoxaline (XXIV) (*2, 140*).] Kidani, however, in his study of the chelate compounds of phenazine derivatives (*146*) has come to the conclusion that copper forms one-to-one derivatives with a polymeric structure with both the 1,4- and 1,6-dihydroxyphenazines (XXV) and (XXVI) and the nitrogen oxide of the latter. The products are

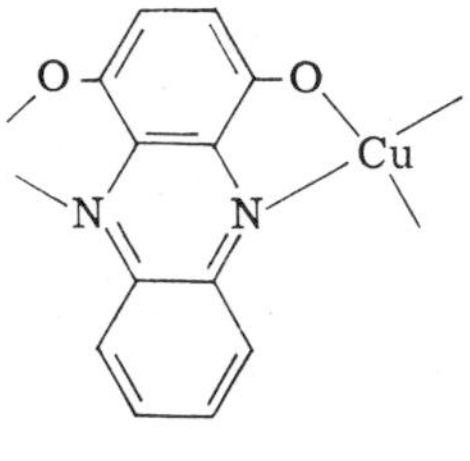

(**XXV**) 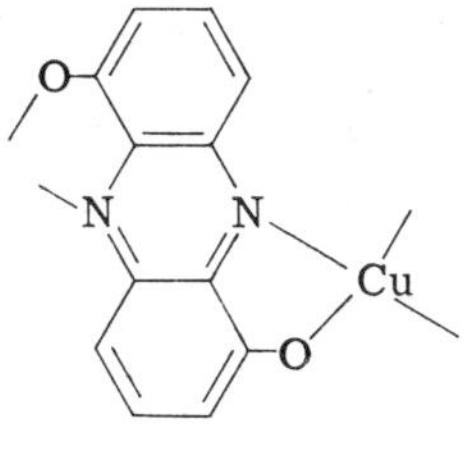   (**XXVI**)

described as amorphous solids. By means of heterocondensation reactions Kanda and Saito have prepared coordination compounds from metal salts of copper(II), silver(I), iron(III), and mercury(II), with 1,6-dihydroxy-phenazine as part of their study of high molecular weight coordination compounds. In a preliminary communication (*139*) they report that the analyses indicate the products to be polymeric, but they give few details.

Another approach to 8-quinolinolate-type polymers is to link two 8-quinolinol molecules and use the resulting compound as a catenating group. This approach has been investigated by Judd, who has prepared (XXVII) with X a single bond, CH_2, or SO_2 (*138*). The heterocondensation of these compounds with metal acetates has led to the formation of pre-cipitates that analyze fairly close to the expected values for infinite poly-mers except in the case of the sulfone, which corresponds to a trimer with solvent end groups. The products are all powders with decomposition temperatures varying from 240° to 320°C.

Korshak and his co-workers have studied the compounds formed by bis(8-hydroxyquinolyl)methane [(XXVII), X = CH_2] when substitution-

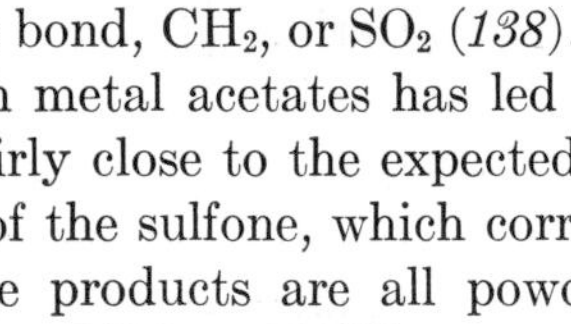

(**XXVII**)

addition reactions between it and metal acetylacetonates are run with melt polymerization techniques or by solution heterocondensation between the bischelate and metal acetates (*164*). They report that nickel and copper yield dimers and trimers but that zinc, manganese, cobalt, and cadmium form polymers. Their products are also stable to 250° to 320°C and are mostly crystalline, according to their X-ray diffraction powder patterns. Making mixed metal products with zinc and copper or cadmium, or mixed ligand products with bis(8-hydroxyquinolyl)methane and quinizarin, yielded products with similar properties.

K. Bis-β-Diketones

Perhaps one of the most investigated systems involving bischelating groups is the area embracing the bis-β-diketones. There has been much interest in the possibilities for these compounds because of the reported thermal stability of the metal complexes of acetylacetone. It now appears that the simple complexes are nowhere near as stable as some statements in the literature lead one to believe. Although it is true that some of the complexes can be distilled, there is definitely some decomposition during the distillation (*303*). There are two ways that β-diketones can be linked together to form bis-β-diketones, through the methylene group between the keto groups or through one of the carbonyl carbon atoms, i.e., $(RCO)_2$-CH—X—CH$(OCR)_2$ or $RCOCH_2CO$—X—$COCH_2COR$. Both types have been investigated.

The initial report of polymers made from bis-β-diketones is in the patent issued to Wilkins and Wittbecker (*314*). In the examples they report the preparation of beryllium derivatives of $CH_3COCH_2COC_6H_4COCH_2COCH_3$, $CH_3COCH_2COC_6H_4OC_6H_4COCH_2COCH_3$, $(CH_3CO)_2CHCH_2C_6H_4CH_2CH$-$(COCH_3)_2$, and $(C_6H_5CO)(CH_3CO)CH(CH_2)_6CH(COC_6H_5)(COCH_3)$ by melt polymerization of the appropriate bis-β-diketone with beryllium acetylacetonate in a substitution-addition reaction and also the preparation of the beryllium derivative of the last bis-β-diketone by heterocondensation using solution techniques. No analytical data are given, but the products are reported to have fiber-forming properties and to be mouldable. The polymers are said to be of lower molecular weight and softer when formed by solution techniques. They are stable for extended periods at temperatures below 300°C.

Holst has studied similar systems with the following bis-β-diketones: $(CH_3CO)_2(CH)_2(COCH_3)_2$, $CH_3COCH_2CO(CH_2)_8COCH_2COCH_3$, $CH_3COCH_2COC_6H_4COCH_2COCH_3$, $C_6H_5COCH_2CO(CH_2)_nCOCH_2COC_6H_5$ with $n = 2$ or 8, and $(CH_3CO)(C_2H_5OOC)CHCOC_6H_4COCH(COOC_2H_5)$-$(COCH_3)$ (*125*). He also investigated both melt and solution polymerization techniques for substitution-additions and heterocondensations and concluded that melt polymerization gave a maximum molecular weight of about 4000 (n about 10), whereas solution techniques (heterocondensation) employing homogeneous precipitation gave higher molecular weight polymers. The maximum degree of polymerization measured was about 16, although some products too insoluble to measure may have had higher values. Relatively low melting, fiber-forming products were isolated from $C_6H_5COCH_2CO(CH_2)_8COCH_2COC_6H_5$ with several different metals, including beryllium, cobalt, nickel, copper, uranium, vanadium, and zinc. With other co-workers Fernelius has investigated a number of other bis-β-diketones but has not found any promising leads to the development of high molecular weight polymers from bis-β-diketones (*92, 93*).

In their study of the application of various techniques to the preparation of inorganic polymers (*152, 153*) Knobloch and Rauscher found that they could make the polymeric copper(II) derivative of $(CH_3CO)_2CHCH(COCH_3)_2$ by interfacial heterocondensation using a methylene chloride solution of the latter and an aqueous solution containing a relatively unstable copper(II) complex such as $Cu(NH_3)_4^{++}$. They were not concerned with the nature of the product other than that it analyzed fairly well for an infinite polymer.

Charles, on the other hand, has looked quite carefully at the properties of copper chelate polymers derived from $(CH_3CO)_2CHCH(COCH_3)_2$ by solution heterocondensation techniques (*63*). His analytical data indicate a degree of polymerization of about five, but he found direct determination of molecular weight impossible. The failure to obtain higher molecular weights is linked to the insolubility of the products when n becomes about 5. X-ray diffraction showed the products to be crystalline. Thermogravimetric analysis and sealed tube pyrolyses show detectable weight losses starting at about 150°C, with most of the weight loss occurring between 250° and 350°C. This is about the same thermal stability that copper(II) acetylacetonate exhibits but somewhat less than for acetylacetone. The decomposition was found to be zero order, and a mechanism was suggested that involves initial dehydrogenation followed by elimination of methane with further polymerization accompanying each step. Metallic copper is ultimately formed, but the residue also contains substantial amounts of copper(II).

The conversion of these typical low molecular weight materials to high molecular weight, linear polymers has been reported by Kluiber and Lewis (*150*). It is generally believed that one of the major reasons for the low degrees of polymerization found for the polymers of metals with bis-chelates is that the insolubility of the low molecular weight fractions prevents the polymers from growing to a large size during the polymerization process. In the work under discussion this difficulty has been overcome by the rearrangement of macrocyclic beryllium compounds. Sublimation of the low molecular weight products obtained by solution copolymerization gave either cyclic monomers (XXVIII) or dimers (XXIX), depending on the nature of R. For methylene chains containing more than six carbon

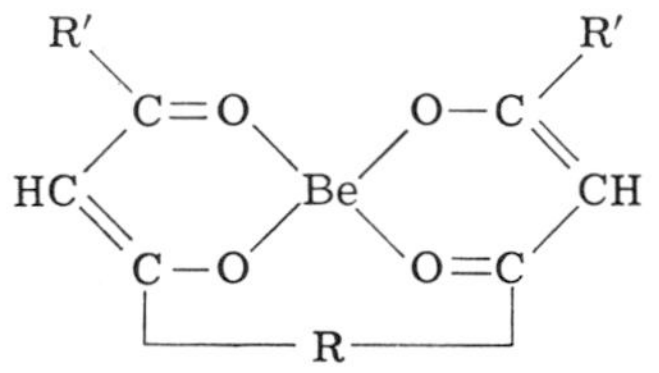

(XXVIII) 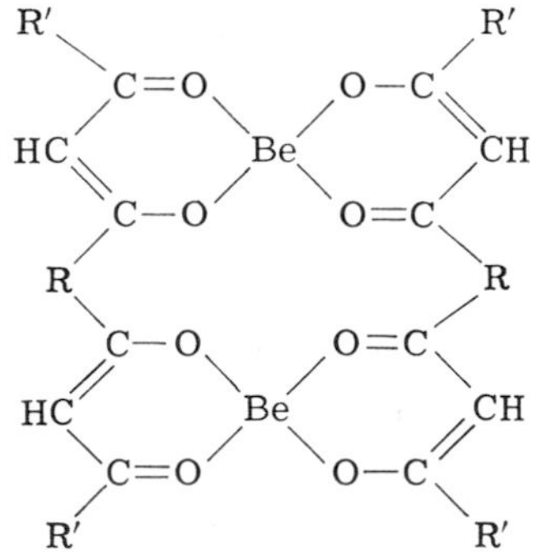   (XXIX)

atoms the monomer is isolated, for $(CH_2)_6$ both monomer and dimer, for shorter chains only dimers. Analytical data and cryoscopic molecular weight determinations support the structures assigned. Heating these macrocyclic products above their melting points produces spontaneous polymerization to amorphous materials with intrinsic viscosities in the range 0.1 to 2.7, interpreted to indicate that they are high molecular weight polymers. The mechanical properties, i.e., flexibility, tensile modulus and strength, and melt index flow rate, are characteristic of high polymers. The polymers, however, were found to revert to the macrocyclic form upon further heating, so it is concluded that polymers and macrocycles are in equilibrium. Attempts to prevent the thermal depolymerization by forming copolymers or by partial crosslinking were not successful. Replacement of the polymethylene chain by a dioxy or diimino polymethylene chain also permitted isolation of macrocyclic species and polymers; however, prolonged heating of these polymers apparently led to much cross-linking, preventing good recovery of the macrocyclic form. The higher glass-transition temperature of the dioxy type is explained in terms of less freedom of rotation about an oxygen than about a methylene group because of participation of the oxygen in resonance stabilization.

Korshak and co-workers have also investigated polymeric metal derivatives of bis-β-diketones (*161, 162*), looking at both the $(RCOCH_2CO)_2Y$ and $[(RCO)_2CH]_2Z$ types with a number of bivalent, tetracoordinate metals. They find a certain degree of parallelism between thermal stability of their products and the formation constants of the corresponding acetylacetone complexes. Korshak and co-workers used both melt polymerization (substitution-addition) and solution heterocondensation techniques. By the use of interfacial polymerization between water and chloroform solutions Koton and co-workers made polymers with Y and Z aromatic groups (*104*). Their products were the same as the corresponding polymers reported by Korshak *et al.* Kenney has investigated the thermal stability of a number of metal derivatives of $C_6H_5COCH_2CO(CH_2)_8$-$COCH_2COC_6H_5$ (*142*) and finds that in three hours at 300°C in air the zinc and copper derivatives are most stable, losing 16% in weight. Weight losses up to 43% for the nickel polymer are observed for other derivatives. The melting points of the polymers vary from 70° for beryllium to 300°C for iron. Drinkard has also reported the preparation of the copper and nickel derivatives of $(CH_3CO)_2CHCH(COCH_3)_2$ (*77*) and, with Ross *et al.* (*80*), examined the thermal properties of a series of bis-β-diketone-copper(II) polymers as a function of the length of the methylene chain. There is a linear decrease in thermal stability with increasing chain length comparable to the behavior of long chain organic compounds. This indicates that simple cleavage of the metal-ligand bonds is not the mode of decomposition. On the other hand no unusual thermal properties are conferred on the materials by the coordination sites. Oh has also prepared polymers from a number of bis-β-diketones of the $[(RCO)_2CH]_2Z$ type by a variety of techniques (*229a*). He finds that their thermal stability is related to the nature of the central atom (Be > Cu > Ni > Zn > Co) and to the nature of Z (single bond > CH_2 > C_2H_4 > $CH(C_6H_5)$ > $CH_2C_6H_4CH_2$).

In their study of polymers containing chelated aluminum (*100, 234*) Frank and co-workers prepared a different type of bis-β-diketone metal polymer that Holst apparently had prepared by substitution-addition or heterocondensation reactions in which the ratio of aluminum to bis-β-diketone was one-to-one. In order to make a linear polymer from tervalent, hexacoordinate aluminum it is necessary to block two of the positions on the aluminum. This was accomplished by first preparing $Al(CH_3COCH$-$COCH_3)(O\text{-}i\text{-}C_3H_7)_2$ and then treating it with bischelating agents in heterocondensation reactions. The bis-β-diketones used were $(CH_3CO)_2$-$CH\text{—}Y\text{—}CH(COCH_3)_2$, $(C_6H_5CO)_2CH(CH_2)_nCH(COC_6H_5)_2$, (CH_3CO)-$(C_2H_5OOC)CHCH_2CH(COOC_2H_5)(COCH_3)$, 2,4-diacetylresorcinol, and α,α'-bisethylacetoacetate. Molecular weights were low, running from 450 to 1860, and there was slow decomposition above 200°C with the evolution of aluminum acetylacetonate, indicating disproportionation. The low molecular weights appear to be caused chiefly by steric hindrance and low thermal stability. The latter factor is the result of facile interchange of chelate ligands upon heating. Similar products resulted when monomers of the type $Al(CH_3COCHCOCH_3)(CH_3COCHCOOC_2H_5)_2$ were treated with diols to yield polymers formulated as $[(CH_3COCHCOCH_3)Al(CH_3COCHCOOYOOCCHCOCH_3)]_x$.

L. Catenating Diols

During the same study Frank and his co-workers investigated the use of diols for bridging the monochelated aluminum species, assuming that aluminum might also show a coordination number of four. They were not able to isolate the hoped for polymers $(—Al(RCOCHCOR')OYO—)_x$, however, but instead obtained only one-to-one addition products when monomers of the type $(RCOCHCOR')AlX_2$ were treated with HOYOH. Schlenker, on the other hand, has apparently obtained polymers from similar systems (*266*). By the treatment of "stabilized" aluminum alkoxide solutions with both aliphatic and aromatic dihydroxy compounds he has prepared low melting products which he describes as cross-linked resins. The stabilized aluminum alkoxide solution is obtained by the treatment of an aluminum alkoxide with a keto-enol capable of chelating. The solution is presumed to contain a molecule of the type $Al(RCOCHCOR')(OR'')_2$. Solution heterocondensation with an appropriate dihydroxy compound, followed by vacuum distillation to remove the solvent and side products leaves a thermoplastic product that is soluble in organic solvents. Apparently the characterization of the products as polymers rests primarily on their physical appearance, especially their viscous nature. In this connection it is interesting to note that McCloskey *et al.* concluded on the basis of the viscosity of the reaction mixtures that the products of the reactions of aluminum alkoxides with pyrocatechol are polymers, formulated as $(—Al(OR)OC_6H_4O—)_x$ (*184*). A coordination number of three is extremely unlikely for aluminum, and it would seem that there must be extensive association between such units to give aluminum a coordination number of four or six.

M. Bis(Schiff Bases) and Related Bisazomethines

Studies of bis(Schiff bases) as catenating chelates were first reported by Pfeiffer and Pfitzner (*238*), who investigated a number of different bis(Schiff bases) made from aromatic diamines and salicylaldehyde. The copper derivatives were found to be one-to-one on the basis of elemental analyses, and the derivatives that were soluble in organic solvents gave cryoscopic molecular weights corresponding to dimers. By analogy the insoluble derivatives were also assumed to be dimers, but recent workers have suggested that a polymeric nature would be more in accord with the insolubility since the established dimers are soluble (*91*).

In a very interesting approach to this type of polymer Bailar and his students have investigated the reaction of monomeric coordination compounds with one another through reactive groups contained in the ligands. Their first study (*244*) led only to limited condensation with the formation of trinuclear and dinuclear species when copper(II) lysinate and bis(salicylaldehydo)nickel(II) were combined. Longer reaction times apparently led to some increase in molecular weight, but without yielding the desired polymers (*202*). In a related system the reaction of phthalic anhydride with the zinc, copper, and nickel derivatives of the Schiff base (**XXX**) apparently led to the formation of polymers, but all the products decom-

(**XXX**)

posed below 200°C, so the work was discontinued (*12*). Drinkard and Chakravarty have also examined this approach (*79*) and were able to make a brittle yellow solid stable to 290°C by the reaction of benzidine with bis(salicylaldehydo)nickel(II). Because of the insolubility of the product, they were unable to measure its molecular weight.

The approach to these polymers via reaction of the preformed bis(Schiff base) with metal compounds has also been studied. Fernelius has reported the results of his attempts to prepare the copper, zinc, nickel, and uranyl derivatives of a large number of such ligands. Because of the difficulties encountered the investigation was discontinued (*91*). In a study of inner complex chelates Martell and co-workers examined the metal derivatives of a number of analogues of $CH_3COCH_2C(CH_3)=NC_2H_4N=C(CH_3)-CH_2COCH_3$ (*129*). When $—(CH_2)_5—$ or $—C_2H_4NHC_2H_4—$ was substituted for $—C_2H_4—$ and phenyl groups for the terminal methyl groups, the copper derivatives were found to be tarry products. They were consequently assumed to be polymers but were not studied further.

Quite similar to the bis(Schiff bases) are the thiopicolinamides investigated by Bailar and co-workers (*12, 193*) and the ketoimides investigated by Nesmeyanov and co-workers (*225*). In each of these studies the bis-chelating ligand was prepared and then converted to polymeric metal derivatives by substitution-addition or heterocondensation reactions. The analytical data for the thiopicolinamide-based polymers (XXXI, X = a single bond, CH$_2$, or SO$_2$, M = Cu, Ni, or Zn) indicate molecular weights

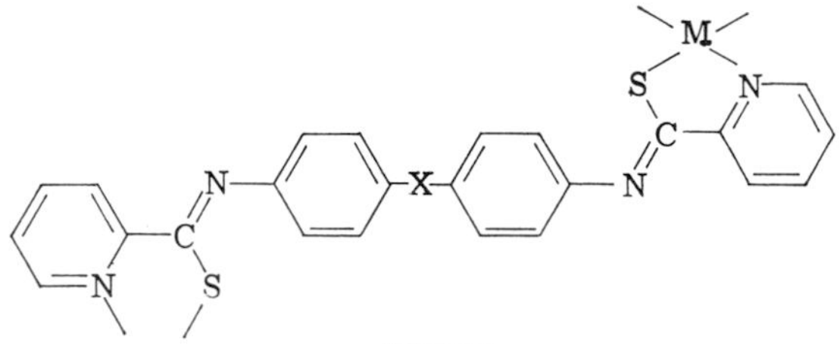

(XXXI)

over 5000. The powders obtained were thermally stable to temperatures of 250° to 410°C, the zinc derivative being the most stable with each ligand. The ketoimide polymers (XXXII) were prepared by treating an aromatic diamine with β-chlorovinyl phenyl ketone in the presence of trimethylamine

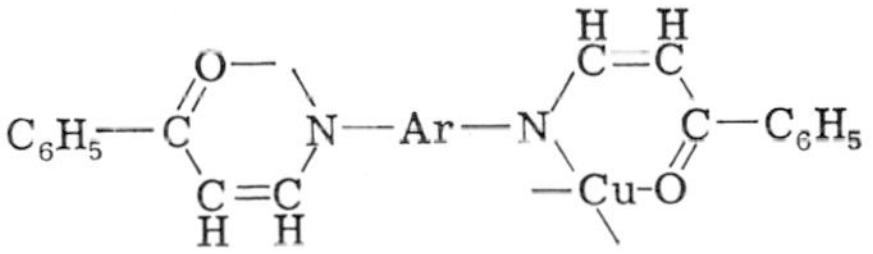

(XXXII)

and then treating the resulting ligand with copper(II) acetate in N,N-dimethylformamide or else using the interfacial condensation technique between chlorobenzene and aqueous solutions. The products are insoluble, finely dispersed powders stable to 400°C for p-phenylenediamine and to 350°C for benzidine.

Drinkard and Chakravarty (79) have prepared bis(thiosemicarbazones) of naphthazarin and terephthalaldehyde and examined their zinc and nickel complexes. The infusible black powders from the former gave no indication of decomposition by differential thermal analysis up to 400°C, whereas the yellow infusible powders from the latter were stable to 250°C. Insolubility prevented the determination of molecular weights. The studies involving the thiosemicarbazone of naphthazarin have been reported separately in more detail (62a).

N. Bis(Amino Acids) and Related Chelating Ligands

Metal derivatives of bis(amino acids) have also been in the literature for some time. Some of them are almost certainly monomers, but it seems likely that others are polymeric. In particular the anhydrous copper salt of HOOCCH(NH$_2$)C$_2$H$_4$CH(NH$_2$)(COOH) is reported to be insoluble in water although the dihydrate is soluble (*290*). Models indicate that a quadridentate monomer cannot be made, suggesting that the product is a polymer. Bailar and his students have been interested in this kind of system for some time. They have prepared metal derivatives of $(HOOC)$-$(H_2N)CH(CH_2)_6CH(NH_2)COOH$, (XXXIII), (XXXIV), N,N'-benzidine-diacetic acid, and α,α'-benzidinedisulfonic acid and found them to be, in general, insoluble precipitates which could not be characterized beyond

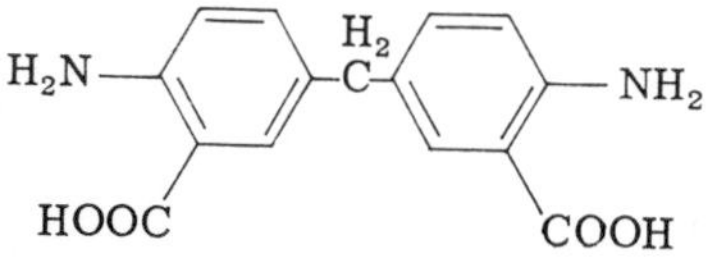

(XXXIII) 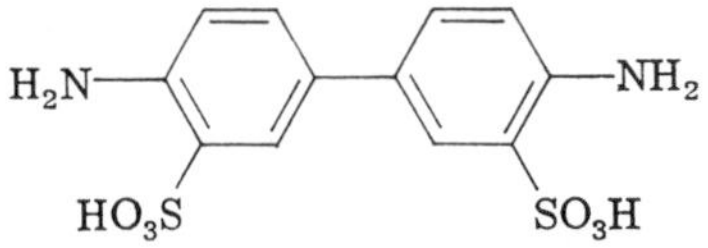   (XXXIV)

elemental analyses (*86*, *138*). Closely related are the bis(aminophenols) (*138*) and bis(hydroxy acids) (*188*) investigated by this same group. The metal derivatives of (XXXV) with Y representing a single bond, $(CH_3)_2C$, or SO_2 are also insoluble powders. All these products were less stable than

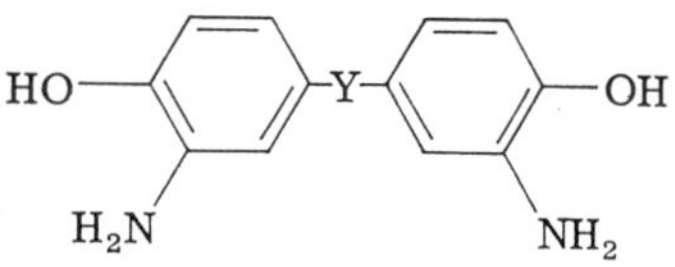

(XXXV)

the bis(8-quinolinols) mentioned earlier and consequently of less interest to the investigators. Similar results were obtained with (XXXVI) where Y represents CH_2 or $C(CH_3)_2$.

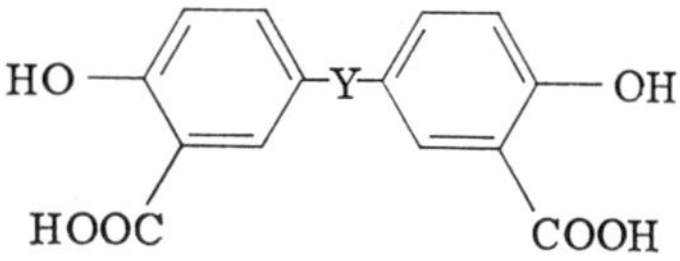

(XXXVI)

In his study of N-substituted 2,5-diaminoterephthalic acid (*297*) Uhlig isolated a one-to-one copper derivative of (XXXVII) which he suggests is

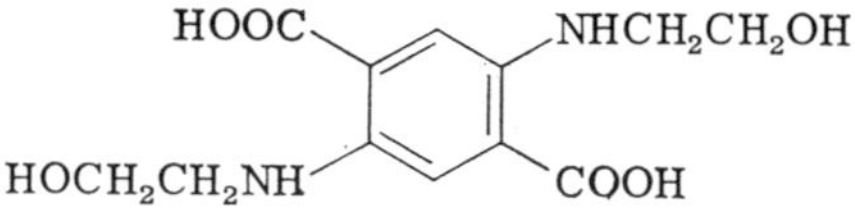

(XXXVII)

a high polymer of the type under consideration. The one-to-one cobalt(II) derivative of (XXXVIII) is also postulated to be a polymer, in this case a

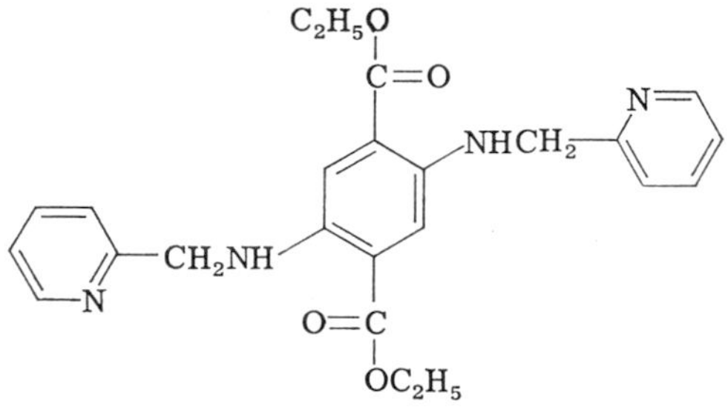

$$C_2H_5O$$
$$C=O$$
NHCH₂—(pyridine)
(pyridine)—CH₂NH
$$O=C$$
$$OC_2H_5$$

(**XXXVIII**)

cation, with, however, a coordination number of six for the cobalt(II), assuming that all the potential donors act as such.

An interesting variation has been investigated by Mattison and co-workers (*204a*). They have prepared the bischelating ligand p-CH₃-COCH₂COC₆H₄NHCH₂COOH which has an amino acid function on one side and a β-diketone function on the other side. One-to-one derivatives, presumably polymers, were made with this ligand and beryllium, copper(II), magnesium, nickel, uranyl ion, and zinc. All were powders which decomposed in the temperature range 300° to 450°C.

O. Double-Bridged Polymers

A preliminary report has been made of an entirely different kind of polymer from those constituting the goal of most research in the field of coordination polymers. Block *et al.* have found that chromium(III) acetylacetonate reacts with diphenylphosphinic acid in a substitution-addition reaction to yield a product from which they were able to isolate fractions with molecular weights from 5,000 to 11,000 having the composition [Cr(CH₃COCHCOCH₃)(OP(C₆H₅)₂O)₂]ₓ (*26b*). The structure of this polymer appears to be of the type shown in Fig. 6 and discussed in Section II,B,5,*b*. Surprisingly it has been possible to make fibers and films from the soluble fractions, which seems to indicate that the double-bridged backbone is not completely rigid. This is due to the spiral nature of the backbone imposed on it by the *cis* configuration of the bridging groups and to the flexibility of the 8-membered rings formed by the double bridges. Polymers with somewhat similar double bridges have been suggested to be present in systems containing the anion $(C_4H_9O)_2PO_2^-$ and copper(II), uranyl ion, or zirconium(IV) (*13a, 115a*).

P. Miscellaneous

Fiber-forming substances have also been made by Karipides by the reaction of KSSCOYOCSSK and nickel(II) with Y representing $(CH_2)_4$, $(CH_2)_6$, $(CH_2OCH_2)_n$, *m*- or *p*-C_6H_4, or $C_2H_4SC_2H_4$ (*139a*). These polymers exhibit low thermal stability.

Bailes and Calvin isolated a yellow powder from the reaction of cobalt(II) acetate with 4-hydroxy-5-formylsalicylaldehyde, which proved to be the dihydrate of the one-to-one compound (*13*). This product they formulated to be a linear polymer containing octahedral cobalt(II), (XXXIX). It easily loses water.

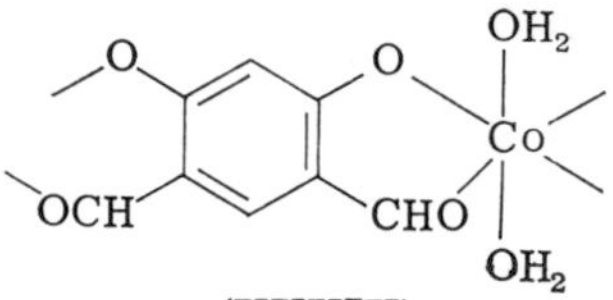

(XXXIX)

Stability at 500°C is reported by Johns and DiPetro for the zinc and beryllium derivatives of tris(2-hydroxyphenyl)-*s*-triazine (*136a*). The former is a one-to-one derivative assumed to be a linear polymer, the latter a three-to-two crosslinked species. One-to-one derivatives were also isolated for copper(II), nickel, manganese(II), iron(II), cobalt(II), and magnesium. These are presumably linear polymers also, although not as stable thermally. Linear polymers were also made with zinc and copper(II) using the catenating ligand made by blocking one of the hydroxy groups in tris(2-hydroxyphenyl)-*s*-triazine with a methyl or acetyl group. All the products are powders which cannot be worked or characterized beyond elemental analysis and spectra.

Polymers made from an unusual bischelating ligand based on ferrocene have been patented by Berlin and Kostroma (*20a*). The reaction of ferrocene with diazotized *p*-aminosalicylic acid or *p*-aminosalicylaldehyde was carried out to give the corresponding tetrasalicyl derivatives of ferrocene. These derivatives then acted as bischelating ligands with various metal salts to produce polymers that exhibited ferromagnetic properties upon being heated to 120° to 150°C.

Some interesting mixed species based on aluminum were prepared by Fujikawa (*101a*). Because of the tervalence of aluminum symmetrical bischelating agents will not lead to neutral chains. Consequently he attempted to prepare neutral chains by first making a compound between aluminum and $(CH_3CO)_2CHCH(COCH_3)_2$, naphthazarin, or 2,5-dihydroxy-*p*-benzoquinone and then carrying out a reaction between that product and 3,3′,4,4′-tetrahydroxybiphenyl, 1,2,4,5-benzenetetrol, or 5,5′-methylenedisalicylic acid. The polymers formed did not have very high stability and appeared to contain hydroxy and oxo groups.

Sacconi has found an interesting kind of coordination polymer in his study of hydrazones (*260, 261*). He has synthesized several hydrazones containing four donor sites arranged sterically so that only three can coordinate to one central atom. By substitution-addition these hydrazones yield nickel derivatives which are diamagnetic, do not melt or decompose up to 350°C, and are insoluble in most solvents. It is also interesting to note that although these products are prepared in aqueous ammoniacal systems they do not retain NH_3 during their isolation. It thus appears that intermolecular coordination is very strong in these materials. The magnetic properties suggest that they are typical planar nickel(II) compounds, and the remaining properties suggest they are polymers. A typical formulation is (XL). Although there are no supporting molecular weight data, such a structure seems quite probable.

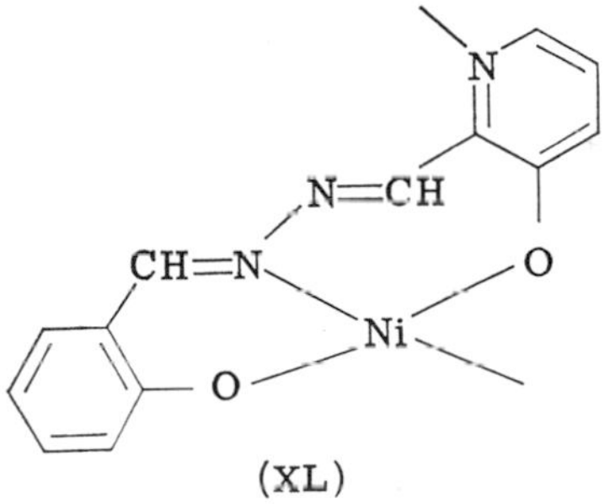

(XL)

The bis(Schiff base) prepared from hydrazine and salicylaldehyde is reported to give products of the same type with nickel, copper, cadmium, cobalt, and zinc by substitution-addition reaction in solution (*195*). They are very insoluble and have fairly good thermal stability at 250°C in air.

In their investigation of inorganic polymers Laubengayer and his students have prepared some aluminum-nitrogen compounds which they formulate as polymers containing tetracoordinated aluminum (*170*). These materials were made by the reaction of triethylaluminum with methylammonium chloride followed by the thermal elimination of ethane. The resulting CH_3NAlCl is an amorphous, insoluble, nonvolatile solid for which a network structure is postulated. Molecular weights could not be determined.

V. Polymeric Ligands

A. General Discussion

A quite different kind of coordination polymer remains to be considered. Several materials are known in which metals are bound to polymeric ligands in such a fashion that coordination is not directly involved in the backbone of the polymer. No attempt will be made to include all the pertinent data in the broad area implied here, for it is beyond the scope of the present work to give a detailed discussion of ion exchange systems, etc. Those investigations directed toward the synthesis of coordination polymers will be reviewed, whereas those studies which have not led to the isolation and characterization of polymeric systems containing coordinated metals will not be discussed. This somewhat arbitrary decision results in the omission of all work involving polymeric ligands and their uptake capacity for metal ions. Millar reviewed such work in 1957 and published an annotated bibliography covering work up to 1956 (*208*).

B. Polyazomethines

There have been several investigations into the use of polymers containing azomethine linkages as polymeric ligands. Although it appears that they did not recognize what they had, Dubský and co-workers were probably the first to make such polymers (*81*). In their study of ketimines for microchemical detection of magnesium and beryllium they made a one-to-one derivative of naphthazarin and ethylenediamine which they formulated as (XLI). This is sterically impossible, and the conclusion of Drinkard and

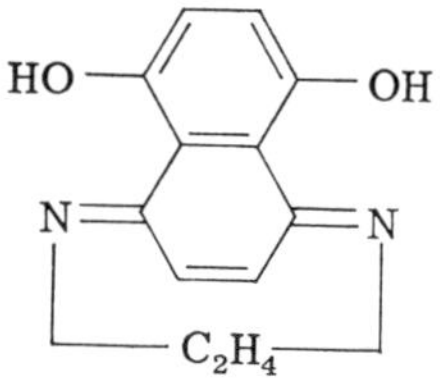

(XLI)

Chakravarty that the product is a polymer with a degree of polymerization of about five (*79*) certainly is more reasonable. The earlier workers prepared a beryllium derivative of the product, whereas the later investigators isolated a copper derivative that appeared to have the same degree of polymerization as the ligand.

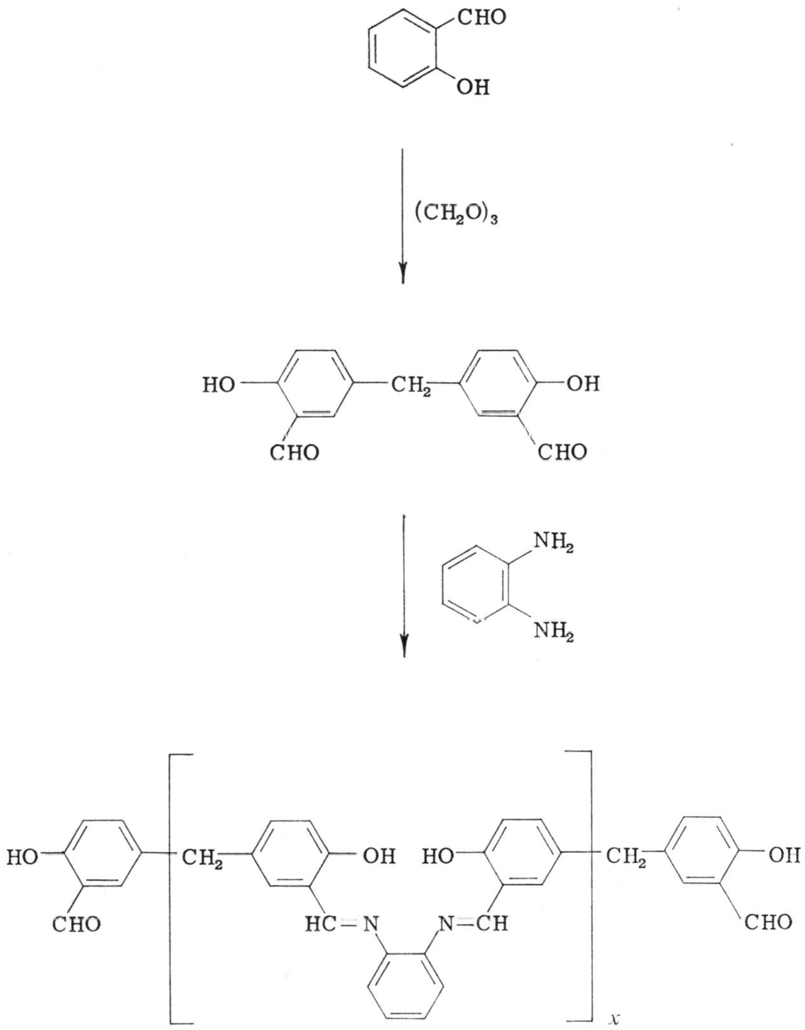

Marvel and his students have examined a number of poly(Schiff bases). The first of their efforts led to resinous, metal-containing materials that were not very well characterized (9). These experiments concerned polymeric ligands made by the condensation of monomeric Schiff bases with formaldehyde. A more satisfactory procedure for the preparation of polymeric Schiff bases proved to be a stepwise process (shown below) in which a dialdehyde is made and then treated with a diamine to give a polymeric Schiff base (199). Attempts to determine its molecular weight were not successful. It reacted with metal acetates in tetrahydrofuran to incorporate the metal ion into the polymer. The analytical data are in accord with a degree of polymerization of 45 for these metal derivatives with copper, cobalt, zinc, nickel, iron, and cadmium. The heat stability increased in the order of the metals listed, but none was as stable as the prototype monomer (XLII). All lost 11–26% of their weight in three hours in air at 250°C, and all were essentially completely destroyed by heating at 250°C for twenty-eight hours in air. In an attempt to increase the stability (*200*) the dialdehyde (XLIII) was used to give (XLIV) with a molecular weight of about 10,000 (intrinsic viscosity). This polymer

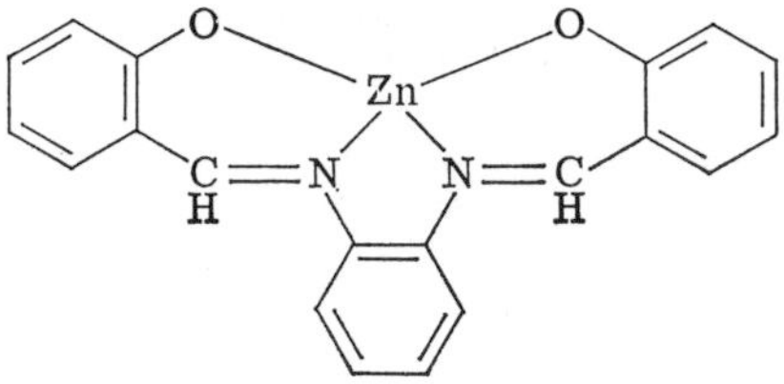

(XLII)

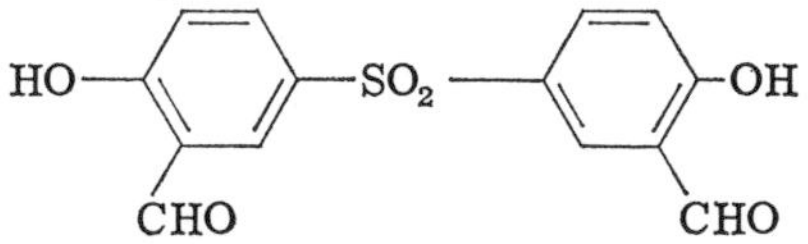

(XLIII)

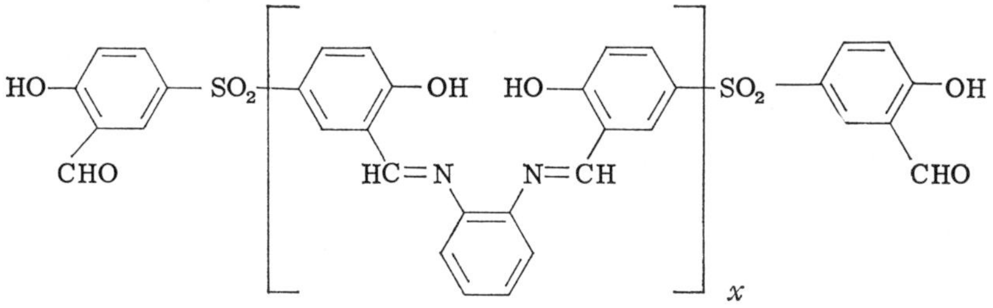

(XLIV)

formed derivatives with cobalt, iron, nickel, copper, and cadmium that showed enhanced thermal stability over the methylene series. It is suggested that the stability relationship is a consequence of the greater electron-withdrawing power of the SO_2 group, which increases the phenol acidity. The relative independence of the thermal stability values from the atmosphere suggests the degradation is thermal rather than oxidative.

Further attempts to increase the molecular weight of the polymeric Schiff base proper by emulsion techniques did not give sufficiently higher values to alter the properties (*195*). Substitution of hydrazine for *o*-phenylene-diamine in the synthesis of the polymeric Schiff base led to low degrees of polymerization, and clear-cut metal derivatives were not formed. Quite similar polymers have been reported by Terentev *et al.* (*294a*).

Polymeric Schiff bases containing sexidentate sites of a similar sort have been made from (XLIII) or the corresponding methylene dialdehyde and triethylenetetramine by Goodwin and Bailar (*106a*). The polymeric Schiff bases, however, did not react readily with metal compounds, and the direct reaction of the metal-triethylenetetramine complex with the dialdehyde proved to be a superior method of synthesis. Elements investigated were copper(II), cobalt(II), nickel, iron(III), aluminum, and chromium(III). Thermogravimetric analysis of the resulting insoluble products indicated greater stability with the bivalent metals and with the Schiff base containing SO_2.

Another of Bailar's students has explored the use of polymeric Schiff bases prepared from bis-β-diketones and ethylenediamine (*229a*). Indications are that the copper(II) derivative of the 1,1,2,2-tetraacetylethane-ethylenediimine polymer is more stable thermally than the copper polymer of the bis-β-diketone, whereas the opposite is true for nickel. The copper(II) derivative of the 1,1,3,3-tetrabenzoylpropane-ethylenediimine polymer, however, is less stable than the copper polymer with the corresponding bis-β-diketone.

In their study of tridentate chelates (*176*) Lions and Martin have made polymeric Schiff bases which can act only as neutral ligands. The reactions of (XLV) with ethylenediamine, hexamethylenediamine, and benzidine have been found to give solid, infusible polymers. The latter two readily

(XLV)

form derivatives with iron(II) sulfate in which there are two polymer units bound per iron atom. It is thus probable that the iron is hexaco-ordinated. The iron-containing polymers have the unusual magnetic property of being ferromagnetic. It is suggested that coupling between iron atoms may be responsible. The iron derivatives are insoluble and do not melt below 300°C. Because of the neutral nature of the Schiff base the polymer with coordinated iron is a cation, and there are discrete anions present to give electrical neutrality. This ionic nature undoubtedly affects the properties of the polymers. With cobalt(II) chloride there is only one polymer unit per cobalt, so it is suggested that there is chloride bridging between two chains to satisfy the coordination number of the cobalt. Although the benzidine-based polymeric Schiff base has little capacity for iron(II), it combines readily with copper(II) chloride. This is related to the different stereochemistries of the two elements, i.e., octahedral vs. planar. The more facile binding of iron(II) by the ethylenediamine- and hexamethylenediamine-based polymers is also probably due to steric relationships. The authors suggest that with the latter polymers it is possible for two successive tridentate units to act as an octahedral sexidentate chelate.

C. Polyvinyl Backbones

Some polyvinyl-type polymers with coordinated groups bonded to the backbone have been investigated. Arimoto and Haven prepared vinylferrocene by the reduction and dehydration of acetylferrocene and then studied its polymerization (7). Homopolymerization yielded oils with acid or persulfate catalysis, but a solid melting at 280° to 285°C with azodiisobutyronitrile catalysis. Copolymerization with methyl methacrylate and with styrene also yielded solids with this catalyst. All the solids could be made into clear brittle films from benzene solution. Copolymerization with chloroprene (persulfate catalysis) gave an elastomer. Formaldehyde readily crosslinked all the polymers and copolymers. It should be noted that the exact nature of these products is not established by the data given. There are no molecular weight data; at most iron analyses are reported. The polymeric nature of these products, however, seems unquestionable in the light of the study of the same system by Chen, Fernandez-Refojo, and Cassidy (66). Although they were not able to establish the electron exchange nature of the polymer, they did analyze samples of polyvinyldicyclopentadienyliron (made by Arimoto and Haven's method) more completely and determined the molecular weight, osmometry giving a number-average molecular weight of 48,600. Sulfonation of the polymer, although not complete so that the product was not clear-cut, led to greater instability to oxidation than found for alkyl-substituted ferrocenes.

Cinnamoylferrocene was made and studied by Coleman and Rausch (68). Homopolymers could not be prepared using bulk or solution techniques in conventional free radical processes. On the other hand bulk or solution techniques with azobisisobutyronitrile initiation were successful for making copolymers with vinyl monomers, and emulsion techniques led to copolymers with dienes. Various substances used successfully for copolymerization were styrene, acrylonitrile, methyl methacrylate, 1,1-dihydroperfluorobutyl acrylate, ethyl acrylate, butadiene, and isoprene. The copolymers softened from 130° to above 275°C and had inherent viscosities ranging from 0.1 to 1.2. They do not offer any advantage over conventional polymers for high temperature use.

In a brief note Sansoni and Sigmund have reported the synthesis of a ferrocene-containing polystyrene via a diazo reaction (*263a*). They were particularly interested in the redox behavior of the iron in the system and found a normal redox potential of 415 mv. The polymer acts as a sink for or a reservoir of electrons.

The free radical polymerization of acrylate-containing basic beryllium carboxylates by benzoyl peroxide initiation was attempted by Marvel and Martin (*196*). Both basic beryllium acrylate and basic beryllium penta-propionate monoacrylate gave insoluble products although it had been thought that the latter would yield a soluble, linear polymer. It is suggested that the insolubility is due to cross-linking in both cases, either disproportionation or the initial presence of more than one acrylate per beryllium accounting for the cross-linking with the latter. The products were both white powders which decomposed extensively at 200°C; the thermal stability is thus not outstanding.

D. Miscellaneous

Materials have been prepared by transchelation between a metal chelate based on a volatile chelating agent and a polymer containing chelating sites (*126*). These products are polymers that contain coordination centers serving as cross links between the preformed organic polymer. The reaction of poly(allyl acetoacetate) with bis(methyl salicylato)beryllium yields a hard film after the product is baked at 120°C. Several different polymers have been used involving chelating sites of the salicylate, ketoxime, dioxime, and Schiff base types as well as the β-diketone pattern, and copper, aluminum, iron, and nickel have been used for the metal. The products can be shaped into films, sheets, or fibers before they are hardened by heating.

An investigation of silicon-nitrogen polymers has also led to the isolation of polymeric ligands (*209*). The reaction of dimethyldichlorosilane with ethylenediamine yields the polymer $(\text{—Si}(CH_3)_2NHC_2H_4NH\text{—})_x$, which was separated into an insoluble fraction not further investigated and a xylene-soluble portion with molecular weight 1940. Refluxing a xylene solution of the latter with copper(II) chloride under nitrogen caused ethylenediamine to be split out as the complex ion $Cu(NH_2C_2H_4NH_2)_2^{2+}$ + and converted the polymer to the ladder-type (XLVI) which can coordinate with copper(II) chloride to yield a xylene-insoluble gel. Washing out the xylene leaves a powder that melts at 240°C and then hardens to a solid resinous material on cooling. These facts are interpreted to indicate that the gel is a swelled polymer, probably crosslinked by the copper. The original polymeric silylamine reacts with beryllium chloride also, but in a different fashion, to form a product in which beryllium is coordinated to about one third of the nitrogen. Evaporatoin of a xylene solution of the

$$
\begin{array}{ccc}
-\text{Si}(\text{CH}_3)_2\!-\!\text{N}\!-\!\text{Si}(\text{CH}_3)_2\!-\!\text{N}\!-\!\\
\mid \qquad\qquad \mid \\
\text{CH}_2 \qquad\quad \text{CH}_2 \\
\mid \qquad\qquad \mid \\
\text{CH}_2 \qquad\quad \text{CH}_2 \\
\mid \qquad\qquad \mid \\
-\text{Si}(\text{CH}_3)_2\!-\!\text{N}\!-\!\text{Si}(\text{CH}_3)_2\!-\!\text{N}\!-\!\\
\end{array}
$$

(XLVI)

product leaves a hard, brittle, transparent, resinous material. Analyses indicated that there was very little rearrangement to the ladder-type polymer with beryllium chloride. The relative rates of hydrolysis of the various polymers shows that coordination with beryllium almost eliminates the tendency of the silicon-to-nitrogen bond to hydrolyze at room temperature and that the Si—N—Si pattern hydrolyzes less readily than the N—Si—C pattern. The latter observation is a reflection of the greater involvement in d_π, p_π bonding of the free electron pair on a nitrogen when it is bonded to *two* silicon atoms, resulting in reduced availability of the electron pair and concomitant reduced chemical activity. Although the copper(II) complex of the ladder-type polymer could not be studied under homogeneous hydrolysis conditions as could the other products, qualitative observations indicate that it hydrolyzes least readily of all. The difference in behavior between copper and beryllium is linked to the different stereochemistry of the two, a planar pattern leading to a structure for the coordinated polymer made from the silylamine which is suceptible to ready elimination of ethylenediamine, the tetrahedral pattern not giving the same favorable relationship. It should be noted, however, that the difference in behavior might be due to stronger bonding between ethylenediamine and copper than with beryllium.

There has been much investigation of the interaction of poly(methyl acrylate), poly(acrylic acid), and related polymers with metal ions. Most of this work has been from an ion exchange point of view and was not directed toward the isolation of products; however, Berlin has suggested that the compounds formed between acrylic acid polymers and copolymers and bi- and polyvalent metals could be useful thermally stable plastics (*20*). In their extensive study of polymers containing reactive groups Kern and co-workers converted poly(methyl acrylate) to poly(acrylo-hydroxamic acid) by treating it with hydroxylamine (*143*). A low molecular weight form of the product was found to form complexes with many metallic cations. A detailed study of the reaction with iron(III) ions showed that an insoluble derivative with three polymer units per iron(III) was formed. The structure suggested involves the chelation of the iron(III) by three —CH₂CH(CO(NO))— units, leading to extensive cross-linking.

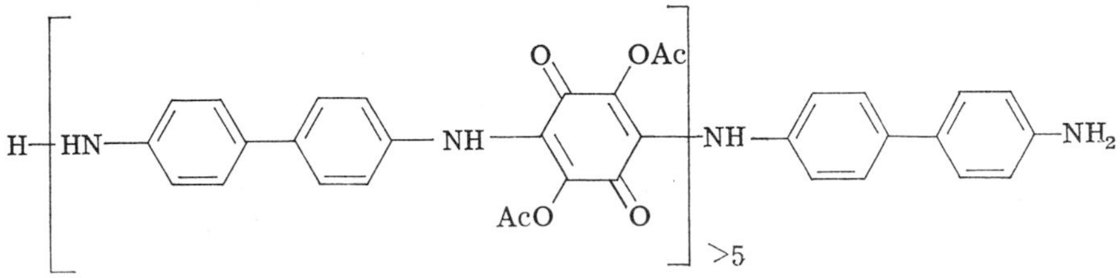

(XLVII)

A polyaminoquinone with chelating properties (XLVII) has been made by Berlin and co-workers via the reaction of benzidine with chloranil in the presence of sodium acetate (*21*, *27*). This polymer, which has a molecular weight of about 2000 or a degree of polymerization of about 5, has strong internal hydrogen bonding and also contains unpaired electrons. It forms insoluble, infusible complexes with copper and other metals; the copper-containing product has about the same electron paramagnetic resonance as the uncomplexed polymer.

Another rather low molecular weight, polymeric coordinating agent has been prepared by Drinkard and Chakravarty (*79*). The reaction of salicylaldehyde with HSC₂H₄SH in either dioxane or ethanol leads to polymeric (XLVIII), with number-average molecular weight about 5000. Addition

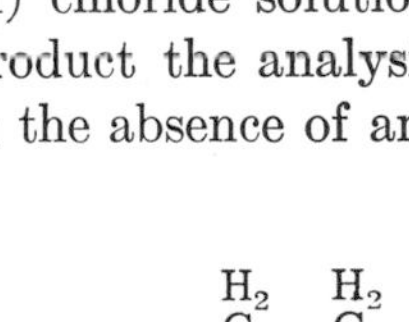

(XLVIII)

of an ammoniacal copper(II) chloride solution to an alcohol solution of the polymercaptal gave a product the analysis of which corresponded to (XLIX) with n about 12. In the absence of ammonia a second copper(II)

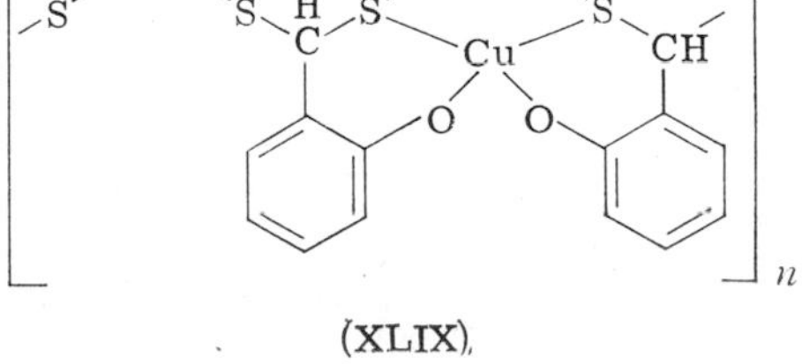

(XLIX).

can be coordinated to the two sulfur atoms. Both copper complexes were obtained as precipitates; they undergo at 110°C an endothermic change the nature of which is not clear, and a second change at about 200°C.

VI. Conclusion

In summary it can be said that the development of coordination polymers as useful materials is in its infancy, with primary activity centering on the synthesis and characterization of systems heavy in organic ligands. Present evidence seems to indicate that such systems will be less stable thermally than the prototype monomers and suggests that their study will primarily be useful in the development of polymerization techniques. The characterization of products is very troublesome because of solubility problems, a factor which also seems to cause difficulty in attempts to increase the degree of polymerization to the larger values attained with useful organic polymers.

The existence of a large number of purely inorganic coordination systems with some polymeric character leaves no doubt that completely inorganic coordination polymers can be made, and it seems only a matter of time until they are synthesized and developed to the point of usefulness. There is also little doubt that a number of semiorganic coordination polymers have been made, albeit of low molecular weight and rather poor characterization. Many of the results reported are not very soundly based because of the extreme difficulties encountered in the characterization of the products. In some instances the nature of the product is based on little more than educated guesses. These guesses will probably prove approximately correct more often than not, but the foundation in fact of any given polymer should be considered quite critically before extensive plans are made for it.

ACKNOWLEDGMENTS

I am greatly indebted to Dr. G. Barth-Wehrenalp, my other colleagues at Pennsalt Chemicals Corporation, and to Dr. L. W. Butz for much valuable discussion and advice on the subject of coordination polymers, to my wife Viola for the preparation of the manuscript, and to the Office of Naval Research for partial support of my studies in this area.

REFERENCES

1. Abel, E. W., Bennett, M. A., and Wilkinson, G., *J. Chem. Soc.* p. 3178 (1959).
2. Adachi, J., *Nippon Kagaku Zasshi* **76,** 311 (1955).
3. Adams, D. M., Chatt, J., Guy, R. G., and Sheppard, N., *J. Chem. Soc.* p. 738 (1961); *Proc. Chem. Soc.* p. 179 (1960).

4. Aebi, F., *Helv. Chim. Acta* **31**, 369 (1948).
5. Amma, E. L., *Dissertation Abstr.* **18**, 1992 (1958).
6. Amon, W. F., Jr., and Kane, M. W., *U. S. Patent* 2,505,085 (1950).
6a. Andrianov, K. A., and Pichkhadze, S. V., *Vysokomolekulyarnye Soedineniya* **3**, 577 (1961); *Chem. Abstr.* **56**, 1585g (1962).
6b. Andrianov, K. A., Pichkhadze, S. V., and Bochkareva, I. V., *Vysokomolekulyarnye Soedineniya* **3**, 1321 (1961).
7. Arimoto, F. S., and Haven, A. C., Jr., *J. Am. Chem. Soc.* **77**, 6295 (1955).
8. Arora, S. D., Lipscomb, W. N., and Sneed, M. C., *J. Am. Chem. Soc.* **73**, 1015 (1951).
9. Aspey, S. A., *Dissertation Abstr.* **15**, 2008 (1955).
10. Babaeva, A. V., and Baranovskii, I. B., *Russ. J. Inorg. Chem.* **5**, 360 (1960).
11. Bailar, J. C., Jr., "Advances in Chelate Chemistry—Abstracts of Symposium," p. 45. Department of Chemistry, Polytechnic Institute of Brooklyn, New York, 1955.
12. Bailar, J. C., Jr., Martin, K. V., Judd, M. L., and McLean, J. A., Jr., *WADC (Wright Air Develop. Center) Tech. Rept. No.* **57**/391, Pt. II (1958).
13. Bailes, R. H., and Calvin, M., *J. Am. Chem. Soc.* **69**, 1886 (1947).
13a. Baldwin, W. H., and Higgins, C. E., *J. Inorg. & Nuclear Chem.* **17**, 334 (1961).
14. Balthis, J. H., *U. S. Patent* 2,621,194 (1952).
15. Balz, D., and Plieth, K., *Z. Elektrochem.* **59**, 545 (1955).
16. Bandyopadhayay, D., *J. Indian Chem. Soc.* **34**, 798 (1957).
17. Bannister, E., and Wilkinson, G., *Chem. & Ind. (London)* p. 318 (1960).
18. Barceló, J. R., *Spectrochim. Acta* **10**, 245 (1958).
19. Bergerhoff, G., *Z. anorg. u. allgem. Chem.* **299**, 328 (1959).
20. Berlin, A. A., *Uspekhi Khim. i Tekhnol. Polimerov Sbornik* **2**, 13 (1957); *Chem. Abstr.* **52**, 21214b (1958).
20a. Berlin, A. A., and Kostroma, T. V., *Russian Patent* 129,018 (1960); *Chem. Abstr.* **55**, 3612e (1961).
21. Berlin, A. A., and Matveeva, N. G., *Izvest. Akad. Nauk S.S.S.R. Otdel. Khim. Nauk* p. 2260 (1959); *Chem. Abstr.* **54**, 10946d (1960); *Vysokomolekulyarnye Soedineniya* **1**, 1643 (1959); *Chem. Abstr.* **54**, 16899i (1960).
22. Berlin, A. A., Matveeva, N. G., and Sherle, A. I., *Izvest. Akad. Nauk S.S.S.R. Otdel. Khim. Nauk* p. 2261 (1959); *Russian Patent* 126,612 (1959).
22a. Berlin, A. A., Boguslavski, L. I., Burshtein, R. K., Matveeva, N. G., Sherle A. I., and Shurmovskaya, N. A., *Doklady Akad. Nauk S.S.S.R.* **136**, 1127 (1961).
23. Bever, A. K. van, *Rec. trav. chim.* **57**, 1259 (1938).
24. Bijvoet, J. M., Claassen, A., and Karssen, A., *Verslag. Akad. Wetenschappen (Amsterdam)* **35**, 111 (1926); *Chem. Abstr.* **20**, 2264² (1926).
25. Blake, D., Calvin, G., and Coates, G. E., *Proc. Chem. Soc.* p. 396 (1959).
26. Block, B. P., *in* "The Chemistry of the Coordination Compounds" (J. C. Bailar, Jr., ed.), p. 354 ff. Reinhold, New York, 1956.
26a. Block, B. P., and Barth-Wehrenalp, G., *J. Inorg. & Nuclear Chem.* (in press).
26b. Block, B. P., Simkin, J., and Ocone, L. R., *J. Am. Chem. Soc.* **84**, 1749 (1962).
27. Blyumenfel'd, L. A., Berlin, A. A., Matveeva, N. G., and Kalmanson, A. E., *Vysokomolekulyarnye Soedineniya* **1**, 1647 (1959); *Chem. Abstr.* **54**, 25948b (1960).
28. Boon, J. W., and MacGillavry, C. H., *Rec. trav. chim.* **61**, 910 (1942).
29. Bottei, R. S., and Gerace, P. L., *Abstr. Papers, 139th Meeting Am. Chem. Soc., St. Louis, Missouri 1961*, p. 16M.

30. Bozorth, R. M., *J. Am. Chem. Soc.* **44**, 2232 (1922).
31. Braekken, H., *Kgl. Norske Videnskab. Selskabs Forh. II, 1929, Medd. No.* **48**, 169 (1930); *Chem. Abstr.* **24**, 5559 (1930).
32. Braekken, H., *Kgl. Norske Videnskab. Selskabs Forh.* **5**(11) (1932).
33. Braekken, H., *Z. Krist.* **74**, 67 (1930).
34. Braekken, H., *Z. Krist.* **83**, 222 (1932).
35. Brasseur, H., and Pauling, L., *J. Am. Chem. Soc.* **60**, 2886 (1938).
36. Brasseur, H., and de Rassenfosse, A., *Nature* **143**, 332 (1939); *Z. Krist.* **101**, 389 (1939).
37. Breed, L. W., and Haggerty, W. J., Jr., *WADC (Wright Air Develop. Center) Tech. Rept.* **57/143**, Pt. IV (1960).
37a. Breed, L. W., and Haggerty, W. J., Jr., *WADC (Wright Air Develop. Center) Tech. Rept.* **57/143**, Pt. V (1960).
38. Brehler, B., *Fortschr. Mineral.* **38**, 198 (1960).
39. Brehler, B., and Winkler, H. G. F., *Heidelberger Beitr. Mineral. u. Petrog.* **4**, 6 (1954); *Chem. Abstr.* **48**, 7384c (1954).
40. Brink, C., and Arkel, A. E. van, *Acta Cryst.* **5**, 506 (1952).
41. Brink, C., and Kroese, H. A. S., *Acta Cryst.* **5**, 433 (1952).
42. Brink, C., and MacGillavry, C. H., *Acta Cryst.* **2**, 158 (1949).
43. Brink, C., Binnendijk, N. F., and Linde, J. van der, *Acta Cryst.* **7**, 176 (1954).
44. Brisi, C., *Ann. chim. (Rome)* **42**, 356 (1952); *Chem. Abstr.* **47**, 3648h (1953).
45. Brodersen, K., *Acta Cryst.* **8**, 723 (1955).
46. Brodersen, K., *Z. anorg. u. allgem. Chem.* **285**, 5 (1956).
47. Brodersen, K., *Z. anorg. u. allgem. Chem.* **298**, 142 (1959).
48. Brodersen, K., and Kunkel, L., *Chem. Ber.* **91**, 2698 (1958).
49. Brodersen, K., and Kunkel, L., *Z. anorg. u. allgem. Chem.* **298**, 34 (1959).
50. Brodersen, K., and Rüdorff, W., *Z. Naturforsch.* **9b**, 164 (1954).
51. Brosset, C., *Z. anorg. u. allgem. Chem.* **235**, 139 (1937).
52. Brosset, C., *Z. anorg. u. allgem. Chem.* **239**, 301 (1938).
53. Brosset, C., *Arkiv Kemi Mineral. Geol.* **25A**, (19) (1948).
54. Brown, H. A., *U. S. Patent* 2,934,450 (1960).
55. Brown, I. D., and Dunitz, J. D., *Acta Cryst.* **13**, 28 (1960).
56. Bucher, A., *U. S. Patent* 2,492,732 (1949).
57. Burg, A. B., and Mahler, W., *J. Am. Chem. Soc.* **80**, 2334 (1958).
58. Cambi, L., *Gazz. chim. ital.* **77**, 575 (1947).
59. Cavalca, L., Nardelli, M., and Coghi, L., *Nuovo cimento* **6**, 278 (1957).
60. Cavalca, L., Nardelli, M., and Fava, G., *Acta Cryst.* **13**, 125 (1960); *Proc. Chem. Soc.* p. 159 (1959).
61. Cavalca, L., Nardelli, M., and Fava, G., *Acta Cryst.* **13**, 594 (1960).
62. Cavell, R. G., and Clark, H. C., *J. Inorg. & Nuclear Chem.* **17**, 257 (1961).
62a. Chakravarty, D. N., and Drinkard, W. C., Jr., *J. Indian Chem. Soc.* **37**, 517 (1960).
63. Charles, R. G., *J. Phys. Chem.* **64**, 1747 (1960).
64. Charles, R. G., and Pawlikowski, M. A., *J. Phys. Chem.* **62**, 440 (1958).
65. Charles, R. G., Hickam, W. M., and Von Hoene, J., *J. Phys. Chem.* **63**, 2084 (1959).
66. Chen, Y. H., Fernandez-Refojo, M., and Cassidy, H. G., *J. Polymer Sci.* **40**, 433 (1959).
67. Cohen, A. J., and Davidson, N., *J. Am. Chem. Soc.* **73**, 1955 (1951).
68. Coleman, L. E., Jr., and Rausch, M. D., *J. Polymer Sci.* **28**, 207 (1958).
69. Colton, R., Levitus, R., and Wilkinson, G., *J. Chem. Soc.* p. 4121 (1960).

70. Cox, E. G., Shorter, A. J., and Wardlaw, W., *Nature* **139,** 71 (1937).

70a. Craven, B. M., and Hall, D., *Acta Cryst.* **14,** 475 (1961).

71. Cromer, D. T., *J. Phys. Chem.* **61,** 1388 (1957).

72. Cromer, D. T., and Larson, A. C., *Abstr. Papers 138th Meeting Am. Chem. Soc. N.Y. 1960,* p. 7N.

73. Dahl, L. F., and Wampler, D. L., *J. Am. Chem. Soc.* **81,** 3150 (1959).

74. Davey, W. P., *Phys. Rev.* **19,** 248 (1922).

75. Deeley, C. M., and Richards, R. E., *J. Chem. Soc.* p. 3697 (1954).

76. Drago, R. S., Kwon, J. T., and Archer, R. D., *J. Am. Chem. Soc.* **80,** 2667 (1958).

77. Drinkard, W. C., Jr., *Dissertation Abstr.* **17,** 499 (1957).

78. Drinkard, W. C., Jr., and Bailar, J. C., Jr., *J. Am. Chem. Soc.* **81,** 4795 (1959).

79. Drinkard, W. C., Jr., and Chakravarty, D. N., *WADC (Wright Air Develop. Center) Tech. Rept.* **59/761,** p. 232 (1960).

80. Drinkard, W. C., Jr., Ross, D., and Wiesner, J., *J. Org. Chem.* **26,** 619 (1961).

81. Dubský, J. V., Langer, A., and Wagner, E., *Mikrochemie* **22,** 108 (1937).

82. Dunitz, J. D., *Acta Cryst.* **10,** 307 (1957).

83. Dwiggins, C. W., Jr., *Dissertation Abstr.* **18,** 1634 (1958).

84. Earwicker, G. A., *J. Chem. Soc.* p. 2620 (1960).

85. Edwards, A. J., and Peacock, R. D., *J. Chem. Soc.* p. 4126 (1959).

86. Elliott, J. R., Doctoral Dissertation, University of Illinois, Urbana, Illinois, 1943.

87. Elvidge, J. A., and Lever, A. B. P., *Proc. Chem. Soc.* p. 195 (1959).

87a. Elvidge, J. A., and Lever, A. B. P., *J. Chem. Soc.* p. 1257 (1961).

88. Epstein, A., and Wildi, B. S., *J. Chem. Phys.* **32,** 324 (1960).

89. Falqui, M. T., and Rollier, M. A., *Ann. chim. (Rome)* **48,** 1154 (1958).

90. Felmayer, W., and Wolf, I., *J. Electrochem. Soc.* **105,** 141 (1958).

91. Fernelius, W. C., *WADC (Wright Air Develop. Center) Tech. Rept.* **56/203** (1956).

92. Fernelius, W. C., Shamma, M., Garofano, N. R., Goldberg, D. E., Martin, D. F., and Thomas, F. D., III, *WADC (Wright Air Develop. Center) Tech. Rept.* **56/203,** Pt. II (1957).

93. Fernelius, W. C., Shamma, M., Davis, L. A., Goldberg, D. E., Martin, B. B., Martin, D. F., and Thomas, F. D., III, *WADC (Wright Air Develop. Center) Tech. Rept.* **56/203,** Pt. III (1958).

94. Ferrari, A., and Baroni, A., *Atti accad. nazl. Lincei* [6] **6,** 418 (1927); *Chem. Abstr.* **22,** 1257⁵ (1928).

95. Ferroni, E., and Bondi, E., *J. Inorg. & Nuclear Chem.* **8,** 458 (1958).

96. Fisher, P. J., Taylor, N. E., and Harding, M. M., *J. Chem. Soc.* p. 2303 (1960).

97. Flumiani, G., and Bajić, V., *Monatsh. Chem.* **72,** 368 (1939).

98. Forsberg, H. E., *Acta Chem. Scand.* **10,** 1287 (1956).

99. Frank, R. L., Clark, G. R., and Coker, J. N., *J. Am. Chem. Soc.* **72,** 1827 (1950).

100. Frank, R. L., Baldoni, A. A., and Patterson, T. R., Jr., *AFOSR Tech. Rept.* **58–18** (1958).

101. Frevel, L. K., and Rinn, H. W., *Acta Cryst.* **9,** 626 (1956).

101a. Fujikawa, C. Y., *Dissertation Abstr.* **21,** 3621 (1961).

102. Geller, S., and Bond, W. L., *J. Chem. Phys.* **29,** 925 (1958).

103. Gibson, C. S., *Proc. Roy. Soc.* **A173,** 160 (1939).

103a. Giffen, W. M., *Dissertation Abstr.* **22,** 1399 (1961).

104. Glukhov, N. A., Koton, M. M., and Mitin, Y. V., *Vysokomolekulyarnye Soedineniya* **2,** 791 (1960).

105. Goebel, M. T., and Iler, R. K., *U. S. Patents* 2,544,666–8 (1951).

106. Goldsztaub, S., *Compt. rend. acad. sci.* **198,** 667 (1934).

106a. Goodwin, H. A., and Bailar, J. C., Jr., *J. Am. Chem. Soc.* **83**, 2467 (1961).
107. Goremykin, V. I., and Gladyshevskaya, K. A., *Zhur. Obshchei Khim.* **14**, 13 (1944); *Chem. Abstr.* **39**, 880² (1945).
108. Gorsich, R. D., *J. Am. Chem. Soc.* **82**, 4211 (1960).
109. Gorskii, V. S., *Physik Z. Sowjetunion* **5**, 367 (1934); *Chem. Abstr.* **28**, 3636³ (1934).
110. Grdenic, D., and Kamenar, B., *Proc. Chem. Soc.* p. 312 (1960).
110a. Grdenić, D., and Kamenar, B., *Proc. Chem. Soc.* p. 304 (1961).
111. Grigor'yev, A. I., Novoselova, A. V., and Semenenko, K. N., *Zhur. Neorg. Khim.* **2**, 2067 (1957); *Chem. Abstr.* **52**, 12639d (1957).
112. Guggiari, P. B., *Ber.* **45**, 2442 (1912).
113. Gutmann, V., and Jack, K. H., *Acta Cryst.* **4**, 244 (1951).
114. Handy, L. L., and Gregory, N. W., *J. Am. Chem. Soc.* **74**, 891 (1952).
115. Hardt, H. D., *Z. anorg. u. allgem. Chem.* **286**, 254 (1956); **292**, 53, 224, 257 (1957).
115a. Hardy, C. J., and Scargill, D., *J. Inorg. & Nuclear Chem.* **17**, 337 (1961).
116. Harmsen, E. J., *Z. Krist.* **100**, 208 (1938).
117. Haslam, J. H., *Advances in Chem. Ser.* **23**, 272 (1959).
118. Haslam, J. H., *U. S. Patent* 2,621,195 (1952).
119. Hauserman, F. B., *Advances in Chem. Ser.* **23**, 338 (1959).
120. Helmholz, L., *J. Am. Chem. Soc.* **69**, 886 (1947).
120a. Hendra, P. J., and Powell, D. B., *J. Chem. Soc.* p. 5105 (1960).
121. Hepworth, M. A., Jack, K. H., Peacock, R. D., and Westland, G. J., *Acta Cryst.* **10**, 63 (1957).
122. Hesse, R., *cited in* Åkerström, S., *Arkiv Kemi* **14**, 387 (1959).
123. Hoard, J. L., and Grenko, J. D., *Z. Krist.* **87**, 110 (1934).
124. Hoffman, C. J., Holder, B. E., and Jolly, W. L., *J. Phys. Chem.* **62**, 364 (1958).
125. Holst, E. H., Doctoral Dissertation, Pennsylvania State University, University Park, Pennsylvania, 1955.
126. Hoover, F. W., and Miller, H. C., *U. S. Patent* 2,933,475 (1960); *British Patents* 791,325 (1958), and 807,198 (1959), presumably by the same authors.
127. Hoppe, R., *Angew. Chem.* **71**, 457 (1959).
128. Hoshino, S., *J. Phys. Soc. Japan* **7**, 560 (1952); *Chem. Abstr.* **47**, 8455a (1953).
129. Hovey, R. J., O'Connell, J. J., and Martell, A. E., *J. Am. Chem. Soc.* **81**, 3189 (1959).
130. Huggins, M. L., and Magill, P. L., *J. Am. Chem. Soc.* **49**, 2357 (1927).
131. Hume, D. N., and Kolthoff, I. M., *J. Am. Chem. Soc.* **72**, 4423 (1950).
132. Hurd, R. N., DeLaMater, G., McElheny, G. C., and Pfeiffer, L. V., *J. Am. Chem. Soc.* **82**, 4454 (1960).
133. Iler, R. K., *U. S. Patent* 2,273,040 (1942).
134. Iler, R. K., and Hanthorn, H. E., *U. S. Patent* 2,307,045 (1943).
135. Irving, R. J., *J. Chem. Soc.* p. 2879 (1956).
135a. Jack, K. H., and Gutmann, V., *Acta Cryst.* **4**, 246 (1951).
135b. Jain, B. D., and Singhal, S. P., *J. Inorg. & Nuclear Chem.* **19**, 176 (1961).
136. Jensen, K. A., *Z. anorg. Chem.* **252**, 227 (1944).
136a. Johns, I. B., and DiPetro, H. R., *J. Org. Chem.* **27**, 592 (1962).
137. Joyner, R. D., and Kenney, M. E., *J. Am. Chem. Soc.* **82**, 5790 (1960).
138. Judd, M. L., *Dissertation Abstr.* **19**, 2456 (1959).
138a. Kanda, S., *Nippon Kagaku Zasshi* **81**, 1347 (1960); *Chem. Abstr.* **55**, 22994e (1961).
139. Kanda, S., and Saito, Y., *Bull. Chem. Soc. Japan* **30**, 192 (1957).
139a. Karipides, D. G., *Dissertation Abstr.* **22**, 59 (1961).

140. Kawai, S., Hamaguchi, H., and Tatsumoto, M., *Bunseki Kagaku* **5**, 165 (1956); *Chem. Abstr.* **51**, 9401h (1957).
141. Keggin, J. F., and Miles, F. D., *Nature* **137**, 577 (1936).
142. Kenney, C. N., *Chem. & Ind.* (*London*) p. 880 (1960).
143. Kern, W., and Schulz, R. C., *Angew. Chem.* **69**, 153 (1957).
144. Ketelaar, J. A. A., *Z. Krist.* **80**, 190 (1931); **87**, 436 (1934).
145. Kharasch, M. S., and Beck, T. M., *J. Am. Chem. Soc.* **56**, 2057 (1934).
146. Kidani, Y., *Chem. & Pharm. Bull.* (*Tokyo*) **6**, 563 (1958); **7**, 68 (1959).
147. Kinoshita, Y., Matsubara, I., Hibuchi, T., and Saito, Y., *Bull. Chem. Soc. Japan* **32**, 1221 (1959).
148. Kinoshita, Y., Matsubara, I., and Saito, Y., *Bull. Chem. Soc. Japan* **32**, 741 (1959).
149. Kinoshita, Y., Matsubara, I., and Saito, Y., *Bull. Chem. Soc. Japan* **32**, 1216 (1959).
150. Kluiber, R. W., and Lewis, J. W., *J. Am. Chem. Soc.* **82**, 5777 (1960).
151. Knobler, C. B., Okaya, Y., and Pepinsky, R., *Z. Krist.* **111**, 385 (1959).
152. Knobloch, F. W., *Dissertation Abstr.* **20**, 1171 (1959).
153. Knobloch, F. W., and Rauscher, W. H., *J. Polymer Sci.* **38**, 261 (1959).
154. Knox, K., *J. Chem. Phys.* **30**, 991 (1959).
155. Kohlschütter, V., *Ber. deut. chem. Ges.* **36**, 1151 (1903).
156. Kolditz, L., and Haage, K., *Z. anorg. u. allgem. Chem.* **301**, 36 (1959).
157. Kolditz, L., and Rehak, W., *Z. anorg. u. allgem. Chem.* **300**, 322 (1959).
158. Kolkmeijer, N. H., and Hengel, J. W. A. van, *Z. Krist.* **88**, 317 (1934).
159. Kondo, M., and Kubo, M., *J. Phys. Chem.* **61**, 1648 (1957).
160. Korshak, V. V., I.U.P.A.C. Macromolecular Chemistry Symposium, Moscow, June 14–18, 1960. Apparently published as Nesmeyanov, A. N., Korshak, V. V. *et al.*, *Doklady Akad. Nauk S.S.S.R.* **137**, 1370 (1961); *Chem. Abstr.* **55**, 21082a (1961).
161. Korshak, V. V., Krongauz, E. S., and Sheina, V. E., *Vysokomolekulyarnye Soedineniya* **2**, 662 (1960).
162. Korshak, V. V., Krongauz, E. S., Sladkov, A. M., Sheina, V. E., and Luneva, L. K., *Vysokomolekulyarnye Soedineniya* **1**, 1764 (1959); *Chem. Abstr.* **54**, 20285a (1960). Korshak, V. V., and Vinogradova, S. V., *Doklady Akad. Nauk S.S.S.R.* **138**, 1353 (1961); *Chem. Abstr.* **55**, 21646d (1961).
163. Korshak, V. V., Vinogradova, S. V., and Artemova, V. S., *Vysokomolekulyarnye Soedineniya* **2**, 492 (1960).
164. Korshak, V. V., Vinogradova, S. V., and Babchinitser, T. M., *Vysokomolekulyarnye Soedineniya* **2**, 408 (1960).
165. Krause, R. A., and Busch, D. H., *J. Am. Chem. Soc.* **82**, 4830 (1960).
166. Krug, J., and Sieg, L., *Z. Naturforsch.* **7a**, 369 (1952).
167. Kugler, V., *Czechoslovakian Patent* 85,300 (1955); *Farbe u. Lack* **65**, 378 (1959); *J. Polymer Sci.* **29**, 637 (1958).
168. Kugler, V., *Czechoslovakian Patent* 89,453 (1959); *Chem. Abstr.* **54**, 8154h (1960).
169. Langkammerer, C. M., *U. S. Patents* 2,489,651 (1949) and 2,621,193 (1952).
170. Laubengayer, A. W., Smith, J. D., and Ehrlich, G. G., *J. Am. Chem. Soc.* **83**, 542 (1961).
171. Lawton, E. A., *J. Phys. Chem.* **62**, 384 (1958).
172. Lawton, E. A., and McRitchie, D. D., *WADC* (*Wright Air Develop. Center*) *Tech. Rept.* **57/642** (1957).
173. Leussing, D. L., and Tischer, T. N., *J. Am. Chem. Soc.* **83**, 65 (1961).
173a. Lever, A. B. P., Lewis, J., and Nyholm, R. S., *Nature* **189**, 58 (1961).
174. Lewis, J., Machin, D. J., Nyholm, R. S., Pauling, P., and Smith, P. W., *Chem. & Ind.* (*London*) p. 259 (1960).

175. Lindqvist, I., *Acta Cryst.* **10**, 29 (1957).
176. Lions, F., and Martin, K. V., *J. Am. Chem. Soc.* **79**, 2733 (1957).
177. Lipscomb, W. N., *Acta Cryst.* **4**, 156 (1951).
178. Lipscomb, W. N., *Acta Cryst.* **4**, 266 (1951).
179. Long, F. A., *J. Am. Chem. Soc.* **73**, 537 (1951).
180. Low, B. W., Hirshfeld, F. L., and Richards, F. M., *J. Am. Chem. Soc.* **81**, 4412 (1959).
181. Ludekens, W. L. W., and Welch, A. J. E., *Acta Cryst.* **5**, 841 (1952).
182. Lüttringhaus, A., and Kullick, W., *Angew. Chem.* **70**, 438 (1958); *Makromol. Chem.* **44–46**, 669 (1961).
183. Lux, H., *in* "Handbuch der Präparativen Anorganischen Chemie" (G. Brauer, ed.), p. 1126. Ferdinand Enke, Stuttgart, 1954.
184. McCloskey, A. L., Brotherton, R. J., Woods, W. G., English, W. D., Boone, J. L., Campbell, G. W., Jr., Goldsmith, H., Iverson, M. L., Newsom, H. C., Manasevit, H. M., and Petterson, L. L., *WADC (Wright Air Develop. Center) Tech. Rept.* **59/761** (1960).
185. MacGillavry, C. H., and Bijvoet, J. M., *Z. Krist.* **94**, 231 (1936).
186. MacGillavry, C. H., Wilde, J. H. de, and Bijvoet, J. M., *Z. Krist.* **100**, 212 (1938).
187. MacGillavry, C. H., Nijveld, H., Dierdorp, S., and Karsten, J., *Rec. trav. chim.* **58**, 193 (1939).
188. McLean, J. A., Jr., *Dissertation Abstr.* **20**, 3065 (1960).
189. Malatesta, L., *Gazz. chim. ital.* **72**, 484 (1942).
190. Malatesta, L., *J. Chem. Soc.* p. 3924 (1955); *Rec. trav. chim.* **75**, 644 (1956).
191. Malatesta, L., and Turner, F., *Gazz. chim. ital.* **72**, 489 (1942).
192. Mangini, A., and Stratta, R., *Gazz. chim. ital.* **62**, 686 (1932).
193. Martin, K. V., *J. Am. Chem. Soc.* **80**, 233 (1958).
194. Martin, R. L., and Waterman, H., *J. Chem. Soc.* p. 2960 (1959).
195. Marvel, C. S., and Bonsignore, P. V., *J. Am. Chem. Soc.* **81**, 2668 (1959).
196. Marvel, C. S., and Martin, M. M., *J. Am. Chem. Soc.* **80**, 619 (1958).
197. Marvel, C. S., and Martin, M. M., *J. Am. Chem. Soc.* **80**, 6600 (1958).
198. Marvel, C. S., and Rassweiler, J. H., *J. Am. Chem. Soc.* **80**, 1197 (1958).
199. Marvel, C. S., and Tarköy, N., *J. Am. Chem. Soc.* **79**, 6000 (1957).
200. Marvel, C. S., and Tarköy, N., *J. Am. Chem. Soc.* **80**, 832 (1958).
201. Marvel, C. S., Aspey, S. A., and Dudley, E. A., *J. Am. Chem. Soc.* **78**, 4905 (1956).
202. Marvel, C. S., Audrieth, L. F., Moeller, T., and Bailar, J. C., Jr., *WADC (Wright Air Develop. Center) Tech. Rept.* **58/51**, Pt. III (1960).
203. Mashovets, V. P., Beletskii, M. S., Saksonov, Y. G., and Svoboda, R. V., *Doklady Akad. Nauk S.S.S.R.* **113**, 1290 (1957); *Chem. Abstr.* **51**, 17377e (1957).
204. Mathews, F. S., and Lipscomb, W. N., *J. Am. Chem. Soc.* **80**, 4745 (1958); *J. Phys. Chem.* **63**, 845 (1959).
204a. Mattison, L. E., Phipps, M. S., Kazan, J., and Alfred, L., *J. Polymer Sci.* **54**, 117 (1961).
205. Meisel, K., *Z. anorg. u. allgem. Chem.* **207**, 121 (1932).
206. Mellor, D. P., and Coryell, C. D., *J. Am. Chem. Soc.* **60**, 1786 (1938).
207. Meriwether, L. S., Colthup, E. C., Fiene, M. L., and Cotton, F. A., *J. Inorg. & Nuclear Chem.* **11**, 181 (1959).
208. Millar, J. R., *Chem. & Ind. (London)* p. 606 (1957).
209. Minné, R., and Rochow, E. G., *J. Am. Chem. Soc.* **82**, 5625, 5628 (1960).
210. Moeller, R. D., Schonfeld, F. W., Tipton, C. R., Jr., and Weber, J. T., *Trans. Am. Soc. Metals* **43**, 39 (1951).

211. Møller, C. K., *Kgl. Danske Videnskab. Selskab. Mat. fys. Medd.* **32**(2), 1 (1959); *Nature* **180**, 981 (1957).
212. Møller, C. K., *Nature* **182**, 1436 (1958).
213. Müller, W., *German Patent* 936,332 (1955).
214. Muetterties, E. L., *J. Am. Chem. Soc.* **82**, 1082 (1960).
215. Nardelli, M., and Chierici, I., *Gazz. chim. ital.* **87**, 1478 (1957).
216. Nardelli, M., and Fava, G., *Acta Cryst.* **12**, 727 (1959).
217. Nardelli, M., and Fava, G., *Gazz. chim. ital.* **88**, 536 (1958).
218. Nardelli, M., and Fava, G., *Proc. Chem. Soc.* p. 194 (1959).
219. Nardelli, M., Braibanti, A., and Fava, G., *Gazz. chim. ital.* **87**, 1209 (1957).
220. Nardelli, M., Cavalca, L., and Fava, G., *Gazz. chim. ital.* **87**, 1232 (1957).
221. Nardelli, M., Coghi, L., and Azzoni, G., *Gazz. chim. ital.* **88**, 235 (1958).
222. Nardelli, M., Fava, G., and Branchi, G., *Acta Cryst.* **13**, 898 (1960).
223. Nast, R., and Rückemann, H., *Chem. Ber.* **93**, 584 (1960).
224. Natta, G., *Atti accad. nazl. Lincei* [6] **5**, 1003 (1927); *Chem. Abstr.* **22**, 337[8] (1928).
224a. Natta, G., Corradini, P., and Allegra, G., *J. Polymer Sci.* **51**, 339 (1961).
225. Nesmeyanov, A. N., Rybinskaya, M. I., and Slonimskii, G. L., *Vysokomolekuly-arnye Soedineniya* **2**, 526 (1960).
225a. Newman, G., and Powell, D. B., *J. Chem. Soc.* p. 477 (1961).
226. Nieuwenkamp, W., and Bijvoet, J. M., *Z. Krist.* **84**, 49 (1933).
227. Nijssen, L., and Lipscomb, W. N., *Acta Cryst.* **5**, 604 (1952).
228. Nijssen, L., and Lipscomb, W. N., *Acta Cryst.* **7**, 103 (1954).
229. O'Brien, T. D., *in* "The Chemistry of the Coordination Compounds" (J. C. Bailar, Jr., ed.), p. 382 ff. Reinhold, New York, 1956.
229a. Oh, J. S., *Dissertation Abstr.* **22**, 61 (1961).
230. Olson, M. H., *Canadian Patents* 579,270–1 (1959); *U. S. Patent* 2,693,458 (1954).
231. Oswald, H. R., *Helv. Chim. Acta* **43**, 77 (1960).
232. Oswald, H. R., and Jaggi, H., *Helv. Chim. Acta* **43**, 72 (1960).
233. Owen, J. E., Joyner, R. D., and Kenney, M. E., *Abstr. Papers 139th Meeting Am. Chem. Soc., St. Louis, Missouri 1961*, p. 17M.
234. Patterson, T. R., Pavlik, F. J., Baldoni, A. A., and Frank, R. L., *J. Am. Chem. Soc.* **81**, 4213 (1959).
235. Pauling, L., *Proc. Natl. Acad. Sci. U.S.* **15**, 709 (1929).
236. Pauling, L., "The Nature of the Chemical Bond," 3rd ed. Cornell Univ. Press, Ithaca, New York, 1960.
237. Pauling, L., and Hoard, J. L., *Z. Krist.* **74**, 546 (1930).
238. Pfeiffer, P., and Pfitzner, H., *J. prakt. Chem.* **145**, 243 (1936).
239. Porai-Koshits, M. A., *Izvest. Akad. Nauk S.S.S.R. Ser. Fiz.* **20**, 740 (1956); *Russ. J. Inorg. Chem.* **4**, 332 (1959).
240. Powell, H. M., and Brewer, F. M., *J. Chem. Soc.* p. 197 (1938).
241. Powell, H. M., and Rayner, J. H., *Nature* **163**, 566 (1949).
242. Prasad, S., and Srivastava, K. P., *J. Indian Chem. Soc.* **35**, 793 (1958).
243. Prosen, R. J., and Trueblood, K. N., *Acta Cryst.* **9**, 741 (1956).
244. Rau, R. L., *Dissertation Abstr.* **16**, 232 (1956).
245. Rây, P., and Rây, R. M., *J. Indian Chem. Soc.* **3**, 118 (1926).
246. Rây, P., and Sahu, H., *J. Indian Chem. Soc.* **23**, 161 (1946).
247. Rayner, J. H., and Powell, H. M., *J. Chem. Soc.* p. 319 (1952).
248. Rayner, J. H., and Powell, H. M., *J. Chem. Soc.* p. 3412 (1958).
249. Reid, T. S., *British Patent* 802,962 (1958); *Canadian Patents* 568,082–3 (1958); *German Patent* 958,831 (1957); *U. S. Patent* 2,662,835 (1953).

250. Rigamonti, R., *Gazz. chim. ital.* **68,** 803 (1938).
251. Rollier, M. A., and Arreghini, E., *Gazz. chim. ital.* **69,** 499 (1939).
252. Rüdorff, W., and Brodersen, K., *Z. anorg. u. allgem. Chem.* **270,** 145 (1952); *Z. Naturforsch.* **7b,** 56 (1952).
253. Rüdorff, W., and Brodersen, K., *Z. anorg. u. allgem. Chem.* **274,** 323 (1953).
254. Rüdorff, W., and Kändler, J., *Naturwissenschaften* **44,** 418 (1957).
255. Rüdorff, W., and Stegemann, K., *Z. anorg. u. allgem. Chem.* **251,** 376 (1943).
256. Rüdorff, W., Ruston, W. R., and Scherhaufer, A., *Acta Cryst.* **1,** 196 (1948).
257. Rüdorff, W., Kändler, J., Lincke, G., and Babel, D., *Angew. Chem.* **71,** 672 (1959).
258. Rundle, R. E., and Goring, J. H., *J. Am. Chem. Soc.* **72,** 5337 (1950).
259. Rust, J. B., Segal, C. L., and Takimoto, H. H., Research on high temperature Polymers. Tech. Rept. No. 3 to the Office of Naval Research, March 1 to September 1, 1959.
259a. Ryan, T. D., and Rundle, R. E., *J. Am. Chem. Soc.* **83,** 2814 (1961).
260. Sacconi, L., *Gazz. chim. ital.* **83,** 894 (1953); *Z. anorg. u. allgem. Chem.* **275,** 249 (1954).
261. Sacconi, L., and Caroti, G., *Z. anorg. u. allgem. Chem.* **271,** 176 (1953).
262. Saito, Y., and Kanda, S., *Japanese Patent* 7241 (1959).
263. Sands, D. E., Zalkin, A., and Elson, R. E., *Acta Cryst.* **12,** 21 (1959).
263a. Sansoni, B., and Sigmund, O., *Angew. Chem.* **73,** 299 (1961).
264. Šćavničar, R., *Acta Cryst.* **9,** 956 (1956).
265. Šćavničar, S., *Acta Cryst.* **8,** 379 (1955).
265a. Schäfer, H. L., and Kling, O., *Z. anorg. u. allgem. Chem.* **309,** 245 (1961).
266. Schlenker, F., *German Patents* 1,018,624 (1957) and 1,045,093 (1958); *Kunststoffe* **47,** 7 (1957).
267. Schmitz-DuMont, O., *Z. Elektrochem.* **47,** 221 (1941).
268. Schmitz-DuMont, O., and Bornefeld, H., *Z. anorg. u. allgem. Chem.* **287,** 120 (1956).
269. Schmitz-DuMont, O., and Fischer, R., *Z. anorg. u. allgem. Chem.* **285,** 303 (1956).
270. Schmitz-DuMont, O., and Füchtenbusch, F., *Z. anorg. u. allgem. Chem.* **284,** 278 (1956).
271. Schmitz-DuMont, O., and Hilger, W., *Z. anorg. u. allgem. Chem.* **300,** 175 (1959).
272. Schmitz-DuMont, O., and Kron, N., *Z. anorg. u. allgem. Chem.* **280,** 180 (1955).
273. Schmitz-DuMont, O., and Ohler, K. H., *Z. anorg. u. allgem. Chem.* **306,** 63 (1960).
274. Schmitz-DuMont, O., and Schulte, H., *Z. anorg. u. allgem. Chem.* **282,** 253 (1955).
275. Schmitz-DuMont, O., Pilzecker, J., and Piepenbrink, H. F., *Z. anorg. u. allgem. Chem.* **248,** 175 (1941).
276. Schmitz-DuMont, O., Simons, P., and Broja, G., *Z. anorg. Chem.* **258,** 307 (1949).
277. Schmitz-DuMont, O., Broja, H., and Piepenbrink, H. F., *Z. anorg. Chem.* **253,** 118 (1947).
278. Schmitz-DuMont, O., Broja, H., and Piepenbrink, H. F., *Z. anorg. Chem.* **254,** 329 (1947).
279. Schmitz-DuMont, O., Nagel, F., and Schaal, W., *Angew. Chem.* **70,** 105 (1958).
280. Schwarzenbach, G., and Zobrist, A., *Helv. Chim. Acta* **35,** 1291 (1952).
281. Scouloudi, H., *Acta Cryst.* **6,** 651 (1953); see also Scouloudi, H., and Carlisle, C. H., *Nature* **166,** 357 (1950).
282. Sears, D. R., *Dissertation Abstr.* **19,** 1225 (1958).
283. Shugam, E. A., and Zhdanov, G. S., *Acta Physicochim. U.R.S.S.* **20,** 247 (1945).
284. Simkin, J., and Block, B. P., *Abstr. Papers 136th Meeting Am. Chem. Soc. Atlantic City, New Jersey 1959* p. 18N.
285. Simkin, J., and Block, B. P., *J. Inorg. & Nuclear Chem.* **23,** 253 (1961).
286. Smirnova, L., Breger, A. K., and Zhdanov, G. S., *Acta Physicochim. U.R.S.S.* **15,** 255, 276 (1941).

287. Smith, H. G., and Rundle, R. E., *J. Am. Chem. Soc.* **80**, 5075 (1958).

288. Sowerby, D. B., and Audrieth, L. F., *J. Chem. Educ.* **37**, 134 (1960).

289. Sprague Electric Co., High temperature dielectric films. Final Report to Signal Corps (1952). PB 114,096.

290. Stephen, H., and Weizman, C., *J. Chem. Soc.* **103**, 269 (1913).

291. Stratton, W. J., and Busch, D. H., *J. Am. Chem. Soc.* **82**, 4834 (1960).

292. Strock, L. W., *Z. physik. Chem.* **B25**, 441 (1934); **B31**, 132 (1935).

293. Stroganov, E. V., and Ovchinnikov, K. V., *Vestnik Leningrad. Univ.* **12**(22) *Ser. Fiz. i Khim.* (4), 152 (1957); *Chem. Abstr.* **52**, 13356i (1958).

294. Takimoto, H. H., and Rust, J. B., *J. Org. Chem.* **26**, 2467 (1961).

294a. Terentev, A. P., Rode, V. V., and Rukhadze, E. G., *Vysokomolekulyarnye Soedineniya* **2**, 1557 (1960); *Chem. Abstr.* **55**, 19303d (1961).

295. Tishchenko, G. N., *Trudy Inst. Krist. Akad. Nauk S.S.S.R. No.* **11**, 93 (1955).

296. Tobolsky, A. V., Personal communication to R. A. Florentine.

296a. Turova, N. Y., Novoselova, A. V., and Semenenko, K. N., *Russ. J. Inorg. Chem.* **5**, 828 (1960).

297. Uhlig, E., *Z. anorg. u. allgem. Chem.* **306**, 71 (1960); **312**, 332 (1961).

298. Underwood, A. L., Toribara, T. Y., and Neuman, W. F., *J. Am. Chem. Soc.* **72**, 5597 (1950).

299. Vaïnshteïn, B. K., *Doklady Akad. Nauk S.S.S.R.* **68**, 301 (1949); *Chem. Abstr.* **44**, 17h (1950).

300. Vaïnshteïn, B. K., *Doklady Akad. Nauk S.S.S.R.* **83**, 227 (1952); *Chem. Abstr.* **47**, 10307g (1953).

301. Vaïnshteïn, B. K., *Zhur. Fiz. Khim.* **26**, 1774 (1952); *Chem. Abstr.* **49**, 2147d (1955).

302. Verweel, H. J., and Bijvoet, J. M., *Z. Krist.* **77**, 122 (1931).

303. Von Hoene, J., Charles, R. G., and Hickam, W. M., *J. Phys. Chem.* **62**, 1008 (1958).

304. Vorres, K. S., and Donohue, J., *Acta Cryst.* **8**, 25 (1955).

305. Watt, G. W., and McCarley, R. E., *J. Am. Chem. Soc.* **79**, 4585 (1957).

306. Weiser, H. B., Milligan, W. O., and Bates, J. B., *J. Phys. Chem.* **46**, 99 (1942).

307. Weiss, A., and Damm, K., *Z. Naturforsch.* **9b**, 82 (1954).

308. Weiss, A., and Weiss, A., *Z. Naturforsch.* **11b**, 604 (1956).

309. Wells, A. F., *Z. Krist.* **100**, 189 (1938).

310. Wells, A. F., *J. Chem. Soc.* p. 1662 (1947).

311. Wells, A. F., *J. Chem. Soc.* p. 1670 (1947).

312. Wells, A. F., "Structural Inorganic Chemistry," 2nd ed. Oxford Univ. Press, London and New York, 1950.

313. West, C. D., *Z. Krist.* **88**, 173 (1934); **90**, 555 (1935).

314. Wilkins, J. P., and Wittbecker, E. L., *U. S. Patent* 2,659,711 (1953).

315. Wilsdorf, H., *Acta Cryst.* **1**, 115 (1948).

316. Wilsey, R. B., *Phil. Mag.* **42**, 262 (1921); *Chem. Abstr.* **15**, 3937[5] (1921).

317. Wilsey, R. B., *Phil. Mag.* **46**, 487 (1923); *Chem. Abstr.* **18**, 2[8] (1924).

318. Wooster, N., *Z. Krist.* **74**, 363 (1930).

319. Wooster, N., *Z. Krist.* **83**, 35 (1932).

320. Wyckoff, R. W. G., and Posnjak, E., *J. Am. Chem. Soc.* **44**, 30 (1922).

321. Wymore, C. E., and Bailar, J. C., Jr., *J. Inorg. & Nuclear Chem.* **14**, 42 (1960).

322. Zachariasen, W. H., *Acta Cryst.* **1**, 265 (1948); *J. Chem. Phys.* **16**, 254 (1948).

323. Zakharkin, L. I., and Savina, L. A., *Izvest. Akad. Nauk S.S.S.R., Otdel. Khim. Nauk* p. 1039 (1960); *Chem. Abstr.* **54**, 24346i (1960).

324. Zhdanov, G. S., *Compt. rend. acad. sci. U.R.S.S.* **31**, 352 (1941).

325. Zhdanov, G. S., and Shugam, E. A., *Acta Physicochim. U.R.S.S.* **20**, 253 (1945).

Electron-Deficient Polymers

AMOS J. LEFFLER

Arthur D. Little, Inc., Cambridge, Massachusetts

TABLE OF CONTENTS

I. Historical

The history of compounds which are polymeric by virtue of electron deficiency is perhaps rather typical of the history of scientific advances. A discovery is made and published, sometimes in an obscure journal, but little interest is created and it becomes known as an odd fact that is swept under the rug of the prevalent theory in the field. From time to time later investigators reexamine the problem and either explain away the facts or deny the existence of any anomaly. Two very good examples of this process are electron-deficient compounds and the arene chromium complexes. Both of these classes of materials were recognized in the first two decades of this century, but it was only a quarter of a century later that the basic chemical bonding principles began to be understood.

The first clear example of an electron-deficient compound to be discovered was diborane, B_2H_6, which is one of the series of boron hydrides that occupies so large a portion of the scientific work of Stock (53). Actually, diborane was not the first of this class of hydrides to be prepared but it is the simplest of the series and its structure presented the most direct challenge to the then existing theories of chemical valence. There was no doubt as to its empirical formula and molecular weight, but there was also no question as to the number of electrons available for bonding by boron and hydrogen. The only conclusion reached at that time was that there were not enough electrons available to hold two boron and six hydrogen atoms together with electron-pair bonds, as required by classical theories of bonding. Sidgwick (*51*) suggested that electron pairs were used for the boron-boron bonding and for four of the boron-hydrogen bonds, while one-electron bonds were formed between the boron atoms and the two remaining atoms. Resonance of six electron pairs among seven positions was later suggested by G. N. Lewis (*26*). These theories are reviewed by Pauling in the second edition of "The Nature of the Chemical Bond" (*37*).

Actually, one of the greatest impediments to a recognition of the true nature of the bonding in diborane was an incorrect picture of the geometry of the molecule. The results of an early electron diffraction study of diborane were interpreted in terms of an erroneous, ethane-like structure (*4*). The correct structure of diborane is shown in Fig. 1. This bridged structure, surprisingly, was first suggested as early as 1921 by Dilthey (*16*), but was not seriously considered until 1943, when available physical measurements were reconsidered (*31*). Confirmation of the bridge structure was afforded by new electron diffraction measurements (*20*), and by spectroscopic studies (*41*). A comparison of the second and third editions of "The Nature of the Chemical Bond" (*37*), as well as a study of recent review articles (*28*, *54*), shows how radically this field altered between 1940 and 1900.

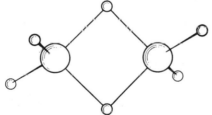

Fig. 1. Structure of diborane.

The discovery of other examples of chemical bonding inexplicable on the basis of electron-pair bonds increasingly challenged existing valence theory. Although examples were known of association in solution, for example, the tetrameric nature of trimethylindium in benzene (*15*), the 1941 discovery by Laubengayer and Gilliam (*24*) that trimethylaluminum was dimeric in the *gas phase* was of particular importance; the reported heat of dissociation of Al_2Me_6 was 20.2 kcal/mole, and could hardly be explained as a vague sort of association.

It was apparent that a more general theory was required to explain the diverse examples of what came to be known as *electron-deficient compounds*, in recognition of the fact that there were not enough valence electrons to hold adjacent atoms together with electron-pair bonds. In a classic 1947 paper, Rundle (44) discussed these compounds from a general point of view, advancing the concept of the "half-bond," in which one atom forms more than one bond with a single bond orbital, using a single electron pair. The idea of half-bonds, now usually known as *three-center bonds*, accounts satisfactorily for the majority of the electron-deficient compounds (55).

II. Requirements for Electron-Deficient Bonding

The term "electron-deficient," as noted above, was applied to molecules with more bonds than bonding electron pairs. Rundle (44) pointed out that in electron-deficient molecules there is one set of atoms A, with fewer valence electrons than stable bond orbitals (i.e., a metal), and another set B, which can be regarded as deficient in stable orbitals (i.e., a nonmetal). Maximum use of stable orbitals can be achieved only if B uses some of its bonding orbitals to form more than one bond, and this tendency to use all low energy orbitals is the underlying principle of electron-deficient bonding (45).

The simplest and most useful way of regarding these compounds is in terms of three-center bonds. In a "normal" B—H bond, for example, which could be called a two-center bond, each atom supplies one (atomic) orbital; these orbitals interact to form one bonding and one antibonding orbital. The B and H each contribute one electron, which exactly fills the bonding molecular orbital, forming a covalent bond. In a B—H—B bridge, each atom supplies one atomic orbital, the three of which interact to form one bonding, one nonbonding, and one antibonding orbital; two electrons fill the bonding orbital, forming the three-center bond. A description of the bonding can also be given in terms of resonance among single bond structures (37) but is perhaps less useful.

This discussion is rather easily generalized (17): if the atoms of a molecule provide n orbitals and m electrons, then for $m = n$, normal electron-pair bonds are favored; for $m > n$, electrons in excess of those permitted in bonding orbitals will be present as lone pairs, as in ammonia; and for $m < n$, as in the boron hydrides, some three-center bonding will take place.

These formal conditions for electron-deficient bonding are necessary but by no means sufficient. A number of other factors such as electronegativity differences, π bonding, and steric factors play an important part in determining the nature of the bonding. For example, the boron hydrides and beryllium hydride are electron deficient, but lithium hydride has an ionic, sodium chloride type of structure.

The methyl derivatives of metals of the third main periodic group are of particular interest (*10*). All meet the formal requirements for electron-deficient bonding, but only trimethylaluminum is dimeric in the gas phase; trimethylboron, trimethylgallium, and trimethylindium are monomeric as gases. Trimethylindium, however, is tetrameric in benzene solution and in the solid state, while trimethylthallium is monomeric in benzene solution.

Steric factors have been suggested as the reason why trimethylboron does not dimerize (*44*). According to this viewpoint, the radius of boron is sufficiently small that boron-boron interaction would be very slight at the bridge bond angle found for Al_2Me_6; the instability of B_2Me_6 is attributed to this factor since calculations for Al_2Me_6 show that metal-metal bonding is rather substantial (*27*). An alternative explanation was put forward by Mulliken (*34*), who attributed the monomeric character of trimethylboron to hyperconjugation involving C—B π bonding (*14*), in the same way that boron halides are monomeric and planar due to conjugation with the lone-pair electrons on the halogen atoms; the monomer of trimethylaluminum would be less stabilized, since double bonding to second row elements is weaker. It has been suggested that metal-metal inner shell repulsions play a part with trimethylgallium and trimethylindium (*27*).

III. Types of Electron-Deficient Polymers

All of the metals and the metal hexaborides, MB_6, are electron-deficient substances (*37, 44*). Since they lack the structural features normally associated with the term "polymer," they will not be discussed here. It is worth noting, however, that electron-deficient bonding in metals and borides can give rise to fairly high orders of thermal stability. As will be noted in what follows, the development of increasingly complex boron hydrides suggests that linear polymer molecules with bonding quite similar to that in the borides may eventually be developed. Several of the electron-deficient materials discussed here truly warrant the use of the term polymer, for example dimethylberyllium. Most of them are dimers and trimers, and are included in the expectation that ways will be found to produce higher degrees of polymerization using the same bonding principles.

That this type of bonding is fairly widespread is shown by the following list of elements which are involved in the electron-deficient bonding in isolable compounds: hydrogen, lithium, beryllium, boron, carbon, magnesium, aluminum, indium, zirconium, hafnium, platinum, and uranium; in addition, copper, gallium, gold, and mercury may form unstable electron-deficient compounds. Some examples of electron-deficient polymers are shown in Table I.

TABLE I

SOME EXAMPLES OF ELECTRON-DEFICIENT POLYMERS

Compound	Properties
	Alkyls[a]
$(MeLi)_n$	Nonvolatile white powder, insoluble in hydrocarbons but soluble in ether with n of 3.
$(EtLi)_n$	Crystalline material, m.p. 95°, soluble in benzene with n varying to 6 in the vapor phase.
$(n\text{-}BuLi)_n$	Viscous liquid soluble in hydrocarbons, distillable at 80 to 100° *in vacuo*, n of 7 in benzene and 5 in diethyl ether.
$(Me_2Be)_n$	Colorless sublimable solid with extrapolated v.p. of 760 mm at 217°, soluble in ethers but not hydrocarbons; the value of n varies but is from 1 to 3 in the vapor phase.
$(Et_2Be)_n$	Liquid with extrapolated b.p. 194°, v.p. 4 mm at 93 to 95°, soluble in benzene and ethers.
$(Me_2Mg)_n$	Pyrophoric solid, slightly soluble in ether and difficultly sublimable in vacuum or in a stream of ether vapor.
$(Me_3Al)_2$	Pyrophoric liquid, m.p. 15°, b.p. 126°, appearing to be partly dissociated at 100 to 160° in the vapor phase with heat of dissociation of 20.2 kcal/mole.
$(Et_3Al)_2$	Pyrophoric liquid, m.p. −52.5°, b.p. 185.6°, partly dissociated in the vapor phase.
$(Pr_3Al)_2$	Pyrophoric liquid, m.p. −107°, b.p. 248–252°, dimeric in benzene but monomeric in the vapor phase; the isopropyl isomer is monomeric in benzene.
$(i\text{-}Bu_3Al)_2$	Easily oxidizable liquid, partly dissociated in cyclohexane.
$(Me_3In)_4$	Cryst. material, m.p. 88°, b.p. 136°, tetrameric in benzene but monomeric in the vapor phase—all other alkylindium compounds are monomeric in benzene.
$(Me_4Pt)_4$	Solid that decomposes without melting and is soluble in benzene, ether, acetone, and petroleum ether.
$(BEt_3CO)_n$	B.p. varies from 65° to 110° at 0.1 mm Hg depending on n.
	Hydrides[b]
B_2H_6	Gas m.p. −165.5°, b.p. −92°, soluble in ethers, exists undissociated in the vapor phase.
B_4H_{10}	Liquid m.p. −120°, b.p. 18°, unstable at room temperature.
B_5H_9	Liquid m.p. −46.9°, b.p. 65°, stable to about 150°, reacts explosively with air, stable to pure water.
$B_{10}H_{14}$	Solid m.p. 99.7°, b.p. 214°, extrapolated, stable to air and moisture at ordinary temperature, soluble in alcohol, ether, benzene and carbon disulfide.
$B_{10}H_{16}$	Solid, stable to 170° *in vacuo*, stable in air.
$(AlH_3)_n$	Solid that has not been prepared free from ether, decomposes about 100° into the elements; high polymer.
$Al(BH_4)_3$	Liquid, m.p. 64.5°, b.p. 44.5°, detonates in air, soluble in hydrocarbons, reacts with ethers, amines.

Compound	Properties
$Be(BH_4)_2$	Solid, m.p. 123°, b.p. 91.3°, sublimes, reacts with amines.
$Zr(BH_4)_4$	Solid, v.p. 15 mm at 25°.
$Hf(BH_4)_4$	Solid, v.p. 14.9 mm at 25°, m.p. 29°.
$U(BH_4)_4$	Solid, v.p. 2.15 mm at 54.3°, decomposes to $U(BH_4)_3$ at 70°, soluble in ether, slightly soluble in heptane.
MgH_2	Nonvolatile solid, decomposes to elements above 300°, high polymer.
$(Me_3NAlH_3)_n$	Solid, n is 1.6 in cyclohexane.
	Halides[b]
B_4Cl_4	Solid, v.p. 7.05 mm at 40.8°, 13.0 mm at 52.4°.
$Cs_2B_{10}Cl_{10}$	Solid, stable to 400° in air, stable to OH^- and OCH_3^-.
	Alkyl Hydrides
$(Et_2BH)_2$	Volatile liquid that readily disproportionates into other ethyl diboranes, B_2H_6, and Et_3B.
$(i\text{-PrBeH})_n$	Viscous nonvolatile polymer.
$(Me_2AlH)_n$	Viscous liquid, v.p. 2 mm at 25°, trimeric in pentane, dimer-trimer equilibrium in the vapor phase.
$MeB_{10}H_{13}$	Liquid, m.p. 4–6°, b.p. 223°.
$1,2\text{-Me}_2B_{10}H_{12}$	Liquid, glass at −40°.
$2,4\text{-Me}_2B_{10}H_{12}$	Solid, m.p. 43.5–44.5°.
$1,2,3\text{-Me}_3B_{10}H_{11}$	Solid, m.p. 161–163°.
$1,2,4\text{-Me}_3B_{10}H_{11}$	Liquid, m.p. 12–13°.
$1,2,3,4\text{-Me}_4B_{10}H_{10}$	Solid, m.p. 178–179°.
$1,2,3,5\text{-Me}_4B_{10}H_{10}$	Solid, m.p. 70–71°; may be the 1,2,3,8-isomer.
$B_{12}H_{11}C_3H_7{}^{2-}$	Properties unknown; from $(H_3O)_2B_{10}H_{10}$ and propylene.

[a] See reference (**10**) for a fuller discussion of many of these compounds.

[b] See references (**28**) and (**54**) for a review of boron hydride chemistry and reference to the boron halide structures.

It should be noted that many cases are known in which halogen, carbonyl, or other groups form bridges between metal atoms, as for example in Al_2Cl_6 and $Fe_2(CO)_9$. Such compounds are not electron-deficient, however, since the unshared pairs on the bridging groups provide enough electrons for all bonds to be of the electron-pair type.

A. Organometallic Compounds

Organometallic compounds contain metal-carbon bonds, and may in certain cases form electron-deficient compounds in which the organic radical functions as the bridging group. Several examples have already been cited.

Ethyllithium and higher alkyllithium compounds are the simplest examples. Bonding in these compounds is covalent in character, as judged by their solubility in hydrocarbon solvents, but their low volatility suggests association. In benzene solution, cryoscopic measurements show a degree of association of about 6 (*8*), and according to recent mass spectroscopic studies ethyllithium vapor consists predominantly of a hexamer and tetramer in approximately equal concentrations at 80–95° (*6*). Infrared studies (*59*) are consistent with this view. It was suggested (*6*) that the structures were cyclic and involved an inner lithium core surrounded by ethyl radicals. A possible structure, in which ethyl bridges alternate above and below the ring, is shown in Fig. 2. Some puckering of the ring may occur to minimize strain.

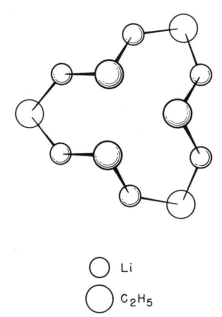

FIG. 2. Suggested structure for ethyllithium hexamer.

The beryllium alkyls constitute an important class of electron-deficient polymers. An X-ray structure determination (*52*) showed that solid dimethylberyllium was made up of linear chains, as shown in Fig. 3. Each beryllium atom is involved in four three-center bonds, displaying a coordination number of six; this is at first surprising, until it is noted that the usual coordination rules are based on electron-pair bonds. In most electron-deficient substances, the ligancy is in fact greater than the number of stable orbitals (*37*). Dimethylberyllium is also associated in the vapor

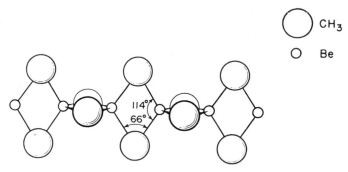

FIG. 3. Structure of dimethylberyllium.

phase, in which it exists as an equilibrium mixture of monomer, dimer, trimer, and of higher polymers when the pressure is near saturation. Study of this equilibrium has shown (*13*) that the heat of formation (ΔH) of one mole of dimer from two of monomer is -24 kcal. This represents mainly the stabilization achieved by conversion of two whole-bonds into four half-bonds. For a similar conversion of two whole-bonds to four half-bonds when monomer goes to "infinite" linear polymer, ΔH is estimated to be -19 kcal (*13*). The lower value is attributed to the distortion of bond angles in a situation in which essentially every beryllium atom forms four half-bonds. When larger alkyl groups replace methyl, the degree of polymerization is much lower. Diisopropylberyllium is dimeric in benzene (*11*), while the volatility of the rather unstable di-*tert*-butylberyllium suggests that it is monomeric (*12*).

As already noted, trialkylborons are monomeric. A carbonyl derivative that may be electron deficient, however, has recently been reported (*42*). Under heat and pressure, substituted boranes react with carbon monoxide to give compounds of the formula $(BR_3CO)_n$, where n may be as high as 10. No structural or spectral information has been reported, and it is an interesting question why these compounds can be polymeric while H_3BCO is a rather unstable monomer.

Much less is known of magnesium dialkyls, but their covalent character and low volatility suggest that electron-deficient bonding is involved. Dimethylmagnesium, for example, is clearly polymeric since it sublimes only with difficulty in high vacuum (*10*), in spite of the fact that the molecular weight of the "monomer" is only 54.3.

It was noted above that trimethylaluminum exists as a dimer in the gas phase (*24*), with $\Delta H = -20.2$ kcal for the formation of Al_2Me_6 from two monomer units. This may be compared with the equivalent figure for dimethylberyllium, $\Delta H = -24$ kcal. As is also the case with beryllium alkyls, dissociation of Al_2R_6 increases with larger alkyl groups, perhaps as a result of steric effects (*27*). Thus triisopropylaluminum is monomeric in benzene solution (*39*). In a recent investigation of trimethylaluminum by the nuclear magnetic resonance (NMR) technique (*33*), it was observed that rapid exchange of bridging and nonbridging methyl groups takes place at room temperature. The exchange was frozen out at $-75°$, and an activation energy of 6 to 14 kcal/mole of dimer was indicated. It is of interest that methyl bridges rather than halogen bridges occur in the halides $MeAlX_2$ and Me_2AlX (*57*).

Elucidation of the tetrameric structure of tetramethylplatinum (*46*) was no doubt of key importance in leading Rundle to formulate his view of electron-deficient bonding (*44*). In this compound (Fig. 4), three of the

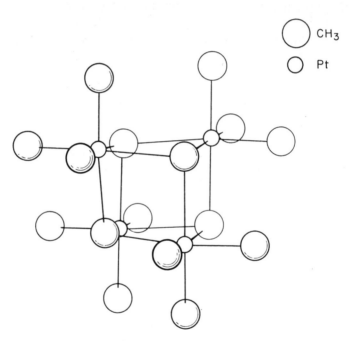

Fig. 4. Structure of tetramethylplatinum.

methyl groups are normally attached to the platinum atoms, while the fourth acts as a bridging group between three platinum atoms. The so-called "hexamethyldiplatinum" appears also to be polymeric and electron deficient. An incomplete X-ray analysis shows that the minimum molecular size corresponds to $(Me_3Pt)_{12}$, and that the structure may in fact consist of infinite chains (*21*).

B. Boron Hydrides and Related Compounds

Diborane is the simplest boron hydride and, as noted above, can be regarded as a dimer of BH_3 units attached by two three-center bonds. For the formation of one mole of B_2H_6 from two BH_3 moieties, ΔH has been estimated (5) as -28 kcal. Boron hydrides of higher molecular weight have been known for some time (53), including B_4H_{10}, B_5H_9, B_6H_{10}, and $B_{10}H_{14}$. With the more complex species, the three-center bond concept accounts satisfactorily for the bridging hydrogens, but bonding of the boron framework is more usefully formulated in terms of molecular orbitals covering the entire framework. This approach has been developed and applied by Lipscomb and his co-workers (17, 28). The most important result is that stable structures have enough electrons, after assigning the necessary electrons to "normal" terminal B—H bonds and to B—H—B bridges, to fill exactly the bonding molecular orbitals of the boron framework.

A recently discovered boron hydride, $B_{10}H_{16}$, provides the first example of a new type of linkage: two B_5H_9 moieties are joined, after removal of hydrogen, at the apical boron atoms (19). This hydride is considered (29) to be intermediate between the previously known boron hydrides and the borides, MB_6. In the latter, each boron atom forms bonds with five other boron atoms, four in its own B_6 octahedron and the fifth in an adjacent octahedron (37). The structure therefore consists of an infinite, three-dimensional framework, with M^{2+} cations in the interstices.

A second way in which boron polyhedra can polymerize is through bridge bonds (29). It is assumed that the electronic structure within the individual polyhedra is not altered, and the polymerization is equivalent to replacement of two B—H bonds, one from each polyhedron, by a B—H—B bridge. Formally, this is equivalent to loss of hydride ion. Thus, as a possible but as yet hypothetical example, two $B_{10}H_{10}^{-2}$ ions would form a $B_{20}H_{19}^{3-}$ ion when joined by a single B—H—B bridge. A very large number of $B_{12}H_{12}^{-2}$ ions, each joined to four others by B—H—B bridges, would yield a $(B_{12}H_{10})_n$ polymer (29). Quite possibly some of the non-volatile higher boron hydrides can be regarded in this way. (See Chapter 4 for a discussion and references on the higher boron hydrides.) The ways in which polymeric species might be built up are outlined by Lipscomb (29).

An indication of the tremendously varied electron-deficient framework structures which can in principle be developed is given by Lipscomb (29). In addition to the replacement of bridging and terminal hydrogens by various groups, many possibilities arise from the substitution of hetero atoms in the boron framework, for example C for B^-, Be for B^+, N for B^{2-}, Al for B. The first examples of such compounds, the carboranes, were recently reported (63). Three compounds were found: $B_3C_2H_5$, and *sym-*

and *unsym*-isomers of $B_4C_2H_6$. The structure proposed (*63*) for *sym*-$B_4C_2H_6$ is shown in Fig. 5. In Lipscomb's view, these are derived from the predicted stable ions $B_5H_5^{-2}$ and $B_6H_6^{-2}$ (*29*).

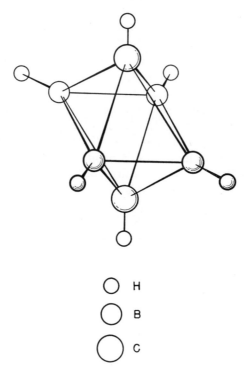

H

B

C

FIG. 5. Structure of *sym*-$B_4C_2H_6$.

A number of electron-deficient hydrides containing more than one type of metal atom is known. These are the borohydrides of aluminum, beryllium, uranium, zirconium, and hafnium. The rather typical structure of aluminum borohydride, in which there are two three-center bonds between each boron and aluminum atom, is shown in Fig. 6. The NMR spectrum shows the equivalence of all hydrogen atoms at room temperature, indicative of a rapid exchange reaction (*35*). When aluminum borohydride is heated to 80° for a considerable period diborane is released and the compound $Al_2B_4H_{18}$ is formed. The structure inferred from NMR studies comprises two $Al(BH_4)_2$ units joined by two AlHAl bridges as shown in Fig. 7. The existence of methylaluminum (*48*) and methylberyllium (*9*) borohydrides should also be mentioned. Alkylmagnesium borohydrides were also reported recently (*3*).

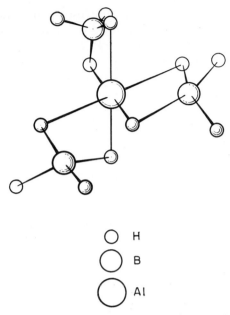

Fɪɢ. 6. Structure of aluminum borohydride.

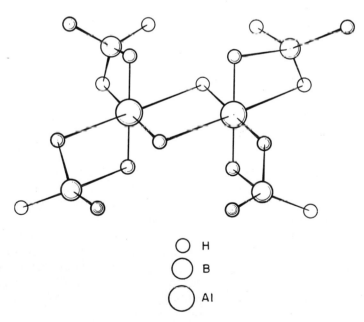

Fɪɢ. 7. Structure of $Al_2B_4H_{18}$.

The BH_4^- group represents the simplest borohydride species. More recently, many other metal borohydrides were discovered, including those containing the ions $B_{12}H_{12}^{2-}$, $B_{10}H_{13}^-$, $B_{10}H_{10}^{2-}$, and $B_2H_7^-$. Stable borohydride species can also be accounted for or predicted by the same technique as is used for predicting the existence of uncharged species (*28*). Terminal B—H bonds in these ions could in principle form bridges to other metal atoms, and one might speculate, for example, that icosohedral $B_{12}H_{12}^{2-}$ ions could be linked by beryllium atoms to form a polymer of composition $(B_{12}H_{12}Be)_n$.

Another class of electron-deficient compounds having a boron framework is the polymeric subhalides of boron, $(BCl_x)_n$. Characterized species are B_4Cl_4 (*56*) and B_8Cl_8, the structures of which are shown in Fig. 8. In B_4Cl_4 (*1*), the boron atoms are located at the corners of a tetrahedron, with one chlorine bonded to each boron. In B_8Cl_8 also, a polyhedron of boron atoms is surrounded by chlorine atoms, each of which is joined to a boron by a single bond (*22*). Linear polymers derived from these polyhedra can be imagined (*28*), such as $(—B_4Cl_2—B_4Cl_2—B_4Cl_2—)_n$, although it would appear that any condensation technique which could be applied would operate in the other dimension as well, forming a cross-linked network. It seems likely that interaction of the lone pairs on chlorine with suitable

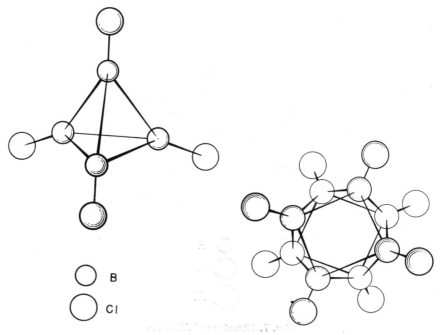

○ B

○ Cl

Fig. 8. Structures of B_4Cl_4 (*top*) and B_8Cl_4 (*bottom*).

orbitals of the boron framework is an important factor in the stability of these compounds (*30*).

Very recently, a group at du Pont has reported briefly on derivatives of the polyhedral anions $B_{10}H_{10}^{2-}$ and $B_{12}H_{12}^{2-}$, at least some of which are remarkably stable (*23a*). Halogens react smoothly with these anions, replacing some or all of the hydrogen to form species such as $B_{10}Cl_{10}^{2-}$, $B_{10}H_3Br_7^{2-}$, $B_{12}F_{12}^{2-}$, and $B_{12}H_3Br_6Cl_3^{2-}$; $Cs_2B_{10}Cl_{10}$ is stable to at least 400° in air, and the B—Cl bonds are inert to hydroxide or methoxide in refluxing water or methanol. Under carefully controlled conditions, $B_{12}H_{12}^{2-}$ can be nitrated with nitric acid to form $B_{12}H_{11}NO_2^{2-}$. Organic derivatives are also formed, and reaction of $B_{10}H_{10}^{2-}$ with dimethyl sulfoxide forms the species $B_{10}H_8(SMe_2)_2$ and $B_{10}H_9SMe_2^-$. This work points the way to much new chemistry of the greatest importance for boron chemistry in general and for boron-containing polymers in particular.

C. Hydrides Other than Boron

The hydrides of beryllium, magnesium, aluminum, gallium, indium, zinc, and cadmium are considered to be electron-deficient polymers, although in some cases the evidence for such a formulation is not entirely convincing. In general, the low stability and high reactivity of these hydrides offer scant reason to hope that they might give rise to useful polymers. Aluminum hydride has perhaps received most attention. Numerous structures have been proposed, of which one is the three-dimensional network shown in Fig. 9 (*60*).

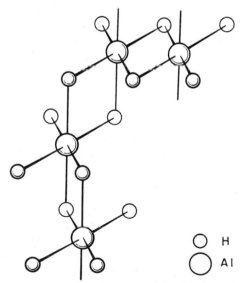

Fɪɢ. 9. Portion of structure proposed for aluminum hydride.

A number of mixed alkylmetallic hydrides are known. A polymeric isopropylberyllium hydride has been prepared (*11*). Dialkylaluminum hydrides are more highly associated than the corresponding trialkyls; dimethylaluminum hydride, for example, is trimeric in isopentane solution (*58*). An alkylmagnesium hydride was recently prepared (*25*) which is probably electron deficient.

IV. Chemistry of Electron-Deficient Polymers

A. Preparation

Electron-deficient organometallic polymers are generally prepared by the action of the standard alkylating agents. For example, dimethylberyllium can be prepared by reaction of beryllium metal with dimethylmercury. Lithium alkyls may also be prepared by direct reaction of the metal with the alkyl halide, and dialkylmagnesium compounds by the Schlenk method (*47*), in which dioxane is added to a Grignard solution. The direct reaction of aluminum with hydrogen and olefins is a modern development of great importance. An excellent general discussion of the preparation of organometallic compounds is given by Coates (*10*).

Methods for the preparation of electron-deficient hydrides have developed remarkably (*54*) since boron hydrides were first obtained by hydrolysis of magnesium boride (*53*). Large scale production methods are based for the most part on the reaction of sodium hydride with a boron halide, or of sodium borohydride with Lewis acids such as the boron halides, ferric chloride, and even sulfuric acid. Diborane is easily separated from ethereal reaction media, a process which is not so simple with the other polymeric metal hydrides. Diborane is normally converted to higher polymers by pyrolysis, but there has been some progress lately in what might be termed the chemically assisted conversion of boron hydrides (*7*). It has also been noted that diborane and decaborane together form BH_x polymer at a lower temperature than either compound alone; it was suggested that the B_2H_6 unit completed the icosahedron structure (*50*). An interesting example of chemical conversion is the reaction of $B_{10}H_{13}I$ with triethylamine to form $[(C_2H_5)_3NH]_2^+B_{12}H_{12}^{2-}$, with $[(C_2H_5)_3NH]_2^+-B_{10}H_{10}^{2-}$ as a by-product (*38*).

The interesting and important carboranes are made at present by the reaction of B_5H_9 with acetylene in a silent electric discharge (*63*) and the recently discovered $B_{10}H_{16}$ is prepared by passing B_5H_9 through a discharge (*19*). Further progress in the conversion of these materials to stable high polymers depends on improved methods of synthesis.

Aluminum borohydride was first prepared by the reaction of diborane with trimethylaluminum (*48*):

$$AlMe_3 + 2 B_2H_6 \rightarrow Al(BH_4)_3 + BMe_3$$

Beryllium borohydride was also prepared in this way (*9*). An improved method is by the following reaction (*49*):

$$3 NaBH_4 + AlCl_3 \rightarrow Al(BH_4)_3 + 3 NaCl$$

Uranium borohydride was prepared by reaction of aluminum borohydride with uranium tetrafluoride, and the borohydrides of zirconium and hafnium with the $NaMF_5$ compound (*23*). All three of these heavy metal borohydrides are remarkably volatile, and the uranium compound was originally investigated for possible use in the gaseous diffusion process for uranium isotope separation.

Hydrides of lithium, beryllium, magnesium, zinc, and cadmium are formed in the reaction of lithium aluminum hydride with the corresponding metal alkyl (*2*). The hydrides cannot be freed entirely from ether, the preferred reaction medium. Magnesium hydride can also be prepared by pyrolysis of diethylmagnesium (*61*), directly from the elements at high temperature and pressure (*62*), and by the hydrogenolysis of diethylmagnesium (*40*). The properties of the material are dependent on the method of preparation, which may be due to the state of subdivision or to a more fundamental structural difference. Beryllium hydride can also be prepared by pyrolysis of di-*tert*-butylberyllium (*12*) and the product is less reactive and more thermally stable than that obtained from the lithium aluminum hydride reaction.

Hydrides of Group III elements, in contrast to those of Groups I and II, are best obtained by reduction of the metal halide with lithium aluminum hydride. The preparation of aluminum hydride has been rather extensively studied. The initially formed AlH_3 is soluble, presumably existing as an etherate; it gradually precipitates from solution as polymerization occurs (*18*). Ether is tenaciously retained, and it has not been possible to remove it below the level of 1 molecule of ether for every 2.3 of aluminum hydride (*32*). Pyrolysis of trialkylaluminum compounds produces the R_2AlH species in certain cases, but metallic aluminum and aluminum carbide result from continued pyrolysis (*64*).

B. Reactions

The most characteristic reaction of electron-deficient substances is with Lewis bases. The course of the reaction depends on the nature and amount of the base, in particular the base strength and whether the base has a reactive proton. Excellent summaries of the reactions of boron hydrides are available (*36, 54*) and some typical reactions of other electron-deficient compounds will be mentioned briefly here.

Trimethylamine, a strong Lewis base, may be used to illustrate the range of possible reactions. With beryllium hydride, there is no reaction; the heat of polymerization of BeH_2 units is apparently large enough to offset the energy released in complex formation (*12*). Dimethylmagnesium takes up trimethylamine reversibly, but no monomeric or volatile compound is formed (*12*). Polymerization of aluminum hydride does not proceed beyond the dimer in its complex with trimethylamine, and Structure I has been suggested (*43*). Dimethylberyllium, on the other hand, is completely depolymerized by trimethylamine, forming the volatile monomeric complex Me_2Be^-——N^+Me_2 (*10*).

(I)   (II)

When the base has a protonic hydrogen, the reaction may be quite different. For example, aluminum hydride with dimethylamine forms a compound (Structure II) which is not electron deficient (*43*).

As noted in Section III,B, it has recently been found (*23a*) that reaction of the polyhedral anions $B_{10}H_{10}^{2-}$ and $B_{12}H_{12}^{2-}$ with electrophilic reagents gives rise to a whole series of new derivatives which promise to be of great importance in the polymer field.

REFERENCES

1. Atoji, M., and Lipscomb, W. N., *Acta Cryst* **6**, 547 (1953).
2. Barbaras, G. D., Dillard, C., Finholt, A. E., Wartik, T., Wilzbach, K. E., and Schlesinger, H. I., *J. Am. Chem. Soc.* **73**, 4585 (1951).
3. Bauer, R., *Z. Naturforsch.* **16b**, 557 (1961).
4. Bauer, S. H., *J. Am. Chem. Soc.* **59**, 1096 (1937).
5. Bauer, S. H., Shepp, A., and McCoy, R. E., *J. Am. Chem. Soc.* **75**, 1003 (1953).
6. Berkowitz, J. L., Bafus, D. A., and Brown, T. L., *J. Phys. Chem.* **65**, 1380 (1961).
7. Boone, J. L., and Burg, A. B., *J. Am. Chem. Soc.* **80**, 1519 (1958).
8. Brown, T. L., and Rogers, M. T., *J. Am. Chem. Soc.* **79**, 1859 (1957).
9. Burg, A. B., and Schlesinger, H. I., *J. Am. Chem. Soc.* **62**, 3425 (1940).
10. Coates, G. E., "Organometallic Chemistry," 2nd ed. Wiley, New York, 1961.
11. Coates, G. E., and Glockling, F., *J. Chem. Soc.* p. 22 (1953).
12. Coates, G. E., and Glockling, F., *J. Chem. Soc.* p. 2526 (1954).
13. Coates, G. E., Glockling, F., and Huck, N. D., *J. Chem. Soc.* p. 4496 (1952).

14. Coyle, T. D., Stafford, S. L., and Stone, F. G. A., *J. Chem. Soc.* p. 3103 (1961).
15. Dennis, L. M., Work, R. W., Rochow, E. G., and Chamot, E. M., *J. Am. Chem. Soc.* **56**, 1047 (1934).
16. Dilthey, W., *Z. angew. Chem.* **34**, 596 (1921).
17. Eberhardt, W. H., Crawford, B., Jr., and Lipscomb, W. N., *J. Chem. Phys.* **22**, 989 (1954).
18. Finholt, A. E., Bond, A. C., and Schlesinger, H. I., *J. Am. Chem. Soc.* **69**, 1199 (1947).
19. Grimes, R., Wang, F. E., Lewin, R., and Lipscomb, W. N., *Proc. Natl. Acad. Sci. U. S.* **47**, 996 (1961).
20. Hedberg, K., and Schomaker, V., *J. Am. Chem. Soc.* **73**, 1482 (1951).
21. Illuminati, G., and Rundle, R. E., *J. Am. Chem. Soc.* **71**, 3575 (1949).
22. Jacobson, R. A., and Lipscomb, W. N., *J. Am. Chem. Soc.* **80**, 5571 (1958).
23. Katz, J. J., and Hoekstra, H., *J. Am. Chem. Soc.* **71**, 2488 (1949).
23a. Knoth, W. H., Miller, H. C., England, D. C., Parshall, G. W., and Muetterties, E. L., *J. Am. Chem. Soc.* **84**, 1056 (1962).
24. Laubengayer, A. W., and Gilliam, W. F., *J. Am. Chem. Soc.* **63**, 477 (1941).
25. Leffler, A. J., and Gatti, A. R., unpublished results.
26. Lewis, G. N., *J. Chem. Phys.* **1**, 17 (1933).
27. Lewis, P. H., and Rundle, R. E., *J. Chem. Phys.* **21**, 986 (1953).
28. Lipscomb, W. N., *Advances in Inorg. Radiochem.* **1**, 117 (1959).
29. Lipscomb, W. N., *Proc. Natl. Acad. Sci. U. S.* **47**, 1791 (1961).
30. Longuet-Higgins, H. C., *Quart. Revs. (London)* **11**, 121 (1957).
31. Longuet-Higgins, H. C., and Bell, R. P., *J. Chem. Soc.* p. 250 (1943).
32. McLure, I., and Smith, T. D., *J. Inorg. & Nuclear Chem.* **19**, 170 (1961).
33. Muller, N., and Pritchard, D. E., *J. Am. Chem. Soc.* **82**, 248 (1960).
34. Mulliken, R. S., *Chem. Revs.* **41**, 207 (1947).
35. Ogg, R. A., Jr., and Ray, J. D., *Discussions Faraday Soc.* **19**, 239 (1955).
36. Parry, R. W., and Edwards, L. J., *J. Am. Chem. Soc.* **81**, 3554 (1959).
37. Pauling, L., "The Nature of the Chemical Bond," 2nd ed., p. 259 ff. Cornell Univ. Press, Ithaca, New York, 1948; 3rd ed. p. 363 ff., 1960.
38. Pitochelli, A. R., and Hawthorn, M. F., *J. Am. Chem. Soc.* **82**, 3228 (1960).
39. Pitzer, K. S., and Gutowsky, H. S., *J. Am. Chem. Soc.* **68**, 2204 (1946).
40. Podall, H. E., Petree, H. E., and Zeitz, J. R., *J. Org. Chem.* **24**, 1222 (1959).
41. Price, W. C., *J. Chem. Phys.* **15**, 614 (1947); **16**, 894 (1948).
42. Reppe, W., and Magin, A., U. S. Patent 3,006,961, October 31, 1961, to BADSFAG
43. Ruff, J. K., and Hawthorn, M. F., *J. Am. Chem. Soc.* **82**, 2141 (1960).
44. Rundle, R. E., *J. Am. Chem. Soc.* **69**, 1327 (1947).
45. Rundle, R. E., *J. Chem. Phys.* **17**, 671 (1949).
46. Rundle, R. E., and Sturdivant, J. H., *J. Am. Chem. Soc.* **69**, 1561 (1947).
47. Schlenk, W., *Ber. deut. chem. Ges.* **64**, 734 (1931).
48. Schlesinger, H. I., Sanderson, R. T., and Burg, A. B., *J. Am. Chem. Soc.* **61**, 536 (1939); **62**, 3421 (1940).
49. Schlesinger, H. I., Brown, H. C., and Hyde, E. K., *J. Am. Chem. Soc.* **75**, 209 (1953).
50. Shapiro, I., and Williams, R. E., *J. Am. Chem. Soc.* **81**, 4787 (1959).
51. Sidgwick, N. V., "The Electronic Theory of Valency," p. 103. Oxford Univ. Press (Clarendon), London and New York, 1927.
52. Snow, A. I., and Rundle, R. E., *Acta Cryst.* **4**, 348 (1951).
53. Stock, A., "Hydrides of Boron and Silicon." Cornell Univ. Press, Ithaca, New York, 1933.

54. Stone, F. G. A., *Advances in Inorg. Chem. Radiochem.* **2,** 279 (1960).
55. Stone, F. G. A., *Endeavour* **20,** 61 (1961).
56. Urry, G., Wartik, T., and Schlesinger, H. I., *J. Am. Chem. Soc.* **74,** 5809 (1952).
57. van der Kelen, G. P., and Herman, M. A., *Bull. soc. chim. Belges* **65,** 362 (1956).
58. Wartik, T., and Schlesinger, H. I., *J. Am. Chem. Soc.* **75,** 835 (1953).
59. West, R., and Glaze, W., *J. Am. Chem. Soc.* **83,** 3580 (1961).
60. Wiberg, E., *Angew. Chem.* **63,** 485 (1951).
61. Wiberg, E., and Bauer, R., *Chem. Ber.* **85,** 593 (1952).
62. Wiberg, E., Goeltzer, H., and Bauer, R., *Z. Naturforsch.* **6b,** 394 (1951).
63. Williams, R. E., *140th Meeting Am. Chem. Soc., Chicago,* **1961,** *Abstr.* p. 14N; *cf. Chem. Eng. News.* Vol. 39, No. 37, p. 55 (1961).
64. Ziegler, K., Nagel, K., and Pfohl, W., *Ann. Chem. Liebigs* **629,** 210 (1960).

Author Index

Numbers in parentheses are reference numbers and indicate that an author's work is referred to although his name is not cited in the text. Numbers in italic show the page on which the complete reference is listed.

Subject Index

Acetamide, cadmium chloride complexes of, 464
Acetic acid, polysiloxanes and, 255
Acetic anhydride, chlorosilanes and, 212
N-(Acetoacetylphenyl)glycine, metal derivatives of, 511
Acetone,
  metaphosphate precipitation by, 54
  poly(dimethylsiloxanes) and, 272
Acetonitrile, boron polymers and, 167–168
Acetoxysilanes,
  preparation of, 212
  polysiloxanes from, 215
Acetylacetonatoaluminum(III), formation of, 491
Acetylacetonatocyanopyridinezinc, polymerization of, 488
Acetylacetonatodiisopropoxoaluminum (III), bis-β-diketones and, 506
Acetylacetone,
  derivatives, pyrolysis of, 488–489
  stability of, 504
  titanium isopropoxide and, 491
  zinc cyanide and, 487
Acetyl chloride, polysilmethylenes and, 324
Acetylene,
  derivatives, organolead compounds and, 390
  pentaborane and, 546
  silicon hydrides and, 328
  siloxanes and, 338
  triethylgermane and, 362
Acetylenebis(magnesium bromide), triorganobromogermanes and, 361
Acetylferrocene, polyvinyl polymers and, 518
Acetyl peroxide, polymers and, 337
Acid(s), siloxanes and, 222–224, 226, 227, 254–255
Acid anhydrides, phthalocyanine polymers and, 493
Acrylic acid,
  lead salts, polymerization of, 389
  triphenyltin hydride and, 376
  esters, tetraallylsilane and, 342

Acrylonitrile,
  allylsilanes and, 343
  cinnamoylferrocene and, 518
  copolymers of, 13, 339, 387
  cyanoalkylsiloxanes and, 294
  diborane and, 168
  silanes and, 208
Acryloxymethylsilane, preparation of, 292–293
Acryloxysilanes, hydrolysis of, 214
Activation energy, viscous flow and, 276–279
S-Acylthiomalic acid, dibutyltin compounds and, 370
Additions, coordination polymers and, 486–487
Adipic acid, dibutyltin compounds and, 370
Adipic acid chloride, basic beryllium carboxylates and, 496
Adiponitrile, copper nitrate complex, structure of, 482
Air, solubility of, 274, 275
Alcohol(s),
  chlorosilanes and, 212
  dialkyltin oxides and, 370
  metaphosphate precipitation by, 54, 68
  polysiloxanes and, 255
  siloxanes and, 222
  surface tension of, 283
Aldehydes, dialkyltin oxides and, 372
Alkali,
  siloxanes and, 222, 224, 226–227, 254–255
  sulfones and, 110
Alkali sulfides,
  organic tetrasulfanes from, 118
  sulfur and, 153–154
  thiokols and, 136
Alkanes,
  cyclic,
    boiling point of, 248
    viscosity-molecular weight and, 276
  surface tension of, 283
1-Alkenes, silanes and, 206, 208
Alkoxysilanes,
  Grignard reagents and, 200

578